Computers & Information Systems:

Tools for an Information Age

THIRD EDITION

COMPUTERS & INFORMATION SYSTEMS

Tools for an Information Age

THIRD EDITION

H. L. Capron and John D. Perron

The Benjamin/Cummings Publishing Company, Inc.

Redwood City, California • Menlo Park, California
Reading, Massachusetts • New York • Don Mills, Ontario
Wokingham, U.K. • Amsterdam • Bonn
Singapore • Tokyo • Madrid • San Juan

Sponsoring Editor	**Michelle Miceli-Baxter**
Developmental Editor	**Jamie Spencer**
Production Editors	**Bonnie Grover, Betty Gee**
Art Supervisor	**Betty Gee**
Cover, Text and Desktop Designer	**Mark Ong**
Illustrations	**Illustrious, Inc.**
Photo Editor	**Cecilia Mills**
Photo Researcher	**Sarah Bendersky**
Copyeditor	**Toni Murray**
Composition and Film	**Black Dot Graphics**
Printing and Binding	**R. R. Donnelley & Sons Company**

Library of Congress Cataloging-in-Publication Data

Capron, H. L.
    Computers and information systems: tools for an information age /
H. L. Capron, John D. Perron. —3rd ed.
      p.   cm.
    Rev. ed. of: Computers, 2nd ed. 1990.
    Includes index.
    ISBN 0-8053-1100-9
    1. Computers. I. Perron, John D. II. Capron, H. L. Computers.
III. Title. IV. Title: Computers and information systems.
QA76.C358   1993
004—dc20   92-41114
                                                CIP

SE   ISBN 0-8053-1100-9
AIE   ISBN 0-8053-0973-X

1 2 3 4 5 6 7 8 9 10   DO 97 96 95 94 93

The Benjamin/Cummings Publishing Company, Inc.
390 Bridge Parkway
Redwood City, CA 94065

H. L. Capron—

For the Morgans: Mary, Jack, Tim, and Joel

J. D. Perron—

For my wife, Jacqueline

The Capron Collection

A Complete Supplements Package

- ***Instructor's Edition with Annotations.*** Written by B. Peacock with H. L. Capron and J. D. Perron, this special edition contains annotations for lecture preparation and includes supplementary material not found in the Instructor's Guide. The annotations include chapter outlines with key terms (for lecture preparation), lecture objectives, lecture activities, discussion questions, lecture hints, global perspectives, test bank references, transparency references, and answers to end-of-chapter true/false questions.

- ***Instructor's Guide and Transparency Masters*** by J. D. Perron (250pages). Each chapter contains learning objectives, a chapter overview, a detailed lecture outline, and a list of key words. The Instructor's Guide also includes 50 transparency masters, and a reference guide to lecture support software screens.

- *Lecture Support Software* by J. Huhtala and G. Novotny. This eight-disk package for the IBM PC, PS/2, or compatible machine provides 280 color screens containing animation and text that summarize the key concepts in each section of the book. The accompanying student workbook (300 pages) supports the software by offering additional text, learning objectives, key terms, review questions, and completion questions. The software and workbook can be used in lecture or lab. A reference guide for the support software is included in the Instructor's Guide.

- *Test Bank* by S. Langman. The test bank contains approximately 2000 items. There are five types of questions: multiple choice, true/false, matching, fill-in-the-blank, and situational essay. Each question is referenced to the text by page number and the answers are provided. The test bank is available both as hard copy and in a computerized format for the IBM PC (and any compatible machine), IBM PS/2, and Macintosh computers.

- *Color Transparency Acetates.* 100 full-color transparency acetates include artwork and diagrams taken directly from the text as well as other sources.

- **Videotapes**. Benjamin/Cummings will make available, to qualified adopters, free videos from our library of commercially produced videos. Use this valuable resource to enhance your lectures about concepts presented in the text. Your sales representative has details about this offer.

Technology Solutions. Today's classroom experience can be enhanced by a variety of information-delivery systems. Consult your Benjamin/Cummings sales representative for options for your classroom.

Lab Manuals

- **SELECT Editions**. Lab manuals in the SELECT Editions line are applications modules that introduce students to the latest packages. Available as separate books, custom-bound in any combination, or bound with a SELECT Edition of *Computers & Information Systems,* SELECT Editions offer the ultimate flexibility in choosing a text that meets the specific needs of your course. The following modules are available: *Lotus 1-2-3, Release 2.2, Lotus 1-2-3, Release 2.3, MS Works 2.0 for PCs, LotusWorks 3.0, DOS 5.0, DOS and Windows 3.0, dBASE IV, dBASE III PLUS, BASIC, QBASIC, WordPerfect 5.1, Excel 3.0 for PCs, Paradox 3.5,* and *Quattro Pro 4.0.*

- *Mastering Microcomputers* by William Davis, et al. Covers basic hardware and software concepts as well as DOS 5.0, WordPerfect 5.1, Lotus 1-2-3, Release 2.3, and dBASE IV 1.5.

- **The *Computing Fundamentals* Series.** This series consists of brief tutorials. The titles include: *Concepts, 3rd ed., WordPerfect 5.0/5.1, dBASE III PLUS, dBASE IV, Lotus 1-2-3, Release 2.01/2.2, Lotus 1-2-3, Release 2.3, PC-DOS and MS-DOS, DOS 5.0, PageMaker for the Macintosh, PageMaker for the IBM PC,* and *Microsoft Word 5.0.*

Software Options for the Instructor

- **LotusWorks 3.0.** This two-disk integrated package available in PC or PS/2 formats offers a spreadsheet, database, word processing and communications service. The package also includes a tutorial booklet and a reference book with a quick-reference guide.

- **Student Editions.** *The Student Edition of Lotus 1-2-3* (509 pages); *The Student Edition of dBASE IV* (704 pages); *The Student Edition of Framework II* (372 pages).

- **Computer Based Training.** Benjamin/Cummings has a variety of software tutorials available. Contact your sales representative for details about this offer.

Brief Table of Contents

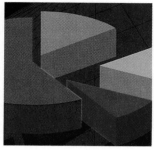

Detailed Table of Contents

Chapter 2

The Central Processing Unit: The Brain of the Machine   51

Chapter 3

Input and Output: Data Given, Information Received   75

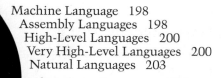

Part 2 Software Tools 187

Chapter 6

Programming and Languages: A Survey 189

Chapter 7

Operating Systems: The Hidden Software 225

Chapter 8

Systems Analysis and Design: Change and the Computer 255

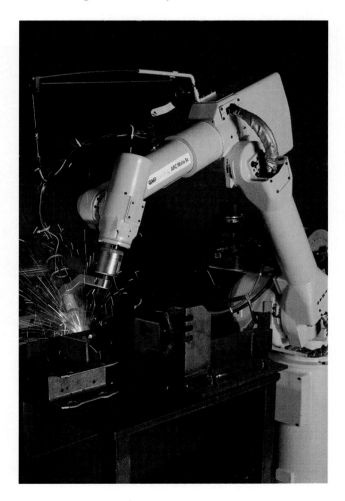

The Galleries and Buyer's Guide

GALLERY 1
MAKING MICROCHIPS (follows page 64)
In this gallery, we take a look at how silicon chips—the "brain" of the computer—are made. We follow the process from the design stage through manufacturing, testing, and packaging the final product.

GALLERY 2
COMPUTERS AROUND US (follows page 224)
This gallery showcases some of the interesting uses for computers in our everyday lives. We examine how computers are being used in science, health and medicine, sports and games, entertainment, music, the service industry, art, and photography.

GALLERY 3
COMPUTERS AT WORK (follows page 448)
The computer has become an essential tool in the world of business and manufacturing. In this gallery, we explore how computers are being used to design, engineer, and manufacture products; to control robots on the job; and to support workers in a variety of fields, from graphic design to finance.

BUYER'S GUIDE: HOW TO BUY YOUR OWN PERSONAL COMPUTER (follows page 320)
This special eight-page section presents issues and questions to consider before buying a personal computer and software. If you are thinking about buying a personal computer now or in the future, read this section carefully.

Preface

In the fast-changing world of computers and information systems technology, giving students an up-to-date introduction to computing can be a challenge. To help instructors meet that challenge, this new edition of ***Computers & Information Systems: Tools for an Information Age*** has been revised and updated throughout. The third edition retains, however, the appealing reading style that has made this text a best-seller. In addition, the accompanying support package provides all the elements instructors need to teach an introductory computer course.

New to this Edition

- **WordPerfect 5.1, Lotus 1-2-3 version 2.3, and dBASE IV,** the most popular software packages, are covered in our revised software applications chapters (Chapters 9-11). We use these packages to demonstrate the basic concepts of word processing, spreadsheets, business graphics, and database management systems. In addition, desktop publishing is now covered along with word processing, reflecting the growing trend toward incorporating desktop publishing features in word processing software.

- **"Computer Graphics: From Art to Animation and Beyond"** (Chapter 12) is a new chapter that provides an overview of computer graphics terminology and describes in basic terms how graphics are created.

- **"Modern Trends: Artificial Intelligence, Expert Systems, and Robotics"** (Chapter 16), new to this edition, focuses on the advances being made on the cutting edge of computing. The chapter introduces students to the concepts of neural networks, natural languages, and fuzzy logic and shows how expert systems and robotics are changing the way businesses operate.

- **Programming concepts** are the focus of a new appendix (Appendix A), which is for those who want to cover structured programming in greater depth.

- **The SELECT System**. With Benjamin/Cummings Publishing Company's SELECT System, you can tailor this text to the needs of your course. The SELECT Edition of *Computers & Information Systems* is custom-bound with your choice of applications modules into one convenient text. Other SELECT options: Applications modules are available as individual books or bound together without *Computers & Information Systems.*

Updated in This Edition

- **Extensive personal computer coverage.** Although we discuss all types of computers, we emphasize personal computers, reflecting their continuing prominence in business and education. Because of the trend toward greater integration of personal computers into schools and work places, we no longer cover PCs in a separate chapter. Instead, we have incorporated a wide variety of new personal computer examples throughout the text.

- **Personal Computers in Action.** Each chapter includes a feature about personal computers that demonstrates the range of tasks personal computers perform. Most of these sections are new to this edition; they include topics such as the use of personal computers on campus, in entertainment, and in business.

- **Buyer's Guide.** Students and their families make important economic decisions when they purchase computers to meet their educational needs. This concise eight-page guide offers the up-to-date information students need to evaluate hardware and software, and a checklist to help them make purchasing decisions.

- **Coverage of mainframes in business.** Although personal computers have become increasingly important in business, large computer systems—supercomputers, mainframes, minicomputers, and the newest superminis—are a critical part of the computer industry. In the third edition we continue to cover large computer systems, and we show how they are affected by personal computers.

- **Management Information Systems.** Reflecting the growing importance of computing systems in the management of information in business, we have expanded and updated coverage of MIS and decision support systems (chapter 14). New topics include the executive support system (ESS), the group decision support system (GDSS), and groupware.

- **Special-topic galleries.** Three revised full-color photo essays vividly illustrate the world of computers. One walks the reader through the manufacture of silicon chips, another marvels at the many uses of computers, and the third shows how computers are used in the business world.

- **Margin notes.** To further engage student attention, margin notes are carefully placed throughout the chapters. The margin notes extend the text by providing additional information and examples of interesting computer applications.

- **Extensive student learning aids.** The third edition features the following pedagogical support: key terms boldfaced in the text; extensive summaries with boldfaced key terms; review questions, discussion questions, and true/false questions; an extensive glossary; and an index.

- **The friendly writing style.** When students enjoy what they read, they remember it. The trademark of this book continues to be the friendly writing style that encourages the reluctant reader and increases the student's comprehension and confidence. For example, stories about computer users engage interest immediately and illustrate key points from the chapter.

Organization of the Text

The text is divided into four parts:

- Part 1 offers an overview of computer systems and explores computer hardware. Hardware topics include updated coverage of the central processing unit and memory, input/output devices, storage mechanisms, and communications technology.

- Part 2 focuses on programming and languages, operating systems, and systems analysis and design. Information about programming and programming languages now appear in a single chapter, and an extended discussion of structured programming concepts has been included in Appendix A. The operating systems chapter includes new information about Microsoft Windows and other graphical user interfaces.

- Part 3 includes three chapters about applications packages: word processing (WordPerfect 5.1) and desktop publishing, spreadsheets and business graphics (Lotus 1-2-3 Release 2.3), and database management systems (dBASE IV PLUS), plus a new chapter on computer graphics.

- Part 4 looks at computers in the workplace; security, privacy, and ethics; and artificial intelligence, expert systems, and robotics.

- Appendix A covers structured programming concepts. Appendix B describes the history of computing. Appendix C offers a review of number systems. These appendices provide material for those who wish to include these topics in their course.

The Capron Collection:
A Complete Supplements Package

- **Instructor's Edition with Annotations.** Written by B. Peacock (North Carolina State University) with H. L. Capron and J. D. Perron, this special edition contains lecture outlines with key terms, learning objectives, lecture hints, discussion questions, lecture activities, global perspective, test bank references, transparency references, and student projects.

- **Instructor's Guide and Transparency Masters.** Written by J. D. Perron, the Instructor's Guide provides learning objectives, a chapter overview, a detailed lecture outline, a list of key words, 50 transparency masters, and a reference guide to lecture support software.

- **Student Study Guide.** Written by H. L. Capron, this study guide contains learning objectives; an overview of each chapter; a chapter outline; a list of key words with space for a student-supplied definition; study hints; self-tests (multiple choice, true/false, matching, fill-in-the-blank, and identification exercises requiring students to label figures from the text); answers to self-tests; additional margin notes; and sections called Close to Home, which provide motivational examples of computer use in everyday life.

- **Test Bank.** The test bank, containing approximately 2000 questions, has been prepared by Shelly Langman. There are four types of questions: multiple choice, true/false, matching, fill-in-the-blank, and situational essay. For your convenience, each question is referenced to the text by page number and answers are provided. The test bank is available both as hard copy and in a computerized format for the IBM PC (and compatible machine), the PS/2, and the Macintosh.

- **Color Transparency Acetates.** 100 full-color transparencies are available to adopters of this text. These transparencies include artwork from this book and from outside sources.

- **Lecture Support Software.** This innovative teaching resource is for use in either lecture or lab. The software provides 280 color screens that use animation and text to summarize the key concepts from each section of the book. A reference guide to help you incorporate the software screens into your lectures is provided in the Instructor's Guide.

- **Videotapes.** Benjamin/Cummings offers free videotapes from our library of commercially produced videos to enhance your lectures. Your Benjamin/Cummings sales representative has details about this offer.

Technology Solutions. Today's classroom experience can be enhanced by a variety of information-delivery systems. Consult your Benjamin/Cummings sales representative for options for your classroom.

Lab Manuals

- **SELECT Editions.** Lab manuals in the SELECT Edition line are applications modules that introduce students to the latest packages. Available as separate books, custom-bound in any combination, or bound with a SELECT Edition of *Computers & Information Systems*, SELECT Editions offer the ultimate flexibility in choosing a text that meets the specific needs of your course. The following are modules available: *Lotus 1-2-3, Release 2.2*, Fox/Metzelaar; *Lotus 1-2-3, Re-*

lease 2.3, Fox/Metzelaar; *MS Works 2.0 for PCs*, Scharpf; *LotusWorks 3.0*, Fox/Metzelaar; *DOS 5.0*, Fox/Metzelaar; *DOS and Windows 3.0*, Fox/Metzelaar/Scharpf; *dBASE IV*, Fox/Metzelaar; *dBASE III PLUS*, Fox/Metzelaar; *BASIC*, Appelt/Whittenhall/Kittner; *QBASIC*, Fenton; *WordPerfect 5.1*, Fox/Metzelaar; *Excel 3.0 for PCs*, Scharpf; *Paradox 3.5*, Fox/Metzelaar; *Quattro Pro 4.0*, Webster.

- *Mastering Microcomputers* by William Davis, Paul Schreiner, Donald Byrkett, and Craig Wood. Covers basic hardware and software concepts, as well as DOS 5.0, WordPerfect 5.1, Lotus 1-2-3, Release 2.3, and dBASE IV 1.5. Students learn problem-solving through the *Solve It Yourself* feature.

- The *Computing Fundamentals* Series. This series consists of brief tutorials that introduce beginners to specific software packages, operating systems, and programming languages. The books cover the fundamental functions necessary to start using a particular application successfully. The titles include: *Concepts, 3rd ed.*, Davis; *WordPerfect 5.0/5.1*, Davis; *dBASE III PLUS*, Davis/Schreiner; *dBASE IV*, Davis/Schreiner; *Lotus 1-2-3, Release 2.01/2.2*, Byrkett; *Lotus 1-2-3, Release 2.3*, Byrkett; *PC-DOS AND MS-DOS*, Wood; *DOS 5.0*, Wood; *PageMaker for the Macintosh*, Davies; *PageMaker for the IBM PC*, Davies; *Microsoft Word 5.0*, Gorman/Haggard.

- The *Hands-On* Series by Larry Metzelaar and Marianne Fox. An ideal introduction to four major software applications for the IBM PC, these books cover the most recent releases: *Hands-On Plus:* MS-DOS, dBASE IV, WordPerfect 5.1, Lotus 1-2-3; *Hands-On, 2nd ed.:* MS-DOS, dBASE III PLUS, WordPerfect 5.0, Lotus 1-2-3, *Hands-On WordPerfect 5.1*; and *Hands-On dBASE IV.*

Software for the Instructor

- **LotusWorks 3.0.** This 2-disk integrated package available in PC or PS/2 formats offers a spreadsheet, database, word processing and communications service. The package also includes a tutorial booklet and a reference book with a quick reference guide.

- **Computer Based Training.** Benjamin/Cummings has a variety of software tutorials available. Contact your sales representative for details about this offer.

Of Related Interest

The Student Edition of Lotus 1-2-3 (509 pages); **The Student Edition of dBASE IV** (704 pages); **The Student Edition of Framework II** (372 pages).

Special Note to the Student

We welcome your reactions to this book. It is written to open up the world of computing for you. Expanding your knowledge will increase your confidence and prepare you for a life that will be influenced by computers. Your comments and questions are important to us. Write to the author in care of Computer Information Systems Editor, Benjamin/Cummings Publishing Company, 390 Bridge Parkway, Redwood City, California 94065. All letters with a return address will be answered by the author.

Acknowledgments

The success of any project as extensive as this one involves the contributions and support of many people. The authors are indebted to all of them, especially the contributors whose expertise inspires many sections of this work: Banks Peacock of North Carolina State University, Mary Allyn Webster of the University of Florida, Melanie Wolf-Greenberg of California State University at Fullerton, and Shelly Langman of Bellevue Community College. We would also like to extend a special thanks to those who helped lift this project out of traditional publishing and into the new electronic world of desktop publishing.

At the top of our list is Jamie Spencer, developmental editor, who spearheaded all parts of the project—one of Benjamin/Cumming's first desktop publishing efforts. Our thanks also go to Bonnie Grover and Betty Gee, production editors, who directed the timely efforts of numerous people and kept those electronic pages pulsing through production stages. A special thanks goes to Toni Murray for extensive copyediting efforts, to Betty Gee for precise and to-the-point illustrations, to Cecilia Mills and Sarah Bendersky for colorful and exacting photo research, and to Larry Olsen for excellent supportive efforts. On the technical side, we wish to thank Ari Davidow for his technical support. For incredible artistry and timeless giving, we extend a special thanks to designer Mark Ong. For keeping all of us communicating smoothly, we wish to thank May Woo, Kathy Galinac and Lisa Weber. And, above all, we wish to thank Michelle Baxter who provided inspired coordination and kept our vision steady.

Reviewers and consultants from both industry and academia have provided many invaluable contributions that continue to improve the quality of this work. Their names follow in a list, and to the reviewers we express our sincere gratitude for helping us provide students with new insights into the ever-changing information age.

Reviewers

Third Edition

Ros Ballantyne
Macquarie University
North Ryde, New South Wales
Australia

Gary Buterbaugh
Indiana University of Pennsylvania
Indiana, Pennsylvania

Mark Ciampa
Volunteer State Community College
Gallatin, Tennessee

William Dorin
Indiana University Northwest
Gary, Indiana

John English
Pittsburg State University
Pittsburg, Kansas

Joyce Farrell
McHenry County College
Crystal Lake, Illinois

Paula Funkhouser
Truckee Meadows Community College
Sparks, Nevada

Gerald Haskins
University of Florida
Gainsville, Florida

Joan Krone
Denison University
Granville, Ohio

Charles Lake
James H. Faulkner Junior College
Bayminette, Alabama

Shelly Langman
Bellevue Community College
Bellevue, Washington

Robert Lover
Belmont Abbey College
Belmont, North Carolina

Randy Marak
Hill College
Cleburne, Texas

William McTammary
Florida Community College at Jacksonville
Jacksonville, Florida

Wes Obst
Deakin University
Warrnambool, Victoria
Australia

Dennis Olsen
Pikes Peak Community College
Colorado Springs, Colorado

Frank Paiano
Southwestern College
Chula Vista, California

Banks Peacock
North Carolina State University
Raleigh, North Carolina

Herb Rebhun
University of Houston-Downtown
Houston, Texas

Dana Roberson
Community College of Southern Nevada
Las Vegas, Nevada

Robert Signorile
Boston College
Chestnut Hill, Massachusetts

Mark Vellinga
Northwestern College
Orange City, Iowa

Karla Vogel
University of New Hampshire at Manchester
Manchester, New Hampshire

Mary Allyn Webster
University of Florida
Gainsville, Florida

Donna Wojcik
Genesee Community College
Batavia, New York

Melanie Wolf-Greenburg
California State University - Fullerton
Fullerton, California

Helen Wolfe
Teikyo-Post University
Waterbury, Connecticuit

Second Edition

Roberta Baber
Fresno City College
Fresno, California

James Boettler
South Carolina State College
Orangeburg, South Carolina

John DaPonte
Southern Connecticut State University
Stratford, Connecticut

Ed Delaporte
Forest City Computer Services
Rockford, Illinois

Linda Denny
Sinclair Community College
Dayton, Ohio

Jeff Frates
Los Medanos Community College
Concord, California

Paul Higbee
University of North florida
Jacksonville, Florida

Usha Jindall
Washtenaw Community College
Ann Arbor, Michigan

Rose Laird
Northern Virginia Community College
Annandale, Virginia

Joyce Little
Towson State University
Baltimore, Maryland

Paul Losleben
Stanford University'
Palo Alto, California

Michael Mehlman
Tennessee State University
Nashville, Tennessee

Patrick Ormond
Utah Valley Community College
Orem, Utah

Charles Prettyman
Mercer County Community College
Trenton, New Jersey

Richard St. Andre
Central Michigan University
Mt. Pleasant, Michigan

Bruce Sophie
North Harris County College
Houston, Texas

Frank R. Wondolowski
East Carolina University
Greenville, North Carolina

First Edition

Kay Arms
Tyler Junior College
Tyler, Texas

Mark Aulick
Louisiana State University
Shreveport, Louisiana

Gary Brown
Santa Rosa Junior College
Santa Rosa, California

Jane Burcham
University of Missouri
Columbia, Missouri

Patricia Clark
Management Information Systems
Seattle, Washington

Carole Colaneri
Mid-Florida Technical College
Orlando, Florida

James Cox
Lane Community College
Eugene, Oregon

Janet Daugherty
Seton Hall University
South Orange, New Jersey

Ralph Duffy
North Seattle Community College
Seattle, Washington

Neil Dunn
Massachusetts Bay
Community College
Wellesley, Massachusetts

John Hamburger
Advanced Micro Devices
Sunnyvale, California

Sharon Hill
Prince George's
Community College
Largo, Maryland

Cary Hughes
Middle Tennessee State
University
Murfreesboro, Tennessee

Marcy Kittner
University of Tampa
Tampa, Florida

Mary Kohls
Austin Community
College
Austin, Texas

Cliff Layton
Rogers State College
Claremore, Oklahoma

Vicki Marney-Petix
Marpet Technical Services
Fremont, California

Spencer Martin
North Shore Community
College
Beverly, Massachusetts

Doug Meyers
Des Moines Area
Community College
Ankeny, Iowa

Jeff Mock
Diablo Valley Community
College
Pleasant Hill, California

Charles Moulton
Beaver College
Glenside, Pennsylvania

Linda Moulton
Montgomery County
Community College
Blue Bell, Pennsylvania

Mike Nakoff
Cincinnati Technical
College
Cincinnati, Ohio

Robert Oakman
Le Conte College,
University of South
Carolina
Columbia, South Carolina

Dennis Olsen
Pikes Peak Community
College
Colorado Springs, Colorado

James Payne
Kellogg Community
College
Battle Creek, Michigan

Gordon Robinson
Forest Park Community
College
St. Louis, Missouri

Gerald Sampson
Brazosport College
Lake Jackson, Texas

Fred Scott
Broward Community
College
Ft. Lauderdale, Florida

Lenny Siegal
Advanced Micro Devices
Sunnyvale, California

Debbie Smith-Hemphill
AT&T Information
Systems
Honolulu, Hawaii

Bruce Sophie
North Harris County
College
Houston, Texas

Rod Southworth
Laramie County
Community College
Cheyenne, Wyoming

Sandra Stalker
North Shore Community
College
Beverly, Massachusetts

Dave Stamper
University of Northern
Colorado
Greeley, Colorado

Sandy Stephenson
Southwest Virginia
Community College
Richlands, Virginia

Greg Swan
Mesa Community College
Mesa, Arizona

Earl Talbert
Central Piedmont
Community College
Charlotte, North Carolina

J. Langdon Taylor
Ohio University
Athens, Ohio

Tim Vanderwall
Joliet Junior College
Joliet, Illinois

Kenneth Walter
Weber State College
Ogden, Utah

William Wells
Sacramento City College
Sacramento, California

The SELECT System

The Benjamin/Cummings Publishing Company is pleased to announce its new SELECT System, an innovation in publishing. SELECT is our response to your request for textbooks tailored to your course. We believe the system offers an unprecedented opportunity for educators to evaluate flexible text components and build them into a customized teaching support system.

A Text with Concepts and Customized Application Coverage

With the SELECT System you can combine this text with your choice of hands-on applications modules. The modules you select are bound with **Computers & Information Systems** into one convenient, durable volume. Modules are also available separately, or without **Computers & Information Systems.** We offer the following selection of modules:

Operating Systems
DOS and Windows 3.0 (128 pages)
DOS 5.0 (128 pages)
Word Processing
WordPerfect 5.1 (128 pages)
Spreadsheets
Lotus 1-2-3, Release 2.2 (143 pages)
Quattro Pro 4.0 (160 pages)
Excel for PCs (160 pages)

Databases
dBASE III PLUS (138 pages)
dBASE IV (182 pages)
Paradox 3.5 (170 pages)
Integrated Packages
MS Works 3.0 for PCs (450 pages)
LotusWorks 3.0 (450 pages)
Programming Languages
Structured BASIC (89 pages)
QBASIC (128 pages)

Each module is written by experienced authors and instructors and follows a consistent, pedagogically sound format. The modules begin with basic concepts, such as how to get help and how to understand the conventions used in the modules. Students learn how to use the software by solving problems in increasingly challenging projects.

These projects which are based on general-interest examples and business documents, are the core of the students' learning process. They are challenged to learn the concepts behind the keystrokes as they work through the projects.

Each project includes objectives, keystroke instructions, screen captures, and sample documents; and each project ends with a summary, a list of key terms, study questions (true/false, completion and discussion) and review exercises. Each module concludes with additional projects, a command reference, an extensive glossary, and an index. The modules are intended for the first-time computer user and contain selected advanced topics for the more experienced student.

Advantages of the SELECT System

The SELECT System brings you and your students many advantages:

- **Flexibility.** Now you can adapt your textbook to your curriculum instead of the other way around. You can choose any combination of modules. And, if your course should change next term, you can choose a new selection of modules to meet your new course needs. Benjamin/Cummings will introduce additional modules that cover new and upgraded software and programming applications. If we don't currently publish modules for the specific software packages you teach, please contact your Benjamin/Cummings sales representative or call the SELECT System Hotline at 800/854-2595. We will be happy to work with you to address your textbook requirements.

- **Convenience.** The SELECT System gives you computer concepts plus the exact lab coverage you want, all in one text and from one publisher. With our low minimum-order policy, we can offer this convenience to almost every educator. Your students will like not having to carry more than one text to lecture and lab.

- **Affordability.** Each module is individually priced. Because you select just the ones you plan to teach, your students pay only for what they need. And because we offer the text and modules bound into one volume, students won't have to pay for costly binders.

- **Improved instructional package.** With computers so much a part of our daily lives, your students deserve the best preparation possible. The SELECT System and *Computers & Information Systems* give you up-to-date coverage of computer concepts by the best-known author in Computer Information Systems; pedagogically consistent, customized lab instruction; and the most complete instructional support available.

In addition to the complete instructional support package for the *Computers & Information Systems* textbook, qualified adopters can order an instructor's manual with tests and transparency masters, for each module. The study questions in the modules can serve as a student study guide if you provide your students with the answer key from the instructor's guide. Also available to module adopters is an instructor's data disk with tests. The disk provides test files, selected answers to review questions and additional projects, and student data files.

Complimentary Review Copies

We have prepared the following materials for review and adoption consideration:

- **The Instructor's Edition with Annotations.** This edition of *Computers & Information Systems* contains the complete contents of the student text plus ten types of margin annotations to support instruction. The student version of the SELECT edition of *Computers & Information Systems* contains this complete text without the blue annotations.

- **The Applications Modules.** Sample modules are bound separately for your review. Once adopted, the modules you have selected will be bound with *Computers & Information Systems*. The instructor's manuals with tests and transparency masters are also available for review purposes.

Ordering and Pricing Information

Your Benjamin/Cummings representative will be happy to provide you and your bookstore manager with information about ordering, pricing, and delivery. You may also call the SELECT System Hotline at 800/854-2595 if you have questions or need complimentary review or desk copies.

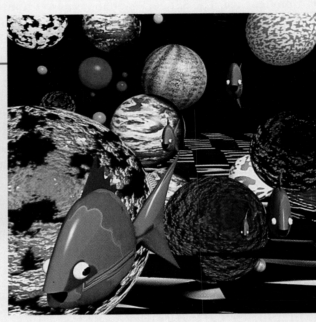

The Age of Information
Reaching for New Tools

The dawn of a new age—the Information Age—glows before us with the promise of new ways of thinking, living, and working. The amount of information in the world is said to be doubling every six to seven years. Can we keep up? We can, but not without an understanding of how computers work and the ability to control them for our own purposes. Used to creating documents with typewriters or crunching numbers with calculators, we now sit before one machine—the computer—that can do these tasks and many, many more. We need to come to terms with this expanding technology and adjust our vision to a whole new world.

"It's a Whole New World!"

Mrs. Lilly Nance, of Oakland, California, has lived through both the Industrial and Information ages and witnessed numerous changes. Born in 1908 on a small farm in North Dakota, she recalls: "One day, my dad came in quite excited. He told mother: 'You know, I heard they have these boxes now that can play music from way off. It's all done with electricity. It's a whole new world.'"

"It wasn't long before we had one of those boxes—a radio—sitting in our living room. Everyone would gather around each evening after dinner and listen to it. I remember one day being outside in a field. I heard this droning sound coming from above. I was frightened at first. I didn't know what it might be. I saw my first aeroplane that day. It was an incredible sight, passed right over me."

"I first began working as a typesetter at the weekly newspaper in Kenmare in 1928. I worked hard to make sure all the words were typed up and lined up just right. It was a big Linotype and made the letters from hot lead—awful hot and smelly sometimes. When I see how today a computer writes on the screen, and how you can change things so quickly, I'm just amazed. What we could have done with such machines back then! Why . . . it's a whole new world."

Stepping Out

Your first steps toward joining the Information Age include understanding how we got to where we are today. Perhaps you recall from history books how the Industrial Age gradually took its place in our world. In less than 100 years, human society changed on a massive scale. To live between 1890 and 1920, for instance, was to live with the dizzying introduction of electricity, telephones, radio, automobiles, and airplanes. The start of the Information Age might be traced to many events earlier this century, including the invention of television. Slow and steady marked its pace up through the 1950s, when the miniaturization of electronic components such as transistors enabled production of the first personal computers—also called microcomputers—in the 1970s. From that point the pace of the Information Age increased to fast and furious, and its impact extended to each individual in our society.

Compared to the Industrial Revolution, the Information Age is evolving much more rapidly. It is likely to continue to evolve well into the twenty-first century. Nevertheless, we can glimpse the future now and see how far we have come, first in society and then on a more personal level.

Forging a Computer-Based Society

Computers are not a fad, like the latest hairstyle or Teenage Mutant Ninja Turtles. Few fads result in hundreds of magazines, thousands of books, as well as weekly radio and TV news shows. Only a major trend has the momentum to sustain these classic indicators of acceptance. But computers have gone beyond mere acceptance—they are remolding society in fundamental ways.

Traditional economics courses define the cornerstones of an economy as land, labor, capital, and the entrepreneurial spirit. That traditional definition is now being challenged. Today you find references to a fifth key economic element: information. As we evolve from an industrial to an information society, our jobs are changing from physical to mental labor. Just as people moved physically from farms to factories in the Industrial Age, so today people are shifting muscle power to brain power in a new, computer-based society (Figure 1).

You are making your move, too, taking your first steps by signing up for this computer class and reading this book. But should you go further and get your own computer? We look next at some of the reasons why you might.

A Computer in Your Future

The television ads appeal: Computers are a *must* for work and play. Your livelihood depends on them, your children's future demands them, your family's hopes and dreams are tied to them. "A tool for modern times,"

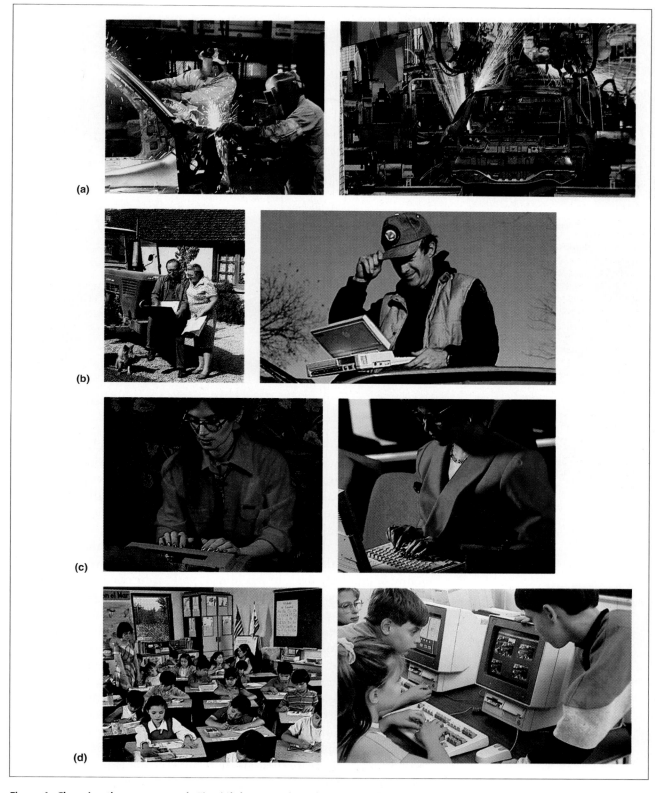

Figure 1   Changing the way we work. The shift from an Industrial Age to an Information Age has changed the way we work. (a) Factory workers doing repetitive tasks have been replaced by robots. (b) Farmers who toiled to till the land now control modern machinery that does it for them. (c) Office workers once limited to one-application typewriters now utilize multi-application computers. (d) Classrooms have changed from lecture halls to hands-on centers.

Figure 2　Personal computer users. All these people—whether at home, at work, or at school—are making good use of the personal computer.

the ads proclaim. "If you can point, you can use a computer." "A computer for the rest of us." The commercials feature celebrities, families, even dogs—or all three—urging us to buy a personal computer. Small enough to sit on a desk top, personal computers (often called PCs) have been hustled like encyclopedias: "For the price of a bicycle, you can help your child's future. . . ."

The growth of the personal computer market has been incredible, perhaps in spite of the ads. Computers have moved into every nook and cranny of our daily lives. In our homes, various forms of the new technology are used not only as playthings but also for keeping track of bank accounts; turning on lawn sprinklers or the morning coffee; monitoring inside temperature and humidity; and teaching math, reading, and other skills to children. At work, they help run our business or do our job—whether that's in a corporate office or on a farm. Personal computers are extremely useful for almost everything we do: writing letters and reports; forecasting and updating budgets; creating and maintaining files; producing charts or graphs; and creating newspapers, newsletters, and magazines. The influence of computers continues to grow as artists, musicians, photographers, and even video and movie makers find ways to use computers to create their art more quickly and efficiently. Almost any career you map out for your future will involve a computer in some way. Clearly, the computer user no longer has to be a Ph.D. in a laboratory somewhere. We are all computer users (Figure 2).

But just how happy are we with such newfound sophistication?

Worry About Computers? Me?

Don't be Afraid to Question

Q: I'm not really interested in computers. I just don't want to be left behind. What should I do?

A: You're right to be concerned. None of us wants to be left behind. Try to learn more about computers. You may become more interested as you gain information. This does not mean you have to become a computer expert. But you do need to understand what computers are able to do and how they might affect your future career.

Q: I'm a student studying in the field of (*fill in the blank*). Could it be possible that computers are going to make the career I'm planning obsolete?

A: Not likely. Some factory workers with repetitive jobs are being replaced, but most jobs won't be lost because of computers. The key is incorporating the computer: Can it enhance your job as opposed to eliminating it? Computers generally change the way jobs are performed, rather than eliminating positions.

Q: Will computers eventually become smarter than human beings and take over, as I have seen in some movies?

A: Who gets to pull the plug? Computers get only, and exactly, the control we humans decide to give them. The real question is *How might other humans use computers to control you?*

A middle-aged woman sat down at a personal computer for the first time in her life. She placed her hands above the keyboard, ready to type—but hesitated. Turning to the instructor, she asked warily: "It won't know what I'm thinking, will it?" Such concerns abound among people whose knowledge of computers comes from movies like *2001: A Space Odyssey* (in which Hal, the computer with the sticky-sweet voice, tries to takes control of the spaceship). Terms such as **computer anxiety** and **computer phobia** have entered our language to describe such wariness. Many people try to avoid situations in which they might be forced into contact with computers. Even businesspeople who deal with computers daily may experience a form of **cyberphobia**—fear of computers. As a result of their fear, some office workers who are cyberphobic suffer nausea, sweaty palms, and high blood pressure. Young people who have grown up with computers may not understand these reactions.

What are such people afraid of? Some may worry about the mathematical implications of the word *computer*. It seems to suggest that only a person with strong analytical and quantitative skills can use the machine. In fact, as we see more and more often, even very young children whose math skills have yet to form can use computers.

Some people are fearful of the computing environment. The movies love to portray old-fashioned, large computer systems—sanitized rooms walled by machines alive with blinking lights and spinning reels; it all looks intimidating. There is a notion that computers are temperamental gadgets and that, once a glitch gets into a computer system, it may wreak all kinds of havoc—from fouling up bank statements to launching nuclear missiles by mistake. Indeed, computer billing and banking errors are problems; however, most errors blamed on computers are the result of mistakes made by people. Computers do not put in the data they must work with, people do. Even so, correcting an error can be frustratingly slow.

Many people worry about computers in relation to their jobs. Some people doubt they have the skills to find jobs and keep them in a technological labor market. Many feel that keeping up with the swift pace of technological change is impossible because it requires costly and continuous training and development. A good many present-day executives whose companies have installed computer terminals in their offices also worry about typing—either they do not know how to type or they are afraid they will lose status if they use a keyboard.

Interestingly, there is another side to computer anxiety: the fear of being left out or left behind. If everyone around you is talking about, living with, and working around computers, how can you keep from revealing your limited understanding?

People are also nervous that computers might fall into the wrong hands. As examples of electronic wrongdoing, try these for size: An "error" purposefully introduced into your computerized credit report by someone who wanted to cause you trouble might do irreparable damage to your

P E R S P E C T I V E S

FIGHTING UNSOLICITED MAIL

Computers have led to many paper-saving measures in the workplace. But they have also allowed lists of addresses to be easily compiled, inadvertently encouraging the modern scourge of unsolicited—junk—mail. Many people fed up with this deluge are starting to fight back.

- Henry Keultjes, an Ohio investor, is lobbying Congress and the U.S. Postal Service to create a kind of unlisted address system, similar to the unlisted phone number system used by the telephone companies. He wants the postal service to redesign its plan to build an electronic database of U.S. addresses so that people can request that junk mailers not target them, and he wants to make sure their requests will be honored.

- James Smith, a Connecticut computer professional, has proposed in *ComputerWorld* magazine a fee-paying strategy. Householders can contribute as much data to a direct marketing database as they want, and junk mailers would have to pay them a royalty each time they use it.

- Dorcas Miller, a Maine author, offers useful tips on who to contact in *The Stop Junk Mail Book*. Others have suggested that mail carriers be allowed to dump all their junk mail in one local bin, so people can pick out what they want instead of having it delivered to each house.

- The Direct Marketing Association offers its own service for households that don't want to receive unsolicited mail. At the same time, however, the association criticizes the concept of the sanctity of the mailbox, arguing that to limit mail access could decrease the education and cost savings that marketers offer, as well as limit the many other positive aspects of direct mail.

financial standing, ending any hopes you might have for owning a home someday. An easily obtainable computerized list might carry personal information that could lead to an invasion of your privacy—or, at the least, a pile of junk mail. Think of all the forms you have filled out for schools, jobs, doctors, credit services, government offices, and so on. There is scarcely one fact related to you that is not on record in a computer file somewhere. Could unauthorized persons obtain this information?

Computer fraud and computer security are not simple issues; they are concerns that society must take seriously. Should we, as computer columnist John Dvorak advocates, let things work themselves out in the courts? Or, should legislators be encouraged to create laws for society's protection?

Computer Literacy for All

Fortunately, fewer and fewer people are suffering from computer anxiety. The availability of inexpensive, powerful, and easier-to-use personal computers is reducing the intimidation factor. As new generations grow up in the Information Age, they are perfectly at home with computers.

Join the Majority

How important is it to be computer literate? Very. You know it, educators know it, the general public knows it. Society is heading in the direction of a computer-literate majority. But it was not always so. The average person learned about computers through science-fiction paperbacks and movies like *2001: A Space Odyssey*. He or she may have worried about the disadvantages and failed to see the advantages.

This situation brings to mind the early 1900s, when cars were first introduced. Historians tell us that the reaction to those horseless carriages was much the same as the reaction to computers. Today's traffic crush, however, is a good indication that attitudes changed somewhere along the way.

The analogy fits, because people who refuse to have anything to do with computers may soon be as inconvenienced as people who refuse to learn to drive.

Why are you studying about computers? In addition to curiosity (and perhaps a course requirement!), you probably recognize that it will not be easy to get through the rest of your life without knowing about computers. Let us begin with a definition of **computer literacy** that encompasses three aspects of the computer's universal appeal:

- **Awareness.** Studying about computers will make you more aware of their importance, their versatility, their pervasiveness, and their potential for fostering good and (unfortunately) evil.

- **Knowledge.** Learning what computers are and how they work requires coming to terms with some technical jargon. In the end, you will benefit from such knowledge, but at first it may be frustrating. Don't worry, no one expects you to become a computer expert.

- **Interaction.** There is no better way to understand computers than through interacting with one. So being computer literate also means being able to use a computer for some simple applications. By the end of this course, you should feel comfortable sitting down at a computer and using it for some suitable purpose.

Note that no part of this definition suggests that you must be able to create the instructions that tell a computer what to do. That would be tantamount to saying that anyone who plans to drive a car must first become an auto mechanic. Someone else can write the instructions for the computer; you simply use the instructions to get your work done. For example, a bank teller might use a computer to make sure that customers really have as much money in their account as they wish to withdraw. Or an accountant might use one to prepare a report, a farmer to check on market prices, a store manager to analyze sales trends, and a teenager to play a video game. We cannot guarantee that these people are computer literate, but they have at least grasped the "hands-on" component of the definition—they can interact with a computer.

The Haves and the Have-Nots

Is it possible for everyone to be computer literate? Computer literacy is not a question of human abilities. Just about anyone can become computer literate. The question of literacy may relate more closely to school budgets than personal talent. Consider the debate about the "haves" and the "have-nots."

Computer experts, social commentators, and even politicians see a future divided between the haves, who are information-rich, and the have-nots, who are information-poor. The source of that information, of course, is the computer. Some have even suggested that, in the near future, people who do not understand computers will have the same status as people today who cannot read. There is a growing chasm between the rich and the poor because children who grow up with advantages have better access to computers. These children live in school districts that have the money to promote computers and computer literacy. In addition, they may have access to computers at home. Children in poorer areas, how-

Literacy Skill Number 1: Typing

Any number of ways exist to communicate with computers: typing on a keyboard, pointing with a handheld device, touching the screen, or speaking directly into a microphone. For the disabled there are special devices for entering information. For those who prefer to write by hand, specialized tablets called pen systems are available.

For most computer users, typing remains the first computer literacy skill they need. Those who do not know how to type would do well to learn by taking a typing course. Ironically, the computer itself can also be your typing teacher—typing lessons are one of the many computer applications.

ever, may never have the opportunity to deal with computers as part of their education. And so another social gap is defined at an early age.

Several politicians have proposed to alter the social equation by providing federal funds for computers in schools. Other efforts have been made by the computer manufacturers. For example, IBM recently provided millions of dollars' worth of computers and other equipment to schools and colleges through its IBM Partnership Program. Apple Computer has given away thousands of computers to schools through a cooperative tie-in with Safeway Stores, Inc. Apple provides free computers in exchange for grocery store receipts collected by students, parents, and teachers. There are many other efforts under way throughout the world, but the problem of unequal access to computers remains worrisome.

So Here You Are in a Computer Class

If this is your first computer class, you might wonder whether using a computer is really as easy as the commercials say. Some students think so, but many do not. In fact, some novice computer users can be confused and frustrated at first. Indeed, a few are so frustrated in the early going they think they never will learn. To their surprise, however, after a couple of lessons they not only are using computers but enjoying the experience.

Some students may be taken aback when the subject matter turns out to be more difficult than they expected—especially if their only computer experience involved the fun of video games. They are confused by the special terms used in computer classes, as if they had stumbled into some foreign-language course by mistake. A few students may be frustrated by the hands-on nature of the experience, in which they have a one-to-one relationship with the computer. Their previous learning experiences, in contrast, have been shared and sheltered—they have been shared with peers in a classroom and sheltered by the guiding hand of an experienced person. Now they are faced with a first: They are one-on-one with a machine, at least part of the time. The experience is different, and maybe slightly scary. But keep in mind that others have survived and even triumphed. So can you.

And don't be surprised to find that some of your fellow students already seem to know quite a bit about computers. As in many areas, some people learn to speak a better game than they play; in other words, some who have been raised in computer-literate environments may have learned the vocabulary without learning much more. Computer literacy courses are required by many schools and colleges and include students with varying degrees of understanding. That mix often allows students to learn from one another—and provides a few with the opportunity to teach others what they know.

Since part of the challenge of computer literacy is awareness, let us now look at what makes computers worthy of our efforts. Let us turn to the various ways computers can be useful. Then we will turn to the various ways they are used.

Figure 3 Service means speed. The speed of a computer helps provide the fast service that customers expect.

Everywhere You Turn

Everywhere you turn nowadays computers are at work—in stores, cars, homes, offices, hospitals, banks, theaters, and even coffee shops. To understand their prevalence in society, we must first look at the traits that make computers so useful.

The Nature of Computers

Human beings are workers, but they also need rest. The computer is a worker that needs no rest whatsoever. Computers can work 24 hours a day. In fact, it is said that the on-off switch on a computer is more likely to wear out than the computer itself; most computers are replaced because they become outmoded, not because they break down.

Humans also get bored with repetitious activities—but not computers. We demand coffee breaks and salary raises; computers do the job exactly the same every time without letup; they will do the ten-thousandth task exactly the way they did the first—and without a break or complaint.

There are three key factors that determine why the computer has become such an indispensable part of our lives:

- **Speed.** Computers provide the processing speed essential to our fast-paced society. We grow restless over long waits for service, becoming temperamental when our expectations are not met. In fact, such quick service has been made possible by computers. A return to the days of long lines and wearisome waits would be most aggravating. When we see television reports about long lines in foreign countries, we wonder how the citizens put up with the situation. We depend on the split-second processing computers provide to handle the large amounts of data involved in handling our paychecks, grades, telephone calls, travel reservations, bank balances, and so many other things (Figure 3).

- **Reliability.** Computers are extremely reliable. Of course, you might not think this from some of the stories you may have seen in the press about "computer errors." What is seldom brought out in those stories is the human side of the mistakes. True, there are times when the electricity fails or the equipment breaks; however, most errors supposedly made by computers are really a person's mistakes. Although one hears the phrase "computer error" quite frequently, the blame usually lies elsewhere.

- **Storage capability.** Computer systems can store tremendous amounts of data—efficiently sorting, finding, and retrieving at lightning speed. The capability to store volumes of data is especially important in an information age.

  These three—speed, reliability, and storage capability—are fundamental characteristics of computers. But there are by-products of computers that are just as important. Consider these three:

- **Productivity.** Computers can increase productivity, especially where dangerous, boring, or routine tasks are involved. Jobs like punching holes in metal or monitoring water levels can be more capably performed by computer. Labor unions that once considered computers a threat, today manage their offices with them; they recognize that, although computers may eliminate some jobs, they also free workers for jobs more suited to human capabilities. Think about what it would mean if we abolished computers from the workplace entirely: We would have to hire millions of workers to do very tedious tasks with little compensation. When computers move into business offices, for example, the first hoped-for change is increasing productivity, as workers learn to use computers to do their jobs better and faster (but many argue that this is not what happens).

- **Decision making.** Because of the huge amounts of information created by our expanding technology and communications capabilities, we suffer from an information explosion. Since the computer is mainly responsible for the problem, its powers should be enlisted to solve it. To make essential business and governmental decisions, managers need to take into account a large variety of financial, geographical, logistical, and other factors. Using problem-solving techniques originally developed by humans, the computer helps decision makers sort things out, analyze the implications, and make better choices.

- **Cost reduction.** Finally, because it improves productivity and aids decision making, the computer helps us eliminate wasteful practices and hold down the costs of labor, energy, and paperwork. As a result, computers help reduce the costs of goods and services in our economy. Take the airline industry, for example: Without computers for reservations, scheduling, traffic control, check-in, seating, and so many other tasks, the price of a ticket to ride might be ten times what it is today.

With so many wonderful traits, it is not hard to see why computers have moved so quickly into every facet of our lives. Next we look at some of the ways we use them to make the workday more productive and our personal lives more rewarding.

Where Computers Are Used

Computers can do just about anything imaginable, but they really excel in certain areas. This section lists some of the principal areas of computer use.

- **Graphics.** One of the most important areas of computer use is the field of graphics. Computer graphics help us envision change. Computers can show how a city's skyline would look with the addition of a new skyscraper. In the field of medicine, brain-scan computers produce color-enhanced maps to help diagnose mental illness. Biochemists use computers to examine, in three dimensions, the structure of molecules. Architects use computer-animated graphics to experiment with possible exteriors, to give clients a visual walk-through of proposed

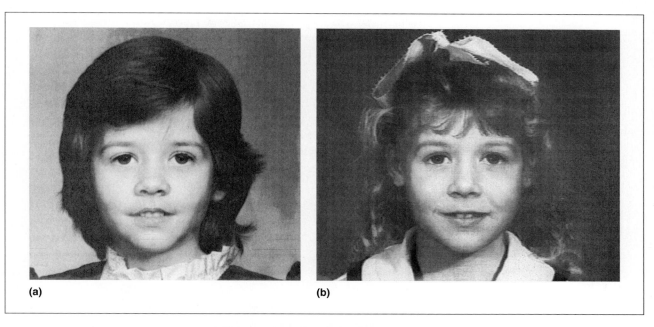

(a)   (b)

Figure 4 Computers continue the hunt. Image-enhancing computer programs can help searchers locate missing children years after their disappearance. (a) Parents can usually provide a recent photo to aid law enforcement officials at the time of the child's disappearance. (b) With computer enhancement, the photo can be "aged" to show how the child might look years later as the search continues.

buildings, and to subject buildings to hypothetical earthquakes. When missing children cannot be found for months or years, computers are called upon to enhance their photos and show us how they might look today, giving searchers a better chance of locating them (Figure 4).

Business executives can utilize computer graphics too, by making bar graphs and pie charts out of tedious figures and using color to convey information with far more impact than numbers alone can do. They can even add a fourth dimension, time, by following the rise and fall of these three-dimensional bars across the years.

Finally, a whole new kind of artist has emerged who uses computers to create cartoon animation, landscapes, television logos, and still lifes (Figure 5).

- **Commerce.** Products from meats to magazines are packaged with zebra-striped bar codes that can be read by scanners at supermarket checkout stands to determine prices. The stripes on each product represent the product's Universal Product Code. The code system is one of the more highly visible uses of computers in commerce; however, there are numerous others. Modern-day warehousing and inventory management could not exist without computers. Take your copy of this book, for instance. From printer to warehouse to bookstore, its movement was tracked with the help of computers and the bar code on the back cover.

- **Energy.** Energy companies use computers to locate oil, coal, natural gas, and uranium. Electric companies use computers to monitor vast power networks. In addition, meter readers use handheld computers

Figure 5 Computer-generated art. Computers give artists a new creative tool.

to record how much energy is used each month in homes and businesses.

- **Transportation.** Computers are used to help run rapid transit systems, load containerships, track railroad cars across the country, safeguard airport takeoffs and landings, monitor air traffic, and schedule travel. They are also used in cars and motorcycles to monitor fluid levels, temperatures, and electrical systems and even improve fuel mileage.

- **Paperwork.** One of the early promises of computers was the so-called paperless society: Newspapers and magazines would leave paper consumption behind and move to electronic editions. But our society still depends on paper—and probably will for decades to come. In some ways the computer contributes to paper use by adding to the amount of junk mail you find in your mailbox. However, in many ways it cuts down on paper handling. Take, for instance, the number of drafts you might go through in creating a term paper. Using a computer and word processing, for example, you might type and edit two or three on-screen drafts before printing anything. Instead of a trash can filled with scraps of draft copies, you print only the final version of your paper. Computerized bookkeeping, record keeping, and document sending have also made paperwork more efficient.

- **Money.** Computers have revolutionized the way we handle money. Once upon a time it was possible to write a check for the rent on Tuesday and cover it with a deposit on Thursday, knowing it would take a few days for the bank to process everything. Not anymore. Computers speed up record keeping and allow banks to offer same-day services, do-it-yourself banking over the phone, and remote transactions via automated teller machines (ATMs). Computers have helped fuel the cashless economy, enabling the widespread use of credit cards and

Computers as Toll Collectors

State officials are trying out new ways of collecting tolls to speed up traffic and cut down air pollution. Although at first this may appear to be great for the environment, some people believe such systems may take a new toll on privacy.

The new systems require that drivers purchase tags that can be checked by a computerized toll system. The tags, placed in a position on the car that can be detected by the computer, allow the cars to pass through the toll plaza without stopping. The computer reads the ID number on the tag and then, at the end of the month, bills the driver for the tolls.

Texas, Louisiana, and Oklahoma currently have such systems in place; California, New Jersey, New York, Pennsylvania, and other states are considering installing them. Advocates say these computer-based systems cut down on traffic and smog because cars do not have to stop. But opponents say the systems could be used to track citizens and monitor their whereabouts. "They'll know when you've gone, and which way you're traveling," said Chris Hibbert, a member of Computer Professionals for Social Responsibility.

A maker of such systems, Amtech of Dallas, Texas, denies such charges, claiming that the systems are optional and that drivers can still choose to pay the toll by hand. However, that choice may cost more. Oklahoma, for example, charges drivers who do not have a tag 25 to 30% more.

instantaneous credit checks by banks, department stores, and other retailers. Some banks now provide ATM card receptacles at the teller's window inside the bank; this allows your name and account information to be recorded automatically so the teller does not have to type it in (thus eliminating possible typing errors). Some oil companies even use credit-card activated, self-service gasoline pumps.

- **Agriculture.** It is no longer low tech down on the farm. Farmers now use small computers—purchased for less than the price of a tractor—to help with billing, crop information, cost per acre, feed combinations, and market price checks. A Mississippi cotton grower, for example, boosted his annual profit 50% by using a computer to determine the best time to fertilize. Cattle ranchers can also use computers for information about livestock breeding and performance. Furthermore, sheep can be sheared by a computerized robotic shearing arm. The arm is guided by sensors and computer memory, which stores the dimensions of a typical sheep. In addition, computers can give people the option of working at home instead of in city offices. The result could lessen the isolation of country living and perhaps even stem the movement of youth from farms to cities.

- **Government.** The largest single user of computers is the federal government. As one bureaucrat put it, the only way you can survive in the government is to learn to use computers. The Social Security Administration, for example, produces more than 36 million benefit checks a month with the help of computers. Computers are also used for forecasting weather (Figure 6), for servicing parks, for processing immigrants, for meting out justice, and—of course—for collecting

Figure 6 When will the storm get here? To improve the science of weather forecasting, researchers program various weather conditions into a computerized global weather model. They can then see what kind of weather develops from those conditions.

Personal Computers in Action

VIRTUAL REALITY: STRAP ON SOME EYEPHONES AND YOU ARE VIRTUALLY THERE

One of the most exciting new areas of computer research is *virtual reality.* Having been featured in TV sitcoms as well as public television documentaries, virtual reality is merely an ambitious new style of computer interface. Virtual reality creates the illusion of being in an artificial world—one created by computers.

Virtual reality visitors strap on a set of eyephones, 3-D goggles that are really individual computer screens for the eyes. Slipping on the rest of the gear allows you not only to see and hear, but also to sense your voyage. The world of virtual reality has been called *cyberspace,* a computer-enhanced fantasy world in which you move around and manipulate objects to your mind's content.

When you move your head, magnetic sensors instruct the computer to refocus your eyephones to your new viewpoint. Sounds surround you, and a fiber-optic glove allows you to "manipulate" what you see. You may seek out strange new worlds, fight monsters in computer combat, or strap yourself into the seat of a *Star Wars*–type jet and scream through cyberspace, blasting all comers to oblivion (computer oblivion, at least). Or, with your stomach appropriately settled, you might even try out the most incredible roller coaster ride you will ever take in your life.

For the disabled, virtual reality promises a new form of freedom. Consider the wheelchair-bound paraplegic child who is suddenly able to use virtual reality gear to take part in games like baseball or

basketball. Research funded by the government takes a military point of view, investigating the possibility of sending robots into the real conflict while human beings don cyberspace gear to guide them from back in the lab.

Spectrum Holobyte, a computer games development company, announced its first virtual reality computer game for the home during the 1991 Christmas season. Imagine yourself suddenly clutching your hand-held laser pistol as a giant bird swoops right at you from the age of dinosaurs! Your laser shot goes astray, and you feel yourself suddenly lifted off the ground and carried higher and higher. That's enough—for some of us it can be virtually too real.

taxes. The FBI keeps track of suspected criminals, compiling separate bits of information into elaborate dossiers; these have already helped put several organized crime lords behind bars. Of the millions of veterans alive today, any one can walk into a local Veterans Administration office and immediately get a rundown on his or her benefits. During drought years in California, state officials keep track of the amount of snow in the Sierra Nevada Range during the winter, then use computers to predict how much water will be available during the rest of the year, allowing cities to set water-use limits.

- **Education.** Computers have been used behind the scenes for years in colleges and school districts for record keeping and accounting. Many

Figure 7   Cold virus. This computer-produced model of the cold virus culprit named HRV14 raises hopes that a cure for the common cold may be possible after all. With the aid of a computer, the final set of calculations for the model took one month to complete. Researchers estimate that without the computer the calculations might have required ten years of manual effort.

colleges have eliminated long registration lines by using computerized, touch-tone telephone registration. Most schools in the U.S. have computers available for use in the classroom, and some colleges require entering freshman to bring their own. Educators who once considered computers a novelty in the classroom now look at them as necessities. Parents want to be sure that their children are not left behind in the computer age, so the pressure is on school districts to acquire computers and train teachers and students in their use.

- **The home.** Are you willing to welcome a computer into your home? Many people already have, often justifying it as an educational tool for their children. But that is only the beginning. Personal computers are being used at home to keep records, write letters, prepare budgets, draw pictures, prepare newsletters, and connect with other computers and information services like Prodigy and CompuServe via the telephone. The more adventurous use computers to control heating and air conditioning, answer telephone calls, safeguard the house during vacations, and so on. Whether you *need* a home computer remains open to debate, but there is no question that it can make your life easier and more entertaining. Sometimes others bring the computer into your home with them: The United Parcel Service asks you to sign a computerized signature pad when you accept delivery.

- **Health and medicine.** Computers have been used on the business side of medicine for some time. Today they can be the difference between life and death in hospitals and medical centers. Computers help monitor the gravely ill in intensive care units and provide cross-sectional views of the body through ultrasound pictures. Huge amounts of data and processing power are sometimes required to make even the smallest progress in fighting deadly diseases. Recent progress in using computers to test antidotes for various diseases, such as AIDS, have helped save or extend lives that otherwise may have been lost. Physicians can also use computers to identify likely diagnoses. In fact, computers have been shown to correctly diagnose heart attacks more frequently than physicians. If you are one of the thousands who suffer one miserable cold after another, you will be happy to know that computers have been able to map, in exquisite atomic detail, the structure of the human cold virus—the first step toward a cure for the common cold (Figure 7). Computers are also being used for health maintenance, in everything from weight-loss programs to recording heart rates and blood pressure.

- **Robotics.** Computers have paved the way for robots to take over many of the jobs that place human life at risk. These robots are performing tasks too unpleasant, too dangerous, or too critical for humans. Examples include robots that enter areas considered dangerous because of terrorist threats, and robots that open packages believed to contain bombs. Cost-sensitive jobs are also targeted for robots. Pattern-cutting robots in the garment business, for instance, are able to get the most apparel out of bolts of cloth. Robots are used for military purposes when they perform underwater missions to search out mines,

Figure 8 Dainty touch. Robots can be programmed to have just the right touch.

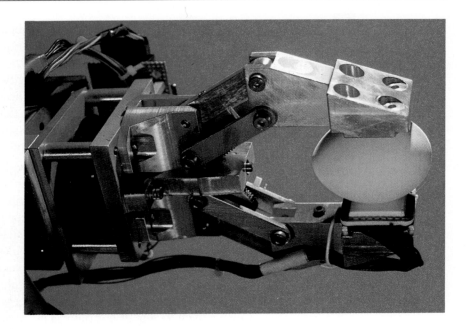

handle surveillance for installations, and do pin-point targeting. Robots can also be used for delicate jobs such as picking fruit, not to mention handling eggs and bananas (Figure 8). Robots are also used to patrol jail corridors at night and report any persons encountered. Especially controversial are the robots that do tedious jobs better than humans do—jobs such as welding or paint spraying in new-car plants. Clearly, these robots have eliminated many jobs for factory workers—a troublesome social problem. Robots are another sign that the Information Age is upon us.

- **The sciences.** For decades scientific research has benefited from the high-speed, massive compilation capabilities of computers. Computers can simulate environments, emulate physical characteristics, and generally allow us to replicate studies and provide proofs in a cost-effective manner. Consider experimentation on animals, that mainstay of scientific research. Many monkeys, mice, cats, and dogs have been spared since computers have been added to the equation. For example, the Food and Drug Administration now has a computer programmed to simulate the reaction of a mouse's digestive system to poisons. Computers are also used to generate models of DNA, the molecule that houses the genetic instructions that determine the specific characteristics of organisms (Figure 9). To test experimental airplanes, aerospace engineers use computers to simulate wind tunnel experiments. In England, researchers have used computers to invent a "bionic nose" that can sniff out subtle differences in fragrances—an invention that could have major benefits for the food, perfume, and distilling industries. On another front entirely, the National Aeronautics and Space Administration has developed a computerized system for use in Arecibo, Puerto Rico, to scan the heavens and listen in on eight million narrow-band radio frequencies in an attempt to find signs of communication from alien beings in outer space. (So far, no messages.)

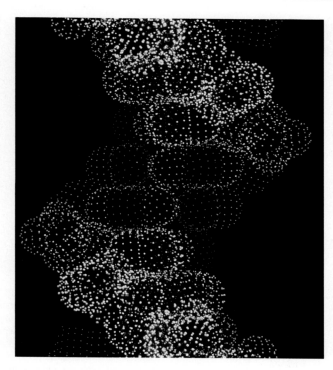

Figure 9   Computer generated model of DNA. Computers are helping scientists to generate models of complex molecules such as DNA, the molecule that determines our genetic makeup.

- **Training.** Computers are being used as training devices in industry and government. It is much cheaper, for instance, to teach aspiring pilots to fly in computerized training "cockpits," or simulators, than in real airplanes. Novice railroad engineers can also be given the experience of running a train with the help of a computerized device. Training simulations are relatively inexpensive and always available on a one-to-one basis, making for very personal learning. Computerized, interactive training gives a new dimension to simulations, allowing the use of full-motion video to put live participants in situations that can be changed quickly.

- **The human connection.** Are computers cold and impersonal? The disabled do not believe it for a moment. Liz Vantrease of Richmond, Virginia, lost the use of her limbs to ALS, or Lou Gehrig's disease. Using a personal computer, she has written an opera, *Liz,* that has been performed at the Virginia Commonwealth University Performance Arts Center (Figure 10). André Alm, paralyzed from his neck down because of an accident, is currently designing a Smart House System for the Swedish company Electrolux. Alm is using computers in his work to allow the disabled to live and work independently. Can the disabled walk again? Some can, with the help of computers. Can dancers and athletes improve their performance? Maybe they can, by using computers to monitor their movements. Can we learn more about our ethnic backgrounds and our cultural history with the aid of computers? Indeed we can.

Figure 10 Opera composer. Stricken with a disease that left her unable to manipulate her limbs, Liz Vantrease put her music skills to work with a personal computer and wrote an opera. Says Liz, "Without my computer, I'd be in a lonely, silent, boring world. Three scenes of my opera, a suite for piano, and a piece for flutes wouldn't exist—because I wouldn't have been able to write them down. Because ALS . . . impairs my speech, I communicate by typing messages on my computer to friends, family, doctors, and my computer bulletin board pals. . . . In short, my computer and modem give me a window to the world into which my feeble legs and arms can no longer carry me."

We hope this discussion has stimulated your interest in computers. For more examples of how computers are used in our lives, see Gallery 2, "Computers Around Us."

 ## *Toward Computer Literacy*

Living in the nineties means living with computers all around us. You have been exposed to computer hype, computer advertisements and discussions, and magazine articles and newspaper headlines about computers. You have interacted with computers in your everyday life—at the grocery store, your school, the library, and more. You know more than you think you do. The beginnings of computer literacy are already apparent.

We have written this book with two kinds of readers in mind. If you are contemplating a computer-related career, you will find a solid discussion of technology, computer applications, and various jobs associated with computers. Even if you are not interested in the technical side of computers, however, most careers involve computers in some way; this book will provide you with a foundation in computer literacy. For if the computer is to help us rather than confound us or threaten us, we must assume some responsibility for understanding it.

The Information Age is still in its infancy and will continue to grow during our lifetimes. Throughout the rest of this book, we will describe its implications in terms of the tasks we must learn.

R E V I E W   A N D   R E F E R E N C E

Summary and Key Terms

- Computers are making life easier and better; most people are optimistic about computers and their place in society.

- Like the Industrial Age, the Information Age is causing massive changes in society. However, changes are occurring more quickly in our time—mainly due to the computer.

- The traditional cornerstones of our economy are land, labor, capital, and entrepreneurship. The Information Age adds a fifth cornerstone, information, to support our move from an industry-based toa computer-based society.

- Personal computers are used in the home and in business for a variety of purposes.

- Some people suffer from **computer anxiety, computer phobia,** or **cyberphobia**—fear of computers. Some people feel intimidated by computers; others fear computer errors, invasion of privacy, job loss or change, and depersonalization.

- **Computer literacy** includes (1) an awareness of computers, (2) knowledge about computers, and (3) interaction with computers. To use a computer, however, you do not need to be able to write the instructions that tell a computer what to do.

- Some experts believe that, unless all students have equal access to computers, the gap between the haves and the have-nots will widen. Major efforts for funding computers in schools and colleges are under way.

- Three key characteristics that make computers an indispensable part of our lives are speed, reliability, and storage capacity. By-products of these characteristics include productivity, decision making, and cost reduction.

- Computers are used in many areas, including graphics, commerce, energy, transportation, paperwork, money, agriculture, govern-ment, education, the home, health and medicine, robotics, the sciences, training, and helping people lead more satisfying lives.

Review Questions

1. In what ways are the Industrial Age and the Information Age similar? In what ways are they different?
2. What are the five cornerstones of the Information Age economy?
3. List four uses of personal computers in the home.
4. List four uses of personal computers in business.
5. What are some fears people have about computers?
6. Name two reasons why computer anxiety will probably decline.
7. What are the three components of computer literacy?
8. List three characteristics that make computers indispensable.
9. Name one use of computers in each of the following areas: graph-ics, commerce, energy, transportation, paperwork, money, agriculture, government, education, the home, health and medicine, robotics, the sciences, and training.
10. Provide an example of how the disabled may benefit from computer use.

Discussion Questions

1. Do you believe that computers make life easier and better? Ex-plain.
2. Do you feel any discomfort or anxiety about computers? Explain why or why not.
3. Why are you taking this class? What do you expect to learn from this class?
4. How do you see society changing—in your daily life—through the use of computers?

True-False Questions

T F 1. Computers are just a fad like spiked hair and Teenage Mutant Ninja Turtles.

T F 2. One difference between the Industrial and Information ages is the speed of the accompanying changes.

T F 3. As the Information Age takes hold, more and more workers will shift from jobs requiring muscle power to jobs requiring mental power.

T F 4. Computers are only used by professors, engineers, and scientists.

T F 5. Cyberphobia is a virus that is passed to people and breaks machines.

T F 6. Computers have had a significant impact on cutting down on junk mail.

T F 7. To be considered computer literate, you need to create the instructions that tell a computer what to do.

T F 8. For most of us, learning to use a computer is harder than learning to drive a car, because we grew up with cars, not computers.

T F 9. The speed of a computer makes it ideal for processing large amounts of data.

T F 10. Most parents and teachers feel that computers are a novelty in schools and only really useful for administrative purposes such as tracking student grades and enrollment.

HARDWARE TOOLS

Overview of a Computer System

Hardware, Software, and People

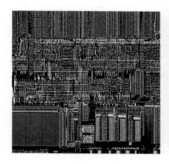   

Reggie decided to buy his first personal computer. At the store, the sales-clerk smiled and asked about Reggie's needs. "I want a personal computer for my home," he replied. "I use one at work to handle orders and letters and stuff. What do you recommend?" The salesperson showed him a computer that looked like the one Reggie used at work. Reggie listened politely to a torrent of terms he did not understand. Then he heard about extras he would need—pieces he had never heard of. Reggie thought all he wanted was a basic machine. But he slowly learned otherwise and saw the price of the machine rise from a few hundred to a few thousand dollars. Reggie left the store without buying; he vowed to learn a lot more before returning.

Reggie's plight is typical of a first-time computer buyer. A personal computer is not an appliance like a toaster. When you make toast, you simply pop a piece of bread into the toaster, wait a minute—and up it pops, ready to eat. Can you imagine a computer as easy to learn to use as a toaster? Computer manufacturers are very serious about making their computers easy to understand, and some of them refer to toasters only partly in jest. In the last few years computers *have* become easier to use, but they are still a long way from being like toasters. There is another comparison that is closer—learning to drive a car. You need training to understand what makes up a car and how to drive it safely. You also need some training to understand and use a computer. As in learning to drive, the average person can learn to use a computer quite readily. It just takes a little explaining and some practical experience. That is what this first chapter is for—to introduce you to the basics so you will be better prepared to sit down "behind the wheel" and learn how to use a computer. Even if you are already somewhat familiar with computers, you will probably pick up some new information as you read this chapter.

 ## The Beginning of What You Need to Know

Essentially, a computer is a system. The purpose of the system is to turn unprocessed data into usable information. This requires four main aspects of data handling: input, processing, output, and storage. Computers as systems have three main components: hardware, software, and people. The equipment associated with a computer system is called **hardware.** A set of instructions called **software** tells the hardware what to do. People, however, are the most important component of a computer system—people apply the powers of the computer for a purpose.

The term **packaged software** refers to software that is literally packaged and sold in stores. Most packaged software is **application software,** software that is *applied*—or put to use—to solve particular problems. There is a great assortment of software to help with a variety of tasks: writing papers, preparing budgets, drawing graphs, playing games, and so forth. The wonderful array of software available is what makes computers so useful.

Software is also referred to as programs. To be more specific, a **program** is a set of step-by-step instructions that directs the computer to do the tasks you want it to do and produce the results you want. A **computer programmer** is a person who writes programs. Most of us do not write programs—we *use* programs written by someone else. This means we are **users**—people who purchase and use computer software. In business, users are often called **end-users** because they are at the end of the "computer line," actually making use of the computer's information. We will emphasize the connection between computers and computer users throughout this chapter and, indeed, throughout this book.

In this chapter, we will first examine hardware, followed by software, and then data. We will consider how these components work together to produce information. Finally, we will devote a separate section to computers and people. As the title of this chapter indicates, what follows is an overview, a look at the "big picture" of a computer system. Then we can zoom in on deeper concerns. Thus, many of the terms introduced in this chapter are defined only briefly here. In subsequent chapters, we will discuss the various parts of a computer system in greater detail.

 ## Hardware: *Meeting the Machine*

What is a computer, anyway? A six-year-old called a computer "radio, movies, and television combined!" A ten-year-old described a computer as "a television set you can talk to." That is closer but still does not recognize the computer as a machine that has the power to make changes. A **computer** is a machine that can be programmed to accept data (**input**), process it into useful information (**output**), and store it away (in a secondary storage device) for safekeeping or later reuse. The processing is directed by the software, but performed by the hardware, which we will examine in this section.

To function, a computer system requires four main aspects of data handling: input, processing, output, and storage (Figure 1-1). The hardware responsible for these four areas operates as follows:

- **Input devices** accept data in a form that the computer can use; they then send the data to the processing unit.

- The **processor,** more formally known as the **central processing unit** (**CPU**), has the electronic circuitry that manipulates input data into the information wanted. The central processing unit actually executes computer instructions.

- **Output devices** show people the processed data—information—in a form they can use easily.

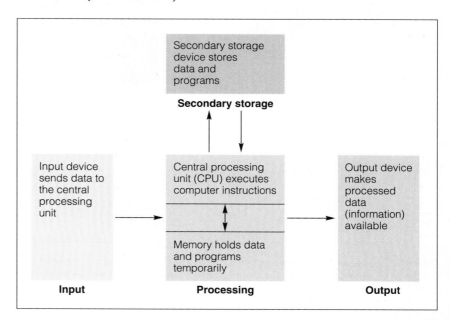

Figure 1-1 Four primary components of a computer system. To function, a computer system requires input, processing, output, and storage.

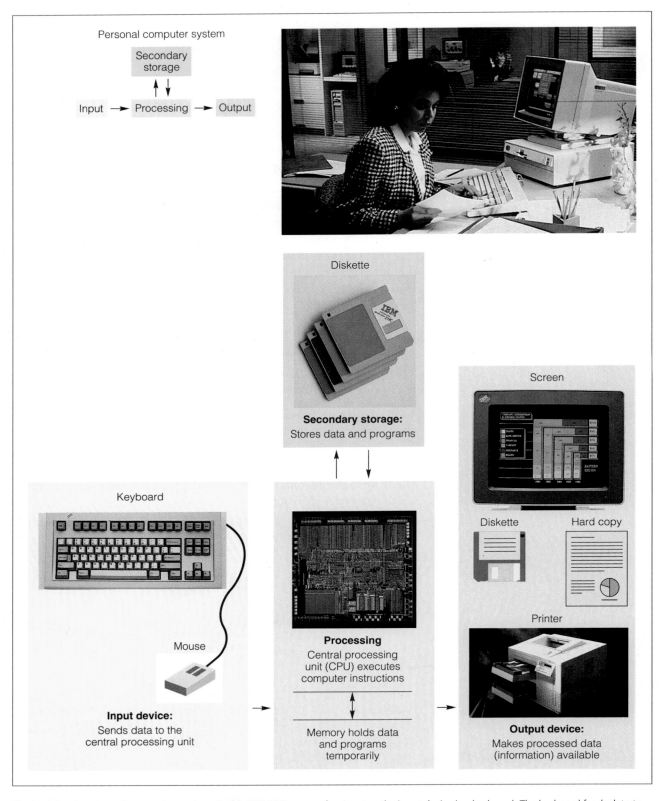

Figure 1-2   A personal computer system. In this IBM PS/2 personal computer, the input device is a keyboard. The keyboard feeds data to the central processing unit, which is inside the computer housing. The central processing unit is an array of electronic circuitry on pieces of silicon. The two output devices in this example are the screen and the printer. The secondary storage device is a 3½-inch disk. These four components of the system operate together to make the computer work for you.

- Storage is usually associated with memory. **Memory** connected to the central processing unit is used to hold temporarily the data and instructions (programs) that the central processing unit needs. This memory is often referred to as **primary storage.** Another kind of storage, **secondary storage,** consists of **secondary storage devices,** which can store additional data and programs. These devices supplement the primary storage memory in ways that will be explained later.

Now let us consider the equipment related to these four aspects of data handling in terms of what you would find on a personal computer.

Your Personal Computer Hardware

Suppose you want to do word processing on a personal computer, using the hardware shown in Figure 1-2. Word processing software allows you to input data such as an essay, save it, revise and resave it, and print it whenever you wish. The *input* device, in this case, is a keyboard, which you use to type in, or key in, the original essay and any changes you want to make to it. All computers, large and small, must have a *central processing unit,* so yours does too—it is within the personal computer housing. The central processing unit uses the word processing software to accept the data you input through the keyboard. Processed data from your personal computer is usually *output* in two forms: on a screen and by a printer. As you key in the essay on the keyboard, it appears on the screen in front of you. After you examine the essay on the screen, make changes, and determine that it is acceptable, you can print the essay on the printer. Your *secondary storage device* is a diskette, a magnetic medium that stores the essay until it is needed again.

Now we will take a general tour of the hardware needed for input, processing, output, and storage. These same components make up all computer systems, whether small, medium, or large. In this discussion we will try to emphasize the types of hardware you are likely to have seen in your own environment. These topics will be covered in detail in Chapters 2, 3, and 4.

Input: What Goes In

Input is the data that you put into the computer system for processing. Some of the most common ways of feeding input data into the system are by:

- *Typing* on a **keyboard** (Figure 1-3a). Computer keyboards operate in much the same way as electric typewriter keyboards. The computer responds to what you enter; that is, it "echoes" what you type by displaying it on the screen in front of you.

- *Pointing* with a **mouse** (Figure 1-3a). A mouse is a device that is moved by hand over a flat surface. As the ball on its underside rotates, the mouse movement causes corresponding movement of a pointer on the computer screen. Pressing buttons on the mouse lets you invoke commands.

(a)

(b)

Desktop MIKE™
*Our unidirectional
microphone looks as
good as it sounds, and
eliminates distracting
background noise.*

Power
Switch

SCSI
Termination
Switch   2.5 mm
            and 3.5 mm   LED
            Mic Jacks   indicators

(c)

(d)

Figure 1-3   Input devices. (a) The keyboard is the most widely used input device, though the mouse has become increasingly popular as use of Microsoft® Windows™ and the Macintosh graphical operating system have increased. Movement of the mouse on a flat surface causes corresponding movement on the screen. (b) Pen systems allow data to be input by writing on a tablet or pad. (c) Voice input systems recognize spoken words as computer input. (d) Scanners can input text and pictures quickly, bypassing the possible introduction of errors by human typists.

- *Writing* with a **pen-based computer** system on a tablet or on a flat pad (Figure 1-3b). You can use print or script, depending on how the system is preset to read your writing. The letters you create are displayed on the screen in a manner similar to keyboard input—without your having to type.

- *Speaking* through a microphone to a **voice input** system (Figure 1-3c). With some voice input systems, also called **speech recognition** systems, it is necessary for the computer to be "trained" to understand a specific voice. In addition, to cut down on the amount of processing involved, speech recognition systems limit the context in which words can be used. Thus, a voice input accounting program would interpret the word "bill" as it relates to an invoice, rather than as a name, a bird's beak, and so forth.

- *Scanning* with a number of input devices. The **wand reader** and **bar code reader** use laser beams to read special letters, numbers, or symbols such as the zebra-striped bar codes on many products. A handheld, flatbed, or overhead **scanner** (Figure 1-3d) can be used to capture photos, art, and text for transfer into digital form for use by your computer. Scanners read data directly from an original document, significantly reducing the cost and potential error associated with manually entering data (for example, from a keyboard). An overhead scanner is used with objects (such as marbles) to provide a 3-D view.

An input device may be part of a **terminal** that is connected to a large computer. A terminal includes (1) an input device (a keyboard, mouse, or wand reader, for instance), (2) an output device (usually a television-like **screen**), and (3) a connection to the main computer. The screen displays what has been input, and, after the computer processes this data, the screen displays the results of the processing—the information wanted.

The Processor and Memory: Data Manipulation

In a computer, the **processor** is the center of activity. The processor, as we noted, is also called the **central processing unit,** or **CPU.** The central processing unit consists of electronic circuits that interpret and execute program instructions, as well as communicate with the input, output, and storage devices.

It is the central processing unit that actually transforms data into information. **Data** is the raw material to be processed by a computer. Such material can be letters, numbers, or facts—such as grades in a class, baseball batting averages, or light and dark areas in a photograph. Processed data becomes **information**—data that is organized, meaningful, and useful. In school, for instance, an instructor enters student grades for each assignment (the data), then obtains final grades, class average, as well as a grading curve (the desired information). Data that is very uninteresting to one person may become very interesting information to another. The raw facts of births, eating habits, and growth rates of calves, for instance, may mean nothing to most people. But the computer-produced relationships among feed, growth, and beef quality are critical information to a cattle breeder.

Computer **memory,** also known as **primary storage,** is closely associated with the central processing unit but separate from it. Memory holds the data after it is input to the system and before it is processed; also, memory holds the data after it has been processed but before it has been released to the output device. In addition, memory holds the programs (computer instructions) needed by the central processing unit. Memory consists of electronic circuits, just as the CPU does. Memory electronically stores letters, numbers, and special characters such as dollar signs and decimal points. Computer memory can even store images and sound in digitized form. Turning on a personal computer activates its memory; turning it off causes anything stored in memory to disappear—thus the need for secondary storage devices for long-term storage.

The central processing unit and memory are usually contained in a cabinet or housing. In the past the cabinets of large computers also contained the computer **console**—a panel of switches and dials, colored buttons, and winking lights that has inspired the control rooms of so many Hollywood-built spaceships. Through the console, the computer system could signal the operator when something needed to be done—for example, when the printer needed to be resupplied with paper. Modern computers are less likely to have dials and lights; operators can communicate with the computer system by using a console terminal. For example, the operator can use the console terminal to determine which programs the system is executing.

Output: What Comes Out

Output, the result produced by the central processing unit is, of course, a computer's whole reason for being. **Output** is usable information—that is, raw input data that has been processed by the computer into information. The most common forms are words, numbers, and graphics. Word output, for example, may be the letters and memos prepared by office people using word processing software. Other workers may be more interested in numbers, such as those found in formulas, schedules, and budgets. In many cases numbers can be understood more easily when output in the form of charts and graphics.

The most common output devices are screens and printers. Others include overhead projectors; plotters; speakers (for sound); and special electronic devices for engineering, research, and other purposes—including specialized medicine. **Screens** can vary in their forms of display. Some may produce lines of written or numeric display only; others may display everything—text, symbols, art, photographs, and even video—in full color (Figure 1-4a).

Printers are machines that produce printed reports at the instruction of a computer program (Figure 1-4b). Some printers form images on paper as typewriters do; they strike a character against a ribbon, which makes an image on the paper. Other printers use lasers, photography, or ink spray. In these types of printers, there is no physical contact between the printer and the paper where the images are being formed. Although originally the reserve of plotters, color printing nowadays can be done by printers that strike the image area and those that do not.

Secondary Storage

Secondary storage provides additional storage separate from the central processing unit and memory. Secondary storage has several advantages. For instance, it would be unwise for a college registrar to try to keep the grades of all the students in the college in memory; if this were done, the computer would probably not have room to store anything else. Also, memory holds data and programs only *temporarily*—hence the need for secondary storage.

The two most common secondary storage mediums are magnetic disk and magnetic tape. A magnetic disk is a flat, oxide-coated disk on which data is recorded as magnetic spots. A disk can be a diskette or a hard disk. A diskette may look like a small stereo record, such as the 5¼-inch diskette (measured by diameter); or like the popular 3½-inch diskette (Figure 1-5a), it may fit into a shirt pocket. Because it has a firm exterior, the smaller version provides more protection to the magnetic surface than the larger version does. Both versions are called floppy disks because the magnetic disk material inside is thin and pliable. The current trend in disk design is toward smaller, more densely packed storage.

(a)

(b)

Figure 1-4   Output devices. Screens and printers are two types of output devices. (a) The graphics displayed on this screen are one form of output. (b) This color laser printer is used to produce professional-quality output.

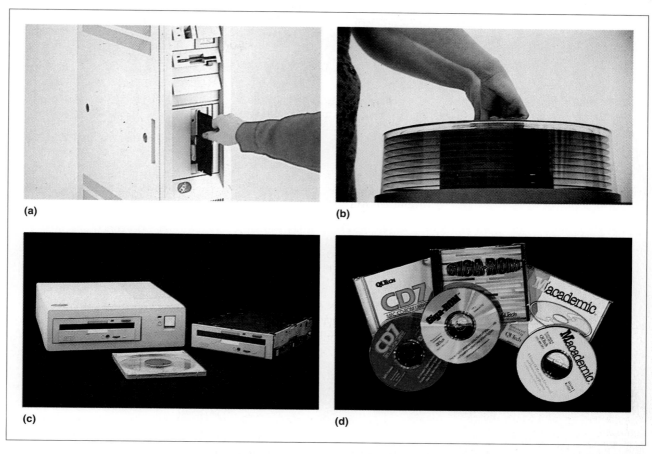

(a)

(b)

(c)

(d)

Figure 1-5   Secondary storage devices. (a) A 3½-inch diskette is being inserted into a disk drive. (b) Disk packs provide large computer systems with unlimited storage space. (c) Removable hard disk cartridges can be loaded like floppies for easy portability. (d) CD-ROM can hold enormous amounts of text, music, graphics—or even video and movies.

Hard disks usually offer more storage capacity than diskettes, although this may be changing; however, hard disks do offer faster access to the data they hold. With large computer systems, hard disks are often contained in disk packs.

Disk data is read by **disk drives.** Personal computer disk drives read diskettes; most personal computers have hard disk drives also. For complex tasks such as desktop publishing and producing memory-hungry graphics, removable cartridge-style hard disks can store enormous amounts of data and still allow for easy portability (Figure 1-5b). On large computer systems, disk packs may be removed from the drives (Figure 1-5c), permitting the use of interchangeable packs and practically unlimited storage capacity.

Magnetic tape, which comes on a reel or cartridge, is similar to tape that is played on a tape recorder. Magnetic tape reels are mounted on **tape drives** when the data on them needs to be read by the computer system or when new data is to be written on the tape (Figure 1-5d). Magnetic tape is usually used for backup purposes—for "data insurance"— because tape is inexpensive.

Macintosh

WATCHING WHILE YOU WORK

The ease of cutting and pasting text, art, and photos from program to program has convinced a number of businesspeople to bring the Macintosh computer into the workplace—especially for desktop publishing. But are you ready for desktop movies? With the same ease with which the machine allows you to cut and paste pictures, the Macintosh now lets you add movies to your programs. Yes, that's right, movies—right on your screen. How will such movies be used?

WordPerfect Corporation recently showed off the ease with which a user can add movies to a document by using the corporation's latest word processing software. Don Sorenson, who works on special projects for WordPerfect, demonstrated an upcoming version of an interactive newspaper, in which movie reviews become movie "trailers," or advertisements, when you press a button. In another example, a business letter describes a new helmet design and includes an animated 360-degree view of the helmet. You can rotate the on-screen image to view the helmet at any angle.

In Switzerland, multimedia designers Thierry Amsallem and Fulvio Massini created an information kiosk for journalists attending the annual Montreux Jazz Festival. For each featured musician at the festival, the kiosk presented biographical text, photographs, and a one-minute movie of a recent performance.

At Northwest Airlines, Macintosh movies help flight schedulers watch worldwide weather changes so they can make the best flight plans. In the past, they could see only one weather image at a time—they had to keep the last image in mind as the next one came up, so they could, for example, figure out which way the wind was

blowing. With the Mac's movie capabilities, the image sequences can be replayed at intervals.

Holland's Veronica Broadcasting has thousands of video clips it is turning into Macintosh movies. The movies will allow news directors to browse the archives on-line and pick just the right video at just the right time.

How does the Macintosh do it? Just like the celluloid variety, Macintosh movies are really thousands of pictures—frames—which, like regular movies, can run at 16 to 32 frames per second. The ability to compress and decompress large amounts of memory on the fly is the key to being able to show movies on the Macintosh screen. A capability called QuickTime allows the Macintosh to compress and decompress any time-based files, including sound, animation, music, and voice. All time-based files have big memory appetites.

Does this mean you may soon be able to watch TV or a movie while working on your personal computer? Stay tuned.

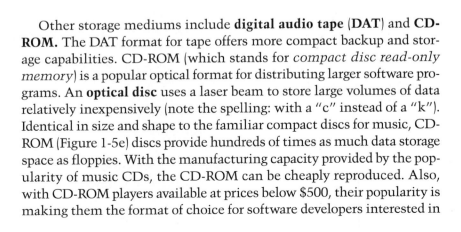

Other storage mediums include **digital audio tape** (**DAT**) and **CD-ROM.** The DAT format for tape offers more compact backup and storage capabilities. CD-ROM (which stands for *compact disc read-only memory*) is a popular optical format for distributing larger software programs. An **optical disc** uses a laser beam to store large volumes of data relatively inexpensively (note the spelling: with a "c" instead of a "k"). Identical in size and shape to the familiar compact discs for music, CD-ROM (Figure 1-5e) discs provide hundreds of times as much data storage space as floppies. With the manufacturing capacity provided by the popularity of music CDs, the CD-ROM can be cheaply reproduced. Also, with CD-ROM players available at prices below $500, their popularity is making them the format of choice for software developers interested in creating large programs with space for extra sound effects, complete musical pieces, and full-color art. Some typeface companies are storing hundreds of type styles on a single CD-ROM disc for use by printers and publishers. Others distribute electronic sources like dictionaries, thesauruses, and other huge collections like the complete works of Shakespeare. In addition, Apple Computer has developed a system called QuickTime which allows Macintosh computers to play movies—complete with sound and multilingual tracks—loaded directly from CD-ROM discs.

The Complete Hardware System

The hardware devices attached to the computer are called **peripheral equipment.** Peripheral equipment includes all input, output, and secondary storage devices. In the case of personal computers, some of the input, output, and storage devices are built into the same physical unit. In many personal computers, the CPU and disk drive are all contained in the same housing; the keyboard and screen are separate.

In larger computer systems, however, the input, processing, output, and storage functions may be in separate rooms, separate buildings, or even separate countries. For example, data may be input on terminals at a branch bank, then transmitted to the central processing unit at bank headquarters (Figure 1-6). The information produced by the central pro-

Figure 1-6 A large computer system. Data is input and then sent to the central processing unit, which may be in an entirely different location. Information can be output on a high-speed printer. Secondary storage may take the form of magnetic tape or, as shown here, magnetic disk.

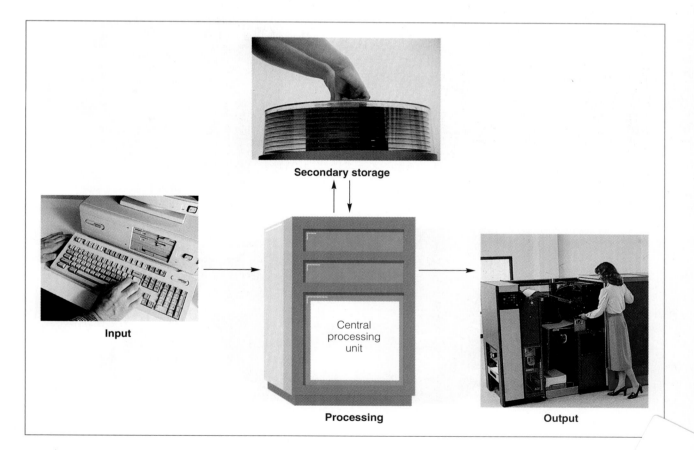

Secondary storage

Input

Central processing unit

Processing

Output

cessing unit may then be transmitted to the international offices, where it is printed out. Meanwhile, disks with stored data may be kept in bank headquarters and duplicate data kept on disk or tape in a warehouse across town for safekeeping.

Although the equipment may vary widely, from the simplest computer to the most powerful, by and large the four elements of a computer system remain the same: input, processing, output, and storage. This was once illustrated in a videotape showing a person holding a $50 Timex wristwatch while standing before a multimillion dollar Cray supercomputer—and telling how they both used the same components. Now let us look at the way computers have been traditionally classified.

Traditional Classification of Computers

Figure 1-7   Computer classifications. (a) The latest IBM mainframe offers 45 to 50% more power than the last generation. (b) The Cray-2 supercomputer has been nicknamed Bubbles because of its bubbling, shimmering coolant liquids. You can own it for a mere $17.6 million. (c) The VAX, a popular minicomputer made by Digital Equipment Corporation (DEC). (d) This popular Sun Microsystems workstation handles heavy-duty graphics demands with ease.

Computers come in sizes from tiny to monstrous, in both appearance and power. The size of a computer that a person or an organization needs depends on the computing requirements. Clearly, the National Weather Service, keeping watch on the weather fronts of many continents, has requirements different from those of a car dealer's service department that is trying to keep track of its parts inventory. And the requirements of both of them are different from the needs of a salesperson using a small laptop computer to record client orders on a sales trip.

(a)

(b)

(c)

(d)

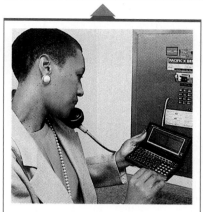

Dick Tracy Would Love This Computer

For years computers have been shrinking in size while gaining in power. First, the room-sized computers were packaged to be about the size of washing machines. Then they became even smaller, to fit on a desk. Soon the desktop computers were compacted into packages called laptop computers—whose batteries alone often weighed more than the computer. Now comes the smallest of them all: the palmtop. The size of a checkbook and weighing in at less than 1 pound, these new computers are finding their own niches—including as combination computer/radio-style pagers that Dick Tracy would love.

Hewlett-Packard's 95LX computer is a handheld machine that weighs a mere 11 ounces. And it is more than just a personal computer. It also has a text pager that allows it to send text over radio paging networks—and for a lot less money than it would cost over cellular radio networks. Paging may soon mean more than tracking someone down. Stuart Lipoff, a vice president at Arthur D. Little, Inc., says things "will soon get to the point where you can call a computer by phone and tell it to send information over the paging network to your hand-held computer." Or, maybe, to your wristwatch?

Mainframes and Supercomputers   In the jargon of the computer trade, large computers are called mainframes (Figure 1-7a). **Mainframes** are capable of processing data at very high speeds—*millions of instructions per second* (MIPS)—and have access to billions of characters of data. The price of these large systems can vary from several hundred thousand to many millions of dollars. With that kind of price tag, you will not buy a mainframe for just any purpose. Their principal use is for processing vast amounts of data quickly, so some of the obvious customers are banks, insurance companies, and manufacturers. But this list is not all-inclusive; other types of customers are large mail-order houses, airlines with sophisticated reservation systems, government accounting services, aerospace companies doing complex aircraft design, and the like.

The mightiest computers—and, of course, the most expensive—are known as **supercomputers** (Figure 1-7b). Supercomputers process *billions* of instructions per second. Most people do not have a direct need for the speed and power of a supercomputer. In fact, for many years supercomputer customers were an exclusive group: agencies of the federal government. The federal government uses supercomputers for tasks that require mammoth data manipulation, such as worldwide weather forecasting, oil exploration, and weapons research.

But now supercomputers are moving toward the mainstream, for activities as varied as creating special effects for movies and analyzing muscle structures. The increasing use of supercomputers is reflected in impressive supercomputer sales: over 25% annual growth in the past ten years.

Minicomputers   The next step down from mainframe computers are **minicomputers** (Figure 1-7c). Minicomputers are generally slower and have less storage capacity than mainframes, and they are less costly. When minicomputers first appeared on the market, their lower price fell within the range of many small businesses, greatly expanding the potential computer market.

Minicomputers were originally intended to be small and serve some special purpose. However, in a fairly short time, they became more powerful and more versatile, and the line between minicomputer and mainframe has blurred. In fact, the appellation *mini* no longer seems to fit very well. The term **supermini** has been coined to describe minis at the top of the size-price scale. Minicomputers are widely used by retail businesses, colleges, and state and city agencies. However, the minicomputer market diminished rapidly as buyers moved toward less expensive personal computers.

Personal Computers   The smallest computers, **personal computers,** are also known as **microcomputers,** or home computers. For many years, the computer industry was on a quest for the next biggest computer. The search was always for more power and greater capacity. Prognosticators who timidly suggested a niche for a smaller computer were

P E R S P E C T I V E S

THE FASTEST COMPUTER SOLD

Danny Hillis, inventor of the Connection Machine, the most powerful supercomputer around, certainly had a lot of fun getting to where he is today—on top of the computer world as far as speed is concerned. But he didn't always cherish speed. He used to tool around Cambridge in a clunky old fire engine. As an undergraduate at MIT, he created a mechanical computer that could play tic-tac-toe—a computer made entirely from Tinkertoys.

His latest feat is a big black cube studded with red blinking lights. The Connection Machine, which can cost as much as $200 million, offers up to 16,000 processors that can handle up to two trillion operations a second. Hillis's company, Thinking Machines Corporation,

builds the Connection Machine in modules that can be combined into a system as big as a small gymnasium.

The concept behind Hillis's supercomputer is simple enough: Use more than one processor. Most computers were designed to do one

thing at a time by channeling all data through the same processor. Hillis proposed to break with that tradition, setting up large numbers of tiny computer chips that could process the data simultaneously. With the Connection Machine, Hillis has legitimized "massively parallel" processing.

Now in its fifth generation, the Connection Machine claims the title as the fastest computer on the market, outperforming the famous Cray supercomputer on some problems by a factor of 100. Some of the organizations shelling out millions for his machine include the Sandia and Los Alamos National Laboratories, the Army High Performance Computing Research Center at the University of Minnesota, Syracuse University, the University of California at Berkeley, and the University of Wisconsin.

subject to ridicule by people who, as it turned out, could not have been more wrong. Today, more than 87 million personal computers have been sold worldwide—31 million to U.S. businesses alone.

Just as the success of minicomputers eventually led to the rise of superminis, so the success of personal computers paved the way for another classification of computers, **supermicros**—or, as they are called today, **workstations** (Figure 1-7d). These upper-end machines, used by workers such as engineers, scientists, financial traders, and graphic designers, are small enough to fit on a desk top but approach the power of a mainframe. As one computer company executive remarked, "What we've done is put the power and capability of an ocean liner into a speedboat."

The subject of personal computers is a major focus throughout this book. When it comes to buying your own personal computer and peripherals, you will probably be interested in the Buyer's Guide, which can help you with purchasing decisions.

Unfortunately, the definitions of *mainframe, minicomputer,* and *personal computer* are not fixed, because computer technology changes so rapidly. One observer noted that trying to distinguish these three different types of computers is like trying to take a picture of three melting ice cubes. However, since these categories still persist throughout the industry, they are worth keeping in mind. Many people often lump mainframes, supercomputers, and minicomputers together as mainframes. In this book, we refer to all three when we use the term *large computer systems.* We use *personal computers* instead of the term *microcomputers.*

Data Communications: Processing Here or There

Originally, a computer user kept all the computer hardware in one place; that is, it was **centralized** in one room. Although this is still sometimes the case, more and more large computer systems are **decentralized.** That is, the computer itself and some storage devices may be in one place, but the devices to access the computer—terminals or even other computers—are scattered among the users. These devices are usually connected to the computer by telephone lines. For instance, the computer and storage that has the information on your checking account may be located in bank headquarters, but the terminals are located in branch banks all over town so a teller in any branch can find out what your balance is. The subject of decentralization is intimately tied to **data communications,** the process of exchanging data over communications facilities. The topic of data communications is so important that we will study it in detail in Chapter 5.

In some systems processing is decentralized as well—the computers and storage devices are in dispersed locations. This arrangement is known as **distributed data processing** because the processing is distributed among the different locations. There are several ways to configure the hardware; one common arrangement is to place smaller computers in local offices but still do some processing on a larger computer at the headquarters office. For example, an insurance company headquartered in Denver with branches throughout the country might process payments and claims through minicomputers or personal computers in local offices. However, summary data could be sent regularly by each office for processing by the mainframe computer in Denver (Figure 1-8).

Many organizations find that their needs are best served by a **network,** a computer system that uses communications equipment to connect computers and their resources. In one type of network, a **local area network (LAN)**, computers are hooked together so that users can communicate and access larger computer systems. Users can operate their personal computers independently or in cooperation with other computers—minis or mainframes—to exchange data and share resources. When smaller computers are connected to larger computers, the result is often referred to as a **micro-to-mainframe link.** This concept has revolutionized the way many businesses operate. Users are able to obtain data directly from the mainframe computer and immediately analyze it on their own personal computers with their own software. People have quick access to more information, which leads to better decision making. This important topic will be discussed further in Chapter 5.

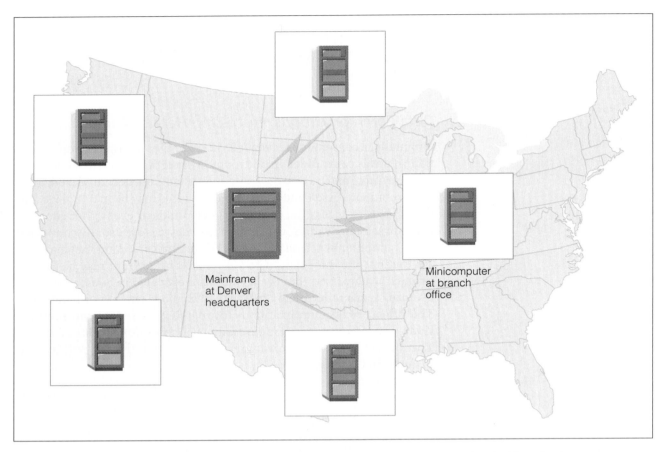

Figure 1-8 **Distributed data processing system.** Branch offices of an insurance company have their own computers for local processing, but they can tie in to the mainframe computer in the headquarters office in Denver.

Software: Telling the Machine What to Do

In the past, when people thought about computers, they thought about machines. The tapping on the keyboard, the clacking of the printers, the rumble of whirling disk drives, the changing flashes of color on a computer screen—these are the attention-getters. However, it is really the software—the planned, step-by-step instructions required to turn data into information—that makes a computer useful.

Software for Your Personal Computer

As we have already noted, you can buy packaged software that is ready for use. Application software for personal computers often comes in a box as colorfully packaged as a video game. Inside the box you may find a diskette or CD-ROM (which stores the software) and an instruction manual, also referred to as a **user's guide,** which carries the printed software **documentation** (Figure 1-9). To use the software, you insert the

Personal Computers in Action

COLLEGE COMPUTING

Although it seems silly today, in the 1950s some people worried that television sets would replace classroom teachers. The same thing was said about computers when they first appeared in colleges. A computer is not a replacement for a teacher or even a textbook. However, a computer is a very effective supplement for lectures and textbooks. Some instructors say they could not teach without it. Consider some of the ways computers are being used in colleges today.

- At the University of Pennsylvania School of Medicine, students use a computer program called Lazy Eye, by Howard Bregman and Dr. Steve Galetta. The software offers a realistic depiction of a physical eye exam. A student can direct a computer "hand" on the screen before a graphic of a face; as the student moves the hand, the on-screen eyes follow it. The student can move the hand out and in, also, and the eyes converge in response. The user can even turn on a little "flashlight" and inspect the pupils as they constrict and dilate. Lazy Eye features diagrams of the underlying anatomy, as well as descriptions of various nerve disorders and relevant treatments.

- At the University of Wisconsin, business students can participate in a multimedia program called "The Manager's Workshop: Motivation," which offers case studies, tutorials, and self-testing modules. Students use interconnected forms of me-

dia—computers, video, text, graphics, and animation—to experience situations based on the experiences of real organizations dealing with workplace problems.

- At the University of California at Santa Barbara, students in professor Brian Fagan's archeology class spend much of their time working on computers and participating in small group discussions regarding computer-based simulations. One of the simulations places them in a subsistence agricultural society along the Zambezi River in Central Africa. There they are faced with issues ranging from what to plant to how to handle floods, marauding animals, and tsetse flies.

- At the University of Washington, "computer-integrated" courses are offered in freshman English composition. Students sit before their own personal computers in three-person clusters. They use the computers to write papers and access bulletin boards—linking the entire class—for assignments and feedback. The instructor may critique their writing online or have them participate in exercises, such as revising a peer's introductory paragraph. Students spend nearly the entire classtime writing and revising.

Because it is easy to erase and rewrite their papers, says instructor Hans Turley, students—who can write anonymously on the bulletin board—find writing their papers and criticizing the work of others challenging. He feels that students express themselves more freely than they do in a traditional classroom. They can ask "dumb" questions, voice nonconformist beliefs, criticize one another without feeling aggressive or rude, and cast off feelings of shyness. "We can't base our teaching on an outdated technology. . . . The reality is, out there in the real world, on the job, they'll be using computers."

- At Harvard University, officials have decided to end the computer literacy test that all students had to pass before graduation. They said the test was no longer necessary, since students were arriving with enough computer experience to make testing obsolete.

The integration of computers into college curriculums has had a positive effect on student morale. Studies indicate that, as students become more adept at using computers, they tend to feel more optimistic about the future.

Figure 1-9 Packaged software. Each of the colorful software packages shown here includes one or more diskettes containing the software needed to run the program and an instruction manual, or documentation, describing how to use the software.

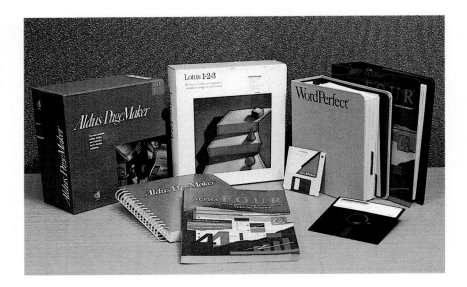

diskette in a disk drive, type a specified instruction on the keyboard, and the software begins to run on the computer.

Most personal computer software is planned to be user friendly. The term **user friendly** has become a cliché, but it usually means that the software is easy for a novice to use, or at least that it can be used with a minimum of training. Although software is usually generalized enough to be marketed to a broad audience, it is possible to customize software by personalizing the data you give it.

Let us consider an example. An educational software package called Where in Time Is Carmen Sandiego? is advertised as a historical chase through time, offering not only fun but also an introduction to history and geography. Sounds easy and educational enough. After you insert the diskette and start your computer, the program begins by displaying the company logo of the software company, then it plays a catchy tune while presenting the program title (Figure 1-10). You start the game in the lobby of a typical office building. You are looking at elevator doors. Above the elevator is a sign. "Acme Detective Agency, Time Crime Division." You must apply for the job of detective, so you ride the elevator to the second floor, the Personnel Department. A woman greets you and asks you to sign a release form. After entering your name, you begin as a Time Cadet and are given your first assignment, along with a "chronoskimmer"—your time travel machine. You must find Carmen Sandiego or one of her gang within a certain number of hours. The program presents clues and lets you search through evidence, inspect criminal dossiers, or travel to various cities worldwide at different time periods. If you find the criminal within the allotted time, you win; if not, you can try a new assignment.

As you play, you press keys or use a mouse to select among various choices. This sets up a dialogue between you and the computer. Note the input-processing-output here. The *input data* consists of what you enter by using the keyboard or mouse. The *processing* involves the computer checking your choices to see if you have caught the time-traveling

A Tool for the Mind

When most people think of tools, they usually think of hand tools such as hammers and saws, or wrenches and screwdrivers. But think of a tool in a broader sense—as anything used to get a job done. Computers are often called *tools for the mind.*

Computers are sophisticated tools, but tools nonetheless. How would you use such a tool? First you would need to know what you wanted to accomplish. If you have no medical plans, it is not likely that you will buy a doctor's tool such as a stethoscope. Or, if you have no plans to play baseball, why buy a bat? On that basis, you probably do not need to purchase a computer until you have a use in mind.

Businesspeople are not interested in buying useless tools. Instead, they plan their purchases to coincide with their business needs. If they have a problem with inventory or sales or even follow-up service, they will purchase a computer and the necessary software to solve those problems.

What job do you need to accomplish? Will your tool be a computer?

Figure 1-10 Personal computer software. This screen from the educational program *Where in Time is Carmen Sandiego?* shows the dialogue between computer and user. The program presents historical and geographical information as you travel the world—and time—in search of arch-criminal Carmen and her gang.

gangster before your time is up. The *output* consists of the displayed facts, pictures, and animations, and the sound effects that occur in response to your choices.

It is a short step, conceptually, from packaged software for your personal use to packaged software for office use. For example, there are many software packages for accounts payable—software to help businesses pay their bills. The principles are the same. You provide input data such as invoice number, vendor name, and amount owed. The computer processes this data to produce output in the form of computer-generated checks and various reports to help you track expenses.

Let us consider some of the popular types of business software for personal computers.

The Big Five: Application Software

The collective set of business problems is limited, and the number of ways to solve these problems is limited too. Thus, the problems and the software solutions fall, for the most part, into just a few categories. These categories can be found in most business environments. We begin with the categories often called, because of their widespread use, the Big Five: word processing/desktop publishing, electronic spreadsheets, database management, graphics, and communications. A brief description of each category follows.

Word Processing/Desktop Publishing   The most widely used personal computer software is **word processing** software. This software lets you create, edit, format, store, and print text and graphics in one document. In this definition, the word that makes word processing different from plain typing is "store." Since you can use a diskette to store the memo or document you type, you can retrieve it another time, change it, reprint it, or do whatever you like with it. You can see what a great time-saver word processing can be: Unchanged parts of the stored document do not need to be retyped; the whole revised document can be reprinted as if new.

As the number of features in word processing packages has grown, word processing has crossed the border into **desktop publishing** territory. Desktop publishing packages are usually better than word processing packages at meeting high-level publishing needs, especially when it comes to typesetting and color reproduction. Many magazines and newspapers today rely on desktop publishing software. Businesses use it to produce professional-looking newsletters, reports, and brochures—both to improve internal communication and to make a better impression on the outside world. Since publishing in one form or another typically consumes up to 10% of a company's gross revenues, desktop publishing has been given a warm welcome by business. We will introduce you to word processing/desktop publishing in more depth in Chapter 9.

Electronic Spreadsheets   Used to organize business data, a spreadsheet is made up of columns and rows. For example, the simple expense spreadsheet in Figure 1-11a shows time periods (months of the year) as columns and various categories (rent, phone, and so forth) as rows. Notice that figures in the rightmost column and in the last row are the results of calculations. Manual spreadsheets have been used as business tools for centuries. But a spreadsheet can be tedious to prepare and, when there are changes, a considerable amount of work may need to be redone. An **electronic spreadsheet** (Figure 1-11b) is still a spreadsheet, but the computer does the work. In particular, spreadsheet software automatically recalculates the results when a number is changed. This capability lets businesspeople try different combinations of numbers and obtain the results quickly. This ability to ask "What if . . . ?" helps businesspeople make better, faster decisions. In addition, modern spreadsheets, like Borland's Quattro Pro have built-in graphics capabilities that let you change raw numbers into charts for faster interpretation of the data. You will learn more about spreadsheets and how to use them in Chapter 10.

Database Management   Software used for **database management**—the management of a collection of interrelated files—handles data in several ways. The software can store data, update it, manipulate it, report it in a variety of views, and print it in as many forms. By the time the data is in the reporting stage—given to a user in a useful form—it has become information. A concert promoter, for example,

EXPENSES	JANUARY	FEBRUARY	MARCH	APRIL	TOTAL
RENT	425.00	425.00	425.00	425.00	1700.00
PHONE	22.50	31.25	17.00	35.75	106.50
CLOTHES	110.00	135.00	156.00	91.00	492.00
FOOD	280.00	250.00	250.00	300.00	1080.00
HEAT	80.00	50.00	24.00	95.00	249.00
ELECTRICITY	35.75	40.50	45.00	36.50	157.75
WATER	10.00	11.00	11.00	10.50	42.50
CAR INSURANCE	75.00	75.00	75.00	75.00	300.00
ENTERTAINMENT	150.00	125.00	140.00	175.00	590.00
TOTAL	1188.25	1142.75	1143.00	1243.75	4717.75

(a)

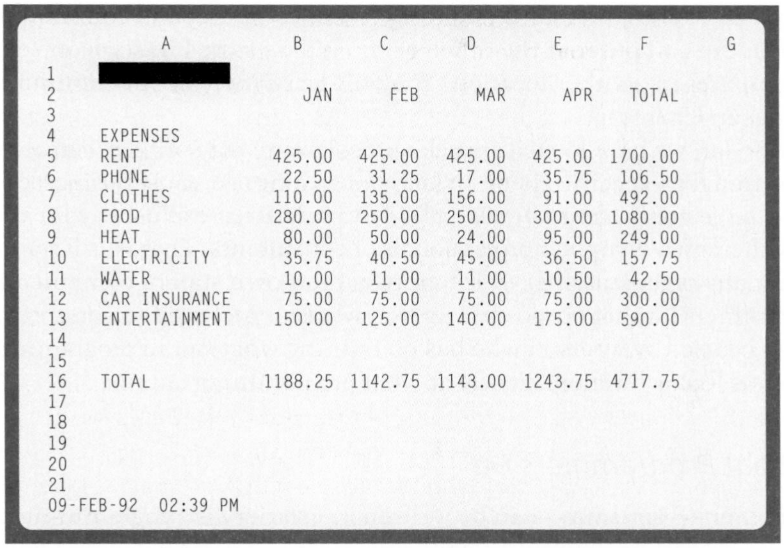

```
            A           B       C       D       E       F       G
  1  ██████████████
  2                   JAN     FEB     MAR     APR    TOTAL
  3
  4   EXPENSES
  5   RENT           425.00  425.00  425.00  425.00 1700.00
  6   PHONE           22.50   31.25   17.00   35.75  106.50
  7   CLOTHES        110.00  135.00  156.00   91.00  492.00
  8   FOOD           280.00  250.00  250.00  300.00 1080.00
  9   HEAT            80.00   50.00   24.00   95.00  249.00
 10   ELECTRICITY     35.75   40.50   45.00   36.50  157.75
 11   WATER           10.00   11.00   11.00   10.50   42.50
 12   CAR INSURANCE   75.00   75.00   75.00   75.00  300.00
 13   ENTERTAINMENT  150.00  125.00  140.00  175.00  590.00
 14
 15
 16   TOTAL         1188.25 1142.75 1143.00 1243.75 4717.75
 17
 18
 19
 20
 21
 09-FEB-92  02:39 PM
```

(b)

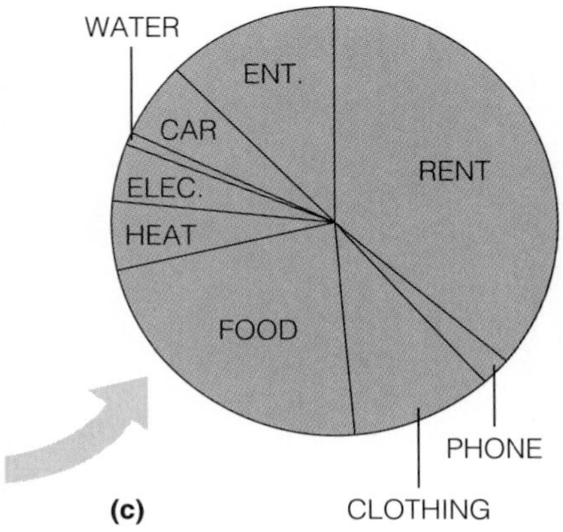

(c)

Figure 1-11   A simple expense spreadsheet. (a) This paper-and-pencil expense sheet is a typical spreadsheet of rows and columns. You have to do the calculations to fill in the totals. (b) This screen shows the same information in Lotus 1-2-3, a computer spreadsheet program, which does the calculations for you. (c) The spreadsheet program can also present the expenses more graphically in the form of a pie chart.

can store and change data about upcoming concert dates, seating, ticket prices, and sales. After this is done, the promoter can use the software to retrieve information, such as the number of tickets sold in each price range or the percentage of tickets sold the day before the concert. Database software can be useful for anyone who must keep track of a large number of facts. You will learn much more about database management in Chapter 11.

Graphics   It might seem wasteful to show **graphics** to businesspeople when standard computer printouts are readily available. However, graphics, maps, and charts can help people compare data and spot trends more easily, and make decisions more quickly (Figure 1-12). Three pages of confusion can be made into a chart that anyone can understand at a glance. In addition, visual information is usually more compelling than a page of numbers. Recently, more and more emphasis has been placed on depicting complex equations and events in a readily comprehensible fashion. For example, a new subject area in engineering, *visualization technology,* uses shape, location in space, brightness, color, and motion to create and manipulate sophisticated graphics representing complex numeric data. You take a closer look at computer graphics in Chapter 12.

Data Communications   We have already described data communications in a general way. From the viewpoint of a worker with a personal computer at home, *data communication* means—in simple terms—that he or she can hook a phone up to the computer and communicate with the computer at the office or get at data stored in someone else's computer in another location. You will learn more about communications in Chapter 5.

So far, we have looked at packaged software, but software can also be written for a specific client. In fact, not so long ago, most businesses using large computer systems had software written exclusively for them by their own computer professionals or consultants. That is still the case in many organizations, which employ their own staff of computer programmers for that purpose. However, whether packaged or not, software can be used by a person who has no training whatever in programming. Let us look a bit more closely at what programming entails.

What Programmers Do

Figure 1-12   Business graphics. Colorful computer-generated graphics can help people compare data and spot trends.

Programs—software—can be written in a variety of programming languages. Most programming languages in common use today are English-

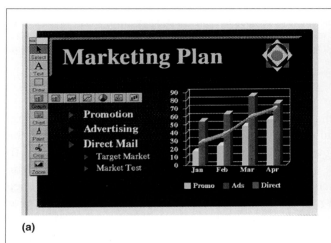
(a)

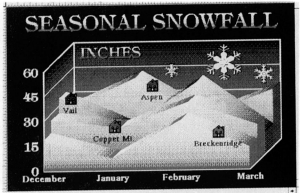
(b)

Help for the SAT

Each year thousands of students work up a full panic at the thought of taking that test of tests, the Scholastic Aptitude Test, not so fondly known as the SAT. The fortunes of many students, including those of the colleges of their choice, ride on the results of the SATs. Small wonder that students seek every mode of assistance. That help has traditionally been in the form of study aids such as special texts and classes.

Now, of course, all that has changed. The most sought-after aid is a computerized preparation course that offers at-home study on your own computer. The system includes diagnostic tests, instructions in the basics of the verbal and math SATs, and plenty of practice tests. Will these computer-tutors raise SAT scores? It looks promising.

like in appearance, and there are very definite rules for using them. Some languages are used specifically for business or scientific applications. One language, BASIC, was designed for beginners but has become popular for use on minicomputers and personal computers. Some languages are relatively easy to learn and are even used by people whose primary occupation is not programming. We will discuss all the varieties of languages in Chapter 6.

Programmers must understand how to use a programming language so that they can convey the logic of a program to the computer in a form the computer understands. Most often, a program is keyed in line by line. It is placed on some form of secondary storage device, such as a disk, from which it can be called into memory for testing and execution. Besides being able to use a programming language, programmers must understand what the program is supposed to do and design it accordingly, test it to remove errors, and document—write about—what they did.

Because of miniaturization, standardization, and the growing popularity of computers, the cost of hardware is going down. The cost of software, however, depends on whether it is packaged or custom-made. Packaged software prices are going down, partly because of increased competition but mostly because volume sales encourage lower prices. The price of custom software, on the other hand, is going up for a variety of reasons. Unlike hardware, the making of software depends chiefly on labor, and labor costs keep rising. In addition, as the information age continues, computers are becoming easier, not harder, for people to use. That is, computers are becoming accessible to more people, and less training is required to use them. But it takes programmers more time to create software that is less complicated to use—thereby providing more people easier access to the computer—another reason why software costs are going up. For those interested in careers in the computer field, then, we suggest that the future lies in understanding software.

 ## People and Computers

We have talked about hardware, software, and data, but the most important element in a computer system is people. Anyone nervous about a takeover by computers will be relieved to know that computers will never amount to much without people—the people who help make the system work and the people for whom the work is done.

Computers and You, the User

As we noted earlier, computer users have come to be called just *users,* a nickname that has persisted for years. Whereas once computer users were an elite breed—high-powered scientists, research-and-development engineers, government planners—today the population of users has broadened considerably. This expansion is due partly to user-friendly software for both work and personal use and partly to the availability of

United Way

For Those in Need

Businesses use computers; everyone knows that. But stretch that point a little further: Everyone who has business applications can make good use of computers. The list of business applications users includes those in education and government, and—perhaps surprisingly—nonprofit agencies.

But think about it. Agencies certainly have to meet payrolls, keep accounting records, write letters, and so forth. What is more, they usually have smaller budgets than private businesses of comparable size; this makes them obvious candidates for the cost savings a computer can provide.

Nonprofit agencies on New York's Long Island have taken this notion forward another step. Led by the United Way agency, 60-plus agencies have banded together to form a computer users' group. The group exchanges information and provides software training. Their efforts have been so successful that they have received a state grant for further growth and nationwide inquiries about how others can do the same thing.

small, low-cost, personal computers. There is a strong possibility that all of us will be computer users, but our levels of sophistication may vary.

A novice is a person with no computer training who is just beginning to learn about computers. This user may be a child playing computer games or a student experimenting with educational software. A more sophisticated user is one who uses a personal computer for term papers, home finances, or as a hobby.

Above this level are those users who, to varying degrees, use the computer for business or professional reasons, although they are not computer professionals themselves. For instance, a person may be trained well enough to make the inquiries required in customer service, banking, or airline reservations. At a slightly higher level, a person may know what data is being entered into the computer and what information being produced would be useful in performing the job at hand.

A more sophisticated user is a person who has written some computer programs, understands computer jargon, and is well equipped to communicate with computer professionals.

Computer People

Another way to think about people and computers is within the context of an organization. Many organizations have a department called **Management Information Systems (MIS)** or **Computer Information Systems (CIS)**, **Computing Services** or **Information Services.** This department is made up of people responsible for the computer resources of an organization. Whether the department is within a university, a government bureau, or a corporation, this department may well be the most important asset of the institution. Most of the institution's data is contained in its computer files: research data, engineering drawings, marketing strategy, accounts receivable, accounts payable, sales facts, manufacturing specifications, transportation plans, warehousing data—the list goes on and on. The guardians of this data are the same people who provide service to the users: the computer professionals. Let us touch on the essential personnel required to run computer systems.

Data entry operators prepare data for processing, usually by keying it in a machine-readable format. **Computer operators** monitor the console, review procedures, and keep peripheral equipment running. **Librarians** catalog the processed disks and tapes and keep them secure.

Computer programmers, as we have noted, design, write, test, and implement the programs that process data on the computer system; they also maintain and update the programs. **Systems analysts** are knowledgeable in the programming area but have broader responsibilities. They plan and design not just individual programs, but entire computer systems. Systems analysts maintain a working relationship with the users in the organization. The analysts work closely with the users to plan new systems that will meet the users' needs. The department manager, often called the **chief information officer (CIO)** must understand more than just computer technology. This person must understand the goals and operations of the entire organization.

The End-User Revolution

In this section, we have distinguished between "users" and "computer professionals." In the most general sense, the professionals provide the computer system and the users use it. But these two camps are not so distinct; in fact, there is common ground between them. In addition to buying and using packaged software, a growing number of users are becoming savvy about hardware—especially personal computers—and are even writing their own software with user-oriented languages. This phenomenon has been called the **end-user revolution.** The fact that many users are taking care of themselves is having a profound effect on the computer industry. We will return to this theme again later in the text as the story unfolds.

The End of the Beginning

In this chapter, we have painted the computer industry with a broad brush, touching on hardware, software, data, and people. We now move on to chapters that explain in more detail the information presented in this chapter.

R E V I E W   A N D   R E F E R E N C E

Summary and Key Terms

- The machines in a computer system are called **hardware.** The **programs,** or step-by-step instructions that run the machines, are called **software.** Software sold in stores, and usually contained in a box or folder, is called **packaged software.** Most packaged software is **application software,** software that is applied to solve a particular problem. **Computer programmers** write programs for **users,** or **end-users**—people who purchase and use computer software.

- A **computer** is a machine that can be programmed to process data (input) into useful information (output). A computer system consists of three main aspects of data handling—input, processing, and output—and is backed by a fourth, storage.

- **Input** is data put into the computer. Common **input devices** include a **keyboard;** a **mouse,** which translates movements on a flat surface to actions on the screen; a **pen-based computer,** which accepts writing on an electronic tablet, or pad; **voice input,** which allows a speaker to control a computer by means of **speech recognition;** a **wand reader,** which scans special letters

and numbers such as those on specially printed price tags in retail stores; a **bar code reader,** which scans the zebra-striped bar codes on store products; and a **scanner,** which reads text, art, and graphics, as well as objects.

- A **terminal** includes an input device, such as a keyboard or wand reader; an **output device,** usually a television-like screen; and a connection to the main computer. A screen displays both the input data and the processed information, **output.**

- The **processor,** or **central processing unit** (**CPU**), organizes raw **data** into meaningful, useful **information.** It interprets and executes program instructions and communicates with the input, output, and storage devices. **Memory,** or **primary storage,** is associated with the central processing unit but is separate from it. Memory holds the input data before processing and after processing, until the data is released to the output device. Traditionally, an operator communicated with a large computer system through the **console.**

- **Output,** raw data processed into usable information, is usually in the form of words, numbers, and graphics.

Users can see output displayed on **screens** and use **printers** to display output on paper.

- **Secondary storage** is needed to store data in a more permanent fashion than the temporary nature of CPU memory. The most common **secondary storage devices** are magnetic disks, but magnetic tape also provides secondary storage. **Magnetic disks** are usually called diskettes or hard disks. **Diskettes** may be 5¼-inch or 3½-inch **floppy disks. Hard disks** may be internal or external units attached to personal computers; on large systems, they are often contained in a **disk pack.** Hard disks hold more data and offer faster access than a diskette. Some hard disks come in removable cartridge form. Disk data is read by **disk drives. Magnetic tape** comes on reels or in cassettes and is mainly used for backup purposes. Magnetic tape reels are mounted on **tape drives. Digital audio tape** (**DAT**) offers a more compact, less expensive format than magnetic tape. An **optical disc** uses a laser beam to store data. **CD-ROM** stands for *compact disc read-only memory*. CD-ROM provides a popular format for distributing large software programs.

- **Peripheral equipment** includes all the input, output, and secondary storage devices attached to a computer. Peripheral equipment may be built into one physical unit, as in many personal computers, or be contained in separate units, as in many large computer systems.

- Computers can be loosely categorized according to their capacity for processing data. Large computers called **mainframes** are used by such customers as banks, airlines, and large manufacturers to process very large amounts of data quickly. The most powerful and expensive computers are called **supercomputers. Minicomputers,** which are widely used by colleges and retail businesses, have become increasingly similar to mainframes in terms of capacity. The largest and most expensive minicomputers are called **superminis.** The smallest computers—such as desktop office computers or home computers—are called **personal computers,** or sometimes **microcomputers. Supermicros,** or **workstations,** combine the compactness of a desktop computer with power that almost equals that of a mainframe. As computer technology changes, distinctions between types of computers will also change.

- A **centralized** computer system does all processing in one location. In a **decentralized** system, the computer itself and some storage devices are in one place, but the devices to access the computer are somewhere else. Such a system requires **data communications**—the exchange of data over communications facilities. In a **distributed data processing** system, a local office usually uses its own small computer for processing local data but is connected to a central headquarters computer for other purposes.

- Often organizations use a **network** of personal computers, which allows users to operate independently or in cooperation with other computers—exchanging data and sharing resources. Such a setup, often called a **local area network** (**LAN**), can even connect personal computers to a mainframe computer to form a **micro-to-mainframe link,** in which users can obtain data from the mainframe and analyze it on their own personal computers. This leads to better decision making.

- Software is accompanied by an instruction manual, or **user's guide,** which holds the printed **documentation.** Software that is easy to use is considered **user friendly.** Software may be packaged for general use or specially written for a specific client.

- Software found in most business environments includes **word processing/desktop publishing, electronic spreadsheets, database management, graphics,** and **data communication.**

- To create software, or programs, computer programmers use a variety of programming languages. Complicated programming is necessary to prepare easily usable software.

- Computer users range from novices with no training to sophisticated users who can deal with computer professionals.

- People are vital to any computer system. An organization's computer resources department—often called **Management Information Services** (**MIS**) or **Computer Information Systems** (**CIS**), **Computing Services,** or **Information Services**—includes **data entry operators** (who prepare data for processing), **computer operators** (who monitor and run the equipment), **librarians** (who catalog disks and tapes), **computer programmers** (who design, write, test, and implement programs), **systems analysts** (who plan and design entire systems of programs), and a **chief** information officer (who coordinates the MIS department).

- In general, a distinction is made between computer professionals, who provide computer systems, and users, who use the systems. However, in a development called the **end-user revolution,** users have become increasingly knowledgeable about computers and less reliant on computer professionals.

Review Questions

1. Define *hardware* and *software*.
2. How do a wand reader and bar code reader differ from a keyboard as input devices?
3. Describe the central processing unit (CPU). What roles does it play in a computer system?
4. Name three common forms of output and two common output devices.
5. Why is secondary storage necessary? Describe the most common forms of secondary storage.
6. Name and describe the three main types of computers.

7. What is distributed data processing?
8. What is documentation?
9. When people call software user friendly, what do they mean?
10. Name at least three things a computer programmer should be able to do.
11. Explain why the cost of custom software is going up.
12. What is the difference between data and information?
13. What is meant by peripheral equipment? Give some examples.
14. State what each of the following computer people does:
    a. data entry operator
    b. computer operator
    c. systems analyst
    d. chief information officer

Discussion Questions

1. What is meant by "system" in the term *computer system?*
2. Consider the terms *input, processing, output,* and *storage* as they relate to computers. How would you use such terms to describe the experience of writing a term paper that involves research? What would be the input? The processing? The output? The storage?
3. Why do you think many large companies prefer decentralized computer systems?
4. How do you think the end-user revolution will affect the computer industry?
5. If you were to consider a career in the computer industry, which of the jobs computer people do would interest you? Why?

True-False Questions

T F 1. The main purpose of a computer is to turn data into useful information.
T F 2. A set of instructions that tells the computer what to do is called hardware.
T F 3. The CPU is the part of a computer that processes raw data into meaningful information.
T F 4. Commercial programs called applications involve software that is put to use to solve particular problems. Word processing software is an example of an application.
T F 5. One type of secondary storage device is a disk drive.
T F 6. Laser printers form images without physically touching the paper where the images are formed.
T F 7. The most important component of a computer system is the person using it.
T F 8. One type of input device used to put data into a computer is a mouse.
T F 9. Mainframes are the fastest, most powerful computers available.
T F 10. Local area networks allow businesses to connect a number of personal computers to mainframes or other computers and permit them to share programs.

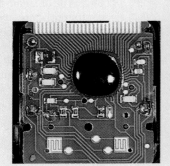

2

The Central Processing Unit

The Brain of the Machine

   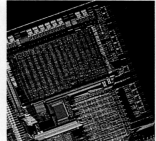

The boy stepped gingerly from key to key. He and a friend were playing on a huge keyboard, part of a gigantic model called "The Walk-Through Computer," a permanent exhibit at the Computer Museum in Boston. Modeled after the walk-through human "Heart Exhibit" at Chicago's Museum of Science and Industry, the two-story–tall computer combines high-tech education with a you-are-there feeling.

Visitors to the Boston museum, a repository of vintage computers and hands-on, interactive exhibits, can touch six-foot–wide disks and even the "brain" of the machine—a 7 1/2-foot–square model of the most popular silicon chip used in personal computers.

You are there. At the Boston Computer Museum, visitors can explore the workings of a computer from the inside out.

In this chapter you will "walk through" a computer. You will learn what the hardware consists of and how the pieces work together. You may be thinking that you do not need to know how a computer operates, but there are rewards for those who probe a little. For one thing, knowledge of how the computer works can help you use it more effectively. For another, knowing what is going on inside the "mysterious" machine you use can give you a great deal of satisfaction. Finally, familiarity with the subject matter in this chapter can help you make more informed choices about selecting options for your own personal computer system.

We begin with a look at the central processing unit—the brain of the machine—and how it works to change raw data into information. This is a complex process, which we will try to simplify here. Even so, you may find this one of the more technical chapters, with a number of new terms. Like Boston's walk-through computer, the components of the process may seem daunting at first. But don't worry; mastering the terms will help shrink the concepts to a manageable size.

The Central Processing Unit

The computer does its primary work in a part of the machine we cannot see, a control center that converts data input to information output. This control center, called the central processing unit (CPU), is a highly complex, extensive set of electronic circuitry that executes stored program instructions. As Figure 2-1 shows, the central processing unit consists of two parts:

- The control unit
- The arithmetic/logic unit

Each part has a specific function.

Before we discuss the control unit and the arithmetic/logic unit in detail, we need to consider data storage and its relationship to the central processing unit. Computers use two types of storage: primary storage and secondary storage. The CPU interacts closely with **primary storage**, or **memory**, referring to it for both instructions and data. For this reason this chapter will discuss memory in the context of the central processing unit. Technically, however, memory is not part of the CPU.

As Chapter 1 discussed, memory holds data only temporarily, at the time the computer is executing a program. **Secondary storage** holds permanent or semi-permanent data on some external magnetic or optical medium. The diskettes that you have seen with personal computers are secondary storage devices. Since the physical attributes of secondary storage devices determines the way data is organized on them, we will discuss secondary storage and data organization together, in Chapter 4.

Now let us consider the components of the central processing unit.

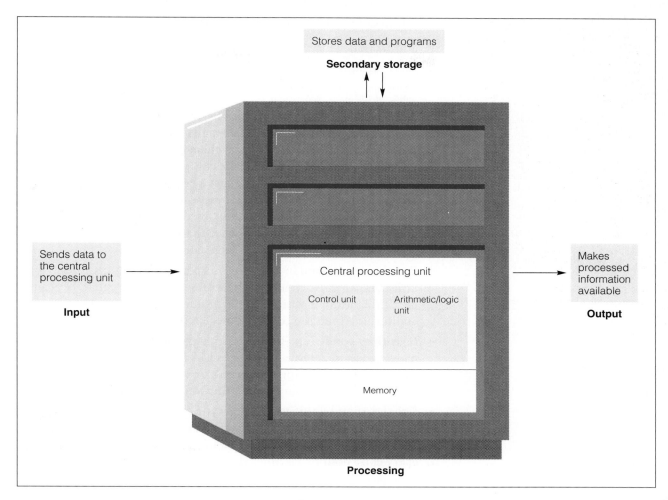

Stores data and programs

Secondary storage

Sends data to
the central
processing unit

Input

Central processing unit

Control unit

Arithmetic/logic
unit

Memory

Makes
processed
information
available

Output

Processing

Figure 2-1   The central processing unit. The two parts of the central processing unit are the control unit and the arithmetic/logic unit. Memory holds data and instructions temporarily, while the program they are part of is being executed. The CPU interacts closely with memory, referring to it for both instructions and data.

The Control Unit

The **control unit** contains circuitry that uses electrical signals to direct the entire computer system to carry out, or execute, stored program instructions. Like an orchestra leader, the control unit does not execute program instructions; rather, it directs other parts of the system to do so. The control unit must communicate with both the arithmetic/logic unit and memory.

The Arithmetic/Logic Unit

The **arithmetic/logic unit** (**ALU**) contains the electronic circuitry that executes all arithmetic and logical operations.

The arithmetic/logic unit can perform four kinds of **arithmetic operations**, or mathematical calculations:

- Addition
- Subtraction
- Multiplication
- Division

As its name implies, the arithmetic/logic unit also performs logical operations. A **logical operation** is usually a comparison. The unit can compare numbers, letters, or special characters. The computer can then take action based on the result of the comparison. This is a very important capability. It is by comparing that a computer is able to tell, for instance, whether there are unfilled seats on airplanes, whether charge-card customers have exceeded their credit limits, and whether one candidate for Congress has more votes than another.

Logical operations can test for three conditions:

- **Equal to condition**. In a test for this condition, the arithmetic/logic unit compares two values to determine if they are equal. For example: If the number of tickets sold *equals* the number of seats in the auditorium, then the concert is declared sold out.

- **Less than condition**. To test for this condition, the computer compares values to determine if one is less than another. For example: If the number of speeding tickets on a driver's record is *less than* three, then insurance rates are $425; otherwise, the rates are $500.

- **Greater than condition**. In this type of comparison, the computer determines if one value is greater than another. For instance: If the hours a person worked this week are *greater than* 40, then multiply every extra hour by 1½ times the usual hourly wage to compute overtime pay.

A computer can simultaneously test for more than one condition. In fact, a logic unit can usually discern six logical relationships: equal to, less than, greater than, less than or equal to, greater than or equal to, and less than or greater than. Note that less than or greater than is the same as not equal to.

Symbols called **relational operators** allow you to define the type of comparison you want the computer to perform. The most common relational operators are the equals sign (=), the less than symbol (<), and the greater than symbol (>).

Registers: Temporary Storage Areas

Registers are temporary storage areas for instructions or data. They are not a part of memory; rather they are special additional storage locations that offer the advantage of speed. Registers work under the direction of the contral unit to accept, hold, and transfer instructions or data and perform arithmetic or logical comparisons at high speed. The control unit uses a data-storage register the way a store owner uses a cash register—as a temporary, convenient place to store what is used in transactions.

Many machines assign special roles to certain registers, including:

- An **accumulator**, which collects the result of computations.
- An **address register**, which keeps track of where a given instruction or piece of data is stored in memory. Each storage location in memory is identified by an **address**, just as each house on a street has an address.
- A **storage register**, which temporarily holds data taken from or about to be sent to memory.
- A **general-purpose register**, which is used for several functions—arithmetic operations, for example.

Consider registers in the context of all the means of storage discussed so far. Registers hold data *immediately* related to the operation being executed. Memory is used to store data that will be used in the *near future*. Secondary storage holds data that may be needed *later* in the same program execution or perhaps at some more remote time in the future. Now let us look at how a payroll program, for example, uses all three types of storage. Suppose the program calculates the salary of an employee. The data representing the hours worked and the data for the rate of pay are ready in their respective registers. Other data related to the salary calculation—overtime hours, bonuses, deductions, and so forth—is waiting nearby in memory. The data for other employees is available in secondary storage. As the computer finishes calculations about one employee, the data about the next employee is brought from secondary storage into memory and eventually into the registers.

Memory

Memory is also known as **primary storage, primary memory, main storage, internal storage,** and **main memory**—all these terms are used interchangeably by people in computer circles. Memory is the part of the computer that holds data and instructions for processing. Although closely associated with the central processing unit, memory is separate from it. Memory stores program instructions or data for only as long as the program they pertain to is in operation. Keeping these items in memory when the program is not running is not feasible for three reasons:

- Most types of memory only store items while the computer is turned on—data is destroyed when the machine is turned off.
- If you share your computer, other people will need the memory space.
- There may not be room in memory to hold the processed data.

How do data and instructions get from an input device into memory? The control unit sends them. Likewise, when the time is right, the control unit sends these items from memory to the arithmetic/logic unit, where an arithmetic operation or logical operation is performed. After being processed, the information is sent to memory, where it is held until it is ready to be released to an output unit.

The chief characteristic of memory is that it allows very fast access to instructions and data, no matter where the items are within it. We will discuss the physical components of memory—memory chips—in this chapter.

How the CPU Executes Program Instructions

Let us examine the way the central processing unit, in association with memory, executes a computer program. We will be looking at how just one instruction in the program is executed. In fact, most computers today can execute only one instruction at a time, though they execute it very quickly. Many personal computers can execute instructions in less than one-*millionth* of a second, whereas those speed demons known as supercomputers can execute instructions in less than one-*billionth* of a second.

Before an instruction can be executed, program instructions and data must be placed into memory from an input device or a secondary storage device. As Figure 2-2 shows, the central processing unit then performs the following four steps for each instruction:

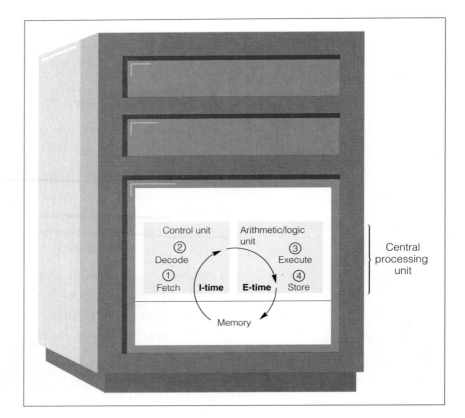

Figure 2-2   The machine cycle. Program instructions and data are brought into memory from an external device, either an input mechanism or secondary storage medium. The machine cycle executes instructions, one at a time, as described in the text.

① The control unit fetches (gets) the instruction from memory.
② The control unit decodes the instruction (decides what it means) and directs that the necessary data be moved from memory to the arithmetic/logic unit. These first two steps are called instruction time, or **I-time.**
③ The arithmetic/logic unit executes the arithmetic or logical instruction. That is, the ALU is given control and performs the actual operation on the data.
④ The result of this operation is stored in memory or a register. Steps 3 and 4 are called execution time, or **E-time.**

The control unit eventually directs memory to release the result to an output device or a secondary storage device. The combination of I-time and E-time is called the **machine cycle**. Figure 2-3 shows an instruction going through the machine cycle.

Each central processing unit has an internal **clock**, which produces pulses at a fixed rate to synchronize all computer operations. A single machine-cycle instruction may be made up of a substantial number of subinstructions, each of which must take at least one clock cycle. Each type of central processing unit is designed to understand a specific group of instructions called the **instruction set**. Just as there are many different languages that people understand, so each different type of CPU has an instruction set it understands. Therefore, one CPU—such as the one for an IBM PS/2—cannot understand the instruction set from another CPU—say, for a Macintosh. What is more, each type of central process-

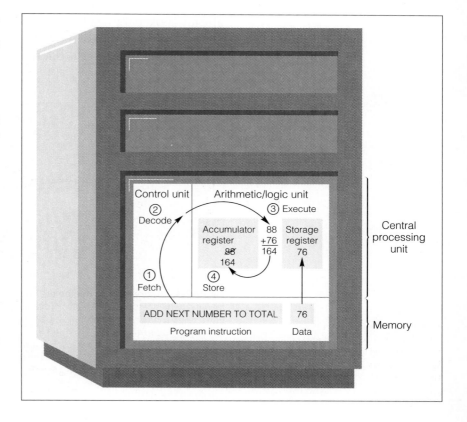

Figure 2-3   The machine cycle in action. Suppose a program must find the average of five test scores. To do this, the five scores must be totaled, then divided by 5. One way to proceed is to set the total to 0 to begin with and then add each of the five numbers, one at a time, to the total. Suppose the scores are 88, 76, 91, 83, and 87. In this figure the total has been set to 0 and 88, the first test score, added to it. It is time to add the next number, 76, to the total. The instruction to do so would be to add the next number to the total. Now follow the steps in the machine cycle. ① The control unit fetches the instruction from memory. ② The control unit decodes the instruction. It determines that addition must take place and gives instructions for the next number (76) to be placed in a storage register for this purpose. The total so far (88) is already in an accumulator register. ③ The ALU does the addition, increasing the total to 164. ④ In this case the new total is stored in the accumulator register instead of memory, since more numbers still need to be added to it. When the new total (164) is placed in the accumulator register, it erases the old total (88).

ing unit has a unique way of following instructions to perform arithmetic, make comparisons, and move input and output.

Storage Locations and Addresses: How the Control Unit Finds Instructions and Data

It is one thing to have instructions and data somewhere in memory and quite another for the control unit to be able to find them. How does it do this?

The location in memory for each instruction and each piece of data is identified by an **address**. That is, each location has an address number, like the mailboxes in front of an apartment house or numbers on bank safe-deposit boxes. And, like the mailbox numbers, the address numbers of the locations remain the same, but the contents (instructions and data) of the locations may change. That is, new instructions or new data may be placed in the locations when the old contents no longer need to be stored in memory. Unlike a mailbox, however, a memory location can hold only a fixed amount of data; an address can hold only one number or one word.

Figure 2-4 shows how a program manipulates data in memory. A payroll program, for example, may give instructions to put the rate of pay in location 3 and the number of hours worked in location 6. To compute the employee's salary, then, instructions tell the computer to multiply the data in location 3 by the data in location 6 and move the result to location 8. The choice of locations is arbitrary—any locations that are not already spoken for can be used. Programmers using programming languages, however, do not have to worry about the actual address numbers—each data address is referred to by a name. The name is called a

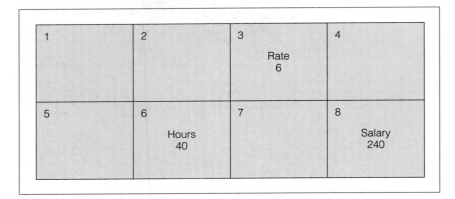

Figure 2-4   Addresses like mailboxes. The addresses of memory locations are like the identifying numbers on apartment-house mailboxes. Suppose we want to compute someone's salary as the number of hours multiplied by the rate of pay. Rate ($6) goes in memory location 3, hours (40) in location 6, and the computed salary ($6×40 hours, or $240) in location 8. Thus, *addresses* are 3, 6, and 8, but *contents* are $6, 40 hours, and $240. Note that the program *instructions* are to multiply the contents of location 3 by the contents of location 6 and move the result to location 8. (A computer language used by a programmer would use some kind of symbolic name for each location, such as R for Rate or Pay-Rate instead of the number 3.) The *data* items are the actual contents—what is stored in each location.

BINARY EQUIVALENT OF DECIMAL NUMBERS 0–15	
Decimal	**Binary**
0	0000
1	0001
2	0010
3	0011
4	0100
5	0101
6	0110
7	0111
8	1000
9	1001
10	1010
11	1011
12	1100
13	1101
14	1110
15	1111

Figure 2-5   Decimal and binary equivalents. Seeing numbers from different systems side by side clarifies the patterns of progression.

symbolic address. In this example, symbolic address names are Rate and Hours.

Data Representation: On/Off

We are accustomed to thinking of computers as complex mechanisms, but the fact is that these machines basically know only two things: on and off. This on/off, yes/no, two-state system is called a **binary system**. Using the two states—which can be represented by electricity turned on or off—the computer can construct sophisticated ways of representing data.

Let us look at one way the two states can be used to represent data. Whereas the decimal number system has a base of 10 (with the ten digits 0, 1, 2, 3, 4, 5, 6, 7, 8, and 9), the binary system has a base of 2. This means it contains only two digits, 0 and 1, which correspond to the two states off and on. Combinations of 0s and 1s represent larger numbers (Figure 2-5).

Bits, Bytes, and Words

Each 0 or 1 in the binary system is called a **bit** (for *bi*nary digi*t*). The bit is the basic unit for storing data in computer memory—0 means off, 1 means on. Notice that since a bit is always either on or off, a bit in computer memory is always storing some kind of data.

Since single bits by themselves cannot store all the numbers, letters, and special characters (such as $ and ?) that must be processed by a computer, the bits are put together in a group called a **byte** (pronounced "bite"). There are usually 8 bits in a byte (Figure 2-6). Each byte usually represents one character of data—a letter, digit, or special character.

Computer manufacturers express the capacity of memory in terms of the number of bytes it can hold. The number of bytes is expressed as **kilobytes.** *Kilo* represents 2 to the tenth power (2^{10}), or 1024. *Kilobyte* is abbreviated **KB** or, simply, **K.** (Sometimes K is used casually to mean 1000, as in "I earned $30K last year.") A kilobyte is K bytes—that is, 1024 bytes. Thus, the memory of a 640K computer can store 640×1024, or 655,360 bytes. Memory capacity may also be expressed in terms of

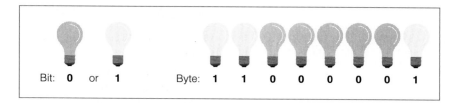

Bit: **0** or **1**   Byte: **1   1   0   0   0   0   0   1**

Figure 2-6   Bit as light bulb. In this illustration a light bulb operates as a binary digit (bit), with off representing 0 and on representing 1. Light bulbs, of course, are not used in computers, but vacuum tubes, transistors, silicon chips, or anything else that can conduct an electrical signal can be used. The group of eight bulbs, each of which can be on or off, represents 1 byte.

megabytes (1024×1024 bytes). One megabyte, abbreviated **MB**, means, roughly, one million bytes. With optical storage devices, computer users start to express memory amounts in terms of **gigabytes** (abbreviated **GB**)—billions of bytes.

Memory in older personal computers may hold between 256K bytes and 640K bytes; in newer machines, memory may hold anywhere from 1MB to 32MB and more. Mainframe memories can hold gigabytes.

A computer **word** is defined as the number of bits that constitute a common unit of data, as defined by the computer system. The length of a word varies by computer. Common word lengths are 16 bits (for traditional minicomputers and some personal computers), 32 bits (for full-size mainframe computers, as well as newer minicomputers and personal computers), and 64 bits (for supercomputers).

The parts of a computer are connected by collections of wires called **buses,** or **bus lines**. Each bus has a certain number of data paths along which bits can travel from one part of the computer to another. Usually, the number of data paths in a bus is related to the number of bits in the word size. For instance, a 32-bit central processing unit has a 32-bit bus, meaning that data can be sent over the bus lines in groups of 32 bits—that is, a word at a time.

The number of bits a computer can store in a word and carry on its buses is very important. In general, the larger the word size or the more bits in a bus, the more powerful the computer. The larger the word or bus size:

- The more data the computer can transfer at a time, making the computer faster.
- The larger the address numbers the computer can reference, allowing more memory.
- The greater the number and variety of instructions that the computer can support.

For example, the Intel 386 central processing unit processes data by using a 32-bit word size, but it comes in two versions. One version uses a 32-bit bus to communicate with memory; the other has only a 16-bit bus for memory. Obviously, sending data 32 bits at a time is more efficient than sending it 16 bits at a time, so the computer with the 32-bit bus is more powerful (and more expensive!).

Coding Schemes: EBCDIC and ASCII

As we said, a byte—a collection of bits—represents a character of data. But just what particular set of bits is equivalent to which character? In theory we could each make up our own definitions, declaring certain bit patterns to represent certain characters. But this would be about as practical as each of us speaking our own special language. Since we need to communicate with the computer and with each other, we must, to be efficient, agree on which groups of bits represent which characters. There are two commonly used coding schemes for representing numbers, letters, and special characters: EBCDIC and ASCII.

Figure 2-7 The EBCDIC and ASCII codes. Shown are binary representations of letters and numbers. The binary representation is in two columns to improve readability.

Character	EBCDIC	ASCII
A	1100 0001	100 0001
B	1100 0010	100 0010
C	1100 0011	100 0011
D	1100 0100	100 0100
E	1100 0101	100 0101
F	1100 0110	100 0110
G	1100 0111	100 0111
H	1100 1000	100 1000
I	1100 1001	100 1001
J	1101 0001	100 1010
K	1101 0010	100 1011
L	1101 0011	100 1100
M	1101 0100	100 1101
N	1101 0101	100 1110
O	1101 0110	100 1111
P	1101 0111	101 0000
Q	1101 1000	101 0001
R	1101 1001	101 0010
S	1110 0010	101 0011
T	1110 0011	101 0100
U	1110 0100	101 0101
V	1110 0101	101 0110
W	1110 0110	101 0111
X	1110 0111	101 1000
Y	1110 1000	101 1001
Z	1110 1001	101 1010
0	1111 0000	011 0000
1	1111 0001	011 0001
2	1111 0010	011 0010
3	1111 0011	011 0011
4	1111 0100	011 0100
5	1111 0101	011 0101
6	1111 0110	011 0110
7	1111 0111	011 0111
8	1111 1000	011 1000
9	1111 1001	011 1001

EBCDIC byte representation	Parity bit	Number of 1 Bits
S 1 1 1 0 0 0 1 0 1		5
U 1 1 1 0 0 1 0 0 1		5
S 0 1 1 0 0 0 1 0 1		4
A 1 1 0 0 0 0 0 1 0		3
N 1 1 0 1 0 1 0 1 0		5

Note error. First bit has been altered.

Figure 2-8   Example of odd parity. A 0 or a 1 is added as a parity bit to the EBCDIC byte so that each byte always comes out with an odd number of 1 bits. Thus, with the second *S* here, the absence of the first 1 produces an even number of bits—which signals the computer that there is an error.

EBCDIC (usually pronounced "EB-see-dick") stands for Extended Binary Coded Decimal Interchange Code. Established by IBM and used in IBM mainframe computers, it uses 8 bits to represent a single character. The letter *A*, for instance, is represented by 11000001.

Another code, **ASCII** (pronounced "AS-key"), which stands for American Standard Code for Information Interchange, uses 7 bits for each character. For example, the letter *A* is represented by 1000001. The ASCII representation has been adopted as a standard by the U.S. government, and it is the standard for a variety of computers—particularly minicomputers and personal computers. Figure 2-7 shows the EBCDIC and ASCII codes.

One code that may be adopted on future computers is called **Unicode**. Unlike the EBCDIC and ASCII codes, Unicode uses 16 bits to represent a character. This allows 65,536 different codes, which may be enough to contain all the characters anyone may want to use—from any language in the world.

The Parity Bit: Checking for Errors

Suppose you just finished transmitting data over a telephone line or even within the computer system itself. How do you know it arrived safely—that is, that nothing was lost or garbled? Sometimes data is lost in transit, owing to timing problems, hardware failure, and the like.

To signal the computer that the bits in a byte have stayed the way they are supposed to, another 0 or 1 bit is added to the byte before transmission. This extra bit is called a **parity bit**, or **check bit**. Thus, in an 8-bit EBCDIC byte, the parity bit is the ninth bit.

Here is how the system works: In an odd-parity system, a 0 or 1 is added to each EBCDIC byte before transmission so that the total number of 1 bits in each byte is an odd number (Figure 2-8). Then, if a 1 bit is lost in a particular byte during transmission, the total number of 1 bits in that byte is even, not odd. Thus, the computer system is alerted that something is wrong with that byte. Some computers use an odd-parity system and others use an even-parity system. The principle behind the two systems is the same, except that, in an even-parity system, the total number of 1 bits is even.

As you might suspect, a parity check is not infallible. For instance, for any of the letters in Figure 2-8, if two 1s were dropped, the number of 1 bits would still add up to an odd number—and the computer would not notice that the byte was erroneous. More advanced schemes have been developed to detect multibit errors. Some not only detect errors, but also correct them.

 Inside Your Personal Computer

Having a look inside most personal computers is easy; all you need is a screwdriver and sometimes not even that. (Caution: Some manufacturers are *not* interested in having you peer under the hood, and doing so

A Family of Chips

The Intel Corporation has provided personal computer makers with four—make that five—generations of microprocessor chips. The first was a standard-setter: the 8088 chip used by the first IBM PC (introduced in 1981) and its many imitators. The next member of the family, the Intel 186, fared less well; this transitional chip was used in just a few products before it was replaced by the Intel 286, which powered the IBM PC AT and, again, a slew of copycats.

Intel moved to increase power and flexibility with the introduction of the Intel 386 chip, first brought to the market in the Compaq 386 computer. The 386 chip lets users run several programs at once—a talent formerly reserved for minicomputers and mainframes. Software developers said this was the chip they had been waiting for. But close on its heels—on the market in 1989—was the Intel 80486 (see Figure 2-9b), a chip whose speed and power make it a veritable mainframe on a chip.

will void your warranty. Check your documentation—your instruction manual—first.) Inside is an impressive array of electronic gear. Part of what you would see before you is related to what we have talked about in this chapter: the central processing unit and memory.

Both the CPU and memory are on silicon chips, which can be smaller than a thumbnail (Figure 2-9a). The word *chip* is bandied about a great deal, but it is not always used properly. There are two basic kinds of chips: one kind corresponds to a central processing unit and another kind corresponds to memory. (For specific applications, such as watches or microwave ovens, both kinds may be combined on a single chip.) A miniaturized central processing unit can be etched on a chip, hence the term *computer on a chip*. A central processing unit, or processor, on a chip is a **microprocessor** (Figure 2-9b), often called a **logic chip** when it is used to control specialized devices (such as the fuel system of a car).

We will present the stories of microprocessors and memory chips in separate sections. Even though we will discuss chips in the context of the personal computer, where they first came to prominence, keep in mind that most large computers also use chips for the central processing unit and memory.

Gallery 1 shows how chips are designed and manufactured.

Microprocessor: Computer on a Chip

Over the years the architecture of microprocessors has become somewhat standardized. Microprocessors usually contain four key components: a control unit and an arithmetic/logic unit, which together form

Figure 2-9   Microprocessor chips. (a) Microprocessors are small enough to fit on the palm of a baby's hand—with room to spare. (b) This is the Intel 80486 microprocessor, which accommodates a 32-bit word. Although the circuitry is complex, the entire chip is smaller than your thumbnail.

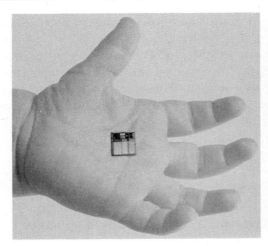

(a)

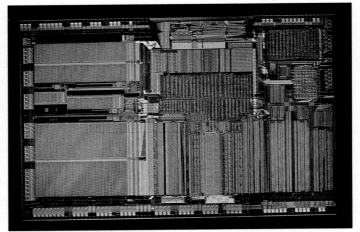

(b)

the central processing unit; registers, buses, and a clock. (Clocks are often on a separate chip in personal computers.) These are exactly the items we have discussed in this chapter, all on one tiny chip. (Notably missing is memory, which comes on its own chip or chips.)

How much smaller? How much cheaper? How much faster? Two decades of extraordinary advances in technology have packed increasingly greater power onto increasingly smaller chips. Engineers can now imprint as much circuitry on a single chip as filled room-size computers in the early days of data processing. But are we approaching the limits of smallness? Current development efforts focus on a three-dimensional chip, built in layers. Chip capacities in the future do seem almost limitless.

 ## Memory Components

Earlier in the chapter we talked about memory and how it interfaces with the central processing unit. Now we will examine the components of memory. Historically, memory components evolved from vacuum tubes to magnetic cores to semiconductors. (For more information on the development of these components, see Appendix B.)

Semiconductor Storage: Let the Chips Fall Where They May

Most modern computers use semiconductor storage because it has several advantages: reliability, compactness (hence increased speed), low cost, and low power usage. Since mass production of semiconductors became economical, the cost of memory has been considerably reduced. Chip prices have fallen and risen and fallen again, based on a variety of economic and political factors, but chips remain a bargain. Semiconductor storage has one major disadvantage: It is **volatile**. That is, semiconductor storage requires continuous electric current to represent data. If the current is interrupted, the data is lost.

Semiconductor storage is made up of thousands of very small circuits—pathways for electric currents—on a silicon chip. Each circuit etched on a chip can be in one of two states: either conducting an electric current or not—on or off. The two states can be used to represent the binary digits 1 and 0. As we noted earlier, these digits can be combined to represent characters, thus making the memory chip a storage bin for data and instructions.

Memory chips that hold up to one million data bits at any one time (or the equivalent of about 80 typed pages) are common. Two companies, IBM and Siemens, are cooperating on the creation of a chip capable of storing 64 million bits (64 megabits) or more of data (the equivalent of 800 typed pages). Such a superchip would be miniaturized in the extreme, with circuits smaller than half a micron, or approximately seven-thousandths of the diameter of a human hair.

Personal Computers in Action

CARVER MEAD: ART IN ENGINEERING

You would think that art would not enter into the design of such exacting entities as microprocessors. But to Carver Mead, a California Institute of Technology electrical engineering professor, beauty is basic. "It took half a day to get this circuit right," he points out while working on a new chip design. "Of course, I could have made it work by brute force. But then it would have been ugly—and that tells you there must be a better way to do it."

For decades, Mead has been working with silicon, the primary element of sand. In pure form, silicon allows engineers to shrink a roomful of computers onto a chip the size of a fingertip. One of his most important contributions is a method for designing microchips by computer. Before Mead, chips were made by engineers who traced the intricate connections on plastic sheets that were then photographed and used as templates for etching electrical connections in silicon. The complexity of the many layers involved made the task so complex that only a handful of the brightest designers were up to it. Therefore, the number of chip designs was limited. To make an analogy between designing chips and publishing, it was as if only those who owned printing presses could write books.

Mead put the computer to work designing chips while at Xerox's Palo Alto Research Center. His process captured the knowledge of the high-tech design priesthood, allowing anyone with a personal computer to create new chip designs. What is more, engineers now create and test circuits on the computer screen and get immediate results. If changes are necessary, they can be made on-screen. This capability is a significant time-saver.

In designing chips, Mead says he cannot stop until he has created something that derives its beauty in part from its technological function. "There are things that are nice to look at but don't do anything. And there are things that do nice things but are ugly. Then, there are the few, rare things whose beauty is related to their function, like in the classic designs of furniture and architecture."

Trying to merge the artificial world of electronics with the natural world of biology has set Mead on a new technological path involving *neural networks*, or *neural nets*. Neural nets involve a grid-like pattern processing that some believe will eventually allow computers to learn like humans learn. Mead investigated the possibility of creating silicon circuits with the same powers as the nerve cells in our eyes, ears, and brains—to provide computers with semblances of hearing, seeing, and thinking. He and his Cal Tech students have already made a chip that mimics an essential structure of the ear, the cochlea; one day it may be used as an implant for the deaf.

Software based on neural networks has been used commercially by Chase Manhattan Bank to help reduce costs from stolen credit cards. But the simplicity of early software efforts has helped to undermine interest in the approach. Mead has pressed on, however, and with Federico Faggin, co-inventor of the microprocessor, he founded Synaptics, Inc., to create microprocessors based on neural net technology. Synaptics' first neural net chip was introduced in 1992 and is being used by such companies as Verifone in its check-reading equipment.

If you are unsure about the existence of art in engineering design, you can decide for yourself. In the accompanying photo, Mead stands before a color image of one of his chip designs—enlarged thousands of times—while on display at New York's Metropolitan Museum of Art.

Making Microchips

Computer power in the hands of the people—we take it for granted now, but not so long ago computers existed only in enormous rooms behind locked doors. The revolution that changed all that was ignited by chips of silicon smaller than your fingernail: microchips. Silicon is one of the most common elements on earth, but there is nothing commonplace about designing, manufacturing, testing, and packaging silicon chips. In this gallery we will explore the key elements in the process by which those marvels of miniaturization—microchips—are made.

The Idea Behind the Microchip

Microchips form the lightning-quick "brain" of a computer. These devices, though complex, work on a very simple principle: They "know" when electric current is on and when it is off. They can process information because it is coded as a series of "on-off" electric signals. Before the invention of microchips, these signals were controlled by thousands of separate devices laboriously wired together to form a single circuit. Because one or more circuits can be embedded on a microchip, a microchip is often called an integrated circuit.

Silicon is a semiconductor—it conducts electricity only "semi" well. This does not sound like such an admirable trait, but the beauty of silicon is that it can be doped, or treated, with different materials to make it conduct electricity well or not at all. By doping various areas of a silicon chip differently, pathways can be set up for electricity to follow. The pathways consist of grooves that are etched into layers placed over silicon substrate. The silicon is doped so the pathways conduct electricity. The surrounding areas do not conduct electricity at all.

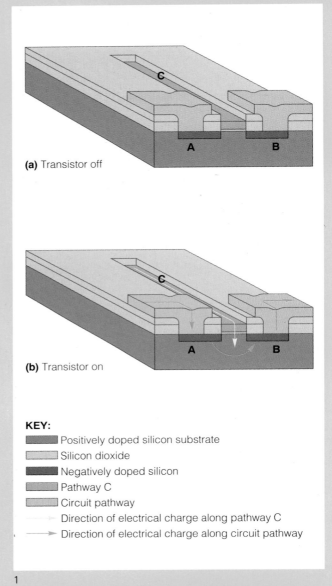

(a) Transistor off

(b) Transistor on

KEY:
- Positively doped silicon substrate
- Silicon dioxide
- Negatively doped silicon
- Pathway C
- Circuit pathway
- → Direction of electrical charge along pathway C
- → Direction of electrical charge along circuit pathway

1

(1) This simplified illustration shows the layers and grooves within a transistor, one of thousands of circuit components on a single chip. Pathway C controls the flow of electricity through the circuit.
(a) When no electric charge is added to pathway C, electricity cannot flow along the circuit pathway from area A to area B. Thus, the transistor is "off." (b) A charge added to pathway C temporarily allows electricity to travel from area A to area B. Now the transistor is "on," and electricity can continue to other components in the circuit. The control of electricity here and elsewhere in the chip makes it possible for the computer to process information coded as "on-off" electric signals.

Preparing the Design

2

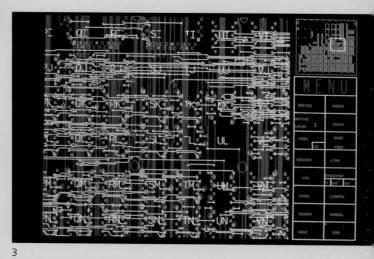

3

4

5

Try to imagine figuring out a way to place thousands of circuit components next to each other so that all the layers and grooves line up and electricity flows through the whole integrated circuit the way it is supposed to. That is the job of chip designers. Essentially, they are trying to put together a gigantic multi-layered jigsaw puzzle.

The circuit design of a typical chip requires over a year's work by a team of designers. Computers assist in the complex task of mapping out the most efficient pathways for each circuit layer. **(2)** By drawing with an electronic pen on a digitizing tablet, a designer can arrange and modify circuit patterns and display them on a screen. Superimposing the color-coded circuit layers allows the designer to evaluate the relationships between them. The computer allows the designer to electronically store and retrieve previously designed circuit patterns.

(3) Here the designer has used computer graphics software to display a screen image of the circuit design. **(4)** The computer system can also provide a printed version of any or all parts of the design. This large-scale printout allows the design team to discuss and modify the entire chip design.

(5) The final design of each circuit layer must be reduced to the size of the chip. Several hundred replicas of the chip pattern are then etched on a chemically coated glass plate called a photomask. Each photomask will be used to transfer the circuit pattern to hundreds of chips. One photomask is required for each layer of the chip. A typical design requires 7 to 12 photomasks, but more complex chips may require as many as 20.

Manufacturing the Chip

The silicon used to make computer chips is extracted from common rocks and sand. It is melted down into a form that is 99.9% pure silicon and then doped with chemicals to make it either electrically positive or electrically negative. **(6)** The molten silicon is then "grown" into cylindrical ingots in a process similar to candledipping. **(7)** A diamond saw slices each ingot into circular wafers 4 or 6 inches in diameter and $\frac{5}{1000}$ of an inch thick. The wafers are sterilized and polished to a mirror-like finish. Each wafer will eventually contain hundreds of identical chips. In the photo, an engineer is holding an experimental 8-inch wafer that can comprise over 2000 chips.

7

6

8

Since a single speck of dust can ruin a chip, chips are manufactured in special laboratories called clean rooms. The air in clean rooms is filtered, and workers dress in "bunny suits," to lessen the chance of chip contamination. A manufacturing lab is 100 times cleaner than a hospital operating room.

(8) Chip-manufacturing processes vary, but one step is common: Electrically positive silicon wafers are placed in an open glass tube and inserted in a 1200° Celsius oxidation furnace. Oxygen reacts with the silicon, covering each wafer with a thin layer of silicon dioxide, which does not conduct electricity well. Each wafer is then coated with a gelatin-like substance called photoresist, and the first photomask pattern is placed over it. Exposure to ultraviolet light hardens the photoresist, except in the areas concealed by the dark circuit pattern on the photomask.

9

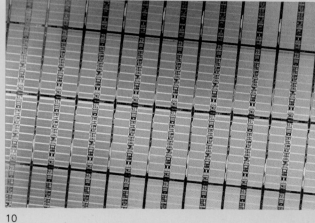

10

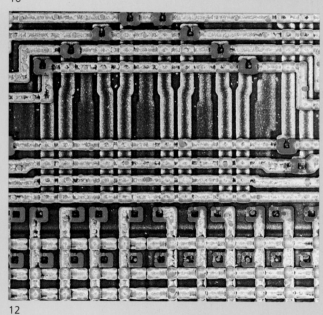

12

11

(9) The wafer is then taken to a washing station in a specially lit "yellow room," where the wafer is washed in solvent to remove the soft photoresist. Next the silicon dioxide revealed by the washing is etched away by hot gases. The silicon underneath, which forms the circuit pathway, is then doped to make it electrically negative. In this way, the circuit pathway is distinguished electrically from the rest of the silicon. This process is repeated for each layer of the wafer, using a different photomask each time. In the final step, aluminum is deposited to connect the circuit components and form the bonding pads to which wires will later be connected. **(10)** The result: a wafer with hundreds of chips. **(11)** Photographic lighting enhances this close-up view of a wafer with chips. **(12)** This close-up of a memory chip shows details of the surface architecture.

Testing the Chip

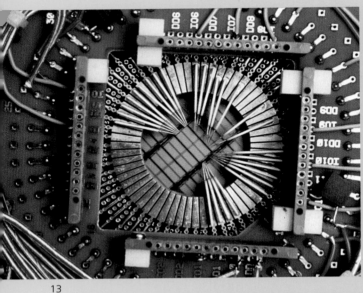

13

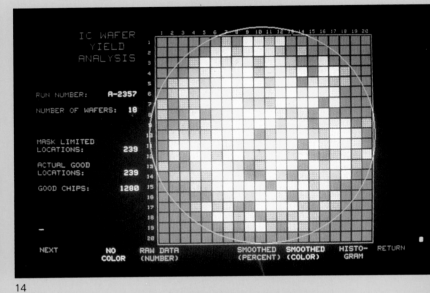

IC WAFER
YIELD
ANALYSIS

RUN NUMBER: A-2357

NUMBER OF WAFERS: 10

MASK LIMITED
LOCATIONS: 239

ACTUAL GOOD
LOCATIONS: 239

GOOD CHIPS: 1280

NEXT   NO   RAW DATA   SMOOTHED SMOOTHED HISTO-   RETURN
            COLOR   (NUMBER)   (PERCENT) (COLOR)   GRAM

14

Although chips on a particular wafer may look identical, they do not perform identically. **(13)** A probe machine must perform millions of tests on each chip, to determine whether it conducts electricity in the precise way it was designed to. The needle-like probes contact the bonding pads, apply electricity, measure the results, and mark ink spots on defective chips. **(14)** A defect review performed by a computer finds and classifies defects in order to eliminate them from the wafer. **(15)** After the initial testing, a diamond saw cuts each chip from the wafer, and defective chips are discarded.

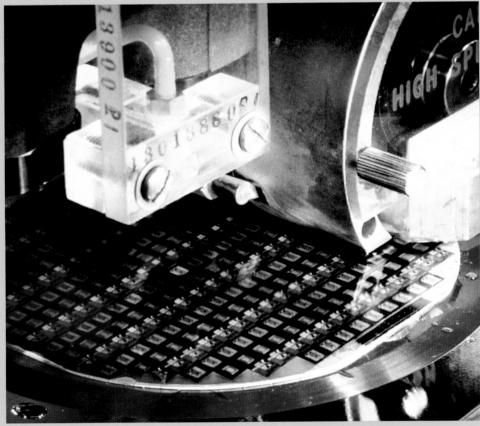

15

Packaging the Chip

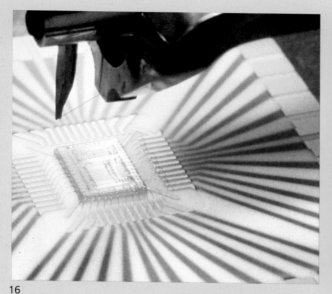

16

18

17

19

Each acceptable chip is mounted on a protective package. **(16)** An automated wire-bonding device wires the bonding pads of the chip to the electrical leads on the package, using aluminum or gold wire thinner than a human hair.

A variety of packages are in use today. **(17)** Dual in-line packages have two rows of legs that are inserted into holes in a circuit board. **(18)** Square pin-grid array packages, which are used for chips requiring many electrical leads, look like a bed of nails. The pins are inserted into holes in a circuit board. In this photo, the protective cap has been cut away, revealing the ultrafine wires connecting the chip to the package. **(19)** This photo shows a dual in-line package (top) compared to two surface-mount packages (bottom). Surface-mount packages do not have to be inserted in circuit board holes. Instead, a machine drops the package on the board, and a laser or infrared beam bonds the package into place. Another advantage of surface-mount packages is that they are smaller than other packages, allowing more computing power in less space.

From Chip to Computer

20

21

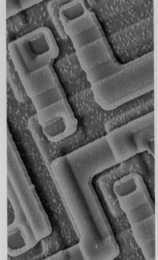

22

23

(20) At the factory that manufactures the NeXT Computer, a robotic arm inserts a pin-grid package into holes in a circuit board. Several surface-mount packages have already been placed on the board. **(21)** Dual in-line packages of various sizes have been attached to this circuit board. **(22)** Metal lines on the board form electrical connections to the legs of the package, as shown in this color-enhanced close-up of some packages on a circuit board. **(23)** In the final step, the board is inserted into one of the many personal computers that owe their existence to the chip.

Chips Inside Everything

So popular is the tiny chip that people participate in the computer revolution every day by simple acts such as using a telephone, looking at a wristwatch, or going through a supermarket checkout line. Furthermore, chips are in cameras, blood pressure devices, microwave ovens, cars, and many other everyday devices. Homeowners can monitor heat, smoke, and security with strategically placed microprocessor chips.

Consider the bicycle odometer above. This little chip-driven device can pick up data from sensors placed on your bicycle wheels and pedals and produce the following information: current speed, average speed, maximum speed, distance, and cadence. If you were to pry the odometer open—not recommended—you would see the microprocessor revealed here.

One important type of semiconductor design is called (**complementary metal oxide semiconductor**), or **CMOS**. This design is noted for using little electricity. This makes it especially useful for computers requiring low power consumption, such as portable computers.

RAM and ROM

The two basic types of memory chips in every computer are popularly known as **random-access memory** (**RAM**) and **read-only memory** (**ROM**). These terms are actually a little misleading, since every chip, RAM or ROM, provides random-access storage. That is, the computer has access to all locations on each type of chip.

The real difference between RAM and ROM is that the data on ROM chips cannot easily be replaced with new data. ROM contains programs and data that are recorded into the memory at the factory. The contents of ROM can be read and used, but they cannot be changed by the user. ROMs are used to store programs, sometimes called **firmware**, that will not be altered. For example, a pocket calculator might have a program for calculating square roots in ROM; a personal computer might have a BASIC-interpreting program in ROM. ROM is nonvolatile—its contents do not disappear when the power is turned off.

With specialized tools called **ROM burners**, the instructions within some ROM chips can be changed. These changeable chips are known as **programmable read-only memory** chips, or **PROM** chips. Other variations on ROM chips are designed and classified according to the methods used to alter them. The business of programming and altering ROM chips is the province of the computer engineer. The rest of us are safe if we just leave ROM alone.

The memory designed for our use is RAM, the temporary storage compartments of the computer. They hold the instructions and data for whatever programs we happen to be using. RAM chips could accurately be described as read-write chips: A user can read the data stored there as well as write new data to replace what is there. The data can be accessed in an easy and speedy manner. RAM is usually volatile—that is, the data is lost once the power is shut off. This is one of the reasons, you recall, that we need secondary storage.

RAM is often divided into two types: **static** RAM (or **SRAM**) and **dynamic** RAM (or **DRAM**). SRAM memory chips are generally faster that DRAM, but their design requires more microscopic electronic components to store each bit. For the same amount of storage, SRAM is both more costly and physically larger than DRAM. On the other hand, DRAM must be constantly refreshed (recharged) by the central processing unit or it will lose its contents—hence the name *dynamic*. Because of the size and cost advantages, most personal computer memory is DRAM, though forms of SRAM are used in computers requiring low power consumption or higher speed.

The more RAM in your computer, the more powerful the programs you can run. In recent years the amount of RAM storage in a personal computer has increased dramatically. An early personal computer, for example, was advertised as including "a full 4K RAM." By 1980, however, most personal computers came with a standard RAM of 64K. Now, to hold larger programs with increasingly sophisticated capabilities, much larger memories are needed. From 640K to 1MB of RAM is usually considered the minimum, and 4MB to 8MB of RAM—or more—may be needed to work with most programs. Many personal computers now allow the user to shift quickly among several programs stored in memory at the same time. Extra memory is required to take advantage of this capability.

You can often augment the RAM of a personal computer by buying extra memory chips to add to the memory board or by buying another memory boardful of chips. A popular style of memory expansion, **single in-line memory modules (SIMM)**, is a circuit board containing 1MB, 2MB, 4MB, or 16MB memory chips that plug into SIMM sockets on the main circuit board of the computer. It is easier to buy SIMMs or extra memory boards since they slip into place more readily than individual chips do.

 ## Computer Processing Speeds

We have saved the discussion of speed until last. Although speed is basic to computer processing, speed is also an ever-changing facet and a good jumping-off point to the future.

The characteristic of speed is universally associated with computers. Certainly all computers are fast, but there is a wide diversity of computer speeds. The execution of an instruction on a very slow computer may be measured in less than a **millisecond,** which is one-thousandth of a second (see Table 2-1). Most computers can execute an instruction measured in **microseconds,** one-millionth of a second. Some modern computers have reached the **nanosecond** range—one-billionth of a second. Still to be broken is the **picosecond** barrier—one-trillionth of a second.

The speed of a computer system might be measured in several ways. For personal computers, **clock speed** is often used. Clock speed is generally expressed in **megahertz,** which represents one million ticks per second. Remember that the clock synchronizes the opera-

Table 2-1 Units of Time: How Fast Is _Fast?_

Unit of Time	Fraction of a Second	Mathematical Notation
Millisecond	Thousandth: 1/1000	10^{-3}
Microsecond	Millionth: 1/1,000,000	10^{-6}
Nanosecond	Billionth: 1/1,000,000,000	10^{-9}
Picosecond	Trillionth: 1/1,000,000,000,000	10^{-12}

How Fast Is a Nanosecond?

If one nanosecond is . . .	Then one second is equivalent to . . .
one mile	2000 trips to the moon and back
one person	the population of China and the United States
one minute	1900 years
one square mile	17 times the land area of the entire world

tion of the computer. Other things being equal, the faster the clock, the faster the computer.

Another measure of computer speed is **MIPS,** which stands for *one million instructions per second.* MIPS is often a more accurate measure than clock speed, because some computers can use each tick of the clock more efficiently than others. For example, when the Intel 486 processor was first introduced, it used a clock speed of 25 megahertz; the older Intel 386 used a clock speed of 33 megahertz. But even at the slower speed, the 486 could perform over 50% faster because of the increased efficiency of its design. Intel has released 33-and 50-megahertz versions—for a speed increase of over 100%.

A third measure of speed is the **megaflop,** which stands for *one million floating-point operations per second.* It measures the ability of the computer to perform complex mathematical operations.

More Speed? What's the Rush?

Computer speeds are beyond anything that we mortals can relate to physically. The blink of an eye takes about half a second—500 times slower than a millisecond, the measuring stick of the *slow* computers. The fastest computers, it would seem, ought to be fast enough for even the most sophisticated computer users. But this is not so. This is not just a greed-for-speed scenario—some people really need still more computer speed.

Just who needs all that speed? A physicist at New York University, for one. He coaxed a big, powerful computer to simulate the behavior of helium atoms at -459° Fahrenheit—that is, near absolute zero. Each time he ran the program, it took all weekend to grind away. At that rate the scientist had to wait two years to get the first satisfactory results. Scientists often work this way. A scientist has an idea of how something works—atoms or ocean currents or prime numbers—and can describe it in terms of numbers and equations. Then the scientist plays elaborate "What if . . . ?" games by changing the numbers and recalculating the equations. These new calculations, of course, are done on the computer. A lot of data means a lot of computer time—even on supercomputers.

The traditional approach to increased speed has been to decrease the distances that electric signals must travel, because the limiting factor is the speed of electricity. Computer designers have packed circuits closer together, making tighter and tighter squeezes in the same space. All these electronic devices humming together in such proximity produce an overheating problem, which must be attacked with elaborate cooling systems.

Modern approaches to increased computer speed include two other strategies: RISC technology and parallel processing. These topics are so important that they deserve sections of their own.

RISC Technology: Less Is More

It flies in the face of computer tradition: Instead of reaching for more variety, more power, more everything-for-everyone, proponents of **RISCs—**

reduced instruction set computers—suggest that we could get by with a little less. In fact, reduced instruction set computers offer only a small subset of instructions; the absence of bells and whistles increases speed. So we have a radical back-to-basics movement in computer design.

RISC supporters say that, on conventional computers (called **CISCs**, or **complex instruction set computers**), a hefty chunk of built-in instructions—the instruction set—is rarely used. Those instructions, they note, are underused, inefficient, and impediments to performance. RISC computers, with their stripped-down instruction sets, zip through programs like racing cars—at speeds four to ten times those of CISC computers. This is heady stuff for the merchants of speed who want to attract customers by offering more speed for the money.

Several considerations contribute to the speed of RISC computers:

- The simplified format of the instructions allows central processing units to be more efficient in carrying them out.

- Because registers are faster to access than memory, RISC computers have many more registers than older designs. Whereas an older machine might have 10 to 20 registers, a RISC computer might have hundreds.

- Instead of fetching one instruction at a time from memory, RISC computers can bring several instructions to the central processing unit at once, keeping them in special registers where they can be accessed quickly.

- In a process called **pipelining**, the central processing unit can start executing one or more instructions before finishing the previous one. For instance, while the result of one instruction is being stored, the arithmetic/logic unit within the central processing unit can be performing the arithmetic in another instruction, and the control unit can be decoding a third.

Does this mean that CISC computers will be a thing of the past? As the old saying goes, If you can't beat 'em, join 'em. Many manufacturers of CISC computers are incorporating the design strategies associated with RISC computers. However, some computers in the RISC camp are edging back toward CISC design. For example, the IBM RS/6000, a RISC computer, has 184 instructions—more than some computers considered to be in the CISC category. Perhaps the end result will be computers that combine the best features of both types of design.

Meanwhile, some people are looking in a different direction altogether. They are actually changing computer architecture to achieve another solution: parallel processing.

Parallel Processing: The Ultimate Speed Solution

A wave of technological change is sweeping over the computer industry. Far-reaching claims such as this are not new in the computer business, so perhaps we could emphasize this point by saying that this change is akin to reinventing the computer. Consider the description of computer processing you have seen so far in this chapter: The processor gets an instruction from memory, acts on it, returns processed data to memory, then repeats the process. Even RISC computers still use one processor that carries out instructions in order. This is conventional **serial processing.**

The problem with the conventional computer is that the single electronic pathway, the bus line, acts like a bottleneck. The computer has a one-track mind because it is restricted to handling one piece of data at a time. For many applications, such as simulating the air flow around an entire airplane in flight, this is an exceedingly inefficient procedure. A better solution? Many processors, each with its own memory unit, working at the same time: **parallel processing** (Figure 2-10).

Some early computer inventors saw that parallel processors working in tandem were preferable, but the limited technology of the day made parallel processing out of the question. Inventors have been tinkering with parallel processors in the lab ever since. Now years of research are

Figure 2-10   Serial vs. parallel processing. (a) Serial processing involves one processor working with one piece of data at a time. (b) Parallel processing involves a number of processors working in concert.

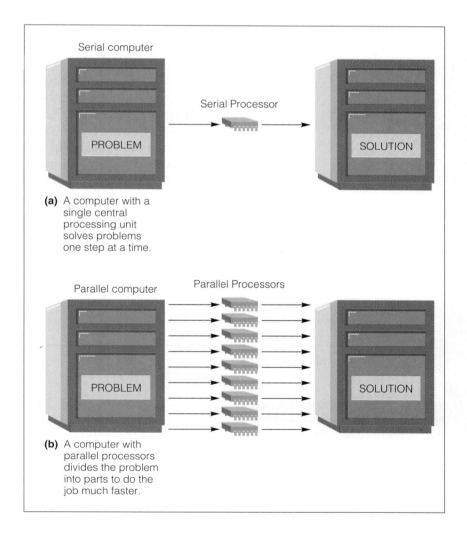

Serial computer

Serial Processor

PROBLEM

SOLUTION

(a) A computer with a single central processing unit solves problems one step at a time.

Parallel computer   Parallel Processors

PROBLEM

SOLUTION

(b) A computer with parallel processors divides the problem into parts to do the job much faster.

starting to pay off: A number of parallel processors are being built and sold commercially. (See the essay "Perspectives: The Fastest Computer Sold" in Chapter 1.)

Let us return to the example of the airplane flight simulation. Using a single conventional processor, the computer could calculate flow between two points on the surface of the plane. Since there are millions of such pairs of points, this calculation method is inefficient. A serial computer would waste most of its time repeatedly retrieving and storing vast amounts of data and devote relatively little time to actual computation. In contrast, a parallel processor could take several pieces of data and perform a series of operations on them in parallel.

Eight processors working together are not necessarily eight times as fast, however. The saying that "Too many cooks spoil the broth" can apply to computers as well. Just as it is difficult to get a group of people to work together, creating programs that can keep more than one processor fully utilized is difficult. If some processors have to wait for the information being processed by others, parallel processing is operating less efficiently than we might expect.

Next: Future Chip Talk

The future holds some exciting possibilities. New speed breakthroughs certainly will continue. One day we may see computers that operate using light (photonics) rather than electricity (electronics) to control their operation. Light travels faster and is less likely to be disrupted by electrical interference. Also, light beams can pass through each other, alleviating some of the problems that occur in the design of electronic components, in which wires should not cross.

And would you believe computers that are actually grown as biological cultures? So-called biochips may replace today's silicon chip. As research continues, so will the surprises.

Whatever the design and processing strategy of a computer, its goal is the same: to turn raw input into useful output. Input and output are the topics of the next chapter.

R E V I E W   A N D   R E F E R E N C E

Summary and Key Terms

- The **central processing unit (CPU)** is an extensive, complex set of electronic circuitry that executes program instructions. It consists of two parts: a control unit and an arithmetic/logic unit.

- The central processing unit interacts closely with **primary storage**, or **memory**. Memory provides temporary storage of data while the computer is executing the program. **Secondary storage** holds the data that is permanent or semi-permanent.

- The **control unit** of the central processing unit coordinates execution of the program instructions by communicating with the arithmetic/logic unit and memory—the parts of the system that actually execute the program.

- The **arithmetic/logic unit (ALU)** contains circuitry that executes the arithmetic and logical operations. The unit can perform four **arithmetic operations:** addition, subtraction, multiplication, and division. Its **logical operations** are usually making comparisons that test for three conditions: the **equal to condition,** the **less than condition,** and the **greater than condition.** The computer can test for more than one condition at once, so it can discern three other conditions as well: less than or equal to, greater than or equal to, and less than or greater than.

- Symbols called **relational operators** (=, <, >) allow you to define the comparison you want the computer to perform.

- **Registers,** areas for temporary storage, quickly accept, hold, and transfer instructions or data. A register might be an **accumulator,** which collects the result of computations. A **storage register** temporarily holds data taken from or about to be sent to memory. Each storage location in memory is identified by an **address.** (Address numbers remain the same, but the contents of the locations change.) An **address register** keeps track of where data is stored in memory, and a **general-purpose register** is used for several functions.

- Registers hold data that will be processed immediately, and memory stores the data that will soon be used in operations. Secondary storage holds data that may be needed for operations later.

- **Memory** is the part of the computer that temporarily holds data and instructions before and after they are processed by the arithmetic/logic unit. Memory is also known as **primary storage, primary memory, main storage, internal storage,** and **main memory.** Most types of memory keep data only when the computer is turned on.

- The central processing unit follows four main steps when executing an instruction: It (1) gets the instruction from memory, (2) decodes the instruction and gives instructions for the transfer of appropriate data from memory to the ALU, (3) directs the ALU to perform the actual operation on the data, and (4) directs the result of the operation to be stored in memory or a register. The first two steps are called **I-time** (instruction time), and the last two steps are called **E-time** (execution time).

- A **machine cycle** is the combination of I-time and E-time. The internal **clock** of the central processing unit produces pulses at a fixed rate to synchronize computer operations. A machine-cycle instruction may include many subinstructions, each of which must take at least one clock cycle. Each central processing unit has a set of commands it can understand. This group is called an **instruction set.**

- Since a computer can recognize only whether electricity is on or off, data is represented by an on/off **binary system.** Two digits, 0 and 1, correspond to off and on.

- Combinations of 0s and 1s represent numbers, letters, or special characters.

- Each 0 or 1 in the binary system is called a **bit** (*bi*nary dig*it*). A group of bits (usually 8 bits) is called a **byte.** Each byte usually represents one character of data, such as a letter, digit, or special character. Memory capacity is expressed in **kilobytes (KB** or **K).** One kilobyte equals 1024 bytes. A **megabyte (MB),** equals about one million bytes, and a **gigabyte (GB),** equals about one billion bytes.

- A computer **word** is the number of bits that make up a unit of data, as defined by the computer system. Common word lengths are from 8 bits to 64 bits. Word length is usually related to the capacity of the computer's **buses,** or **bus lines.** These are collections of wires that provide data paths for transferring bits from one part of the computer to another. In general, a larger word length means a more powerful computer—the computer can transfer more information at one time, can have a larger memory, and can support a greater number and variety of instructions.

- Commonly used coding schemes for representing characters are **EBCDIC** (Extended Binary Coded Decimal Interchange Code), which uses 8-bit characters, and **ASCII** (American Standard Code for Information Interchange), which uses 7-bit characters. One possible code for future use is **Unicode,** which will be a 16-bit code designed to store the characters of all the world's languages.

- A **parity bit,** or **check bit,** is an extra bit added to each byte; it may alert the computer if data has been damaged in transmission.

- A central processing unit on a chip is called a **microprocessor,** or **logic chip.** Microprocessors usually contain a control unit and an ALU, registers, bus lines, and a clock. For memory, most modern computers use **semiconductor storage,** thousands of circuits on a silicon chip. Semiconductor storage is compact and economical, but it is also **volatile**—if the power is shut off, the data is lost. One important type of semiconductor design is called **CMOS (complementary metal oxide semiconductor).**

- There are two basic types of memory chips, **random-access memory (RAM)** and **read-only memory (ROM).** RAM provides volatile storage for data and instructions and can be increased by adding extra memory chips. Data in RAM must be saved in secondary storage before the computer is turned off. ROM is nonvolatile—ROM programs (or **firmware**), which are recorded into the memory at the factory, remain after the computer is turned off. The data and instructions on **programmable read-only memory (PROM)** chips can be changed with **ROM burners.**

- RAM is often divided into two types: **static RAM (SRAM)** and **dynamic RAM (DRAM).** SRAM is generally faster than DRAM, but SRAM needs more microscopic electronic components to store each bit. For the same amount of storage, SRAM is both more costly and physically larger than DRAM. DRAM is dynamic, therefore, the central processing unit must constantly refresh (recharge) it or it will lose its contents.

- A **single in-line memory module (SIMM)** is a memory board of extra RAM. SIMMs can hold 1 MB, 2MB, 4MB, or 16MB modules of memory that plug easily into SIMM sockets on the main circuit board of the computer.

- Computer speed can be measured in **milliseconds** (one-thousandth of a second), **microseconds** (one-millionth of a second), and even **nanoseconds** (one-billionth of a second). The **picosecond** barrier (one-trillionth of a second) is yet to be broken.

- The speed of a computer system can be measured in several ways. For personal computers, the **clock speed** is often used. Clock speed is generally expressed in **megahertz,** which represents one million ticks per second. Another measure of computer speed is **MIPS,** which stands for *one million instructions per second.* MIPS is often a more accurate measure than clock speed, because some computers use each tick more efficiently than others. A third measure, the **megaflop,** stands for *one million floating-point operations per second.*

- One way to increase computer speed is to decrease the distance electric signals must travel by packing circuits closer together. Another way to increase speed is by building a **reduced instruction set computer** (**RISC**). This contrasts with a **complex instruction set computer** (**CISC**). RISC computers increase their speed by simplifying the format of the instructions, using more registers; fetching several instructions from memory at one time; and using **pipelining,** in which the CPU can start executing one or more instructions before finishing the previous ones. Design features of RISC computers are now being used in the design of CISC computers as well. Finally, **parallel processing** uses many processors working at the same time—a method that could replace traditional **serial processing**. Unlike serial processing, parallel processing allows the computer to handle more than one piece of data at a time.

Review Questions

1. Name and describe the functions of the two parts of the central processing unit.
2. How does memory differ from secondary storage?
3. Name and describe the functions of the four types of registers.
4. What is the function of computer memory?
5. Describe the steps in the execution of a program instruction.
6. How does the control unit find instructions and data?
7. Explain why the binary system is used to represent data for the computer.

8. Define the following: bit, byte, kilobyte, megabyte, gigabyte, and word.
9. Why is the word size of a computer important?
10. What is a bus line?
11. Name and describe the two main coding schemes.
12. Explain how a parity bit alerts the computer to errors.
13. What are the advantages of semiconductor storage?
14. Define the following: RAM, ROM, and PROM.
15. Define the following: millisecond, microsecond, nanosecond, and picosecond.
16. Describe ways of increasing computer speed.
17. What is an instruction set?
18. For what kind of applications is a CMOS design especially useful?
19. What are three differences between SRAM and DRAM?
20. Describe ways of measuring the speed of a central processing unit.
21. What are some of the methods used to increase the speed of RISC computers?

Discussion Questions

1. Give an example of a practical application of each of the three basic logical operations.
2. Why is writing instructions for a computer more difficult than writing instructions for a person?
3. Do you think there is a continuing need to increase computer speed? Explain your answer.
4. Some people believe we will have chips implanted in our bodies someday. Such chips might help to replace injured limbs or impaired senses. Do you think this is a good or bad idea? Defend your answer.
5. Look into the future. How might photonic computers be used?

True-False Questions

T F 1. Storage locations that are part of the design of the central processing unit are called addresses.
T F 2. The clock is the component of the computer that produces pulses at a fixed rate to synchronize all computer operations.
T F 3. Computer memory stores data in bits, or binary digits.
T F 4. A megabyte stores more information than a gigabyte.
T F 5. The two most common codes for storing computer information are EBCDIC and ASCII.
T F 6. The parity bit shows whether an error has occurred during transmission of data.
T F 7. The parts of a computer are connected by collections of wires called conduits.
T F 8. The ALU is the part of the central processing unit that decodes instructions and directs the operation of the CPU.

T F   9. A RISC computer would generally have a smaller instruction set than a CISC computer.

T F 10. Of RAM and ROM, the type of memory that is normally volatile is ROM.

T F 11. Each central processing unit has a pre-defined group of commands that it understands; this group is called the instruction set.

T F 12. The type of processing in which several central processing units work together to solve a problem is called serial processing.

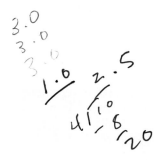

Input and Output

Data Given, Information Received

How input and output relate to a computer system was not what Paul
Yen had in mind when he thumbed through the catalog from Lands' End,
a mail-order firm in Wisconsin that offers quality casual and sports clothing. Paul simply wanted to order a few knit shirts and a leather belt.
Whether he knew it or not, however, when Paul wrote these items on
the order form, he started the computer action rolling.

The items on his order form would become input data for the computer system. In this example, the input is the data related to the customer order—customer name, address, and (possibly) charge-card number—as well as the data for each item—catalog number, quantity,

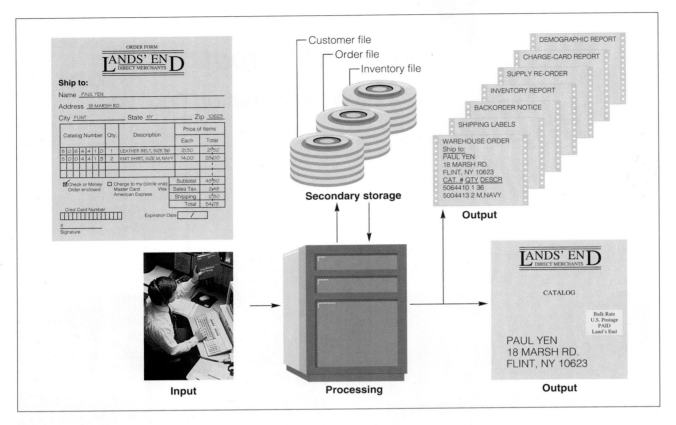

Figure 3-1   Lands' End. At this mail-order house, customer order data is input, processed, and used to produce a variety of outputs.

description, and price. Keyed into the Lands' End computer system as soon as it arrives, this data is placed in customer and order files to be used with files containing inventory and other related data.

What Paul provided as input can be processed into a variety of outputs, as shown in Figure 3-1. Some outputs are for individual customers, and some show information combined from several orders: warehouse orders, shipping labels (to send the shirts and belt), backorder notices, inventory reports, supply reorder reports, charge-card reports, demographic reports (showing which merchandise sells best where), and so forth. And—to keep the whole process going—Lands' End also prints out Paul's name and address on a label for the next catalog.

Input and Output: The People Connection

We have already pointed out how the central processing unit is the unseen part of a computer system. But users are very much aware—and in control—of the input data given to the computer. They submit data to the computer to get processed information, the output. Output is what makes the computer useful to people.

Sometimes the output is an instant reaction to the input. Consider these examples:

- Zebra-stripe bar codes on supermarket items provide input that permits instant retrieval of outputs—price and item name—right at the checkout counter.

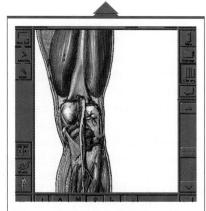

Twenty-First Century Anatomy Lessons

If you ever considered studying medicine—then changed your mind when you thought about dissecting things—well, a computer program might convince you to reconsider. A.D.A.M., which stands for Animated Dissection of Anatomy for Medicine, is a new software application that is being called a twenty-first–century version of *Gray's Anatomy,* the classic anatomy textbook used by almost all medical students.

The program is designed for use with a mouse instead of a knife. You can use A.D.A.M. to peel away layers of skin and study the underlying muscles and bones. You can even try your hand at "surgery"—without shedding a drop of blood.

"No one has ever illustrated anatomy in this kind of detail," says Greg Swayne, the medical illustrator who is president of A.D.A.M. Software, Inc. of Marietta, Georgia. Swayne believes the software will revolutionize the way medicine is taught and practiced by taking anatomy out of the textbook. Medical students can dissect without cutting into real cadavers, and doctors can show patients exactly what is wrong—or right—with them.

- You use a joy stick—a kind of hand-controlled lever—to input data to guide the alien spacecraft—or whatever—in a computer game. The output is the desired movement of the spacecraft.

- A medical student studies the human body on a computer screen, inputting changes to the program to show a close-up of the leg, then to "tear" away several layers of skin and reveal the bone and muscles underneath. The screen outputs the changes, allowing the student—without donning a mask, sanitary gloves, or operating gown—to try "surgery" for the first time right on the computer.

- A bank teller queries the computer through the small terminal at the window by giving a customer's account number as input. The same screen immediately provides the customer's account balance as output.

- A forklift operator speaks to a computer directly, through a microphone. Words like *left, right,* and *lift* are the actual input data. The output is the computer's instant response, which causes the forklift to operate as requested.

- A sales representative uses an instrument that looks like a pen to enter an order on a special pad. The handwritten characters are displayed as "typed" text and are stored in the pad, which is actually a small computer.

You may have participated in or witnessed most of these practical applications without recognizing them as examples of instantaneous input/output.

Input and output may sometimes be separated by time and/or distance. Some examples:

- Factory workers input data by punching in on a time clock as they go from task to task. The time clock is connected to a computer. The outputs are their weekly paychecks and management reports that summarize hours per project on a quarterly basis.

- A college student writes checks. The data on the checks is used as input to the bank computer, which eventually processes the data to prepare a bank statement once a month.

- Charge-card transactions in a retail store provide input data that is processed monthly to produce customer bills.

- Water-sample data is collected at lake and river sites, keyed in at the environmental agency office, and used to produce reports that show patterns of water quality.

The examples in this section show the diversity of computer applications, but, in all cases, the process is the same: input-processing-output. We have already had an introduction to processing. Now, in this chapter, we will examine input and output methods in detail. We begin with a description of types of input; then consider computer screens (displays used for both input and output); and, finally, we examine devices that are used for output only.

Types of Input

Some input data can go directly to the computer for processing. Input in this category includes bar codes; speech that enters the computer through a microphone; and data entered by means of a device that converts motions to on-screen action. (This section will discuss all these options.) Some input data, however, goes through a good deal of intermediate handling, such as when it is copied form a **source document** (jargon for the original written data) and translated to a medium that a machine can read, such as a magnetic disk. In either case the task is to gather data to be processed by the computer—sometimes called *raw data*—and convert it into some form the computer can understand. The evolution of input devices is toward equipment that is easy to use, fast, and accurate.

Keyboard Entry

The most popular input device is the keyboard. A keyboard, which usually is similar to a typewriter, may be part of a personal computer or part of a terminal that is connected to a computer somewhere else (Figure 3-2a). Not all keyboards are traditional, however. A fast-food franchise like McDonald's, for example, uses keyboards whose keys each represent an item, such as large fries or a Big Mac (Figure 3-2b). Even less traditional is the keyboard shown in Figure 3-2c, which is used to enter Chinese characters.

Keyboards and Personal Computer Users Users of personal computers find that familiarity with a keyboard breeds productivity. Consider

Figure 3-2 **Keyboards.** (a) A traditional computer keyboard. (b) Workers at McDonald's press a key for each item ordered. The amount of the order is totaled by the computer system, then displayed on a small screen so the customer can see the amount owed. (c) Chinese characters are significantly more complicated than the letters and digits found on a standard keyboard. To enter Chinese characters into the computer system, a person uses a special keyboard. Each letter key shows the characters available by holding down other keys while typing (as you would hold down a shift key to make capitals).

(a)

(b)

(c)

the traditional flow of paperwork in an office: A manager writes a memo by hand or dictates it, then a secretary types it. The manager checks the typed memo; if there are changes to be made, the secretary must retype it. With a personal computer on the manager's desk, however, the manager can enter the memo by using the keyboard, proofread it on the screen, and make any necessary changes before it is printed. This greatly reduces the lag time between writing a memo and getting it in the mail.

Keyboards and Data Entry Operators   Entering large amounts of data via keyboard calls for the services of data entry operators. **Data entry operators** use computer terminals or perhaps personal computers to enter data from some nonautomated form, usually handwriting on paper (see the photo labeled "Input" in Figure 3-1). Such a system is often used to process large quantities of data that can be handled in groups, or batches, such as engineering drawing data, customer payments, or bank transactions received in the mail.

The data that operators enter into the system can be stored on either tape or magnetic disk. The tapes or disks are then sent to the main computer for processing. In many systems, the data can be entered directly into the computer.

The Mouse

The **mouse,** popularized by the Macintosh computer, is a computer input device that actually looks a little bit like a mouse (Figure 3-3a). The mouse, which has a ball on its underside, is rolled on a flat surface, usually the desk on which the computer sits. The rolling movement that results when you push the mouse causes the related output, a corresponding movement on the screen. Moving the mouse allows you to reposition the **pointer,** or **cursor,** an indicator on the screen that shows where the next interaction with the computer will take place. The cursor can also be moved by pressing various keyboard keys. You can communicate commands to the computer by pressing a button on top of the mouse.

Figure 3-3   Mouse. (a) As the ball on the underside of the mouse moves over a smooth surface such as a desktop, the pointer on the screen makes a corresponding movement. (b) Once the pointer is in position, a user can select an option from a list of choices by pressing a button on the mouse.

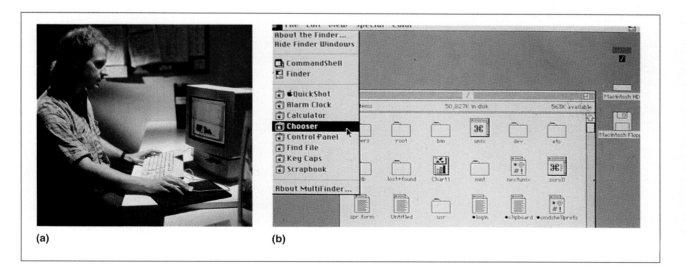

(a)   (b)

Personal Computers in Action

FINDING YOUR WAY AROUND A KEYBOARD

Most personal computer keyboards have three main parts: function keys, the main keyboard in the center, and numeric keys to the right. Extended keyboards, such as the IBM PS/2 keyboard shown here, have additional keys between the main keyboard and the numeric

keys and status lights in the upper-right corner.

Function Keys

The function keys (highlighted in green on the diagram) are an easy way to give certain commands to the computer. What each function key does is defined by the particular software you are using. For instance, using WordPerfect, a popular word processing program, you press function key F4 to indent and F8 to underline text. Function keys can be located across the top of the keyboard, as shown here, or on the left side of the keyboard.

Main Keyboard

The main keyboard includes the familiar keys found on a typewriter keyboard (dark blue), as well as some special command keys (light blue). The command keys have different uses that depend on the software being used. Some of the most common uses are listed here.

 The Escape key, Esc, is used in different ways by different programs; often it allows you to "escape" to the previous screen of the program.

 The Tab key allows you to tab across the screen and set tab stops as you would on a typewriter.

 When the Caps Lock key is pressed, upper-case letters are produced. Numbers and symbols are not affected—the number or symbol shown on the bottom of a key is still produced. When the Caps Lock key is pressed, the status light under "Caps Lock" lights up.

 The Shift key allows you to produce uppercase letters and the upper symbols shown on the keys.

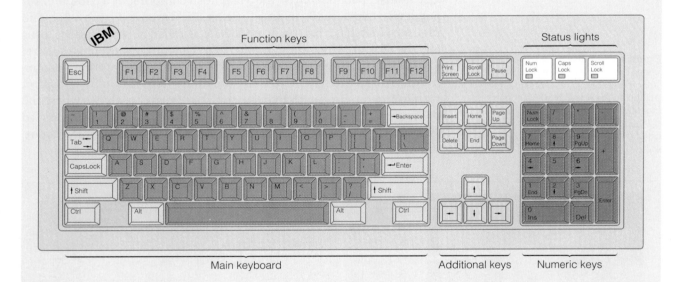

Main keyboard   Additional keys   Numeric keys

Some people who write software for personal computers have made the mouse an important part of using the software. For example, some software displays pictorial symbols called **icons** (Figure 3-3b). One icon might be a picture of a sheet of paper; the symbol represents a memo you have stored. If you want to retrieve the memo, roll the mouse on the desk surface until the pointer is over the picture of the paper. Then signal the

The Control key, Ctrl, is pressed in combination with other keys to initiate commands as specified by the software.

 The Alternate key, Alt, is also used in combination with other keys to initiate commands.

 The Backspace key is most often used to delete a character to the left of the cursor, moving the cursor back one position. (The cursor is the flashing indicator on the screen that shows where the next character will be inserted.)

 The Enter key moves the cursor to the beginning of the next line. It is used at the end of a paragraph, for instance.

Numeric Keys

The numeric keys (purple) serve one of two purposes, depending on the status of the Num Lock key. When the computer is in the Num Lock mode, these keys can be used to enter numeric data and mathematical symbols (/ for "divided by," * for "multiplied by," -, and +). In the Num Lock mode, the status light under "Num Lock" lights up. When the computer is not in the Num Lock mode, the numeric keys can be used to move the cursor and perform other functions. For example:

 The End key moves the cursor to the bottom-left corner of the screen.

 This key moves the cursor down.

 The Page Down key, PgDn, advances one full screen while the cursor stays in the same place.

 This key moves the cursor to the left.

 This key moves the cursor to the right.

 The Home key moves the cursor to the top-left corner of the screen.

 This key moves the cursor up.

 The Page Up key, PgUp, backs up to the previous screen while the cursor stays in the same place.

 The Insert key, Ins, can be used to insert additional characters within a line.

 The Delete key, Del, deletes a character or space.

Additional Keys

Extended keyboards include additional keys (yellow) that duplicate the cursor movement functions of the numeric keys. Users who enter a lot of numeric data can leave their computers in the Num Lock mode and use these additional keys to control the cursor.

The Arrow keys, to the left of the numeric keys, move the cursor position, just as the numeric keys 2, 4, 6, and 8 do when they are not in the Num Lock mode.

Just above the arrow keys are six keys—Insert, Delete, Home, End, Page Up, and Page Down—which duplicate functions of the numeric keys 0, decimal point (Del), 7, 1, 9, and 3.

At the top of the keyboard, to the right of the function keys, are keys that perform additional tasks. For example:

 The Print Screen key, when pressed with the Shift key, causes the current screen display to be printed.

 The Scroll Lock key causes lines of text—not the cursor—to move when cursor keys are used. When the computer is in the Scroll Lock mode, the status light under "Scroll Lock" lights up.

 The Pause key causes the screen to pause when information is appearing too fast to read.

computer that you wish to work with the memo by rapidly pressing the mouse button twice (this action is known as a **double-click**). These actions replace typing commands on the keyboard.

With the introduction of the *Microsoft*® *Windows*™ graphical environment—Windows, for short—in the IBM world, many users have converted to the mouse method of interacting with their personal computers. Recent mouse models have rubber-coated control balls for smoother, near-silent operation on all surfaces. A variation on the mouse is the **trackball.** You may have used a trackball to play a video game. The trackball is like an upside-down mouse—you roll the ball directly with your hand. The trackball has two advantages: It does not require a clear surface to roll on, and it can be attached firmly to the keyboard or computer case (it is often built in on portable computers).

Source Data Automation: Collecting Data Where It Starts

The challenge to productive data entry is clear: Cut down the number of intermediate steps required between data and processing so data processing becomes more efficient. This is best accomplished by **source data automation**—the use of special equipment to collect data at the source and send it directly to the computer. Source data automation is an enticing alternative to typing, because by eliminating the keying it reduces costs and the opportunities for human-introduced mistakes. Since data about a transaction is collected when and where the transaction takes place, source data automation also improves the speed of the input operation.

One characteristic of source data automation is that the data entry equipment needs to be fairly easy to use, reliable, and maintenance-free. The people who use it are often data entry personnel who do not receive much computer training—meter readers, shop clerks, and grocery clerks, for example.

For convenience we will divide this discussion into four areas related to source data automation: magnetic-ink character recognition, optical recognition, data collection devices, and voice input. Let us consider each of these in turn.

Magnetic-Ink Character Recognition   Abbreviated **MICR, magnetic-ink character recognition** is a method of machine-reading characters made of magnetized particles. The most common example of magnetic characters is the array of futuristic-looking numbers on the bottom of your personal check. Figure 3-4 shows what some of these numbers and attached symbols represent.

The MICR process is, in fact, used mainly by banks for processing checks. Checks are read by a machine called a **MICR reader/sorter,** which sorts the checks into different compartments and sends electronic signals—read from the magnetic ink on the check—to the computer.

Most magnetic-ink characters are pre-printed on your check. If you compare a check you wrote that has been cashed and cleared by the bank with those that are still unused in your checkbook, you will note that the amount of the cashed check has been reproduced in magnetic characters in the lower-right corner. These characters were added by a person at the bank by using a **MICR inscriber.** (If you find a discrepancy between the amount you wrote on your check and the amount given on your bank statement, look at the inscribed number. Maybe someone had trouble reading your handwriting.)

Figure 3-4 The symbols on your check.
Magnetic-ink numbers and symbols run along the bottom of a check. The symbols on the left are pre-printed; the MICR characters in the lower-right corner of a cashed check are entered by the bank that receives it. Note that the numbers should correspond to the amount of the check.

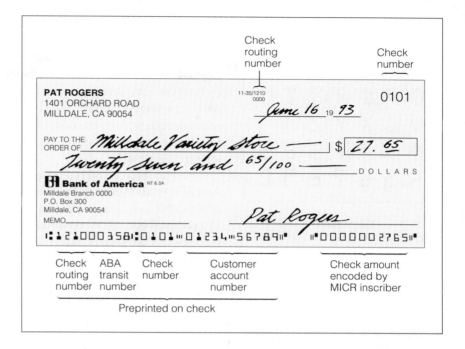

When your check is run through the reader/sorter, it is sorted by account number so that it can be stored along with all of your checks and returned to you with your statement at the end of the month. (Some banks, however, keep the checks themselves in the interest of saving handling and postage.) Torn and otherwise mutilated checks that cannot be read by the machine are sent to a separate compartment of the machine. The banking transaction is later recorded by a person who handles the check manually.

Optical Recognition Systems that use **optical recognition** can read numbers, letters, special characters, and marks by "looking" at them. An electronic scanning device converts the data into electrical signals and sends the signals to the computer for processing. Various optical recognition devices can read these types of input:

- Optical marks
- Optical characters
- Handwritten characters
- Bar codes

Optical Mark Recognition Abbreviated **OMR, optical mark recognition** is sometimes called *mark sensing,* because a machine senses marks on a piece of paper. As a student, you may immediately recognize this approach as the technique used to score certain tests. Using a pencil, you make a mark in a specified box or space that corresponds to what you think is the answer. The answer sheet is then graded by a device that uses a light beam to recognize the marks and convert them to electrical signals, which are sent to the computer for processing.

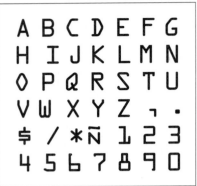

Figure 3-5   OCR-A typeface. This is a common standard font for optical character recognition.

Figure 3-6   Wand reader. The photo shows a clerk using a wand reader to scan a price tag printed with OCR-A characters. The price and merchandise number are entered into the computer through the point-of-sale (POS) terminal. The computer retrieves a description of the merchandise from secondary storage and calculates the total price of the purchase. A printer in the terminal produces a receipt for the customer. Later, computer reports can be generated for store personnel to use.

Optical Character Recognition   Abbreviated **OCR, optical character recognition** devices also use a light source to read special characters and convert them into electrical signals to be sent to the central processing unit. The characters—letters, numbers, and special symbols—can be read by both humans and machines. They are often found on sales tags in department stores or imprinted on credit-card slips in gas stations after the sale has been written up. A standard typeface for optical characters, called **OCR-A,** has been established by the American National Standards Institute (Figure 3-5).

The handheld **wand reader** is a popular input device for reading OCR-A. There is an increasing use of wands in libraries, hospitals, and factories, as well as in retail stores. In retail stores the wand reader is connected to a **point-of-sale (POS) terminal** (Figure 3-6). This terminal is like a cash register in many ways, but it performs many more functions. When a clerk passes the wand reader over the price tag, both the price and the merchandise number are entered into the computer system. Given the merchandise number, the computer can retrieve a description of the item from a file. This description is displayed on the screen of the point-of-sale terminal along with the price. (Some systems, by the way, input only the merchandise number and retrieve both price and description.) A small printer produces a customer receipt that also shows both the item description and the price. The computer calculates the subtotal, the sales tax (if any), and the total. This information is displayed on the screen and printed on the receipt.

The raw purchase data becomes valuable information when it is summarized by the computer system. This information can be used by the accounting department to keep track of how much money is taken in each day, by buyers to determine what merchandise should be reordered, and by the marketing department to analyze the effectiveness of their ad campaigns. Thus, capturing data at the time of the sale provides many benefits beyond giving the customer a fancy computerized receipt.

Some OCR readers are less finicky than others. The Postal Service uses scanners that can handle 30,000 letters an hour. The human eye can barely follow individual envelopes as they are sucked out of a feeder, run through the OCR scanner, and dispatched to one of several slots. Eleven people using conventional equipment and their own eyes cannot sort as fast as one machine. However, not all the letters mailed end up on the scanner. Most handwritten zip codes are sent to human sorters.

Handwritten Characters   Machines that can read handwritten characters are yet another means of reducing the number of intermediate steps between capturing data and processing it. There are many instances where it is preferable to write the data and immediately have it usable for processing rather than having data entry operators key it in later. However, not just any kind of handwritten scrawl will do; the rules as to the size, completeness, and legibility of the handwriting are fairly rigid (Figure 3-7). The Internal Revenue Service uses optical scanners to read handwritten numbers on some income tax forms. Taxpayers must follow the directions for forming numbers, however.

Figure 3-7   Handwritten characters.
Legibility is important in making handwritten characters readable by optical recognition.

	Good	Bad
1. Make your letters big	*TAPLEY*	*TAPLEY*
2. Use simple shapes	*25370*	*25370*
3. Use block printing	*STAN*	*STAN*
4. Connect lines	*B5T*	*135T*
5. Close loops	*9068*	*9068*
6. Do not link characters	*LOOP*	*LOOP*

Bar Codes   Each product on the store shelf has its own unique number, which is part of the **Universal Product Code** (**UPC**). This code number is represented on the product label by a pattern of vertical marks, or bars, called **bar codes.** You need only look as far as the back cover of this book to see an example of a bar code. These zebra stripes can be sensed and read by a **bar code reader,** a photoelectric scanner that reads the code by means of reflected light. As with the wand reader in a retail store, the bar code reader in a bookstore or grocery store is part of a point-of-sale terminal. When you buy, say, canned corn in a supermarket, the checker moves it past the scanner that reads the bar code (Figure 3-8a). The bar code merely identifies the product to the store's computer; the code does not contain the price, which may vary. The price is stored in a file that can be accessed by the computer. (Obviously, it is easier to change the price once in the computer than to have to repeatedly restamp the price on each can of corn.) The computer automatically tells the point-of-sale terminal what the price is; a printer prints the item description and price on a paper tape for the customer.

There are a great many benefits using the UPC system—benefits that help slow the rise of grocery prices:

- Prices determined at the point-of-sale terminal by scanning are more accurate than those rung up by human checkers.

- Checkout is faster.

- Checkout training is easier, since the machine does most of the work previously done by people punching keys.

- Cash register tapes are more complete, since they identify not only prices but also name the corresponding purchases.

- Labor costs are reduced.

- Inventory control and marketing are easier. As goods are moved through the checkout stand, the computer can keep a tally of what is left on the shelves and signal the store manager when restocking and reordering are necessary. Marketing personnel receive instant data on what shoppers are buying.

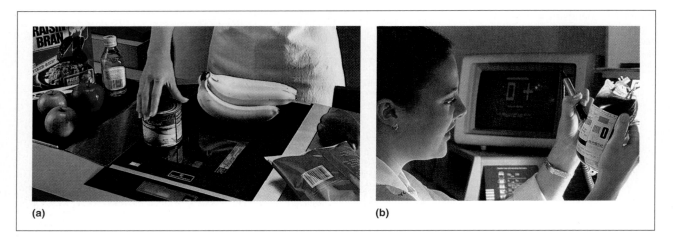

(a) (b)

Figure 3-8   Bar Codes. (a) This photoelectric bar code scanner, often seen at supermarket checkout counters, reads the product's zebra-stripe bar code. The bar code identifies the product for the store's computer, which retrieves price information. The price is then automatically rung up on the point-of-sale terminal. (b) The Australian Red Cross combines personal computers and handheld bar code readers to verify blood-type labels.

Although bar codes were once found primarily in the supermarket, there are a variety of other interesting applications. Bar coding has been described as an inexpensive and remarkably reliable way to get data into a computer. It is no wonder that virtually every industry has found a niche for bar codes. In Brisbane, Australia, bar codes help the Red Cross manage their blood bank inventory (Figure 3-8b). Also consider the case of Federal Express. The management attributes a large part of the corporation's success to the bar-coding system it uses to track packages. A ten-digit bar code uniquely identifies each package. As each package wends its way through the transportation system, the bar code is read at each point, and the bar-code number is fed to the computer. An employee can use a computer terminal to query the location of a given shipment at any time; the sender can request a status report on a package and receive a response within 30 minutes. The figures are impressive: In regard to controlling packages, the company has an accuracy rate of better than 99%.

Data Collection Devices   Another source of direct data entry is a **data collection device,** which may be located in a warehouse or factory or wherever the activity that is generating the data is located (Figure 3-9). As we noted earlier in the chapter, for example, factory employees can use a plastic card to punch job data directly into a computerized time clock. This process eliminates intermediate steps and ensures that the data will be more accurate.

Such devices must be sturdy, trouble-free, and easy to use, since they are often located in dusty, humid, or hot or cold locations. They are used by people such as warehouse workers, packers, forklift operators, and others whose primary work is not clerical. Examples of remote data collec-

Figure 3-9   A data collection device. Such devices are designed for use in demanding factory environments for collection of data at the source.

tion devices are machines for taking inventory, reading shipping labels, and recording job costs.

Voice Input   Have you talked to your computer recently? Has it talked to you? Both feats are possible with current technology, even though there are some limitations. In this chapter, we will examine the parts played by both you and the computer. Since we are presenting input here, we will begin with you, as you talk to your computer. What could be more direct than speaking to a computer?

Voice input is more formally known as **speech recognition,** the process of presenting input data to the computer through the spoken word (Figure 3-10). Voice input is about twice as fast as keyboard input by a skilled typist. **Speech recognition devices** accept the spoken word through a microphone and convert it into binary code (0s and 1s) that can be understood by the computer. There are a great many uses for this process, quite apart from being an aid to status-conscious executives who hate to type. In fact, voice input is creating new uses for computers. Typical users are those with "busy hands," or hands that are too dirty for the keyboard, or hands that must remain cleaner than using a keyboard would permit. Among current uses are:

- Controlling inventory in an auto junkyard
- Reporting analysis of pathology slides viewed under a microscope
- Making phone calls from a car
- Calculating a correct anesthetic dosage for a patient in surgery
- Changing radio frequencies in airplane cockpits
- Asking for stock-market quotations over the phone
- Sorting packages
- Inspecting items moving along an assembly line
- Allowing physically disabled users to enter commands

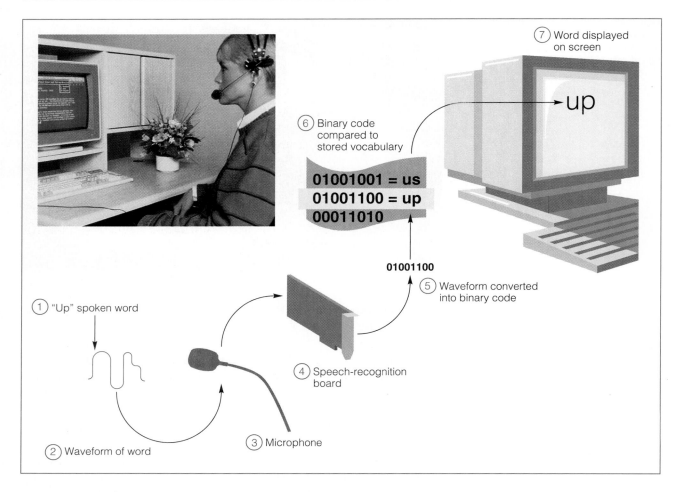

Figure 3-10   How voice input works.
The user speaks into a microphone or telephone. A chip on a board inside the computer analyzes the waveform of the word and changes it to binary numbers the computer can understand. These digits are compared with the numbers in a stored vocabulary list; if a match is found, the corresponding word is displayed on the screen.

- Starting the motor, locking the doors, or turning on the windshield wipers of a car

In each of these cases, the speech recognition system "learns" the voice of the user, who speaks isolated words repeatedly. The voiced words the system "knows" are then recognizable in the future. The package sorter, for instance, speaks digits representing zip codes. The factory inspector voices the simple words *good* or *bad,* or *yes* or *no.* A biologist tells a microscope to scan "Up," "Down," "Right," and "Left." Today voice input is even available on personal computers. Video games that anyone can talk to will be here soon, accepting verbal commands like "Bombs away!," "Dive! Dive! Dive!," and other important instructions.

What are the problems of voice recognition? First of all, speech communication is a very subtle process. Computers are not yet discerning enough to cope with all the ambiguities of spoken language. For example, will the computer know the difference between a *pair* of shoes and a *pear* on a tree? (Some systems are indeed this sophisticated, recognizing the true word from its context.) Second, most speech recognition systems are speaker dependent—that is, they must be separately trained for each individual user. Speech technologists are still wrestling with the wide range of accents and tonal qualities, although a system developed at Carnegie-Mellon can recognize about 1000 English words spoken by anyone. Third, there is the problem of distinguishing voice from background noise and other interfering sounds. Finally, voice input systems usually have a relatively small vocabulary.

Many speech recognition systems, called **discrete word systems,** are limited to isolated words, and speakers must pause between words. Some systems can interpret sustained speech, so users can speak normally. This type of system is called a **continuous word system,** which can be used, for instance, in the automatic transcription of spoken English into typed text. We can assume that this will eventually lead to word processors that take dictation.

Experts have tagged speech recognition as one of the most difficult things for a computer to do. Some of the world's largest companies—AT&T, IBM, Exxon—have been developing speech technology for years without the hoped-for degree of success. Recently National Semiconductor introduced a **digital signal processor (DSP)** chip that gives speech recognition a hardware boost. With this chip in your phone, answering machines will become outmoded, and you will be able to command your phone by voice (instead of touch-tone key presses). Soon people will routinely talk to their computers, toys, TV sets, refrigerators, ovens, automobiles, and door locks. And no one will stare at them when they do.

Computer Screens: Input/Output Devices

The relationship between input and output is an important one. Although some people naively think that the computer wields magical power, the truth is that the output produced is directly related to the input given. Many users call this relationship *garbage in, garbage out* (or **GIGO**). That is, the quality of the information the computer produces can be no better than the quality and accuracy of the data given to it in the first place. That fact is most obvious when input and output devices are closely related. For instance, computer screens are involved in both input and output: When data is entered, it appears on the screen; the computer response to that data—the output—also appears on the screen. Thus, if a mistake is made in entering data or if there is a problem with the computer program, the mistake shows up right away on the screen.

Computer screens come in many different shapes, sizes, and colors. The most common type of screen is the **cathode ray tube,** or **CRT.** Color monitors are available for displaying color graphics (Figure 3-11a). Some screens are **monochrome**—characters and graphics appear in only one color. Some common monochrome screens display green or amber letters and numbers on a dark background, but newer monitors use black on white—or vice versa (Figure 3-11b).

A screen you have probably seen often is the one that is part of the automated teller machine (ATM) at your bank. You can insert your plastic card and type in a personal identification number (PIN), then give the machine your instructions. You can tell it to make a cash withdrawal,

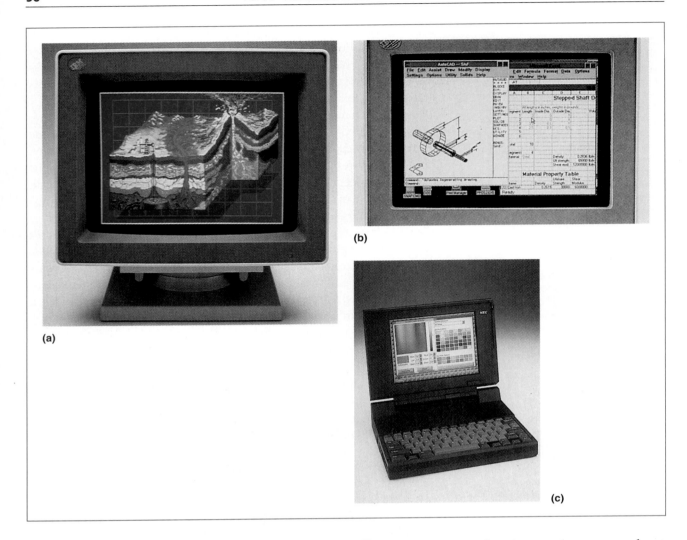

(a)

(b)

(c)

Figure 3-11   A variety of screens. (a) This high-resolution brilliance is available only on a color graphics display. (b) Monochrome screens can use black on white to simulate a paper-like environment. (c) Laptop and notebook computers can use thin-film-transistor (TFT) active matrix technology for their small, lightweight screens.

for example. A small computer screen gives instructions to you about how to use the machine, and it responds to your requests. When you make a routine transaction, you probably do not pause to ponder the fact that this machine can accept your input and, almost instantly, produce an output response and follow your instructions.

CRT Screen Technology

Most CRT screens use a technology called **raster-scan technology.** The image to be displayed on the screen is sent electronically from the computer to the cathode ray tube, which directs a beam of electrons to the screen. The beam causes the phosphor-coated screen to emit a light, which causes an image on the screen. But the light does not stay lit very long, so the image must be **refreshed** often. If the screen is not refreshed often enough, the fading screen image appears to flicker. A **scan rate**—the number of times the screen is refreshed—of 60 times per second is usually adequate to retain a clear screen image.

P E R S P E C T I V E S

TO YOUR HEALTH

Can all this computing be good for you? Are there any unhealthy side effects? The computer seems harmless enough. How bad can it be, sitting in a padded chair in a climate-controlled office?

How Bad Is It?

Health questions have been raised by the people who sit all day in front of the video display terminals (VDTs) of their computers. Are computer users getting bad radiation? What about eyestrain? And what about the age-old back problem, updated with new concerns about workers who hold their hands over a keyboard? What about repetitive-action injury, also known as *carpal tunnel syndrome?*

VDT Radiation

In 1991, the U.S. government said its four-year study of 2430 telephone operators—in which half used VDTs and half did not—revealed that women in the two groups had about the same rate of miscarriage. Along with similar recent findings, the result of the government study seems to undermine as an anomaly a 1988 conclusion that VDTs increase the risk of miscarriage. Still, many remain unconvinced. In San Francisco, a city requirement that all businesses must install radiation protection devices over VDTs was struck down by a judge who said such laws must be dealt with on the state level. Unions and legislators in many other communities continue to push for laws limiting exposure to video screens. Many manufacturers now offer screens with built-in protection.

Ergonomics

Meanwhile, there are a number of things workers can do to take care of themselves. A good place to begin is with an ergonomically designed workstation. *Ergonomics* is the study of human factors related to computers. A properly designed workstation takes a variety of fac-

tors into account, such as the distance from the eyes to the screen and the angle of the arms and wrists.

How We Cope

Experts recommend these steps as coping mechanisms:

- Turn the screen away from the window to reduce glare, and cover your screen with a glare deflector (see photo). Turn off overhead lights; illuminate your work area with a lamp.

- Put your monitor on a tilt-and-swivel base.

- Get a pneumatically adjustable chair. Position the seat back so your lower back is supported.

- Place the keyboard low enough to avoid arm and wrist fatigue. Do not bend your wrists when you type. Use an inexpensive, raised wrist rest. Do not rest your wrists on a sharp edge.

- Sit with your feet firmly on the floor.

- Exercise at your desk occasionally rotating your wrists, rolling your shoulders, and stretching. Better yet, get up and walk around at regular intervals.

The Name Sticks

In engineering as in many other fields, mistakes sometimes stick around for many years after they have been un-masked. Take, for instance, the name of a semiconductor technology called *ferroelectronics*.

It wasn't long after the introduction of the semiconductor that its ability to hold a charge was questioned. Although the semiconductor was revolutionary in being able to store data, the device required a constant supply of energy to retain it; if the battery died, the data soon disappeared. An alternative semiconductor technology called ferro-electronics soon emerged. Ferroelectronics offered the ability to hold data for up to 10 years without recharging the storage components. The technology took its name from the material thought to be responsible for its power—ferrous, or iron-related, compounds.

It was later shown that ferrous material was not responsible for the improved performance. Nevertheless, the name *ferroelectronics* stuck—partly because the technology lay dormant for some time. However, it re-emerged in late 1991, when Canon Inc. of Japan announced that it had a better way to make flat, high-resolution screens.

Most companies use a semiconductor technology called TFT, or thin-film transistors active matrix, to create flat-screen displays. TFT involves hundreds of transistors that require constant recharging to show a picture. One flawed transistor can ruin the whole screen, and the failure rate in making flat TFT screens can run as high as 95%. In contrast, according to Canon, the ferroelectronic technology requires far fewer transistors and could cut the failure rate to 35%. Hiroshi Tanaka, a senior Canon managing director, says its new ferroelectronics technology makes full-size, flat-screen TV a reality. And the name *ferroelectronics* lives on.

A computer display screen that can be used for graphics is divided into dots that are called addressable because they can be *addressed* individually by the graphics software. These displays are called **dot-addressable displays,** or **bit-mapped displays.** The capacity to illuminate each dot individually on the screen makes each dot a potential *pic*ture *el*ement, or **pixel.** The **resolution** of the screen—its clarity—is directly related to the number of pixels on the screen: The more pixels, the higher the resolution. Some computers, such as the Macintosh, come with built-in graphics capability. Others need an extra device, called a **graphics card** or **graphics adapter board,** that has to be added. To display graphics, you need both a color monitor and color graphics circuitry, either built-in or on a board.

As the resolution of CRT screens increases, it becomes more difficult for manufacturers to design screens that can handle the extra pixels. Manufacturers speak of pixels as laid out in horizontal lines down the screen. Many companies have used a technique by which every other line is scanned in one pass, with the remaining lines scanned on a second pass. Such screens are called **interlaced**. Though interlacing allows high-resolution screens to be built at a lower cost, viewing the screens for long periods is more likely to cause eyestrain. On some screens the resolution can be selected by the user, so interlacing may be used only in the highest resolutions.

Another important class of displays are **flat-panel displays.** These screens are usually much thinner and lighter than CRTs and generally consume much less power, which makes them a popular choice for laptop computers. The most common flat-panel display is the **liquid crystal display (LCD).** LCD screens do not emit light themselves, but rather use reflected light or light transmitted from behind (called backlighting). **Backlighting** allows viewing the screen in poor light and improves readability. Unfortunately, backlighting also requires more power, reducing one advantage of having a flat-panel display. Though early LCD screens were of poor quality, modern screens are much easier to read. Most LCDs are monochrome, but color screens are available. A flat-panel screen gaining popularity is the **thin-film-transistor (TFT) active matrix** screen(Figure 3-11c), featured on the NEC 486SX/C color laptop and Macintosh PowerBook 170. Every pixel on the screen is powered by its own transistor, which results in resolution as sharp as that of a regular CRT.

Terminals

A screen may be the monitor of a self-contained personal computer or it may be part of a terminal that is one of many terminals attached to a larger computer. A **terminal** consists of an input device, an output device, and a communications link to the main computer. Most commonly, a terminal has a keyboard for an input device and a screen for an output device, although there are many variations on this theme. A terminal with a screen is called a **video display terminal (VDT).**

There are three kinds of terminals: dumb, smart, and intelligent. A

The Instamatic Goes Digital

Until recently there was no easy, inexpensive way to input a photograph into your computer. The only available methods have been time-consuming and expensive: You could scan the photograph; you could use a camcorder with a still-video interface; or you could use a disk-based camera like Canon's Xapshot which requires extra analog-to-digital conversion equipment. Now one-piece digital cameras are available. Called the Instamatic of digital cameras, Fotoman needs no film—it captures up to 32 pictures in digital form. You connect it to your PC and transfer the pictures to your hard disk. Then you can take another 32 pictures—without having to load a new roll of film. With the software that comes with Fotoman, you also can touch up, size, and adjust the brightness and contrast of your "photos" right on your computer screen. What kind of new output devices does this cry out for? How about inexpensive machines that can produce commercial-quality photographs and slides from those digital pictures? As they say, one thing leads to another.

dumb terminal does not process data; it is merely a means of entering data into a computer and receiving output form it. Far more common is the **smart terminal,** which can do some processing, usually to edit data it receives. In contrast, an **intelligent terminal** can be programmed to perform a variety of processing functions. Most supermarket point-of-sale terminals are smart. They have central processing units in them that can edit data right at the checkout stand.

The keyboard is an important component of a terminal. To communicate with the main computer through a terminal keyboard, you make what is called an **inquiry.** An inquiry is a request for information. In most cases, you don't have to wait long before the result is displayed on the CRT screen. Sometimes the computer, in turn, requests data or a command of you, the user of the computer. This request is known as a **prompt.** Suppose you work in police communications and receive a report that a police officer has sighted a suspicious-looking car with a license plate beginning with *AXR*. You make an inquiry: You ask the computer to display a list of all stolen cars in your state with license plates beginning *AXR*. The computer does this, then provides a prompt:

```
DO YOU WISH DETAILS FOR A SPECIFIC NUMBER FROM THIS
LIST?
YES (Y) OR NO (N)
```

You type Y, and the computer provides another prompt:

```
TYPE SPECIFIC LICENSE NUMBER
```

You do so, and you receive details about the make and the year of the car, its owner, address, and so on.

Pen-Based Computers and Interactive Tablets

Sometimes it is just not practical to use a keyboard or mouse. You might not have enough deskspace or the input device might be too bulky to carry around. Or, you may feel more comfortable writing with a pen than typing. The answer is a **pen-based computer system,** (Figure 3-12), also called a **notepad computer** or **interactive tablet.** These devices have special screens that can both sense the touch of a special stylus and display graphics and text the same way a screen can.

The pen-based computer is designed to take advantage of a skill most people already have—writing with a pen on paper. With such a computer, the user writes directly on the computer screen. Pen-based computers employ special software that can sense not only touch, but also motion. As a result, the user can make specific gestures on the screen to indicate specific actions. For example, one system allows the user to delete an item on the screen by scratching it out, to select an action from a menu by writing a check mark, and to insert data at a given location by drawing a caret (^). Pen-based computers can also recognize handwriting and can re-display the handwritten characters as regular printed text, to allow users to verify what they have written.

Figure 3-12   Pen-based computer. In overalls, a Southern Pacific rail worker may not strike you as the typical high-tech person. However, with pen-based computers like Radio Shack's GridPad (shown here), the worker can keep better track of railroad cars.

The capabilities of pen-based computers have introduced computers to new environments and new users. Sales representatives can take them along when calling on clients, for example, and enter orders directly on the graphic image of an order form which is displayed on the notepad screen. In addition, a pen-based input device brings the power of the computer to people who do not type.

So far, we have looked at types of input and at screens, which are input/output devices. Now it is time to examine output devices.

Types of Output

Output can take many forms, such as screen output, paper printouts, microfilm and voice. Output that includes graphics, such as overhead transparencies and 35mm slides, will be reviewed in Chapter 12. One computer system may be designed to produce several different kinds of output. You can see this the next time you go to a travel agency that uses a computer system. If you ask about airline connections to Toronto, Calgary, and Vancouver, say, the travel agent will probably make a few queries to the system and receive on-screen output indicating availability on the various flights. After the reservations have been confirmed, the agent can ask for printed output of three kinds: the tickets, the traveler's itinerary, and the invoice. The agency may also keep records of your travel plans, which may be output on microfilm. In addition, agency manage-

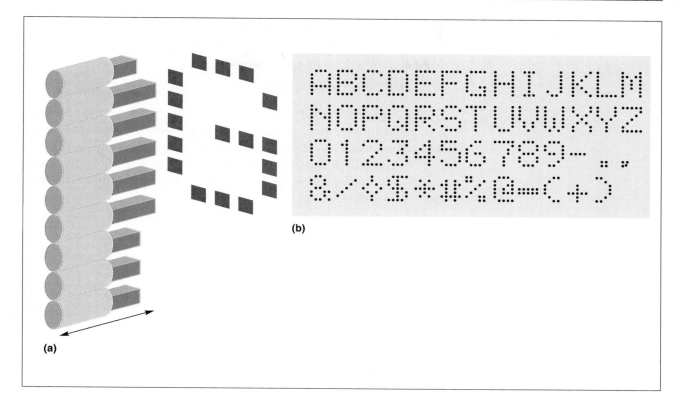

(b)

(a)

Figure 3-13   Forming dot-matrix characters. (a) The letter *G,* is being printed as a 5 × 7 dot-matrix character. The moving matrix head has nine vertical pins, which move back and forth as necessary to form each letter. (b) Letters, numbers, and special characters are formed as 5 × 7 dot-matrix characters. Although not shown in this figure, dot-matrix printers can print lowercase letters too. The two lower pins are used for the parts of lowercase letters *g, j, p,* and *y* that go below the line.

ment may periodically receive printed reports and charts, such as monthly summaries of sales figures or pie charts of regional costs.

As you might already suspect, the printer is one of the principal devices used to produce computer output.

Printers: The Image Makers

A **printer** is a device that produces printed paper output—known in the trade as **hard copy** because it is tangible and permanent (unlike soft copy, which is displayed on a screen). Some printers produce only letters and numbers, whereas others are also able to produce graphics.

Printers form letters and numbers as solid characters or as dot-matrix characters. **Dot-matrix printers** create characters in the same way that individual lights in a pattern spell out words on a basketball scoreboard. Dot-matrix printers construct a character by activating a matrix of pins that produces the shape of the character. Figure 3-13 shows how this works. A typical matrix is 5 × 7—that is, five dots wide and seven dots high. These printers are sometimes called 9-pin printers, because they have two extra vertical dots for creating the parts of lowercase letters *g, j, p,* and *y* that go below the text line. The 24-pin dot-matrix printer uses a series of overlapping dots—the more dots, the better the quality of the letter produced. This printer is the dominant dot-matrix printer. Some dot-matrix printers can produce color images.

Categorizing printers according to whether they produce dot-matrix or solid characters is one way to distinguish them. But the two principal ways of classifying printers are according to the

- Means of making an image on the paper
- Amount of information they print at a time

There are two ways of making an image on paper: the impact method and the nonimpact method. An **impact printer** is much like a typewriter. It forms characters by physically striking paper, ribbon, and print hammer together. A **nonimpact printer** forms characters by using a noncontact process—that is, there is never physical contact between the printing mechanism and the paper.

Let us take a closer look at these differences.

Impact Printers   The term *impact* refers to the use of some sort of physical contact with the paper to produce an image. The impact may be produced by a character-shaped print hammer striking a ribbon against the paper or by a print hammer hitting paper and ribbon against a character. Impact printers are of two kinds: character and line.

Character printers are like typewriters. They print character by character across the page from one margin to the other. A typical character printer is the **daisy wheel printer.** Although not used much outside business, daisy wheel printers are noted for high-quality printing; this kind of printer is useful for word processing and professional correspondence, especially when pre-printed forms or carbon copies are involved. The daisy wheel consists of a removable wheel with a set of spokes, each containing a raised character. The entire wheel rotates to line up the appropriate character, which is then struck by a hammer. The user can change type styles (fonts) by changing wheels. Most new electronic typewriters use the daisy-wheel technique.

Line printers assemble all characters on a line at one time and print them out practically simultaneously. There are several types of impact line printers. The **band printer,** the most popular type of impact printer, uses a horizontally rotating band that contains characters, as shown in Figure 3-14a. The characters on the band are struck by hammers through paper and ribbon. The **chain printer** consists of characters on a chain that rotate past all print positions (Figure 3-14b). Hammers are aligned with each position, and when the appropriate character goes by, a hammer strikes paper and ribbon against it. The **drum printer** consists of a cylinder with embossed rows of characters on its surface (Figure 3-14c). Each print position has a complete set of characters around the circumference of the drum. As the drum turns, a hammer strikes paper and ribbon against the drum. The drum printer is considered a dinosaur among printers, but many can still be found hard at work in computer installations.

Nonimpact Printers   There are many advantages to nonimpact printers, but there are two main reasons for their growing popularity: They

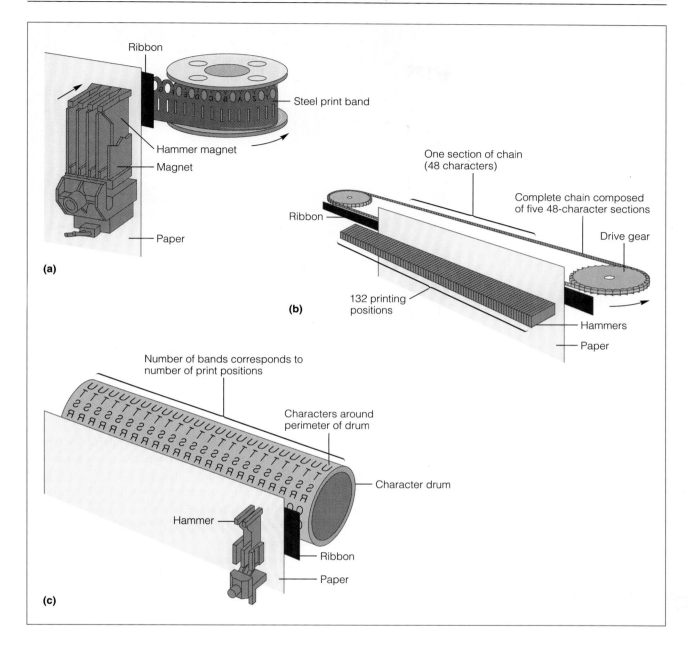

Figure 3-14 Three kinds of impact line-printer mechanisms. (a) Band printer mechanism. The band or belt can be easily changed to print different styles of type. Some band printers can print up to 600 lines per minute. (b) Chain printer mechanism. Some print up to 3000 lines per minute. (c) Drum printer mechanism. Some of these also print up to 3000 lines per minute.

are faster and quieter. Speed derives from the fact that nonimpact printers have fewer moving parts than impact printers; they have no type elements or hammers that move around. The lowering of the noise level results from the absence of the impact—the striking of print hammers against ribbon and paper.

Other advantages of nonimpact printers over conventional mechanical printers are their ability to change typefaces automatically and their graphics capacity.

The major technologies competing in the nonimpact market are ink jet and laser. They use the dot-matrix concept to form characters. Let us briefly consider each of these.

Printer Speeds

This list of printers is not all-inclusive, but these speeds are typical. Characters per second is represented by *cps,* lines per minute by *lpm.*

Daisy wheel—50 to 80 cps

Dot-matrix character—50 to 500 cps

Dot-matrix line—300 to 900 lpm

Band—400 to 3600 lpm

Ink jet—110 to 400 cps

Laser—10,000 to 20,000 lpm

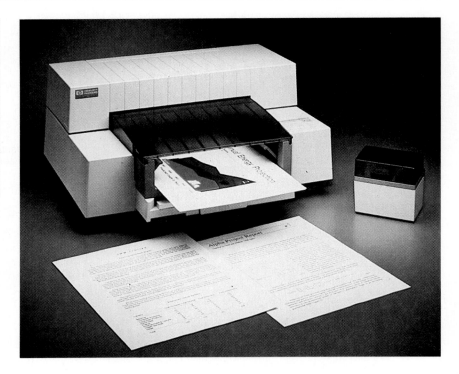

Figure 3-15   Ink-jet printer. Ink-jet printers are noted for high-quality and inexpensive color graphics output.

Ink-Jet Printers   Spraying ink from jet nozzles, **ink-jet printers** are up to ten times faster than impact printers. The ink, which is charged, passes through an electric field, which deflects it to produce a dot-matrix character. Ink-jet printers, by using multiple nozzles, can print in several different colors of ink. Color ink-jet printers, as shown in Figure 3-15, produce excellent graphics. However, these printers often produce poor-quality text and at relatively slow speeds.

One variation of the ink-jet printer is the **bubble-jet printer.** This printer uses a rising and falling bubble to force a droplet of ink onto the paper.

Laser Printers   A generation of children has watched movies in which space travelers use a laser, a powerful beam of bright light, to cut a hole through a wall or zap a flying target. Lasers have a real home, however, with computers, where **laser printers** use a light beam to help transfer images to paper (Figure 3-16). A laser beam "writes" an image onto the surface of a rotating metal drum. Then ink-like toner is deposited on the drum; it adheres where the image was "written." The toner is then transferred to paper. The result is an extremely high-quality image. A laser printer can print a page at a time at record-breaking speeds.

Laser printers have been around for a number of years, but their initial high cost—hundreds of thousands of dollars—limited their use to companies whose need for speed made the machines cost-effective. Technological advancements, however, have now significantly reduced cost. The Oregon legislature, for example, has taken advantage of the new af-

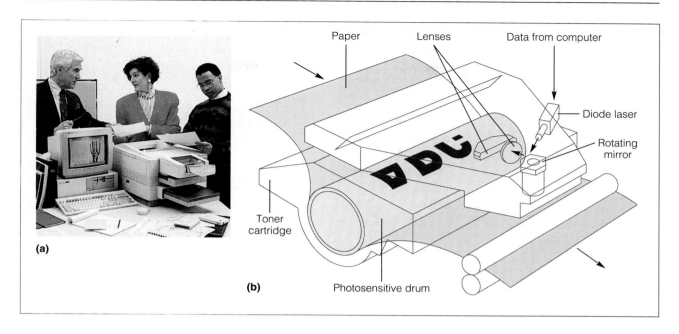

Paper   Lenses   Data from computer

Diode laser

Rotating mirror

Toner cartridge

(a)

(b)   Photosensitive drum

Figure 3-16   Laser printers. (a) Even though they are at the high end of the price scale, the high-quality print and durability of the Hewlett-Packard LaserJet series printers make them best-sellers. (b) A laser printer works like a photocopy machine. Using patterns of small dots, a laser beam conveys information from the computer to a positively charged drum inside the laser printer. Wherever an image is to be printed, the laser beam is turned on, causing the drum to become neutralized. As the drum passes by a toner cartridge, toner sticks to the neutral spots on the drum. The toner is then transferred from the drum to a piece of paper. In the final printing step, heat and pressure fuse the toner to the paper. The drum is then cleaned for the next pass.

fordability by placing laser printers in key administrative areas. Legislators who used to wait hours for drafts of new legislation to be delivered by courier now have easy access to draft bills from a nearby printer. "It's as quiet as the copy machine," marveled one politician. "All you can hear is the paper moving."

The price of a good laser printer is now low enough—some models cost less than $1000—to tempt people who care about first-rate printing. The rush to laser printers has been influenced by the trend toward desktop publishing—using a personal computer, a laser printer, and special software to make professional-looking publications. We will examine desktop publishing in detail in Chapter 9.

Which Type of Printer?   A lot has been said about nonimpact printers. The trade press and industry consultants have embraced nonimpact technology, and market acceptance increases with every price decrease. But impact printers will not necessarily be swept aside by the onrushing wave of nonimpact machines. A key reason is the seeming invincibility of impact printers: They chatter away day after day, year after year, without missing a beat—and rarely need repair. Another reason: multiple-part forms. Companies that print W-2 forms, stock certificates, mass-mailing cards, legal documents—anything requiring copies—will continue to use impact printers.

As Table 3-1 shows, printers made especially for personal computers come in just about all the varieties we have already discussed. People are often surprised to discover that it is as difficult to choose a printer as it is to choose the computer itself. Some people are also startled to find that the printer they want may cost twice as much as the computer.

Paper   Now that you know something about printers, you can appreciate the fact that they use a variety of papers. Some printers use ordinary paper; others require special paper.

Table 3-1   Personal computer printer comparison chart.

Suit your convenience and your pocketbook when you choose a printer.

	Daisy wheel	Dot-matrix 9-pin	Dot-matrix 24-pin	Ink-jet	Laser
Speed	Slow	Medium	Fast	Medium	Very fast
Versatility	Low	Medium	Medium	Medium	High
Quality	Good	Fair	Good	Good	Excellent
Cost	Medium	Low	Medium	High	High
Graphics	No	Yes	Yes	Yes	Yes
Color	No	No	Some	Yes	No
Noise	Loud	Loud	Loud	Quiet	Quiet

Computer output may be produced on a variety of different kinds of paper—cheap newsprint, lined-stock tabulating paper (called **stock tab**), shaded-band paper (called **green-bar paper**), or even fancy preprinted forms with institutional logo and address.

Paper may come in a letter-size sheet; this size is becoming more common with the growing popularity of laser printers. But just as common is paper that comes in a roll or in one continuous folded form called **continuous form** (Figure 3-17). Continuous form paper has sprocket holes along the sides, which help feed the paper rapidly through the printer without slippage. A computer operator puts a box of continuous paper under the printer, feeds the paper through the printer, and allows the printer output to accumulate—folded—in another box. The continuous paper must then be separated, a process called **bursting.**

Figure 3-17   Continuous form paper.
Some printout paper is a continuous form, as shown here. Many printers can use single sheets of paper.

If multiple copies are required, carbon paper for computer printers is available. The process of removing the carbon paper from between the layered copies is called **decollating**. A special paper called **NCR paper** (*NCR* stands for *no carbon required*) allows several copies to be made without carbon paper. NCR paper is more convenient but more expensive than carbon paper.

Computer Output Microfilm

How many warehouses would it take to store all the census data for this country? How many rooms in an insurance company would be required to hold all the printed customer records? To save space, **computer output microfilm** (generally referred to by its abbreviation, **COM**) was developed (Figure 3-18). For COM, output takes the form of very small images on sheets or rolls of film. A microfilm record can be preserved on rolls of film (usually 35mm) or on 4 × 6-inch sheets of film called **microfiche;** users often call them just fiche.

COM has many advantages, not the least of which is space savings. At 200 pages per microfiche, this book, for instance, could be stored on four 4 × 6-inch microfiche. The major disadvantage of COM is that it cannot be read without the assistance of a microfilm reader. COM may soon disappear, however, in favor of disk storage—when everyone has a computer to access disks.

Numbers and pictures are—by far—the most common output forms, but voice output is growing.

Voice Output: Your Master's (Digital) Voice

We have already examined voice input in some detail. As you will see in this section, however, computers are frequently like people in the sense

Figure 3-18   Computer output microfilm. One 4 × 6-inch microfiche sheet can hold the equivalent of over 200 pages.

that they find it easier to talk than to listen. **Speech synthesis**—the process of enabling machines to talk to people—is much easier than speech recognition.

"The key is in the ignition," your car says to you as you open the door. Machine voices are not real human voices. They are the product of **voice synthesizers** (also called **voice-output devices** or **audio-response units**), which convert data in main storage to vocalized sounds understandable to humans.

There are two basic approaches to getting a computer to talk. The first is **synthesis by analysis,** in which the device analyzes the input of an actual human voice speaking words, stores and processes the spoken sounds, and reproduces them as needed. The process of storing words is similar to the digitizing process we discussed earlier when considering voice input. In essence, synthesis by analysis uses the computer as a digital tape recorder.

The second approach to synthesizing speech is **synthesis by rule,** in which the device applies a complex set of linguistic rules to create artificial speech. Synthesis based on the human voice has the advantage of sounding more natural, but it is limited to the number of words stored in the computer. Synthesis by rule has no vocabulary restriction, but the spoken product is often mechanical and sounds like no voice from this planet.

Voice synthesizers can be relatively inexpensive ($200 or so) and connect to almost any computer. Most synthesizers plug into the computer where the printer does and, rather than print the output, they speak it. Speed and pitch can usually be adjusted.

Eager candidates for voice synthesizers are often those who have speech impairments. Several software packages exist that let people communicate on the phone by typing their messages, which are then converted to synthetic speech. For example: "Hello. I am not able to speak, but I am able to hear you, and my computer is doing the talking for me. Would you please tell me if you have tickets for the Beethoven concert on Friday, the 18th?" This message can be keyed before the phone call. After the call is dialed and someone answers, the user pushes the Speak button, and the message goes out over the phone.

In addition, a reading machine has been devised that is of considerable help to the blind. Scanning a page, it recognizes letters and words, applies phonetic rules, and produces spoken sentences. The machine can even put in stresses and accents.

Voice output has become common in such places as airline and bus terminals, banks, and brokerage houses. It is typically used when an inquiry is followed by a short reply (such as a bank balance or flight time). Many businesses have found other creative uses for voice output as it applies to the telephone. Automatic telephone voices ("Hello, this is a computer speaking . . .") take surveys, inform customers that catalog orders are ready to pick up, and remind consumers that they have not paid their bills. (By using voice output one utility company saves the cost of hiring people to call the thousands of customers who do not pay on time.)

One more note. Perhaps it has occurred to you that voice input and voice output systems can go together. Today's technology permits combined voice input and output—consider the car system that you can talk to and get responses from.

Yet to Come

Almost weekly, new forms of computer input and output are announced, with an array of benefits that promise to have an enormous impact on our lives. The effectiveness of all such new input or output, however, depends on two components that we have not yet discussed: storage and software. We will study the first of these in the next chapter.

R E V I E W   A N D   R E F E R E N C E

Summary and Key Terms

- Inputting is the procedure of providing data to the computer for processing.

- The keyboard is a common input device used by owners of personal computers, as well as by **data entry operators,** who use computer terminals to enter large amounts of data from **source documents.** The data that operators enter can be stored on magnetic tape or disk before being sent to a main computer for processing, or the main computer may be updated directly.

- A **pointer,** or **cursor,** is a flashing indicator on a screen that shows where the next user-computer interaction will take place. The cursor can be moved by pressing certain keys on the keyboard or by rolling a **mouse** on a flat surface. A mouse has a button that can be pressed to give certain commands to the computer. To press the mouse button twice in rapid succession is to **double-click.** A variation on the mouse is the **trackball.** To move the cursor, the user rolls a ball that is embedded in the top of the trackball device.

- An **icon** is a pictorial symbol on a screen. A computer user can interact with an icon by using a mouse.

- **Source data automation,** the use of special equipment to collect data and send it directly to the computer, is a more efficient method of data entry than keyboarding. Four means of source data automation are magnetic-ink character recognition, optical recognition, data collection devices, and voice input.

- **Magnetic-ink character recognition** (**MICR**) involves characters made of magnetized particles, such as the preprinted characters on a personal check. The characters are put on documents by **MICR inscribers** and are read by **MICR reader/sorters.**

- **Optical recognition** converts optical marks, optical characters, handwritten characters, and bar codes into electrical signals to be sent to the computer. **Optical mark recognition** (**OMR**) devices use a light beam to recognize marks on paper. **Optical character recognition** (**OCR**) devices use a light beam to read special characters, such as those on price tags. These characters are often in a standard typeface called **OCR-A.** A commonly used OCR device is the handheld **wand reader,** which is often connected to a **point-of-sale** (**POS**) **terminal** in a retail store. Some optical scanners can read precise handwritten characters. A **bar code reader** is a stationary photoelectric scanner used to input a **bar code,** the pattern of vertical marks that represents the **Universal Product Code** (**UPC**) that identifies a product.

- **Data collection devices** allow direct, accurate data entry in places such as factories and warehouses.

- **Voice input,** or **speech recognition,** is the process of presenting input data to the computer through the spoken word. **Speech recognition devices** convert spoken words into a digital code that a computer can understand. **Digital signal processor** (**DSP**) chips change sound into the digital form understood by computers. The two main types of devices are **discrete word systems,** which require speakers to pause between words, and **continuous word systems,** which allow a normal rate of speaking.

- **GIGO** stands for *garbage in, garbage out,* which means that the quality of the output depends on the quality of the input.

- Some computer screens are **monochrome**—the characters appear in one color on a black background, or they can be black on white. Color screens are also available to display color text and graphics. The most common type of screen is the **cathode** ray tube (**CRT**).

- CRT images are usually created through **raster-scan technology,** in which electron beams cause the screen to emit light, and the result is the screen image. The screen image is **refreshed,** or kept lit, at a particular **scan rate.**

- **Dot-addressable displays,** or **bit-mapped displays,** are graphics display screens that are divided into dots, each of which can be illuminated as a *picture* **el**ement, or **pixel.** The greater the number of pixels, the greater the **resolution,** or clarity, of the image.

- To display graphics, you need both a color monitor and color graphics circuitry, either built-in or on a **graphics card** or **graphics adapter board.**

- Some screens are called **interlaced** when every other line is scanned, and it takes more than one pass to refresh the screen. Such screens produce high resolution at a low cost.

- An important class of displays is the **flat-panel display,** which is lighter and uses less power than CRTs. The most common type is the **liquid crystal display** (**LCD**) found on laptop computers. A type gaining popularity because of its clarity is the **thin-film-transistor (TFT) active matrix** screen. Flat-panel displays do not emit their own light, so they are often used with **backlighting.**

- A screen may be the monitor of a self-contained personal computer, or it may be part of a **terminal,** an input-output device linked to a main computer. A terminal with a screen is called a **video display terminal** (**VDT**).

- Terminals can be classified as dumb, smart, or intelligent according to their processing power. A **dumb terminal** does not process data; it only enters data and receives output. A **smart terminal** can do some processing (usually data editing), but it cannot be programmed by the user. An **intelligent terminal** can be programmed to perform a variety of processing tasks.

- An **inquiry** is a user's request for information from the computer. A **prompt** is a computer request for data or a command from the user.

- One special class of computer is the **pen-based computer,** also called an **interactive tablet** or **notepad computer.** These computers have a special screen that the user can write on like a sheet of paper. The computers can recognize handwriting and also special gestures, including actions such as inserting, selecting, and deleting.

- **Printers** produce **hard copy,** or printed paper output. Some printers produce solid characters; others, **dot-matrix printers,** construct characters by producing closely spaced dots.

- Printers can also be classified as being either **impact printers,** which form characters by physically striking the paper, or **nonimpact printers,** which use a noncontact printing method.

- Impact printers include **character printers** (such as the **daisy wheel printer**) and **line printers.** (Line printers can be **band, chain,** or **drum printers**).

- Nonimpact printers, which include **ink-jet, bubble-jet,** and **laser printers,** are faster and quieter than impact printers.

- The main types of computer paper for business are lined-stock tabulating paper (**stock tab**) and shaded-band paper (**green-bar paper**). Computer paper may also be **continuous form** paper, which has sprocket holes along the sides. **Bursting** is the process of separating the folded paper after printing. **Decollating** is the process of removing carbon paper from layered copies. **NCR paper** (*no carbon required*) is a more convenient but more expensive alternative to carbon paper. Laser printers use regular letter- and legal-size paper.

- With **computer output microfilm** (**COM**), output is stored on 35mm film or 4 × 6-inch sheets called **microfiche.**

- Computer **speech synthesis** has been accomplished through **voice synthesizers** (also called **voice-output devices** or **audio-response units**). One approach to speech synthesis is **synthesis by analysis,** in which the computer analyzes stored tapes of spoken words. In the other approach, called **synthesis by rule,** the computer applies linguistic rules to create artificial speech.

Review Questions

1. Explain what magnetic-ink character recognition is and how it is used by banks to process checks.
2. Name the types of optical character recognition devices and explain how each one works.
3. Describe the two types of speech recognition systems and discuss the problems involved in speech recognition.
4. What is the difference between an inquiry and a prompt?
5. What is hard copy?
6. How does a dot-matrix printer differ from a solid-character printer?
7. How do character printers differ from line printers?
8. What are the advantages of nonimpact printers? What are the advantages of impact printers?
9. Explain what COM is and why it was developed.
10. Give an advantage and disadvantage of backlighting a liquid crystal display screen.
11. In speech synthesis, how do *synthesis by rule* and *synthesis by analysis* differ? What are the benefits of one over the other?

Discussion Questions

1. Do you think that continued research into voice input is worthwhile? In your answer discuss the practicality of current and potential uses.
2. What should a buyer consider when comparing different models of printers?
3. Some people predict that offices of the future will rely on soft copy output rather than hard copy. Explain why you agree or disagree with this prediction.
4. How might businesses benefit from using speech synthesizers?

True-False Questions

T F   1. An LCD screen generally uses more power than a CRT screen of the same size.
T F   2. GIGO stands for *guaranteed input, guaranteed output.*
T F   3. A discrete word system is a type of speech recognition device.
T F   4. A digitizer allows you to see the text written with a special pen appear as printed characters on the screen.
T F   5. A source document is the piece of paper where data is originally written before being entered into a computer.
T F   6. A bubble-jet printer is an impact type of printer.
T F   7. Impact printers are faster than nonimpact printers because they have fewer moving parts.
T F   8. Bursting continuous paper means to separate individual sheets.
T F   9. Voice output and voice input cannot be used together.
T F 10. Higher resolution means fewer pixels on a screen.
T F 11. An input device called a joystick is used by rolling a ball which in turn moves the cursor on the screen.

CHAPTER

4

Storage Devices and File Processing

Electronic Facts

When airline executive Pete James finally bought a personal computer for his own office, it was with some reluctance. He had one at home that, for the most part, his children used, and he had taken an evening course that introduced word processing, database, and spreadsheet programs. Several members of his staff seemed to be computer hotshots, but Pete was not sure that a computer belonged on his desk. Still, he realized that the old saw—Executives aren't supposed to be the technical people—no longer held; there were many ways he could use a computer.

Pete took a little time to investigate his choice. He wanted a machine that had growth potential. Working with a professional from the Management Information Systems Department of his company, Pete decided on a mid-priced model with 6MB of RAM, a mouse for graphics input, and a high-resolution color monitor. To produce professional correspondence and business charts, he chose a low-priced laser printer.

Pete hesitated about the storage, however. He knew he would need a diskette drive for transferring software, and the MIS advisor convinced him that a tape backup unit would be efficient. But he had some misgivings about the capacity of the hard disk. Could he really use the 220MB disk the advisor recommended? How could he possibly come up with 220 million characters of data? Pete chose a 100MB hard disk, which seemed more than adequate.

The choices for storage, whether for a large or small computer, are complicated. Pete did not choose too badly. We will check back with him later in the chapter to see how his choices worked out. We switch now from personal computer storage to the broader needs of a large corporation or government agency.

 ## Why Secondary Storage?

Picture, if you can, how many filing-cabinet drawers would be required to hold the millions of files of, say, criminal records held by the U.S. Justice Department or employee records kept by General Motors. The record storage rooms would have to be enormous. Computer storage—the ability to store many records in extremely compressed form and to have quick access to them—is unquestionably one of the most valuable assets of the computer.

The Benefits of Secondary Storage

Secondary storage, you will recall, is necessary because memory, or primary storage, can be used only temporarily: If you are sharing your computer, you must yield memory to someone else after your program runs; if you are not sharing your computer, your programs and data will probably disappear from memory when you turn the computer off. However, you probably want to store the data you have used or the information you have derived from processing, and that is why secondary storage, or **auxiliary storage,** is needed. Also, memory is limited in size, whereas secondary storage media can store as much data as necessary.

The benefits of secondary storage are:

- **Economy.** It is less expensive to store data on magnetic tape or disk, the principal means of secondary storage, than in filing cabinets. Optical storage media are also relatively low in cost. Inexpensive storage space permits the storage of vast amounts of data, with increased accuracy in filing and retrieving it.

- **Reliability.** Data in secondary storage is basically safe, since secondary storage is physically reliable. Also, the data in it is stored in such a way that data tampering is difficult.

- **Convenience.** With the help of a computer, authorized people can locate and access data quickly.

These benefits apply to all the various secondary storage devices, but—as you will see—some devices are better than others.

What Are the Choices and Which Is Best?

We will spend most of the chapter answering these questions. At this point, however, consider this summary: The magnetic hard disk is the primary means of storage, because of its relatively low cost, its ease of use, and the speedy access it provides to any file or record. Diskettes are useful for transferring software and data and for removing data from a computer for safekeeping. Magnetic tape, though still important, is now used mostly for backup, archiving, and transferring data from one machine to another.

There are other choices. Will we stick with traditional magnetic media or consider optical technology, which can store vast amounts of data—usually in a highly portable and secure form?

What about the personal computer user? We have already hinted that storage decisions in that arena require thoughtful planning. We will examine all the possibilities. And, of course, we will return to Pete James, to see if he is happy with his disk decision.

First, though, we will consider how data is organized and how it is processed. These topics are intimately related to our choice of a storage medium.

 ## Data: Getting Organized

Data cannot be dumped helter-skelter into a computer. The computer is not a magic box that can bring order out of chaos. In fact, submitting data to a computer cannot be chaotic in the least—it must be carefully planned.

To be processed by the computer, raw data is organized into characters, fields, records, files, and databases. We will start with the smallest element, the character.

- A **character** is a letter, number, or special character (such as $, ?, or *). A character is essentially the same as a byte, which we described in the last chapter as consisting of 8 bits. One or more related characters constitute a field.

- A **field** contains a set of related characters. For example, suppose a health club is making address labels for a mailing. For each person, it might have a member-number field, a name field, a street-address field, a city field, a state field, a zip-code field, and a phone-number field (Figure 4-1).

- A **record** is a collection of related fields. Thus, on the health club mailing list, one person's member number, name, address, city, state, zip code, and phone number constitute a record.

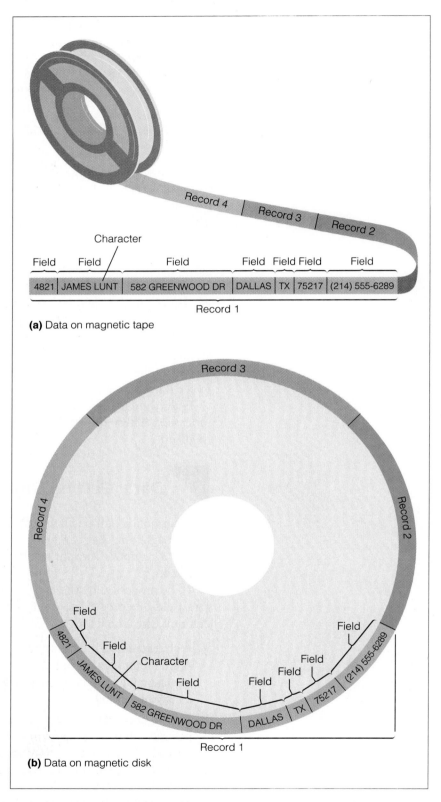

(a) Data on magnetic tape

(b) Data on magnetic disk

Figure 4-1   How data is organized. Whether stored on tape or on disk, data is organized into characters, fields, records, and files. A file is a collection of related records.

- A **file** is a collection of related records. All the member records for the health club compose a file.
- A **database** is a collection of interrelated files stored together with minimum redundancy. Specific data items can be retrieved for various applications. For instance, if the health club is opening a new outlet, it can pull out the names and addresses of all the people with specific zip codes that are near the new club. The club can then send a special announcement about opening day to those people. The concept of a database is complicated; we will return to it in detail in Chapter 11.

Processing Data into Information

There are several methods of processing data in a computer system. The two main methods are batch processing (processing data transactions in groups at a more convenient—usually later—time) and transaction processing (processing the transactions immediately, "in real time"). A combination of these two techniques is also used. We will now look at these methods and give examples of their use.

Batch Processing

Batch processing is a technique in which transactions are collected into groups, or batches, to be processed at a time when the computer may be less expensive to use or more accessible. Let us suppose that we are going to update the health club address-label file. The **master file,** a semipermanent set of records, is, in this case, the list of all members of the health club and their addresses. The **transaction file** contains all changes to be made to the master file: additions (transactions to create new master records for new names added), deletions (transactions with instructions to delete master records of people who have resigned from the health club), and revisions (transactions to change items such as street addresses or phone numbers in fields in the master records). Each month, the master file is **updated** with the changes called for in the transaction file. The result is a new, up-to-date master file (Figure 4-2).

In batch processing, before a transaction file is matched against a master file, the transaction file must be **sorted** (usually by computer) so that all the transactions are in sequential order according to a field called a key. The **key** is a unique identifier for a record. It is usually a number; since two or more people may have the same name, names are not good keys. Social Security numbers are commonly used as keys. In updating the health club address-label file, the key is the member number assigned by the health club. The records on the master file are already in order by key. Once the changes on the transaction file are sorted by key, the two files can be matched and the master file updated. Note that keys are also used to locate specific records within a file; that is why you always need to provide your account number when paying a bill or inquiring about a

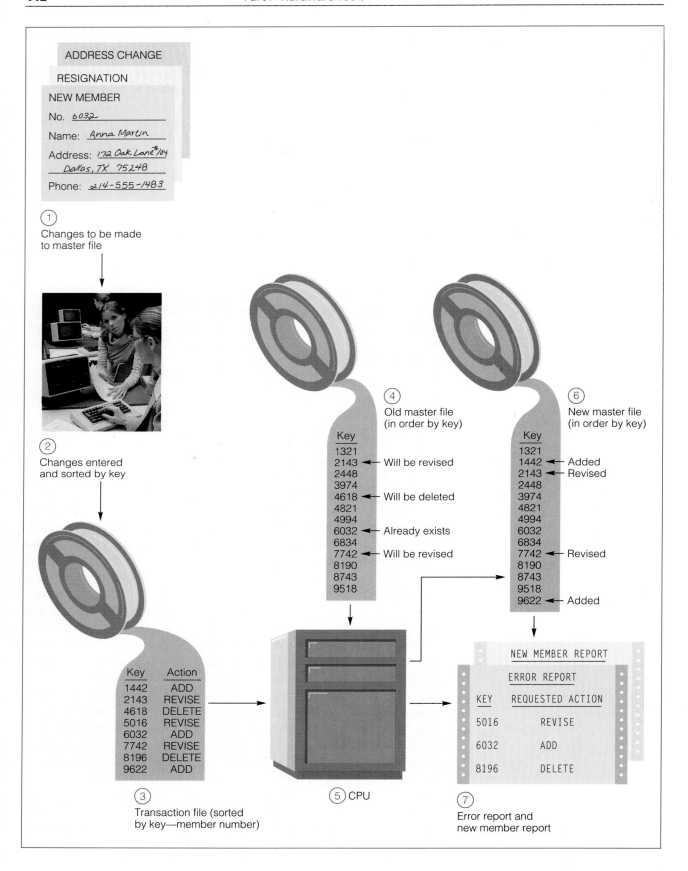

ADDRESS CHANGE

RESIGNATION

NEW MEMBER

No. *6032*

Name: *Anna Martin*

Address: *172 Oak Lane #104*
Dallas, TX 75248

Phone: *214-555-1483*

① Changes to be made
to master file

② Changes entered
and sorted by key

Key	Action
1442	ADD
2143	REVISE
4618	DELETE
5016	REVISE
6032	ADD
7742	REVISE
8196	DELETE
9622	ADD

③ Transaction file (sorted
by key—member number)

④ Old master file
(in order by key)

Key	
1321	
2143	← Will be revised
2448	
3974	
4618	← Will be deleted
4821	
4994	
6032	← Already exists
6834	
7742	← Will be revised
8190	
8743	
9518	

⑤ CPU

⑥ New master file
(in order by key)

Key	
1321	
1442	← Added
2143	← Revised
2448	
3974	
4821	
4994	
6032	
6834	
7742	← Revised
8190	
8743	
9518	
9622	← Added

NEW MEMBER REPORT

ERROR REPORT

KEY	REQUESTED ACTION
5016	REVISE
6032	ADD
8196	DELETE

⑦ Error report and
new member report

Figure 4-2 How batch processing works. The purpose of this system is to update the health club's master address-label file. ① Changes to be made (additions, deletions, and revisions) are input with ② a keyboard and sent to a tape. The computer sorts the list of changes according to member number and puts the sorted list onto ③ another tape, which is a transaction tape. The transaction file contains records in sequential order, according to member number, from lowest to highest. The record element used to identify the record is called the key. In this case the key is the member number. ④ The master file is also organized by member number. ⑤ The computer matches transaction file data and master file data by member number to produce ⑥ a new master file and ⑦ an error report and a new member report. The error report lists member numbers in the transaction file that were not in the master file and member numbers that were included in the transaction file as additions that were already in the master file.

to provide your account number when paying a bill or inquiring about a bill. Your record is located by your number, not by your name.

During processing, the computer matches the keys from the master and transaction files, carrying out the appropriate action to add, revise, or delete. At the end of processing, a newly updated master file is created; in addition, an error report is usually printed. The report shows such actions as an attempt to delete a nonexistent record or an attempt to add a record that already exists.

Batch processing of transaction and master files is becoming outmoded in many organizations. However, it still offers some advantages. One advantage of batch processing is that it is usually less expensive than other types of processing because it is more efficient: A group of records is processed at the same time. The main disadvantage of batch processing is that you have to wait. It does not matter that you want to know what the gasoline bill for your car is now; you have to wait until the end of the month when all your credit-card gas purchases are added up. Batch processing cannot give you a quick response to your question.

Transaction Processing

Transaction processing is a technique of processing transactions in random order—that is, in any order they occur. No pre-sorting of the transactions is required.

Transaction processing is real-time processing. **Real-time processing** can obtain data from the computer system in time to affect the activity at hand. In other words, a transaction is processed fast enough for the result to come back and be acted upon right away. For example, a teller at a bank (or you at an automatic teller machine) can find out immediately what your bank balance is. You can then decide right away how much money you can afford to withdraw. For processing to be real-time, it must also be **on-line**—that is, the terminals must be connected directly to the computer.

The great leap forward in the technology of real-time processing was made possible by the development of the magnetic disk as a data storage medium. With magnetic tape it is not possible to go directly to the particular record you are looking for—the tape might have to be advanced several feet first. However, with disk you can move directly to one particular piece of data, just as a CD player can go directly to a particular song on a compact disc.

There are several advantages to transaction processing. The first is that you do not need to wait. For instance, a department store salesclerk using a point-of-sale terminal can key in a customer's charge-card number and a code that asks the computer, Is this charge card acceptable? With transaction processing, the clerk gets an immediate reply. Immediacy is a distinct plus, since everyone expects fast service these days. Second, transaction processing permits continual updating of a customer's record. Thus, the salesclerk can not only verify the customer's credit, but also record the sale in the computer; the customer will eventually be billed through the computerized billing process.

Transaction processing systems are usually time-sharing systems. **Time-sharing** is a system in which two or more users can, through individual terminals, share the use (the time) of a central computer and, because of the computer's speed, receive practically simultaneous responses. Thus, an airline can have reservation clerks in far-flung cities interact with the same computer at the same time to keep informed about what flights are scheduled and how many seats are available on each.

Transaction processing does have some drawbacks. One is expense. Unlike batch processing, which uses the computer only for the amount of time needed to get the job done, transaction processing allows access to the computer at all times. Because transaction processing uses more computer resources, it costs more. However, when weighed against the alternative, such as lack of quick service, the added expense may be a minor matter.

A more serious drawback is security risk. If many users have access to the same data, it is more difficult to protect that data from theft, tampering, destruction by disgruntled employees, or unauthorized use. It has become necessary, therefore, for the computer industry to take greater precautions to protect the security of computer files. We will discuss security issues in detail in Chapter 15.

An example of transaction processing is given in Figure 4-3, which shows what happens when a patient submits a prescription for processing.

Batch and Transaction Processing: The Best of Both Worlds

Numerous computer systems combine the best features of both of these methods of processing. A bank, for instance, may record your withdrawal transaction during the day at the teller window whenever you demand your cash. However, the deposit that you leave in an envelope in an "instant" deposit drop may be recorded during the night by means of batch processing. Many oil company credit-card systems also combine both methods: A credit-card machine at the pump can instantaneously register the amount of your purchase, but for billing purposes all your gasoline purchases may be batched and totaled at one time.

Police license-plate checks for stolen cars work the same way. As cars are sold throughout the state, the license numbers, owners' names, and so on, are updated in the motor vehicle department's master file, usually via batch processing on a nightly basis. But when police officers see a car they suspect may be stolen, they can radio headquarters, where an operator with a terminal checks the master file immediately to see if the car was reported missing.

Both batch and transaction processing can also be used in a store. Using point-of-sale terminals, inventory data is captured as sales are made; this data is processed later in batches to produce inventory reports.

As we have mentioned, two primary media for storing data are magnetic tape and magnetic disk. Since these media have been the staples of the computer industry for three decades, we will begin with them.

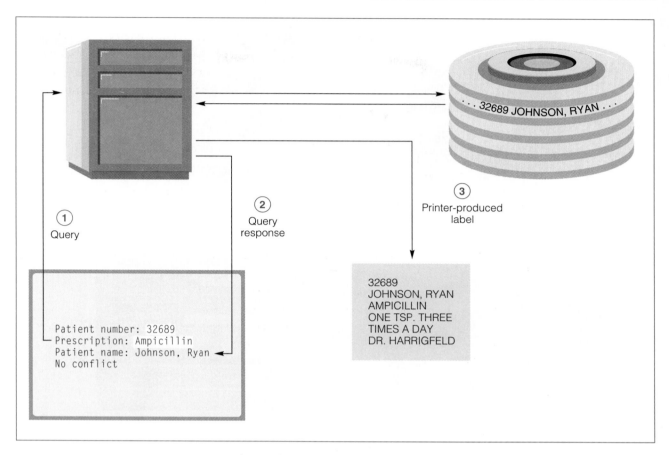

Figure 4-3 How transaction processing works. The purposes of this pharmacy system are to verify that a patient's prescription is safe, produce a prescription label for the medication bottle, and update the patient's medical records. Because of the possibility of patients having the same name, the file is organized by patient number rather than by name. Here Ryan Johnson, patient number 32689, brings his prescription to the pharmacist. ① Through the terminal the pharmacist asks the computer system whether the ampicillin prescribed is apt to conflict with other medication the patient is taking. ② The computer screen shows that 32689 is Ryan Johnson and displays the message "No conflict." The computer then updates Johnson's file so other physicians can see later that ampicillin was prescribed for him. ③ A printer attached to the computer system prints a prescription label that the pharmacist can place on the ampicillin bottle. All this is done while the patient is waiting.

 Magnetic Tape Storage

Magnetic tape looks like the tape used in music cassettes—plastic tape with a magnetic coating. (Figure 4-4). Data is stored as extremely small magnetic spots, which a tape unit can read into the main storage of a computer. Tapes come in a number of forms, including ½-inch–wide tape wound on a reel, ¼-inch–wide tape in data cartridges and cassettes, and tapes that look like ordinary music cassettes but are designed to store data instead of music.

Figure 4-4   Magnetic tape. Magnetic tape comes in several forms, including the work-horse of the large computer system, (a) ½-inch tape reels. Other forms of magnetic tape are (b) ¼-inch cartridges; (c) cassettes; and (d) DAT, digital audio tape, which uses helical scan recording technology. Cartridges, cassettes, and DAT are becoming more common for personal computers.

The amount of data on a tape is expressed in terms of **density,** which is the number of **characters per inch (cpi)** or **bytes per inch (bpi)** that can be stored on the tape. For tape cartridges, the amount of data might be expressed in megabytes or even gigabytes.

Data Representation on Tape

How is data represented on tape? As Figure 4-5 shows, one character is represented by a cross section of a tape. As the figure also shows, the tape contains **tracks,** or **channels,** that run the length of the entire tape. On most modern computer tapes, one cross section of the tape, representing one character, contains 9 bits, one on each of the tracks. There are nine locations. Each location has either a magnetized spot, which represents the 1 bit, or no magnetization, which represents the 0 bit.

Figure 4-5 describes how the tracks are used. Note that the tracks that have the most magnetized spots are clustered toward the middle. This

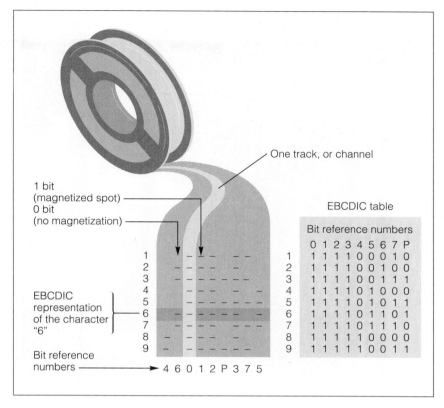

Figure 4-5 How data is represented on magnetic tape. This shows how the numbers 1 through 9 are represented on tape in EBCDIC code, using combinations of 1 bits and 0 bits. For each character there are 8 bits. The ninth bit is a parity bit represented by the letter *P.* In the odd-parity system illustrated here, each byte is always made up of an odd number of 1 bits. In an odd-parity system, an even number of 1 bits suggests that something is wrong with the data. Note that the parity-bit track appears close to the middle of the tape. The bits are out of order on the tape because the most commonly used bit locations are placed toward the center of the track, as far from dirt and grime as possible.

is to protect the data from dirt and damage, which are more apt to affect the edges of the tape.

The Magnetic Tape Unit

Figure 4-6a shows a **magnetic tape unit** that might be used on a minicomputer or mainframe. (A unit that uses cartridges or cassettes might be much smaller, even small enough to fit into a personal computer.) The purpose of the tape unit is to write and to read—that is, to record data on and retrieve data from—magnetic tape. This is done by a **read/write head** (Figure 4-6b), an electromagnet that reads the magnetized areas on the tape and converts them into electrical impulses, which are sent to the processor. The reverse procedure is called writing. When the machine is writing on the tape, the **erase head** first erases any data previously recorded on the medium.

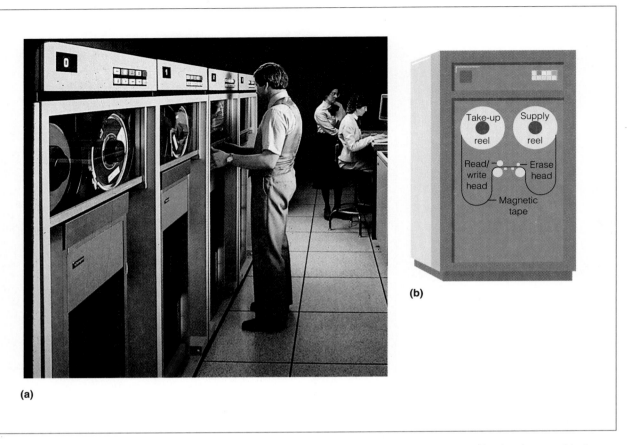

(a)

(b)

Figure 4-6   Magnetic tape units. Tapes are always protected by glass from outside dust and dirt. (a) Magnetic tape on reels is run on these tape drives. (b) This diagram highlights the read/write head and the erase head found in magnetic tape units.

Two reels are used, a **supply reel** and a **take-up reel.** The supply reel, which has the tape with data on it or on which data will be recorded, is the reel that is changed. The take-up reel always stays with the magnetic tape unit. Many cartridges and cassettes have the supply and take-up reels built into the same case.

Blocking

Speed of access to records is important; therefore, magnetic tape units are designed to provide fast access to records processed one after another on tape. However, just as you cannot stop a car on a dime, you cannot stop a tape instantly. Thus, it is necessary to have some room between records for stopping space. This space is called an **interblock gap (IBG),** or **interrecord gap (IRG).** Typically, it is blank space on the tape 3/5 inch long.

However, having many IRGs on a tape wastes space and adds to processing time. To avoid this, records are grouped together, using a process

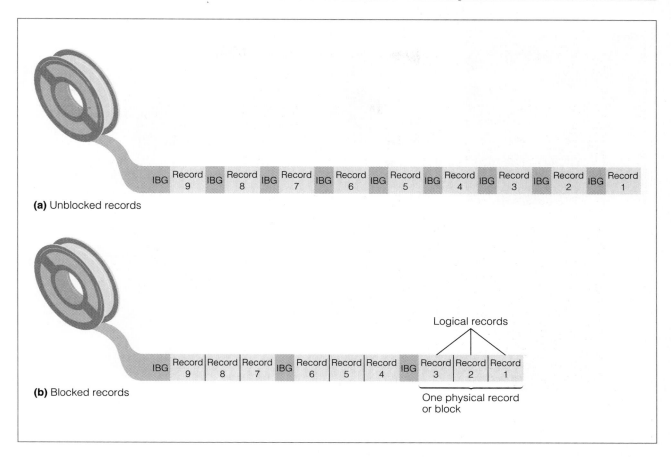

(a) Unblocked records

(b) Blocked records

Logical records

One physical record
or block

Figure 4-7   Blocking. (a) In unblocked records, each record is a physical record and also a logical record. Each physical record (block) is separated from the next by an interblock gap (IBG). (b) In blocked records, three logical records are grouped into one physical record. This saves space, because there are fewer interblock gaps (IBGs), and it increases processing speed.

called blocking. Figure 4-7 shows how this works. **Blocking** consists of putting together logical records into one physical record, or block, followed by an interblock gap. By **logical record,** we mean the record written by an application program; it is called logical because it is related to the logic of the program. A **physical record,** otherwise known as a **block,** is the collection of logical records grouped together on a tape. Programmers use the term **blocking factor** to refer to the number of logical records in one physical record. Files on disk can be blocked too. Although blocking saves time and space, there are costs involved: the cost of the time spent blocking and deblocking as well as the cost of the extra memory needed to hold the larger records.

DAT and Helical Scan Recording

Tape technology used at home for video or music is now being used with computers. For example, **digital audio tape,** or **DAT,** uses **helical scan**

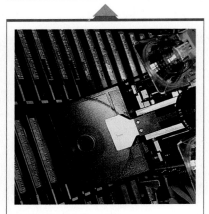

Jukebox for Tape Cartridge Libraries

A tape library system from Storage Technology Corporation can store and retrieve 6000 cartridge data tapes in much the same way that a jukebox plays records. STC says it controls about 90% of the market for such cartridge libraries, which, the corporation reports, are a must for big government and business. The libraries are used for storing data such as Social Security files, land-title records, engineering files, and historical files—sources that may be voluminous but not often referenced.

Company representatives say the 18-track tape used in its most popular cartridge libraries is about to be replaced by a 36-track tape. Systems with the new tape will be faster and cost less. A new smaller system, capable of handling 500 cartridges, is also being introduced. Ryal Poppa, STC chairman, says the trend is for high-speed disk array systems to feature stacks of smaller disks that can store data and preserve it even if some disks fail.

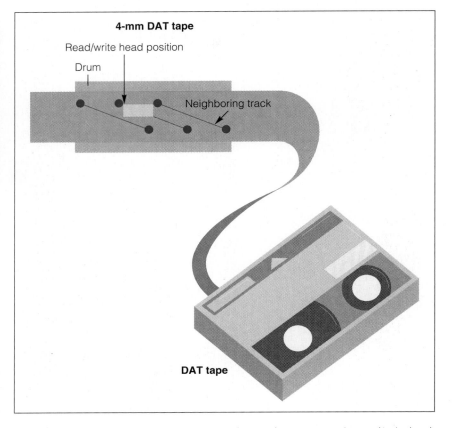

Figure 4-8   **Helical scan recording.** This is a technique that uses a rotating read/write head to write data in diagonal tracks across a tape. The advantages of helical scanning include high data density and long tape life. One format that uses helical scan recording is digital audio tape, or DAT, which uses technology developed for music recording.

recording (Figure 4-8). DAT wraps around a rotating read/write head that spins vertically as it moves. This places the data in diagonal bands that run across the tape rather than down its length. Some advantages of helical scan recording are high data density; fast transfer rates; fast, direct access to data; and long tape life.

One DAT format consists of 4mm–wide tape in a cartridge similar in size to a music cassette. Another system uses 8mm–wide tape, similar to that used in some video recorders. Some formats of DAT can store over 2GB of data.

Magnetic Disk Storage

Magnetic disk storage is another common form of secondary storage. A **hard magnetic disk,** or **hard disk,** is a metal platter coated with magnetic oxide that looks something like a stereo record but does not act like one. Hard disks come in a variety of sizes; 8, 5¼, and 3½ inches are typical diameters. Several disks are assembled together in a **disk pack**

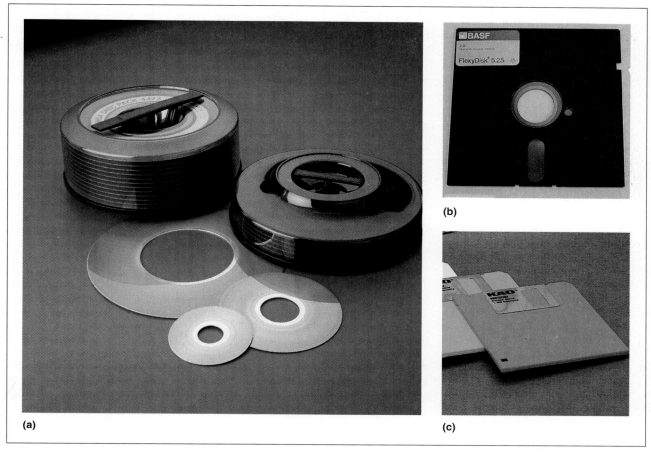

(a)

(b)

(c)

Figure 4-9 Magnetic disks. (a) Hard magnetic disks come in a variety of sizes, as shown by these three individual disks. Also, disk packs can vary in the number of disks they contain, as illustrated by the two disk packs shown here. (b) This 5¼-inch diskette is in a square protective paper jacket. (c) This 3½-inch diskette is protected by a firm plastic exterior cover.

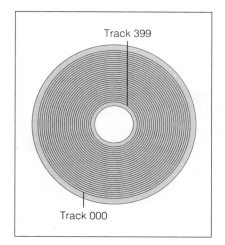

Track 399

Track 000

Figure 4-10   Surface of a disk. Note that each track is a closed circle, unlike the tracks on a phonograph record. This drawing is only to illustrate the location of the tracks; you cannot actually see the tracks on the disk surface.

(Figure 4-9a). A disk pack looks like a stack of stereo records, except that daylight can be seen between the disks. There are different types of disk packs, with the number of platters varying by model. Each disk has a top and bottom surface on which to record data. Many disk devices, however, do not record data on the top of the top platter or on the bottom of the bottom platter. Disk packs are still in use but are no longer manufactured.

Another form of magnetic disk storage is the **diskette,** which is a round piece of plastic coated with magnetic oxide (Figure 4-9b,c). Diskettes and small hard disks are used with all sizes of computers, but keep in mind that the principles of disk storage that will be discussed regarding disk packs in the next several sections also apply to hard disk storage.

How Data Is Stored on a Disk

As Figure 4-10 shows, the surface of each disk has tracks on it. Data is recorded as magnetic spots on the tracks. The number of tracks per surface varies with the particular type of disk.

But note how a disk differs from a stereo record: The track on a long-playing record allows the arm of the stereo to move gradually from the outside toward the center; a track on a disk is a closed circle—when the arm is on a particular track, it always stays the same distance from the center. All tracks on one disk are concentric; that is, they are circles with the same center.

The same amount of data is stored on every track, from outermost (track 000) to innermost (track 399 of a 400-track disk), and it takes the same amount of time to read the data on the outer track as on the inner, even though the outer track moves faster. (The disk can be compared to a chain of ice skaters playing crack the whip: The outside skater is racing, but the inside skater is only inching around—but both take the same amount of time to circle.) Disks rotate at a constant speed.

A magnetic disk is a **direct-access storage device (DASD).** With such a device you can go directly to the record you want. With tape storage, on the other hand, you must read all preceding records on the file until you come to the record you want. Data can be stored either sequentially or randomly on a direct-access storage device.

The Disk Drive

A **disk drive** is a machine that allows data to be read from a disk or written on a disk. A diskette is inserted into a disk drive that is part of a personal computer. A disk pack, however, is mounted on a disk drive that is a separate unit connected to the main computer (Figure 4-11). Some disks are permanently mounted inside a disk drive. Generally, these are used in personal computers or in cases where several users are sharing data. A typical example is a disk with files containing flight information that is used by several airline reservation agents.

In the disk drive a diskette rotates at speeds of 300 to 400 revolutions per minute. Typically, hard disks rotate 3600 revolutions per minute. In a disk pack, all disks rotate at the same time, although only one disk is being read or written on at any one time.

Figure 4-11   Disk drive units. Looking like cake covers, these disk-pack containers are sitting atop disk drive units. The disk packs themselves sit beneath the top-loading glass doors when the machine is running. Disk packs are rapidly fading into history.

Figure 4-12   Read/write heads and access arms. (a) This photo shows a read/write head on the end of an access arm poised over a hard disk. (b) When in operation, the read/write head comes very close to the surface of the disk. On a disk, particles as small as smoke, dust, a fingerprint, and a hair loom large. If the read/write head crashes into such a particle, data is destroyed and the disk damaged. You can see why it is important to keep disks and disk drives clean. (c) Note that there are two read/write heads on each access arm. Each arm slips between two disks in the pack. The access arms move simultaneously, but only one read/write head operates at any one time.

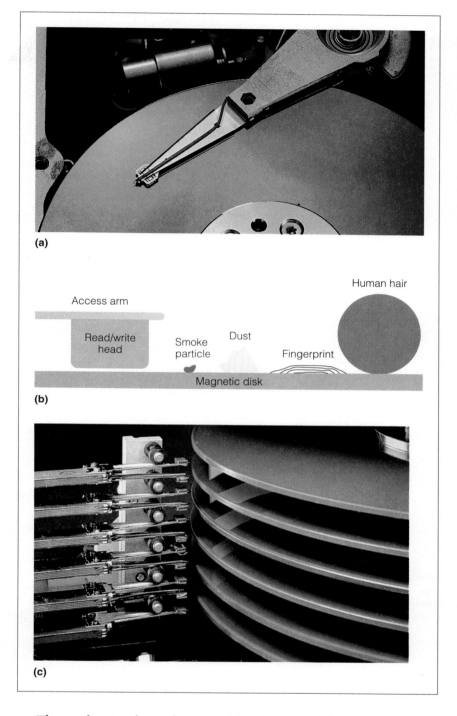

The mechanism for reading or writing data on a disk is an **access arm;** it moves a read/write head into position over a particular track (Figure 4-12a). The access arm acts somewhat like the arm on a stereo, although it does not actually touch the surface. A disk pack has a series of access arms, which slip in between the disks in the pack (Figure 4-12c). Two read/write heads are on each arm, one facing up for the surface above it, one facing down for the surface below it. However, only one read/write head can operate at any one time.

Winchester Disks

In some disk drives the access arms can be retracted; then the disk pack can be removed from the drive. In other cases, however, the disks, access arms, and read/write heads are combined in a **sealed module** called a **Winchester disk.** (These devices were named by IBM after the Winchester 30-30 rifle because the company planned to produce a dual-disk system with 30MB of storage each. IBM later abandoned the dual-disk idea, but the name *Winchester* remained.) Winchester disk assemblies are put together in clean rooms so even microscopic dust particles do not get on the disk surface. Many Winchester disks are built-in, but some are removable in the sense that the entire module can be lifted from the drive. The removed module, however, remains sealed and contains the disks and access arms.

Winchester disks were originally 14 inches in diameter, but now smaller versions are made. Hard disks on personal computers—5¼- and 3½-inch disks—usually employ Winchester technology. The principal reasons for their popularity are that Winchester disks cost about half as much but last twice as long as removable disk packs. This increased reliability is because operators do not handle the Winchester disk at all and because the sealed module keeps the disks free from contamination.

How Data Is Organized on a Disk

There is more than one way of physically organizing data on a disk. The methods we will consider here are the sector method and the cylinder method.

The Sector Method   In the **sector method,** each track is divided into sectors that hold a specific number of characters (Figure 4-13). Data on the track is accessed by referring to the surface number, track number, and sector number where the data is stored. The sector method is used for diskettes as well as disk packs.

Figure 4-13   Sector data organization. When data is organized by sector, the address is the surface, track, and sector where the data is stored.

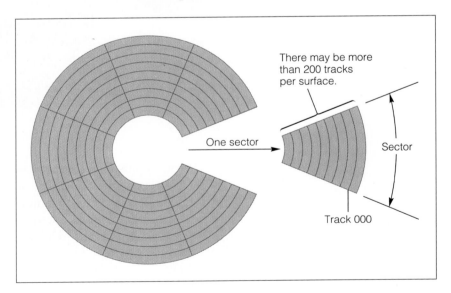

There may be more than 200 tracks per surface.

One sector

Sector

Track 000

Diskettes seldom have the same number of tracks and sectors, even if they are physically the same size. This is why diskettes from one computer may not work in another.

The Cylinder Method   Another way to organize data on a disk is the **cylinder method,** shown in Figure 4-14. Most hard disks use the cylinder method. The organization in this case is vertical. The purpose is to minimize seek time, the time it takes to move the access arms into position. It is clear that once the access arms are in position, they are in the same vertical position on all disk surfaces.

To appreciate this, suppose you had an empty disk pack on which you wished to record data. You might be tempted to record the data horizontally—to start with the first surface, fill track 000, then track 001, track 002, and so on and then move to the second surface and again fill tracks 000, 001, 002, and so forth. Each new track and new surface, however, would require movement of the access arms, a relatively slow mechanical process. Recording the data vertically, on the other hand, substantially reduces access arm movement: The data is recorded on the tracks that can be accessed by one positioning of the access arms—that is, on one **cylinder.** To visualize cylinder organization, pretend a cylinder (like a tin can) were dropped straight down through all the disks in the disk pack. The access arms mechanism has equal access to track 000 of all surfaces. The cylinder method, then, means all tracks of a certain cylinder on a disk pack are lined up one beneath the other, and all the vertical tracks of one cylinder are accessible by the read/write heads with one positioning of the access arms mechanism. Tracks within a cylin-

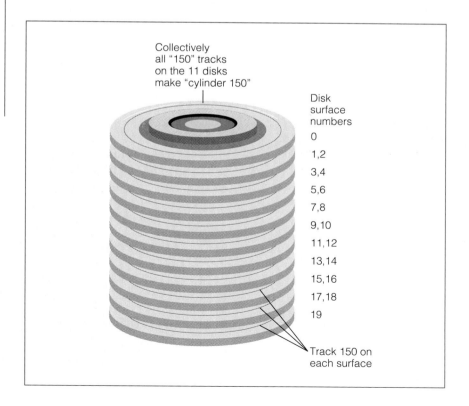

Figure 4-14   Cylinder data organization. To visualize the cylinder form of organization, imagine that a cylinder such as a tin can were dropped straight down through all the disks in the disk pack. Within cylinder 150, the track surfaces are numbered (except for the top and bottom surfaces) as shown. This is a vertical system of track numbering.

der are numbered according to this vertical perspective: A 20-surface disk pack contains cylinder tracks numbered 0 through 19, top to bottom.

Now that you have seen how data can be written vertically on disk with the cylinder method, you can also see how to establish a disk address for a particular record. The disk address is the cylinder number, surface number, and record number, in that order. For example, the disk address of a record might be cylinder 150, surface 16, record 4. Now consider access to data on disk.

Disk Access to Data

Four primary factors determine the time needed to access data:

- **Seek time.** This is the time it takes the access arm to get into position over a particular track. Keep in mind that all the access arms move as a unit, so they are simultaneously in position over a series of tracks.
- **Head switching.** The access arms on the access mechanism do not move separately; they move together, all at the same time. However, only one read/write head can operate at any one time. Head switching is the activation of a particular read/write head over a particular track on a particular surface. Since head switching takes place at the speed of electricity, the time it takes is negligible.
- **Rotational delay.** With the access arm and read/write head in position, ready to read or write data, the read/write head waits in position for a short period until the record on the track moves under it.
- **Data transfer.** This activity is the transfer of data between memory and the place on the disk track—to the track if you are writing, from the track to memory if you are reading.

With these four motions users can quickly get at any particular record any place on a disk, provided they have a method of finding where it is.

One measure for the performance of disk drives is the average access time, which is usually measured in **milliseconds (ms).** Access time is the speed with which a disk can find the data being sought. For many disks the access time is less than 15 milliseconds. Another measure is the **data transfer rate,** which tells how fast data can be transferred once it has been found. This usually will be stated in terms of megabytes per second.

 ## File Organization: Three Methods

There are three major methods of storing files of data in secondary storage:

- **Sequential file organization,** in which records are organized in sequential order by key.
- **Direct file organization,** in which records are organized randomly—not in any special order.

- **Indexed file organization,** which is a combination of sequential and direct organization. Indexed records are organized sequentially, but indexes built into the file allow a record to be accessed either sequentially or directly.

We will study each of these file organization methods in turn.

Sequential File Processing

In **sequential file processing,** records are usually in order according to a key field. If it is an inventory file, the key might be the part number. A file describing people might use a Social Security number or credit-card number as the key. We have already seen an example of sequential file processing in our discussion of batch processing (see Figure 4-2).

Direct File Processing

Direct file processing, or **direct access,** allows you to go directly to the record you want by using a record key; the computer does not have to read all preceding records in the file as it does if the records are arranged sequentially. (Direct access is sometimes called **random access** because the records can be in random order.) It is this ability to access any given record instantly that has made computer systems so convenient for people in service industries—for travel agents checking a flight for available seats, for example, and bank tellers determining individual bank balances.

Obviously, if we have a completely blank area on the disk and can put records anywhere—in other words, place them randomly—then there must be some predictable system for placing a record at a disk address and for retrieving the record at a subsequent time. In other words, once the record has been placed on a disk, it must be possible to find it again. This is done by choosing a certain formula to apply to the record key, thereby deriving a number to use as the disk address. **Hashing,** or **randomizing,** is the name given to the process of applying a formula to a key to yield a number that represents the address (Figure 4-15). An example of how direct processing works is provided in Figure 4-16.

Indexed File Processing

Indexed file processing, or **indexed processing,** is the third method of file organization, and it represents a compromise between the sequential and direct methods. It is useful in cases where files need to be in sequential order but where, in addition, you need to be able to go directly to specific records.

An indexed file works as follows: Records are stored in the file in sequential order, but the file also contains an index. The index contains entries consisting of the key to each record stored on the file and the corresponding disk address for that record. The index is like a directory, with

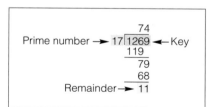

Figure 4-15   A hashing scheme. Dividing the key number 1269 by the prime number 17 yields remainder 11, which can be used to indicate track location on a disk.

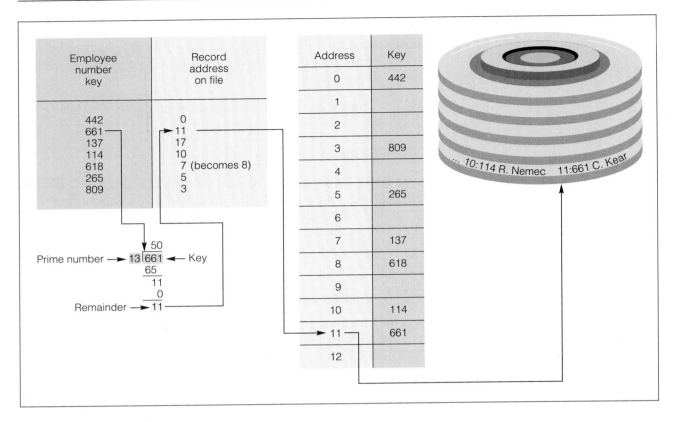

Figure 4-17 illustrates how this works.

Figure 4-16   An example of direct processing. Assume there are 13 addresses (0 through 12) available in the file. Dividing the key number 661, C. Kear's employee number, by the prime number 13 yields remainder 11. Thus, 11 is the address for key 661. However, for the key 618, dividing by 13 yields remainder 7—and this address has already been used (by the key 137). Hence, the address becomes the next location—that is, 8. Note, incidentally, that keys (and therefore records) need not appear in any particular order. (The 13 record locations available are, of course, too few to hold a normal file; a small number was used to keep the example simple.)

the keys to all records listed in order. To access a record directly, the record key must be located in the index; the address associated with the key is then used to locate the record on the disk. Figure 4-17 illustrates how this works.

You can access a record sequentially in two different ways. To retrieve an entire file of records, begin with the first record and proceed through the rest of the records. A second method for sequential retrieval is to begin with the retrieval of a record with a certain key—that is, to begin somewhere in the middle of the file—and then proceed through the file as before.

A disadvantage of indexed processing is that the process of looking up the key in the index adds one more operation to retrieval. It is therefore not as fast as direct file processing.

Disk Storage: Still the King

Why is disk storage still the primary means of storage for all sizes of computers? One reason might be historical: The disk has been an important storage medium for many years, and people do not drop too quickly something that works so well. Disk storage does indeed seem the very model of a good storage medium:

- Data on disk is very reliable.

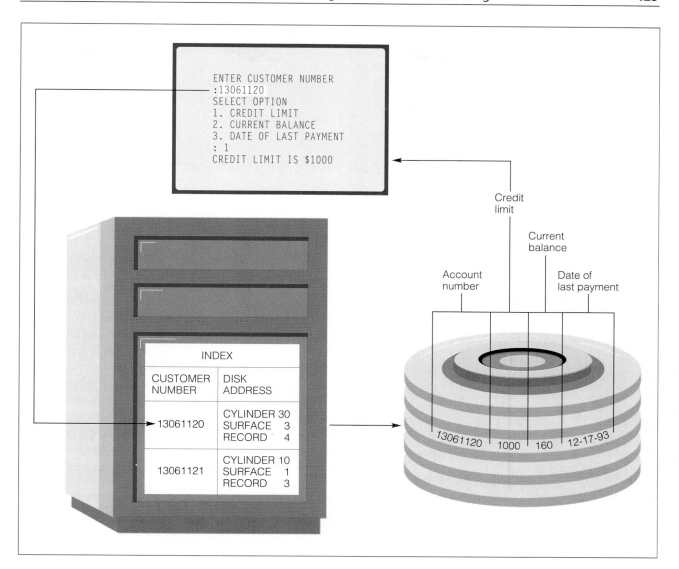

```
ENTER CUSTOMER NUMBER
:13061120
SELECT OPTION
1. CREDIT LIMIT
2. CURRENT BALANCE
3. DATE OF LAST PAYMENT
: 1
CREDIT LIMIT IS $1000
```

Credit
limit

Current
balance

Account
number

Date of
last payment

INDEX	
CUSTOMER NUMBER	DISK ADDRESS
13061120	CYLINDER 30 SURFACE 3 RECORD 4
13061121	CYLINDER 10 SURFACE 1 RECORD 3

13061120   1000   160   12-17-93

Figure 4-17   An example of indexed processing. In a credit department a terminal operator can make an inquiry about a customer's account by using the terminal to type in the customer number. The index then directs the computer to the particular disk address where the customer information is stored.

- Disk files may be organized directly, which allows immediate access and updating of any given record. This is the biggest advantage and is basic to real-time systems that facilitate instant credit checks and airline reservations.

- Using direct access, data may be updated easily. In contrast to a sequentially processed record, a single direct-access record may be read, updated, and returned to the disk, without the necessity of rewriting the entire file (this is called being updated in place.)

So why is tape still around? We have seen that records cannot be processed directly on tape. Even so, tape has certain advantages that make it a viable storage medium. It is portable—a reel of tape can be carried or mailed. It is relatively inexpensive: The cost to store a megabyte of data on tape is measured in pennies, whereas the cost for storage on a hard disk is measured in dollars. The chief uses of magnetic tape today include archiving information, transporting data, and backup—all involving a great need for high storage capacity but where direct access is less important.

What about other storage methods? Improvements in the cost and storage capacity of memory chips has allowed them to replace disks in some applications. And as you will see at the end of the chapter, optical storage combines many of the advantages of both tape and disk.

Improving Disk Drive Performance

Many techniques have been introduced to improve the performance and storage capacity of disk drives. Some of these techniques are useful in other types of storage as well.

Caching

Caching is a technique that uses a relatively small amount of semiconductor memory, called a **cache,** to speed up the performance of a disk. Caching takes advantage of the fact that most disk accesses occur in some pattern. For example, if you ask the computer to read one sector on a disk, you will probably ask it to read an adjacent sector next. The cache tries to "guess" which data you will want and have it available in the cache, where it will be thousands of times faster to access than on the disk. When the computer looks for data, it looks first in the cache, avoiding the relatively slow process of a disk access. The percentage of time that the computer finds what you want in the cache is called the **hit rate.**

Two forms of caching are write-through and write-back (Figure 4-18).

Figure 4-18   How a cache works. When data is needed, the central processing unit requests it first from the cache. If the data is not there, the CPU requests it from the disk. After the data is found and loaded from the disk, it is also loaded to the cache. The next time the central processing unit wants the data, it finds it in the cache—immediately. Write-back caching is faster than write-through caching. (a) In write-back caching, data is written to the cache immediately; writing to the disk may be delayed until the disk is idle. (b) In write-through caching, data is written simultaneously to the cache and the disk.

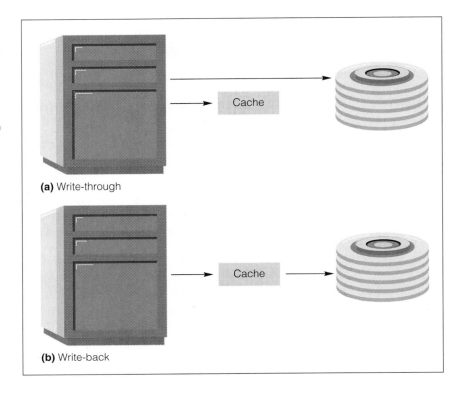

(a) Write-through

(b) Write-back

In **write-through caching,** when data is saved (written) on the disk, it is written to the cache and the disk at the same time. This has the advantage of always keeping the disk up-to-date, but writing takes a fairly long time. **Write-back caching** first writes only to the cache, without updating the disk immediately. This saves time but involves a risk that the disk will not be updated correctly should a problem occur.

Caching can also be used between the registers of the central processing unit and the main memory. In this case, a small amount of very high speed memory is used as a cache, which the CPU searches before looking in the slower main memory.

Zone Recording

The fact that a disk is circular presents a problem: The distance around the tracks on the outside of the disk is greater than that of the tracks on the inside. A given amount of data that takes up 1 inch of a track on the inside of a disk might be spread over several inches on a track near the outside of a disk. This means that the tracks on the outside are not storing data as efficiently.

Zone recording involves dividing a disk into zones to take full advantage of the amount of storage available on all tracks. Figure 4-19 shows how zone recording differs from traditional recording. Tracks in outer zones have more sectors than those in inner zones. Since each sector on the disk holds the same amount of data, more sectors mean more data storage than if all tracks had the same number of sectors. One disadvantage of zone recording is that the disk drive motor has to change speeds when moving to a zone with a different number of sectors. Therefore, the disk mechanism for zone recording is more complicated to design than the mechanism for traditional recording.

Figure 4-19   Zone vs. traditional recording. (a) If a disk is divided into recording zones, the farther from the center, the more sectors to the zone. Each sector holds the same amount of data, but since the outer zones have more sectors, the disk as a whole holds more data. (b) If a disk is divided into traditional sectors, each track has the same number of sectors. Sectors near the outside of the disk are wider, but they hold the same amount of data.

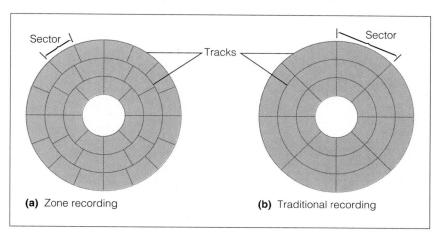

(a) Zone recording   **(b)** Traditional recording

Data Compression

When big things come in small packages on computers, data compression may be involved. Computer data consists of 0s and 1s—how can they be squeezed into smaller packages? If you say by writing smaller, you are on the wrong track. Rather than thinking in terms of size, think in terms of patterns.

Data compression takes advantage of the fact that data falls into patterns. Various techniques can exploit these patterns to encode them more efficiently (Figure 4-20a). As you will see in the next chapter, compression is also useful when transmitting data through a computer network. The result is transmission that is faster and cheaper. Though compression saves storage space, it is usually offset by the amount of time it takes

Figure 4-20   Data compression. (a) On a disk, space is normally allocated to files in units of a fixed size, often by sector. This means that, unless the file is the same size as a sector or a multiple of that size, there will be wasted space. Before compression, the files in each sector occupy the darkly shaded regions. The lightly shaded space of those sectors is wasted. One way to save space is to combine the individual files into a larger file. After compression, the combined files take up only three sectors rather than four. Note that space is wasted only in the last sector of the third file. (b) Another data compression method takes advantage of repeated patterns. Before compression, the text is represented by a two-bit code for each of four possible letters; the sentence takes up 24 bits of space in memory. After compression, by assigning the most frequent letter, *a,* a shorter code, the sentence uses only 16 bits of data—one-third less space.

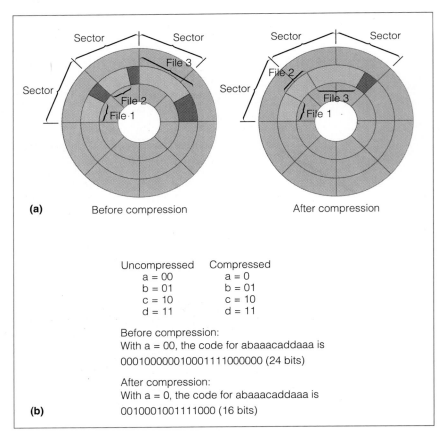

(a)   Before compression   After compression

Uncompressed	Compressed
a = 00	a = 0
b = 01	b = 01
c = 10	c = 10
d = 11	d = 11

Before compression:
With a = 00, the code for abaaacaddaaa is
000100000010001111000000 (24 bits)

After compression:
With a = 0, the code for abaaacaddaaa is
0010001001111000 (16 bits)

(b)

to compress the data when written, as well as the time it takes to decompress it when read.

There are many possible data compression techniques. One allocates file space in chunks of a predetermined size. For example, files might consist of blocks of 1024 bytes. If you create a file that uses only 300 bytes, the disk still takes 1024 bytes to store it, wasting 724 bytes. You might compare this example of inefficient storage to a term paper that is 5½ pages long—the last half page is wasted blank space. By combining several files into one large file, however, space is wasted in only one sector, at the end of the large file rather than in many sectors between individual files. This technique is especially useful for storing files that are accessed infrequently.

Another data compression technique takes advantage of the fact that certain words or characters are more likely to be used than others. For example, *and, of,* and *the* occur over and over in text. Assigning shorter codes to these frequent combinations of characters can slim down text considerably (Figure 4-20b).

Using Several Disks Together

The old cliché that two heads are better than one can apply to disk drives. If one disk is good, why not use several disks? There are many ways that multiple disks can work together, both for increased security and faster access.

Disk mirroring uses two identical disks that are updated simultaneously. If anything happens to one disk, the data is stored on the other. An expansion of this idea is called **RAID (redundant array of inexpensive disks).** This involves a group of connected disks that all operate as a single unit, allowing options not available from a lone disk. One problem with this concept is that it is more difficult to design devices that will control and coordinate several disks acting together.

One possible use of multiple disks involves assigning one disk as a *parity disk.* In Chapter 3 we looked at how parity helps detect errors in a byte. In an array of several disks, one disk might contain the parity bits for several other disks. In another use of multiple disks, the records of a file are spread over several disks. This means that while one disk is reading a record, the next disk can be moving into place to read the next record. This negates the time lost to seek time and rotational delay.

Personal Computer Storage

The market for data storage devices surged with the popularity of personal computers. Though optical disks are increasing their share of the market and tape is useful for backup purposes, we will focus first on the most prominent storage media: diskettes and hard disks.

HOW TO HANDLE DISKETTES

Do not lock your diskette in the trunk of the car on a hot day, or leave it on the dashboard in the sun, or pin it to the door of your refrigerator with a magnet. Avoid smoking cigarettes around your computer, since particles deposited on the diskette will cause the head to scratch the diskette surface. Keep diskettes away from subways and telephones, which have magnetic coils.

These are only a few of the rules for taking care of diskettes. The main forces hostile to diskettes are dust, magnetic fields, liquids, vapors, and temperature extremes. Although 3½-inch diskettes have plastic jackets and are thus less fragile than 5¼-inch diskettes, all require care in handling.

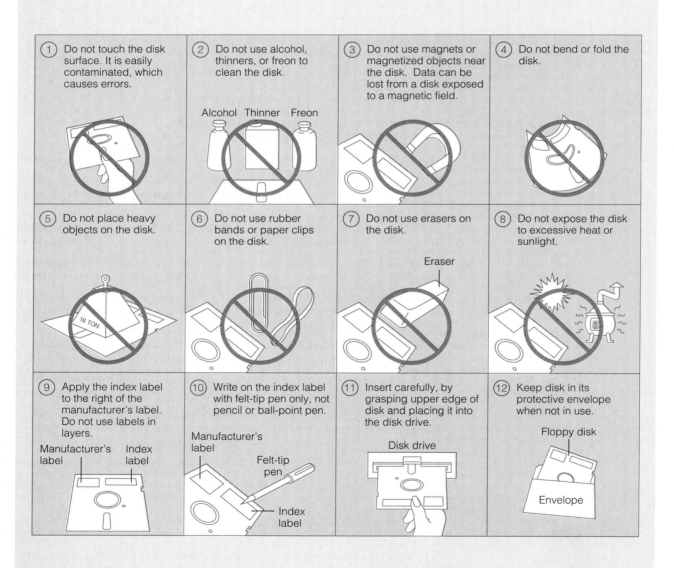

1. Do not touch the disk surface. It is easily contaminated, which causes errors.

2. Do not use alcohol, thinners, or freon to clean the disk.

3. Do not use magnets or magnetized objects near the disk. Data can be lost from a disk exposed to a magnetic field.

4. Do not bend or fold the disk.

5. Do not place heavy objects on the disk.

6. Do not use rubber bands or paper clips on the disk.

7. Do not use erasers on the disk.

8. Do not expose the disk to excessive heat or sunlight.

9. Apply the index label to the right of the manufacturer's label. Do not use labels in layers.

10. Write on the index label with felt-tip pen only, not pencil or ball-point pen.

11. Insert carefully, by grasping upper edge of disk and placing it into the disk drive.

12. Keep disk in its protective envelope when not in use.

Figure 4-21   Diskettes. (a) A cutaway view of a 5¼-inch diskette. (b) A cutaway view of a 3½-inch diskette.

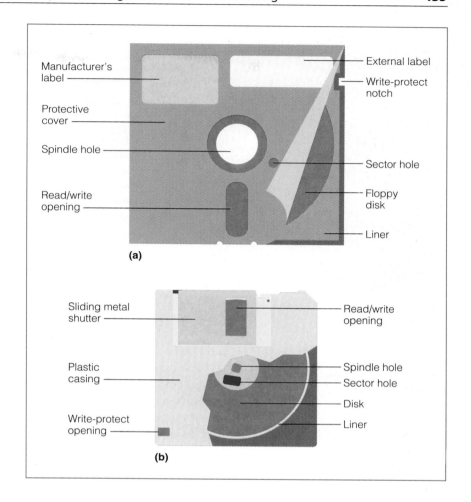

Manufacturer's label
Protective cover
Spindle hole
Read/write opening

External label
Write-protect notch
Sector hole
Floppy disk
Liner

(a)

Sliding metal shutter
Plastic casing
Write-protect opening

Read/write opening
Spindle hole
Sector hole
Disk
Liner

(b)

Diskettes

Diskettes have been popular since shortly after personal computers entered the market. The older, 5¼-inch diskette is still in use; it can hold from 360K to over 2MB of data. The 3½-inch diskette is usually used with newer computers. It can hold from 720K to more than 20MB of data (Figure 4-21).

Apple Computer set the 3½-inch standard for diskettes with its popular Macintosh computer. The 3½-inch diskette comes in a hard plastic housing and offers several advantages. It is sturdier and easier to store—fitting into a shirt pocket or purse. It weighs less and consumes less power. Its higher capacity allows companies to offer several applications programs on a single diskette, so users do not have to shuffle so many diskettes around.

Hard Disks

Hard disks are 5¼-inch or 3½-inch Winchester disks in sealed modules (Figure 4-22). Their cost has come down substantially: A hard disk with 80MB of storage may now cost less than $200, down from several thou-

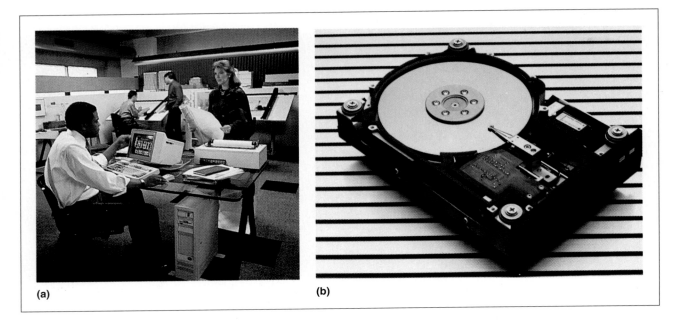

(a)   (b)

Figure 4-22   Hard disks. (a) Hard disks. (b) Innards of a hard disk. This drive stores about 20 million characters on a pair of 3½-inch disks.

sand just a few years ago. Hard disks are extremely reliable, since they are sealed against contamination by outside air or human hands.

Hard disks can save you time as well as space. You may not need all the storage a hard disk provides, but the way it speeds up your computing can make having one more than worthwhile. Accessing files on a hard disk is significantly faster than accessing files on a diskette—up to 20 times faster. The convenience of a hard disk is a factor, too—a hard disk helps you start work quickly, with all your programs and data conveniently at your disposal. Today most personal computers come with a hard disk installed.

Removable Storage

It is often said that you cannot have enough storage space. No matter how much you start with, eventually you want more. Hard disks are internal or external devices of a fixed size. They cannot be transported without a tangle of cables. To combat these disadvantages, distributors now offer **removable hard disk cartridges**, units that provide portability and an unlimited capacity.

Whenever you fill up a removable hard disk cartridge, you remove it and place a fresh one in its place. In effect, a removable cartridge works like a regular floppy disk—but the cartridge holds much more data. Two of the most popular removable hard-disk cartridge systems are by Iomega and Syquest (Figure 4-23). Iomega's Bernoulli system offers 44MB and 90MB cartridges. Syquest removable cartridges also come in two sizes: 44MB and 88MB. Ricoh offers cartridges similar to Syquest's, but Ricoh claims its product is more secure when transported. Still others offer portable hard disk units that "dock" on less expensive devices that stay with the personal computer. Removable units are very important to businesses concerned with security, because the units can be placed in se-

World's Tiniest Hard Drive

Hewlett-Packard has introduced the world's tiniest hard disk drive—about the size of a matchbox and weighing one ounce—that can hold more than 20MB, or the equivalent of about 20 long novels. The new Kittyhawk Personal Storage Module is a 1.3-inch disk drive—a third smaller than the previous record-holder, a 1.8-inch drive. It is shown here resting on a 5¼-inch diskette (capacity: 360K—or ⅟₆₀ of Kittyhawk's capacity.

The little storage device is seen as providing important portable memory for pen-based and notebook computers, cellular phones, video games, and other small machines like microwave ovens. The current competition for the Kittyhawk—chips that can compete in size and storage capabilities but that cost much more to manufacture. The popular disk drives used in computers today measure 2.5 inches and 3.5 inches and can provide three to four times the amount of built-in memory as the smaller drives. However, the Kittyhawk will appeal to computer users and manufacturers because of its durability, since larger drives have moving parts that often malfunction if bumped, according to Bruce Spenner, general manager of H-P's Disk Memory division in Boise, Idaho. He said the 1.3-inch disk drive is rugged enough to hold its data even if dropped.

cure places overnight or on weekends, then brought out for use during business hours.

Notwithstanding the advantages of removable cartridges, most hard-disk personal computer systems include at least one floppy disk drive to allow users access to software and data stored on diskettes.

Hardcards

Most people, especially in business, are surprised at how fast a hard disk fills with data. Removable cartridges offer one answer, but before they came along there was another alternative: the hardcard. The hardcard is still a popular option. Instead of buying another hard-disk drive and attaching it to your machine (and taking up more desk space), you can in-

Figure 4-23 Removable storage. (a) The Syquest drive—the standard removable hard disk drive for Macintosh computers—allows you to access and carry from place to place a special hard disk cartridge in either of two sizes: 44MB or 88MB. For IBM computers the most popular removable hard disk drive is (b) Bernoulli, which offers cartridges with capacities of 44MB or 90MB.

(a)

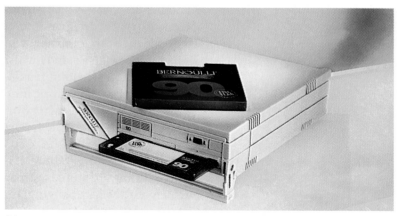

(b)

Figure 4-24 **Hardcard.** (a) This disk drive on a card—a hardcard—is being inserted into a slot inside a personal computer. (b) The interior of a hardcard, showing the disk.

(a)

(b)

stall a **hardcard** (Figure 4-24) in a slot inside your computer. Hardcards offer various capacities, from 20MB up to 100MB and more. The primary advantage of a hardcard is that it is out of sight and does not clutter up your desk.

RAM Disks

It is called a **RAM disk,** but it is not really a disk at all. A RAM disk uses random-access memory—call it semiconductor storage—as if it were just another disk drive. The RAM disk might be a part of the computer's main memory that is designated for this purpose, or it might be a separate device added to the computer. The advantage of a RAM disk is that it works much faster than a standard disk. It is often used for temporary files, and it is particularly helpful if a user is sending data from one computer to another. Instead of waiting for the diskette or hard disk to send data, the user can send data directly from the RAM disk.

So why not put all files on RAM disk and enjoy the pure speed? RAM disk, alas, is volatile—its contents are lost if the computer is turned off or if there is a power failure. It is acceptable to lose program files in such a way if they are stored permanently on a disk somewhere. Data files, which are always changing, must be saved on disk before you turn off your computer. (In fact, it is a good idea to save your files periodically as you are working on them, to avoid data loss due to power surges or power

Figure 4-25 Flash memory. Combining the high speed and low power use of main memory with the permanent data storage of disk, flash memory is often used in portable computers.

failures.) So, in summary, you can load your programs onto RAM disk for the day, but you must save new data on storage devices before shutting off the computer.

Flash Memory

Disk storage is also getting competition from a type of semiconductor storage other than RAM disk: flash memory (Figure 4-25). **Flash memory** is a special type of programmable read-only memory (PROM), a type of memory you studied in Chapter 2. Access time is normally not as fast as with RAM but still thousands of times faster than with a disk. Data in flash memory is nonvolatile—that is, like data on a disk, data in flash memory is not lost when the power goes off. Also like the contents of a disk, the contents of flash memory can be altered. Because flash memory has no moving parts to draw power, it is a good substitute for disk storage where power use is critical, such as with laptop computers. Flash memory can also be placed on removable cards. However, due to its higher cost and physical size per megabyte, flash memory is not likely to replace disks for everyday use.

Backup Systems

Figure 4-26 Tape backup systems. These tape backup units—one for external and the other for internal use—permit backup of part or all of a hard disk for security or archival purposes.

Although a hard disk is an extremely reliable device, a hard disk drive is subject to electromechanical failure. With any method of data storage, a **backup system**—a way of storing data in more than one place to protect it from damage and loss—is vital. There are inexpensive solutions that can store data on diskettes, and these are appropriate for small hard drives of, say, 10MB to 20MB. But such solutions are too slow and cumbersome for larger systems. Personal computer users often use **tape backup systems** to copy the data from their disks onto cassettes or cartridges (Figure 4-26). A cartridge might store hundreds of megabytes, and a DAT cartridge several gigabytes—plenty of capacity to back up even the most storage-rich computers. Data thus saved can be restored to the hard disk later if needed. A key advantage of a tape backup system is that it can copy the entire hard disk in minutes, saving you the trouble of swapping diskettes in and out of the machine. Such systems are sometimes called *streaming tape backup systems* because the tape does not stop and start; it moves in a continuous stream.

Checking an Earlier Decision

We left Pete James with his personal computer equipped with a 100MB hard drive. The capacity of the machine was just fine for Pete's original purposes—writing notes, letters, outlines, speeches, and position papers and producing business charts. But he soon began branching out in other directions, using various types of software. He tracked names and phone numbers, analyzed financial data, and even produced some complex graphics. He used the computer as a system for filing ideas that he could access instantaneously. All these activities used data files, and Pete eventually found that his hard drive was getting crowded.

A rule of thumb among computer professionals is to estimate disk needs generously and then double that amount. But estimating future needs is rarely easy. Many users, therefore, make later adjustments. Pete chose a Syquest removable cartridge disk unit to accommodate his expanding storage needs. To quote Pete, "Before, I just couldn't envision how computers could be used. Now I think of my computer as an extension of my brain."

 ## Optical Storage: Superdisc Takes Off

Now that you have a thorough grounding in traditional magnetic media, you can better appreciate the technology called **optical disc.** The explosive growth in storage needs has driven the computer industry to provide cheaper, more compact, and more versatile storage devices with greater capacity. This demanding shopping list is a description of the optical disc.

How Optical Discs Work

The technology works like this. A laser hits a layer of metallic material spread over the surface of a disc. When data is being entered, heat from the laser produces tiny spots on the disc surface. To read the data, the laser scans the disc, and a lens picks up different light reflections from the various spots.

Optical storage technology is categorized according to its read/write capability. **Read-only media** are recorded on by the manufacturer and can be read from but not written to by the user. Such a disc cannot, obviously, be used for your files, but manufacturers can use it to supply software. Current multiple-application packages—a package that includes

P E R S P E C T I V E S

THE WHOLE WORLD ON CD-ROM

Why is CD-ROM optical technology revolutionary? It is certainly revolutionizing the way data is stored and made available to personal computer users. Government agencies, insurance firms, and banks are transferring their microfilm data to CD-ROM and other optical forms of storage, and many commercial publishers are making entire libraries available on CD-ROM discs. Consider a few of the thousands of titles now available for just about everyone:

- For students and researchers, there's *Compton's Multimedia Encyclopedia* (shown here). Or take the content of the *Encyclopedia Britannica*, whose 450 million characters reside in 30 book volumes, and would require 1250 standard 360K diskettes. But the entire set of volumes can fit quite nicely, with room to spare, on a single optical disc. Grolier Electronic Publishing has put an entire 20-volume encyclopedia onto a CD-ROM disc; Microsoft has collected a number of works on its *Bookshelf* disc, including the *American Heritage Dictionary, Roget's Thesaurus, Bartlett's Familiar Quotations, The World Almanac, A Manual of Style, Business Information Sources,* and a zip code directory. An increasing number of publishers are collecting libraries on one disc.

- For newspaper, magazine, and other print publishers, entire collections of photographs and illustrations have been made available on CD-ROM discs such as *PhotoBank, Volume 1,* which contains 500MB of high-resolution color photos, each available in a variety of formats for most publishing needs. Numerous CD-ROM disc

publishers are jumping on the graphics library bandwagon.

- For multimedia and movie makers, a firm called CD Technology offers several CD-ROM discs featuring movie-making tutorials; animation instruction; libraries of video, animation, and movie clips; as well as sounds, photos, and backgrounds. As

multimedia expands, more such offerings from such top film companies as Disney, Paramount, and others should help desktop movie-making take off.

- For historians, The Bureau of Electronic Publishing's *U.S. History on CD-ROM* contains the full text of 107 books relating to U.S. history. The CD-ROM provides details, from a variety of viewpoints, on U.S. political, social, military, and economic history. The disc includes over a thousand photos, maps, and tables of historical events.

- For educators, Quantum Leap CD Software offers *Macademic,* a disc covering pre-school through graduate school subjects from anatomy to zoology—including art, music, math, science, and foreign languages—and even educational games. The disc provides help for teachers, and

lesson plans, too. In addition, the company's *Giga-ROM* CD features 11,000 Macintosh shareware programs, its *CD7* CD-ROM includes some 15,800 files of art, games, demos, and utilities.

- Newshounds can have it all too: *The Washington Times* and *Insight on the News* CD-ROM captures the news of the world from June 1989 through June 1991, including the full text of headline articles as well as commentary and sports, financial, and weather news. The publisher, Wayzata, also offers *Front Page News,* a research tool CD-ROM providing the complete news offerings of ten domestic and international wire services and featuring more than 200,000 articles.

One likely new product is the modular library that can be updated quarterly to provide pressing news and information. One of the first such offerings, *Stat-Ref,* is published by Teton Data Systems for doctors. Each quarter, a new disc is sent to any physician requesting it. The CD-ROM contains 20 "locked"

volumes that can only be opened by calling in a credit-card number to obtain the password. Cost is based on the volumes unlocked.

The Blistering Speed of Holostore

Optical storage may be just a stepping-stone into the future when it comes to secondary storage. As central processing units get faster, we will need faster ways to store data—and optical media may not be able to keep up. Some engineers believe the answer lies in a completely new direction, with lasers storing data in the form of holographs.

You may be familiar with holographs as the 3-D pictures on credit cards. Holographic storage, or holostore, for short, can move data at blistering speeds—up to 10,000 times faster than what we know today. A holostore device could hold over 100GB in one module and could transfer data at a rate of more than one trillion bytes per second.

word processing, spreadsheet, graphics, and database programs—sometimes encompass as many as 16 diskettes; all these could fit on one optical disc with plenty of room to spare.

Write-once, read-many media, also called **WORM media,** may be written to once. Once filled, a WORM disc becomes a read-only media. A WORM disc is nonerasable. For applications demanding secure storage of original versions of valuable documents or data, the primary advantage of nonerasability is clear: Once they are recorded, no one can erase or modify them. Write-once optical media can provide a secure comparison base for auditing changes to original data—an invaluable function in, say, geophysical applications where a difference of a few bits can signal the presence of oil. Optical disc has opened up a wide range of new capabilities and novel applications.

Another variation of optical technology is the **CD-ROM,** for **compact disc read-only memory.** CD-ROM has a major advantage over other optical disc designs: The disc format is identical to that of *audio* compact discs, so the same dust-free manufacturing plants that are now stamping out digital versions of Bach or Madonna can easily convert to producing anything from software to the *Encyclopedia Britannica.* Since producing CD-ROM is simply a matter of pressing out copies from a master disc, it is much more economical than traditional magnetic storage, which makes copies byte by byte.

The Future Approaches

Early optical discs could not be written on, but that has changed. Today, optical discs can be written to and erased many times. Two competing technologies are magneto-optical discs and phase-change discs. **Magneto-optical discs** use a laser to heat a spot on a disc while magnetizing it. This magnetism can then be read by changing the laser light reflected from the spot. **Phase-change media** use two laser beams of different powers to melt a spot on a disc. One power creates a 0, the other creates a 1. The difference in power results in a difference in the way the spots reflect light, which can be detected by the reading laser. Though magneto-optical arrived first, it has the disadvantage of having to first erase a spot before writing it, thereby doubling the time required to write.

Optical disc storage will continue to take over some of the work now being done by magnetic disk and tape. The high data density of optical storage gives it an edge for storing large amounts of data, and the ability of optical technology to provide direct access may make it more useful than tape for backup.

Onward

What is the future of storage? Perhaps holographic storage, which would provide gigabytes of capacity and be much faster than even the fastest hard drives. Whatever the technology, it seems likely that we will be seeing greater storage capabilities in the future. Such capabilities have awesome implications; think of the huge data files for law, medicine, science, education, government, and ultimately . . . you.

To have access to all that data from any location, we need data communications, to which we turn in the next chapter.

R E V I E W   A N D   R E F E R E N C E

Summary and Key Terms

- **Secondary storage,** or **auxiliary storage,** is necessary because memory, or primary storage, can only be used temporarily. The benefits of secondary storage are economy, reliability, and convenience. Two common means of secondary storage are magnetic tape and magnetic disk; optical storage is a newer technology.

- To be processed by a computer, raw data is organized into characters, fields, files, and databases. A **character** is a letter, number, or special character (such as $). A **field** is a set of related characters, a **record** is a collection of related fields, a **file** is a collection of related records, and a **database** is a collection of interrelated files.

- The two main methods of data processing are **batch processing** (processing data transactions in groups) and **transaction processing** (processing data transactions one at a time). Many computer systems combine features of both types of processing.

- Batch processing involves a **master file,** which contains semi-permanent data, and a **transaction file,** which contains additions, deletions, and changes to be made to **update** the master file. These new transactions are **sorted** sequentially by a **key,** or a field that identifies records. The master file, which is already in order, is then updated by being compared against the transaction file.

- An advantage of batch processing is the economy of processing records in groups. Disadvantages include both the delay in receiving the initial output and the additional time needed later to locate a particular record in a group.

- In transaction processing, the transactions are processed in the order they occur, without any pre-sorting. This is **real-time processing** because the results of the transactions are available quickly enough to affect the activity at hand. For real-time processing, the user's terminals must be **on-line** (directly connected to the computer).

- Transaction processing systems are usually **time-sharing** systems, in which users share access to a central computer that can process their transactions almost at the same time.

- Advantages of transaction processing include quick results and continual updating. Disadvantages include the expense of continual access to the computer and the difficulty of protecting the security of computer files.

- The amount of data on a **magnetic tape** is expressed in terms of **density,** as the number of **characters per inch (cpi)** or **bytes per inch (bpi)** that can be stored on a tape.

- **Tracks,** or **channels,** run the length of the magnetic tape. On most tapes a cross section representing one character contains 9 bits, one for each track. A magnetized spot represents a 1 bit; a location with no magnetization represents a 0 bit.

- A **magnetic tape unit** records and retrieves data by using a **read/write head,** an electromagnet that can convert magnetized areas into electrical impulses (to read) or reverse the process (to write). When the machine is writing, the **erase head** erases any previously recorded data.

- The magnetic tape is inserted into the unit on a **supply reel,** passed through the read/write head, and attached to the **take-up reel.** During processing the tape moves back and forth between the two reels, then is rewound onto the supply reel when the processing is complete.

- Since fast-moving magnetic tape cannot stop instantly, some blank stopping space is necessary between records. This space is called an **interblock gap (IBG),** or **interrecord gap (IRG).** To avoid wasting space on a tape, **blocking** is used. In other words, **logical records,** the records written by the applications program, are blocked, or put together, into **physical records,** or **blocks.** The term **blocking factor** refers to the number of logical records in one physical record.

- **Helical scan recording** is a technique that uses a rotating read/write head to write the data in diagonal tracks across the tape. Its advantages are high data density and long tape life. One format that uses helical scan recording is **digital audio tape, DAT,** which uses technology developed for music recording.

- A **hard magnetic disk,** or **hard disk,** consists of a metal platter coated with magnetic oxide. The surface of a magnetic disk has tracks on which data is recorded as magnetic spots. All the tracks are closed circles having the same center, and the same amount of data is stored on each track. When more than one hard disk is assembled as a unit, the group is called a **disk pack.** A **diskette** is a round piece of plastic coated with magnetic oxide.

- A disk or diskette storage device is a **direct-access storage device (DASD)** because it locates a record directly (unlike magnetic tape, which requires the read/write head to read all the preceding records on the file). With a DASD, data can be stored either sequentially or randomly.

- A **disk drive** rapidly rotates a disk, diskette, or disk pack as an **access arm** moves a read/write head that detects the magnetized data.

- A **Winchester disk** combines disks, access arms, and read/write heads in a **sealed module.** Some disk modules are built-in; others are removable.

- The two main methods of writing data on a disk or diskette are the sector method and the cylinder method. In the **sector method,** each track is divided into sectors and data is identified by surface, track, and sector number. The cylinder method accesses a set of tracks lined up one under the other, one from each surface. Such a set of vertically aligned tracks is called a **cylinder.** The cylinder method means fewer movements of the access arms mechanism and faster processing.

- The time needed to access data is determined by four factors: (1) **seek time,** the time it takes the access arm to get into position over the track; (2) **head switching,** the small amount of time needed to activate the appropriate read/write head; (3) **rotational delay,** the time necessary for the appropriate record to get into position under the head; and (4) **data transfer,** the time required for data to be transferred between memory and the disk track.

- Two common measures of the speed of a disk drive are the **average access time** (which is usually measured in **milliseconds, ms)** and the **data transfer rate.**

- The three main methods of storing files of data in secondary storage are **sequential file organization, direct file organization,** and **indexed file organization.**

- In **sequential file processing,** records are usually in order according to a key field.

- **Direct file processing** (also called **direct access** or **random access)** allows direct access to a record by using a record key; the user does not have to wait for the computer to read preceding records in the file. **Hashing,** or **randomizing,** is the process of applying a formula to a key to yield a number that represents the address.

- In **indexed file processing,** or **indexed processing,** records are stored in sequential order, but the file also contains an index of record keys so an individual record can be located.

- Disk storage provides high-volume data capacity and allows direct file processing, which enables the user to immediately find and update records. Tape storage does not allow direct file processing, but it is portable and less expensive than disk storage.

- Several methods have been used to improve the performance of disk drives. **Caching** uses memory called a cache that the computer can search for data before looking on the disk. The success of finding data in the cache is called the **hit rate.** Caching can be **write-back,** in which data is not written back to the disk immediately, or **write-through,** in which the cache and disk are written to at the same time.

- **Zone recording** puts more sectors on the longer outer tracks of a disk, allowing more data to be stored. **Data compression** uses several techniques to decrease the amount of space required to store data. **Disk mirroring** updates two disks simultaneously. **RAID (redundant array of inexpensive disks)** technology uses a number of methods involving multiple disks to improve data access and security.

- Common storage media for personal computers are diskettes and hard disks. **Diskettes** include 5¼-inch and 3½-inch sizes. A **hard disk** is more expensive than a floppy disk and cannot easily be moved from computer to computer, but it does provide more storage and faster processing.

- The storage capacity of a personal computer with a built-in hard disk can be increased through the addition of another hard disk drive, a **removable cartridge disk drive,** or a **hardcard.**

- A **RAM disk** is not a disk at all. It is a part of random-access memory as if it were a disk drive for storing programs and data. A RAM disk works much faster than a standard disk drive and is useful for sending data from computer to computer. The disadvantage of RAM is that it is volatile.

- **Flash memory** is a type of writable, nonvolatile semiconductor memory that can take the place of disks in applications where low power use is important.

- Despite the reliability of data storage devices, a **backup system**—a way of protecting data by copying it and storing it in more than one place—is vital. Hard disks can be backed up efficiently with a **tape backup system,** which can hold many megabytes of data. Such backup units can copy an entire hard disk in minutes, and—if needed—restore it just as quickly.

- In **optical disc** technology, a laser beam records data by producing tiny spots on the metallic surface of an optical disc. Data is read by having the laser scan the disc surface while a lens picks up different light reflections from the spots.

- Optical storage technology is categorized according to its read/write capability. A **read-only medium** is recorded on by the manufacturer. A **write-once, read-many medium (WORM)** can be written to once; then it becomes read-only.

- A variation on the optical technology is the **CD-ROM,** which stands for **compact disc read-only memory.** CD-ROM has the same format as audio compact discs.

- The latest optical disc technology allows data to be stored, moved, changed, and erased—just as on magnetic media. Two technologies vie for the upper hand: **Magneto-optical discs** combine magnetic and optical technologies and work faster than its competition; **phase-change disks,** require lasers to melt a spot on a disc to alter data content.

Review Questions

1. Describe the benefits of secondary storage.
2. Define the following: character, field, record, file, and database.
3. Explain how batch processing differs from transaction processing.
4. Provide one advantage and one disadvantage of batch processing.
5. Provide one advantage and one disadvantage of transaction processing.
6. Explain how batch and transaction processing may be combined.
7. Explain how data is represented on magnetic tape.
8. Describe how a disk drive works.
9. Explain how the sector method differs from the cylinder method.
10. Describe the three major methods of file organization.
11. How do hard disks differ from diskettes?
12. Describe methods used to improve disk performance.
13. Describe how optical discs work.
14. Describe two uses of semiconductor memory that replace disk drives.

Discussion Questions

1. Provide your own example to illustrate how characters of data are organized into fields, records, files, and databases. If you wish, you may choose one of the following examples: department-store data, airline data, or Internal Revenue Service data.

2. Give your own examples to illustrate the use of each of the following types of processing: batch processing, transaction processing, and a combination of batch processing and transaction processing.
3. Imagine that you are buying a personal computer. What would you choose for secondary storage and why?

True-False Questions

T F 1. The RAM disk is a way of using computer memory as if it were a disk.

T F 2. When searching for data on a disk, seek time occurs after rotational delay.

T F 3. Of CD-ROM and WORM, the one the computer can write to is CD-ROM.

T F 4. DAT stands for *digital audio tape,* and refers to a method of sound reproduction that can also be used for computer backup.

T F 5. A Winchester disk is a type of hard disk in which the disks are sealed to prevent contamination.

T F 6. An advantage of batch processing is that the data stored in the computer is always up to date.

T F 7. The method of file organization that allows the fastest access to an individual record is direct file organization.

T F 8. A field is a collection of related records.

T F 9. The data on the surface of a disk is divided into concentric circles called sectors.

T F 10. Caching is another term for backing up a computer.

T F 11. The method of file organization most closely associated with tape is indexed file organization.

T F 12. For most computer storage applications, tape is still used as frequently as disk.

5

Communications

Linking Computers Worldwide

Shortly after Kevin Costelloe donated a kidney to help save his sister

Patty's life, his heart stopped beating. Both lives were suddenly in dan-

ger. The large Costelloe family—eight family groups—overwhelmed the

hospital phone lines for condition reports. So another brother, Terry, set

up a laptop computer in his sister's hospital room and signed onto the

Prodigy Services computer network. With a few keystrokes, he sent eight

copies of condition updates through electronic mail. When family mem-

bers signed onto Prodigy from their own personal computers, each re-

ceived a flashing "New Mail" alert, indicating another message had ar-

rived. Finally Terry sent a long-awaited message: Both patients were out

of danger and would recover fully.

This example of one family's experience with telecommunications reflects a change in the direction of electronic mail. It is no longer just a business tool but a burgeoning new medium for personal communication.

Potentially, any two computers in the world can be linked together using existing telephone lines and communications equipment. Although potential abuses accompany any new technology, the merger of communications and computers—**telecommunications**—is an exceptional benefit, helping people get full value from each technology. Telecommunications gives people access to on-line information, brings services like banking and shopping into the home, and links professionals together in complex computer networks. People who use telecommunications technology are just as casual about linking up with a computer in another state or country as they are about using the telephone. This chapter will highlight these topics and the technology that makes them possible. We will begin with a look at the past.

 ## Data Communications: How It All Began

Mail, telephone, TV and radio, books, and periodicals—these are the principal ways we send and receive information, and they have not changed appreciably in a generation. However, **data communications systems**—computer systems that transmit data over communications lines such as public telephone lines or private network cables—have been gradually evolving since the mid-1960s. Let us take a look at how they came about.

In the early days, large computers were often found in several departments of large companies. There could be, for example, different computers to support engineering, accounting, and manufacturing. However, because department managers generally did not know enough about computers to use them efficiently, expenditures for computers were often wasteful. The response to this problem was to centralize computer operations.

Centralization provided better control, and the consolidation of equipment led to economies of scale—that is, hardware and supplies could be purchased in bulk at cheaper cost. **Centralized data processing** placed everything—all processing, hardware, software, and storage—in one central location. Computer manufacturers responded to this trend by building even larger, general-purpose computers so that all departments within an organization could be serviced efficiently.

Eventually, however, total centralization proved inconvenient. All input data had to be physically transported to the computer, and all processed material had to be picked up and delivered to the users. Insisting on centralized data processing was like insisting that all conversations between people occur face-to-face in one designated room. The next logical step was to connect users via telephone lines and terminals to the central computer. Thus, in the 1960s, the centralized system was made more flexible by the introduction of time-sharing through **teleprocessing systems**—terminals connected to the central computer via communications lines. Teleprocessing systems permitted users to have remote access to the central computer from their terminals in other buildings and even other cities. However, even though access to the computer system was decentralized, all processing was still centralized—that is, performed by one central computer.

In the 1970s, businesses began to use minicomputers, which were often at a distance from the central computer. These were clearly decentralized systems because the smaller computers could do some processing on their own, yet some also had access to the central computer. This new setup was labeled **distributed data processing (DDP).** It is similar to teleprocessing, except that it accommodates not only remote *access* but also remote *processing.*

Processing is no longer done exclusively by the central computer. Rather, the processing and files are dispersed among several remote locations and can be handled by computers—usually minicomputers or personal computers—all hooked up to the central host computer and sometimes to each other as well. A typical application of a distributed data processing system is a business or organization with many locations, branch offices, or retail outlets. DDP communications systems are more complex and usually more expensive than exclusively centralized computer systems, but they provide many more benefits to users.

The whole picture of distributed data processing has changed dramatically with the advent of networks of personal computers. By **network,** we mean a computer system that uses communications equipment to connect two or more computers and their resources. DDP systems are networks. Of particular interest in today's business world are **local area networks (LANs),** which are designed to share data and resources among several individual computers (Figure 5-1). We will examine networking in more detail in later sections of the chapter.

Figure 5-1   Local area network. Businesses can use shared resources to their advantage with a local area network.

Another type of connection is the **micro-to-mainframe link.** Although users have a variety of business software available for their microcomputers, or personal computers, they often want to use that software to process corporate data that resides in the mainframe files. Giving users access to that data is a hot issue. The connection itself is a problem because the two computers—mainframe and personal—may not be compatible. But a more serious problem is the security and integrity of the data after it has been released.

In the next section we will preview the components of a communications system to give you an overview of how these components work together.

Communications: The Complete System

The components are few. The complications are many. The basic configuration—how the components are put together—is pretty straightforward, but there is a great variety of components to choose from and the technology is ever changing. Assume that you have some data—a message—to transmit from one place to another. The basic components of a data communications system used to transmit that message are (1) a sending device, (2) a communications link, and (3) a receiving device. Suppose, for example, that you work at a sports store. You might want to send a message to the warehouse to inquire about a Wilson tennis racquet, an item you need for a customer. In this case the sending device is your computer terminal at the store, the communications channel is the phone line, and the receiving device is the central computer at the warehouse. As you will see, however, there are many other possibilities.

Figure 5-2 Communications system components. Data originated from (1) a sending device is (2) converted by a modem to data that can be carried over (3) a link and (4) reconverted by a modem at the receiving end before (5) being sent to the computer.

There is another often-needed component that must be mentioned in this basic configuration, as you can see in Figure 5-2. This component is a modem, which is sometimes needed to convert computer data to signals that can be carried by the communications channel and vice versa.

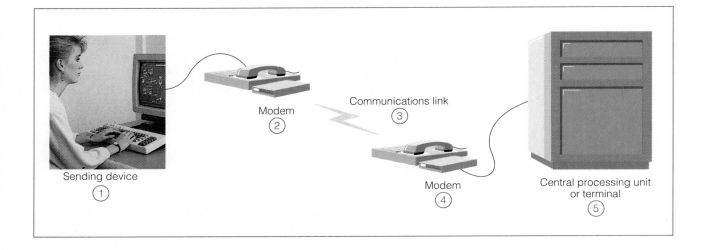

Large computer systems may have additional components. At the computer end, data may travel through a communications control unit called a **front-end processor,** which is actually a computer itself. Its purpose is to relieve the central computer of some of the communications tasks and so free it for processing applications programs. In addition, a front-end processor usually performs error detection and recovery functions. Small computers, we should note, usually perform communications functions by using a special logic board in the computer itself.

Let us see how the components of a communications system work together, beginning with how data is transmitted.

Data Transmission

A terminal or computer produces digital signals, which are simply the presence or absence of an electric pulse. The state of being on or off represents the binary number 1 or 0. Some communications lines accept digital transmission directly, and the trend in the communications industry is toward digital signals. However, most telephone lines through which these digital signals are sent were originally built for voice transmission, and voice transmission requires analog signals. We will look at these two types of transmission and then study modems, which translate between them.

Digital and Analog Transmission

Digital transmission sends data as distinct pulses, either on or off, in much the same way that data travels through the computer. This means that computer-generated data can be transmitted directly over digital communications media. However, most communications media are not digital. Communications devices such as telephone lines, coaxial cables, and microwave circuits are already in place for voice transmission. The easiest choice for most users is to piggyback on one of these. The most common communications devices all use **analog transmission,** a continuous electric signal in the form of a wave.

To be sent over analog lines, a digital signal must first be converted to an analog form. It is converted by altering an analog signal, which is called a **carrier wave** (Figure 5-3a). An analog carrier waveform has several alterable characteristics. One such characteristic is the **amplitude,** or height of the wave, as shown in Figure 5-3b. In this case, the height of the wave can be increased to represent the binary number 1, or left the same to represent 0. You might imagine this as a loud sound representing the 1 and a soft sound representing the 0. Another characteristic that can be altered is the **frequency,** or number of times a wave repeats during a specific time interval.

Conversion from digital to analog signals is called **modulation,** and the reverse process—reconstructing the original digital message at the other end of the transmission—is called **demodulation.** (You probably know amplitude and frequency modulation by their abbreviations, AM

Figure 5-3   Analog signals. (a) An analog carrier wave moves up and down in a continuous cycle. (b) The analog waveform can be converted to digital form through amplitude modulation. As shown, the wave height is increased to represent a 1 or left the same to represent a 0.

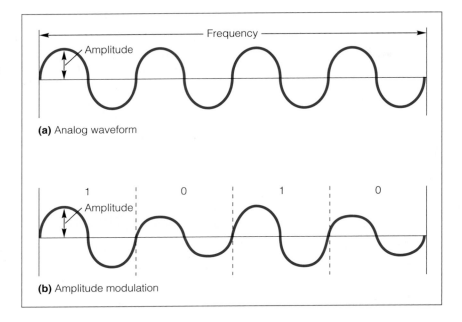

and FM, the methods used for radio transmission.) So we see that the marriage of computers to communications is not a perfect one. Instead of just "joining hands," a third party may be needed in between. This extra device is called a modem.

Modems

A **modem** is a device that converts a digital signal to an analog signal and vice versa (Figure 5-4a). *Modem* is short for *mo*dulate/*dem*odulate.

Types of Modems   Modems vary in the way they connect to the telephone line. There are two main types: direct-connect modems and acoustic coupler modems.

A **direct-connect modem** is directly connected to the telephone line by means of a telephone jack. An **external direct-connect modem** is separate from the computer (Figure 5-4b). Its main advantage is that it can be used with a variety of computers. If you buy a new personal computer, for example, you can probably keep the same modem. For those personal computer users who regard a modem as one more item taking up desk space new modem-on-a-chip designs have produced a modem that is so small you will hardly notice it (Figure 5-4c). For a modem that is out of sight—literally—**internal modem boards** can be inserted into the computer by users; they might even come installed in a personal computer as standard equipment.

An **acoustic coupler modem** is connected to a telephone receiver rather than directly to a telephone line. Some acoustic couplers are connected to the computer by a cable, but others are built-in. The advantage of acoustic couplers is that they can be connected to any phone, but the transmission quality may suffer since they are not connected directly to the telephone line. This type of modem may be especially useful for

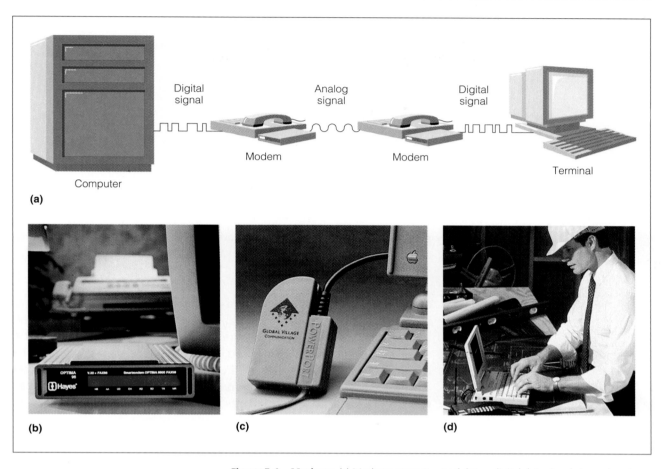

Figure 5-4   Modems. (a) Modems convert—modulate—digital data signals to analog signals for traveling over communications links, then reverse the process—demodulate—at the other end. (b) This external modem rests under the telephone that hooks the computer to the outside world. (c) New modem-on-a-chip designs have allowed modems to shrink. The one shown here is designed to work with a notebook computer. (d) A cellular phone connection allows you to send and receive information from anywhere in the world.

portable computer users (Figure 5-4d), allowing remote access to a main computer from many locations, including pay telephones.

Modem Features   Most modems come with features that make communication as automatic and natural as possible. For example, most modems include **auto-answer,** whereby the modem answers all incoming calls. With **auto-disconnect** a modem disconnects a call automatically whenever the other party hangs up or a disconnect message is received. The **auto-dial** feature allows you to call another computer with a minimum of action on your part. The **automatic redial** feature allows a modem to redial a call that resulted in a busy signal. Finally, a **time delay** allows your computer to call another computer and transfer a file at a future time of your choosing—presumably at night, when rates are lower. Many of these functions can also be carried out by the software program that controls the modem. Many modems are called **Hayes com-**

Table 5-1   Data transfer rates compared.

Data transfer rate (bps)	Time to transmit a 20-page single-spaced report
300	40.00 min.
1,200	10.00 min.
2,400	5.00 min.
4,800	2.50 min.
9,600	1.25 min.
14,400	50.00 sec.
19,200	37.50 sec.

patible because they include the features mentioned. These features were originally used in the Hayes Smartmodem, one of the first modems designed for personal computers.

Modem Data Speeds   In addition to offering new features, modems are moving into the fast lane. In general, modem users use normal telephone lines to connect their computers and pay telephone charges based on the time the computers are connected. Thus, there is a strong incentive to transmit as quickly as possible. The old standard modem speeds of 100 and 300 bits per second (bps) have now been superseded by modems that transmit at 1200, 2400 or 9600 bits per second. Despite the limitations of standard telephone lines, modems that transmit at 14,400 or 19,200 bits per second or more are also becoming available for some applications. That is good news for users ever in search of speed and for everyone who wants to save money by saving time when transmitting. Note the transmission time comparisons in Table 5-1.

Asynchronous and Synchronous Transmission

Sending data off to a far destination works only if the receiving device is ready to accept it. By "ready" we mean more than just available; the receiving device must be able to keep in step with the sending device. Two techniques commonly used to keep the sending and receiving units dancing to the same tune are asynchronous and synchronous transmission.

When **asynchronous transmission** (also called the **start/stop method**) is used, a special start signal is transmitted at the beginning of each group of message bits—a group is usually a character. Likewise, a stop signal is sent at the end of the group of message bits (Figure 5-5a). When the receiving device gets the start signal, it sets up a timing mechanism to accept the group of message bits.

Synchronous transmission is a little trickier because characters are transmitted together in a continuous stream (Figure 5-5b). There are no call-to-action signals for each character. Instead, the sending and receiving devices are synchronized by having their internal clocks put in time with each other by a bit pattern transmitted at the beginning of the message.

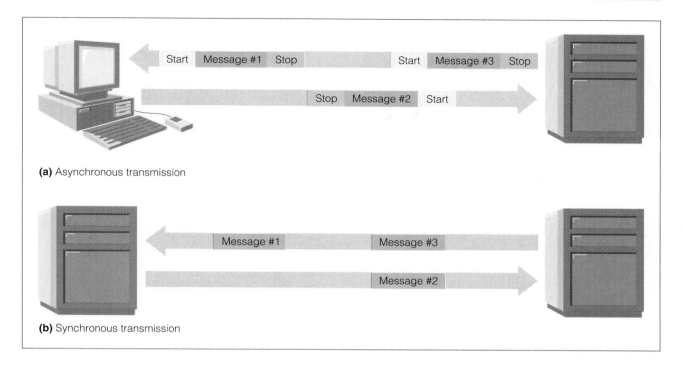

(a) Asynchronous transmission

(b) Synchronous transmission

Figure 5-5   Asynchronous and synchronous transmission. (a) Asynchronous transmission uses start/stop signals surrounding each character. (b) Synchronous transmission uses a continuous stream of characters.

Synchronous transmission equipment is more complex and more expensive than the equipment required for start/stop transmission. The payoff, however, is speedier transmission that is free from the bonds of the start/stop signals.

Simplex, Half-Duplex, and Full-Duplex Transmission

As Figure 5-6 shows, data transmission can be characterized as simplex, half duplex, or full duplex, depending on permissible directions of traffic flow. **Simplex transmission** sends data in one direction only; everyday examples are television broadcasting and arrival/departure screens at airports. A simplex terminal can send or receive data, but it cannot do both. It would seem that data collection—say, sending data from a deposit slip to computer storage at a bank—is a good application for simplex transmission. But the operator would want some sort of response, at least a confirmation that the data was received and, probably, error indications as well. Simplex transmission cannot handle even this limited type of situation.

Half-duplex transmission allows transmission in either direction, but only one way at a time. An analogy is talk on a CB radio. Using half-duplex transmission, the operator in the bank deposit example can send the data and, after it is received, the program in the computer can send a confirmation reply. **Full-duplex transmission** allows transmission in both directions at once. An analogy is a telephone conversation in which, good manners aside, both parties can talk at the same time.

We have discussed data transmission at some length. Now it is time to turn to the actual media that transmit the data.

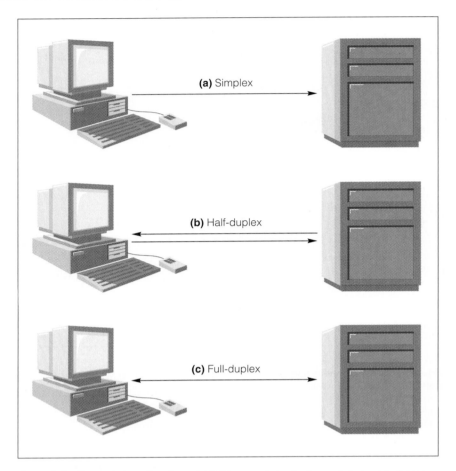

Figure 5-6   Transmission directions. (a) Seldom-used simplex transmission sends data in one direction only. (b) Half-duplex transmission can send data in either direction, but only one way at a time. (c) Full-duplex transmission can send data in both directions at once.

 ## Communications Links

As we have seen, computers are no longer islands unto themselves. The cost for linking widely scattered machines can be substantial (as much as one-third of the data processing budget), so it is worthwhile to examine the communications options. Telephone lines are the most convenient communications channel because an extensive system is already in place, but there are many other options. A communications **link** is the physical medium used for transmission.

Types of Communications Links

There are several kinds of communications links. Some may be familiar to you already.

Wire Pairs   One of the most common communications media is the **wire pair,** also known as the **twisted pair.** Wire pairs are wires twisted together to form a cable, which is then insulated (Figure 5-7a). Wire pairs are inexpensive and frequently used to transmit data over short distances. They are often used because they had already been installed in a building for other purposes. However, they are susceptible to electrical interference, or noise. **Noise** is anything that causes distortion in the signal when it is received, including high-voltage equipment and even the sun.

Coaxial Cables   Known for contributing to high-quality transmission, **coaxial cables** are bundles of insulated wires within a shielded enclosure (Figure 5-7b) that can be laid underground or undersea. These cables can transmit data much faster than wire pairs and are less prone to noise.

Fiber Optics   Traditionally, most phone lines transmitted data electrically over wires made of metal, usually copper. These wires, being metal, had to be protected from water and other corrosive substances. **Fiber optics** technology was developed by Bell Laboratories to eliminate this requirement (Figure 5-7c). Instead of using electricity to send data, fiber optics uses light. The cables are made of glass fibers, each thinner than a human hair, that can guide light beams for miles. Fiber optics transmits data faster than some technologies, yet the materials are lighter and less expensive than wire cables. Because it uses light rather than electricity, fiber optics is less likely to cause fires (no sparks), is harder to wiretap, and is not affected by electrical interference. It can also send and receive a wider assortment of data frequencies at one time. The range of frequencies that a device can handle is known as its **bandwidth.** The broad bandwidth of fiber optics translates into promising multimedia possibilities, since fiber optics is well suited for handling all types of data—voice, pictures, music, and video—at the same time.

Microwave Transmission   Another popular medium is **microwave transmission** (see Figure 5-8a), which uses what is called line-of-sight transmission of data signals through the atmosphere. Since these signals cannot bend around the curvature of the earth, relay stations—usu-

Figure 5-7   Communications links. (a) Wire pairs are pairs of wires twisted together to form a cable, which is then insulated. (b) A coaxial cable. (c) Fiber optics consists of hair-like glass fibers that carry voice, television, and data signals.

(a)

(b)

(c)

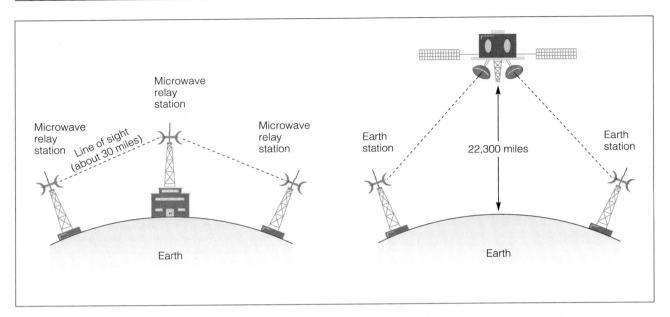

Figure 5-8   Microwave transmission. (a) To relay microwave signals, dish-shaped antennas such as these are often located atop buildings, towers, and mountains. Microwave signals can follow a line-of-sight path only, so stations must relay this signal at regular intervals to avoid interference from the curvature of the earth. (b) In satellite transmission, a satellite acts as a relay station and can transmit data signals from one earth station to another. A signal is sent from an earth station to the relay satellite, which changes the signal frequency before transmitting it to the next earth station.

ally, antennas in high places such as the tops of mountains, towers, and buildings—are positioned at points approximately 30 miles apart to continue the transmission. Microwave transmission offers speed, cost-effectiveness, and ease of implementation. Unfortunately, there are some real problems with interference in microwave transmission. In major metropolitan areas, for instance, intervening tall buildings can sometimes jam signals.

Satellite Transmission   Although it is often said to be getting crowded up there, communications satellites are still being launched into space where they are suspended about 22,300 miles above the earth. Why 22,300 miles? That is where satellites reach geocentric orbit—the orbit that allows them to remain positioned over the same spot on the earth. The basic components of **satellite transmission** are earth stations, which send and receive signals, and a satellite component called a transponder. The **transponder** receives the transmission from an earth station, amplifies the signal, changes the frequency, and retransmits the data to a receiving earth station (Figure 5-8b). (The frequency is changed so that the weaker incoming signals will not be impaired by the stronger outgoing signals.) This entire process takes a matter of a few seconds.

Protocols

Can we talk? A line **protocol** is a set of rules for the exchange of data between a terminal and a computer or between two computers.

AP Transmits Graphically

The Associated Press, the member-owned wire service, now transmits whole newspaper pages. The wire services are not just sharing news items and photos anymore. The company whose name is synonymous with the clack of old Teletype machines, has updated its image with high-end news gathering and distribution.

In 1991, AP began combining its wire services—text, news photographs, and information graphics—into full pages, and transmitting them via the AP GraphicsNet satellite system. According to Vice President and Executive Editor Bill Ahearn, "We see telling a news story as more than just words. . . . These pages offer us the opportunity to present something comprehensively as well as comprehensible."

Newspaper members usually cover their own local and regional areas, allowing the AP to share materials with all members. In turn, they get enough national news and features to fill up their news pages. The full-page service is expected to be used by about half the membership—in several ways. The full page can be reproduced as one or chopped up and used in pieces. Member papers can also modify the pages, using a local angle or selected elements. AP decided to use the page layout program QuarkXpress as a standard so that all members can cut and paste as they like, as well as make font changes and other style revisions. For graphics, AP has used Aldus Freehand as a standard. The first page AP transmitted, "The Heart—a User's Guide," covered the prevention and treatment of heart disease.

Protocol Communications   Two devices must be able to ask each other questions (Are you ready? Did you get my last message? Is there trouble at your end?) and to keep each other informed (I am sending data now). In addition, the two devices must agree on how data is to be transferred, including data transmission speed and duplex setting. But this must be done in a formal way. When communication is desired among machines from different vendors (or even different models from the same vendor), the software development can be a nightmare because different vendors use different protocols. Standards would help.

Setting Standards   Standards are important in the computer industry; it saves money if we can all coordinate effectively. Nowhere is this more obvious than in data communications systems, where many components must "come together." But it is hard to get people to agree to a standard.

Communications standards exist, however, and are constantly evolving and being updated for new communications forms. Standards provide a framework for how data is transmitted. The International Standards Organization (ISO) has defined a set of communication protocols called the **Open Systems Interconnection (OSI) model.** (Yes, that is ISO giving us OSI.) Individual companies have developed other standards, including **Systems Network Architecture (SNA)** from IBM. But there is another player in this cast of characters, a player whose name we would not bother to trip over if it were not so important: In 1984, the **Consultative Committee on International Telegraphy and Telephony (CCITT)**, an agency of the United Nations with tremendous worldwide clout, endorsed the OSI model. IBM has attempted to make SNA compatible with OSI networks.

Line Configurations

There are two principal line configurations, or ways of connecting terminals with a computer: point-to-point and multipoint.

The **point-to-point line** is simply a direct connection between each terminal and the computer, as Figure 5-9 shows, or computer to computer. The **multipoint line** contains several terminals connected on the same line to the computer. In many cases a point-to-point line is sufficient; in other cases it is not efficient, convenient, or cost-effective. For instance, if the computer is at the head office in Dallas, but there are several branch offices with terminals in Houston, it does not make sense to connect each terminal individually to the computer in Dallas. It is usually better to run one line between the two cities and hook all the terminals on it in a multipoint arrangement. On a multipoint line, only one terminal can transmit at any one time, although more than one terminal can receive messages from the computer simultaneously.

When two computers are connected by a communications link, that link might consist of an entire circuit. A *circuit* can be thought of as a gate through which an electric current can flow. If that gate is closed or cut off, it causes an interruption of the transmission. So a complete com-

Figure 5-9   Point-to-point and multi-point lines. (a) In point-to-point lines, each terminal is connected directly to the central computer. (b) In multipoint lines, several terminals share a single line, although only one terminal can transmit at a time.

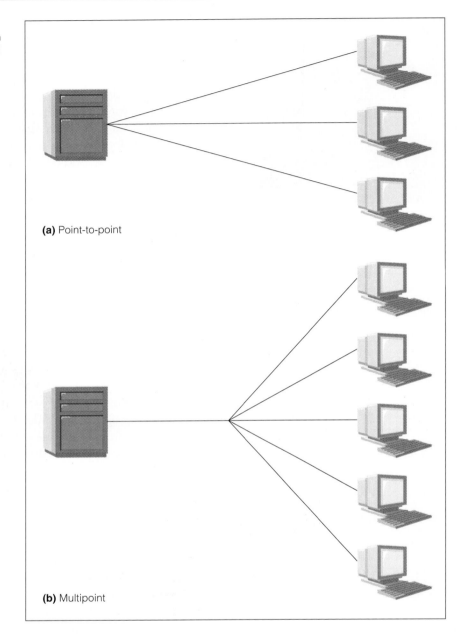

(a) Point-to-point

(b) Multipoint

munications link must be established and continuously maintained for any transmission to be successfully carried out (Figure 5-10a). Both computers are tied up for the duration. If the messages are short, more time may be spent creating the connection than sending the message.

An alternative to this method is called **packet switching,** in which the communication is broken into units called packets (Figure 5-10b). This is especially useful when computers communicate in short bursts. Each packet contains not only data, but also instructions about the destination of the packet. The sending computer places a packet on the network, then directs it through a series of links until it reaches its destination. If a transmission requires several packets, each packet might move through a network along different paths and at different speeds. A packet

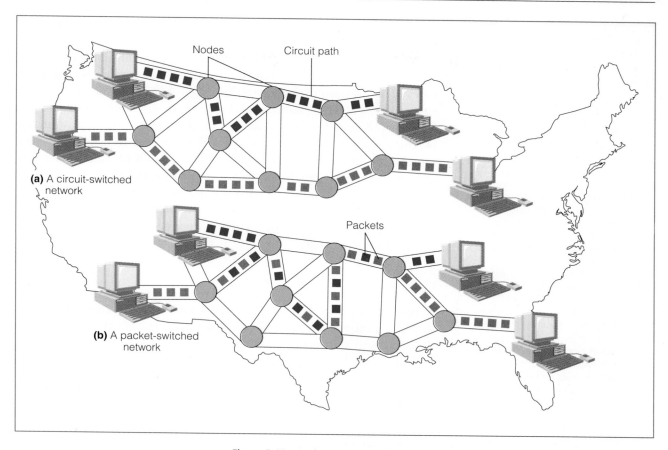

Nodes   Circuit path

(a) A circuit-switched network

(b) A packet-switched network

Packets

Figure 5-10 Packet switching. (a) When two computers are connected by a circuit, a continuous path (darker line) connecting the machines is kept open as long as they are communicating. (b) In a packet-switched network, the data is sent in individual packets, which are directed through the network from node to node until they reach their destination. No continuous circuit has to be kept open. If necessary, the packets can even be stored at a node until transmission can continue.

might even be temporarily stored before it reaches its destination, until such time as it is reasonable to continue its transmission.

Packet switching has its disadvantages. Packets might possibly arrive at their destination out of order, requiring reassembly at their destination. A network might also get too congested with packets, possibly resulting in packets that never reach their destination.

Carriers and Regulation

A company wishing to transmit messages can consider various communications facilities. In the United States the facilities are regulated by an agency of the federal government, the **Federal Communications Commission (FCC),** and by state regulatory agencies. Any organization wishing to offer communications services must submit a tariff to the FCC. A **tariff** is a list of services and the rates to be charged for those ser-

Telephone Translations

No matter whom you want to phone anywhere in the world nowadays, it is likely that a native speaker is available to translate for you. AT&T has an army of translators standing by—for more than 160 languages. Just call 1-800-628-8486.

To overcome language barriers, companies like Westin Hotels & Resorts, Dollar Rent A Car, and Philadelphia Gas Works have dialed AT&T's Language Line Services number. Ready to translate around the clock, the interpreters who answer can help you speak in any language from Arabic to Yiddish, including some fairly obscure languages, such as Sioux and Fanti.

The cost is $3.50 a minute, plus long-distance charges. Customers can set up a conference call or pass the phone back and forth with the foreign speaker. Besides a contingent of full-time foreign-language speakers, AT&T also employs more than 1000 part-time interpreters who work out of their homes and are paid for time on-line. One part-timer is not sure his services will be required: Prince Yaw Nimako, a native of Ghana, Africa, is now a doctoral student in telecommunications living in East Lansing, Michigan. He can translate to English both the Twi and Fanti languages spoken in Ghana and the Ivory Coast. After eight months, he is still awaiting his first call.

vices. The FCC commissioners' view of the public good determines whether the FCC grants a license to the organization.

An organization that has been approved to offer communications services to the public is called a **common carrier.** The two largest common carriers are American Telephone & Telegraph (AT&T) and Western Union.

Public as well as commercial networks also exist. One of the largest of these is **Internet.** Evolving from a system originally founded by the government as a network for defense research, Internet has grown into an international system with millions of users in over 30 countries. Internet provides services for private, government, and academic institutions. Internet reached a degree of notoriety in the fall of 1988, when many computers on the network were attacked by a "worm" program written by a college student—a story we will relate in detail in Chapter 15.

Carrier Lines

Common carriers offer two types of lines: switched and private. **Switched lines,** like those used for your phone service, connect through switching centers to a variety of destinations. You as the user pay only for the services used, but, as with ordinary phone use, you may find the line busy or the connection poor. **Private** (or **leased**) **lines** offer communication to fixed destinations. A private line is dedicated to one customer. The key advantage of this service is that the line is always available. Another important advantage is security—that is, the private line is indeed private, unshared by others and thus less subject to snooping. Private lines may be conditioned (improved) by the carrier to reduce noise and can accommodate very high transmission rates.

One service offered by many carriers is **integrated services digital network (ISDN).** Though ISDN has been under development for two decades, recent efforts at standardization may finally bring it into widespread use. ISDN provides channels for both voice and data communication, and it can be used to send data for videoconferencing. ISDN can also provide standard functions such as automatic number identification, call waiting, and call forwarding. The regional Bell companies have announced their intentions to increase the number of ISDN lines in the coming years, creating nationwide ISDN services.

Ma Bell Changes Everything

In 1968, the FCC handed down the landmark **Carterfone decision,** the first in a series of decisions that have permitted competitors—many from the data processing industry—to enter the formerly regulated domain of AT&T. The gist of the decision is that other companies can interface independent equipment with the public telephone network. These decisions spurred all kinds of independent activity in the communications industry. In 1972, communications companies were even permitted to launch their own satellites.

An outgrowth of this trend is the **value-added network (VAN).** In this type of system, a value-added carrier leases communications lines from a common carrier. These lines are then enhanced by adding error detection or improving response time, for example.

For many years AT&T and the U.S. government locked horns in an antitrust suit. Finally, in January 1982, the government agreed to drop its charges if the corporation would divest itself of the 22 local operating companies that then made up the Bell System. AT&T got to keep Bell Laboratories, its research arm; Western Electric, which makes equipment; and the long-distance telephone service. Most important, it was allowed to enter areas from which it was formerly barred by federal regulations—namely, data processing, computer communications, and the manufacture of computer equipment. Recently, AT&T won the right to compete in the dissemination of electronic information.

Overview of Networks

Computers that are connected so that they can communicate among themselves are said to form a **network.** Wide area networks send data over long distances by using the telephone system. Local area networks send data among computers linked together in one building or in buildings that are close together. Let us consider each of these types of networks.

Wide Area Networks

A **wide area network (WAN)** is a network of geographically distant computers and terminals. In business, a personal computer sending data any significant distance is probably sending it to a minicomputer or mainframe computer. Since these larger computers are designed to be accessed by terminals, a personal computer can communicate with a minicomputer or mainframe only if the personal computer emulates, or imitates, a terminal. This is accomplished by using **terminal emulation software** on the personal computer. The larger computer then considers the personal computer or workstation as just another user input/output communications device—a terminal. However, if a personal computer presents itself as a terminal, it is then subject to the limitations of a terminal.

The larger computer to which the terminal is attached is called the **host computer.** A user can use the terminal to type keystrokes to the host computer, and the host computer can display output on the terminal screen. Terminals usually do not have their own disk drives or central processing units, so programs and data files are stored on the host computer's disk drives. Since terminals cannot store files, files cannot be sent from the terminal to the host. For the same reason, the terminal can display a file sent to it by the host, but it cannot store the file. When using a personal computer or workstation as a terminal, these limitations can be overcome by **file transfer software.** With file transfer pro-

Personal Computers in Action

THE NEW ELECTRONIC UNIVERSITY CULTURE

Networking and communications have begun to change higher education throughout the world. Whether a network offers access to electronic mail, library catalog and reference services, registration, administrative information, or everyday campus activities, students, faculty, and staff are increasingly finding themselves operating inside a new electronic university culture.

Networks may link computer labs that are physically separated around campus and provide access to even wider-ranging, outside, networks. As an example, San Francisco State University offers the Fiber Optic Gateway Network (FOGNET) for its community to share campus information resources. Once connected, students might access the Journalism Department's Macintosh computers to submit an article they have com-

pleted, the Computer Science Department's NeXT computer cluster to pick up a programming assignment, or the Chemistry Department's Sun workstations to review information on chemical reactions. There are a multitude of other campus computer systems, including mainframes, minicomputers, and personal computers.

SF State is one of 19 campuses in the California State University (CSU) system—and one link in the California State University Network (CSUNET). Through CSUNET, a student at the CSU-Fullerton campus might access the Geographic Information System (GIS) Center at SF State to generate

maps with information on flood zones or earthquake faults. Or a student conducting basic research at CSU-Sacramento might find necessary information in a thesis available in the on-line library catalog at CSU-Hayward.

Students at any CSU campus can also travel electronic pathways to the hallowed halls of campuses in other parts of the world. One of the most popular higher education networks providing nationwide links is BITNET (Because It's Time NETwork). An international pathway is INTERNET, a network that allows government, research, and education organizations to share information resources. Another network that is beginning to find an international audience is the National Research and Education Network (NREN), a collaborative effort in higher education, government, and industry.

Students who tap into electronic links in college are learning to work in ways that will help them when entering the "real world" after graduation.

grams, you can **download** files—retrieve files from another computer and store them in your computer's memory—or **upload** files—send files from your computer to another computer.

When uploading and downloading files, the data compression methods discussed in Chapter 4 are often useful. They can save both time and connection charges for transmitting a file. Each computer must have corresponding software or hardware to handle the compression, so that data compressed before transmitting can be correctly decompressed when received.

An intermediate network is the **metropolitan area network (MAN)**, which operates over the distance of a city, possibly avoiding long-distance phone charges. Next is the local area network, which can communicate data much faster than most wide area networks.

Local Area Networks

A **local area network (LAN)** is a collection of computers, usually personal computers, that share hardware, software, and data. In simple terms, LANs hook personal computers together through communications media so that each personal computer can share the resources of the others. All the devices—personal computers and other hardware, such as printers—attached to the LAN are called **nodes** on the LAN. As the name implies, LANs cover short distances, usually one office or building or a group of buildings that are close together.

Here are some typical tasks for which LANs are especially suited:

- A personal computer can read data from a hard disk belonging to another personal computer as if it were its own. This allows users who are working on the same projects to share word processing, spreadsheet, and database data.

- A personal computer may print one of its files on the printer of another personal computer. (Since few people need a laser printer all the time, this relatively expensive type of printer can be hooked to only a few computers.)

- One copy of an application program, when purchased with the proper license from the vendor of the program, can be used by everyone on the LAN. This is less expensive than purchasing a copy of the program for each user.

As any or all of these activities are going on, the personal computer whose resource is being accessed by another can continue doing its own work.

These advantages go beyond simple convenience; some applications require that the same data be shared by coworkers. Consider, for example, a company that sends catalogs to customers, who can then place orders over the telephone. Waiting at the other end of the phone line are customer-service representatives, who key the order data into the computer system as they are talking to the customer.

Each representative has a personal computer on which to enter orders, but all representatives share common computer files that provide information on product availability and pricing. It is not practical to provide a separate set of files for each representative because then one representative would not know what the others had sold. One representative, for example, could accept an order for 20 flannel shirts when there are only 5 shirts in stock because other representatives had already accepted orders for that product.

In this kind of application, workers must have access to one central master file that reflects the activities of other workers. Then, when a representative checks the file to see whether there is enough of a product available to accept an order, he or she can be confident that the quantity on hand has been updated and is correct. You might recognize this as an example of real-time processing, which was discussed in Chapter 4.

Local Area Network Components

Not all networks of computers in an office or building are LANs. LANs do not use the telephone network. Networks that are LANs are made up of a standard set of components.

- All networks need some system for interconnection. In some LANs, the nodes are connected by a shared **network cable.** Low-cost LANs are connected with twisted wire pairs like those used to connect the telephones in a building. However, many LANs use coaxial cable or fiber optics cable; these are more expensive but allow faster transmission. For some local area networks, infrared or radio wave transmissions are used instead of cables. Wireless networks have the advantage of being easy to set up and reconfigure, as there are no cables to connect and disconnect. They may be especially useful in situations in which the computers are portable or must be moved frequently. Wireless networks have the disadvantage of being prone to interference, and the security of the transmissions is difficult to ensure.

- LANs use a hardware device called a **cable interface unit,** a set of electronic components in a box outside the computer, to send and receive signals on the network cable.

- A **network interface card,** inserted into a slot inside the personal computer, contains the electronic components needed to send and receive messages on the LAN. A short cable connects the network interface card to the cable interface unit.

- If there is some degree of similarity between networks, they might be interconnected by a repeater, bridge, router, or brouter, depending on the level of the protocol. A **repeater** relays a physical signal to another network. A **bridge** recognizes the packets on a network and passes on those addressed to nodes in other networks. A **router** operates at a higher level than a bridge and attempts to route a packet toward its correct destination. A **brouter** combines the functions of a bridge and a router, acting as a bridge when it does not understand the destination protocol and as a router when it does.

- A **gateway** is a hardware device—sometimes even a separate computer—that connects two dissimilar networks. A gateway, for example, can connect a wide area network to a local area network. Users on both networks can share devices and exchange data.

Local Area Network Topology

The physical layout of a local area network is called a **topology.** LANs come in three basic topologies: star, ring, and bus networks. A **star network** has a host computer that is responsible for managing the LAN. It is to this central computer that the shared disks and printers are usually attached (Figure 5-11a). All messages are routed through the central computer. A **ring network** links all nodes together in a circular manner, usually without benefit of a central computer (Figure 5-11b). To prevent the

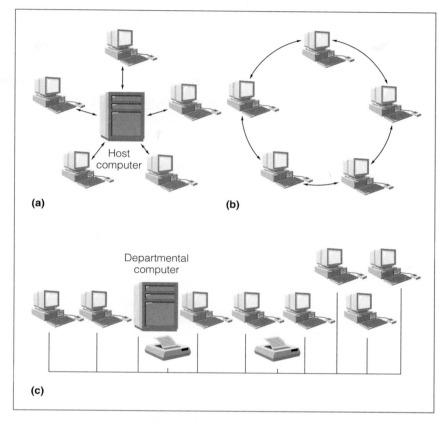

(a)   (b)

(c)

Figure 5-11   LAN topologies. (a) The star topology has a central host computer that runs the LAN. (b) The ring topology connects computers in a circular fashion. (c) The bus topology assigns a portion of network management to each computer but preserves the system if one computer fails.

ring network from failing if a computer or link should fail, nodes are often linked with a double ring. Disks and printers are scattered throughout the system. A **bus network** assigns a portion of network management to each computer but preserves the system if one component fails (Figure 5-11c). The majority of LANs are bus-structured. All of the preceding topologies can be organized in different ways; two of the most popular ways are described next.

Local Area Network Models

Two models for organizing the resources of a LAN are client/server and peer-to-peer. A **client/server** arrangement involves a **server,** a dedicated computer that controls all the programs and peripherals in a network and offers access to all personal computers or workstations that have a **client** program. This arrangement can be very economical. Since a server-based network takes the load off local resources needed for each connected computer and because the server is usually faster and more powerful than other computers in the network, client/server arrangements do not slow down under heavy use. Such slowing is a problem with the second model, the peer-to-peer setup.

All computers in a **peer-to-peer** arrangement share each other's resources. No one computer controls things. With all files and peripheral devices distributed across several computers, users share each other's data and devices as needed. An example might involve a corporate building in which marketing wants its files kept on its own computer, communications wants its files kept on its own computer, personnel wants its files kept on its own computer, and so on; all can still gain access to the other's files when needed. The main disadvantage is lack of speed—most peer-to-peer networks slow down under heavy use. Many networks are hybrids, containing elements of both client/server and peer-to-peer arrangements.

Types of Local Area Networks

The two most common types of LANs are popularly known as Ethernet and the IBM Token Ring Network.

Ethernet is the most popular type of local area network. Ethernet uses a high-speed network cable. Since all the nodes in a LAN use the same cable to transmit and receive data, the nodes must follow a set of rules about when to communicate; otherwise, two or more nodes could transmit at the same time, causing garbled or lost messages. Before a node can transmit data, it must check the cable to see whether or not it is being used. If the cable is in use, the node must wait. When the cable is free from other transmissions, the node can begin transmitting immediately. This transmission method is called by the fancy name of **carrier sense multiple access with collision detection,** or **CSMA/CD.** Some personal computers, including the NeXt and Macintosh Quadra, come with Ethernet connectors built-in.

The IBM **Token Ring Network** connects nodes in a ring topology by using a network cable of twisted wire pairs. The protocol for controlling access to the shared network cable is called **token passing.** The idea is similar to the New York City subway: If you want to ride—transmit data—you must have a token. The token is a special signal that circulates from node to node along the ring-shaped LAN.

Only one token is available on the network. When a node on the network wishes to transmit, it first captures the token; then it can transmit data. When the node has sent its message, it releases the token back to the network (Figure 5-12). Since only one token is circulating around the network, only one device is able to access the network at a time.

The Work of Networking

Think of it: There are more than 500 million telephones installed throughout the world and, theoretically, you can call any one of them. Further, every one of these phones has the potential to be part of a networking system. Although we have discussed other communications media, it is still the telephone that is the basis for action for the user at home or in the office. Revolutionary changes are in full swing in both places, but

Figure 5-12   The IBM Token Ring Network. This type of network connects nodes in a ring. An electronic signal, or token, circles the ring. (a) The sender waits for the token to pass by and then (b) captures the token to transmit data. (c) The receiver retrieves the data and sends the token back to the sender.

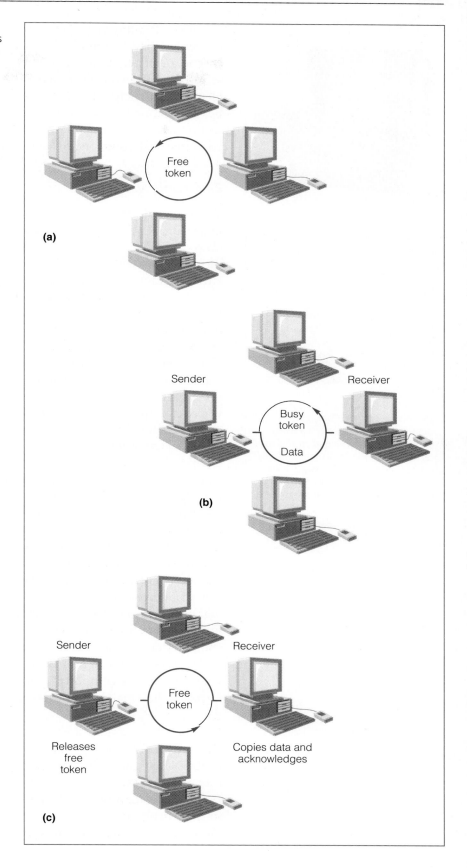

(a)

Sender   Receiver

Busy
token

Data

(b)

Sender   Receiver

Free
token

Releases   Copies data and
free   acknowledges
token

(c)

Le Minitel Est Arrivé

The Minitel phone system, known in France for pioneering personal telecommunications, has arrived in the U.S. Designed in 1976 as the world's first online phone directory, Minitel adds a small computer terminal to your regular phone and provides such services as electronic mail, sports and entertainment news, dating, education, classifieds, banking, travel, shopping, news, and weather.

In San Francisco Minitel is called 101 On Line, advertised as "your local French connection." 101 On Line turns your phone into a mailbox, grocery store, or bank deposit slot. All charges for the service are included on your local phone bill. The small monthly fee includes World Connection which links you with the Minitel service in France. *Et voilà!* Worldwide service at a reasonably small price!

the office. Revolutionary changes are in full swing in both places, but particularly in the office.

The use of automation in the office is as variable as the offices themselves. As a general definition, however, **office automation** is the use of technology to help achieve the goals of the office. Much automated office innovation is based on communications technology. We begin this section with several important office technology topics—electronic mail, voice mail, teleconferencing, and facsimile.

Electronic Mail

You know all about telephone-tag. From your own phone you call Ms. Jones. She is not in, so you leave a message. You leave your room for a class, and when you return you find a message from Ms. Jones; she returned your call while you were out—and so it goes. Few of us, it seems, are sitting around waiting for the phone to ring. It is not unusual to make dozens of calls—or attempts at calls—to set up a meeting among just a few people. **Electronic mail** is the process of sending messages directly from one terminal or computer to another. Electronic mail releases workers from the tyranny of the telephone.

Perhaps a company has employees who find communication difficult because they are geographically dispersed or are too active to be reached easily. Yet these may be people who need to work together frequently, whose communication is valuable and important. These people are ideal candidates for electronic mail.

A user can send messages to a colleague downstairs; a query across town to that person who is never available for phone calls; even memos simultaneously to regional sales managers in Chicago, Raleigh, and San Antonio (Figure 5-13). The beauty of electronic mail, or **e-mail**, as it is also called, is that a user can send a message to someone and know that the person will receive it.

Electronic mail works, of course, only if the intended receiver has the electronic mail facility to which the sender is connected. There are several electronic mail options. A user can enlist a third-party service bureau that provides electronic mail service for its customers. Another popular option is to use a public data network such as CompuServe. Or, a user may purchase an electronic mail software package for a personal computer or large computer system.

The service bureau creates as many electronic "mailboxes"—space allotments on its computer's disk—as needed for each user company. Users get their mail by giving proper identification from their own computers.

Public data services offer their own version of electronic mail. CompuServe users can send e-mail messages to any other CompuServe subscriber. Users get flashing messages when they turn on their machines if mail awaits them.

Finally, you could consider putting your own custom electronic mail software in place. Major hardware manufacturers are becoming more communications-oriented and are offering software or office systems pack-

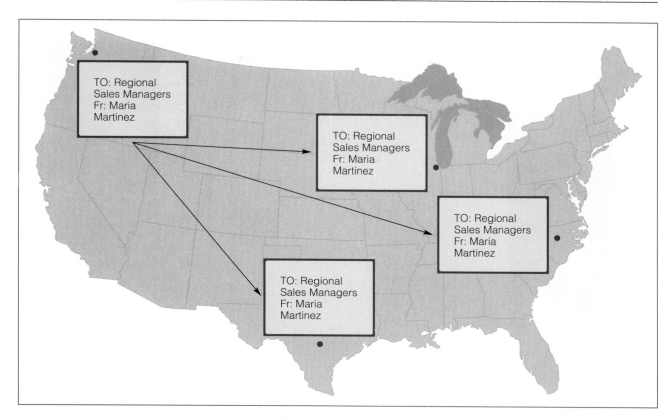

Figure 5-13   Simultaneous memo transmission with electronic mail. From company headquarters in Seattle, Maria Martinez is able to send a memo simultaneously to sales managers in Chicago, Raleigh, and San Antonio. This is made possible by an electronic mail system linking the computers in the home office and the regional offices.

ages that support e-mail. A key advantage of such a package is that the buyer pays for it just once; a subscriber must pay for a third-party service on a continual basis.

Electronic mail users shower it with praise. It crosses time zones, can reach many people with the same message, reduces the paper flood, and does not interrupt meetings the way a ringing phone does. It has its limitations, however. The current problem is similar to the problem faced by telephone users a hundred years ago: It is not of much use if you have the only one. No one knows exactly how many people use e-mail, but Link Resources Corporation, a market research group, estimates there are 11.5 million e-mail users across the U.S., with about 1.5 million using it from their home computer systems. Prodigy, mentioned in our introductory story about the Costelloes, estimates that 30,000 e-mail messages flow through its system each day.

Voice Mail

Here is how **voice mail** typically works. A user dials a special number to get on the voice mail system. If the recipient does not answer, the caller can then dictate his or her message into the system. The voice mail com-

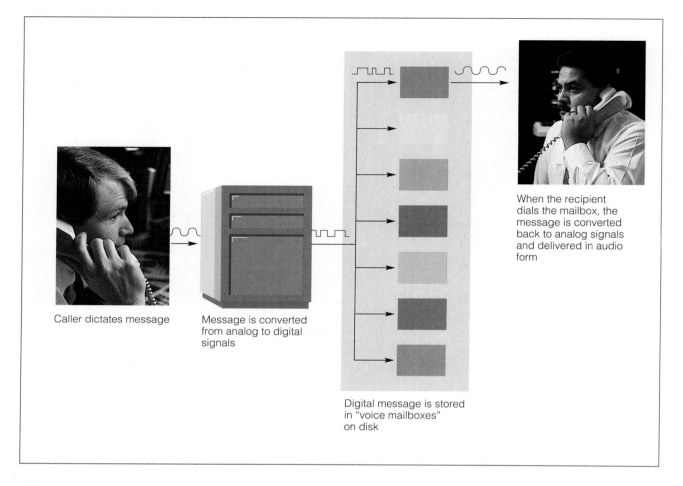

Caller dictates message

Message is converted from analog to digital signals

Digital message is stored in "voice mailboxes" on disk

When the recipient dials the mailbox, the message is converted back to analog signals and delivered in audio form

Figure 5-14   A voice mail system. The caller's message is stored in the recipient's voice mailbox on disk. Later, the recipient can check his mailbox to get the message.

puter system translates the words into digital impulses and stores them in the recipient's "voice mailbox." Later, when the recipient dials the mailbox, the system delivers the message in audio form (Figure 5-14).

This may sound like a spoken version of electronic mail. There is one big difference between electronic mail and voice mail, however. To use electronic mail, you and the mail recipient must have compatible devices with a keyboard and be able to use them. In contrast, telephones are everywhere and everyone already knows how to use them.

Senders can instruct some voice mail systems to re-dial specific numbers at regular intervals to deliver urgent messages or simply set one delivery time and date. Another useful feature allows users to circulate messages among associates for comment. This method is far more efficient than circulating the traditional paper intraoffice memo.

There are some problems, however—not with the technology, but with user acceptance of the technology. Some people do not like talking to a machine. Others will not tell a machine anything important. A more serious problem is the lack of editing capability—most users simply cannot organize their thoughts as well when they speak as they do when they write.

But electronic "meetings" are more spontaneous and less demanding of writing perfection. That brings us to teleconferencing.

Some people keep in touch the easy way, using electronic mail through a combination of the phone system and their personal computers. Some examples:

- **E-Mail in space.** When the space shuttle *Atlantis* rocketed into space in August 1991, one of the computers on board was a portable Macintosh. Astronauts used e-mail to send messages back to earth. One of the goals of the experiment was to test the viability of e-mail for communications with the Freedom space station, scheduled for deployment in the middle of the decade. One of the problems encountered was keeping a constant connection going with the orbiting space station. Astronaut David Low is optimistic about using electronic mail for communication, since it let them avoid carrying as much as 100 pounds of paper. On a more personal level, he says, "It would be great if we could leave a message for our spouses and kids."

- **Electronic house calls.** Patients with high blood pressure, each equipped with a home blood pressure kit, call their doctor's talking computer. Patients respond to the computer's questions by pressing keys on their touch-tone phones. The computer system replies with an appropriate comment, such as this gentle scolding to a patient who admitted not taking her medication: "Your blood pressure is not so good today. If you took your medication, it might be lower."

- **Application and registration.** Applying to some colleges by computer is pretty simple: From a local personal computer, you dial into the school's network and fill out an application "form" right on the computer screen. The application is then submitted directly to the school's computerized admissions files. The whole process takes about ten minutes. In addition, many universities now use computerized registration procedures that allow students to avoid the long lines that used to plague the start of every semester. Students are assigned a time period in which they can phone the computer and use touch-tone keys to register for their classes.

Teleconferencing

An office automation development with great promise is **teleconferencing**, a method of using technology to bring people and ideas "together" despite geographic barriers. The technology has been available for years, but the acceptance of it is quite recent. The purpose of teleconferencing is to let people conduct meetings with others in different geographic locations.

There are several varieties of teleconferencing. The simplest, computer conferencing, is a method of sending, receiving, and storing typed messages within a network of users. Computer conferences can be used to coordinate complex projects over great distances and for extended periods of time. Participants can communicate at the same time or in different time frames, at the users' convenience. Conferences can be set up for a limited period to discuss a particular problem, as in a traditional office gathering. Or they can be ongoing networks for weeks or months or even years.

A **computer conferencing system** is a single software package designed to organize communication. The conferencing software runs on a network's host, either a minicomputer or a mainframe. In addition to the host computer and the conferencing software, each participant needs a personal computer or word processor, a telephone, a modem, and data communications network software.

Computer conferencing is a many-to-many arrangement—everyone is able to "talk" to anyone else. Messages may be sent to a specified individual or set of individuals or "broadcast" to all receivers. Recipients are automatically notified of incoming messages.

Would you like your picture broadcast live across the miles for meetings? Add cameras to computer conferencing, and you have another form of teleconferencing called **videoconferencing** (Figure 5-15). The technology varies, but the pieces normally put in place are a large screen (possibly wall size), cameras that can send "three-dimensional" pictures, and an on-line computer system to record communication among participants.

Although this setup is expensive to rent and even more expensive to own, the costs seem trivial when compared to travel expenses for in-person meetings. Airfare, lodging, and meals for a group of employees are very costly.

But there are drawbacks to videoconferencing. Consider that picture of you. Most people do not like the way they look on camera. We tend to be uncomfortable about our appearance, and balk when we envision slouching posture, crooked tie, or fidgeting fingers. There is also fear that the loss of personal contact will detract from some business functions, especially those related to sales.

But employees are overcoming their reluctance. Videoconferencing may be an idea whose time has come.

Figure 5-15   A videoconferencing system. Geographically distant groups can hold a meeting with the help of videoconferencing. A camera transmits images of local participants for the benefit of distant viewers.

Facsimile Technology

One alternative to meetings is to use computers and data communications technology to transmit drawings and documents from one location to another. **Facsimile technology,** operating something like a copy machine connected to a telephone, uses computer technology to send quality graphics, charts, text, and even signatures almost anywhere in the world. The drawing—or whatever—is placed in the facsimile machine at one end, as shown in Figure 5-16, where it is digitized. Those digits are transmitted across the miles and then reassembled at the other end to form a nearly identical version of the original picture. All this takes only minutes—or less. Facsimile is not only faster than overnight delivery services, it is less expensive. *Facsimile* is abbreviated **fax,** as in "I sent a fax to the Chicago office." Fax has become the norm in many offices.

Fax equipment is becoming standard in many homes and home offices. Some inexpensive fax phones (which cost less than $500) offer automatic dialing, answering, copying (to make single copies), and fax capabilities. Since those who prefer to write with pen and paper can immediately transmit their thoughts with a fax, the popularity of fax technology is growing, as evidenced by these everyday examples:

- A radio station asks listeners to send in faxes of their song requests.

- A television news commentator reads faxes that are sent in immediately after an important news event, to communicate the reactions of viewers.

- A magazine ad displays a phone number you call to have several pages of specific information regarding products faxed back to you.

Figure 5-16   Faxing it. This facsimile machine can send drawings and graphs long distance.

The fax was instrumental in keeping communication flowing among dissidents inside and outside China during the Tiananmen Square massacre. Fax machines also helped keep information flowing to and from the Soviet Union during the failed 1991 coup attempt. If anything contributed to the unraveling of the Soviet Union, according to many experts, it was the introduction of personal computers and fax machines.

Since fax machines are usually standalone devices, how do personal computers interact with them? Software is available that allows fax users to control the sending and receiving of fax documents from their personal computers. Some connect their standalone fax machines to their computers; others use a variation of the fax machine, a **fax board,** which fits inside a personal computer. A user can send computer-generated text and graphics without interrupting other applications programs in use. When a fax comes in, it can be reviewed on the screen and printed out. The only missing ingredient in this scheme is paper; if the document to be sent is on paper, it must be scanned into the computer first. Some modems also combine the functions of a modem and a fax board.

Electronic Fund Transfers: Instant Banking

You may already be handling some financial transactions electronically instead of using checks. In **electronic fund transfers (EFTs),** people pay for goods and services by having funds transferred from various accounts electronically, using computer technology. One of the most visible manifestations of EFT is the ATM—the automated teller machine that many use to obtain cash quickly.

Incidentally, over 650 million Social Security checks have been disbursed by the government directly into the recipients' checking accounts via EFT rather than by mail. Unlike those sent via U.S. mail, no such payment has ever been lost. Moreover, such payments are easily traceable—again, unlike the mail.

Electronic Data Interchange

Businesses use a great deal of paper in transmitting orders. One method devised to cut down on paperwork is **electronic data interchange (EDI).** EDI is a series of standard formats that allow businesses to transmit invoices, purchase orders, and the like electronically. EDI can also help to eliminate errors in transmitting orders that result from transcription mistakes made by people. Many firms use EDI to reduce paperwork and personnel costs. Some large firms have sought to require their suppliers to adopt EDI in order to streamline their purchasing efforts.

Bulletin Boards

Person-to-person data communication is one of the more exhilarating ways of using your personal computer, and its popularity is increasing at breakneck speed. A **bulletin board system (BBS)** uses data communications systems to link personal computers to provide public-access message systems.

Electronic bulletin boards are similar to the bulletin boards you see in Laundromats or student lounges. Somebody leaves a message, but the person who picks it up does not have to know the person who left it. To get access to someone else's computer, all you really have to know is that computer's bulletin board phone number. You can use any kind of computer, but you need a modem so you can communicate over the phone lines. Anyone who has a personal computer can set up a bulletin board: It takes a computer (usually with a hard disk drive), a phone line, a modem, and some software that costs around $50. You just tell a few people about your board, start up your computer using the BBS software, and sit back and watch the messages start scrolling down your screen.

Bulletin boards perform a real service. For example, personal computer hobbyists can obtain advice about a particular vendor's product, find discounts on hardware or software, and discuss programming or other topics. Some people have fun on their BBS, adding their creative touches to growing novels or poems, and playing collaborative games, puzzles, and other activities; others gather on-line for discussions with famous persons or experts on special topics. Even legislators have set up their own BBS for gathering data or disseminating ideas. Of course, many government agencies, magazines, and others use BBSs to post announcements, job offerings, classified ads, business opportunities, and even find dates. Clubs, organizations, and associations are finding BBSs useful in communicating with members beyond their regular meetings.

Data Communications Shopping

In recent years there has been a trend toward nonstore retailing in such forms as telephone- and mail-generated orders to department stores, offerings of records and tapes of popular music through television commercials ("Not available in any store!"), and airline in-flight shopping catalogs. United Airlines recently offered travelers a chance to shop above

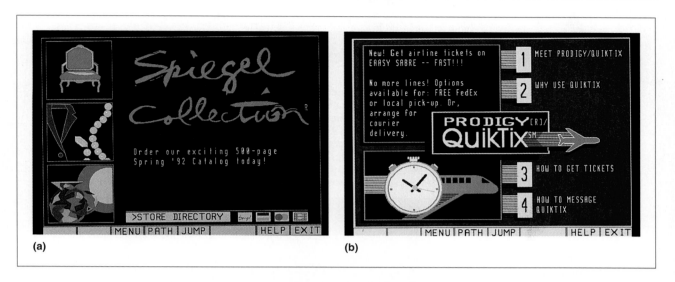

(a)   (b)

Figure 5-17 Catalog shopping. Using on-line services like Prodigy, computer users can "window shop" from the comfort of their homes. Prodigy services include (a) the Spiegel catalog and (b) Quiktix for purchasing airline tickets.

the crowds, providing a new kind of in-flight shopping service. Its "High Street Emporium" program allows passengers to shop through catalogs, using on-board telephones to place orders. For an extra charge, the merchandise will be waiting for them when they arrive at their destination.

One of the newest forms of retailing is interactive two-way cable **videotex**—data communications merchandising. Consumers with accounts with the videotex merchandiser shop at home for a variety of products and services. Using an in-home video display catalog, they can get information about a product or order products from a participating retailer (Figure 5-17). When an order is received in the computer, the retailer assembles the goods from a fully automated warehouse. Simultaneously, funds are transferred from the customer's to the retailer's bank account. A customer chooses between picking up the order at a nearby distribution point or having it delivered to the door.

Commercial Communications Services

Users can connect their personal computers to commercial consumer-oriented communications systems via telephone lines. These services—known as **information utilities**—are widely used by both home and business customers. Two major information utilities are CompuServe and Prodigy.

CompuServe offers program packages, text editors, encyclopedia reference, games, a software exchange, and a number of programming languages. CompuServe services include a travel reservation system, home shopping, banking, weather reports, and even medical and legal advice. Of particular interest to business users are investment information, world news, and professional forums—enough to keep any communications junkie busy. Finally, if you really have nothing to do tonight, you can participate in an on-line auction, interacting with auctioneers electronically.

Prodigy was jointly introduced by Sears and IBM and is aimed primarily at the home user. It is designed to be easy to use—it even allows use of

P E R S P E C T I V E S

SOME THORNS AMONG THE ROSES

A system as powerful as a computer network raises concerns about privacy issues. Here are a few samples:

- **Computer spy ring.** A discrepancy of 75 cents in a Berkeley, California, astronomer's telephone bill helped uncover a major spy operation in Europe. In his book about the ordeal, *The Cuckoo's Egg,* Clifford Stoll tells how he noticed some unusual entries while trying to trace the error in his bill for telecommunications usage. Over a two-year period, this clue eventually led the FBI and CIA to three West German men who were breaking into key military and research computers in the United States and selling stolen codes and data to KGB agents shortly before the fall of Soviet Communism. How could this happen? Did they climb a fence, pick a lock, compromise an insider? Not at all. They obtained everything they wanted by using their own computers and networks—from *inside* West Germany. Then they distributed their costs in small amounts among unsuspecting network users, believing that the small charges would not raise any eyebrows.

- **Computer monitoring.** Some U.S. workers are being watched by their own computers. Many firms are using computer monitoring to collect detailed data on employee performance for management. Nearly seven million workers are currently

being monitored electronically, including data and word processing specialists, insurance claims adjustors, telemarketers, telephone operators, and airline reservation clerks. Data collected by computers may include the number of

keystrokes, customers served, length of time on each call, minutes of inactivity, number of inaccuracies, changes, and so on. It has caused many unions, civil libertarians, and legislators to express concern about possible violations of workers' rights to privacy.

- **Privacy surprises.** Business users are attracted to electronic mail by its speed, relatively low cost, and even its high-tech status. However, many employees are surprised to discover their e-mail is subject to inspection by their employer. Some workers have been fired

for mail they did not know management was reading. In addition, managers are less than pleased to discover some employees using e-mail for personal purposes. Perhaps the most offensive use, from management's point of view, is

the use of e-mail to distribute chain letters, which is (among other things) illegal.

- **Telephone tag weirdness.** You might have known this would happen. The story goes that two clerks changed offices for a day. Leslie switched offices with Kathy and decided to forward her calls to Kathy's office. Kathy thought that was a good idea, so she put her phone on call forwarding to Leslie's office. The infinite loop created within the phone system resulted in all kinds of random and bizarre error messages to anyone trying to call either of the women.

a mouse for data entry. Among the many services offered are news and financial services, product reviews, and home shopping. Users can also play games and interact through bulletin boards and personal messages.

Other commercial communications facilities offer specialized services: Knowledge Index (general-interest information), NewsNet (news),

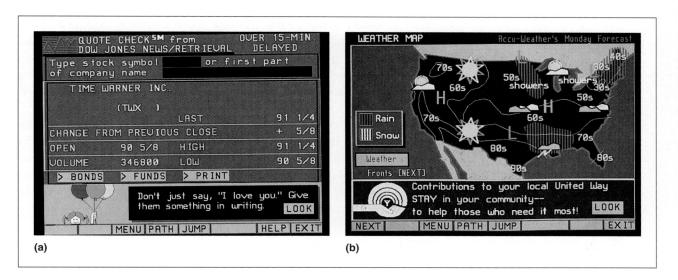

Figure 5-18 Commercial services. Computer users can use their personal computers to get information on (a) Dow Jones averages or (b) the national weather forecast through services such as Prodigy.

Official Airline Guide (travel), and Grassroots (agriculture) (Figure 5-18).

These commercial services usually charge an initiation fee and a monthly fee, neither of which is insignificant. The charges on your phone bill are additional. Some communities, however, have local-line access to informational utilities like Prodigy and CompuServe, so users do not have to pay long-distance charges.

Computer Commuting

A logical outcome of computer networks is **telecommuting,** the substitution of telecommunications and computers for the commute to work. Many in the work force are information workers; if they do not need face-to-face contact in their work, they are candidates for using telecommuting to work at home.

Although the original idea was that people would work at home all the time, telecommuting has evolved into a mixed activity. That is, most telecommuters stay home two or three days a week and come into the office the other days. Time in the office permits the needed personal communication with fellow workers and also provides a sense of participation and continuity.

Some companies also use a variation on telecommuting in which workers drive to nearby offices linked to the main office. Workers from several different companies might share the same satellite office. This method has the advantage of placing the worker in an office environment with support staff, away from the distractions of home. The long commute time to a distant office is still avoided.

Potential benefits of telecommuting include savings in fuel costs and commuting time, an opportunity to work at your own pace, increased productivity, and an opportunity for workers to work in an undisturbed environment. Some problems arise when employers create what might be called at-home sweatshops for data processing, word processing, and other kinds of repetitive work. Employers can claim the workers are part-time consultants, independent contractors, and the like, and avoid paying for benefits like insurance and medical plans, not to mention payroll and other taxes. Unions, worker advocates, and lawmakers are working to pass zoning laws that forbid such sweatshop-style work outside certain areas.

There are, of course, other problems. One associated with telecommuting is the strain on families that results when a family member works at home. A more common complaint is that at-home employees miss the interaction with co-workers at the office. At the head of the list, however, is this, from the telecommuters themselves: They work too much!

Workgroup Computing

Many of the previously mentioned topics can be loosely grouped in a category called workgroup computing, or groupware. **Groupware** encompasses a number of different techniques and technologies for allowing several people to work together, often when they are separated by time or space. Groupware might include electronic mail, voice mail, teleconferencing, and facsimile technology. Other techniques include:

- Calendaring systems that coordinate the calendars and schedules of the members of a group, often automatically finding openings when meetings can be scheduled. Project coordination tools can keep track of each member's responsibilities in a group project.

- Document annotation systems that allow several individuals to edit the same document (Figure 5-19). Document annotation programs can store the suggestions from different individuals and eliminate the need to shuffle papers covered with editing marks. Some of these systems might allow several people to work on the same document simultaneously at different locations, with each person seeing changes

Figure 5-19   **Document annotation software.** This application uses networking hardware and specialized software to encourage students and teachers to work together on writing development. Packages such as Aspects and Conference Writer allow a student to see, on the screen, reactions to his or her writing. The student can then revise the document.

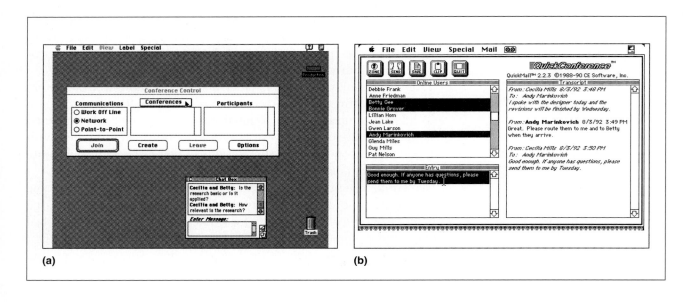

(a)   (b)

Groupware Conferencing

Teleconferencing and groupware technology are normally put in action when the participants are separated by time or space. But could they be of use when the group is located in the same place and time?

That idea came to a leading computer industry analyst when confronted by large conferences in which participants had only a limited amount of time for interaction. Those attending such conferences often complained that it was physically impossible to contact all the people they wanted to.

The analyst decided to use a groupware product at a conference to allow messages between the participants on a one-to-many and one-to-one basis. General guidelines were suggested, but users were free to comment on any topic they wished.

The result? Thousands of messages of all types were passed among the participants. The experiment was considered a success, since the most frequent complaint from the participants involved the lack of sufficient terminals for accessing the system.

proposed by others on his or her own screen. Some systems are taking advantage of the pen-based technology discussed in Chapter 3.

- Conferencing by computer does not have to take place at different times and places. Individuals in the same location might all have their own terminals, sending messages to individual participants as well as the group at large. A person does not have to wait until he or she "has the floor" to communicate.

Group interaction on computers can change the way people look at working as a group. Certain pressures of person-to-person confrontation disappear. Individuals who are less assertive vocally might feel free to speak out on a computer. Members may also feel less constrained from inserting long or irrelevant remarks into a group session. Some studies have shown that, though people may harbor fewer reservations about voicing their opinions through a computer, it may take longer to reach a decision.

Educational programs are emerging that apply the workgroup concept. Called **collaborative software,** this type of educational tool allows students to work together in both cooperative and competitive ways. In Oregon Trail—1848, from MECC, students start the program by "joining" the wagon train; in effect, each student's computer becomes a separate wagon on the trail west, undergoing all the hardships and contributing to the success or failure of the trek. Reading Maze, from Great Wave Software, is a program for younger children. Regardless of their reading abilities, students see the same game screen but play at their own reading level. The end result is a collaborative goal—finding their way *together* out of the maze.

Can entertainment be far behind? No. It's way out front. One of the many fascinating networked games is Vette! Two or more personal computers on the same network participate in a car race. Participants can choose a "track," such as the streets of San Francisco. As they race through changing scenes (with authentic street names), others participating over the network may suddenly race their cars by them or fall in behind and jockey for position. Players say it adds excitement to the race when they see other cars driven by real people suddenly appear on the screen to challenge them.

Networks and Security

Networks mean that access to data is dispersed. Valuable files are in many locations, data is transmitted over different kinds of communications lines, and many people have access to the system. Clearly, the question of security arises: If it is so easy for authorized people to get data, what is to stop unauthorized people from tapping it? Many people, dazzled by the expanded capabilities offered by data communications, are complacent about the security of their data. Even though warned of weaknesses in their security, many companies and government agencies have done little to prevent even the most unsophisticated criminals from breaking into their files. The safety of data is of paramount importance and deserves a chapter by itself. We will address this topic more fully in Chapter 15.

Our Crystal Ball

The near future in data communications is not difficult to see. The demand for services is just beginning to swell. Electronic mail already pervades the office, the campus, and the home. Expect instant access to all manner of databases from a variety of convenient locations. Prepare to be blasé about automated services available in your own home and everywhere you go.

Next we venture into Part Two for a closer look at software, focusing on what it is that programmers do, how programming languages work, how operating systems control things, and what it means for computers to change. In other words, we will examine systems analysis and design.

REVIEW AND REFERENCE

Summary and Key Terms

- **Telecommunications** is the merger of communications and computers.
- **Data communications systems** are computer systems that transmit data over communications lines such as public telephone lines or private network cables.
- **Centralized data processing** places all processing, hardware, software, and storage in one central location.
- In **teleprocessing systems,** terminals at various locations are connected by communications lines to the central computer that does the processing.
- Businesses with many locations or offices often use **distributed data processing (DDP),** which allows both remote access and remote processing. Processing can be done by the central computer and the other computers that are hooked up to it.
- In a connection called a **micro-to-mainframe link,** personal computer users can process data from the files of a mainframe computer.
- The basic components of a data communications system are a sending device, a communications link, and a receiving device. Some large systems also have a **front-end processor,** a computer that functions as a commu-

nications control unit, which frees the central computer to process applications programs.

- **Digital transmission** sends data as distinct on or off pulses. **Analog transmission** uses a continuous electric signal in a waveform having a particular **amplitude** and **frequency.**
- Computers produce digital signals, but most types of communications equipment use analog signals. Therefore, transmission of computer data involves altering the analog signal, or **carrier wave.** Digital signals are converted to analog signals by **modulation** (changé) of a characteristic, such as the amplitude of the carrier wave. **Demodulation** is the reverse process; both processes are performed by a device called a **modem.** Radio transmissions are made by altering amplitude or frequency—that is, by amplitude modulation or frequency modulation.
- A **direct-connect modem** is connected directly to the telephone line by means of a telephone jack. An **external direct-connect modem** is not built-in to the computer and can therefore be used with a variety of computers. An **internal modem** is on a board that fits inside a personal computer. An **acoustic coupler modem** allows a standard telephone receiver to be coupled to a computer terminal.

- Most modems include **auto-answer, auto-disconnect, auto-dial, automatic redial,** and **time-delay** features. Many modems understand commands that are **Hayes compatible.**

- Two common methods of coordinating the sending and receiving units are **asynchronous transmission** and **synchronous transmission.** The asynchronous, or **start/stop,** method keeps the units in step by including special signals at the beginning and end of each group of message bits—a group is usually a character. In synchronous transmission, the internal clocks of the units are put in time with each other at the beginning of the transmission, and the characters are transmitted in a continuous stream.

- **Simplex transmission** allows data to move in only one direction (either sending or receiving). **Half-duplex transmission** allows data to move in either direction but only one way at a time. With **full-duplex transmission,** data can be sent and received at the same time.

- A communications **link** is the physical medium used for transmission. Common communications links include **wire pairs (twisted pairs), coaxial cables, fiber optics, microwave transmission,** and **satellite transmission.** In satellite transmission a **transponder** ensures that the stronger outgoing signals do not interfere with the weaker incoming ones. **Noise** is anything that causes distortion in the received signal. **Bandwidth** refers to the number of frequencies that can fit on one link at the same time.

- A line **protocol** is a set of rules for exchanging data between a terminal and a computer or between two computers. Two standard sets of protocols are the **Open Systems Interconnection** model **(OSI),** developed by the International Standards Organization, and **Systems Network Architecture (SNA),** developed by IBM. Since the **Consultative Committee on International Telegraphy and Telephony (CCITT)** endorsed the OSI model, IBM has ensured that SNA networks can communicate with OSI networks.

- A **point-to-point line** is a direct connection between a terminal and a computer or between two computers. In a **multipoint line** several terminals are connected on the same line to a computer.

- One method of computer communication is called **packet switching.** This method breaks a communication down into units called packets, which can be routed to their destination by various links or even stored for a time. Packet switching does not require a continuous connection between the sending and receiving computers.

- Any organization wishing to become a **common carrier,** or supplier of communications services to the public, must apply to the **Federal Communications Commission (FCC)** by submitting a **tariff,** or list of services and rates. Common carriers can provide both **switched lines,** which are connected through switching centers, and **private** (or **leased**) **lines,** which are used exclusively by one customer for communication to a fixed destination. **Internet** is a public network used by many government and academic institutions. **Integrated services digital network (ISDN)** is a service that provides digital voice and data communication.

- The 1968 **Carterfone decision** opened the door for other communications companies to use the public telephone network. This development led to the **value-added network (VAN),** in which a communications company leases communications lines from a common carrier and adds improvements.

- Computers that are connected so that they can communicate among themselves are said to form a **network.** A **wide area network (WAN)** is a network of geographically distant computers and terminals. In a situation in which a personal computer or workstation is being used as a network terminal, **file transfer software** enables a user to **download** files (retrieve them from another computer and store them) and **upload** files (send files to another computer). To communicate with a workstation or mainframe, a personal computer must employ **terminal emulation software.** Intermediate in size is a **metropolitan area network (MAN),** which covers an area about the size of a city.

- A **local area network (LAN)** is smaller than a WAN or MAN. It is usually a network of personal computers that share hardware, software, and data. All the devices—personal computers and other hardware—attached to the LAN are called **nodes** on the LAN. The nodes on some LANs are connected by a shared **network cable** or by wireless transmission. LANs use a hardware device called a **cable interface unit,** a set of electronic components in a box outside the computer, to send and receive signals on the network cable. A **network interface card** may be inserted into a slot inside the computer to allow it to send and receive messages on the LAN.

- A **gateway** is a hardware device—sometimes even a separate computer—that connects two dissimilar networks. If two LANs are similar, they might be able to send messages to each other by using a **repeater, bridge, router,** or **brouter.**

- The physical layout of a local area network is called a **topology.** A **star network** has a central computer that is responsible for managing the LAN; it is to this central computer that the shared disks and printers are usually attached. A **ring network** links all nodes together in a circular manner without benefit of a server. A **bus network** assigns a portion of network management to each computer but preserves the system if one component fails.

- The larger computer to which the terminal is attached, known as the **host computer,** controls the network. A

client/server setup involves a **server** that controls the network and a **client** that accesses the network and its services. Clients are programs that run on personal computers or workstations, allowing communication with the server. A second setup is the **peer-to-peer** arrangement, in which there is no controlling computer; all computers on the network share their programs and resources.

- **Ethernet** is the most popular type of local area network; this system accesses the network by listening for a free cable, or carrier. The method the computer uses to determine if the cable is free for transmission is called **carrier sense multiple access with collision detection,** or **CSMA/CD.** The IBM **Token Ring Network** controls access to the shared network cable by using **token passing.**

- **Office automation** is the use of technology to help achieve the goals of the office. **Electronic mail (e-mail)** and **voice mail** allow workers to transmit messages to the computer files of other workers. **Teleconferencing** includes **computer conferencing**—in which typed messages are sent, received, and stored—and **videoconferencing**—computer conferencing combined with cameras and large screens. **Facsimile technology (fax)** can transmit graphics, charts, and signatures. **Fax boards** can be inserted inside computers.

- In **electronic fund transfers (EFTs),** people pay for goods and services by having funds transferred from various checking and savings accounts electronically, using computer technology. **Electronic data interchange (EDI)** allows businesses to send common business forms electronically—without paper.

- **Bulletin board systems (BBS)** use data communications to link personal computers into public-access message systems. People can shop at home by using a **videotex,** a video display catalog.

- CompuServe and Prodigy are two major commercial communications services, or **information utilities.**

- **Telecommuting** is the substitution of telecommunications and computers for the commute to work. Many communications technologies might be used in workgroup computing or **groupware,** which uses computers to make it easier and more productive for people to work in teams, even if they are separated by time or space. **Collaborative software** uses networked computers to allow students to cooperate or compete in learning activities.

- A problem with dispersed data is securing it against unauthorized persons.

Review Questions

1. What is telecommunications?
2. Discuss the advantages and disadvantages of centralized data processing.
3. Explain how distributed data processing and teleprocessing differ.
4. What are the functions of a front-end processor?
5. Explain what modems are used for.
6. Why is a high modem speed important?
7. Why is synchronous transmission faster than asynchronous transmission?
8. Differentiate the following types of transmission: simplex, half duplex, and full duplex.
9. Describe the advantages of each of the following: wire pairs, coaxial cables, fiber optics, microwave transmission, and satellite transmission.
10. What is a protocol, and why are protocol standards important?
11. Describe how packet switching works.
12. How do wide area networks, metropolitan area networks, and local area networks differ?
13. How does a star network differ from a ring network?
14. Describe electronic mail, voice mail, teleconferencing, and facsimile.
15. What is a bulletin board system, and how is it useful?
16. Describe how networking systems can be used for banking and shopping.
17. Define telecommuting and discuss its advantages and disadvantages.
18. Describe several types of groupware.

Discussion Questions

1. Describe two situations, one in which a point-to-point line is preferable and one in which a multipoint line is preferable.
2. Discuss the advantages and disadvantages of teleconferencing versus face-to-face business meetings.
3. Discuss your opinion of telecommuting. Do you think you would like to telecommute? Why or why not?
4. What do you perceive as problems that might arise in the use of groupware or collaborative software?

True-False Questions

T F 1. Coaxial cable is generally faster than cable made of wire pairs.

T F 2. Digital transmission sends data in a continuous wave.

T F 3. The asynchronous mode of transmission is also called the start/stop method.

T F 4. A device used to hook a modem to a telephone line is called a transponder.

T F 5. Transmissions that run in two directions simultaneously are called simplex.

T F 6. A protocol is a set of rules for transmitting data between a terminal and a computer or between two computers.

T F 7. VAN stands for *value-added network.*

T F   8. Networks that are similar might be connected by a bridge or router.

T F   9. Nodes on an Ethernet control communication by passing a set of bits called a token to each node on the network in turn.

T F   10. A public-access computer message service is called an EFT.

T F   11. A communications method that uses a continuous link between the sending and receiving computers is called packet switching.

T F   12. In the history of data communications, centralized data processing came before distributed data processing.

SOFTWARE TOOLS

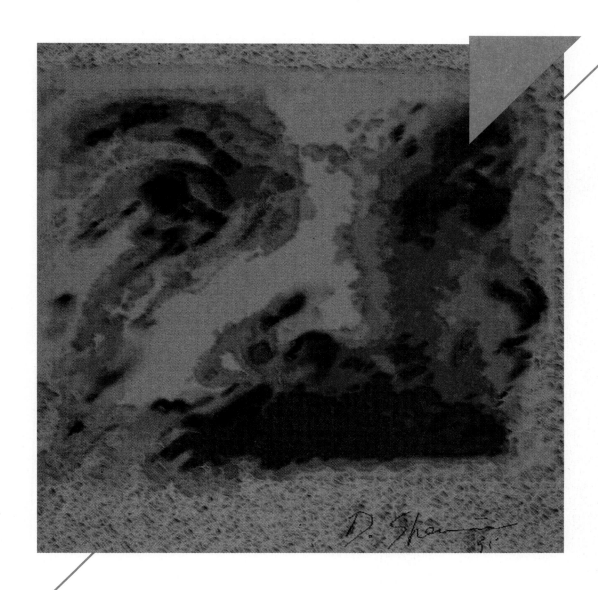

6

Programming and Languages

A Survey

The TV comedy skit goes something like this: A man in a trench coat walks up to a bank teller's window. He slides a note across and peers menacingly at the person behind the counter. Suddenly, the teller points at the writing on the paper and snaps: "This is incorrect. 'Handover' should be two words! And 'mony' is spelled with an *e*. Next!" The would-be bank robber slinks away sadly. The joke lies in the surprising reaction of the teller. The robber expected the teller to react to the *semantics,* or meaning, of the message; instead, the teller reacted to the *form* of the message.

To communicate, everyone involved must agree on the semantics and the form of the language used. Agreement must extend to grammar, word order, and symbol systems as well as to the definitions of the words themselves. Despite the amount of agreement required to use language meaningfully, however, humans can tolerate a good deal of imprecision, or ambiguity, in communication. Consider two friends discussing their dogs. One tells the other that her dog is black and white. The listener may visualize a black dog with a white face, a white dog with a black face, a black dog with white spots, or any number of other combinations of black and white. The dog's actual appearance may not matter, unless the dog is lost.

Computers, in contrast to humans, require absolute precision in communication. Remember that computers can make only two distinctions: whether electricity is on or off. Therefore, a computer language can allow none of the ambiguity that humans can accommodate. Though a word in human language can have several meanings, a word used in communication with a computer must be limited to only one meaning. Even though a language for computers is limited in this way, it can still be used in step-by-step fashion to solve complex problems.

A set of rules that provides a way of telling a computer what operations to perform is called a **programming language.** There is not, however, just one programming language; there are many. In this chapter, you will learn about controlling a computer through the process of programming. You may even discover why you might want to become a programmer.

 ## *Why Programming?*

You may already have used software to solve problems. But perhaps now you are curious to learn how programmers write software. As we noted earlier, a **program** is a set of step-by-step instructions that directs the computer to do the tasks you want it to do and produce the results you want.

There are at least two good reasons for learning programming:

- Programming helps you understand computers. The computer is only a tool. Learning to write simple programs as you master the machine increases your confidence level. Most people find great personal satisfaction in creating a set of instructions that solve a problem.

- Learning programming lets you find out quickly whether you like programming and whether you have the analytical turn of mind programmers need. Even if you decide that programming is not for you, understanding the process certainly will increase your appreciation of what programmers and computers can do.

An important point before we proceed, however: You will not be a programmer when you finish reading this chapter or even when you finish reading the final chapter. Programming proficiency takes practice and

A Programming Pioneer: Grace M. Hopper

When Grace M. Hopper died in 1992 at the age of 85, she left behind the legacy of a true programming pioneer—involvement with the first computers and the first business programming language.

As a Phi Beta Kappa graduate of Vassar College with an M.A. and Ph.D. from Yale University, Hopper joined the U.S. Naval Reserve in 1943. She was assigned to the Bureau of Ordinance Computation Project at Harvard, where she learned to program the first large-scale digital computer, the Mark I. In 1948, Hopper became senior mathematician at the Eckert-Mauchly Computer Corporation. Later she became senior programmer on the team that created the first commercial large-scale electronic computer, UNIVAC I. In the 1950s, she co-authored the COBOL compiler and programming language. Among all of her achievements, the one she liked best was her promotion to the rank of Rear Admiral in the U.S. Naval Reserve.

training beyond the scope of this book. But you will be able to understand how programmers develop solutions to a variety of problems.

What Programmers Do

In general, the programmer's job is to convert problem solutions into instructions for the computer. That is, the programmer prepares the instructions of a computer program and runs, tests, and corrects the program. The programmer also writes a report on the program. These activities are all done for the purpose of helping a user fill a need—to pay employees, bill customers, admit students to college, and so forth. Programmers help the user develop new programs to solve problems, weed out errors in existing programs, or perform changes on programs as a result of new requirements (such as a change in the payroll program to make automatic union dues deductions).

The activities just described could be done, perhaps, as solo activities. But a programmer typically interacts with a variety of people. For example, if a program is part of a system of several programs, the programmer coordinates with other programmers to make sure that the programs fit together well. If you were a programmer, you might also have coordination meetings with users, managers, and with peers who evaluate your work—just as you evaluate theirs.

Let us turn now from programmers to the programming process.

The Programming Process

Developing a program involves steps similar to any problem-solving task. There are five main ingredients in the programming process:

1. Defining the problem
2. Planning the solution
3. Coding the program
4. Testing the program
5. Documenting the program

Let us discuss each of these in turn.

1. Defining the Problem

Suppose that, as a programmer, you are contacted because your services are needed. You meet with users from the client organization to analyze the problem, or you meet with a systems analyst who outlines the project. Specifically, the task of defining the problem consists of identifying what it is you know (input—given data), and what it is you want to obtain (output—the result). Eventually, you produce a written agreement that, among other things, specifies the kind of input, processing, and output required. This is not a simple process. It is closely related to the process of systems analysis, which is discussed in Chapter 8.

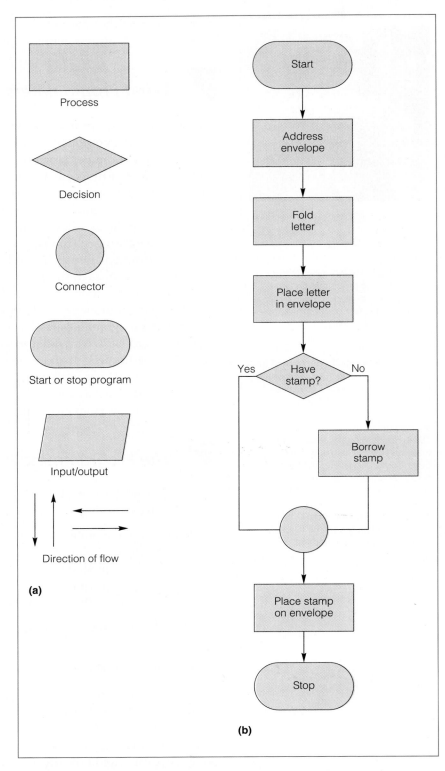

Figure 6-1   Flowchart symbols and a simple flowchart. (a) The ANSI standard flowchart symbols. (b) A flowchart shows how the standard symbols might be used to prepare a letter for mailing. There can be as many flowcharts to represent the task as there are ways of mailing a letter.

2. Planning the Solution

Two common ways of planning the solution to a problem are to draw a flowchart and/or write pseudocode. Essentially, a **flowchart** is a pictorial representation of a step-by-step solution to a problem. It consists of arrows representing the direction the program takes and boxes and other symbols representing actions. It is a map of what your program is going to do and how it is going to do it. The American National Standards Institute (ANSI) has developed a standard set of flowchart symbols. Figure 6-1 shows the symbols and how they might be used in a simple flowchart of a common everyday act—preparing a letter for mailing. **Pseudocode** is an English-like language that lets you state your solution with more precision than you can in plain English but with less precision than is required when using a formal programming language. In addition, **structure charts,** which diagram the hierarchical relationship between logical elements in a program, may be used to supplement these two diagramming tools. We will illustrate all three later in this chapter, when we focus on language examples. A detailed look at flowcharting and psuedocode is offered in Appendix A.

3. Coding the Program

As the programmer, your next step is to code the program—that is, to express your solution in a programming language. You will translate the logic from the flowchart or pseudocode—or some other tool—to a programming language. A programming language is a set of rules that provides a way of instructing the computer what operations to perform. There are many programming languages: BASIC, COBOL, Pascal, FORTRAN, and C are some examples. You may find yourself working with one or more of these. Although such languages operate grammatically, somewhat like the English language, they are much more precise. To get your program to work, you have to follow exactly the rules—the **syntax**—of the language you are using. Of course, using the language correctly is no guarantee that your program will work, any more than speaking grammatically correct English means you know what you are talking about. The point is that correct use of the language is the required first step. Then your coded program must be keyed, often at a terminal, in a form the computer can understand. We will discuss the different types of languages in detail later in this chapter.

One more note here: An experienced programmer can often write code for simple programs directly at a terminal or personal computer, skipping the coding-on-paper step. However, we do not recommend that beginners skip any steps. Even experienced programmers can get into trouble and waste a lot of time when they do not define the problem and plan the solution carefully before beginning to code.

4. Testing the Program

Some experts forcefully support the notion that a well-designed program can be written correctly the first time. In fact, they assert that there are mathematical ways to prove that a program is correct. However, the imperfections of the world are still with us, so most programmers get used to the idea that there are a few errors in their newly written programs. This is a bit discouraging at first, since programmers tend to be precise, careful, detail-oriented people who take pride in their work. Still, there are many opportunities to introduce mistakes into programs, and you, like those who have gone before you, will probably find several of them.

Eventually, after coding and keying the program, you must prepare to run it on the computer. This step involves these phases:

- **Desk-checking.** This phase, similar to proofreading, is sometimes avoided as a shortcut by the programmer who is eager to run the program on the computer, now that it is written. However, with careful desk-checking you may discover several errors and possibly save yourself several computer runs. In **desk-checking,** you simply sit down and mentally trace, or check, the logic of the program to ensure that it is error-free and workable.

- **Translating.** A **translator** is a program that translates your program into a form the computer can understand. Programs are most commonly translated by a compiler or an interpreter. A **compiler** translates your entire program at one time, giving you all the syntax-error messages—these messages are called **diagnostics**—at once. As shown in Figure 6-2, the translation involves a **source module,** which is transformed by a compiler into an **object module.** Prewritten programs

Figure 6-2   Preparing a program for execution. An original program, the source module, is translated by the compiler into an object module, which represents the program in a form the machine can understand. The compiler may produce diagnostic messages, indicating syntax errors. A listing of the source program may also be output from the compiler. After the program successfully compiles, the object module is linked in the link-load phase with system library programs as needed, and the result is a load module, or executable program.

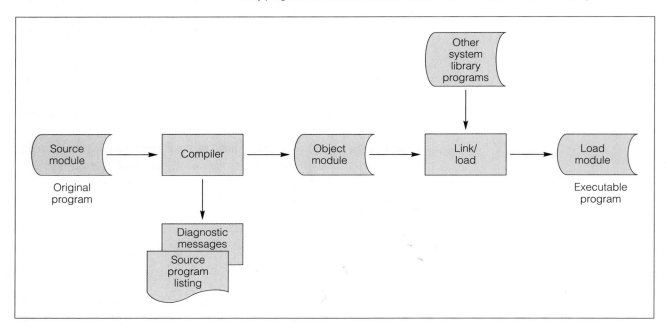

The First "Bug" was Real

Computer literacy books are bursting with bits and bytes and disks and chips and lessons on writing programs in BASIC. All this is to provide quick enlightenment for the computer illiterate. But the average newly literate person has not been told about the bugs.

It is a bit of a surprise, then, to find that the software you are using does not always work quite right. Or, perhaps the programmer who is doing some work for you cannot seem to get the program to work correctly. Both problems are "bugs," errors that were introduced unintentionally into a program when it was written.

The term *bug* comes from an experience in the early days of computing. One summer day in 1945, according to Grace M. Hopper (see the essay "A Programming Pioneer," earlier in this chapter), the Mark I computer came to a halt. Working to find the problem, computer personnel actually found a moth inside the machine (see photo above). They removed the offending bug, and the computer was fine. From that day forward, any mysterious problem or glitch was said to be a bug.

from a system library may be added during the **link/load phase,** which results in a **load module.** The load module can then be executed by the computer. A by-product of the process is that the translator tells you if you have improperly used the programming language in some way. These types of mistakes are called **syntax errors.** The translator produces descriptive error messages. For instance, if in FORTRAN you mistakenly write N = 2*(I + J))—which has two closing parentheses instead of one—you will get a message that says, "UNMATCHED PARENTHESES." (Different translators may provide different wording for error messages.) An **interpreter,** often used for the BASIC language, translates your program one line at a time; some interpreters signal syntax errors as each line is keyed in.

- **Debugging.** A term used extensively in programming, **debugging** means detecting, locating, and correcting "bugs" (mistakes) by running the program. These bugs are **logic errors,** such as telling a computer to repeat an operation but not telling it how to stop repeating. In this phase, you run the program against test data, which you devise. You must plan the test data carefully to make sure you test every part of the program.

5. Documenting the Program

Documenting is an ongoing, necessary process-although, like many programmers, you may be eager to pursue more exciting computer-related activities. **Documentation** is a written detailed description of the programming cycle and specific facts about the program. Typical program documentation materials include the origin and nature of the problem, a brief narrative description of the program, logic tools such as flowcharts and pseudocode, data-record descriptions, program listings, and testing results. Comments in the program itself are also considered an essential part of documentation. Many programmers document as they code. In a broader sense, program documentation can be part of the documentation for an entire system, as you will learn in Chapter 8, which discusses systems analysis and design.

The wise programmer continues to document the program throughout its design, development, and testing. Documentation is needed to supplement human memory and to help organize program planning. Also, documentation is critical to communicate with others who have an interest in the program, especially other programmers who may be part of a programming team. And, since turnover is high in the computer industry, written documentation is needed so that those who come after you can make any necessary modifications in the program or track down any errors that you missed.

Programming Languages

At present, there are over 200 programming languages—and these are the ones that are still being used. We are not counting the hundreds of

P E R S P E C T I V E S

YOUR CAREER: IS THE COMPUTER FIELD FOR YOU?

There is a shortage of qualified personnel in the computer field but, paradoxically, there are many people at the front end trying to get entry-level jobs. Before you join their ranks, consider the advantages of the computer field and what it takes to succeed in it.

The Joys of the Field

Although many people make career changes into the computer field, few choose to leave it. In fact, surveys of computer professionals consistently report a high level of job satisfaction. There are several reasons for this contentment. One is the challenge—most jobs in the computer industry are not routine. Another is security, since established computer professionals can usually find work. And that work pays well—you will probably not be rich, but you should be comfortable. The computer industry has historically been a rewarding place for women and minorities. And, finally, the industry holds endless fascination since it is always changing.

What It Takes

You need, of course, some credentials, most often a two- or four-year degree in computer information systems or computer science. The requirements and salaries vary by the organization and the region, so we will not dwell on these here. Beyond that, the person most likely to land a job and move up the career ladder is the one with excellent communication skills, both oral and written. These are also the qualities that can be observed by potential employers in an interview. Promotions are sometimes tied to advanced degrees (an M.B.A. or an M.S. in computer science).

Open Doors

The outlook for the computer field is still promising, despite the downsizing of the industry that occurred in the early 1990s. Using the Bureau of Labor Statistics as its source, the *Wall Street Journal* reported that throughout the 1990s the need for programmers will increase 72% and the need for systems analysts by 69%. These two professions are predicted to be the number two and number three high-growth jobs. (In case you are curious, the number one high-growth job area is predicted to be

the paralegal profession.) The reasons for continued job increase in the computer field are more computers, more applications of computers, and more computer users.

Career Directions

Traditional career progression in the computer field was a path from programmer to systems analyst to project manager. This is still a popular direction, but it is complicated by the large number of options open to computer professionals. Computer professionals sometimes specialize in some aspect of the industry, such as data communications, database management, personal computers, graphics, or equipment. Others may specialize in the computer-related aspects of a particular industry, such as banking or insurance. Still others strike out on their own, becoming consultants or entrepreneurs.

Keeping Up

Your formal education is merely the beginning. In the ever-changing computer field, you must take responsibility for your ongoing education. There are a variety of formal and informal ways of keeping up: college or on-the-job classes, workshops, seminars, conventions, exhi-

languages that for one reason or another have fallen by the wayside over the years. Some of the languages have rather colorful names: INTELLECT, DOCTOR, UFO. Where did all these languages come from? Do we really need to complicate the world further by adding programming languages to the Tower of Babel of human languages?

Initially, programming languages were created by people in universities or in government and were devised for special functions. Some languages endured because they served special purposes in science, engineering, and the like. However, it soon became clear that some standardization was needed. It made sense for those working on similar tasks to use the same language.

There are several languages in common use today, and we will discuss the most popular ones later in the chapter. Before we turn to the hit parade of languages, however, we need to discuss levels of language.

bitions, trade magazines, books, and professional organizations.

Organizations are particularly important; by attending a monthly meeting you can exchange ideas with other professionals, make new contacts, and hear a speaker address some current topic. Some of the principal professional societies are:

- **AFIPS.** The American Federation of Information Processing Societies is an umbrella federation of organizations relating to information processing.
- **ACM.** The Association for Computing Machinery is a worldwide society devoted to

developing information processing as a discipline.

- **ASM.** The Association for Systems Management keeps members current on developments in systems management and information processing.
- **AWC.** The Association of Women in Computing is open to professionals interested in promoting the advancement of women in the computer industry.
- **DPMA.** The Data Processing Management Association, one of the largest of the professional societies in the computer field,

is open to all levels of information management personnel. The group seeks to encourage high standards and a professional attitude toward data processing.

- **IEEE** Computer Society. The Institute of Electrical and Electronic Engineers Computer Society is an organization devoted to the advancement of the theory, practice, and application of computer processing and technology.

You should also consider becoming a Certified Data Processor (CDP), Certified Systems Professional (CSP), or Certified Computer Programmer (CCP). These certifications are granted upon passing an examination that tests mastery of a core curriculum and one of the following subspecialties: business information systems, communications, office information systems, scientific programming, software engineering, systems programming, or systems security.

There are other certifications available for computer professionals, including the ACP (Associate Computer Professional) to measure entry-level programmers. For information, write to ICCP (Institute for Certification of Computer Professionals), Suite 268, 2200 East Devon Avenue, Des Plaines, Illinois 60018-4503.

Levels of Language

Programming languages are said to be "lower" or "higher," depending on how close they are to the language the computer itself uses (0s and 1s—low) or to the language people use (more English-like—high). We will consider five levels of language. All these languages are considered traditional programming languages, since they use **structured programming,** a technique for organizing and coding programs. They are numbered 1 through 5 to correspond to level, or generation. In terms of ease of use and capabilities, each generation is an improvement over its predecessors. The five generations of languages are:

1. Machine language
2. Assembly languages

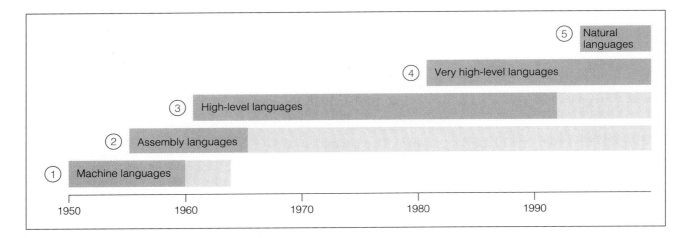

1950   1960   1970   1980   1990

Figure 6-3 Language generations on a time line. The darker shading indicates the period of greater use by applications programmers; the lighter shading indicates the time during which a generation faded from primary use.

```
FD      71      431F    4153
F3      63      4267    4321
96      F0      426D
F9      10      41F3    438A
47      40      40DA
47      F0      4050
```

Figure 6-4 Machine language. True machine language is all binary—only 0s and 1s—but since an example would take too much space here, we are showing an example of machine language in the hexadecimal (base 16) numbering system. (The letters A through F in hexadecimal represent the numbers 10 through 15 in the decimal system.) The computer commands shown, taken from machine language for the IBM 360/370 series computers, are operation codes instructing the computer to divide two numbers, compare the quotient, move the result into the output area of the system, and set up the result so it can be printed.

3. High-level languages
4. Very high-level languages
5. Natural languages

Note the time line for the language generations in Figure 6-3. Let us look at each of these categories.

Machine Language

Humans do not like to deal in numbers alone—they prefer letters and words. But, strictly speaking, numbers are what machine language is. This lowest level of language, **machine language,** represents data as 1s and 0s—binary digits corresponding to the "on" and "off" electrical states in the computer.

An example of machine language is shown in Figure 6-4. This is a language taken from a mainframe computer. In the early days of computing, each computer had its own machine language, and programmers had rudimentary systems for combining numbers to represent instructions such as *add* and *compare*. Primitive by today's standards, the programs were not convenient for people to read and use. The computer industry quickly moved to develop assembly languages.

Assembly Languages

Today, **assembly languages** are considered very low level—that is, they are not as convenient for people to use as more recent languages. At the time they were developed, however, they were considered a great leap forward. Rather than using simply 1s and 0s, assembly language uses mnemonic codes, abbreviations that are easy to remember, to replace the numbers: A for Add, C for Compare, MP for Multiply, STO for storing information into memory, and so on. Although these codes are not English words, they are still—from the standpoint of human convenience—preferable to numbers (0s and 1s) alone.

The programmer who uses an assembly language requires a translator to convert the assembly language program into machine language.

```
                 PRINT   NOGEN
PROG8            START   0
CARDFIL          DTFCD   DEVADDR=SYSRDR,RECFORM=FIXUNB,IOAREA1=CARDREC,C
                         TYPEFLE=INPUT,BLKSIZE=80,EOFADDR=FINISH
REPTFIL          DTFPR   DEVADDR=SYSLST,IOAREA1=PRNTREC,BLKSIZE=132
BEGIN            BALR    3,0                   REGISTER 3 IS BASE REGISTER
                 USING   *,3
                 OPEN    CARDFIL,REPTFIL       OPEN FILES
                 MVC     PRNTREC,SPACES        MOVE SPACES TO OUTPUT RECORD
READLOOP         GET     CARDFIL               READ A RECORD
                 MVC     OFIRST,IFIRST         MOVE ALL INPUT FIELDS
                 MVC     OLAST,ILAST           TO OUTPUT RECORD FIELDS
                 MVC     OADDR,IADDR
                 MVC     OCITY,ICITY
                 MVC     OSTATE,ISTATE
                 MVC     OZIP,IZIP
                 PUT     REPTFIL               WRITE THE RECORD
                 B       READLOOP              BRANCH TO READ AGAIN
FINISH           CLOSE   CARDFIL,REPTFIL       CLOSE FILES
                 EOJ                           END OF JOB
CARDREC          DS      0CL80                 DESCRIPTION OF INPUT RECORD
IFIRST           DS      CL10
ILAST            DS      CL10
IADDR            DS      CL30
ICITY            DS      CL20
ISTATE           DS      CL2
IZIP             DS      CL5
                 DS      CL3
PRNTREC          DS      0CL132                DESCRIPTION OF OUTPUT RECORD
                 DS      CL10
OLAST            DS      CL10
                 DS      CL5
OFIRST           DS      CL10
                 DS      CL15
OADDR            DS      CL30
                 DS      CL15
OCITY            DS      CL20
                 DS      CL5
OSTATE           DS      CL2
                 DS      CL5
OZIP             DS      CL5
SPACES           DC      CL132''
                 END     BEGIN
```

Figure 6-5   Assembly language. This example shows the IBM assembly language BAL used in a program for reading a record and writing it out again. The left column contains symbolic addresses of various instructions or data. The second column contains the actual operation codes to describe the kind of activity needed; for instance, MVC stands for *Move characters*. The third column describes the data on which the instructions are to act. The far right column contains English-like comments related to the line or lines opposite. This entire page of instructions could be compressed to a few lines in a high-level language.

A translator is needed because machine language is the only language the computer can actually execute. The translator is an **assembler program,** also referred to as an assembler. It takes the programs written in assembly language and turns them into machine language. Programmers need not worry about the translating aspect; they need only write programs in assembly language. The translation is taken care of by the assembler.

Although assembly languages represent a step forward, they still have many disadvantages. A key disadvantage is that assembly language is detailed in the extreme, making assembly programming repetitive, tedious, and error prone. This drawback is apparent from Figure 6-5. Assembly language may be easier to read than machine language, but it is by no means crystal clear.

High-Level Languages

The first widespread use of **high-level languages** in the early 1960s transformed programming into something quite different from what it had been. The harried programmer working on the nitty-gritty details of coding and machines became a programmer who could pay more attention to solving a client's problems. Programs could now direct much more complex tasks. In addition, the programs were written in an English-like manner, thus making them more convenient to use. As a result of these changes, the programmer could accomplish more with less effort.

These so-called third-generation languages spurred the great increase in data processing that characterized the '60s and '70s. During that time the number of mainframes in use increased from hundreds to tens of thousands. The impact of third-generation languages on our society has been enormous.

Of course, a translator is needed to translate the symbolic statements of a high-level language into computer-executable machine language; this translator is usually a compiler. There are many compilers for each language and one for each type of computer. Since the machine language generated by one computer's COBOL compiler, for instance, is not the machine language of some other computer, it is necessary to have a COBOL compiler for each type of computer on which COBOL programs are to be run.

Some languages are created to serve a specific purpose, such as controlling industrial robots or creating graphics. Many languages, however, are extraordinarily flexible and are considered to be general-purpose. In the past, the majority of programming applications were written in BASIC, FORTRAN, or COBOL—all general-purpose languages. In addition to these three, other popular high-level languages today are Pascal and C—and their derivatives, which we will discuss later.

We noted that high-level languages relieve the programmer of burdensome details. However, with this convenience comes an inevitable loss of flexibility. A few high-level languages like C and FORTH offer some of the flexibility of assembly language together with the power of high-level languages, but these languages are not well suited to the beginning programmer.

We will discuss and demonstrate several high-level languages later in the chapter.

Very High-Level Languages

Languages called **very high-level languages** are often known by their generation number. That is, they are called **fourth-generation languages,** or—more simply—**4GLs.** But though the name is easy, the definition is not.

Definition   Will the real fourth-generation languages please stand up? There is no consensus about what constitutes a fourth-generation language. The 4GLs are essentially shorthand programming languages. An operation that requires hundreds of lines in a third-generation language such as COBOL typically requires only five to ten lines in a 4GL. However, beyond the basic criterion of conciseness, 4GLs are difficult to describe.

Characteristics   Fourth-generation languages share some characteristics. The first is that they make a true break with the prior generation—they are basically nonprocedural. A **procedural language** tells the computer *how* a task is done: Add this, compare that, do this if something is true, and so forth—a very specific step-by-step process. The first three generations of languages are all procedural. In a **nonprocedural language,** the concept changes. Here, users define only *what* they want the computer to do; the user does not provide the details of just how it is to be done. Obviously, it is a lot easier and faster to just say what you want rather than how to get it. This leads us to the issue of productivity, a key characteristic of fourth-generation languages.

Productivity   Folklore has it that fourth-generation languages can improve productivity by a factor of 5 to 50. The folklore is true. Most experts say the average improvement factor is about 10—that is, you can be ten times more productive in a fourth-generation language than in a third-generation language. Consider this request: Produce a report showing the total units sold for each product, by customer, in each month and year, and with a subtotal for each customer. In addition, each new customer must start on a new page. A 4GL request looks something like this:

```
TABLE FILE SALES
SUM UNITS BY MONTH BY CUSTOMER BY PRODUCT
ON CUSTOMER SUBTOTAL PAGE BREAK
END
```

Even though some training is required to do even this much, you can see that it is pretty simple. The third-generation language COBOL, however, typically requires over 500 statements to fulfill the same request. If we define productivity as producing equivalent results in less time, then fourth-generation languages clearly increase productivity.

The Downside of 4GLs   Fourth-generation languages are not all peaches and cream and productivity. The 4GLs are still evolving, and that which is still evolving cannot be fully defined or standardized. What is more, since many 4GLs are easy to use, they attract a large number of new users, who may then overcrowd the computer system. One of the main criticisms is that the new languages lack the necessary control and flexibility when it comes to planning how you want the output to look. A common perception of 4GLs is that they do not make efficient use of machine resources; however, the benefits of getting a program finished more quickly can far outweigh the extra costs of running it.

It's Too Easy To Be Programming!

You have learned to do a job and do it well. You put in the time, went through the training, and now you are a respected professional with a salary to match. A programmer. But now your hard-earned skills are being eroded in the marketplace: There are new languages that anyone can use. A quiet panic sweeps over you.

This little scene is common across the land. Programmers sometimes resist the new tools. Managers complain about underutilization of fourth-generation languages by professional programmers. There is another reason besides the fear of obsolescence: Old habits die hard. When someone has worked in a traditional language for many years, it is hard to make a switch to something new. There is the element of culture shock, and what is more, programmers sometimes think that if a language is easy to use, it must be for someone else. "Real" programmers have to use a language that is difficult.

What many forget is the "turn of mind" involved in programming. Some people call it *algorithmic thinking.* Others believe it is a knack for problem solving. Still others feel programming is an art. No matter how we interpret excellence in programming, we have to realize it involves a certain mindset—no matter how "easy" or "natural" programming languages may become.

4GL Benefits   Fourth-generation languages are beneficial because:

- They are results-oriented; they emphasize *what* instead of *how*.
- They improve productivity because programs are easy to write and change.
- They can be used with a minimum of training by both programmers and nonprogrammers.
- They shield users from needing an awareness of hardware and program structure.

It was not long ago that few people believed that 4GLs would ever be able to replace third-generation languages. These 4GL languages

Figure 6-6   An example of Focus. (a) The code here produces (b) the Foster University roster for a differential equations class. To print field names in the heading, you must use angle brackets (<>) as delimiters. The sequence "< / 2" tells Focus to skip two lines after the heading. The program begins a new page every time the course number (CNUM) changes. The IF clauses print records only if they pertain to the fall semester of 1988.

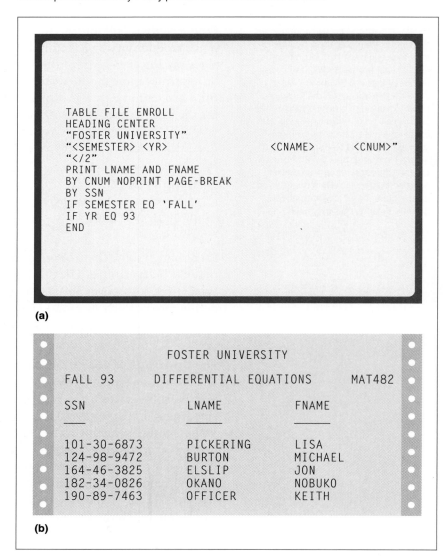

```
TABLE FILE ENROLL
HEADING CENTER
"FOSTER UNIVERSITY"
"<SEMESTER> <YR>                    <CNAME>        <CNUM>"
"</2"
PRINT LNAME AND FNAME
BY CNUM NOPRINT PAGE-BREAK
BY SSN
IF SEMESTER EQ 'FALL'
IF YR EQ 93
END
```

(a)

```
                    FOSTER UNIVERSITY

   FALL 93        DIFFERENTIAL EQUATIONS        MAT482

   SSN                 LNAME           FNAME
   ___                 _____           _____

   101-30-6873         PICKERING       LISA
   124-98-9472         BURTON          MICHAEL
   164-46-3825         ELSLIP          JON
   182-34-0826         OKANO           NOBUKO
   190-89-7463         OFFICER         KEITH
```

(b)

Mining by Computer

PROSPECTOR is an expert system developed by SRI International. The system predicts the potential for finding mineral deposits in a certain area. PROSPECTOR was developed by interviewing experienced prospectors—geologists who are experts in locating underground mineral deposits. In the photo, geologist Dennis Cox (*left*), an authority on copper deposits, is being interviewed by an SRI knowledge engineer, who will convert Cox's knowledge about geology into thousands of rules a computer can use. By formalizing the rules that expert geologists follow and putting them into a computer system, the expert's knowledge is available to more people.

are being used, but in a very limited way. Figure 6-6 illustrates a 4GL called Focus.

Natural Languages

The word *natural* has become almost as popular in computing circles as it has in the supermarket. But fifth-generation languages are, as you may guess, even more ill-defined than fourth-generation languages. They are most often called **natural languages** because of their resemblance to the "natural" spoken English language. And, to the manager new to computers for whom these languages are now aimed, *natural* means human-like. Instead of being forced to key correct commands and data names in correct order, a manager tells the computer what to do by keying in his or her own words.

A manager can say the same thing any number of ways. For example, "Get me tennis racket sales for January" works just as well as "I want January tennis racket revenues." Such a request may contain misspelled words, lack articles and verbs, and even use slang. The natural language translates human instructions—bad grammar, slang, and all—into code the computer understands. If it is not sure what the user has in mind, it politely asks for further explanation.

Natural languages are sometimes referred to as knowledge-based languages because natural languages are used to interact with a base of knowledge on some subject. The use of a natural language to access a knowledge base is called a **knowledge-based system.** A species of knowledge-based systems is the expert system, although the terms for each type are often used interchangeably. An **expert system** offers the computer as an expert on some topic. The expertise of the system is usually equivalent to that of a human expert and can be queried—asked questions—in a similar way. We will examine expert systems for business in Chapter 16.

The use of natural language to access a knowledge base is the foundation of **artificial intelligence.** Bill Gates, founder of the Microsoft Corporation, can be credited with a common-sense definition of artificial intelligence: "anything that makes software softer." In other words, the goal is to let the user focus on the task rather than the computer.

Consider this request that could be given in the 4GL Focus: "SUM ORDERS BY DATE BY REGION." If we alter the request and, still in Focus, say something like "Give me the dates and the regions after you've added up the orders," the computer will spit back the user-friendly version of "You've got to be kidding" and give up. But some natural languages can handle such a request. Users can relax the structure of their requests and increase the freedom of their interaction with the data.

Here is a typical natural-language request:

```
REPORT THE BASE SALARY, COMMISSIONS AND YEARS OF SERVICE
BROKEN DOWN BY STATE AND CITY FOR SALESCLERKS IN NEW
JERSEY AND MASSACHUSETTS.
```

You can hardly get closer to conversational English than that.

Figure 6-7   A natural language. This package, called Cash Management System, uses a language that is so "natural" that some might think it a little too cute, as in "Just a sec."

```
Hello
How may I help you?
Who are my customers in Chicago?
Just a sec.  I'll see.
The customers in that city are:
I.D.                    Name
_____
Ballard            Ballard and Sons, Inc.
Fremont            Henry Fremont Associates
Greenlake          Greenlake Consortium
Wallingford        Wallingford, Inc.
What can I do for you now?
What is Fremont's balance?
Hang on.  I'll see.
Accounts Receivable    563.47
Unapplied Credit        79.16
           Balance     484.31
What else can I do for you?
Give me Fremont's phone number!
Please wait while I check the files.
   (312) 789-5562
What can I do for you now?
```

An example of a natural language is shown in Figure 6-7. Natural languages excel at easy data access. Indeed, the most common application for natural languages is interacting with databases.

If we limit our needs to data queries, some programs **query by example (QBE)** instead of using natural languages; once a query is made, it acts as an example for later queries. Developed by IBM in the late 1970s, QBE is now used by such programs as Paradox by Borland. Paradox also has an option that translates QBE into **structured query language (SQL)** 4GL commands. In addition, computer-aided software engineering (CASE) systems are often utilized with 4GL languages. We will learn more about CASE tools when we discuss systems analysis and design, in Chapter 8.

Choosing a Language

How do you choose the language in which to write your program? Perhaps you will use a particular language because it is the only one available at your installation. Perhaps your manager has decreed that everyone on your project will use a certain language. Perhaps you know only one language!

A sensible approach is to pick the language that is most suitable for your particular programming task. The following sections on individual languages will give you an overview of the languages in common use. We describe these third-generation languages: FORTRAN, COBOL, BASIC, Pascal, Ada, and C. Then we discuss several object-oriented languages, which create a computing environment different than that of third-generation languages. The text will note special features of each third-generation and object-oriented language and state the types of applications for which each is often used. Table 6-1 summarizes these applications.

Table 6-1   Applications of some important programming languages.

Language	Application
FORTRAN—FORmula TRANslator (1954)	Scientific
COBOL—Common Business-Oriented Language (1959)	Business
BASIC—Beginner's All-purpose Symbolic Instruction Code (1965)	Education, business
Pascal—named after French inventor Blaise Pascal (1971)	Education, systems, scientific
Turbo Pascal—an enhanced version of Pascal	
Ada—named after Ada, the Countess of Lovelace (1980)	Military, general
C—evolved from the language B, from Bell Labs (1972)	Systems, general
C++ (1980)—an enhanced version of C	
Smalltalk—first object-oriented language (1970)	Systems, business
LISP—first artificial intelligence language, developed at MIT (1958)	Artificial intelligence

This chapter will present programs written in FORTRAN, COBOL, BASIC, Pascal, Ada, and C. You will also see output produced by each program. All these programs are designed to average numbers; each sample output shows the average of three numbers. Since all six programs perform the same task, you will see some of the differences and similarities between the languages. We do not expect you to understand each line of these programs; they are here merely to let you see what each language looks like. Figure 6-8 presents the flowchart, pseudocode, and structure chart for the task of averaging numbers. As we discuss each language, we will provide a program for averaging numbers that follows the logic shown.

FORTRAN: The First High-Level Language

Developed by IBM and introduced in 1954, **FORTRAN**—for FORmula TRANslator—was the first high-level language. FORTRAN is a scientifically oriented language—in the early days use of the computer was primarily associated with engineering, mathematical, and scientific research tasks. FORTRAN is still the most widely used language in the scientific community.

FORTRAN is noted for its brevity, and this characteristic is part of the reason why it remains popular. This language is very good at serving its primary purpose, which is execution of complex formulas such as those used in economic analysis and engineering. Although in the past it was considered limited in regard to file processing or data processing, its capabilities have been greatly improved.

Not all programs are organized in the same way. Organization varies according to the language used. In many languages (such as COBOL), programs are divided into a series of parts. FORTRAN programs are not composed of different parts (although it is possible to link FORTRAN programs together); a FORTRAN program consists of statements one after the other. Different types of data are identified as the data is used.

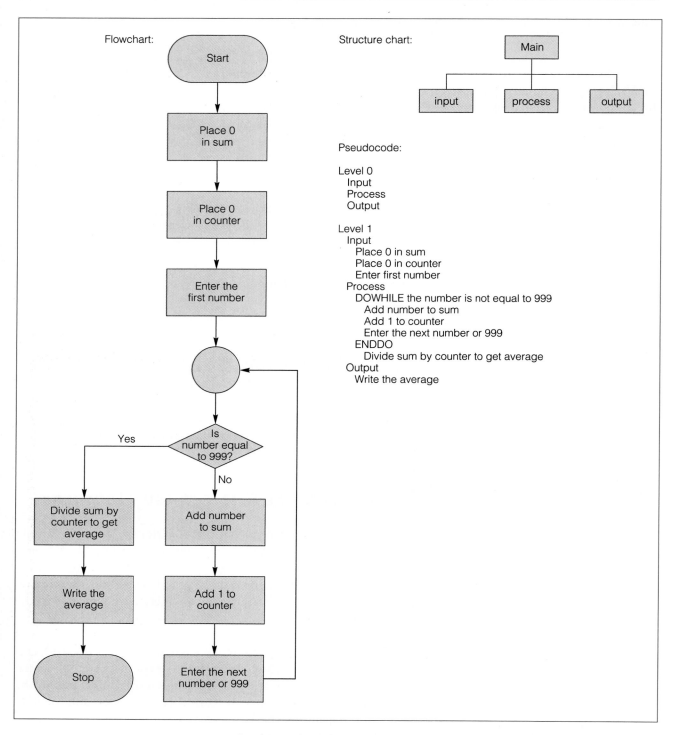

Figure 6-8   Flowchart, structure chart, and psuedocode for averaging numbers. This flowchart—along with its matching structure chart and pseudocode—shows the logic for a program to let a user enter numbers through the keyboard; the program then averages the numbers. The user can make any number of entries, one at a time. To show when he or she is finished making entries, the user enters 999. The logic to enter the numbers forms a loop: entering the number, adding it to the sum, and adding 1 to the counter. When 999 is keyed, the loop is exited. Then the machine computes the average and displays it on the screen. This logic is used for thè programs, in various languages, that follow.

Figure 6-9 FORTRAN program and sample output. This program is interactive, prompting the user to supply data. (a) The first two lines are comments, as they are in the rest of the programs in this chapter. The WRITE statements send output to the screen in the format called for by the second numeral in the parentheses. The READ statements accept data from the user and place it in location NUMBER, where it can be added to the accumulated total, SUM. The IF statement checks for 999 and, when 999 is received, diverts the program logic to statement 2, where the average is computed. The average is then displayed. (b) This screen display shows the interaction between program and user.

```
C       FORTRAN PROGRAM
C       AVERAGING INTEGERS ENTERED THROUGH THE KEYBOARD
        WRITE (6,10)
        SUM = 0
        COUNTER = 0
        WRITE (6,60)
        READ (5,40) NUMBER
   1    IF (NUMBER .EQ. 999) GOTO 2
        SUM = SUM + NUMBER
        COUNTER = COUNTER + 1
        WRITE (6,70)
        READ (5,40) NUMBER
        GO TO 1
   2    AVERAGE = SUM / COUNTER
        WRITE (6,80) AVERAGE
  10    FORMAT (1X, 'THIS PROGRAM WILL FIND THE AVERAGE OF ',
        'INTEGERS YOU ENTER ',/1X, 'THROUGH THE ',
        'KEYBOARD. TYPE 999 TO INDICATE END OF DATA.',/)
  40  * FORMAT (13)
  60  * FORMAT (1X, 'PLEASE ENTER A NUMBER ')
  70    FORMAT (1X, 'PLEASE ENTER THE NEXT NUMBER ')
  80    FORMAT (1X, 'THE AVERAGE OF THE NUMBERS IS ',F6.2)
        STOP
        END
```

(a)

```
THIS PROGRAM WILL FIND THE AVERAGE OF INTEGERS YOU ENTER
THROUGH THE KEYBOARD.  TYPE 999 TO INDICATE END OF DATA.
PLEASE ENTER A NUMBER    6
PLEASE ENTER THE NEXT NUMBER      4
PLEASE ENTER THE NEXT NUMBER     11
PLEASE ENTER THE NEXT NUMBER    999
THE AVERAGE OF THE NUMBERS IS     7.00
```

(b)

Descriptions for data records appear in format statements that accompany the READ and WRITE statements. Figure 6-9 shows a FORTRAN program and a sample output from the program.

COBOL: The Language of Business

In the 1950s FORTRAN had been developed, but there was still no accepted high-level programming language appropriate for business. The

U.S. Department of Defense in particular was interested in creating such a standardized language, and so it called together representatives from government and various industries, including the computer industry. These representatives formed **CODASYL**—COnference of DAta SYstem Languages. In 1959 CODASYL introduced **COBOL**—for COmmon Business-Oriented Language. The U.S. government offered encouragement by insisting that anyone attempting to win government contracts for computer-related projects had to use COBOL. The American National Standards Institute first standardized COBOL in 1968 and, in 1974, issued standards for another version known as **ANSI-COBOL.** And, after more than seven controversial years of industry debate, the standard known as **COBOL 85** was approved, making COBOL a more usable modern-day software tool. The principal benefit of standardization is that COBOL is relatively machine independent—that is, a program written for one type of computer can be run with only slight modifications on another for which a COBOL compiler has been developed.

The principal feature of COBOL is that it is English-like—far more so than FORTRAN or BASIC. The variable names are set up in such a way that, even if you know nothing about programming, you can still understand what the program does. For example:

```
IF SALES-AMOUNT IS GREATER THAN SALES-QUOTA
        COMPUTE COMMISSION = MAX-RATE * SALES-AMOUNT
ELSE
        COMPUTE COMMISSION = MIN-RATE * SALES-AMOUNT.
```

Once you understand programming principles, it is not too difficult to add COBOL to your repertoire. COBOL can be used for just about any task related to business programming; indeed, it is especially suited to processing alphanumeric data such as street addresses, purchased items, and dollar amounts—the data of business. However, the feature that makes COBOL so useful—its English-like appearance and easy readability—is also a weakness because a COBOL program can be incredibly verbose. A programmer seldom knocks out a quick COBOL program. In fact, there is hardly such a thing as a quick COBOL program; there are just too many program lines to write, even to accomplish a simple task. For speed and simplicity, BASIC, FORTRAN, and Pascal are probably better bets.

As you can see in Figure 6-10, a COBOL program is divided into four parts called divisions. The *identification division* identifies the program by name and often contains helpful comments as well. The *environment division* describes the computer on which the program will be compiled and executed. It also relates each file of the program to the specific physical device, such as the tape drive or printer, that will read or write the file. The *data division* contains details about the data processed by the program, such as type of characters (whether numeric or alphanumeric), number of characters, and placement of decimal points. The *procedure division* contains the statements that give the computer specific instructions to carry out the logic of the program.

It has been fashionable for some time to criticize COBOL: It is old-fashioned, cumbersome, inelegant, and has none of the most important

Figure 6-10   COBOL program and sample output. The purpose of the program and its results are the same as those of the FORTRAN program, but (a) the look of the COBOL program is very different. Note the four divisions. In particular, note that the logic in the procedure division uses a series of PERFORM statements, which divert action to other places in the program. After a prescribed action has been performed, the computer returns to the procedure division, to the statement after the one that was just completed. DISPLAY writes to the screen and ACCEPT takes user input. (b) This screen display shows the interaction between program and user.

```
****************************************************************
IDENTIFICATION DIVISION.
****************************************************************
PROGRAM-ID.  AVERAGE.
* COBOL PROGRAM
* AVERAGING INTEGERS ENTERED THROUGH THE KEYBOARD.
****************************************************************
ENVIRONMENT DIVISION.
****************************************************************
CONFIGURATION SECTION.
SOURCE-COMPUTER.             H-P 3000.
OBJECT-COMPUTER.             H-P 3000.
****************************************************************
DATA DIVISION.
****************************************************************
FILE SECTION.
WORKING-STORAGE SECTION.
01 AVERAGE          PIC ---9.99.
01 COUNTER          PIC 9(02)        VALUE ZERO.
01 NUMBER-ITEM      PIC S9(03).
01 SUM-ITEM         PIC S9(06)       VALUE ZERO.
01 BLANK-LINE       PIC X(80)        VALUE SPACES.
****************************************************************
PROCEDURE DIVISION.
****************************************************************
100-CONTROL-ROUTINE.
    PERFORM 200-DISPLAY-INSTRUCTIONS.
    PERFORM 300-INITIALIZATION-ROUTINE.
    PERFORM 400-ENTER-AND-ADD
            UNTIL NUMBER-ITEM = 999.
    PERFORM 500-CALCULATE-AVERAGE.
    PERFORM 600-DISPLAY-RESULTS.
    STOP RUN.
200-DISPLAY-INSTRUCTIONS.
    DISPLAY
      "THIS PROGRAM WILL FIND THE AVERAGE OF INTEGERS YOU ENTER".
    DISPLAY
      "THROUGH THE KEYBOARD. TYPE 999 TO INDICATE END OF DATA.".
    DISPLAY BLANK-LINE.
300-INITIALIZATION-ROUTINE.
    DISPLAY "PLEASE ENTER A NUMBER".
    ACCEPT NUMBER-ITEM.
400-ENTER-AND-ADD
    ADD NUMBER-ITEM TO SUM-ITEM.
    ADD 1 TO COUNTER.
    DISPLAY "PLEASE ENTER THE NEXT NUMBER".
    ACCEPT NUMBER-ITEM.
500-CALCULATE-AVERAGE.
    DIVIDE SUM-ITEM BY COUNTER GIVING AVERAGE.
600-DISPLAY-RESULTS.
    DISPLAY "THE AVERAGE OF THE NUMBERS IS ",AVERAGE.
```

(a)

```
      THIS PROGRAM WILL FIND THE AVERAGE OF
      INTEGERS YOU ENTER THROUGH THE KEYBOARD.
      TYPE 999 TO INDICATE END OF DATA.

      PLEASE ENTER A NUMBER
      6
      PLEASE ENTER THE NEXT NUMBER
      4
      PLEASE ENTER THE NEXT NUMBER
      11
      PLEASE ENTER THE NEXT NUMBER
      999
      THE AVERAGE OF THE NUMBERS IS    7.00
```

(b)

features of a modern language. But this golden oldie is still with us. And all the criticism does not alter the fact that, if you are interested in making money as a business programmer, COBOL is still your best bet.

BASIC: For Beginners and Others

BASIC—Beginners' All-purpose Symbolic Instruction Code is a common language that is easy to learn. Developed at Dartmouth College,

Figure 6-11   BASIC program and sample output. (a) A BASIC program looks very much like a FORTRAN program. The main difference is in the input and output statements. Here, PRINT displays data right in the statement on the screen. INPUT accepts data from the user. (b) This screen display shows the interaction between program and user.

```
 10 REM  BASIC PROGRAM
 20 REM  AVERAGING INTEGERS ENTERED THROUGH THE KEYBOARD.
 30 PRINT "THIS PROGRAM WILL FIND THE AVERAGE OF INTEGERS YOU ENTER"
 40 PRINT "THROUGH THE KEYBOARD.  TYPE 999 TO INDICATE END OF DATA."
 50 PRINT
 60 SUM=0
 70 COUNTER=0
 80 PRINT "PLEASE ENTER A NUMBER"
 90 INPUT NUMBER
100 IF NUMBER=999 THEN 160
110 SUM=SUM+NUMBER
120 COUNTER=COUNTER+1
130 PRINT "PLEASE ENTER THE NEXT NUMBER"
140 INPUT NUMBER
150 GOTO 100
160 AVERAGE=SUM/COUNTER
170 PRINT "THE AVERAGE OF THE NUMBERS IS";AVERAGE
180 END
```

(a)

```
THIS PROGRAM WILL FIND THE AVERAGE OF INTEGERS YOU ENTER
THROUGH THE KEYBOARD. TYPE 999 TO INDICATE END OF DATA.

PLEASE ENTER A NUMBER
?6
PLEASE ENTER THE NEXT NUMBER
?4
PLEASE ENTER THE NEXT NUMBER
?11
PLEASE ENTER THE NEXT NUMBER
?999
THE AVERAGE OF THE NUMBERS IS    7
```

(b)

BASIC was introduced by John Kemeny and Thomas Kurtz in 1965 and was originally intended for use by students in an academic environment. In the late 1960s, it became widely used in interactive time-sharing environments in universities and colleges. The use of BASIC has extended to business and personal computer systems.

The primary feature of BASIC is one that may be of interest to many readers of this book: BASIC is easy to learn, even for a person who has never programmed before. Thus, the language is used often to train students in the classroom. BASIC is also used by nonprogramming people, such as engineers, who find it useful in problem solving. For many years, BASIC was looked down on by "real programmers," who complained that it had too many limitations and was not suitable for complex tasks. Newer versions such as True BASIC (by originators Kemeny and Kurtz), Power-BASIC (Spectra), and QuickBASIC (Microsoft) include substantial improvements. Programs written by professionals in these newer BASICs are said to resemble Pascal or C programs. An example of a BASIC program and its output are shown in Figure 6-11.

Pascal: The Language of Simplicity

Named for Blaise Pascal, the seventeenth-century French mathematician, **Pascal** was developed as a teaching language by a Swiss computer scientist, Niklaus Wirth, and first became available in 1971. Since that time it has become quite popular, first in Europe and now in the United States, particularly in universities and colleges offering computer science programs.

The foremost feature of Pascal is that it is simpler than other languages—it has fewer features and is less wordy than most. In addition to the popularity of Pascal in college computer science departments, the language has also made large inroads in the personal computer market as a simple yet sophisticated alternative to BASIC. Over the years new versions have improved on the original capabilities of Pascal. Today Turbo Pascal (by Borland) leads the Pascal world—the designers of the program succeeded in eliminating most of the drawbacks of the original Pascal. Turbo Pascal is used by the business community and is often the choice of nonprofessional programmers (usually individuals from other professions) who need to write their own programs. An example of a Turbo Pascal program and its output are shown in Figure 6-12.

Ada: The Language of Standardization?

Is any software worth over $25 billion? Not any more, according to Defense Department experts. In 1974 the U.S. Department of Defense had spent that amount on all kinds of software for a hodgepodge of languages for its needs. The answer to this problem turned out to be a new language called **Ada**—named for Countess Ada Lovelace, "the first programmer" (see Appendix B). Sponsored by the Pentagon, Ada was originally intended

```
PROGRAM AverageofNumbers;
(*Pascal Program
  averaging integers entered through the keyboard*)

USES
   crt;

VAR
   counter, number, sum : integer;
    average : real ;

BEGIN (*main*)
    WRITELN ('THIS PROGRAM WILL FIND THE AVERAGE OF INTEGERS YOU ENTER');
    WRITELN ('THROUGH THE KEYBOARD. TYPE 999 TO INDICATE END OF DATA.' );
    WRITELN;
    sum :=0;
    counter :=0;
    WRITELN ('PLEASE ENTER A NUMBER');
    READLN (number);
    WHILE number <> 999 DO
        Begin  (*while loop*)
            sum := sum + number;
            counter := counter + 1;
            WRITELN ('PLEASE ENTER THE NEXT NUMBER');
            READ (number);
        END; (*while loop*)
    average := sum / counter;
    WRITELN ('THE AVERAGE OF THE NUMBERS IS ', average:6:2);
END.  (*main*)
```

(a)

```
THIS PROGRAM WILL FIND THE AVERAGE OF INTEGERS YOU ENTER
THROUGH THE KEYBOARD. TYPE 999 TO INDICATE END OF DATA.

PLEASE ENTER A NUMBER
6
PLEASE ENTER THE NEXT NUMBER
4
PLEASE ENTER THE NEXT NUMBER
11
PLEASE ENTER THE NEXT NUMBER
999
THE AVERAGE OF THE NUMBERS IS   7.00
```

(b)

Figure 6-12   Pascal program and sample output. (a) Comments are from (* to *). Each variable name must be declared. The symbol := assigns a value to the variable to its left; the symbol <> means not equal to. WRITELN by itself puts a blank line on the screen. (b) This screen display shows the interaction between program and user. The program was written in Turbo Pascal.

to be a standard language for weapons systems, but it has also been used successfully for commercial applications. Introduced in 1980, Ada has the support not only of the defense establishment but also of such industry heavyweights as IBM and Intel, and Ada is even available for some personal computers. Although some experts have said Ada is too complex (futurist Charles Lecht describes it as a klutz), others say that it is easy to learn and that it will increase productivity. Indeed, some experts believe that it is by far a superior commercial language to such standbys as COBOL and FORTRAN.

Widespread use of Ada is considered unlikely by many experts. Although there are many reasons for this (the military services, for instance, have different levels of enthusiasm for it), probably its size—which may hinder its use on personal computers—and complexity are the greatest barriers. Although the Department of Defense is a market in itself, Ada has not caught on to the extent that Pascal and C have, especially in the business community. An example of an Ada program and its output are shown in Figure 6-13.

C: A Portable Language

A language that lends itself to systems programming (operating systems and the like) as well as to more mundane programming tasks, **C** is credited to Dennis Ritchie at Bell Labs. It evolved from the BCPL language in 1969, through an early version called B, which eventually led to its release as C in 1972. C produces code that approaches assembly language in efficiency while still offering high-level language features such as structured programming. C contains some of the best features from other languages, including PL/I and Pascal. C compilers are simple and compact. A main attraction is that it is independent of the architecture of any particular machine, a fact that contributes to the portability of C programs—that is, C programs can be run on more than one type of computer.

Although C is simple and elegant, it is not simple to learn. It was developed for gifted programmers, and the learning curve is steep indeed. Straightforward tasks may be solved easily in C, but complex problems require mastery of the language.

An interesting sidenote is that the availability of C on personal computers has greatly enhanced the value of personal computers for budding entrepreneurs. A cottage software industry can use the same basic tool—the language C—used by established software companies like Microsoft and Borland. Today C is fast being replaced by its enhanced cousin, C++ (which will be discussed later). An example of a C++ program and its output are shown in Figure 6-14.

Some Other Languages

The languages just described are probably the major ones used today—albeit in various forms through several generations. Many of them oc-

(Continued on page 215)

```
-- ADA PROGRAM
-- AVERAGING INTEGERS ENTERED THROUGH THE KEYBOARD.
with TEXT_IO; use TEXT_IO;
procedure AVERAGE is
    package INT_IO is new INTEGER_IO (INTEGER);
    AVERAGE:                FLOAT                        ;
    COUNTER:                INTEGER         :=         0;
    NUMBER:                 INTEGER                     ;
    SUM:                    INTEGER         :=         0;
begin
    PUT_LINE("THIS PROGRAM WILL FIND THE AVERAGE OF INTEGERS YOU ENTER");
    PUT_LINE("THROUGH THE KEYBOARD. TYPE 999 TO INDICATE END OF DATA.");
    NEW_LINE;
    PUT("PLEASE ENTER A NUMBER");
    INT_IO.GET(NUMBER);
    while NUMBER /= 999 loop
        SUM := SUM + NUMBER;
        COUNTER := COUNTER + 1;
        PUT("PLEASE ENTER THE NEXT NUMBER");
        INT_IO.GET(NUMBER);
    end loop;
    AVERAGE := SUM/COUNTER;
    PUT("THE AVERAGE OF THE NUMBERS IS");
    FLO_IO.PUT(AVERAGE);
end AVERAGE;
```
(a)

```
THIS PROGRAM WILL FIND THE AVERAGE OF INTEGERS YOU ENTER
THROUGH THE KEYBOARD.  TYPE 999 TO INDICATE END OF DATA.
PLEASE ENTER A NUMBER      6
PLEASE ENTER THE NEXT NUMBER     4
PLEASE ENTER THE NEXT NUMBER    11
PLEASE ENTER THE NEXT NUMBER   999
THE AVERAGE OF THE NUMBERS IS      7.00
```

(b)

Figure 6-13   Ada program and sample output. (a) Comments begin with a double hyphen. Ada requires that each variable be declared before the logic begins. NEW_LINE displays a blank line, and PUT_LINE displays data on the screen. The symbol /= means is not equal to. (b) This screen display shows the interaction between program and user.

```
// C++ PROGRAM
// AVERAGING INTEGERS ENTERED THROUGH THE KEYBOARD

#include <iostream.h>
main ()
{
  float average;
  int number, counter = 0; int sum = 0;
  cout << "THIS PROGRAM WILL FIND THE AVERAGE OF INTEGERS YOU ENTER \ n";
  cout << "THROUGH THE KEYBOARD.  TYPE 999 TO INDICATE END OF DATA. \ n \ n";
  cout << "PLEASE ENTER A NUMBER";
  cin >> number;
  while (number !=999)
    {
      sum := sum + number;
      counter ++;
      cout << "\nPLEASE ENTER THE NEXT NUMBER";
      cin >> number;
    }
  average = sum / counter;
  cout << "\nTHE AVERAGE OF THE NUMBERS IS " << average
}
```

(a)

```
THIS PROGRAM WILL FIND THE AVERAGE OF INTEGERS YOU ENTER
THROUGH THE KEYBOARD.  TYPE 999 TO INDICATE END OF DATA.
PLEASE ENTER A NUMBER    6
PLEASE ENTER THE NEXT NUMBER     4
PLEASE ENTER THE NEXT NUMBER     11
PLEASE ENTER THE NEXT NUMBER    999
THE AVERAGE OF THE NUMBERS IS     7.00
```

(b)

Figure 6-14   C++ program and sample output. (a) The symbol ≠≠ marks comment lines. All variable names, such as number, must be declared. The command cout sends output to the screen and cin takes data from the user. (b) This screen display shows the interaction between program and user. The program was written in Turbo C++.

cupy their privileged positions for no reason other than they got there first or they were backed by powerful organizations. But other languages, though not as popular as the most common ones, have still managed to flourish. You are apt to see these mentioned, and it is important to know about them. Notice that many of them are special-purpose languages, a fact that helps to account for their more limited use. Here, in alphabetical order, are some other noteworthy languages.

ALGOL   Standing for ALGOrithmic Language, **ALGOL** was introduced in 1960. Though popular in Europe, it has never really caught on in the

United States. ALGOL was developed primarily for scientific programming and is considered the forerunner of PL/I and Pascal.

APL Introduced by IBM in 1968, **APL**—short for *A Programming Language*—was conceived by Kenneth Iverson. APL is powerful, interactive, and particularly suited to table handling—that is, to processing groups of related numbers in a table. APL has a score of funny symbols, and that is one reason you would have trouble running the language on your home computer—it uses many symbols that are not part of the familiar ASCII character set. Some of these symbols represent very powerful operations. To perform all these operations, the APL compiler must be rather large, so it is apt to be available only on systems with huge memories, such as mainframes.

FORTH Released by Charles Moore in 1975, **FORTH** was designed for real-time control tasks (such as guiding astronomical telescopes) as well as assorted business and graphics programs. But it was also designed to make the best possible use of computer memory and speed. Thus, FORTH is an excellent language for personal computers; a typical FORTH program runs much faster and uses much less memory than an equivalent BASIC program. Today FORTH is available on almost every kind of computer, from micros to mainframes. FORTH requires little computer memory, but only skilled programmers can use it properly.

LISP Developed in 1958 at the Massachusetts Institute of Technology by John McCarthy, **LISP**—short for list processing—is designed to process nonnumeric data—that is, symbols, such as characters or words. LISP can be used interactively at a terminal. It is a popular language for writing programs dealing with artificial intelligence.

LOGO If you overhear a couple of programmers (or even schoolteachers) using the word *turtle* in conversation, it is a fair guess they are talking about **LOGO.** A dialect of LISP and developed at the Massachusetts Institute of Technology by Seymour Papert, LOGO became popular as a language that even children can use. The original LOGO turtle was a mechanical drawing device that rolled about the floor. It was built to look like a turtle—to the delight of young children—and it had a drawing pen attached. The "turtle" on the computer screen is actually a triangular pointer that responds to a few simple commands such as FORWARD and LEFT. The language is interactive, which means that a person can learn to use LOGO through dialogue sessions with the computer. Figure 6-15 gives an example of LOGO program design.

Modula-2 Pascal programmers have no trouble recognizing **Modula-2** because the two languages look almost identical. Perhaps this should not be surprising, since both languages were invented by Niklaus Wirth. Pascal was intended to be a teaching language, a task it performs very well. But Modula-2 shines where Pascal does not—it is specifically designed to write systems software.

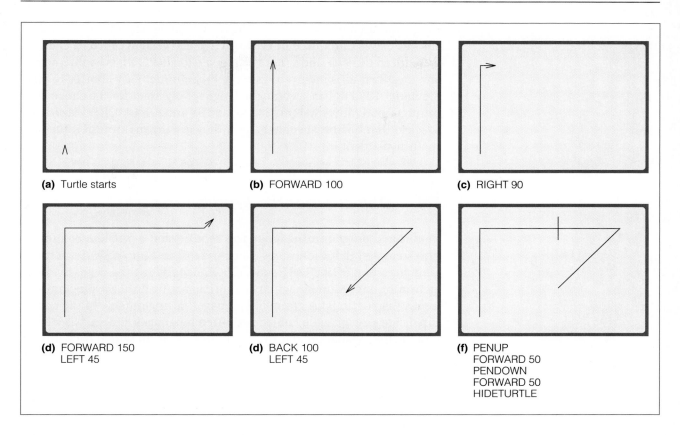

(a) Turtle starts

(b) FORWARD 100

(c) RIGHT 90

(d) FORWARD 150
LEFT 45

(d) BACK 100
LEFT 45

(f) PENUP
FORWARD 50
PENDOWN
FORWARD 50
HIDETURTLE

Figure 6-15 LOGO logic. The "turtle," or triangular pointer, can be moved with a simple sequence of LOGO commands. FORWARD moves the turtle in the direction the apex is facing; BACK moves the turtle backward. The number following a LOGO command indicates the length of the line to be drawn. RIGHT and LEFT followed by a number indicates the direction and the number of degrees the turtle is to be rotated. PENUP and PENDOWN raise and lower the "pen"—the turtle leaves a trace when it moves with the pen down. HIDETURTLE causes the turtle to disappear from the screen.

PILOT   Invented in 1973, **PILOT** was originally designed to introduce children to computers. PILOT is now most often used to write computer-aided instruction in all subjects. It is especially suited for such instructional tasks as drills and tests. PILOT is not a good choice for complex computational problems.

PL/I   Introduced in 1964, **PL/I**—for Programming Language One—was sponsored by IBM. It was designed as a compromise for both scientific and business use. PL/I is quite flexible; in fact, it is easy to learn the rudiments by studying examples. However, being all things to all people, some critics claim, makes the language so loaded down with options that it loses some of its usefulness.

PROLOG   Probably the most popular of a short list of artificial-intelligence programming languages, **PROLOG** (PROgramming in LOGic) received attention as a tool for natural-language programming. It was invented in 1972 by Alan Colmerauer at the University of Marseilles, but it did not attract widespread attention until 1979, after a more efficient version was introduced. PROLOG was selected by the Japanese as the official language of their fifth-generation computer project.

RPG   The problem-oriented language **RPG**—for Report Program Generator—was designed to solve the particular problem of producing business reports. It is also capable of doing some file updating. Developed at

IBM—and used today almost exclusively by IBM AS/400 minicomputers—RPG was introduced in 1964. An updated version called RPG II was introduced in 1970, and a more recent version, RPG III, is an interactive language that uses menus to give the programmer easy choices to plan programs. RPG III has become the language of choice for the entire IBM minicomputer line (Systems 34, 36, and 38 and AS/400). RPG is so easy to learn that businesspeople believe they get the maximum return on their investment.

 Object-Oriented Programming

Traditional programming languages require that a problem be broken into steps and that these steps then be translated into code. Structured languages like FORTRAN and COBOL usually involve a passive programming environment, with nothing happening until the programmer issues instructions. A group of languages falling outside of the structured category are called **object-oriented languages** and are based on a more active, visual programming environment, in which background **messages** continually convey instructions. Structured languages treat data and tasks (instructions) separately; object-oriented languages view data and tasks together for each object. **Objects** are software entities that contain their own programming code. Because of this independence, objects are easy to revise. Objects that share a common structure and behavior may be grouped in **classes.** (Read more about objects in the "What's an Object?" essay in this chapter.) Corporations that require large teams to build huge programs find object-oriented languages appealing, especially when it comes to updating or maintaining programs; in the past, such tasks could be involved and costly. The use of objects speeds up productivity and cuts down on program maintenance.

Current examples of object-oriented programming languages include: Smalltalk, C++, and Object-oriented Pascal, as well as some more popular and more visually enhanced hybrids like HyperCard and Toolbook. There are also visual programming languages, such as Visual Basic and ObjectVision.

Smalltalk   Object-oriented languages arrived with **Smalltalk,** a dramatic departure from traditional computer science because it supports an especially visual system. Invented in 1970 by Alan Kay at the Palo Alto Research Center in California and developed by Xerox Corporation, Smalltalk works by using a keyboard to enter text, but all other interaction takes place through a mouse and icons.

C++   The object-oriented version of **C++** is a superset of the programming language C. As early as 1980, the first versions of C++ were called C with Classes. The object-oriented version of C is not only more portable but also more easily maintained. Versions of C++ are available for large systems and personal computers.

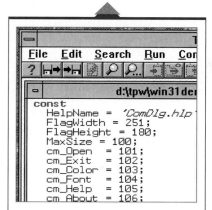

What's an Object?

You hold an object in your hand. It is small and round. You throw it and someone uses a bat to hit it. Your object carries with it all our knowledge of what we mean by *baseball*. There are many other kinds of balls—softballs, beach balls, soccer balls, and the like. We need only change certain features of our baseball to magically convert it into one of those other types of balls. The object we call *ball* has the potential to become any of them.

Software objects are like that. Each contains its own code, or description, of what exactly it is or does. On a Macintosh personal computer, for example, you can use electronic objects called file folders to hold electronic documents you pound out on your word processor, just as you might in the physical world. But you can also use those objects to hold data files from your database program.

In business, an object-oriented computer system might have objects called employees, which would include data about each worker in the company, as well as the programming needed to calculate salary, raises, vacation pay, and payroll deductions. Because an object is "intelligent," it knows when it is called by the computer, perhaps to update the record of an employee's number of dependents or to issue a payroll check.

Objects are important to modern programming because they can be reused in different programs. The object in an electronic mail system that alphabetizes messages can also be used in a billing program to alphabetize invoices. This means that programs can be built quickly from prefabricated—and already tested—pieces by changing certain features. Later, programs can be updated by simply adding new objects.

Object-Oriented Pascal   The object-oriented version of Pascal has the capability of defining data and its operation on that data (procedures and functions) as objects. As you have read, objects are entities that can be swapped in and out when it comes to changing the program at a later time. A popular version of object-oriented Pascal is Borland's Turbo Pascal.

Hybrids   **Hybrid object-based programming languages** are visual like object-oriented languages, but the hybrids lack certain features of their object-oriented cousins. The *hybrids* are called object-*based* languages because they do not offer, among other things, classes. The first hybrid to receive wide attention was **HyperCard** on the Macintosh, which allows users to point and click their way into program development. HyperCard uses **stacks,** index card–like screens that utilize a limited set of objects and offer "scripting" capabilities to carry out instructions. An object can hold both text and graphics. Scripts with each object control the flow of the program. HyperCard caused quite a stir when nonprogrammers suddenly found they could use it to create their own programs, including graphics, sound, and animation. HyperCard was followed by SuperCard (from Aldus), which added full-color pictures to HyperCard-like capabilities, and Plus (Spinnaker), which mimicked HyperCard but could run on IBM personal computers. The first HyperCard work-alike programs designed for IBM personal computers included HyperPad (Brightbill-Roberts & Co.) and LinkWay (IBM). They were followed by others, including the popular Toolbook (Asymetrix).

Recently, object-based versions of BASIC have been suggested. Some consider Visual Basic from Microsoft one of the first such languages. Others call it another type of hybrid object-based language classified as a **visual programming language.** Figure 6-16 illustrates the graphical programming environment of Visual Basic. Most visual programming languages are distinguished by their ability to build programs by connecting links between various objects. In such languages, scripting is unnecessary. One of the popular visual programming languages, ObjectVision (Borland), has no scripting language. You "program" in ObjectVision by connecting icons and using diagrams to control the logic.

Some Advice

If you plan to become an application programmer, there is a good chance that you will take your first steps in BASIC or Pascal, then receive more formal training in a business-oriented language—possibly COBOL. Perhaps you will be able to add another language such as C++. Many new programmers go into the job world with these language tools. But notice something: All these are third-generation languages.

This chapter has addressed the direction of language use. It seems clear that fourth-generation languages are not just the wave of the future, they are here now. But they are offered at only a few schools. Why is this? There are several reasons. No 4GL has emerged as number one, the way COBOL

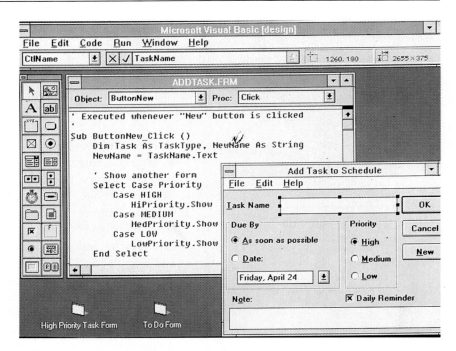

Figure 6-16   A visual programming environment. This screen shows the graphical programming environment of Visual Basic from Microsoft. Compare this to the command line environment of regular BASIC in Figure 6-11. In Visual Basic, you use a mouse or other device to manipulate icons and pull-down menus to build or run programs.

did for business. Could a school dare to turn out 4GL programmers without a clear signal from the community of local employers? (The schools that have replaced their COBOL course with a 4GL class are almost all in large urban environments where, presumably, some of everything is needed.) Other obstacles—lack of a 4GL compiler or the money for one, the need for teacher training, and the difficulty of fitting a 4GL into the existing curriculum—can be overcome once the big question is answered: Which 4GL?

Meanwhile, where does this leave you? Your training in third-generation languages is valuable because it teaches you to think analytically and gives you skills in languages that are still in demand. But you must be alert for opportunities on the job to learn a 4GL. Most people who program in 4GLs learned to do so from employer-sponsored classes. Be ready to take the opportunity when it comes your way.

 ## Is Programming for You?

In this chapter you have seen just an overview of the programming process. The is-this-for-me question can be answered only after you have given programming a try. There are many stories—and books—about early personal computer programmers who gave programming an aura of individualism. Many of those early pioneers are now leaders in the field of computer engineering, entrepreneurs whose early efforts have evolved into huge corporations (see Appendix B); others believe in programming as a way of life.

Personal Computers in Action

THE FIRST HACKERS

The first "hackers" were students at the Massachusetts Institute of Technology (MIT) who belonged to the TMRC (Tech Model Railroad Club). Some of the members really built model trains, but many were more interested in the wires and circuits underneath the track platform. Spending hours at TMRC creating better circuitry was called "a mere hack." Those members who were interested in creating innovative, stylistic, and technically clever circuits called themselves (with pride) *hackers.*

During the spring of 1959, a new course was offered at MIT, a freshman programming class. Soon the hackers of the railroad club were spending days, hours, and nights hacking away at their computer, an IBM 704. Instead of creating a better circuit, their hack became creating a faster, more efficient program—with the least number of lines of code. Eventually they formed a group and created the first set of hacker's rules, called the Hacker's Ethic.

Steven Levy, in his book *Hackers,* presented the rules:

Rule 1: Access to computers— and anything which might teach you something about the way the world works—should be unlimited and total.

Rule 2: All information should be free.

Rule 3: Mistrust authority— promote decentralization.

Rule 4: Hackers should be judged by their hacking, not bogus criteria such as degrees, race, or position.

Rule 5: You can create art and beauty on a computer.

Rule 6: Computers can change your life for the better.

These rules made programming at MIT's Artificial Intelligence Laboratory a challenging, all-encompassing endeavor. Just for the exhilaration of programming, students in the AI Lab would write a new program to perform even the smallest tasks. The program would be made available to others who would try to perform the same task with fewer instructions. The act of making the computer work more elegantly was, to a bonafide hacker, awe-inspiring.

Hackers were given free reign on the computer by two AI Lab professors, "Uncle" John McCarthy and Marvin Minsky, who realized that hacking created new insights. Over the years, the AI Lab created many innovations: Life, a game about survival; LISP, a new kind of programming language; the first computer chess game; The Cave, the first computer adventure; and Spacewar, the first video game.

The essential power of any computer is found in its operating system, and those who program operating systems are likely to be held in great esteem by programmers in general. In the next chapter we describe operating systems, the programs that allow computers to control resources, execute programs, and manage data.

R E V I E W A N D R E F E R E N C E

Summary and Key Terms

- A **programming language** is a set of rules for instructing the computer what operations to perform. A programming language has a limited vocabulary, has a precise meaning for each word, and can be used to solve complex problems in a step-by-step manner.

- A programmer converts solutions to the user's problems into instructions for the computer. These instructions are called a **program.** Writing a program involves defining the problem, planning the solution, coding the program, testing the program, and documenting the program.

- Defining the problem means discussing it with the users or a systems analyst to determine the necessary input, processing, and output.

- Planning can be done by using a **flowchart** or **structure chart,** which are pictorial representations of the step-by-step solution, and by using **pseudocode,** which is an English-like outline of the solution.
- Coding the program means expressing the solution in a programming language.
- Testing the program consists of desk-checking, translating, and debugging. The rules of a programming language are referred to as its **syntax. Desk-checking** is a mental checking or proofreading of the program before it is run. In translating, a **translator** program converts the program into a form the computer can understand and in the process detects programming language errors, which are called **syntax errors.** Two types of translators are **compilers,** which translate the entire program at one time and give all the error messages (**diagnostics**) at once, and **interpreters,** which translate the program one line at a time. The original program, called a **source module,** is translated to an **object module,** to which prewritten programs may be added during the **link/load phase** to create an executable **load module. Debugging** is running the program to detect, locate, and correct mistakes—**logic errors.**
- Typical **documentation** contains a detailed written description of the programming cycle and the program along with the test results and a printout of the program.
- Programming languages are described as being "lower" or "higher," depending on how close they are to the language the computer itself uses (0s and 1s—low) or to the language people use (more English-like—high). There are five main levels, or generations, of languages: (1) machine language, (2) assembly language, (3) high-level language, (4) very high-level language, and (5) natural language. All are considered to be traditional programming languages, using **structured programming**—a technique for organizing and coding programs.
- **Machine language,** the lowest level, represents data as 1s and 0s—binary digits corresponding to the "on" and "off" electrical states in the computer.
- **Assembly languages** use letters as mnemonic codes to replace the 0s and 1s of machine language. An **assembler program** is used to translate the assembly language into machine language. Although assembly languages provide great flexibility in tapping a computer's capabilities, they have disadvantages. For instance, assembly languages vary according to the type of computer and are extremely detailed.
- **High-level languages** are written in an English-like manner. Each high-level language requires a different compiler, or translator program, for each type of computer on which it is run.
- **Very high-level languages,** also called **fourth-generation languages (4GLs),** are basically nonprocedural. A **nonprocedural language** defines only *what* the computer should do, without detailing the procedure. A **procedural language** tells the computer specifically *how* to do the task.
- Although fourth-generation languages still require further standardization, they have a number of clear benefits, including primary emphasis on results (*what*) rather than procedure (*how*); improved productivity, and less training for both programmers and users.
- Fifth-generation languages are often called **natural languages** because they resemble "natural" human language.
- A system that uses a natural language to access a knowledge base is called a **knowledge-based system.** One type of knowledge-based system, the **expert system,** offers the computer as an expert on some topic.
- Knowledge-based systems are closely related to **artificial intelligence,** with its emphasis on easy interaction between users and computers. However, natural languages are not yet able to handle complicated logic.
- Some programs **query by example (QBE),** or model new queries on past ones, without your having to write the new query from scratch. A **structured query language (SQL)** is a standard interface that allows access to data on all systems.
- The first high-level language, **FORTRAN** (FORmula TRANslator), is a scientifically oriented language that was introduced by IBM in 1954. Its brevity makes it suitable for executing complex formulas.
- **COBOL** (COmmon Business-Oriented Language) was introduced in 1959 by **CODASYL** (COnference of DAta SYstem Languages) as a standard programming language for business. The American National Standards Institute (ANSI) standardized COBOL in 1968, again in 1974 (in a version called **ANSI-COBOL),** and more recently in a version known as **COBOL 85.** Since COBOL is English-like, it is useful for processing business data such as street addresses and purchased items, but the wordiness of COBOL programs means a sacrifice of speed and simplicity.
- A COBOL program has four divisions: identification, environment, data, and procedure.
- When **BASIC** (Beginners' All-purpose Symbolic Instruction Code) was developed at Dartmouth and introduced in 1965, it was intended for instruction. Now its uses include business and personal computer applications.
- **Pascal,** named for the French mathematician Blaise Pascal, first became available in 1971. It is popular in college computer courses.
- **Ada,** named for Countess Ada Lovelace, was introduced in 1980 as a standard language for weapons systems. Although it also has commercial uses, experts disagree regarding how easy it is to learn.
- Invented at Bell Labs, **C** offers high-level language features such as structured programming. C code is almost

as efficient as assembly language, and it is suitable for writing "portable" programs that can run on more than one type of computer.

- Other important languages include **ALGOL,** popular in Europe for scientific programming; **APL,** used for processing related numbers in tables; **FORTH,** known for its very efficient use of computer memory and speed; **LISP,** used for nonnumeric data processing and artificial intelligence programs; **LOGO,** designed as an interactive language that children can use; **Modula-2,** a Pascal look-alike designed for writing systems software; **PILOT,** used for computer-aided instruction; **PL/I,** designed for scientific and business uses; **PROLOG,** popular for natural language programming; and **RPG** (for Report Program Generator), a problem-oriented language for producing business reports.

- **Object-oriented languages** fall outside the category of structure programming languages and allow programmers to create **objects, messages,** and **classes.** Code reuse and ease of program modifications are the chief advantages of an object-oriented language.

- Popular object-oriented languages include **Smalltalk, Turbo Pascal,** and **C++.**

- **Hybrid object-based programming languages** such as **HyperCard** and Toolbook have placed the ability to develop relatively sophisticated software programs into the hands of nonprogrammers. HyperCard uses **stacks,** index card–like screens that employ objects to carry out instructions. Some hybrids, such as **Visual Basic** and **ObjectVision,** are classified as **visual programming languages.**

Review Questions

1. Name the five steps in the programming process.
2. Describe the two common ways of planning a program, and discuss their advantages and disadvantages.
3. Describe the phases in testing a program.
4. Why is documentation important?
5. In general, how do programming languages differ from human languages?
6. What do *high* and *low* mean in reference to programming languages?
7. Explain how the following types of languages differ: machine language, assembly language, and high-level language.
8. Explain why fourth-generation languages represent increased productivity when compared to third-generation languages.
9. Discuss the advantages and limitations of natural languages.
10. How does COBOL differ from FORTRAN and BASIC?
11. How are BASIC and Pascal similar? How do they differ?
12. Discuss the appropriate and inappropriate uses of each of the following languages: FORTRAN, COBOL, and Pascal.

13. Discuss the advantages of the C language.
14. Briefly identify the uses of each of the following languages: ALGOL, LISP, PROLOG, PL/I, APL, LOGO, PILOT, FORTH, Modula-2, and RPG.
15. Describe the main difference between an object-oriented programming language and a structured programming language.

Discussion Questions

1. Should students taking a computer literacy course be required to learn some programming? Why?
2. Do you think you might like to become a computer programmer or some other computer professional?
3. In your opinion what kind of person makes a good programmer? Discuss specific characteristics and explain why they are important.
4. Discuss the advantages of standardizing a programming language.
5. Discuss why a particular language stays in use or goes out of use.
6. Do you think there will be less demand for programmers as languages become easier to use? Explain.
7. Consider the six program examples (Figures 6-9 through Figure 6-14) that find the average of three integers. How would you change the programs to find the sum of only two integers?
8. Why do you think object-oriented programming languages were developed? What types of needs do they fulfill that are not met by other kinds of programming languages?

True-False Questions

T F   1. Flowcharts and structure charts perform the same task.

T F   2. A programmer chooses a language solely on the basis of its ease of use.

T F   3. Programs are written correctly the first time.

T F   4. A compiler and interpreter perform the task of translating a program into a form the computer can understand.

T F   5. Fourth-generation languages are slower and more cumbersome than third-generation languages.

T F   6. Documentation is the part of a software program that is printed.

T F   7. Debugging is one process of locating program errors.

T F   8. All languages can perform text manipulation easily.

T F   9. High-level languages are closer to the English language than low-level languages.

T F   10. There is only one way to solve a programming problem.

Computers Around Us

In this gallery, we will look at how computers are used in a variety of settings. In the photo shown here, a head-mounted display enables the user to interact with the computer in the world of virtual—artificial—reality.

Science

(1) This large tablet appears to be a drawing board, but it is actually an oversized digitizer attached to a computer. With a handheld device, a user can scan whatever is on the tablet—in this case a map—and press a button to input the image as data.
(2) These astrophysicists use a multimedia approach to viewing the galaxies, projecting the digitized computer vision onto a nearby screen.
(3) Researchers use supercomputer graphics to simulate the formation and evolution of a galaxy over its lifetime. This "landscape" plots the density of the interstellar matter.

1

2

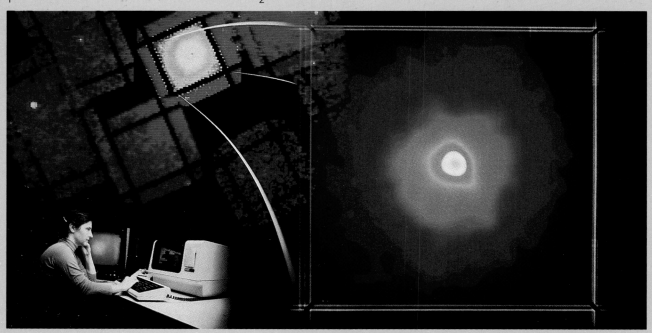

3

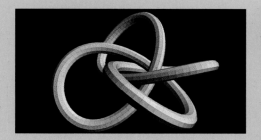

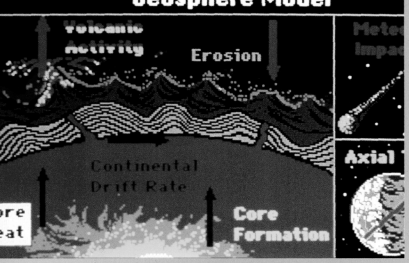

(4) Knot theory, a branch of pure mathematics, has recently been applied in such diverse areas as molecular biology and theoretical physics. This torus knot can be produced quite easily using special graphics software. **(5)** Computer scientists who work for oil-exploration companies feed topographical data into computers to analyze the possibility of finding an oil reservoir. **(6)** Computers under water? What next! In this case, a scientist puts a "wet suit" on his laptop computer to record his underwater explorations for the National Geographic Society. **(7)** This colorful software lets users model geologic influences, such as volcanic eruptions, on the Earth's surface. **(8)** Chemists and molecular biologists are aided in the laboratory by computers that can create 3-D models of complex chemical structures.

Health and Medicine

9

(9) This computer-enhanced image of an ultrasound test shows the baby quite clearly. (10) Medical students use this "electric cadaver" for computerized anatomy lessons. The system includes a laser disc of images and a Macintosh computer. Using the mouse attached to the computer, a student can point to a part of the body, press the mouse button, and obtain detailed information about that part.

10

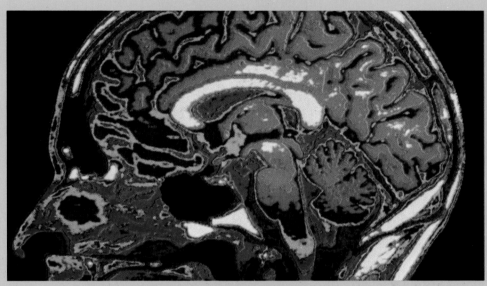

11

12

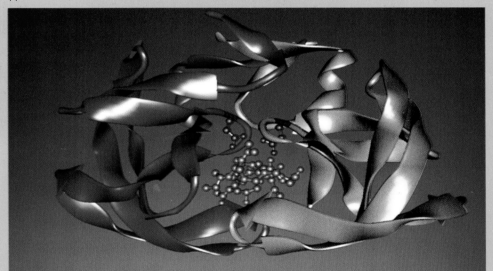

13

(11) Doctors use PET (positron emission tomography) diagnostic images of the brain to look for indications of abnormal activity. **(12)** This computer-produced image shows how a human antibody (red) attaches to a common cold virus (blue). **(13)** This free-flowing illustration is actually a sophisticated computer model of the AIDS-related human immunodeficiency virus (HIV). Such models are helping researchers understand how the virus interacts with the body's immune system—and to speed their search for a cure.

Sports and Games

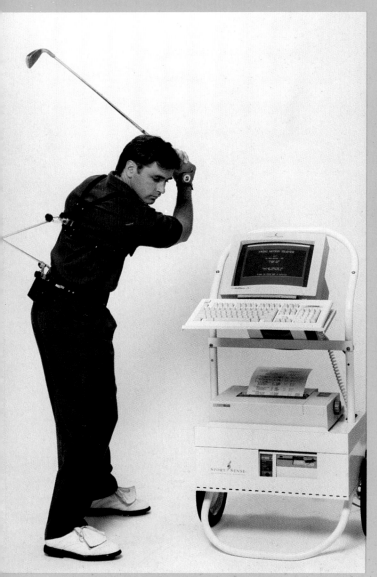

14

File Game Options Scores Help

pring Fire (April) Evening Star
and Score   0   Hand 2   Deal 12   Game Score   5,000

15

16

(14) Does your golf game need improvement? Try this on for size: In this demonstration, a golfer is fitted with a device that is wired to a computer to record and analyze the body motions of his golf swing. **(15)** There are computer games to satisfy all interests. This sophisticated imagery is from a computer game called "Heaven and Earth". **(16)** The Mario Brothers continue their adventures in the latest version of the popular computer game developed by Nintendo.

17

(17) Track athletes in training use starting blocks hooked to computers to measure the force of their getaway. **(18)** Playing virtual reality racquetball: Special goggles block out a player's view of the real world and replace it with a computer-generated view of a racquetball court, a ball, and a racket. The player moves around an empty room, smashing an imaginary ball. **(19)** Cross-country skiers in training for the Olympics wear computerized devices that record data from the soles of their feet. Computer graphical analysis helps skiers improve their performance.

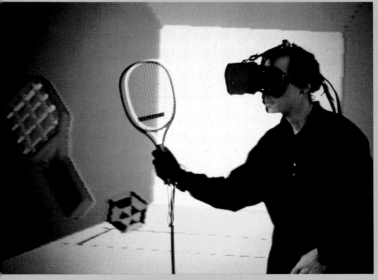

18

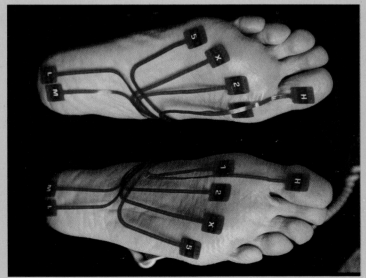

19

Entertainment

20

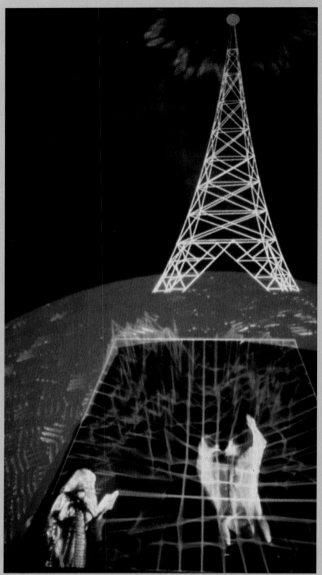

21

(20) The Coca-Cola Company put computers to work in kiosks that function as interactive television sets. Visitors can touch the screen to follow world events that match the evolution of Coca-Cola.
(21) This scene is from a 45-minute performance artwork called "Invisible Site," which features a mixture of computer animation with live action, light, music, and magic. Viewers in the audience must wear 3-D glasses.

22

23

24

(22) Computer animation was used to create the opening and closing animated screens for MTV's *Liquid Television*. **(23)** This special-effects scene from the movie *Terminator 2* was not a real fire at all, but the output of a computer program. **(24)** The astonishing special effects in the movie *Death Becomes Her*, including the stretching of actress Meryl Streep, were achieved frame by frame with the help of a computer. **(25)** The rock band U2 enhances its performance by using computer-controlled lighting. Even the suspended cars are carefully controlled by computers.

25

Music

26

(26) Using an electronic glove, Todd Machover—a musician, computer scientist, and professor at MIT—conducts computer-generated music in conjunction with live musicians. **(27)** Dartmouth music students use personal computers to study notation in an electronic music studio. All Dartmouth students take a "computer survival skills" course when they first arrive on campus.

27

Service

28

29

30

(28) At this sports store, a customer accesses product information with the help of a user-friendly computer system. This is equivalent to being able to go directly to a particular page in a printed catalog. **(29)** Ready for a "makeover"? You can experiment directly by placing a variety of products on your skin and checking the effect in the mirror. Or, you can save yourself the trouble by having a computerized makeover. First your face is photographed. Then the photograph is digitized for the computer and displayed on the screen. From that point it is a straightforward matter for the makeup artist to use the computer to simulate makeup. In this case, the artist has chosen a blush color, which he "applies" by using a mouse-like pen. **(30)** Many mechanics have a computer helper nearby. This mechanic uses database software to pull information about a particular problem—and its solution—up on the screen. **(31)** By pressing just a few buttons that activate a computer-controlled system, customers can see sample music videos right in the store.

31

Computer Art

(32) This "string art" image is generated by combining curved lines representing mathematical equations. **(33)** The computer artist who developed this colorful image gave it the fanciful title *Memories of Home*.

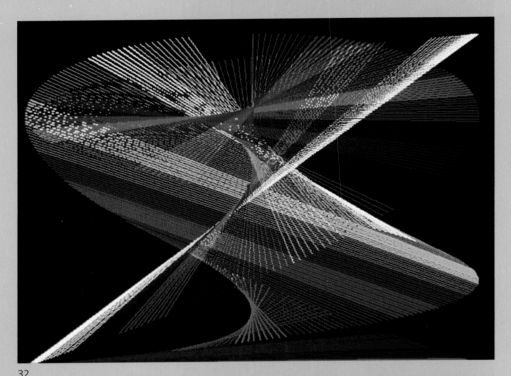

32

33

(34) This fractal art image is based on the principle of self-similarity—in other words, the large form is composed of smaller, similar shapes. This repetitive approach is particularly suited to computer art. **(35)** This spectacular work looks more like a photograph than art, but it was generated entirely on the computer.

34

35

More Computer Art

(36) A water strider photographed gliding over a rocky streambed? No, another example of realistic computer artwork. **(37)** Computer graphics can store images of real-life art, as shown here. This capability is useful for museum curators, who can easily summon to the computer screen electronic versions of any work in their collections. Furthermore, educators can use computers to choose and organize images for lectures; the selected images can be projected directly onto classroom display screens. **(38, 39, 40)** These three images, by computer artist Gregory MacNichol, demonstrate both his artistic and computer skills in portraying color, form, and dimension.

36

37

38

39

40

Photography

41

43

42

(41) To create the eye-catching graphic at top left for his business card, the artist used the computer to superimpose a digitized photo of Earth over a separate photo, also digitized, of a man in a chair. **(42, and 42 inset)** This photo of several past and present San Francisco 49ers, a team that has won four National Football League Super Bowls, owes much of its drama to the computer's sleight of hand. The trophies themselves (inset) are just 2 feet tall. Computer technicians used a digitizer to convert the original trophy photo to computer-usable form. Shots of the players were also digitized and then superimposed, via computer, on the original photo. **(43)** Just butterflies? Look again. A computer artist has superimposed faces on digitized photographs of real butterflies.

7

Operating Systems
The Hidden Software

  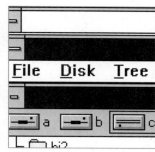 

Sam Adelson fell in love with his first personal computer from the moment it was set up on his desk. His office cubicle took on a new appeal. Here was something worth learning, to help ease the monthly pressure of repetitious forms, tracking, and project analyses that were part of his job at East Coast Pump Company. But the romance was short-lived. Within a few weeks, Sam grew tired of switching from one program to another and spending hours learning the new commands of the latest power-packed program from his boss (a technology freak, as far as Sam was concerned). Every time Sam got used to one program, his boss would find a new one to "help speed things up."

For Sam, the problem disappeared only after his boss presented him with a new program called Windows. This new package saved him from memorizing all the computer commands—Windows let him use a mouse for selecting commands from a menu. From then on, Sam began to relax, knowing each new program from the boss would, for all intents and purposes, work the same way as the last one. Sam even started looking forward to the latest "power packs." He began to wonder if the boss's excitement wasn't rubbing off on him.

Although Sam did not know it, his was a love-hate relationship with **operating systems,** programs that control and manage a computer's resources. In this chapter, we will examine the basic functions of operating systems. We will present the rationale for operating systems and give some idea of how they work. Many operating systems concepts apply mainly to large, multiuser computers, and we will begin there. Then we will turn to a detailed discussion of the ongoing changes in operating systems for personal computers.

Operating Systems: The Wizard of Oz

Inside every computer—like an ever-vigilant wizard of Oz behind the curtain—lies a hidden world of software called the operating system. Consisting of a set of programs that control all computer functions, the operating system is always available but out of view. This hidden software commands the computer's resources, executes its programs, and manages its memory and data.

An operating system allows the computer system to manage its own resources. Those resources include the central processing unit, memory, secondary storage devices, and various input/output devices like printers. In a broader sense, resources also include data, programs, and people. Figure 7-1 gives a conceptual picture of operating system soft-

Figure 7-1 A conceptual diagram of an operating system. Closest to the user are applications programs—software that helps a user compute a payroll or play a game or calculate the trajectory of a rocket. The operating system is the set of programs between the applications programs and the hardware.

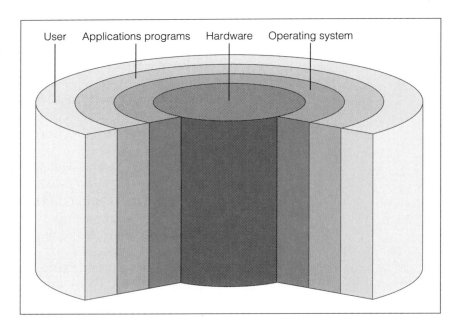

ware as a cushion between the hardware and applications programs, such as a word processing program on a personal computer or a payroll program on a mainframe. In other words, whether or not you are aware of it, using any software application requires that you invoke—call into action—the operating system as well. Whether you are a user of software or a programmer, you will come to appreciate the fact that the operating system takes care of many chores automatically.

Let us pause briefly to trace the beginnings of operating systems and imagine what computer use was like without them. Consider the pre-1960s days of computing, when the primary goal was to get a computer that was bigger and faster. In those days a computer system executed only one program at a time. (This may not seem peculiar in the context of a personal computer, but remember that we are now talking about big, expensive computers.) This meant that all the system's resources—the central processing unit; all the memory and secondary storage at hand; and all peripheral devices, such as printers—were available on demand for that one program. However, it also meant that these components were idle most of the time; while a record was being read from tape, for instance, the central processing unit and printer were inactive.

Time was also wasted while the system waited for the computer operator to finish tasks: to set up tapes, push buttons on the console, and so on. A program came to the end of its run, and the entire system was idle while the operator got the next job ready.

All this was inefficient use of an expensive machine. To improve the efficiency of computer operations, operating systems were introduced in the 1960s.

An operating system, as we have said, is a set of programs. It handles many chores implicitly, without being told to do so by each individual programmer.

An operating system has three main functions:

- To manage the hardware efficiently
- To support applications
- To establish a user interface

The control programs, one part of the operating system, minimize operator intervention in managing the hardware so that the computer operations flow smoothly and without interruption. The most important program in the system is the **supervisor program,** most of which remains in memory. It controls the entire operating system and calls in other operating system programs from disk storage as needed (Figure 7-2). These operating system programs stay in memory while they are executing. But they do not remain in memory all the time; that would be an inefficient use of space. To free up space in memory, the supervisor program releases other operating system programs and hardware when they are not in use, recalling them when they are needed.

The operating system improves efficiency in two ways: (1) It is like a traffic cop, enforcing cooperation among users and helping them make the best use of computer system resources (memory, the central processing

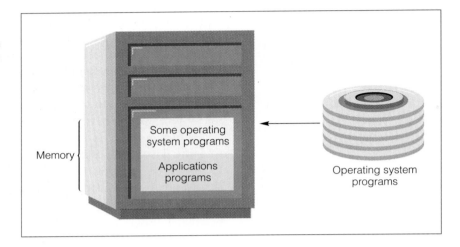

Figure 7-2   Retrieving operating system programs from disk. The supervisor program of the operating system remains in memory and calls in other operating system programs as needed.

unit, peripheral devices, and so on) so that everyone benefits. (2) It is like a subcontractor or specialist, possessing special routines and service utility programs that carry out common tasks related to the hardware, peripherals, and data. This frees applications programmers from time-consuming tasks and lets them concentrate on solving problems for clients. Turning hardware functions over to the operating system also allows it to perform its traffic cop duties better; all of these functions are controlled by the operating system.

Finally, the operating system establishes a way for you to work with the computer. You will learn about several types of operating environments, beginning with the traditional style of typing in commands and moving on to today's more user-friendly styles.

Let us now examine some of the various ways operating systems help in sharing resources.

 ## Sharing Resources

We have noted the inefficiency of running just one program at a time on a big computer and indicated that all that has changed. Indeed it has. Such a computer can now handle many programs at the same time—although we are not saying that the programs necessarily run simultaneously. Before we explain that, let us acknowledge some related questions that often come up when computer users first realize that their applications program is "in there" with all those other programs.

Question: If there are several other programs in memory at the same time as my program, what keeps the programs from getting mixed up with one another?

Answer: The operating system.

Question: And if my program and another program both want to use the central processing unit at the same time, what decides which program gets it?

Answer: The operating system.

Question: But what if one of the other programs gets in an endless loop and won't give up the CPU? Who is going to step in and set things right?

Answer: The operating system.

Question: Well, the printer must be a problem. If we all need it, what prevents our output files from coming out in one big jumble?

Answer: The operating system!

This litany may sound repetitive, but it does make a point: The operating system is programmed to anticipate all these problems so that you, as a user or programmer, can share the computer's resources with minimum concern about the details of how it is done.

We will begin with the basic process of sharing resources, called multiprogramming, then move to a variation called time-sharing.

Multiprogramming

When two or more programs are being executed concurrently on a computer and are sharing the computer's resources, the situation is referred to as **multiprogramming,** or **multitasking.** What this really means is that the programs are taking turns; one program runs for a while, then another one. The key word here is *concurrently* as opposed to *simultaneously.* If there is only one central processing unit, for example (the usual case), it is not physically possible that more than one program use it at the same time—that is, simultaneously. But one program could be using the CPU while another does something else, such as writing a record to the printer. Concurrent processing means that two or more programs are using the central processing unit in the same time frame—during the same hour, for instance—but not at the exact same time. *Concurrent,* in other words, means that one program uses one resource while another program uses another resource. This gives the illusion of simultaneous processing. As a result, there is less idle time for the computer system's resources.

Concurrent processing is effective because CPU speeds are so much faster than input/output speeds. During the time it takes to execute a read instruction for one program, for example, the central processing unit can execute several calculation instructions for another program. If the first program is in memory by itself, however, the CPU is idle during the read time.

We emphasize concurrent processing here because many computers, including personal computers, use concurrent processing today. That is because most computers have only a single CPU. Recall the discussion of parallel processing in Chapter 2 and the "Perspectives" essay in Chapter One regarding the fastest computer sold, the Connection Machine. Parallel processing uses multiple CPUs, a feature that permits *simultaneous* processing.

Multiprogramming is **event-driven.** This means that programs share resources based on events that take place in the programs. Normally, a program is allowed to complete a certain activity (event), such as a calculation, before relinquishing the resource (the central processing unit, in this example) to another program that is waiting for it.

The operating system implements multiprogramming through a system of interrupts. An **interrupt** is a condition that causes normal program processing to be suspended temporarily. This is similar to call waiting on a telephone, a service that alerts you to other calls coming in. For example, suppose you are talking on the phone and suddenly a clicking sound interrupts your conversation; you put the current caller on hold, temporarily switch to the latest phone call, then return to the call that was interrupted. Similarly, your computer may be reading a record when the program is interrupted by the operating system, which takes over to pursue an activity for a second program. The program waiting for the record relinquishes control of the central processing unit; the computer may then proceed to execute calculations in this second program. When it is finished, the second program releases the CPU to return to reading the record for the first program. Thus, although it occurs so quickly that it may go unnoticed, applications are constantly being interrupted as the operating system allocates computer resources among different programs.

In large computer systems, programs that run in an event-driven multiprogramming environment are usually batch programs. Typical examples are programs for payroll, accounts receivable, sales and marketing analysis, financial planning, quality control, and stock reporting.

Time-Sharing

The concurrent use of one machine by several people is called **time-sharing.** Time-sharing, a special case of multiprogramming, is usually **time-driven** rather than event-driven. A common approach is to give each user a **time slice**—typically, a few milliseconds or even microseconds—during which the computer works on a single user's tasks. However, the operating system does not wait for completion of the event; at the end of the time slice, the resources are taken away from that user and given to someone else.

Think of the kindergarten teacher whose students each demand exclusive attention. The first child asks how a shoe is tied. The teacher, who is an adult and therefore very fast at tying shoes, shows her. The child is amazed at the looping and takes time to ponder the knot and try to understand it. Meanwhile the teacher turns to a second child, who asks how to zip a jacket. The teacher is so fast at these things and the young children are so slow, that the teacher can help several children concurrently. The children get instantaneous service and do not notice other children are also being helped.

The operating system in time-sharing environments works like that teacher. Its shifting attention from program to program is hardly noticeable to the user: When you are sitting before a terminal in a time-sharing system, the computer's response time will be quite short—fractions of a second—and it will seem as if you have the computer to yourself. **Response time** is the time between your typed computer request and the computer's reply. Even if you are working on a calculation and the operating system interrupts it, sending you to the end of the line until other users have had their turns, you may not notice that you have been deprived of service. Not all computer systems give ideal service all the time, however; if a computer system is trying to serve too many users at the same time, response time may slow down noticeably.

You should realize that, generally speaking, you as the user do not have control over the computer system. In a time-sharing environment the operating system has actual control because it controls the users by allocating time slices. Giving the users the processor in turns is called **round-robin scheduling;** Figure 7-3 shows this type of operation. However, sometimes a particular user will, for some reason, be entitled to a higher priority than other users. Higher priority translates to faster and better service. A common method of acknowledging higher priority is for the operating system to give that user more turns. Suppose, for example, that there are five users who would normally be given time slices in order: A-B-C-D-E. If user B is assigned a higher priority, the order could be changed to A-B-C-B-D-B-E-B, giving B every other turn.

Typical time-sharing applications are credit checking; point-of-sale systems; engineering design; airline reservation systems; and hospital information systems. Each of these systems has several users who need to share the system resources.

Figure 7-3   Round-robin scheduling.
The computer gives each user a turn.

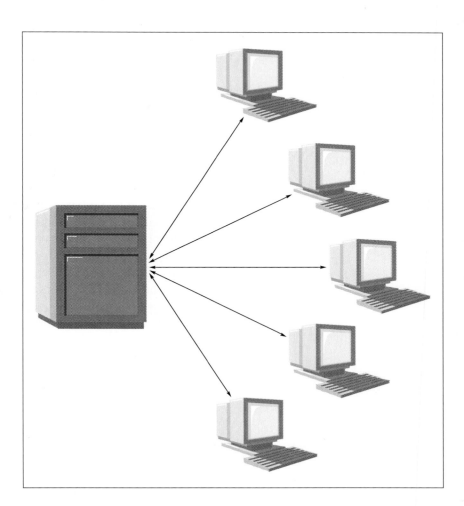

Managing Shared Resources: The Traffic Cop

When several programs share the same computer resources, special problems of control must be considered. Just as a traffic cop controls the flow of vehicles, someone or something must determine which program will be executed next. For example, a given program must be able to access needed devices. Memory space must be available to the program, and that program must be protected from inadvertent interference from other programs. We will now consider how the operating system handles some of these types of problems.

Resource Allocation

How does the operating system fairly allocate various resources of the computer system—such as the central processing unit, memory, secondary storage, and input/output devices—to the various programs as they are needed? **Resource allocation** is the process of assigning resources to certain programs for their use. Those same resources are deallocated—removed—when the program using them is finished, then reallocated elsewhere.

A program waiting to be run by the computer is placed on disk, with other waiting programs. A scheduling program, part of the operating system, selects the next job according to such factors as memory requirements, priority, and devices needed. In other words, the selection is based to some extent on whether available resources can satisfy the needs of the waiting program.

In the course of the resource allocation, the operating system must consider the input/output devices available and their use. For example, at any given moment, the operating system knows which program is using which particular disk drive and knows which devices are free and can be allocated to a program waiting to run. The scheduling program would not allow a job to begin, for example, if it needed three disk drives and only two were currently available.

It is theoretically possible for two programs to need resources during processing that are unavailable to them; each may want a resource held captive by the other. What is more, neither may be willing to give up the resource it is holding until it gets the one the other is holding, a condition known as a **deadlock.** Note the example in Figure 7-4. Most operating systems are able to anticipate and thus prevent deadlocks; others force one of the contenders to back off after the fact.

Memory also needs to be allocated, but this special resource merits its own section.

Memory Management

What if you have a very large program, for which it might be difficult to find space in memory? Or what if several programs are competing for

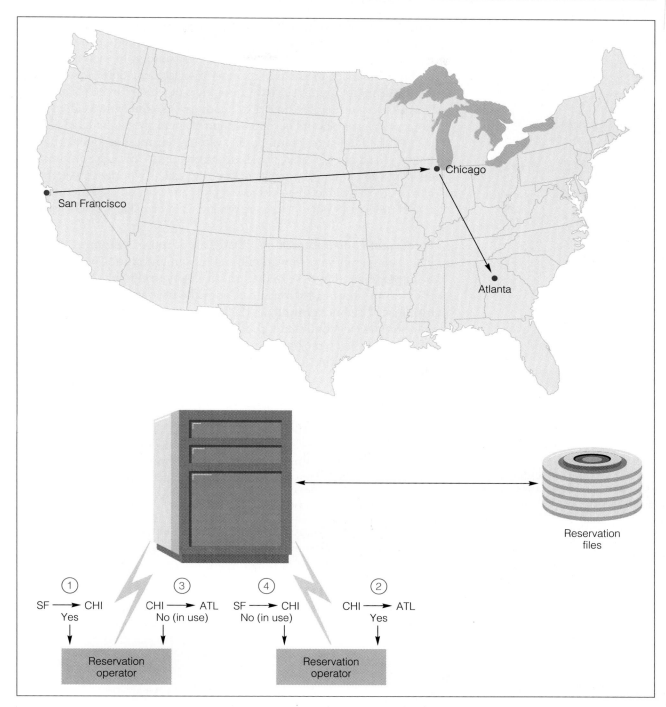

Figure 7-4   A deadlock. Each reservation operator, it just so happens, has a customer who wants to fly from San Francisco to Chicago to Atlanta. When an operator wants to make a reservation for a customer, the flight record must be made temporarily unavailable to other operators, lest one operator wipe out another's updates. In this case, let us suppose that ① one operator takes the record for the San Francisco to Chicago flight, while ② the other operator begins with the Chicago to Atlanta flight. ③ When the first operator tries to get the Chicago–Atlanta segment, it is unavailable because the other operator is using it. If the first operator holds on to the San Francisco–Chicago record while waiting for Chicago–Atlanta, ④ he or she might wait forever because the other operator might not give up Chicago–Atlanta until he or she gets San Francisco–Chicago.

space in memory? These questions are related to memory management. **Memory management** is the process of allocating memory to programs and of keeping the programs in memory separate from each other.

There are many methods of memory management. Some systems simply divide memory into separate areas, each of which can hold a program. The problem is how to know how big the areas, sometimes called partitions or regions, should be; at least one of them should be large enough to hold the largest program. Some systems use memory areas that are not of a fixed size—that is, the sizes can change to meet the needs of the current assortment of programs. In either case—whether the areas are of a fixed or variable size—there is a problem with unused memory between programs. When these are too small to be used, space is wasted.

Foreground and Background   Large all-purpose computers often divide their memory into foreground and background areas. The **foreground** is for programs that have higher priority. A typical foreground program is in a time-sharing environment, with the user at a terminal awaiting response. The **background,** as the name implies, is for programs with less pressing schedules and, thus, lower priorities. Typical background programs are batch programs in a multiprogramming environment. Foreground programs are given privileged status—more turns for the central processing unit and other resources—and background programs take whatever they need that is not currently in use by another program. Programs waiting to run are kept on the disk in **queues** suitable to their job class, as you can see in Figure 7-5.

This discussion has been purposely general, but the principles do apply to many large computers. Another technique is virtual storage, which—as you will see—expands the memory management possibilities.

Virtual Storage   Many computer systems manage memory by using a technique called **virtual storage** (also called **virtual memory**). Virtual storage means that part of the program is stored on disk and is brought

Figure 7-5   Programs waiting in queues. These programs are waiting on disk in queues organized by program class. That is, time-sharing programs (1 through 6) wait in their own queue for a foreground area to open up, and batch programs (A through C) wait in a queue for a background area to be free.

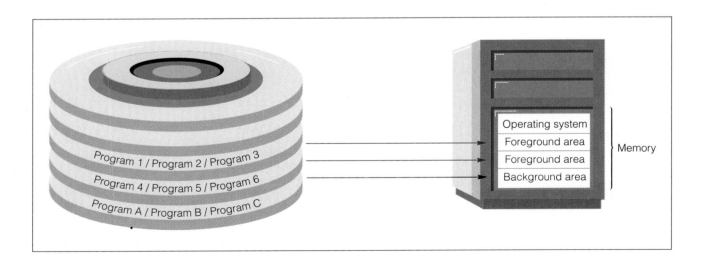

into memory for execution only as needed. (Again, the delay in time may not be noticeable.) The user appears to be using more memory space than is actually the case. Since only part of the program is in memory at any given time, the amount of memory needed for a program is minimized. Memory, in this case, is considered **real storage,** while the secondary storage holding the rest of the program (a disk drive, for example) is considered virtual storage (Figure 7-6). If you remember the virtual reality environment example in Chapter 1, you might recognize that "virtual" objects appear real but are not. For example, the ball we see with our computer-controlled goggles in virtual reality is not physically there. Similarly, virtual storage is not located in memory but on disk.

Virtual storage can be implemented in a variety of ways. Consider the paging method, for example. Suppose you have a very large program, which means there will be difficulty finding space for it in the computer's memory. Remember that memory is shared among several programs. If your program is divided into small pieces, it will be easier to find places to put those pieces. This is essentially what paging does. **Paging** is the process of dividing a program into equal-size pieces called **pages** and storing them in equal-size memory spaces called **page frames.** All pages and page frames are the same fixed size—typically, 2K or 4K bytes. The pages are stored in memory in *noncontiguous* locations—that is, locations not necessarily next to each other.

Even though the pages are not right next to each other in memory, the operating system is able to keep track of them. It does this by using a page table, which lists the number of pages that are part of the program and the beginning addresses of areas in memory where each page has been placed.

Memory Protection   In a multiprogramming environment it is theoretically possible for the computer, while executing one program, to destroy or modify another program by transferring it to the wrong memory locations. That is, without protection, one program might accidentally hop into the middle of another, causing destruction of data and general chaos. To avoid this problem, the operating system confines each pro-

Figure 7-6   Virtual storage. Virtual storage, also known as virtual memory, offers a larger amount of memory than is physically available in your computer by using space on a disk. (a) Virtual memory involves pages of data that can be located with the help of (b) a memory map that references the space on (c) a disk.

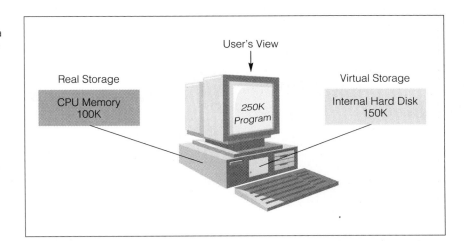

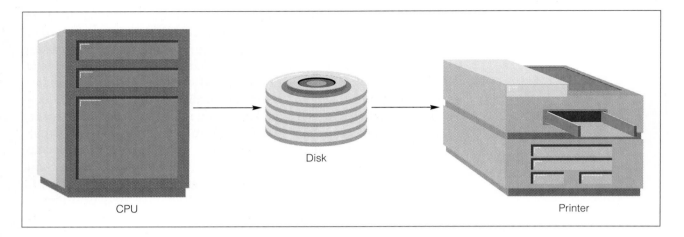

CPU   Disk   Printer

Figure 7-7   Spooling. Program output that is destined for the printer is written first to a disk—spooled—and later transferred to a printer.

gram to certain defined limits in memory. If a program is inadvertently transferred to some memory area outside those limits, the operating system terminates the execution of that program. This process of keeping your program from straying into others' programs and their programs from yours is called **memory protection.**

Spooling

Suppose a half dozen programs are active, but your system has only one printer. If all programs took turns printing out their output a line or two at a time, interspersed with the output of other programs, the resulting printed report would be worthless. To get around this problem, a process called **spooling** is used: Each program writes onto a disk each file that is to be printed. When the entire program is on the disk, spooling is complete, and the disk files are printed intact (Figure 7-7).

Spooling also addresses another problem—relatively slow printer speeds. Writing a record on disk is much faster than writing that same record on a printer. A program, therefore, completes execution more quickly if records to be printed are written temporarily on disk instead. The actual printing can be done at some later time, when printing will not slow program execution. Some installations use a separate (usually smaller) computer dedicated exclusively to the printing of spooled files; some print off-hours or overnight so that smaller, more immediate jobs can use the lone printer during the day.

 ## Service Programs

Most of the tasks just described in the section on sharing resources are done by the operating system, without involvement by an application programmer. Although programmers may need to make requests for input and output devices, they generally do not need to give the operating system specific instructions about how to use these devices. Activities such as paging and spooling go on without explicit commands. Other activities might be special requests to the operating system, known to programmers as *system calls.* When the operating system takes on its specialist role, it may provide separate **service programs** that do "house-keeping" functions; or, service programs may be integrated into applications programs.

Why reinvent the wheel? Duplication of effort is what service programs, better known as **utilities** among personal computer users, are supposed to avoid. Such programs perform many chores, including file conversions and transfers, sort/merge operations, and program translation. Strictly speaking, these utilities are not part of the operating system. They are, however, generally included with the operating system on any computer system. Many types of utility programs might be found with an operating system, including simple text editors, language translators, and backup and restore utilities. Some useful utilities can be purchased separately.

One important type of utility allows the commands of the operating system to be used like the commands of a programming language. This allows several operating system functions to be run in one sequence. These programs are often called **batch files,** or **command files.** For example, a user might want to run the same set of programs—say, to provide the path information necessary for locating files supporting Microsoft Windows—each time he or she booted the computer. Many such commands could be included in one batch file that runs automatically when the computer starts up.

Thus far in this chapter, we have examined general properties and services of operating systems. Now we will turn to some specific trends in operating systems.

UNIX and Generic Operating Systems

Once upon a time when you bought a computer, the operating system came with the hardware. First it was free, later *not.* In the mainframe world, operating systems are usually defined by the vendor, with the user silently acquiescing. But some changes have occurred in recent years. The trend is toward what is called a **generic operating system**—that is, an operating system that works with more than one manufacturer's computer system. In 1991, IBM and Apple joined together in an alliance that promises a future generic operating system on a grand scale. There are several generic operating systems available today, but we will discuss one that is particularly influential: UNIX.

The UNIX Graduates

UNIX was developed in 1971 by Ken Thompson and Dennis Ritchie at AT&T's Bell Laboratories for use on its DEC minicomputers. You might recall Ritchie as the author of the programming language C, discussed in Chapter 6. The designers were surprised to see UNIX become so successful during the late 1970s and early 1980s. How did this come about?

PERSPECTIVES

IBM AND APPLE TEAM UP

Once enemies in the personal computer marketplace, IBM and Apple have joined to create a new generic operating system that promises to make computers easier to use. In teaming up, IBM and Apple effectively declared war on two corporations—Microsoft and Intel—that wield much power over the personal computer industry by controlling, respectively, the most popular operating system and microprocessor.

IBM—the acknowledged standard bearer in hardware—found its leadership position eroded by outside competitors that used inexpensive Intel microchips and Microsoft's MS-DOS to create cheaper, IBM-compatible clones. At the same time, Apple was unable to gain much of a share of the personal computer market because its Macintosh computer required a different operating system. By 1991, the share of the marketplace occupied by the IBM PS/2 had dwindled to 20%, while the share occupied by the Apple Macintosh could grow no larger than 10%. The rest of the marketplace—70%—was owned by manufacturers of IBM clones stocked with Intel's microchips and Microsoft's MS-DOS.

Then the unthinkable happened: The two former adversaries became bedfellows. IBM and Apple struck an alliance to regain control of the marketplace. Here are highlights of the agreement signed by both parties in 1991:

- In the area of network systems, the two companies are cross-licensing technologies and developing a range of products to enable better integration of the IBM and Macintosh operating environments. In effect, IBM licenses the AppleTalk network for inclusion in the IBM OS/2 operating system to allow Macintosh and IBM computers to network more smoothly.

- In the area of multimedia, the two companies are developing, licensing, and making available specifications and technologies to promote the exchange of time-based information (sounds, movies, video, and so on) across a variety of computer and consumer electronics devices.

- In the area of RISC architecture, IBM, Apple, and Motorola (a competitor of Intel's and the maker of the 68000 family of microprocessors that run Macintosh computers) are collaborating on the design and production of the PowerPC, which is based on the IBM RS/6000 microprocessor. The three companies expect the result to serve as the RISC architecture for the next generation of personal computers.

- In the area of operating systems open to all hardware manufacturers, Apple and IBM are working together to create an industry standard UNIX, called PowerOpen. This promises to be the basis for AIX products from IBM and A/UX offerings from Apple.

- In the area of object-oriented systems, the two companies are forming a joint venture to develop and market a completely new object-based operating system that will be available for multiple hardware environments. This system, formerly code-named "Pink" at Apple, is said by insiders to promise a revolutionary new way of developing and using software. It is not expected to be released until the late 1990s.

John Markoff, a *New York Times* columnist, says the glue for such a combination was IBM interest in Apple QuickTime, a tool for developing multimedia products. The Quick-Time standard provides compression techniques for adding full-motion video, sound, and computer animation to current applications—as part of the operating system in all Macintosh systems. Microsoft, the chief competitor in this area, is expected to add multimedia extensions to its Windows environment, which already overlays DOS.

Part of the reason may involve a social factor, not the software itself—namely, the "UNIX graduate" phenomenon. In the late 1970s Bell gave away UNIX to many colleges and universities, and students became accustomed to using it. Consequently, when many of these schools' graduates entered the work force, they began agitating for the acceptance of UNIX in industry.

Though not everyone agrees, many consider UNIX—a multiuser, time-sharing operating system—to be the most sophisticated operating system available.

Is UNIX a Standard?

When something like an operating system is accepted by a majority of users in the computer world, it is said to be a **standard.** Many believe that UNIX is a standard among large system users. An outgrowth of the UNIX graduate phenomenon was that UNIX became the only operating system that was user driven. That is, key UNIX supporters—the scientific community, the federal government, the aerospace industry—often named UNIX in their bid specifications to computer manufacturers. In effect, they said, "If you want our business, you better offer a system that includes UNIX." Vendors who could not offer UNIX-supported hardware were effectively cut out of the bidding process. This was a powerful incentive to offer UNIX with a hardware system. Today UNIX runs on everything from the Cray-2 supercomputer to personal computers.

But UNIX has some drawbacks. It has never been considered very user friendly. Critics point, for example, to capricious use of abbreviations and inadequate documentation. Also, UNIX is said to lack sophisticated security features necessary for many organizations. Still, UNIX supporters take on a fervor that has been described as cult-like. Said one adherent, "Sure it's got problems—but show me something better." Many companies have tried to do just that—within the UNIX environment. Much of the unfriendliness has been replaced by pull-down menus that look much like those of other systems. A few common UNIX instructions are shown, along with those from several other common operating systems, in Table 7-1.

Operating Systems for Personal Computers

We have already indicated that some software packages hide the operating system interface, but others want you to use your own copy of the operating system, probably the one that came with the machine. This is called **booting** the system—that is, loading the operating system into memory. The word *booting* is used because the operating system seems to pull itself up by its bootstraps. A small program (in ROM—read-only memory) "boot-straps" the basic components of the operating system in from a diskette or hard disk.

If you are using the popular operating system called **MS-DOS** (for Microsoft Disk Operating System), the net observable result of booting MS-DOS is an A> or C> on the screen. (See a detailed description of booting in the essay "How to Use MS-DOS," on page 242.) The letter A or C refers to the disk drive; the > symbol is called a **prompt,** a signal that the system is *prompting* you to do something. The prompt indicates that the operating system is waiting for a command. At this point you must give some instruction to the computer. Perhaps all you need to do is insert a

Table 7-1 Comparing common commands.

Different operating systems accomplish similar operations in different ways. MS-DOS and UNIX use a command-line interface to write abbreviated commands. Microsoft Windows and the Macintosh use a mouse to achieve a graphical user interface.

Operation	MS-DOS	UNIX	Windows	Macintosh
Lists all the files on a disk	DIR	LS	Double-click disk icon	Double-click disk icon
Copies a file	COPY	CP	Drag file icon to destination disk	Drag file icon to destination disk
Deletes a file	DEL	RM	Select File icon and press Del	Drag icon to trash can

commercial software disk, then type certain characters to make the application software take the lead. But it could be more complicated than that because the prompt is actually the signal for direct communication between you, the user, and the operating system. If you are connected to a machine that uses UNIX, a dollar sign ($) is the prompt that indicates that the computer is ready for instructions.

Using MS-DOS

To use the computer to run applications programs, you need to understand some basics about your operating system. You will use the operating system whenever you use your computer. Here we will consider MS-DOS, the most entrenched operating system for IBM and IBM-compatible personal computers, in detail. We will refer to MS-DOS by its abbreviated name, DOS, which rhymes with *boss*.

DOS programs are stored on one or more diskettes, which were probably purchased with the computer. These programs are executed by issuing a **command,** a name that invokes the correct program. Whole books have been written about DOS commands; we will consider only the commands you need to use an application program. These DOS commands let you:

- Access DOS files
- Initialize (format) new diskettes for use
- List the names of the files you have on your disk
- Name new files on disk and change the names of old files
- Copy files from one disk to another
- Erase files from a disk

DOS Commands

Although you may not use all DOS commands, certain programs invoked by DOS commands must be in your computer's memory before you can

IBM Seeds Harvard M.B.A.s

Harvard Business School student John Pollock shows off the outdoor possibilities of the IBM PS/2 L40SX notebook computer. IBM provided students with 700 of these notebooks before the machines were released to the general public. The students found some fault with the device, but in general they approved. The Intel 386SX-based unit includes a 60MB hard disk, 2MB to 18MB of memory, a floppy disk drive and built-in modem that can send and receive data and fax messages. Why give them to students? The seeding of the UNIX operating systems throughout the computer world was said to have been carried out by students who took it with them into the business world when they graduated. Do you think IBM might have something similar in mind for its notebooks?

use DOS or an application program such as Lotus 1-2-3. These essential DOS programs are accessed by using commands referred to as the **internal DOS commands.** The internal DOS commands are in programs that must be loaded—placed—into your computer's memory when you turn on your computer. Once the internal DOS programs are in memory, you can remove the DOS disk but still use the internal DOS programs. However, internal DOS must sometimes be reloaded when you stop using one application program and wish to use a different application program. And, of course, since the computer loses whatever is in its memory when you turn off the machine, you must reload internal DOS into memory whenever you turn the computer on to use an application program.

When you want to use an internal DOS program, you tell DOS to execute the program by typing in the appropriate command. Internal DOS commands execute immediately because the internal DOS programs are loaded into the computer when it is booted. Two important internal DOS commands are the *COPY* command, which lets you make copies of files, and the *DIR* (directory) command, which lets you list the names of files stored on a disk.

Most applications programs require a lot of computer memory to run. Therefore, only internal DOS programs, which are necessary to support the work of applications programs, are loaded into memory when the computer is booted. The other DOS programs, which reside in files on the DOS disk, are accessed by using commands referred to as the **external DOS commands.** The external DOS commands are in programs that must be read from disk before they can be executed. One of the most important external commands is the *FORMAT* command, which prepares a disk so that it is capable of storing files.

The point of this discussion is that you must have access to the external DOS programs before you can use them. Therefore, you must have the DOS disk in the proper disk drive or installed on the hard disk before you can use external commands. Usually, however, all you will need are the internal DOS commands.

Now let us consider the hardware you will need to run DOS.

DOS and Disk Drives

As you know from your earlier reading, a computer has several distinct pieces of hardware. The central processing unit executes the instructions in a computer program. The computer's memory contains program instructions and data. Internal DOS programs are loaded into memory. Secondary storage is needed, usually one or more disk drives. Since many DOS commands involve files on disk, we are particularly concerned about disk drives in this section.

Disk Drive Configurations   The two most popular kinds of disk drives are diskette drives and hard disk drives (also called hard drives). If you have two diskette drives, they are called drives A and B. A hard drive is called drive C. (Of course, you may add others, including a sec-

Personal Computers in Action

HOW TO USE MS-DOS

When you learn how to use a computer, you sometimes hear a little voice within you that plants a seed of doubt ("Are you *sure* you want to press *that* key?") and hints that the computer will self-destruct if you make a mistake. Some software saves you from this uncertainty. You simply insert the application program, turn on the computer, and follow the step-by-step instructions on the screen. However, there are times when the computer waits for *you* to give the instructions. For instance, some tasks require knowing how to use an operating system disk like MS-DOS, which prepares the computer for particular applications programs.

Since it was released by Microsoft in 1981, MS-DOS has been used on all IBM and IBM-compatible personal computers. MS-DOS features a command-line interface, which requires the user to remember commands and type them after the prompt. Since the introduction of MS-DOS versions 4.0 and 5.0, however, MS-DOS has also offered a shell environment that eliminates the need to memorize commands by providing menus of commands (see Table 7-2). This essay will cite directions for using the command-line interface to load MS-DOS on an IBM PS/2 using a floppy disk drive and a hard disk drive (for possible configurations, see Figure 7-8). Two common tasks requiring command-line instructions are included: (1) getting a list of the files on a disk and (2) copying files from one disk to another.

Using MS-DOS from a 3½-inch Diskette

As you read these steps, follow along on the drawing.

1. Insert the MS-DOS disk in the 3½-inch disk drive (drive A).
2. Turn the computer on. The light on drive A goes on, and the drive whirs for a few seconds. Then the light goes off.
3. When the screen requests the date, you can either enter today's date (month-day-year; for example, 10-13-93) and press Enter or simply press Enter without entering a new date.

4. When the screen requests the time, you can either enter the current time (military time; for example, 14:30) and press Enter or simply press Enter without entering a new time.
5. When the prompt (A>) appears on the screen, MS-DOS has been loaded in drive A. (If you are going to insert an application program in drive A, you may now remove the MS-DOS disk.)

Using MS-DOS from a Hard Drive

1. Turn the computer on. The light on drive C goes on as the drive whirs for a few seconds. Then the light goes off. (If you are asked for the date and time, you may wish to follow the preceding instructions for the floppy disk drive.)
2. When the prompt (C>) appears, MS-DOS has been loaded into memory. The computer is ready to accept your command.

Getting a List of Files

1. Load MS-DOS as previously described.
2. After the prompt, type the command for a directory, which is

   `DIR`

3. Press Enter
4. A list of the files on the current disk (along with other information, including file size) appears on the screen. If there are more file names than fit on one screen, you can cause the screen to stop at each screenful by adding a forward slash (/) and a P to the directory command. In other words, type

   `DIR/P`

5. Press Enter for the next screenful. When the list is done, the prompt returns. You may also wish to try another parameter: DIR/W (don't forget to include the forward slash mark). This results in a list of file names in columns across the screen.

Copying Files from a Floppy to a Hard Disk

1. Load MS-DOS as previously described.
2. Insert the source disk (the original disk with the files to be copied) in drive A.
3. a. To copy a specific file on the disk in drive A to the hard disk in drive C, after A> type
   `COPY filename C:`
   For example, if the file name is PAYROLL, the screen should read
   `A>COPY PAYROLL C:`
   b. To copy *all* the files on the disk in drive A to the hard disk, use asterisks like so
   `COPY *.* C:`
4. Press Enter
5. When the light in drive A goes off, the computer has completed the copying.

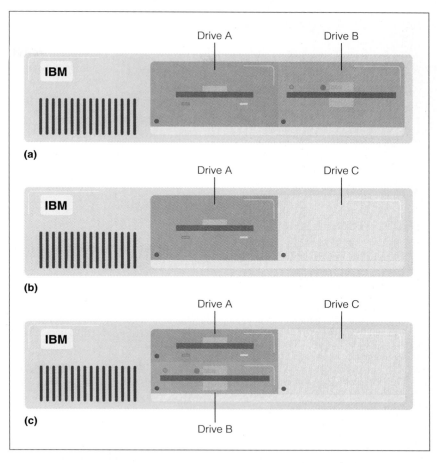

Figure 7-8   Disk drive configurations. As you use different computers, you may see several different types of disk drive combinations. The following are common: (a) 3½-inch diskette drive A on the left, 5¼-inch diskette drive B on the right; (b) 3½-inch diskette drive A on the left, hard-drive C on the right; and (c) 3½-inch diskette drive A and 5¼-inch diskette drive B stacked on the left, hard-drive C on the right. In all cases drive C is inside the computer housing.

ond hard drive, called drive D, and so on.) Configurations vary, but three common arrangements are shown in Figure 7-8.

From now on, to make your reading a little easier, we will use the word *disk* to refer to both diskettes and hard disks. When it is necessary to distinguish between these two storage devices, we will use the terms *diskette* and *hard disk*.

The Default Drive   Since some DOS commands refer to disk files, which store programs and data, we need to pause for a moment to consider where those files are. For example, the DIR command displays a list of files—but how does DOS know which drive contains the disk that the files are stored on? Although DOS commands let you specify a particular drive, it is easier to omit a drive specification, thus permitting DOS to use the default drive.

**An Operating System
Made Bill Richest**

Two people vied for IBM's attention
when it came to producing the operating system for its first personal computer: Bill Gates and Gary Kildall. Of the
two, Kildall was the first to succeed in
promoting an operating system standard for personal computers, having
written and marketed CP/M through his
company, Digital Research. Gates was
known mainly for his version of the
BASIC programming language.

It is not hard to understand why IBM
contacted Kildall first. However, when a
contingent of IBM representatives
showed up for an appointment with
him, Kildall was out. His lawyer, so the
story goes, was reluctant to sign IBM's
standard pretalk nondisclosure agreement. Later, Kildall got involved in the
process and telephoned IBM. But two
weeks later Kildall's IBM contact was off
the project, and Kildall could not reach
the new project leaders.

He never did, because they were in
contact with Gates, president of Microsoft. Gates delivered MS-DOS (which
IBM calls PC-DOS—the two programs
are almost identical) for the IBM PC,
and the rest is history. Microsoft diversi-
fied to applications software and became the leading independent software
house.

In 1991, IBM and Microsoft had a
falling out, and IBM once again approached Digital Research to license
that company's latest operating environment, DR DOS. It is ironic—but not
unusual—that IBM went back to the
people it spurned ten years before to
compete with the fellow they first chose
as their protégé. Business is business. Of
course, by then Bill didn't mind all that
much, since he had just been named by
Forbes magazine as the richest man in
America—he is worth more than $6.3
billion.

The **default drive,** also called the **current drive,** is the drive that the computer is currently using. If your computer does not have a hard disk, DOS assumes that the drive where DOS was loaded is the default drive. DOS will always remind you which drive is currently the default drive by means of the prompt. If you see A>, then the default drive is A. Similarly, B> means the default drive is B, and C> means the default drive is C.

You can change to another default drive if you wish: Type the letter of the desired drive, followed by a colon, and then press Enter. Suppose, for example, that the default drive is currently drive A, but you want to access files on the disk that you have in drive B. To change the default drive to B, type

        B:

and then press Enter. (You can, by the way, type an upper- or lowercase B. DOS recognizes either.) Now the screen shows a B>.

Only one disk drive at a time can be the default drive. If you ask DOS to retrieve a file for you and DOS replies that it cannot find the file, perhaps the file is not on the disk in the default drive. You may need to change the default drive or place another disk in the current default drive.

Diskette Functions   Though most MS-DOS computers can be purchased with hard disks, diskettes still serve several important functions on these computers. Diskettes serve as:

- **System disks.** These disks store the operating system files necessary to boot the computer if you do not wish to boot from the hard disk or if the hard disk is damaged.

- **Program installation disks.** Many large programs require that they be run from a hard disk; often a program takes up numerous diskettes, so manufacturers provide installation diskettes to make the process easier.

- **Backup and archive disks.** Often you will want to copy the data from your hard disk to a diskette. It is a good idea to have a backup or archive copy in case you make a mistake or the hard disk is damaged.

- **Data disks.** Despite the increasing use of networks, diskettes are still used to carry data from one computer to another. Data disks do not require system files for booting, since the files they hold are usually used only in conjunction with programs already running. Often the physical act of carrying data disks from computer to computer is face-tiously referred to as a sneaker net—a human instead of a computer network.

When you create files, you choose a name for the file. When there are several files on the disk, you may want to see a list of all the files. You may want to copy files from one data disk to another so you can have a backup copy. You may want to erase files you no longer need. To do these things, you need to know how to use the appropriate DOS commands (as well as how DOS stores files, which it does in a tree-like structure).

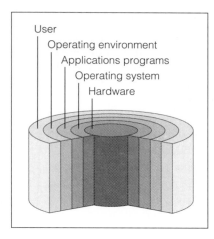

User
Operating environment
Applications programs
Operating system
Hardware

Figure 7-9   Operating environments.
This illustration is identical to Figure 7-1, except that an environment layer has been added to shield the user from having to know commands of the operating system. The four operating environments dealt with in the text include the traditional command-line, shell, graphical user, and gesture-based interfaces.

Although the details of these commands are mostly beyond the scope of this book, you can see how the commands are used by reading, in this chapter, the essay called "How to Use MS-DOS."

Operating Environments: The User Interface

Figure 7-9 tells the story at a glance: Compare Figure 7-9 to Figure 7-1, and you will see that another layer has been added between the operating system and the user. It is called the **operating environment** because it defines the environment in which the user works. This environment is involved when we discuss the **user interface,** or the way you interface with, or use, the computer. Traditionally, operating environments have allowed users to type in commands from a keyboard. However, the hassle of having to remember the specific nature of the commands and their parameters eventually led to the emergence of friendlier operating environments. We now turn to the different user interfaces available on personal computers.

The Command-Line Interface

The traditional environment for MS-DOS or UNIX is called a **command-line interface,** or **CLI,** because the user normally directs the operating system by typing commands. For example, when using a personal computer with a built-in hard disk, you see the prompt C>. It is awaiting your command. To see a list of the files on that disk, you type the command DIR. When you press Enter, the operating system carries out your command, presenting on the computer screen a list of all the files on the disk in drive C. Once you learn all the commands, you may find it convenient and fast to work with a command-line interface. On the other hand, many of the commands require remembering specific symbols—such as backward and forward slashes—which many people confuse. Frustrations with the command-line interface have led operating system producers to come up with environments that handle the memory work for users. Table 7-2 is a sampler of operating system commands and what they do.

Shells

Sometimes an operating environment is called a **shell,** because it appears to form a "coating" around the operating system. These operating environments are designed to make life easier for the average user. The shell environment may come as part of the operating system, or it may be a product that can be added later. Instead of typing commands and their parameters, you select from a list of commands, usually located in a menu. Some of the early shells on IBM-compatible personal computers were programs like Norton Commander, which overlaid DOS and insulated the user from the command-line interface; users worked with

Table 7-2 Two generations of MS-DOS commands.

Some commands used by two generations of Microsoft DOS are listed below. The Operation column shows what a command does. The second column shows the MS-DOS 4.01 command for each operation. The third column shows both the MS-DOS 5.0 command you can type to perform the operation and the MS-DOS 5.0 menu where you can find the command when you use the new, optional shell environment. Note that MS-DOS 5.0 introduced the UNDELETE and UNFORMAT commands.

Operation	MS-DOS 4.01	MS-DOS 5.0
Prepares a disk for use	FORMAT	FORMAT or Disk Utilities
Makes copy of a file	COPY	COPY or File menu choice
Gives a file a new name	RENAME	RENAME or File menu choice
Deletes a file	DEL (also ERASE)	DEL or File menu choice
Lists all files on a disk	DIR (for *Directory*)	DIR or View menu choice
Reverts to previous format	Not available	UNFORMAT or Disk Utilities
Undoes the last command	Not available	UNDELETE or Disk Utilities

a screen that presented two "windows" of file names at a time. A menu bar offered the commands users could select.

For example, to copy a file from one disk to another by using the command-line interface of MS-DOS, you have to type in several items, including the command COPY, correct spaces, the source disk drive location, the file name, and the name of the destination disk drive. With the Norton Commander, you could do the same task by highlighting the file name in one window, selecting the destination disk in the other window, then selecting Copy from the menu bar. Those who worked with MS-DOS continually thought the extra steps of the shell program wasted time. Since they used MS-DOS daily, these people had no trouble remembering the MS-DOS commands. Those who worked intermittently with MS-DOS commands, however, found looking them up to be tedious. Among this group of users, shells became very popular additions to the operating system.

Eventually Microsoft acknowledged the popularity of shell programs by adding one of its own. MS-DOS now allows users to work in either of two ways: by using a command-line interface or a shell environment (Figure 7-10). If users prefer the traditional environment of typing in commands, they opt for the command-line interface. When they prefer to access commands from a menu, they choose the DOSSHELL environment.

The Graphical User Interface

The interface that has quickly become popular for IBM personal computers is the **graphical user interface,** or **GUI** (pronounced "gooey"). The most popular GUI is Microsoft Windows. Instead of having to remember a command to type, Windows users have only to make selections from choices available on the screen. Most graphical user interfaces rely on a mouse with one or more buttons to select items from the screen. The graphical user interface does more than provide basic routines for

Windows Does It Your Way

Microsoft Windows provides an easy-to-use graphical user interface to DOS-based personal computers. Nearly all IBM-compatible software can be made to work in the Windows operating environment, but Windows really shines with applications specifically designed for it.

Most popular software programs have been revised from DOS to Windows versions to take advantage of the most appealing power of Windows: It allows many applications to run at the same time. This is called *multitasking*. In separate windows you can display screens from a spreadsheet program, a word processing program, and an electronic mail session. Depending on the amount of memory installed in your computer, as many as 20 applications can be active at a time. By contrast, only one application at a time can run on a computer that uses standard DOS only.

When you consider how people think and work, the advantage of multitasking becomes clear. For instance, if you are writing a memo at the office and the phone rings, you normally would not put your writing materials in a drawer before answering. If a co-worker walks in while you are on the phone, you would not hang up before you ask your visitor to come back later. Humans are naturally multitasking beings. Windows lets your computer do things your way.

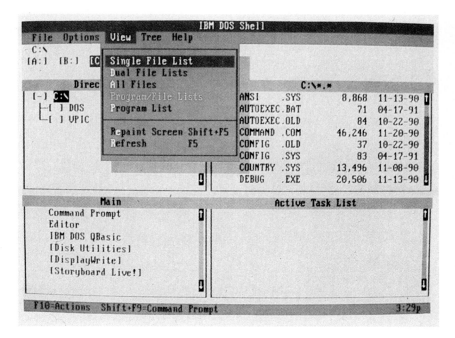

Figure 7-10   A shell for MS-DOS. When Microsoft released MS-DOS version 5.0, the company provided new flexibility for DOS users by allowing both a command-line interface and a shell interface. When users want to type in commands, they can opt for the traditional command-line interface. When they prefer to access commands from a menu, they can work in the shell interface.

controlling the hardware; it provides the programmer with the tools to control many aspects of how the user interacts with a program. In doing so, the graphical interface helps standardize how programs work, so that a user familiar, say, with the way to open a document in a word processing program can open a worksheet in a spreadsheet program the same way. In standardizing such processes, the interface is said to be more *intuitive*—more like the way you might do something in the physical world.

Most graphical user interfaces make use of a mouse for many tasks. When using Windows or the Macintosh, for example, on the screen you see little pictures (called **icons**) instead of a prompt. The icons represent items like disks or files. You point to an icon and click it with the mouse button. The computer highlights the icon to show that it is selected. Then you can perform an operation on what the icon represents. If the icon represents a document, you can double-click the icon to open the document in its own application. The operating system gets the message and starts up the word processing application in which it was created, then loads the document. The document appears, ready for editing. The point-and-click process of the mouse replaces the command-line interface, allowing you to perform actions many consider easier to remember because they mimic the way you do things in the real world.

Apple Computer's Macintosh paved the way for the graphical user interface, but various other GUIs are available for other operating systems (Figures 7-11 and 7-12). Some of the most prominent are Microsoft Win-

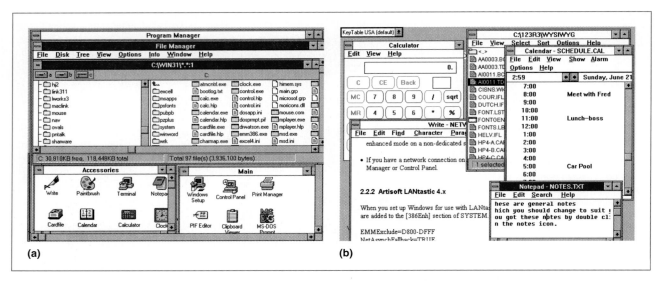

(a)   **(b)**

Figure 7-11   Microsoft Windows in Action. The most popular graphical user interface on IBM personal computers is Microsoft Windows, which lets users run programs concurrently by placing the display from each in a separate window. Windows offers easy-to-use menus and a mouse-based system of pointing and clicking. (a) The icons along the left represent available software tools, several of which are displayed in overlapping windows on the screen. (b) Windows provides users access to several applications programs at one time. The icons at the bottom of the screen represent additional applications.

dows, OS/2 (IBM), DR DOS (Digital Research), New Wave (Hewlett-Packard), and NeXTstep (NeXT). Even UNIX has a GUI called X-Windows. See Table 7-1 for a comparison of commands common to the various operating environments.

The Gesture-Based Interface

GUI is not the last word in interfaces. Pen-based computers use a pen-like stylus to interact with the computer in a way that is natural to most people—by writing on a tablet. The tablet is actually a computer screen that is sensitive to the touch of the stylus. There are icons on the screen as in a GUI; however, the stylus lets the user feel as if he or she is touching and manipulating the computer directly. Many users also find the stylus easier to control than a mouse because they are performing actions more directly on the screen. The interface of the pen-based computers has been called a **gesture-based interface** because it involves gestures made on the tablet with the stylus.

Pen-based computers also have handwriting recognition software. This combines two ways of working with computers—writing and selecting. Thus, it outshines the GUI environment because of that environment's reliance on the mouse. When you write with a word processing program, for example, you must move a hand to the mouse to select menus and icons, then move back to the keyboard to type again. With the stylus, the pen-based computer user can make selections by using the appropriate gestures, then write directly on the screen if characters must be entered. These gestures are designed to reflect the way you would natu-

Figure 7-12 GUI gallery. Several other graphical user interface programs can overlay DOS on IBM personal computers, just as Microsoft Windows does. A few competitors are (a) IBM's own Presentation Manager; (b) Hewlett-Packard's New Wave; and (c) NeXT's NeXTstep, which has been extended beyond NeXT computers to work with IBM machines.

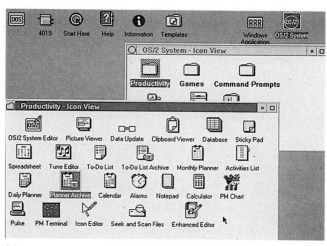

(a)

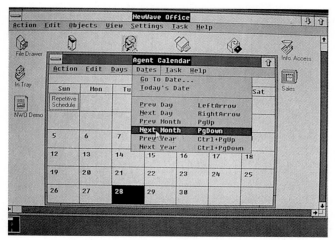

(b)

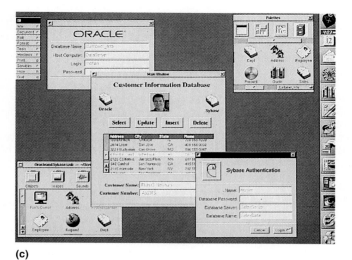

(c)

Macintosh

THE GUI THAT STARTED IT ALL

When Apple introduced its Macintosh computer in a 1984 TV commercial that wowed the advertising world with a witty jab at IBM dominance, the Macintosh market took off. When its next highly acclaimed TV commercial showed its machines being used more than other computers in the business office, sales of the Mac continued onward and upward.

Apple claimed its machine was "the computer for the rest of us," calling the Macintosh graphical user interface (GUI) *intuitive*. Instead of the command line and A prompt (A>) the IBM PC presented, users could move a mouse to manipulate symbols right on the screen. It was not long before the rest of the industry saw the point: Most people could use this computer without much training. Microsoft soon introduced its own GUI called Windows. IBM followed suit with Presentation Manager and OS/2, and many others offered GUI products.

What made the Macintosh so appealing? Apple created its operating system as a metaphor—a computerized desktop that resembled your own physical desktop. As shown in accompanying screen (a), when the Macintosh desktop starts up, you see icons (little pictures of fold-ers, disks, and even a trash can). With the mouse you point and click to manipulate symbols directly. For instance, you place the mouse pointer on the icon of a folder,

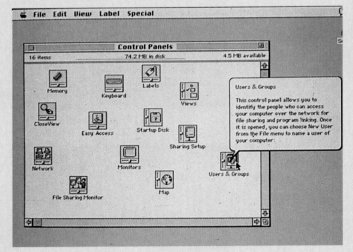

The Macintosh desktop. (a) The original Macintosh desktop. Icons represent disks, folders, files, applications, and even a trash can. You work with a Macintosh by means of a point-and-click mouse and a metaphorical desktop. A document icon called My document is a file that was created in the application, Microsoft Word, whose icon is below it. Beneath that application is the folder MS Word folder, which can hold both the file and the application. You click the file's icon to select it, drag it around to place or copy it, and double-click it to begin work on it. The trash can icon is where you drop off unwanted files—just like in real life. (b) In 1991, Apple introduced its latest version of the Macintosh operating system, System 7, which added 3-D icons, balloons for help messages, file sharing over networks, and other new features.

quickly press the mouse button twice (a double-click), and the folder opens to reveal its contents (files, applications, and even more folders). The words at the top of the screen occupy the menu bar, each choice offering a list of commands when chosen.

The mouse plays a primary role in getting things done on the Mac. First you select something with the mouse, then you act on it. For example, you select a file, then choose the Duplicate command from the File menu; a copy of the file appears on the desktop. All Mac applications programs follow this same procedure whether you are opening, closing, saving, copying, deleting, or printing a file.

When the Mac first appeared, some skeptics called it a toy machine, since it had only limited memory. Over the generations of new machines, however, its ability to handle graphics and printing evolved until it became the most popular desktop publishing computer in the business world. In 1991, with the release of the Apple System 7, which is shown in accompanying screen (b), came a new look and new powers for the desktop: customized labels and balloon help, 3-D icons, 32-bit color, virtual memory, file sharing, multitasking, and a new look and feel for the desktop metaphor.

Table 7-3 GUI vs. pen-based operations.

The GUI mouse and pen-based stylus are used in different ways to accomplish similar tasks. The mouse is called a point-and-click device; the pen (or stylus) is called a gesture device.

Operation	Windows and Macintosh	PenPoint
Selects a file	Position the pointer over the file icon and click once	Tap the file icon once or draw brackets around it
Starts an application	Position the pointer over the application icon and double-click	Tap twice rapidly on the application icon
Shows the files on a disk	Double-click the disk icon	Tap the page icon

rally work with paper and pencil. For example, the PenPoint system lets you tap the screen or draw brackets ([ ]) to select, write an X to delete, and draw a caret (^) to insert. In Table 7-3, GUI and pen-based operations are compared.

Do I Really Need to Know All This?

The answer to that question depends on how you expect to use a computer. If your primary use of a computer is as a tool to enhance your other work, then you may have minimum interaction with an operating system. In that case, whether you are using a personal computer or a mainframe, you will learn to access the application software of choice very quickly.

But there are other options. In fact, there are far more options than we are able to present in this introductory chapter. As a sophisticated user, you can learn your way around the operating system of any computer you might be using. If you plan to be a programmer, then there is no question about whether you need to know everything in this chapter; you will need to know this and much more.

R E V I E W   A N D   R E F E R E N C E

Summary and Key Terms

- An **operating system** is a set of programs through which the computer manages its own resources (the central processing unit, memory, secondary storage devices, input/output devices, and so on). Thus, applications programs do not have to provide all the instructions that the computer requires. This allows programmers to focus on solving problems for clients.

- An operating system has three main functions: (1) to manage the hardware, (2) to support applications, and (3) to establish a user interface.

- The **supervisor program** controls the entire operating system, ensuring that other programs in the system are called into memory as needed and that memory space is used efficiently.

- The operating system improves efficiency in two ways: (1) by helping users get maximum benefit from computer system resources and (2) by providing special routines and programs that take care of certain common tasks.

- **Multiprogramming,** often called **multitasking,** is running two or more programs concurrently on the same computer and sharing the computer's various resources. Multiprogramming is **event driven,** meaning that one program is allowed to use a particular resource (such as the central processing unit) to complete a certain activity (event) before relinquishing the resource to another program. In multiprogramming, the operating system uses **interrupts,** which are conditions that temporarily suspend the execution of individual programs.

- **Time-sharing** is a special case of multiprogramming in which several people use one machine at the same time. Time-sharing is **time driven**—each user is given a **time slice** in which the computer works on that user's tasks before moving on to another user's tasks. **Response time** is the time between the user's typed computer request and the computer's reply. The system of having users take turns is called **round-robin scheduling.**

- Through the **resource allocation** process, the operating system coordinates resource availability with the requirements of the various programs. Most operating systems are able to prevent a **deadlock,** a condition in which two programs come into conflict, with neither one willing to give up the resource it is holding until it gets the resource the other is holding.

- **Memory management** is the process of allocating memory to programs and of keeping the programs in memory separate from each other. Some operating systems divide memory into separate areas of fixed size; others allow variable sizes. Large all-purpose computers often divide memory into a **foreground** area for programs with higher priority and a **background** area for programs with lower priority. Programs waiting to be run are kept on the disk in **queues.**

- In the **virtual storage** (or **virtual memory**) technique of memory management, part of the application program is stored on disk and is brought into memory only when needed for execution. Memory is considered **real storage;** the secondary storage holding the rest of the program is considered virtual storage.

- Virtual storage can be implemented in several ways. **Paging** divides a program into equal-size pieces (**pages**) that fit exactly into corresponding memory spaces (**page frames**).

- In multiprogramming, **memory protection** is an operating system process that defines the limits of each program in memory, thus preventing programs from accidentally destroying or modifying one another.

- **Spooling** prevents printouts that are a combination of the output from concurrently processed programs. Each file to be printed is written temporarily onto a disk instead of being printed immediately. When this spooling process is complete, all the appropriate files from a particular program can be printed intact.

- **Service programs,** also called **utilities,** are prewritten standard programs that perform many repetitive file-handling tasks such as file conversions and sort/merge operations. A **batch file,** or **command file,** is one that automatically loads and runs the same set of programs each time the computer starts up.

- **UNIX,** a multiuser, time-sharing operating system developed in 1971 by researchers at Bell Labs, has been described as a generic operating system. A **generic operating system** is one that works with more than one manufacturer's computer system. Many consider UNIX a **standard,** the operating system accepted by a majority of users of large computer systems.

- **MS-DOS** is the popular operating system written by Microsoft for IBM personal computers and IBM-compatible machines. **Booting** the system is the process of loading the operating system into memory. A **prompt** signals the user when the booting process is complete and the operating system is ready for a command.

- MS-DOS programs are executed by issuing a **command,** a name that invokes the correct program. DOS commands are placed into your computer's memory when you turn on the computer. **Internal DOS commands** must be loaded into memory when the computer is turned on; **external DOS commands** are read from disk before they can be executed. The **default drive,** also called the **current drive,** is the drive that the computer is currently using.

- In general, personal computer software written to be run with one operating system will not run with another one. Therefore, most software developers maximize sales by writing programs for the most widely used operating systems, such as MS-DOS and Windows.

- The **operating environment** describes the area lying between the computer and the user. It involves the concept of **user interface,** or the way the user works with the computer. There are several different operating environments.

- The **command-line interface,** or **CLI,** is a traditional user interface that requires users to remember commands and type them to invoke them. This type of interface is the basis of MS-DOS.

- When a program overlays the operating system in an attempt to provide a friendlier environment, it may be called a **shell,** since it forms a kind of "coating" around the operating system. MS-DOS now offers both a traditional CLI and a friendlier shell in which the user does not have to remember or look up the appropriate commands.

- The most popular operating environment is the **graphical user interface,** or **GUI,** which allows the use of a pointing device like a mouse to command and control the computer. The most popular GUI is Microsoft Windows. Apple paved the way for this type of interface with its Macintosh.

- The operating environment for pen-based computers is called a **gesture-based interface** because it relies on motions or "gestures" of a pen-like stylus on a touch-sensitive computer screen.

Review Questions

1. What is an operating system?
2. What are the three main functions of an operating system?
3. How does an operating system improve efficiency?
4. Describe how multiprogramming works.
5. Explain how time-sharing works.
6. Describe the process of resource allocation.
7. Why is memory management necessary?
8. Why do some computer systems divide the memory into foreground and background areas?
9. Describe paging.
10. In multiprogramming, what prevents one program from destroying or changing another program?
11. Explain how spooling works and why it is useful.
12. What do utility programs do?
13. What is meant by the current drive?
14. Explain the difference between a CLI and a GUI.
15. Why is a GUI considered easier to use?

Discussion Questions

1. How would your access to computers be affected if there were no operating systems?
2. Discuss the advantages and disadvantages of a generic operating system.
3. When might you prefer a shell environment over a command-line interface?
4. How would you explain the rapid acceptance of Microsoft Windows?

True-False Questions

T F 1. Virtual memory is a method used by the operating system to temporarily store programs and data on disks.

T F 2. A mouse, icons, and pull-down menus are associated with a command-line interface.

T F 3. The process of writing a file to be printed to disk before printing is called booting.

T F 4. The first operating system developed for IBM and IBM-compatible personal computers was UNIX.

T F 5. The drive that the operating system of the computer is using is called the foreground drive.

T F 6. Multiprocessing involves two or more programs running on the computer concurrently.

T F 7. The layer of program between the operating system and the user program may be called a shell.

T F 8. Two or more programs holding resources wanted by other programs while waiting for the other programs to give up those resources is called deadlock.

T F 9. A graphical user interface would be considered more intuitive and natural for the user than a command-line interface.

T F 10. The conditions that cause the operating system to temporarily suspend operation of a program are called breakpoints.

Systems Analysis and Design

Change and the Computer

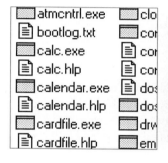

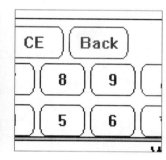
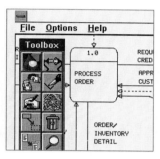

Carly Mack, operations manager of an airport car rental agency, was look-

ing for ways to improve customer service. Surveys showed that customers

put standing in line at the top of their list of annoyances. Interviews with

agency clerks, however, revealed that the reason for the long lines was

geographic uncertainty—most of the customers were from out of town

and needed time-consuming directions.

Brainstorming managers, along with a computer consultant, came up

with the idea of a computer system so simple that the customers could

run it themselves. The system centered on a touch screen that would

display nearby locations; the customer need only touch the desired lo-

cation and the computer would take it from there.

Although the idea was still in the formative stages, Carly was surprised to find resistance from the clerks. They did not like the idea of sharing their expertise and were uneasy about being "replaced" by a computer.

Change has taken on a new immediacy in the Information Age. It is expected. But people continue to sense the stress that surrounds it and try to avoid change. Sometimes change is someone else's idea, an idea forced upon others. So, not only is the change set in motion externally, but it is accompanied by fear of diminished control. When a new computer system supplants an old one, someone must step in to guide the process smoothly and efficiently—not only in respect to equipment and programs, but also with an eye out for the people involved. The person responsible for guiding change in such situations is a systems analyst. This chapter will describe the qualities of a systems analyst and the variety of professional skills needed. The systems analyst—the change agent—moves through five phases—preliminary investigation, systems analysis, systems design, systems development, and implementation—to complete a systems project.

 ## The Systems Analyst

The boss tells you someone is coming to look over the work situation and ask you a few questions, "get a fix on the work flow, maybe see if we can't streamline some things and get them on a computer system." Your ears perk up. A computer? Suddenly you feel very nervous. They're going to take your job and give it to a computer! Congratulations. You are about to be visited by a systems analyst.

A systems analyst with any experience, however, knows that people are uneasy about having their job situations investigated, that they may be nervous about computers, and that they may react adversely by withholding their cooperation (sometimes subtly, sometimes quite aggressively). Attitudes depend somewhat on prior experience with computer systems.

The Analyst and the System

What is a systems analyst? Although we will describe a systems project more formally later in the chapter, let us start by defining what we mean by the words *system, analysis,* and *design.* A **system** is an organized set of related components established to accomplish a certain task. There are natural systems, such as the cardiovascular system, but many systems have been planned and deliberately put into place by people. For example, the lines you stand in, stations you go to, and forms you fill out on your college's registration day constitute a system to get qualified students into the right classes. A **computer system** is a system that has a computer as one of its components.

Systems analysis is the process of studying an existing system to determine how it works and how it meets user needs. Systems analysis lays the groundwork for improvements to the system. The analysis involves

Personal Computers in Action

TRADITIONS CHANGE SLOWLY

Building a publishing system from scratch requires patience, planning, and—in the case of *New Yorker* magazine—a sophisticated sense of tradition. When this legend of the literary world decided to update its publishing system, it was with one foot firmly planted in the past. But not even *New Yorker* could afford to ignore high technology when it came to cutting costs— more than $1 million would be saved during its first year of change.

But how do you deal with change when the old equipment to be replaced would be welcomed— and was—by the Smithsonian Institute? Or where only a handful of the people involved have any experience with computers? That was the job Pamela Older accepted when she moved from *Time,* where she was production director, to the den of literary lions: the *New Yorker* office in Manhattan.

Before installing the $350,000 Macintosh-based system for editorial, production, and art promotion departments in the spring of 1991, some of the aspects that Older had to consider were the tradition-based character of the magazine and the idiosyncratic nature of the staff, the priorities of the publishing system, the hardware and software options available, the bottom-line costs, and the impact of the system on the venerable magazine's office environment.

Older says a main drawback was the low-tech nature of the work environment. "My objective was to do it quietly, behind the scenes, without rocking the boat," she says. She set about by moving computer systems into areas that offered the most immediate opportunity for reducing costs—that is, in the typesetting area and on the desks of a few experienced computer users. The exposure piqued the interest of others. As more and more people saw what the new systems saved in time and energy— not to mention money—it was not long before more staffers wanted to participate in computerization.

Quality control took time. *New Yorker* magazine is famous for its old-fashioned, sophisticated design. Since this design is mainly based on its distinctive typography, no available computer font was acceptable. Some six months were spent digitizing the original fonts and testing the new versions.

As computerization continued, Older realized that moving the electronic publishing system in slowly was not enough; it was decided to move it into an entirely new location. The magazine relocated across the street from its home of 60 years. "The older offices had reached their capacity in terms of electrical outlets; the wiring just wasn't adequate for the Ethernet network," says Older. "Psychologically, it helped to leave the old building and come into the new one with the computers already set up." Besides the Smithsonian, the New York Public Library benefitted from the move. The library received donations of manuscripts and correspondence from such famous writers as E. B. White, Truman Capote, James Thurber, Dorothy Parker, Robert Benchley, and Ogden Nash.

THE NEW YORKER

an investigation, which in turn usually involves establishing a relationship with the client for whom the analysis is being done and with the users of the system. The **client** is the person or organization contracting to have the work done. The **users** are people who will have contact with the system, usually employees and customers. For instance, in a college registration system, the client is the administration, and the users are both the school employees and the students.

Systems design is the process of developing a plan for an improved system, based on the results of the systems analysis. For instance, the analysis phase may reveal that students waste time standing in lines when they register in the closing weeks of the fall semester. The new system design might involve plans for a preregistration process.

Figure 8-1   Impetus for change. Internal and external sources can initiate a system change.

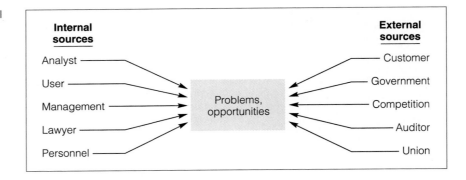

The **systems analyst** normally performs both analysis and design. (The term *systems designer* is not common, although it is used in some places.) In some computer installations a person who is mostly a programmer may also do some systems analysis and have the title **programmer/analyst.** Traditionally, most people who have become systems analysts have done so by way of programming. Starting out as a programmer helps the analyst appreciate computer-related problems that arise in analysis and design work. As you will see, programmers often depend on systems analysts for specifications from which to design programs. But not all programmers eventually become system analysts; a different set of skills is needed for each job. In addition, some analysts come up by way of the management track.

A systems analysis and design project does not spring out of thin air. There must be an *impetus*—motivation—for change and related *authority* for the change. The impetus for change may be the result of an internal force, such as the organization's management deciding a computer could be useful in warehousing and inventory, or an external force, such as government reporting requirements or customer complaints about billing (Figure 8-1). Authority for the change, of course, comes from higher management.

The Systems Analyst as Change Agent

The systems analyst fills the role of **change agent.** That is, the analyst must be the catalyst or persuader who overcomes the natural inertia and reluctance to change within an organization. The key to success is to involve the people of the client organization in the development of the new system. The common industry phrase is **user involvement,** and nothing can be more important to the success of the system. The finest system in the world will not suffice if users do not perceive it as useful. Users must be involved in the process from beginning to end. The systems analyst must monitor the user pulse regularly to make sure that the system being planned is one that will meet user needs.

What It Takes to Be a Systems Analyst

Not every computer professional aspires to the job of systems analyst. Before we can understand what kind of person might make a good systems analyst, we need to look at the kinds of things an analyst does. The systems analyst has three principal functions:

- **Coordination.** An analyst must coordinate schedules and system-related tasks with a number of people: the analyst's own manager; the programmers working with the system; the system's users, from clerks to top management; the vendors selling the computer equipment; and a host of others, such as postal employees handling mailings and carpenters doing installation.

- **Communication, both oral and written.** The analyst may be called upon to make oral presentations to clients, users, and others involved with the system. The analyst provides written reports—documentation—on the results of the analysis and the goals and means of the design. These documents may range from a few pages long to a few inches thick.

- **Planning and design.** The systems analyst, with the participation of members of the client organization, plans and designs the new system. This function involves all the activities from the beginning of the project until the final implementation of the system.

With these as principal functions, the kind of personal qualities that are desirable in a systems analyst must be apparent: an *analytical mind* and good *communication skills.* Perhaps not so obvious, however, are qualities such as *self-discipline* and *self-direction*—a systems analyst often works without close supervision. An analyst must have good *organizational skills* to be able to keep track of all the facts about the system. An analyst also needs *creativity* to envision the new system. Finally, an analyst needs the *ability to work without tangible results.* There can be long dry spells when the analyst moves numbly from meeting to meeting, when it can seem that little is being accomplished.

One other trait should be obvious: *knowledge* or *experience.* The person who knows how a business operates or who has some experience with what is involved has an advantage in dealing with clients in that business. Some consulting firms specialize in analyzing specific types of companies for just this reason.

Let us suppose that you are blessed with these admirable qualities and that you have become a systems analyst. You are given a job to do. How will you go about it?

How a Systems Analyst Works: Overview of the Systems Development Life Cycle

Whether you are investigating how to improve registration procedures at a college or any other task, you will proceed by using the **systems development life cycle (SDLC).** The systems development life cycle has five phases:

1. Preliminary investigation—determining the problem
2. Analysis—understanding the existing system

3. Design—planning the new system
4. Development—doing the work to bring the new system into being
5. Implementation—converting to the new system

These simple explanations for each phase will be expanded to full-blown discussions in subsequent sections; each phase is summarized in Table 8-1. As you read about the phases of a systems project, follow the Swift Sport Shoes inventory case study, which is presented in the adjacent essays. Although space prohibits us from presenting a complete analysis and design project, this case study gives the flavor of the real thing. Let us begin at the beginning.

Table 8-1   Systems development life cycle

Phase	Focus
Phase 1: Preliminary investigation	True nature of problem Problem scope Objectives

Phase 2: Systems analysis	Data gathering
	    Written documents
	    Interviews
	    Questionnaires
	    Observation
	    Sampling
	Data analysis
	    Charts
	    Tables
	    System requirements

Phase 3: Systems design	Alternative candidates Output Input Files Processing Controls Backup
Phase 4: Systems development	Programming Testing
Phase 5: Implementation	Training Equipment conversion File conversion System conversion Auditing Evaluation Maintenance

PRELIMINARY INVESTIGATION

CASE STUDY

You are employed as a systems analyst by Software Systems, Inc., a company offering packaged and custom software as well as consulting services. Software Systems has received a request for a systems analyst; the client is Swift Sport Shoes, a chain of stores carrying a huge selection of footwear for every kind of sport. Your boss hands you this assignment, telling you to contact company officer Kris Iverson.

In your initial meeting with Mr. Iverson, who is vice president of finance, you learn that the first Swift store opened in San Francisco in 1974. The store has been profitable since the second year. Nine new stores have been added in the city and nearby shopping malls. These stores also show a net profit; Swift has been riding the crest of the fitness boom. But even though sales have been gratifying, Mr. Iverson is convinced that costs are higher than they should be.

In particular, Mr. Iverson is disturbed about inventory problems, which are causing frequent stock shortages and increasing customer dissatisfaction. The company has a superminicomputer at headquarters, where management offices are. Although there is a small information systems staff, their experience is mainly in batch processing for financial systems. Mr. Iverson envisions more sophisticated technology for an inventory system and figures that outside expertise is needed to design it. He introduces you to Robin Christie, who is in charge of purchasing and inventory. Mr. Iverson also tells you that he has sent a memo to all company officers and store managers, indicating the purpose of your presence and his support of a study of the current system. Before the end of your visit with Mr. Iverson, the two of you construct the organization chart shown in Figure 8-2.

In subsequent interviews with Ms. Christie and other Swift personnel, you find that deteriorating customer service seems to be due to lack of information about inventory supplies. Together, you and Ms. Christie determine the problem definition, as shown in Figure 8-4. Mr. Iverson accepts your report, in which you outline the problem definition and suggest a full analysis.

Phase 1: Preliminary Investigation

The **preliminary investigation**—often called the **feasibility study,** or **system survey**—is the initial investigation, a brief study of the problem. It consists of the groundwork necessary to determine if the systems project should be pursued. You, as the systems analyst, need to determine what the problem is and what to do about it. The net result will be a rough plan for how—and if—to proceed with the project.

Essentially, this means you must be able to describe the problem. To do this, you will work with the users. One of your tools will be an **organization chart,** which is a hierarchical drawing showing management by name and title. Figure 8-2 shows an example of an organization chart. Constructing such a chart is not an idle task. If you are to work effectively within the organization, you need to understand what the lines of authority through the formal communication channels are.

Problem Definition: Nature, Scope, Objectives

Your initial aim is to define the problem. You and the users must come to an agreement on these points: You must agree on the nature of the problem and then designate a limited scope. In the process you will also determine what the objectives of the project are. Figure 8-3 shows an overview of the problem definition process, and Figure 8-4 (page 263) gives an example related to the Swift Sport Shoes project.

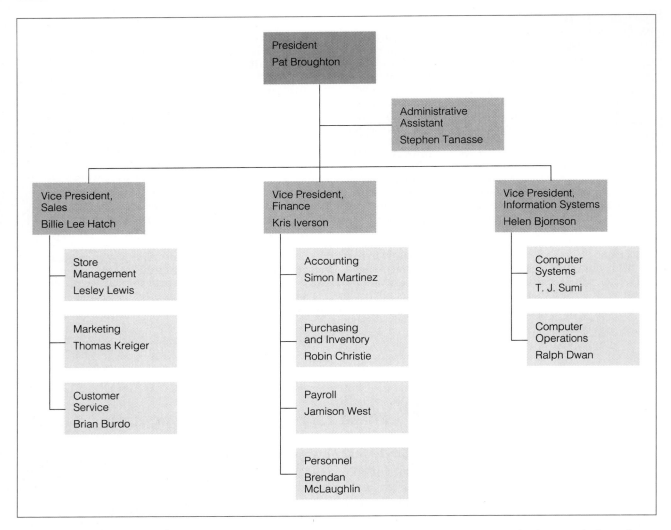

Figure 8-2 An organization chart. The chart shows the lines of authority and formal communication channels. This example shows the organizational setup for Swift Sport Shoes, a chain of stores.

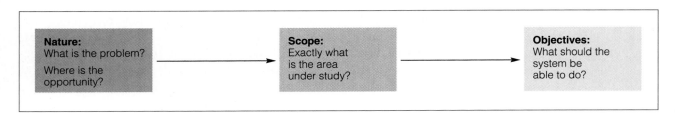

Figure 8-3 Problem definition overview.

Nature of the Problem Begin by determining the true nature of the problem. Sometimes what appears to be the problem turns out to be, on a closer look, only a symptom. For example, suppose you are examining customer complaints of late deliveries. Your brief study may reveal that the problem is not in the shipping department, as you first thought, but in the original ordering process.

Figure 8-4   Problem definition. The nature and scope of the problem along with system objectives are shown for the Swift Sport Shoes system.

SWIFT SPORT SHOES: PROBLEM DEFINITION

True Nature of the Problem

The nature of the problem is the existing manual inventory system. In particular:

–Products are frequently out of stock

–There is little interstore communication about stock items

–Store managers have no information about stock levels on a day-to-day basis

–Ordering is done haphazardly

Scope

The scope of the project will be limited to the development of an inventory system using appropriate computer technology.

Objectives

The new automated inventory system should provide the following:

–Adequate stock maintained in stores

–Automatic stock reordering

–Stock distribution among stores

–Management access to current inventory information

–Ease of use

–Reduced operating costs of the inventory function

Scope   Establishing the scope of the problem is critical because problems tend to expand if no firm boundaries are established. Limitations are also necessary to stay within the eventual budget and schedule. So in the beginning the analyst and user must agree on the scope of the project: what the new or revised system is supposed to do—and not do. If the scope is too broad the project will never be finished, but if the scope is too narrow it may not meet user needs.

Objectives   You will soon come to understand what the user needs—that is, what the user thinks the system should be able to do. You will want to express these needs as objectives. Examine the objectives for the Swift inventory process. The people who run the existing inventory system already know what such a system must do. It remains for you and them to work out how this can be achieved on a computer system. In the next phase, the systems analysis phase, you will produce a more specific list of system requirements, based on these objectives.

Wrapping Up the Preliminary Investigation

The preliminary investigation, which is necessarily brief, should result in some sort of report, perhaps only a few pages long, telling management what you found and listing your recommendations. At this point management has three choices: They can (1) drop the matter; (2) fix the problem immediately, if it is simple; or (3) authorize you to go on to the next phase for a closer look.

Phase 2: Systems Analysis

Let us suppose management has decided to continue. Remember that the purpose of **systems analysis** is to understand the existing system. A related goal is to establish the system requirements. The best way to understand a system is to gather all the data you can about it; this data must then be organized and analyzed. During the systems analysis phase, then, you will be concerned with (1) data gathering and (2) data analysis. Keep in mind that the system being analyzed may or may not already be a computerized system.

Data Gathering

Data gathering is expensive and requires a lot of legwork and time. There is no standard procedure for gathering data because each system is unique. But there are certain sources that are commonly used:

- Written documents
- Interviews
- Questionnaires
- Observation
- Sampling

Sometimes you will use all these sources, but in most cases it will be appropriate to use some and not others. All references to data-gathering techniques assume that you have the proper authority and the cooperation of the client organization before proceeding.

Written Documents   These include procedures manuals, reports, forms, and any other kind of material bearing on the problem that you find in the organization. You may find very few documents and no trail to follow. Sometimes the opposite is true: There are so many documents that it is difficult to know how to sift through them. Thus, judgment is required, or you will spend hours reading outdated reports or manuals that no one follows. In particular, take time to get a copy of each form an organization uses.

Interviews   This method of data gathering has advantages and disadvantages. A key advantage is that interviews are flexible; as the interviewer, you can change the direction of your questions if you discover a valuable area of investigation. Another bonus is that you can probe with open-ended questions that people would balk at answering on paper. You will find that some respondents yield more information in an interview than they would if they had to commit themselves in writing. You can

Some Tips for Successful Interviewing

- Plan questions in advance—even if you vary from them during the interview.

- Listen carefully to the answers and observe the respondent's voice inflection and body movements for clues to evaluate responses.

- Dress and behave in a business-like manner.

- Avoid technical jargon.

- Respect the respondent's schedule.

- Avoid office gossip and discussion of the respondent's personal problems.

also observe the respondent's voice inflection and body motions, which may tell you more than words alone. Finally, of course, there is the bonus of getting to know clients better and establishing a rapport with them—an important factor in promoting user involvement in the system from the beginning.

Interviews have certain drawbacks. They are unquestionably time-consuming and therefore expensive. You will not have the time or the money to interview large numbers of people. If you need to find out about procedures from 40 mail clerks, for example, you are better off using a questionnaire.

There are two types of interviews—structured and unstructured. A **structured interview** includes only questions that have been planned and written out in advance. The interviewer sticks to those questions and asks no others. A structured interview is useful when it is desirable—or required by law—to ask identical questions of several people. However, the **unstructured interview** is often more productive. An unstructured interview includes questions prepared in advance, but the interviewer is willing to vary from the line of questioning and pursue other subjects if they seem appropriate.

Questionnaires   Unlike interviews, questionnaires can be used to get information from large groups. They allow people to respond anonymously—the respondents just complete forms and turn them in—and presumably, they respond more truthfully. Questionnaires do have disadvantages, however. Some people will not return questionnaires because they are wary of putting anything on paper, even anonymously. And the questionnaires you do get back may contain biased answers.

There are many types of questionnaires; the ballot-box type (in which the respondent simply checks off "yes" or "no") and the qualified response (in which one rates agreement or disagreement with the question on a scale from, say, 1 to 5) are two common examples. In general, people prefer a questionnaire that is quick and simple. Analysts also prefer simple questionnaires because their results are easier to tabulate. If you have long, open-ended questions, such as "Please describe your job functions," you should probably save them for an interview. In general, questionnaires should be written by those who are experts in the subject area as well as experienced in the art of questioning.

Observation   As an analyst and observer, you go into the organization and watch how data flows, who interrelates with whom, how paper moves from desk to desk, and how it comes into and leaves the organization. Normally, you make arrangements with a group supervisor, and you return on more than one occasion so that the people under observation become used to your presence. The purpose of your visits is known to the members of the organization. One form of observation is **participant observation;** in this form the analyst temporarily joins the activities of the group. This practice may be useful in studying a complicated organization.

SYSTEMS ANALYSIS

With the assistance of Ms. Christie, you learn more about the current inventory system. She helps set up interviews with store managers and arranges to have you observe procedures in the stores and at the warehouse. As the number of stores has increased, significant expansion has taken place in all inventory-related areas: sales, scope of merchandise, and number of vendors.

Out-of-stock situations are common. The stock shortages are not uniform across all ten stores, however; frequently one store will be out of an item that the central warehouse or another store has on hand. The present system is not effective at recognizing this situation and transferring merchandise. There is a tendency for stock to be reordered only when the shelf is empty or nearly so. Inventory-related costs are significant, especially those for special orders of some stock items. Reports to management are minimal and often too late to be useful. Finally, there is no way to correlate order quantities with past sales records, future projections, or inventory situations.

During this period you also analyze the data as it is gathered. You prepare data flow diagrams of the various activities relating to inventory. Figure 8-6 shows the general flow of data to handle purchasing in the existing system. You prepare various decision tables, such as the one shown in Figure 8-7b.

Your written report to Mr. Iverson includes the list of system requirements in Figure 8-8.

Sampling   You may need to collect data about quantities, costs, time periods, and other factors relevant to the system. How many phone orders can be taken by an order entry clerk in an hour? If you are dealing with a major mail-order organization, such as L. L. Bean in Maine, this type of question may be best answered through a procedure called sampling: Instead of observing all 75 clerks filling orders for an hour, pick a sample of 3 or 4 clerks. Or, in a case involving a high volume of paper output, such as customer bills, you could collect a random sample of a few dozen bills.

Data Analysis

Your data-gathering processes will probably produce an alarming amount of paper and a strong need to get organized. It is now time to turn your attention to the second activity of this phase, data analysis. What, indeed, are you going to do with all the data you have gathered? There are a variety of tools—charts and diagrams—used to analyze data, not all of them appropriate for every system. You should become familiar with the techniques, then use the tools that suit you at the time. We will consider two typical tools: data flow diagrams and decision tables.

The reasons for data analysis are related to the basic functions of the systems analysis phase: to show how the current system works and to determine the system requirements. In addition, data analysis materials will serve as the basis for documentation of the system.

Data Flow Diagrams   A **data flow diagram** (**DFD**) is a sort of road map that graphically shows the flow of data through a system. It is a valuable tool for depicting present procedures and data flow. Although data flow diagrams can be used in the design process, they are particularly useful for facilitating communication between you and the users during the analysis phase. Suppose, for example, you spend a couple of hours with a McDonald's franchise manager, talking about the paperwork that keeps the burgers and the customers flowing. You would probably make copi-

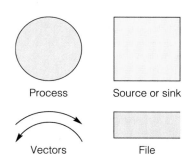

Figure 8-5 Data flow diagram symbols.

Figure 8-6 A data flow diagram. This "map" shows the current flow of data in the purchasing department at Swift Sport Shoes. The diagram (greatly simplified) includes authorization for purchases of goods, purchase-order preparation, and verification of the vendor's invoice against the purchase order. Note that the stores, vendors, and accounts payable are in square boxes because they are outside the purchasing department.

ous notes about what goes on where. But that is only the data-gathering function—now you must somehow analyze your findings. You could come back on another day with pages of narrative for the manager to review or, instead, show an easy-to-follow picture. Most users would prefer the picture.

There are a variety of notations for data flow diagrams. The notation used here has been chosen because it is informal and easy to draw and read.

The elements of a data flow diagram are processes, files, sources and sinks, and vectors, as shown in Figure 8-5. Note also the DFD for Swift Sport Shoes (Figure 8-6) as you follow this discussion.

Processes, represented by circles, are the actions taken on the data—comparing, checking, stamping, authorizing, filing, and so forth. A **file** is a repository of data—a tape or disk file, a set of papers in a file cabinet, or even mail in an in-basket or blank envelopes in a supply bin. In a DFD a file is represented by an open-ended box.

A **source** is a data origin outside the organization. An example is a payment sent to a department store by a charge customer; the customer is a source of data. A **sink** is a destination for data going outside the organization; an example is the bank that receives money from the accounts receivable organization. A source or a sink is represented by a square. **Vectors** are simply arrows, lines with directional notation. A vector must come from or go to a process circle, or bubble.

Decision Tables   A **decision table,** also called a **decision logic table,** is a standard table of the logical decisions that must be made regarding potential conditions in a given system. Decision tables are useful in cases

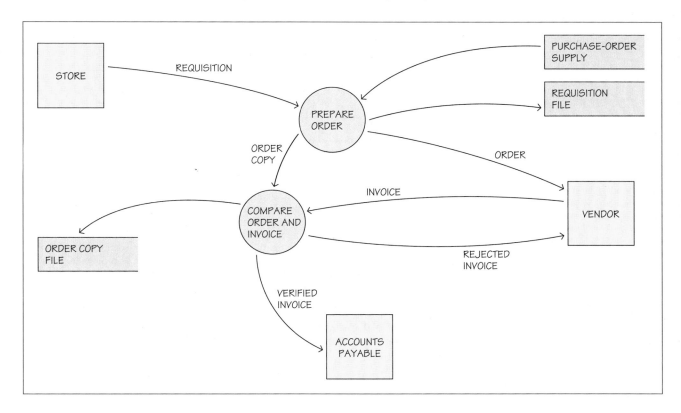

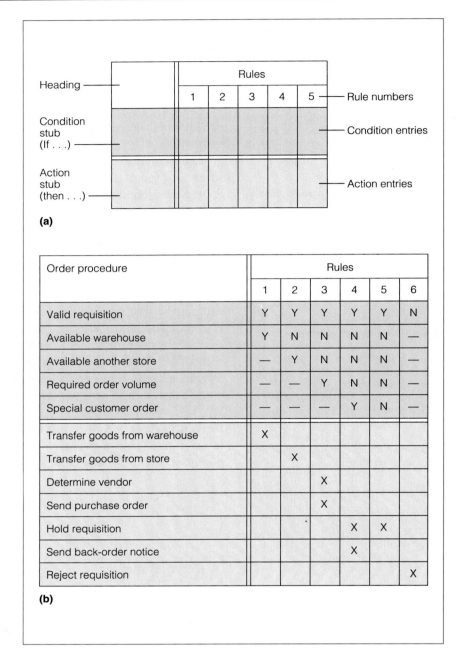

Figure 8-7   Decision tables. (a) The format of a decision table. The table is organized according to the logic that "If this condition exists or is met, then do this." (b) A decision table example. This decision table, which describes the current ordering procedure at Swift Sport Shoes, takes into consideration whether a requisition for goods from a store is valid, the availability of the wanted goods in the warehouse or some other Swift store, whether the quantity ordered warrants an inventory order, and if the order is a special order for a customer. Examine rule 4. The requisition is valid, so we proceed. The desired goods are not available in either the warehouse or in another store, so they must be ordered. However, there is not the required volume of customer demand to place a standard inventory order now, so the requisition is put on hold until there is. (In other words, this order will be joined with others.) And, finally, since this is a special customer order and the order is on hold, a back-order notice is sent.

that involve a series of interrelated decisions; their use helps to ensure that no alternatives are overlooked. Programmers can code portions of a program right from a decision table. Figure 8-7a shows the format of a decision table; Figure 8-7b gives an example of a decision table that applies to the Swift Sport Shoes system.

As you know, data flow diagrams and decision tables are typical data analysis vehicles, but they are by no means the only data analysis tools.

System Requirements

As we mentioned, the purpose of gathering and analyzing data is twofold: to understand the system and, as a by-product of that understanding, to establish the system requirements. The description of the system was quite broad in the preliminary investigation phase, but now you are ready to list precise system requirements. You need to determine and document specific user needs. A system that a bank teller uses, for example, needs to be able to retrieve a customer record and display it on a screen within five seconds. The importance of accurate requirements cannot be overemphasized, because the design of the new system will be based on the system requirements. Note the requirements for the Swift system, in Figure 8-8.

Report to Management

When you have finished the systems analysis phase, you present a report to management. This comprehensive report, part of the continuing process of documentation, summarizes the problems you found in the current system, describes the requirements for the new system, and makes recommendations on what course to take next. If implementing the new system presents significant problems, this might be a good point for management to stop the project, because the investment is still small relative to the amount that will be invested when programming begins. If management decides to pursue the project, you move on to phase 3.

Figure 8-8   System requirements. These are the requirements for an inventory system for Swift Sport Shoes.

SWIFT SPORT SHOES: REQUIREMENTS

The requirements for the Swift Sport Shoes inventory system are as follows:

–Capture inventory data from sales transactions

–Implement automatic inventory reordering

–Implement a standardized interstore transfer system

–Provide both on-demand and scheduled management reports

–Provide security and accounting controls throughout the system

–Provide a user-oriented system whose on-line usage can be learned by a new user in one training class

–Reduce operating costs of the inventory function by 20%

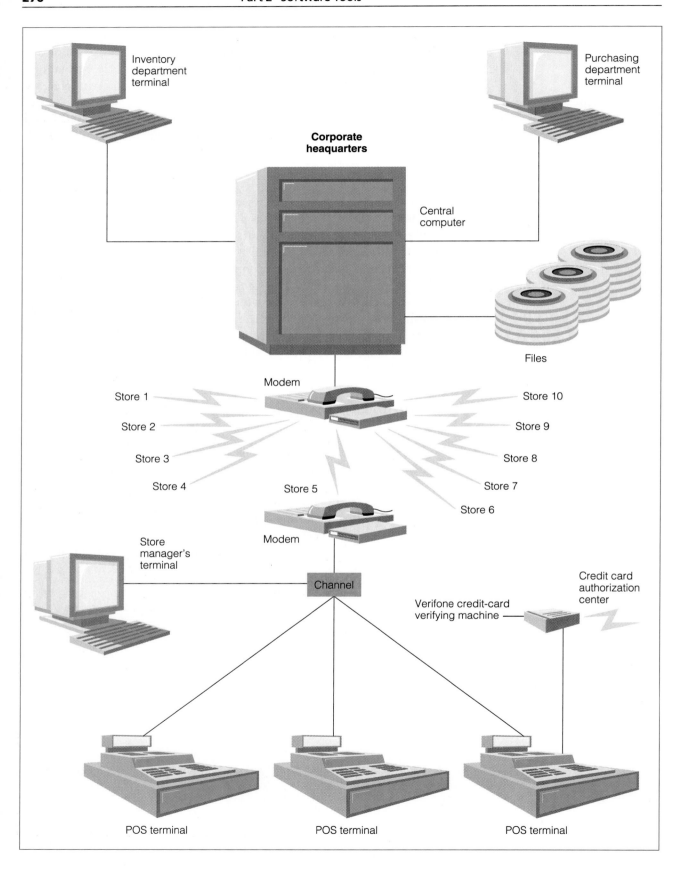

Inventory department terminal

Purchasing department terminal

Corporate heaquarters

Central computer

Files

Modem

Store 1
Store 2
Store 3
Store 4
Store 5

Store 10
Store 9
Store 8
Store 7
Store 6

Modem

Store manager's terminal

Channel

Credit card authorization center

Verifone credit-card verifying machine

POS terminal   POS terminal   POS terminal

Phase 3: Systems Design

The **systems design** phase is the phase in which you actually plan the new system. This phase is divided into two subphases: **preliminary design,** in which the analyst establishes the new system concept, followed by **detail design,** in which the analyst determines exact design specifications. The reason this phase is divided into two parts is that an analyst wants to make sure management approves the overall plan before spending time on details.

Preliminary Design

The first task of preliminary design is to review the system requirements, then to consider some of the major aspects of a system. Should the system be centralized or distributed? Should the system be on-line? Should packaged software be purchased as opposed to having programmers write new software? Can the system be run on the user's personal computers? How will input data be captured? What kind of reports will be needed?

The questions can go on and on. Eventually, together with key personnel from the user organization, you determine an overall plan. In fact, it is common to offer alternative plans, called **candidates.** Each candidate meets the user's requirements but with variations in features and costs. The chosen candidate is usually the one that best meets the user's needs and is flexible enough to meet future needs. The selected plan is expanded and described so that it can be understood by both the user and the analyst.

At this stage it is wise to make a formal presentation of the plan or all the alternatives. The point is that you do not want to commit time and energy to—nor does the user want to pay for—a detailed design until you and the user agree on the basic design. Such presentations often include a drawing of the system from a user's perspective, such as the one shown in Figure 8-9 for the Swift Sport Shoes system. This is the time to emphasize system benefits—see the list in Figure 8-10.

Figure 8-9   Overview of the system. This overview shows the Swift Sport Shoes inventory system from a user's point of view. *Input* data is from point-of-sale (POS) terminals. Except for local editing, *processing* takes place in the central computer. All *storage* files are located at the central site. *Output* is in the form of screen displays and printed reports.

Figure 8-10   Benefits. Benefits are usually closely tied to the system objectives. These are the anticipated benefits of the new Swift Sport Shoes inventory system.

SWIFT SPORT SHOES: ANTICIPATED BENEFITS

–Better inventory control

–Improved customer service

–Improved management information

–Reduced inventory costs

–Improved employee morale

Presentations

Presentations often come at the completion of a phase, especially the analysis and design phases. They give you an opportunity to formalize the project in a public way and to look good in front of the brass.

The full range of presentation techniques—using visuals, planning logistics, keeping the audience focused, communicating effectively, and minimizing stage fright—must be topics for another book, but we can consider presentation *content* here.

- **State the problem.** Although you do not want to belabor the problem statement, you do want to show you understand it.

- **State the benefits.** These are a new system's whole reason for being, so your argument here should be carefully planned. Will the system improve accuracy, speed turnaround, save processing time, save money? The more specific you can be, the better.

- **Explain the analysis/design.** Here you should give a general presentation, then be prepared to take questions about details. Remember that higher management will not be interested in hearing all the details.

- **Present a schedule.** How long is it going to take to carry out the plan? Give your audience the time frame.

- **Estimate the costs.** The costs include development costs (those required to construct the system) and operating costs (those ongoing costs of running the system). You will also need to tell your audience how long it is going to be before they get a return on their original investment.

- **Answer questions.** The question-and-answer period will make you appreciate the value of having involved the system user from the very beginning. After all, the audience for the presentation is made up of users (and perhaps their boss), and you should have resolved the stickiest questions well before this point. A good rule of thumb is to save half the allotted time for questions.

Prototyping

The idea of building a prototype—a sort of guinea-pig model of the system—has taken a sharp upward turn in popularity recently. Considered from a systems viewpoint, a **prototype** is a limited working system—or subset of a system—that is developed quickly, sometimes in just a few days. A prototype is a working model, one that can be tinkered with and fine-tuned. The idea is that users can get an idea of what the system might be like before it is fully developed. If they are not satisfied, they can revise their requirements before a lot has been invested in developing the new system.

Could you adopt this approach to systems development? It seems at odds with this chapter's systems development life cycle, which promotes doing steps in the proper order. And yet, some analysts in the computer industry are making good use of prototypes. We need to ask how and why. The "how" begins with prototyping tools.

Prototyping Tools   The prototype approach exploits advances in computer technology and uses powerful high-level software tools. These software packages allow analysts to build quick systems in response to user needs. In particular recall the fourth-generation languages we discussed in Chapter 6. One of their key advantages is that they can be used to produce something quickly. The systems produced can then be refined and modified as they are used, in a continual process, until the fit between user and system is acceptable.

Why Prototyping?   Many organizations use prototyping on a limited basis. For example, an organization may make a prototype to demonstrate a certain data entry sequence, a particular screen output, or an especially complex or questionable part of a design. That is, prototyping does not necessarily have the scope of the final system. Some organizations develop throwaway prototypes that they use only to get a grip on the requirements; then they begin again and go through the systems development life cycle formally. Other organizations start with a prototype and keep massaging it until it becomes the final and accepted version. In either case a prototype forces users to get actively involved.

Prototyping is a possibility if you work in an organization that has quick-build software and management support for this departure from traditional systems procedures.

Prototype Results   What is the net result of making a prototype of a system? What will it produce for users? A prototype of a whole system will initially include minimum input data, no editing checks, incomplete files, limited security checks, sketchy reports, and minimum documentation. But actual software uses real data to produce real output. Remember that prototyping is an iterative process; the system is changed again and again based on the lessons learned by creating the prototype.

The computer industry is looking even beyond prototyping, to a future using CASE tools.

SYSTEMS DESIGN

The store managers, who were uneasy at the beginning of the study, are by now enthusiastic participants in the design of the new system they are counting on for better control of their inventory. As part of the preliminary design phase, you offer three alternative system candidates for consideration. The first is a centralized system, with all processing done at the headquarters computer and batch reports generated on a daily basis. The third takes the opposite approach, placing all processing in the stores on their own minicomputers. The second candidate, the one selected, includes processing at the central site; however, data will be edited locally, at the individual stores, before transmission to the central site.

The chosen alternative makes use of point-of-sale (POS) terminals at the store checkout counters, where inventory data is captured as a by-product of the sale. There will be continuous two-way data transmission between the stores and the central site. All files will be maintained at the central site. Output will be in two forms: printed reports and on-demand status reports on terminal screens available to store managers locally and to department managers in the headquarters office. Figure 8-9 shows the overall design from a user's viewpoint. The key ingredient of the proposed solution is an automatic reorder procedure: The computer generates orders for any product shown to be below the preset reorder mark.

You make a formal presentation to Mr. Iverson and other members of company management. Slides you prepared on a microcomputer (with special presentation software) accent your points visually. After a brief statement of the problem, you list anticipated benefits to the company; these are listed in Figure 8-10. You explain the design in general terms and describe the expected costs and schedules. With the money saved from the reduced inventory expenses, you project that the system development costs will be repaid in three years. Swift Sport Shoes management accepts your recommendations, and you proceed with the detail design phase.

You design printed reports and screen displays for managers; samples are shown in Figures 8-12 and 8-13. There are many other exacting and time-consuming activities associated with detail design. Although space prohibits discussing them, we list some of these tasks here to give you the flavor of the complexity: You must plan the use of wand readers to read stock codes from merchandise tags, plan to download (send) the price file daily to be stored in the POS terminals, plan all files on disk with regular backups on tape, design the records in each file and the methods to access the files, design the data communications system, draw diagrams to show the flow of the data in the system, and prepare structure charts of program modules. Figure 8-15 shows a skeleton version of a systems flowchart that represents part of the inventory processing. Some of these activities, such as data communications, require special expertise, so you may be coordinating with specialists. Several systems controls are planned, among them a unique numbering system for stock items and editing of all data input at the terminal.

You make another presentation to managers and more technical people, including representatives from information systems. You are given the go-ahead.

CASE Tools

CASE tools turn traditional systems approaches upside down. The set of software known as **CASE**—for **computer-aided software engineering**—tools goes beyond the concept of prototyping and has become a significant factor in the development of systems. CASE tools provide an automated means of designing and changing systems (Figure 8-11). In fact, integrated CASE tools can automate most of the systems development life cycle.

These tools let the systems analyst generate designs right on the computer screen. Thus, a key ingredient of a package of CASE tools is a graphics interface. What is more, that screen is usually part of a personal computer. Other important CASE ingredients are a data store—often called a data dictionary or even an encyclopedia—and the ability to generate code automatically, right from the design.

CASE tools have several advantages. Foremost is the ability to note inconsistencies in the system design. Such tools can also make global changes related to a single change; for example, if you change a name in

Figure 8-11   CASE tools. Here is a data flow diagram produced by Excelerator, a commercially available CASE package. Notice that Excelerator uses rounded squares for data flow diagram processes.

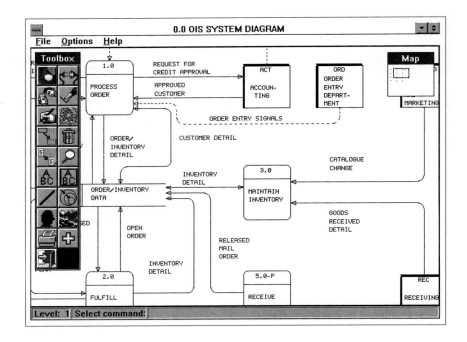

one place, the CASE tool automatically changes it throughout the design specifications. CASE tools provide consistency, speed, increased productivity, and cost savings.

But they are not cure-alls. To begin with, they really have value only for new systems—an estimated 80% of computer organization time is devoted to the maintenance of existing systems. Also, CASE standards have not been established, and the result is a hodgepodge of methodologies from a variety of vendors. Finally, it is the nature of evolving technology to have setbacks—to pursue goals that are eventually proved unworthwhile or implement methods that turn out to be inefficient. But CASE technology will evolve because business demands faster, better ways to create new systems.

Detail Design

Let's say that the users have accepted your design proposal—you are on your way. You must now develop detailed design specifications, or a detail design. This is a time-consuming part of the project, but it is relatively straightforward.

In this phase, every facet of the system is considered in detail. Here is a list of some detail design activities: designing output forms and screens, planning input data forms and procedures, drawing system flowcharts, planning file access methods and record formats, planning database interfaces, planning data communications interfaces, designing system security controls, and considering human factors. This list is not comprehensive, nor will all activities listed be used for all systems. Some analysts choose to plan the overall logic at this stage, preparing program structure charts, pseudocode, and the like.

Normally, in the detail design phase, parts of the system are considered in this order:

- Output requirements
- Input requirements
- Files and databases
- System processing
- System controls and backup

Output Requirements   Before you can do anything, you must know exactly what the client wants the system to produce—the output. This may seem backwards to you, but consider how you might plan for a vacation: You need to know where you are going before you consider how to travel or what clothes to pack. As an analyst, you must also consider the *medium* of the output—paper, computer screen, microfilm, and so on. In addition, you must determine the *type* of reports needed (summary, exception, and so on) and the *contents* of the output—what data is needed for the reports. What *forms* the output will be printed on is also a consideration; they may need to be custom-printed if they go outside the organization to customers or stockholders. You may wish to determine the report format by using a **printer spacing chart,** which shows the position of headings, the spacing between columns, and the location of date and page numbers (Figure 8-12). You may also use screen reports, mockups on paper of how the screen will respond to user queries. A sample screen report is shown in Figure 8-13.

Input Requirements   Once your desired output is determined, you must consider what kind of input is required to produce it. First you must consider the input *medium:* Will you try to capture data at the source via

Figure 8-12 Example of a printer spacing chart. This chart shows how a systems analyst wishes the report format to look—headings, columns, and so on—when displayed on a printer. This example shows discontinued items, a report that is part of the new Swift Sport Shoes system.

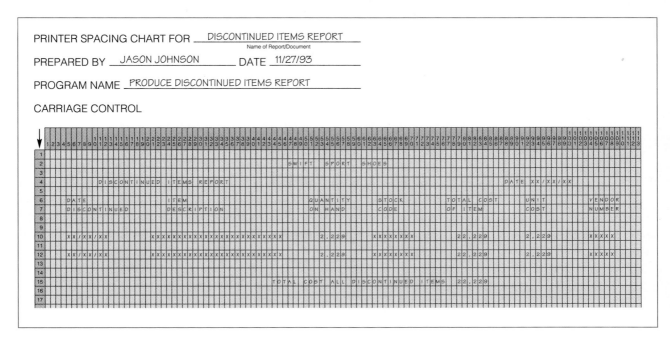

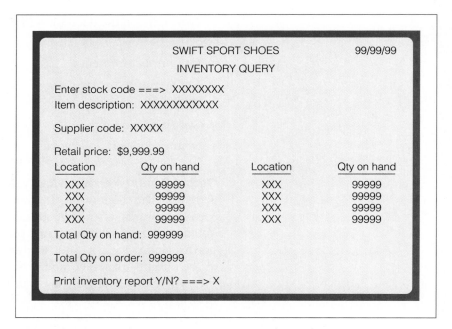

Figure 8-13   Example of a screen report. This screen report has been designed as part of the Swift Sport Shoes system. The purpose of the screen is to give information about how much of a given stock item is in each store. The report shows an approximation of what the user will see after entering a stock code.

point-of-sale (POS) terminals? Will you put it on diskettes? Next you must consider *content* again—what fields are needed, the order in which they come, and the like. This in turn may involve designing *forms* that will organize data before it is entered. You need to plan some kind of input *editing* process, a check that data is reasonable as well as accurate—you would not expect a six-figure salary, for example, for someone who works in the mail room. Finally, you need to consider input *volume*, particularly the volume at peak periods. Can the system handle it? A mail-order house, for instance, may have to be ready for higher sales of expensive toys in the December holiday season than at other times of the year.

Files and Databases   You need to consider how the files in your computer system will be organized: sequentially, directly, with an index, or by some other method. You also need to decide how the files should be accessed. They might be organized as indexed files but be accessed directly or sequentially, for example. You need to determine the format of records making up the data files. If the system has one or more databases, collections of interrelated data (a subject we will cover at length in Chapter 11), then you will have to coordinate your design efforts with the database administrator, the person responsible for controlling and updating databases.

Systems Processing   Just as you drew a flow diagram to describe the old system, now you need to show the flow of data in the new system. One method is to use standard ANSI flowchart symbols (Figure 8-14) to

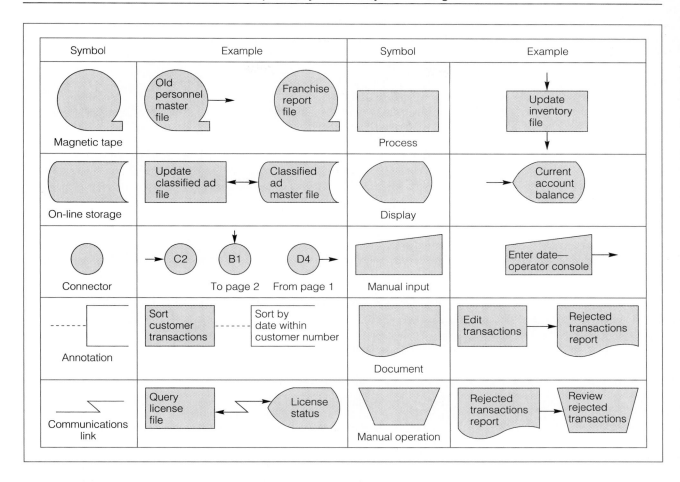

Symbol	Example	Symbol	Example
Magnetic tape	Old personnel master file → Franchise report file	Process	Update inventory file
On-line storage	Update classified ad file ↔ Classified ad master file	Display	→ Current account balance
Connector	→ C2 B1 D4 → To page 2 From page 1	Manual input	Enter date—operator console →
Annotation	Sort customer transactions ----- Sort by date within customer number	Document	Edit transactions → Rejected transactions report
Communications link	Query license file ↔ License status	Manual operation	Rejected transactions report → Review rejected transactions

Figure 8-14   ANSI systems flowchart symbols. These are some of the symbols recommended by the American National Standards Institute for systems flowcharts, which show the movement of data through a system.

illustrate what will be done and what files will be used. Figure 8-15 shows a resulting **systems flowchart.** Another popular way to describe processing is the structure chart mentioned in Chapter 6 and described in Appendix A. Note that a systems flowchart is not the same as the logic flowchart used in programming. The systems flowchart describes only the "big picture"; a logic flowchart represents the flow of logic in a program.

Systems Controls and Backup   To make sure data is input, processed, and output correctly and to prevent fraud and tampering with the computer system, you will need to institute appropriate controls. Begin with the source documents, such as time cards or sales orders. Each document should be serially numbered so the system can keep track of it. Documents are time-stamped when received and then grouped in batches. Each batch is labeled with the number of documents per batch; these counts are balanced against totals of the processed data. The input is controlled to make sure data is accurately converted from source documents to machine-processable form. Data input to on-line systems is backed up by **system journals,** files whose records represent the transactions made at the terminal, such as an account withdrawal through a bank teller. Processing controls include the data editing procedures we mentioned in the section on input requirements.

It is also important to plan for the backup of system files; copies of

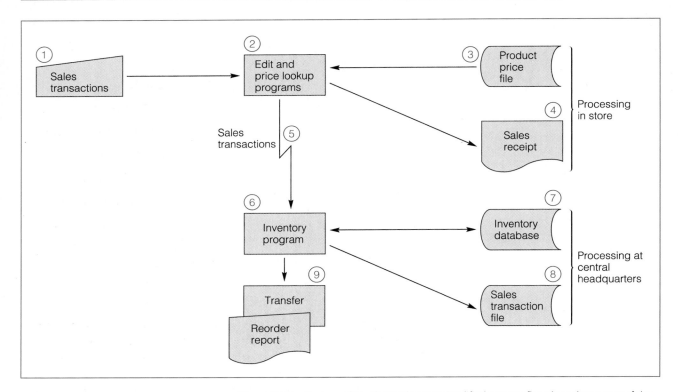

Figure 8-15   Systems flowchart. This very simplified systems flowchart shows part of the processing for the new Swift Sport Shoes inventory system. Note that the top half of the drawing shows processing that occurs in the store. The processing takes place in a POS terminal while the customer waits. The bottom part of the drawing shows processing that is done on the computer at the central headquarters site. The clerk ① inputs sales transaction data, which ② is edited by the POS terminal processor. The POS terminal also looks up the item price from the ③ files downloaded earlier in the day from the central site, then ④ prints a sales receipt. That takes care of the customer. Meanwhile, ⑤ the sales transaction data is sent over data communications lines to the central computer, which ⑥ processes it for inventory purposes by updating the ⑦ inventory database, placing the ⑧ sales transaction on its own file for later auditing and for producing ⑨ transfer and reorder reports as needed.

transaction and master files should be made on a regular basis. These file copies are stored temporarily in case the originals are inadvertently lost or damaged. Often the backup copies are stored off site for added security. We will focus on security in Chapter 15.

As before, the results of this phase are documented. The resulting report, usually referred to as the detail design specifications, is large and detailed and is an outgrowth of the preliminary design document. A presentation often accompanies the completion of this stage. Unless something unexpected has happened, it is normal to proceed now with the development of the system.

Phase 4: Systems Development

Finally, the system is actually going to be developed. As a systems analyst you prepare a schedule to monitor the principal activities in **systems development**—programming and testing.

Figure 8-16   Gantt chart. This bar chart shows the scheduled tasks and milestones of the Swift Sport Shoes project. Notice that some phases overlap.

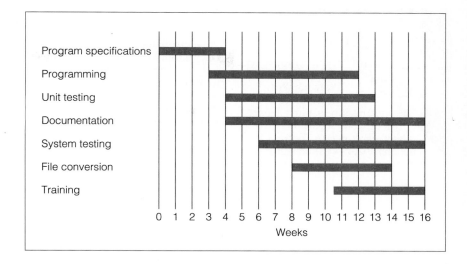

Scheduling

Figure 8-16 shows what is known as a **Gantt chart,** a bar chart commonly used to depict schedule deadlines and milestones. In our example the chart shows the work to be accomplished over a given period. It does not, however, show the number of work hours required. If you were the supervisor, it would be common practice for you to ask others on the development team to produce individual Gantt charts of their own activities.

Programming

Until this point there has been no programming. (Sometimes people jump the gun and start programming early, but the task often has to be done over if started with incomplete specifications.) Before programming begins, you need to prepare detail design specifications. Program development tools must be considered. Some of this work may already have been done as part of the design phase, but usually programmers participate in refining the design at this point. Design specifications can be developed through detailed logic flowcharts and pseudocode, among other tools.

Testing

Would you write a program, then simply turn it over to the client without testing it first? Of course not. Thus, the programmers perform **unit testing,** by which they individually test their own program pieces (units), using test data. This is followed by **system testing,** which determines whether all the program units work together satisfactorily. During this process the development team uses test data to test every part of the programs. Finally, **volume testing** uses real data in large amounts. Volume testing sometimes reveals errors that do not show up with test data—errors in storage or memory usage.

As in every phase of the project, documentation is required. Indeed, documentation is an ongoing activity (as the Gantt chart in Figure 8-16

CASE STUDY

SYSTEMS DEVELOPMENT

Working with Dennis Harrington of the information systems department, you prepare a Gantt chart, as shown in Figure 8-16. This chart shows the schedule for the inventory project.

Program design specifications are prepared using pseudocode, the design tool Mr. Harrington thinks will be most useful to programmers. The programs will be written in COBOL, since that is the primary language of the installation and it is suitable for this business application. Three programmers are assigned to the project.

You work with the programmers to develop a test plan. Some inventory data, both typical and atypical, is prepared to test the new system. You and the programmers continue to build on the documentation base by implementing the pseudocode and by preparing detailed data descriptions, logic narratives, program listings, test data results, and related material.

shows). In this phase documentation describes the program logic and detailed data formats.

Phase 5: Implementation

You may think that implementation means quitting one system and starting the new one. You are not alone. Many companies believe that also, but they find out that there is much more to it. Even though **implementation** is the final phase, a good deal of effort is still required, including the following activities:

- Training
- Equipment conversion
- File conversion
- System conversion
- Auditing
- Evaluation
- Maintenance

Training

Often systems analysts do not give training the attention it deserves, because they are so concerned about the computer system itself. But a system can be no better than the people using it. A good time to start training—for at least a few of the users—is at some point during the testing, so that people can begin to learn how to use the system even as the development team is checking it out.

An important tool in training is the user's manual, a document prepared to aid users not familiar with the computer system. The user's manual can be an outgrowth of the other documentation. But documentation for the user is just the beginning. Any teacher knows that students learn best by doing. Besides, users are as likely to read a thick manual as they are to read a dictionary. The message is clear: Users must receive

A New Entrance for the Louvre

When visitors arrive at the historic Louvre museum in Paris, France, they are greeted by a gleaming, towering pyramid—part of the renowned museum's new public entrance. After a study of the flow of traffic in and around the Louvre's diverse treasures—a study that demanded the skills and approach common for systems analysis, incidentally—the museum redesigned its entranceway to improve accessibility to visitors from around the world.

Designed by I. M. Pei, the eye-catching pyramid complex includes the museum bookstore and a variety of shops supported by an IBM AS/400 minicomputer and 15 IBM point-of-sale (POS) terminals.

hands-on training to learn to use the system. The trainer must prepare exercises that simulate the tasks users will be required to do. For example, a hotel clerk learning a new on-line reservation system is given typical requests to fulfill and uses a terminal to practice. The user's manual is used as a reference guide. Setting all this up is not a trivial task; the trainer must consider class space, equipment, data, and the users' schedules. Experts believe that the person who does the training should not be one of the data processing people who may talk over the heads of the learners; they feel the best trainer may be their own supervisor who knows the learners and can relate to their needs.

Equipment Conversion

Equipment considerations vary from almost none to installing a mainframe computer and all its peripheral equipment. If you are implementing a small- or medium-size system on established equipment in a major information systems department, then perhaps your equipment considerations will involve no more than negotiating scheduled run time and disk space. If you are purchasing a moderate amount of equipment, such as terminals and modems, then you will be concerned primarily with delivery schedules and compatibility. A major equipment purchase, on the other hand, demands a large amount of time and attention.

For a major equipment purchase you will need site preparation advice from vendors and other equipment experts. You may be considering having walls moved! You will need to know the exact dimensions and weight of the new equipment to fit it through doors and locate it in various parts of a building. You may need to protect the systems from damage by dirt, water—leaky plumbing and roofs happen—and even fire. You may even need to consider electrical capacity and wiring hookups as well as new flooring—flooring that is raised to hide cabling and ease access for repairs to large computers and related equipment. Finally, most medium to large machines need air conditioning and humidity control.

Personal computer systems are far less demanding, but they too require site planning in terms of the availability of space, accessibility, and cleanliness. And, as the analyst, you are probably the one who does the actual installation.

File Conversion

This activity may be very tricky if the existing files are handled manually. The data must be prepared in such a way that it is accessible to computer systems. All the contents of the file drawers in the personnel department, for instance, must now be keyed to be stored on disk. Some scheme must be used to input the data files and keep them updated. You may need to employ temporary help. If many files have already been converted to some machine-accessible form—for use in a prior automated system—you may need to write a program to convert the old files to the format needed for the new system. This is a much speedier process than

IMPLEMENTATION

While the system is being developed, you take advantage of this time to write the user's manuals. This is done in conjunction with training store personnel and managers in the use of the system. The training is not a trivial task, but you do not have to do all of it yourself. Training on the new POS cash registers will be done by the vendor. You plan to hold training classes for the people who will use the local micros to run programs and send data to the computer at headquarters. You will have separate classes to teach managers to retrieve data from the system via terminal commands. In both cases training will be hands-on. Company personnel should find the training enjoyable because the on-screen dialogue is user friendly—the user is instructed clearly every step of the way.

File conversion is painful. One evening after closing time, the staff works into the evening to take inventory in the stores. Temporary personnel are hired to key an inventory master file from this data. Transactions for the master file are accumulated as more purchases are made, up until the time the system is ready for use; then the master will be updated from the transactions generated by the POS terminals. After discussing the relative merits of the various system conversion methods, you and Ms. Christie agree that a pilot conversion would be ideal. Together you decide to bring up the original store first, then add other stores to the system one or two at a time.

To evaluate the new system, Mr. Iverson puts together a local team consisting of Ms. Christie, a programmer, and an accountant. Since your documentation is comprehensive, it is relatively easy for the team to check the system completely to see if it is functioning according to specifications. The evaluation report notes several positive results: out-of-stock conditions have almost disappeared (only two instances in one store in one month), inventory transfer among stores is a smooth operation, and store managers feel an increased sense of control. Negative outcomes are relatively minor and can be fixed in a system maintenance operation.

having to key in data from scratch. Nevertheless, it is not unusual for file conversion to take a long time; there are cases where it has gone on for as long as five years.

System Conversion

This is the stage in which you actually "pull the plug" on the old system and begin using the new one. There are four ways of handling the conversion.

Direct conversion means the user simply stops using the old system and starts using the new one—a somewhat risky method, since there is no other system to fall back on if anything goes wrong. This procedure is best followed only if the old system is in unusable condition. A **phased conversion** is one in which the organization eases into the new system one step at a time so that all the users are using some of the system. In contrast, in a **pilot conversion** the entire system is used by some of the users and is extended to all users once it has proved successful. This is most useful when a company has several branch offices or separate divisions. In **parallel conversion**—the most prolonged and expensive method—the old and new systems are operated simultaneously for some time, until users are satisfied that the new system performs to their standards.

System conversion is often a time of stress and confusion for all concerned. As the analyst, your credibility is on the line. During this time users are often doing double duty, trying to perform their regular jobs and simultaneously cope with a new computer system. Problems seem to appear in all areas, from input to output. Clearly, this is a period when your patience is needed.

Auditing

Security violations, whether deliberate or unintentional, can be difficult to detect. Once data is in the system and on media such as disks, it is possible for it to be altered without any trace in the source documents—unless the systems analyst has designed an **audit trail** to trace output back to the source data. In real-time systems security violations can be particularly elusive unless all transactions are recorded on disk or tape for later references by auditors. Modern auditors no longer shuffle mountains of paper; instead, they have computer programs of their own to monitor applications programs and data. Security issues will be discussed further in Chapter 15.

Evaluation

Is the system working? How well is it meeting the original goals, specifications, budgets, schedules, and so forth? Out of such evaluation will come adjustments that will improve the system. Approaches to evaluation vary. Sometimes the systems analyst and someone from the client organization evaluate the system against preset criteria. Some organizations prefer to bring in an independent evaluating team on the assumption that independent members will be free from bias and expectations.

Maintenance

Many consider maintenance to be a separate phase, one that begins only when the initial development effort is complete. In any case, the maintenance process is an ongoing activity, one that lasts the lifetime of the system. Monitoring and necessary adjustments continue so that the computer produces the expected results. Maintenance tasks also include making revisions and additions to the computer system. As more computer systems are implemented, organizations will obviously have an increased number of systems to maintain. In many computer installations a very high percentage of personnel and effort is dedicated to maintenance. This necessarily limits the number of personnel available for systems development. The net result is often a backlog of development projects. Many people picture the average programmer spending most of the time writing new programs; in reality, over 50% of the job involves maintaining and revising existing programs.

 Putting It All Together: Is There a Formula?

The preceding discussion may leave the impression that, by simply following a magical recipe, a system can be developed. In fact, novice analysts sometimes have the impression that there is a formula for developing systems. It would be more correct to say that there are guidelines.

PERSPECTIVES

CAN WE ABSOLUTELY POSITIVELY GUARANTEE THE SYSTEM?

Some jobs have little room for error or second guessing—the job must be done right the first time. An air traffic controller has such a job; directing a plane to the wrong altitude could have fatal consequences. Systems analysts, on the other hand, have many opportunities to ponder, to test, to re-think. Given those opportunities, it seems reasonable to hope that the completed system will be reliable. In fact, some people think that an analyst should be able to absolutely positively guarantee that the system works as it is supposed to.

However, reliability has not historically been the hallmark of computer systems. There are several reasons for this. One is the inherent complexity of most computer systems. A related reason is the failure to understand the complexity at the outset. The most perplexing reason is that, despite the analyst's heroic

efforts to accommodate the client, the client decides to change the nature of the desired system as it is developed. Finally, we must acknowledge the possibility of incompetent computer personnel.

Although many systems are less than perfect when first implemented, computer personnel usually work out the kinks until the system becomes acceptable. Systems that are true disasters are often hidden from view; few organizations want to highlight their own fumbles. However, some unreliable systems are so much in the public eye that the bad news cannot be concealed. When AT&T suffered long-distance system outages in 1991, not only was the East Coast phone system essentially cut off, it also put much of the country on hold—stock markets shut down, airports closed, airline reservations halted, and other industries could not continue business as usual. AT&T finally traced the outage to a software bug caused by a recently upgraded program. The near-disas-

ter spread to so many industries so quickly that AT&T had to revise system backup plans in hopes of preventing a recurrence.

Users stuck with unreliable systems are changing their focus from "What went wrong?" to "Who is going to pay?" That is, they want to know who is liable. Liability concerns also extend to unreliable purchased software. In the rush to be first on the market with innovative software, program bugs seem inevitable. In fact, there is probably no software publisher who could certify that a program is bug-free.

What is an analyst to do? Work harder? Be more careful? There are no simplistic answers. A competent analyst in a professional environment should produce a successful product. But the day may be coming when analysts and software vendors may need to carry liability insurance. If this sounds farfetched, remember that doctors thought liability insurance was a joke just a few decades ago.

Each system is unique, so there can be no one way that fits every project.

Historically, even analysts who followed the guidelines were not always successful in developing systems. Systems analysts have been embarrassed to find that they were not always good at estimating time, so schedules constantly slipped. (Budget overruns are one of the obvious results of sliding schedules.) Some observers, in fact, think that systems analysis is so ambiguous that analysts do not even know when they are finished. Sometimes it seems that the definition of project completion is the point at which analysts have run out of time on the schedule.

Another frequent problem has been imperfect communication between analysts and users. Poor communication results in poorly defined specifications, which, in turn, result in a supposedly complete system that does not do what the user expects. In addition, by-guess-and-by-gosh methods of analysis and design have often been used instead of formal tools. In the 1960s and 1970s, some systems were completed according to plan and schedule, but many others were not.

Out of these experiences, however, have come some solutions. Managers have become more sophisticated—and more realistic—in planning schedules and budgets. Analysts have learned to communicate with users and to recognize the cyclic nature of the systems analysis process. In addition to the analysis and design approach described here (which is considered the traditional way of creating a system), there are other, newer approaches, which are beyond the scope of this book. If you pursue a career in systems analysis, you will no doubt encounter these approaches and find them useful.

Being a systems analyst can be important work; an analyst is in a position to help institute fundamental changes that alter business operations, work habits, and use of time. As we suggested at the beginning of this chapter, however, a systems analyst must be sensitive to the possible effects of his or her work on people's lives. The real danger, it has been remarked, is not that computers will begin to think like people, but that people will begin to think like computers.

Getting Personal with Computers

This chapter has addressed a broad spectrum of systems change, taking into account its effects on the entire organization. But an organization is composed of individuals, and individuals these days are likely to have their own personal computers. This important topic deserves special consideration, so we devote the next chapters to the most popular personal computer applications software for business and the home.

R E V I E W   A N D   R E F E R E N C E

Summary and Key Terms

- A **system** is an organized set of related components established to accomplish a certain task. A **computer system** has a computer as one of its components. A **client** requests a systems analysis, a study of an existing system, to determine both how it works and how well it meets the needs of its **users,** who are usually employees and customers. Systems analysis can lead to systems design, the development of a plan for an improved system. A **systems analyst** normally does both the analysis and design. Some people do both programming and analysis and have the title **programmer/analyst.** The success of the project requires both *impetus* and *authority* within the client organization to change the current system.

- The systems analyst must be a **change agent** who encourages **user involvement** in the development of a new system.

- The systems analyst has three main functions: (1) coordinating schedules and task assignments, (2) communicating analysis and design information to those involved with the system, and (3) planning and designing the system, with the help of the client organization. A

systems analyst should have a creative, analytical mind, good communication and organizational skills; self-discipline and self-direction; and the ability to work without tangible results.

- The **systems development life cycle (SDLC)** has five phases: (1) preliminary investigation, (2) analysis, (3) design, (4) development, and (5) implementation.

- Phase 1, which is also known as the **feasibility study,** or **system survey,** is the **preliminary investigation** of the problem to determine how—and if—an analysis and design project should proceed. Aware of the importance of establishing a smooth working relationship, the analyst refers to an **organization chart** showing the lines of authority within the client organization. After determining the nature and scope of the problem, the analyst expresses the users' needs as objectives.

- In phase 2, **systems analysis,** the analyst gathers and analyzes data from common sources such as written documents, interviews, questionnaires, observation, and sampling.

- The client organization determines what data sources are accessible, but the analyst must then decide which are appropriate. The analyst must evaluate the relevance of written documents such as procedure manuals and reports. Interview options include the **structured interview,** in which all questions are planned and written in advance, and the **unstructured interview,** in which the questions can vary from the plan. Although interviews can allow flexible questioning and the establishment of rapport with clients, they can also be time-consuming. Questionnaires can save time and expense and allow anonymous answers, but response rates are often low. Another method is simply observing how the organization functions, sometimes through **participant observation,** temporary participation in the organization's activities. Statistical sampling is also useful, especially when there is a large volume of data.

- The systems analyst may use a variety of charts and diagrams to analyze the data. A **data flow diagram (DFD)** provides an easy-to-follow picture of the flow of data through the system. The elements of a DFD are processes, files, sources and sinks, and labeled vectors. **Processes** are the actions taken on the data. A **file** is a repository of data. A **source** is a data origin outside the organization; a **sink** is a destination for data going outside the organization. **Vectors** are arrows indicating the direction in which the data travels. Another common tool for data analysis is the **decision table,** or **decision logic table,** a standard table indicating alternative actions under particular conditions.

- Upon completion of the systems analysis phase, the analyst submits to the client a report summarizing the current system's problems and requirements and making recommendations about what course to take next.

- In phase 3, **systems design,** the analyst submits a general preliminary design for the client's approval before proceeding to the specific detail design.

- **Preliminary design** involves reviewing the system requirements before submitting an overall plan or, perhaps, alternative **candidates.** The analyst presents the plan in a form the users can understand. The analyst may also develop a **prototype,** a limited working system or part of a system that gives users a preview of how the new system will work. Software for **CASE—computer-aided software engineering**—provides an automated means of designing systems.

- **Detail design** normally involves considering the parts of the system in the following order: output requirements, input requirements, files and databases, system processing, and system controls and backup. Output requirements include the *medium* of the output, the *type* of reports needed, the *contents* of the output, and the *forms* on which the output will be printed. The analyst might determine the report format by using a **printer spacing chart,** which shows the position of headings, columns, dates, and page numbers. Input requirements include the input *medium,* the *content* of the input, and the design of data entry *forms.* The analyst also plans an input *editing* process for checking whether the data is reasonable, and the analyst makes sure that the sys-

tem can handle variations in input *volume.* The organization of files and databases must be specified. The processing must also be described, perhaps by using a **systems flowchart** that uses ANSI flowchart symbols to illustrate the flow of data or by using the hierarchical organization of a structure chart. The analyst must also spell out system controls and backup. Data input to online systems must be backed up by **system journals,** files that record transactions made at the terminal. Processing controls involve data-editing procedures. Finally, copies of transaction and master files should be made regularly.

- Phase 4, **systems development,** consists of scheduling, programming, and testing. Schedule deadlines and milestones are often shown on a **Gantt chart.** The programming effort involves selecting the program language and developing the design specifications. Programmers then do **unit testing,** (individual testing of their own programs), which is followed by **system testing,** (the assessment of how the programs work together). **Volume testing** tests the entire system with real data. Documentation of phase 4 describes the program logic and the detailed data formats.

- Phase 5, **implementation,** includes training, to prepare users of the new system; equipment conversion, which involves ensuring compatibility and providing enough space and electrical capacity; file conversion, making old files accessible to the new system; system conversion; auditing, the design of an **audit trail** to trace data from output back to the source documents; evaluation, the assessment of system performance; and maintenance, the monitoring and adjustment of the system.

- System conversion may be done in one of four ways: **direct conversion,** immediately replacing the old system with the new system; **phased conversion,** easing in the new system a step at a time; **pilot conversion,** testing the entire system with a few users and extending it to the rest when proved successful; and **parallel conversion,** operating the old and new systems concurrently until the new system is proved successful.

Review Questions

1. What is the distinction between systems analysis and systems design?
2. Describe the main duties of a systems analyst.
3. List some qualities of a good systems analyst, and discuss the importance of each one.
4. Name the five phases of the systems development life cycle.
5. Describe the preliminary investigation phase and explain why it is necessary.
6. Discuss the advantages and disadvantages of the most common sources of data about a system.
7. Describe the use of data flow diagrams.

8. Describe the prototyping approach and explain how it differs from the traditional systems development life cycle. Why is this approach useful?
9. Describe the main activities involved in detail design.
10. Discuss what is involved in systems development.
11. Describe the main activities in the implementation phase.
12. Why is documentation of each phase important?

Discussion Questions

1. Which qualities of a systems analyst do you consider to be the most important? Explain your answer.
2. Does following the traditional guidelines limit the creativity of a systems analyst? Explain your answer.
3. Explain why it is so important that a systems analyst interacts well with others.
4. Should system evaluation be done by the analyst and the client organization or by an independent evaluating team? Explain your answer.

True-False Questions

T F   1. A system analyst's primary job is programming.
T F   2. The system user is a person who enters data.
T F   3. The systems analyst begins the preliminary investigation stage by trying to determine the nature of the problem.
T F   4. The scope of the problem definition should be as broad as possible.
T F   5. In a data flow diagram, a source is a source of data or paper within the organization.
T F   6. In a data flow diagram, a sink is a destination for data or paper within the organization.
T F   7. The last step of the detail design stage is to examine output requirements.
T F   8. Different phases of systems analysis and design can overlap.
T F   9. Once a system is ready, the best training method is to have intended users read and be tested on their understanding of the user's manual.
T F 10. The best person to evaluate how well a system works is a typical user.

PERSONAL
COMPUTING TOOLS

9

Word Processing and Desktop Publishing

The Most Popular Software on Personal Computers

Professor Tony Scossi had taught college business courses for many years, but he had never seen such changes in student writing as had occurred in the last year: All final term papers arrived in high quality, word-processed form. It was pretty impressive—and startling.

Tony had always prided himself on high standards and fair treatment when it came to grading student writing. Suddenly he realized he had been biased. When only 10 to 20% of students had submitted word-processed papers, he would set them aside to correct later, as a group; he would then turn immediately to those that were typewritten. Now he saw that the initial group was graded more harshly. With all papers now word-processed, there were none to set aside. Each looked near-perfect in quality.

With word processing, it is easy to correct errors on the screen before printing out the paper. As a tool, the typewriter has its shortcomings. You produce a permanent mark whenever you press a key. Therefore, if you make a mistake, it is hard to correct without a lot of extra work. Things get even worse when you have to add or delete several sentences. At best, the whole page must be retyped. But the altered document may be longer or shorter than the original text, so the new version may no longer fit on one page. You then have to retype all the pages that follow, too. Using white out keeps you from having to retype whole pages, but your instructor might not tolerate the smudged result. If nothing else, the traditional way of correcting typing errors usually means handing in a less-than-perfect term paper. However, such a result is not acceptable in the workplace. The appearance of a document or letter is crucial to the image of a business. And beyond image, there may be exacting legal demands. Documents submitted in a court of law, for example, have to be originals (not copies), and corrections are not permissible on the document. If the same legal document needs to be sent to different people or offices, each copy has to be typed perfectly again and again.

As a student, you have to be careful when typing a paper to ensure yourself fair treatment—just as you must be careful when typing a resume to seek employment. A poorly typed resume makes a bad impression. If you pay to have it typed for you, you may have to pay again to add more courses and experience. A customized resume for a particular position might require partial or even complete retyping of your original resume.

In this chapter, you will learn about word processing and desktop publishing. First you will focus on word processing and then turn to desktop publishing. Some people are sorely pressed to distinguish the features of some word processing packages from their desktop publishing cousins. Both word processing and desktop publishing offer affordable and perfect copies every time—delivering on a promise of providing time and money benefits.

 ## *Word Processing as a Tool*

Word processing is using a computer for the creation, editing, formatting, storing, and printing of a document. Let us examine each part of this definition. First, a *document* is anything that can be keyed in, such as a letter. *Creation* is the original composing and keying in of the document. *Editing* is making changes to the document to fix errors or improve its content—such as deleting a sentence, correcting a misspelled name, or moving a paragraph. You can edit your work as you create it. *Formatting* refers to adjusting the appearance of the document to make it look appropriate and attractive. For example, you might want to center a heading, make wider margins, or use double spacing. *Storing* the document means saving it on a floppy disk or

Personal Computers in Action

WRITERS THROW OFF THEIR CHAINS

Although some resist, many professionals who design and write publications for a living have taken the plunge into word processing and desktop publishing. So have people who write reports, memos, and so forth, as a component of their jobs. The statements of these people tell the story.

James Michener, novelist. Computers haven't changed my way of writing, only the way things are handled. I write on legal pads, then my secretary types it up on a word processor. When she prints it out, I edit it. The final version goes on disk to the publisher.

Mark Ong, graphic designer. In 1986, I started using computers. It just seemed like there was no way that I could compete unless I knew how to use a computer. I taught myself to use Word and PageMaker. I use the computer primarily for design layouts, word processing, and final output. There are times when I still may make some changes to a design by hand, because I can't do certain things with a computer or because certain things are just faster by hand. I'm using it to express my traditional knowledge, not to shift everything over to a computer-based design approach. So, in a sense, I represent a transitional generation that is making the leap from pencil and paper to the computer.

Susan Yoachum, political writer. I've been in journalism about 15 years. At first I didn't like the idea of computers; they were an invasion into my regular routine. Now I wonder, why was it so hard to give up the Royal typewriter? I work on a terminal that is hooked up to a mainframe computer. I can type my story directly into the computer and then transmit it to another terminal for editing. We also have access to an electronic mail system—it's one of the best things about having a computer on your desk. It allows you to transmit information quickly and efficiently to other people within the main office, and it's fun, too.

Alice Kahn, author. For me, getting a computer meant the difference between being an amateur and a pro. I used to write on yellow pads and scribble the changes into the margins before I would even go near the typewriter. Now I turn out two pieces a week, and my writing income has increased 800%.

Chris Pray, television writer. I have a war with machines. I don't even drive. I have a Stone Age psychology and even have a Stone Age computer: no modem, no hard disk. The first month I had my computer, I found myself thinking like a computer after I turned it off: I'd think about deleting dumb remarks I'd made in a conversation, or inserting things, or moving things around.

Harvey Rosenfield, head of Ralph Nader's Access to Justice. The special interests, with their infinitely greater resources, had access to computerized press lists and word processing. Then came the PC. Sensing vaguely what it could do for us, I took out a loan and bought a PC. It was a revolution among the revolutionaries. Suddenly, a position paper could quickly become legislative testimony; a press release, a newsletter. Most important, it helped even the odds for the consumer movement.

hard disk. *Printing* is producing the document on paper, using a printer connected to the computer.

Some people think of word processing as just another form of typing, but it is much more. Word processing stores your typed words in computer memory, lets you see what you type on the screen before printing, remembers what you type and lets you change it, and prints the typed document at your request.

There are two notable differences between using a word processing program and using a typewriter. The first involves the separation of typing from printing. When you use word processing, typing the document and printing the document do not occur at the same time; you print the document on paper whenever you like. Perhaps you want to print an intermediate draft, just to see how it looks, and then continue making changes. Or you may choose to commit your work to paper only in the final version.

The second difference between word processing programs and typewriters is related to the first: When you use a word processing package you can make changes as you go along, or even at some later time, and print out a revised—and perfect—copy. The point here is that only the changes themselves are retyped, not the entire document.

A word processing package is a sophisticated software tool with many options. We will begin here with an overview of how word processing works. Then we will present an easy-to-follow example so you can see how different word processing features are used.

 ## An Overview: How Word Processing Works

Think of the computer screen as a page of typing paper. On the screen the word processing program indicates the top of the page and the left and right edges (margins) of the typed material. When you type you can see the line of text you are typing on the screen—it looks just like a line of typing on paper. Remember that you are not really typing on the screen; the screen merely displays what you are entering into memory. As you type, the program displays a **cursor** (Figure 9-1) to show where the next character you type will appear on the screen. The cursor is usually a blinking dash or rectangle. If you use a mouse, your screen also displays a pointer on the screen. Pressing the mouse button moves the cursor to the location of the pointer.

Figure 9-1   Entering text with word processing software. As you type in your text, the position of the cursor (the dash just to the right of the last word in the paragraph) shows you where the next character will be placed.

Cursor

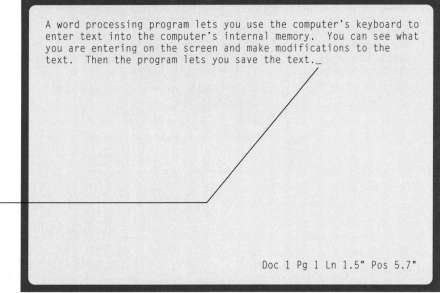

```
A word processing program lets you use the computer's keyboard to
enter text into the computer's internal memory.  You can see what
you are entering on the screen and make modifications to the
text.  Then the program lets you save the text._




                                        Doc 1 Pg 1 Ln 1.5" Pos 5.7"
```

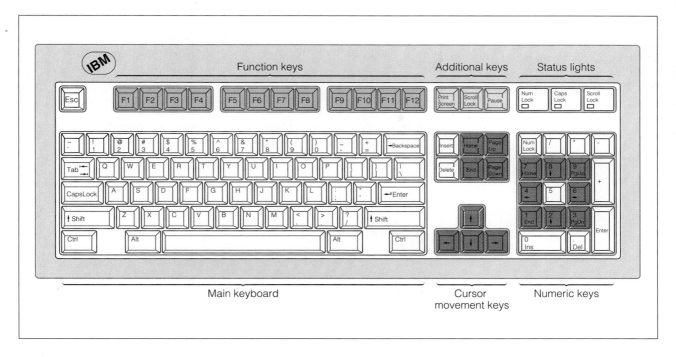

Figure 9-2   A personal computer keyboard. The cursor movement keys, highlighted in blue, let you move the cursor around on the screen. The function keys, at the top of the keyboard, let you accomplish a number of tasks with the press of one key; for example, WordPerfect offers a Help screen when you press F1.

You can also move the cursor around on the screen by using **cursor movement keys** on the right side of the keyboard (Figure 9-2). The Up Arrow and Down Arrow keys move the cursor up or down one line at a time. The **PgUp** and **PgDn** keys let you move the cursor up or down a page at a time.

Scrolling

A word processing program lets you type page after page of material. Most programs show a line of dashes on the screen to mark where one printed page will end and another will begin; this line is not printed when you print your document. Most word processing programs also indicate what page the cursor is on and what line it is on.

A screen can display only about 24 lines of text. Although the screen display size is limited, your document size is not. As you continue to type new lines, the earlier lines you typed move up the screen as each new line is added at the bottom of the screen. Eventually, the first line you typed disappears off the top of the screen. But the line has not disappeared from computer memory.

To see a line that has disappeared from the top of the screen, use the Up Arrow key to move the cursor up to the top of the screen. As you continue to press the Up Arrow key, the line that had disappeared drops back down onto the screen. The program treats the text you are typing as if it were all on a long roll of paper like a roll of paper towels or a scroll. You "roll the scroll" up or down on the screen by moving the cursor. This process, called **scrolling,** lets you see any part of the document on the screen—but only 24 or so lines at a time (Figure 9-3).

Figure 9-3   Scrolling through a document. Although most documents contain many lines of text, the screen can display only about 24 lines at one time. You can use the cursor movement keys to scroll up and down through the document.

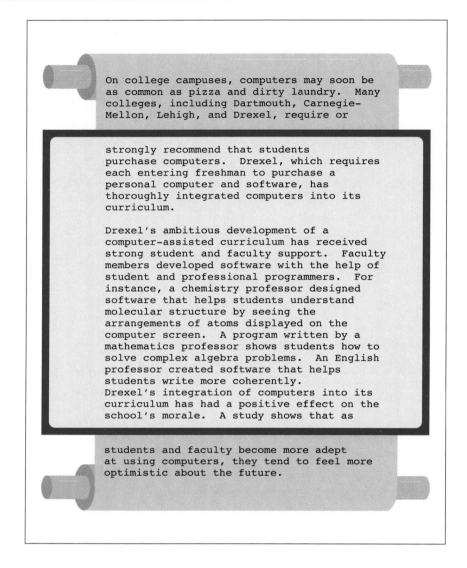

```
On college campuses, computers may soon be
as common as pizza and dirty laundry.  Many
colleges, including Dartmouth, Carnegie-
Mellon, Lehigh, and Drexel, require or
```

```
strongly recommend that students
purchase computers.  Drexel, which requires
each entering freshman to purchase a
personal computer and software, has
thoroughly integrated computers into its
curriculum.

Drexel's ambitious development of a
computer-assisted curriculum has received
strong student and faculty support.  Faculty
members developed software with the help of
student and professional programmers.  For
instance, a chemistry professor designed
software that helps students understand
molecular structure by seeing the
arrangements of atoms displayed on the
computer screen.  A program written by a
mathematics professor shows students how to
solve complex algebra problems.  An English
professor created software that helps
students write more coherently.
Drexel's integration of computers into its
curriculum has had a positive effect on the
school's morale.  A study shows that as
```

```
students and faculty become more adept
at using computers, they tend to feel more
optimistic about the future.
```

No Need to Worry About the Right Side

When you type a line of a document, you eventually get to the right side of the screen. Unlike using a typewriter, however, if you are using a word processing program you do not have to press Enter (an action equivalent to pressing the Carriage Return key on an electric typewriter) at the end of each line. In fact, you should not press Enter; the word processing software watches to see how close you are to the edge of the "paper" (the right margin). If there is not enough room at the end of a line to complete the word you are typing, the program automatically starts that word at the left margin of the next line down. You never have to worry about running out of space on a line; the word processor plans ahead for you. This feature is called **word wrap,** and it will not work properly if you press Enter at the end of each line. However, you *will* use Enter to signal the end of a paragraph or to force the word processing program to begin a new line.

Easy Corrections

What if you make a mistake while you are typing? No problem: Move the cursor to the position of the error and make the correction. Word processing programs let you delete characters or whole words or lines that you have already typed, and they close up the resulting spaces automatically.

You can also insert new characters in the middle of a line or a word, without typing over (and erasing) the characters that are already there. The program moves the existing characters to the right of the insertion as you type the new characters. However, if you wish, the word processing program also lets you *overtype* (replace) characters you typed earlier. We will discuss these correction techniques in more detail later.

Function Keys: Making It Easy

The *function keys* on a keyboard (see Figure 9-2) can save you a lot of time. Most word processing packages make use of the function keys, but the result of pressing each function key differs according to the application program. For example, if you are using one word processing program and you want to underline a word, you can press F8. But if you are using another program, you might have to press another function key or even a combination of keys to do the same task.

To help people remember which function key performs which task, software manufacturers often provide a sheet of plastic or paper that describes the use of each key. This sheet, called a **template,** fits over the function keys (Figure 9-4).

Figure 9-4 A function-key template. This template helps you remember which function keys perform which tasks. Without the template you would have to memorize numerous key combinations. The template is color-coded to match related keys: red for the Ctrl key, blue for the Alt key, green for the Shift key, and black for the function key alone. Examples: Press Shift-F7 to print, Ctrl-F2 to invoke the Spelling Checker, or just F6 for boldface. (To fit on this page the template has been split in half; normally it fits above the function keys.)

WordPerfect®
for IBM® Personal Computers

Column Left/Right	Home, ←/→
Compose	2
Delete to End of Ln/Pg	End/PgDn
Delete Word	Backspace
Hard Page	Enter
← Margin Release	Tab
Pull-Down Menus	=
Screen Up/Down	–/+ (num)
Word Left/Right	←/→

74 – 10– 10
© WordPerfect Corp. 1989 TMUSIWP51XID—7/90

				Ctrl	
Shell	Spell	Screen	Move		Text In/Out
Thesaurus	Replace	Reveal Codes	Block	*Alt*	Mark Text
Setup	← Search	Switch	→ Indent ←	*Shift*	Date/Outline
Cancel	→ Search	Help	→ Indent		List
F1	F2	F3	F4		F5

			Ctrl				
Tab Align	Footnote	Font		Merge/Sort	Macro Define		
Flush Right	Columns/Table	Style	*Alt*	Graphics	Macro		
Center	Print	Format	*Shift*	Merge Codes	Retrieve		
Bold	Exit	Underline		End Field	Save	Reveal Codes	Block
F6	F7	F8		F9	F10	F11	F12

Now you are ready to see how these concepts work in a word processing package.

Getting Started:
Using a Word Processing Package

Carl Wade has just graduated with a business degree and is looking for an entry-level job in an advertising firm. Carl already has a resume, but he wants to use a word processing package to prepare a cover letter. Carl chooses WordPerfect, a popular word processing package. When it is necessary to be specific in this example, we will use commands from Word-Perfect Version 5.1. Many people use Version 5.0; most keystrokes for WordPerfect commands are the same in both versions.

Loading the Program

As always, Carl begins by booting the computer. (For information on booting, refer to Chapter 7.) After Carl boots the computer, he loads his word processing program from hard drive C and places his formatted data disk in drive B. (This scenario assumes that Carl is using a computer with a hard drive and two diskette drives, that the word processing software is already in drive C, and that he will keep his own files on a diskette in drive B.)

At this point, with the C> on the screen, Carl needs to type a command to get the word processing program started. The specific command depends on the program he is using: WP for WordPerfect, WS for Word-Star, and WORD for Microsoft Word. When he types the correct command and presses Enter, the word processing program is loaded from disk drive C into computer memory. Depending on the word processing program used, a set of menu choices may appear on the screen. However, WordPerfect, the program Carl is using, immediately displays an almost blank screen to represent a blank sheet of typing paper (Figure 9-5).

Creating the Cover Letter

The following steps describe, in a general way, how Carl creates (enters), saves, and prints his letter. Although the specific keystroke instructions refer to WordPerfect, the general approach fits any word processing package. Once Carl has loaded the word processing program, he proceeds as follows.

Entering the Letter   Carl starts by typing the letter (Figure 9-6) on the computer keyboard. He uses the keyboard as he would a typewriter. He can see the results of his keystrokes on the screen. If he needs to make corrections, he can use the Backspace key or the Del (Delete) key. To position his address and the date on the right side of the letter, he presses the Tab key several times before he begins typing. Carl knows the letter is being stored in memory as he types so, as he continues to use the

Figure 9-5   Getting started with Word-Perfect. When Carl first loads WordPerfect, the screen is almost as blank as a fresh sheet of paper. Note the cursor in the upper-left corner. The information at the bottom of the screen is called the status line. The status line includes the document number, the page number, the position of the cursor in inches from the top of the page (Ln 1″), and the position of the cursor in inches from the left edge of the paper (Pos 1″).

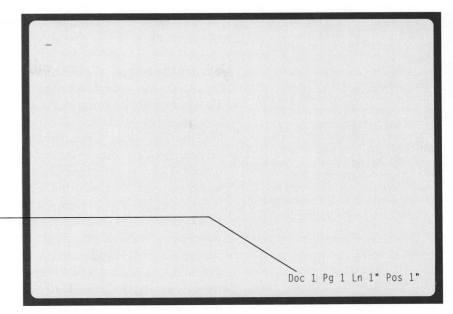

Status line

Doc 1 Pg 1 Ln 1" Pos 1"

Figure 9-6   The first draft of Carl's cover letter. Carl can enter this draft and use WordPerfect to make the changes described in the text.

```
                                          18 Leroy Street
                                          Binghamton, NY 10037
                                          July 13, 1993


Ms. Louise Graham
Director of Personnel
Charnley Advertising, Inc.
1900 Corporate Lane
Baltimore, Maryland 21200


Dear Ms. Graham:

I am writing to inquire about the possibility of a
position in Charnley's accounts department.

I recently graduated from Pennsylvania State University
with a BA in business.  My area of interest was
marketing.

I became acquainted with your company through my intern
work at the Dunhill Agency in New York.  I have always
hoped to combine my background in business and my
interest in marketing.  Charnley Advertising seems to
offer the best opportunity for doing this.

I will be in Baltimore on July 28 and 29.  Would it be
possible for us to meet to discuss this further?  I can
be reached at 600—623—4667.  I look forward to hearing
from you.

Sincerely,

Carl Wade
```

word processing package, he can continue to make changes to any part of the letter.

Saving the Letter   Recall that memory keeps data only temporarily; you must store your documents on disk if you want to keep them. When Carl has finished keying in the letter and has corrected his mistakes, he stores—saves—the letter in a file on his data disk. Carl begins by pressing F10. The words "Document to be saved:" appear at the bottom of the screen, and Carl needs to enter a file name for his document. A file name lets DOS keep track of the file's location on a disk so the file can be found when requested in the future. Carl enters B:CLETTER—the B: tells the program which disk to store the file on, and CLETTER (an abbreviation for *cover letter*) is the name of the file. Carl then presses Enter. If Carl were saving files on the disk in drive A, he would have saved the file by typing A:CLETTER. If he were saving files on his hard disk, he might enter CLETTER and let WordPerfect store the file in the default directory. By saving the letter, Carl has a version of the letter he can use if he needs it again.

Printing the Letter   Carl decides he wants to see a printed copy of what he has written so far. After turning on the printer, he holds down Shift and presses F7. WordPerfect then gives him a list of choices—a menu—related to printing. Carl notices menu item 6—View Document—and selects it. He sees something similar to Figure 9-7, which shows how his document will look on the page when it is printed. To return to the main Print Menu, Carl presses F1 (Cancel). Now he can choose to print the full document (choice 1) or only one page at a time (choice 2). Because he has only a one-page letter, it really makes no difference which he chooses. He presses 1 for choice 1. This activates the printer, and his letter is printed.

Figure 9-7   The View Document screen. By pressing Shift-F7 and then pressing 6 to choose item 6 (View Document) from the menu that appears, Carl can see on the screen what his file will look like before he prints it. He has control over how he views the document too; he can adjust the size of the type, the area of the letter, and even show more than one page at a time.

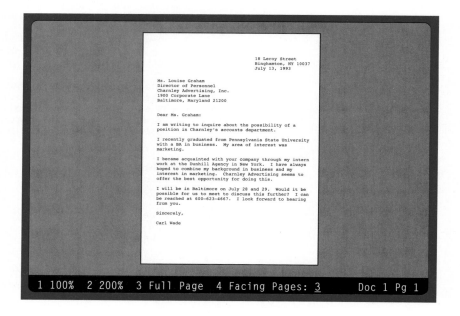

Exiting the Program   Once Carl has finished using the program, he presses F7 to exit the program. WordPerfect then presents a question at the bottom of the screen: "Save document?" Carl types N for *No* since the file has already been saved. WordPerfect then asks "Exit WP?" and Carl types Y for *Yes*. This leads him back to the DOS prompt. If Carl wanted to start a new file without leaving the program, he could clear the screen by typing N in response to the second question.

Editing the Letter

As we said, a significant payoff of word processing is the ease of making corrections to existing documents. Suppose Carl decides, for example, that his cover letter would be more effective if he made several changes. Consider for a moment what Carl would have to do if the letter had been prepared on a typewriter. He would, of course, have to retype the entire letter. Now follow the word processing approach to making changes. Since Carl has already exited to DOS, he must load WordPerfect into memory, as before.

Retrieving the Letter   Carl presses Shift and F10 together to invoke the Retrieve function. When WordPerfect asks for the name of the document to retrieve, he types B:CLETTER (or whatever is appropriate for his drive), as illustrated in Figure 9-8. When he presses Enter, the current version of his letter, just as he last saved it on his data disk, is loaded into memory and then displayed on the screen.

Making the Changes   We have already described how existing text can be moved over to allow new text to be inserted. To do this, the computer must be in the **Insert mode,** the standard mode for inserting corrections when you are using word processing. For example, suppose Carl wants

Figure 9-8   Retrieving the letter. To retrieve a document, Carl must type in the name of the file he wants. B: tells the computer the drive that holds the diskette with the file; CLETTER tells the computer the name of the file that holds the document.

```
Document to be Retrieved:  B:CLETTER_
```

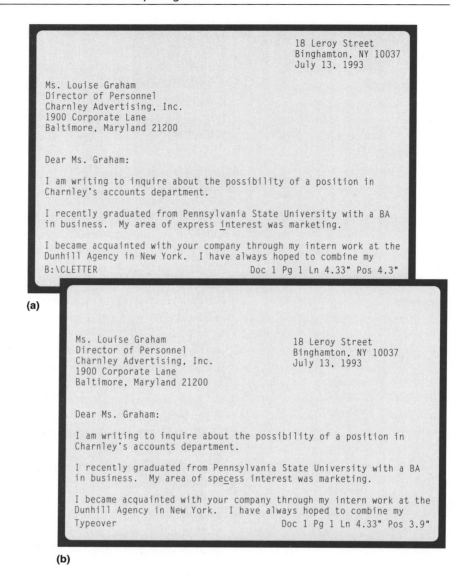

```
                                              18 Leroy Street
                                              Binghamton, NY 10037
                                              July 13, 1993

      Ms. Louise Graham
      Director of Personnel
      Charnley Advertising, Inc.
      1900 Corporate Lane
      Baltimore, Maryland 21200


      Dear Ms. Graham:

      I am writing to inquire about the possibility of a position in
      Charnley's accounts department.

      I recently graduated from Pennsylvania State University with a BA
      in business.  My area of express interest was marketing.

      I became acquainted with your company through my intern work at the
      Dunhill Agency in New York.  I have always hoped to combine my
      B:\CLETTER                              Doc 1 Pg 1 Ln 4.33" Pos 4.3"
```

(a)

```
      Ms. Louise Graham                       18 Leroy Street
      Director of Personnel                   Binghamton, NY 10037
      Charnley Advertising, Inc.              July 13, 1993
      1900 Corporate Lane
      Baltimore, Maryland 21200


      Dear Ms. Graham:

      I am writing to inquire about the possibility of a position in
      Charnley's accounts department.

      I recently graduated from Pennsylvania State University with a BA
      in business.  My area of specess interest was marketing.

      I became acquainted with your company through my intern work at the
      Dunhill Agency in New York.  I have always hoped to combine my
      Typeover                                Doc 1 Pg 1 Ln 4.33" Pos 3.9"
```

(b)

Figure 9-9   Editing the letter. Carl uses the flexibility of word processing to edit his letter. (a) First he uses the Insert mode to add the word "express" in the middle of a line. He positions the cursor and types in the word and a space. (b) Carl decides to use the Typeover mode to change "express" to "special." As Carl keys in the word "special," he types over the word he wants to replace. In the screen shown here, he has typed "spec" so far, so we still see the "ess" of "express."

to add the word "express" before the word "interest" in the second paragraph. All he has to do is move the cursor so it is below the "i" in "interest" and then type the word "express" and press the Spacebar. He has added the word to the sentence (Figure 9-9a).

Another correction option is to type right over the existing text. To do this, the computer must be in **Typeover mode,** which allows you to replace existing text with new text. If Carl wants to replace the word "express" with the word "special," he moves the cursor under the "e" in

Figure 9-10 The corrected letter. Carl prints out the corrected letter, knowing he can make further changes later if he wishes.

```
                                        18 Leroy Street
                                        Binghamton, NY 10037
                                        July 13, 1993


Ms. Louise Graham
Director of Personnel
Charnley Advertising, Inc.
1900 Corporate Lane
Baltimore, Maryland 21200


Dear Ms. Graham:

I am writing to inquire about the possibility of a
position in Charnley's accounts department.

I recently graduated from Pennsylvania State University
with a BA in business.  My area of special interest was
marketing.

I became acquainted with your company through my intern
work at the Dunhill Agency in New York.  I have always
hoped to combine my background in business and my
interest in marketing.  Charnley Advetising seems to
offer the best opportunity for doing this.

While I was in school, I prepared and monitored
advertising campaigns and tracked account budgets.  I
am also familiar with several types of computers and
computer systems.

I will be in Baltimore on July 28 and 29.  Would it be
possible for us to meet to discuss this further?  I can
be reached at 600-623-4667.  I look forward to hearing
from you.

Sincerely,

Carl Wade
```

"express," presses the Ins (Insert) key, and types "special" (Figure 9-9b). Then he presses Ins again to turn off the Typeover mode. It may seem odd that Carl presses the Ins key to both enter and exit the Typeover mode. This occurs because the program starts with the Insert mode as the default mode, and the Ins key acts as a **toggle switch,** allowing you to switch between the Insert mode and the Typeover mode.

Carl also wants to add several sentences that explain his experience. He decides to insert the sentences between the third and fourth paragraphs. To insert the new sentences, Carl uses the cursor movement keys to position the cursor at the point where he wishes to add the new sentences. Then he types them. He may, of course, make any other changes he wishes at this time. When he is finished, he presses Enter to provide the proper spacing at the end of the new paragraph. Compare the final version (Figure 9-10) with the original version (Figure 9-6).

Unlocking His Mind

Imagine that you have something important to say but cannot say it. Suppose, further, that your mind is so dazzling that you could make a significant contribution to the world, if only you could express yourself. This is the situation in which Stephen Hawking, victim of Lou Gehrig's disease, found himself. But this is the age of technology, and technology solved Stephen's problem: His words are channeled from his brain to the rest of us via a computer and a very clever word processing program.

Stephen Hawking is a physicist, an unlikely candidate for making the best-seller charts. But that is exactly what he did with his book *A Brief History of Time.* He wrote the book by using a personal computer and a system called Equalizer, which Stephen can use by wiggling a single finger on a switch. Think of a set of lines on a screen, with several words per line. When Stephen presses the switch to activate the system, the software uses a highlighting bar to scan the words on the screen. Stephen presses the switch again when the highlight bar lands on the word he wants, and the word is selected. The system is actually more powerful than this minimal description would indicate, but never is more than a flick of the switch required.

Stephen Hawking is widely regarded as the most brilliant theoretical physicist since Einstein, but he is not very interested in such descriptions of himself. Says he, "It's media hype. I'm a bit smarter than most, but not exceptional."

Saving the Corrected Letter   As before, Carl presses F10 to save the letter on his disk. WordPerfect asks if Carl wants to replace the earlier version of the letter with the new version. Carl types Y for *Yes,* and the letter is again saved in a file named B:CLETTER. If he had pressed N for *No,* WordPerfect would have asked for the name of the document to be saved, and Carl could have entered a different name.

After you have practiced a bit, you will see that making changes with word processing is swift and efficient, even for a short document such as a letter. Considering the volume of correspondence—or any kind of typing—in an office, the labor savings is significant.

Formatting: Making a Good Impression

Now that you know the basics of creating text with a word processing program, you can turn your attention to the appearance, or **format,** of the document. This is not a trivial matter. In fact, one of the most appealing aspects of word processing is the ability it gives you to adjust the appearance of a document. You can use this capability to present your company—or yourself—attractively on paper.

Image is important. A multimillion-dollar company that relies on public opinion certainly wants to appear at its best on paper. So do little companies that do not have money to spend on fancy typesetting and printing. All these companies, big and small, can afford word processing.

The format of a document is the way the document appears on the page. *Format* refers to the size of the margins, the amount of space between the lines, and all the other factors that affect appearance. To show you how formatting works, we return to Carl Wade. Figure 9-11 shows some format considerations for the first draft of Carl's resume. Word processing software offers many features to control and vary the format of a document.

The Resume Example

Once Carl finishes his cover letter, he decides to polish his resume (Figure 9-11). He sees at a glance that it can use some improvement: The resume is bunched up at the top of the page, giving it a short, squatty look. Carl wonders if the name and address lines would look better if they were centered. And he sees that the text runs together, making it hard to read. As Carl ponders various ways to fix the resume, he retrieves the original version from the disk and studies it on the screen.

Carl decides to try several format changes to make the resume longer and more attractive. These changes are (1) adding a space after each major heading, (2) centering the name and address lines, (3) centering the text vertically on the page, (4) increasing the width of the margins, (5) evening up (justifying) the right margin, and (6) using boldface and underlining to highlight certain words.

Figure 9-11 The first draft of Carl's resume. This is Carl's first draft of his resume. It is a good start, but he can make it much better. If Carl had to rely on a typewriter to make the corrections described in the text, he would have to retype the entire page. With word processing software, Carl can change the look of the document in seconds. He can change the margins, center the heading, use double-spacing, or make dozens of other style changes.

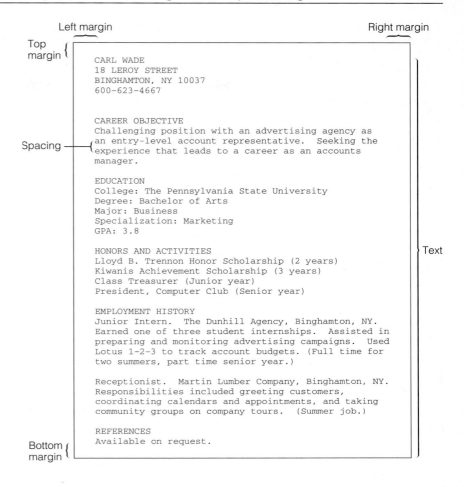

Adding Blank Lines

The first change is easy enough: Carl positions the cursor at the end of each major heading (for example, the heading "CAREER OBJECTIVE") and presses Enter. This moves the cursor one line down and adds a blank line in the text.

Centering Lines

To **center** the name and address lines between the left and right sides of the page, Carl positions the cursor under the leftmost character of a line, presses Shift and F6 simultaneously. This automatically centers the line of text. He repeats this process for each of the next three lines. Figure 9-12 shows the results.

Vertical Centering

Carl's next improvement is to center the resume on the page, a process called vertical centering. **Vertical centering** adjusts the top and bottom margins so the text is centered vertically on the printed page. This eliminates the need to calculate the exact number of lines to leave at the top

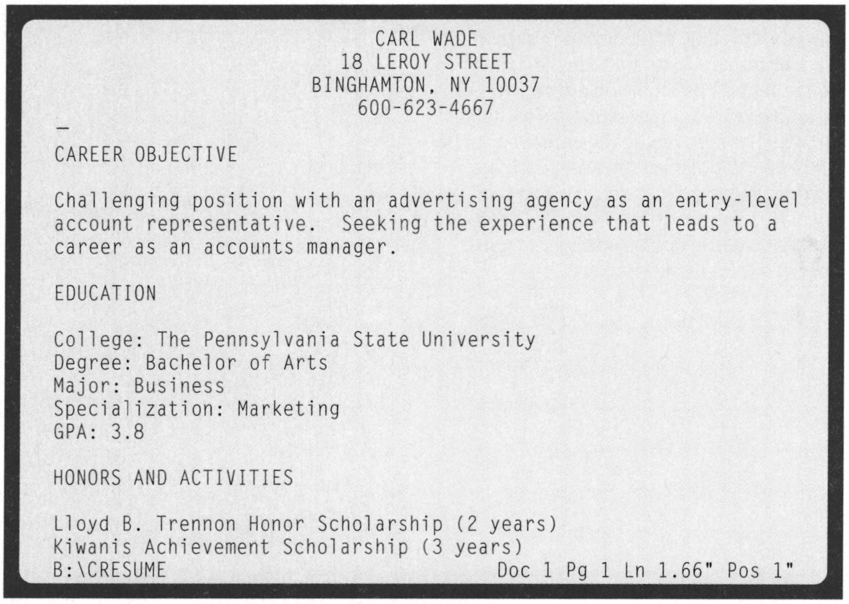

Figure 9-12   Easy centering. Carl can center the top four lines, without the risk of introducing typing errors.

```
                    CARL WADE
                 18 LEROY STREET
               BINGHAMTON, NY 10037
                   600-623-4667
   ‾
CAREER OBJECTIVE

Challenging position with an advertising agency as an entry-level
account representative.  Seeking the experience that leads to a
career as an accounts manager.

EDUCATION

College: The Pennsylvania State University
Degree: Bachelor of Arts
Major: Business
Specialization: Marketing
GPA: 3.8

HONORS AND ACTIVITIES

Lloyd B. Trennon Honor Scholarship (2 years)
Kiwanis Achievement Scholarship (3 years)
B:\CRESUME                              Doc 1 Pg 1 Ln 1.66" Pos 1"
```

and bottom of a page, a necessary process if centering vertically using a typewriter.

To center the whole page vertically, the cursor must be at the top of the page. After Carl moves the cursor, he presses Shift and F8 at the same time to access the format menu. Next he types 2 to see the Page Format menu, and then he types 1 to choose the option for centering the page top to bottom. He finally presses Enter repeatedly until he returns to the document. The document does not look any different on the screen, but when it is printed it will be centered vertically.

Changing Margins

When Carl first typed his resume, he left the margins—left and right, top and bottom—on their original settings. The original settings are called **default settings**—settings used by the word processing package unless the user deliberately changes them. The default left and right margins are usually 1 inch wide; the default top and bottom margins are also usually 1 inch each; allowing about 54 lines of text per page.

Documents are often typed using the default margin settings. However, if the document would look better with narrower or wider margins, the margin settings can be changed. Most packages even allow several different margin settings in various parts of the same document. Carl wants to increase the left and right margins for the entire resume. To do this, he must first move the cursor to the top of the document. He presses Shift and F8 at the same time to access the Format menu, and then presses 1 to get the Line Format menu, and then 7 to choose the Margins Left/Right option. To change the left margin from the default setting of 1 inch to 1.75 inches, he types 1.75 and presses Enter. To change the right margin to 1.5 inches, he types 1.5 and presses Enter. He presses Enter

Figure 9-13   Changing the margins.
When Carl widened the margins, WordPerfect automatically shifted the text to fit into the narrower space. Notice how the CAREER OBJECTIVE paragraph now takes up four lines rather than three.

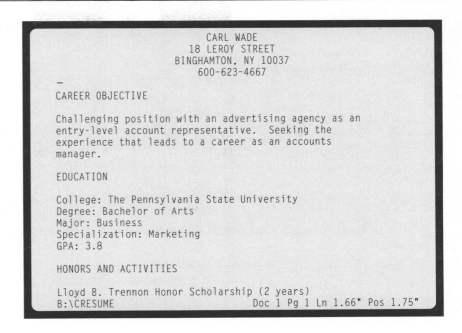

```
                              CARL WADE
                           18 LEROY STREET
                        BINGHAMTON, NY 10037
                            600-623-4667


     CAREER OBJECTIVE

     Challenging position with an advertising agency as an
     entry-level account representative.  Seeking the
     experience that leads to a career as an accounts
     manager.

     EDUCATION

     College: The Pennsylvania State University
     Degree: Bachelor of Arts
     Major: Business
     Specialization: Marketing
     GPA: 3.8

     HONORS AND ACTIVITIES


     Lloyd B. Trennon Honor Scholarship (2 years)
     B:\CRESUME                        Doc 1 Pg 1 Ln 1.66" Pos 1.75"
```

until he gets back to the document. To see the results of his changes, he may have to move the cursor past the centered lines.

When the margin settings are changed, most word processing software automatically adjusts the text to accommodate the new margins. This is called **automatic reformatting.** Figure 9-13 illustrates how WordPerfect automatically reformatted the text so that the resume now has wider margins. With some word processing packages, you may have to press specific keys to initiate reformatting.

Justifying the Right Margin

Carl now wants to make the right margin even. Notice in Figure 9-11 that the left side of the resume is neatly lined up but that the right side is uneven, or ragged. **Ragged right margin** means that the end of each line that calls for word wrapping does not end in the same position on the right side of the document. But Carl wants his right margin to be **justified**—that is, to line up neatly on the right side.

Some word processing software assumes right justification as the default setting, meaning that the right margin is automatically justified unless a user specifically requests a ragged right edge. Many word processing packages, such as WordPerfect, automatically justify the right margin when the document is printed, even though the right margin may appear ragged on the screen. The advantage of this approach is that inadvertent blanks between words can be seen and removed before the document is printed. WordPerfect justifies the right margin by spreading each line of text from margin to margin, leaving some extra spaces between words.

If Carl wanted to print his resume with a ragged right margin, he would first move the cursor to the top of the page. Next, he would press Shift and F8 at the same time to access the Format menu, and then type 1 for

The Biggest Market of Them All

Worldwide competition for the honor of producing the best-selling word processing program continues to heat up between two giant rivals: Microsoft and WordPerfect. In 1986, computer information firm Dataquest, Inc., estimated sales of word processing programs at more than $200,000. Since then, word processing has been considered the largest software market of them all. By 1991, the worldwide market was estimated at $1 billion. WordPerfect is considered the leader, with 60% of the market. The runner-up product is Microsoft Word.

When Microsoft released its Windows operating system, millions of DOS users switched to it, and industry observers watched sales of Microsoft applications for Windows increase. The most lucrative field, word processing, features Microsoft Word for Windows. Although the amount of Windows use is not yet comparable to that of DOS, Windows use is gaining. Unfortunately for WordPerfect, the release of its Windows version was delayed for 12 months. "You can't make people wait a year and not slip," said Dataquest Analyst Peter Francis, who was referring to WordPerfect's loss of market share. His comment recalled what happened to early market leader WordStar. A delay in releasing a new WordStar version in the early 1980s provided WordPerfect with the opening to move up. Today WordStar holds only about 10% of the word processing market.

Willard E. Peterson of WordPerfect Corporation says he is confident that the initial sales of WordPerfect for Windows ensures its leadership position in the market.

---

the Line Format menu. Carl would then type 3 for Justification and type 1 for Left (he wants the document justified—even—on the left side only).

Adding Boldfacing and Underlining

When Carl wants to add a few special touches to his resume, he may decide to use darker or italicized text to emphasize certain parts. Some word processors show text style changes right on the screen, and some do not. When a word processing program can show a character's style change on the screen the program is called **wysiwyg** (pronounced "wiz-ee-wig"), which stands for *what you see is what you get*. If a word processing program is non-wysiwyg, like WordPerfect for MS-DOS, word style changes are denoted by brightness or color changes to the characters on the screen, and the actual style change shows up only when the file is printed on paper. The version of WordPerfect called WordPerfect for Windows is designed for use with Microsoft Windows and is a wysiwyg word processor.

Carl decides to use darker text, or **boldface** text, for the address and name lines and the major headings, and he wants to underline his job titles to emphasize them. If Carl had realized, before typing the words, that he wanted to use boldface, he could have done it easily: He could have pressed F6, typed the text, then pressed F6 again to turn off the boldfacing. To boldface a group of words he has already typed, Carl must use the Block feature (which we will describe in more detail later). He begins by positioning the cursor at the beginning of the first word he wants to be bold. He presses Alt and F4 together. The words "Block on" flash in the lower-left corner of the screen. Then he moves the cursor to the end of the last word in the block he wants to be bold. This highlights the block of words (Figure 9-14a). Next Carl presses F6. The words "Block on" disappear, and the words that will be printed in boldface appear brighter, dimmer, or a different color than the surrounding words on the screen (Figure 9-14b), depending on the word processing package and the monitor. When the resume is printed, the marked words will appear darker than the rest of the text.

Underlining is also easy. To underline his job titles, which have already been typed, Carl positions the cursor at the beginning of the words he wants to underline. Next he presses Alt and F4 simultaneously. He then moves the cursor to the end of the block of words to be underlined. After he has done this, he presses F8. On the screen, the text may be highlighted (as in Figure 9-14c), a different color, or underlined, but it definitely will be underlined when it is printed. If Carl wants to underline text he has not yet typed, he presses F8 to start underlining, types the text, and then presses F8 again when he wants to stop underlining.

Carl's final version of his resume is shown in Figure 9-15. As you can see, the resume is much more attractive and readable than the original version. As before, Carl saves his resume on the data disk, so he has the option of making more changes in the future. The changes can be format changes or changes to the substance of his resume; he can, for example, add job experience as he gains it.

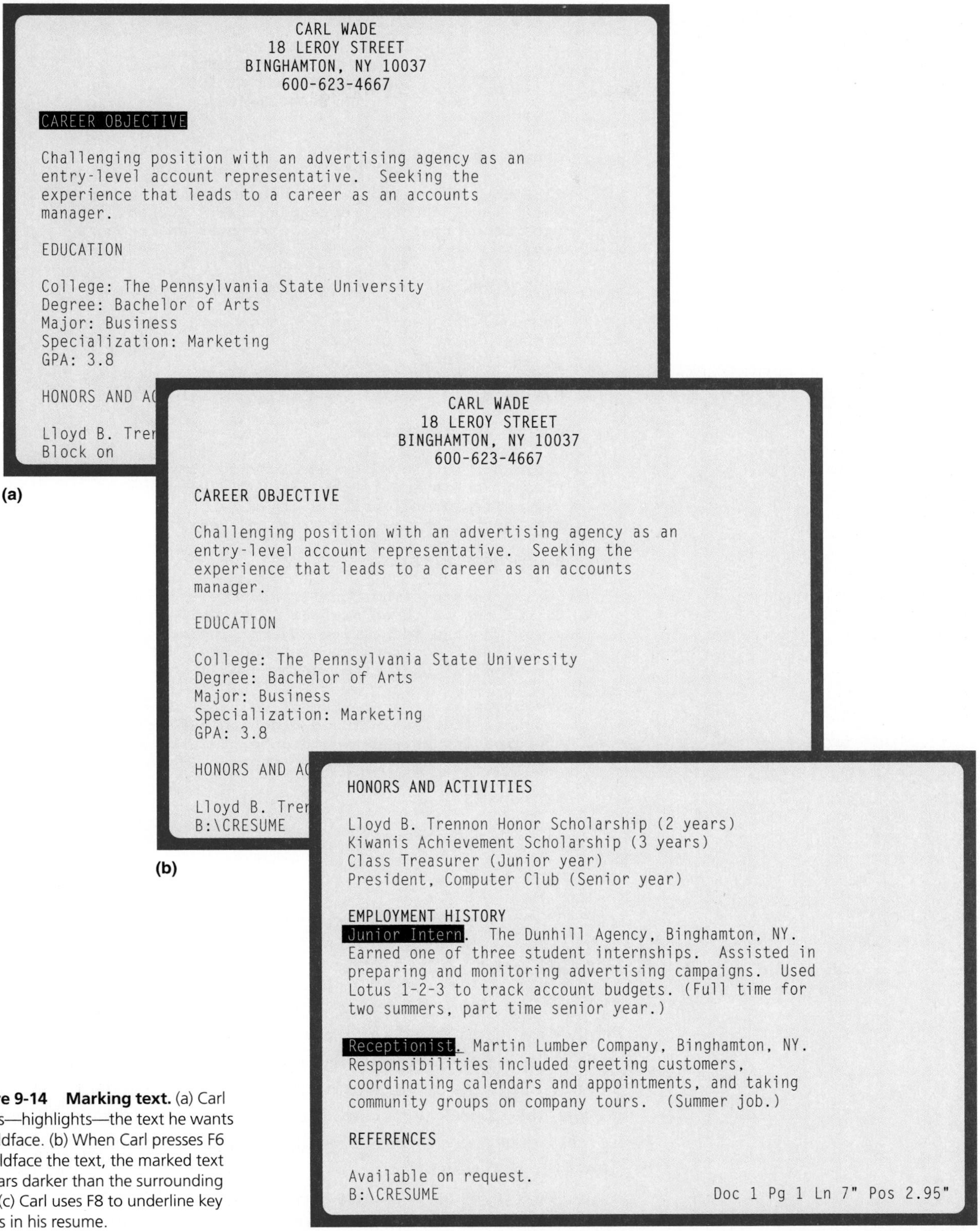

```
                    CARL WADE
                 18 LEROY STREET
               BINGHAMTON, NY 10037
                  600-623-4667

CAREER OBJECTIVE

Challenging position with an advertising agency as an
entry-level account representative.  Seeking the
experience that leads to a career as an accounts
manager.

EDUCATION

College: The Pennsylvania State University
Degree: Bachelor of Arts
Major: Business
Specialization: Marketing
GPA: 3.8

HONORS AND AC

Lloyd B. Tren
Block on
```
(a)

```
                    CARL WADE
                 18 LEROY STREET
               BINGHAMTON, NY 10037
                  600-623-4667

CAREER OBJECTIVE

Challenging position with an advertising agency as an
entry-level account representative.  Seeking the
experience that leads to a career as an accounts
manager.

EDUCATION

College: The Pennsylvania State University
Degree: Bachelor of Arts
Major: Business
Specialization: Marketing
GPA: 3.8

HONORS AND AC

Lloyd B. Tren
B:\CRESUME
```
(b)

```
HONORS AND ACTIVITIES

Lloyd B. Trennon Honor Scholarship (2 years)
Kiwanis Achievement Scholarship (3 years)
Class Treasurer (Junior year)
President, Computer Club (Senior year)

EMPLOYMENT HISTORY
Junior Intern.  The Dunhill Agency, Binghamton, NY.
Earned one of three student internships.  Assisted in
preparing and monitoring advertising campaigns.  Used
Lotus 1-2-3 to track account budgets. (Full time for
two summers, part time senior year.)

Receptionist. Martin Lumber Company, Binghamton, NY.
Responsibilities included greeting customers,
coordinating calendars and appointments, and taking
community groups on company tours.  (Summer job.)

REFERENCES

Available on request.
B:\CRESUME                        Doc 1 Pg 1 Ln 7" Pos 2.95"
```

Figure 9-14 Marking text. (a) Carl marks—highlights—the text he wants in boldface. (b) When Carl presses F6 to boldface the text, the marked text appears darker than the surrounding text. (c) Carl uses F8 to underline key words in his resume.

(c)

Figure 9-15   The final draft. Compare this version of Carl's resume to his first draft, in Figure 9-11.

```
                    CARL WADE
                 18 LEROY STREET
             BINGHAMTON, NY 10037
                  600-623-4667


CAREER OBJECTIVE

Challenging position with an advertising agency as an
entry-level account representative.  Seeking the
experience that leads to a career as an accounts
manager.

EDUCATION

College: The Pennsylvania State University
Degree: Bachelor of Arts
Major: Business
Specialization: Marketing
GPA: 3.8

HONORS AND ACTIVITIES

Lloyd B. Trennon Honor Scholarship (2 years)
Kiwanis Achievement Scholarship (3 years)
Class Treasurer (Junior year)
President, Computer Club (Senior year)

EMPLOYMENT HISTORY

Junior Intern.  The Dunhill Agency, Binghamton, NY.
Earned one of three student internships.  Assisted in
preparing and monitoring advertising campaigns.  Used
Lotus 1-2-3 to track account budgets.  (Full time for
two summers, part time senior year.)

Receptionist.  Martin Lumber Company, Binghamton, NY.
Responsibilities included greeting customers,
coordinating calendars and appointments, and taking
community groups on company tours.  (Summer job.)

REFERENCES

Available on request.
```

Reveal Codes

The monitor shows the results of Carl's work so far. By accessing the Print, View feature, Carl can see what the page will look like when it is printed. In addition, WordPerfect allows him to see the codes that the program put in the document to generate the screen and printed output. We will take a peek with Carl. To see the codes, Carl must access the **Reveal Codes** mode by pressing Alt and F3 simultaneously. Figure 9-16 shows the resulting screen.

You now see what goes on behind the scenes. The odd-looking bracketed commands tell WordPerfect how to display and print the text. While using the Reveal Codes mode, Carl can edit and format the document as usual. He can still use the cursor keys to scroll, for example. When

Figure 9-16   Behind the scenes with Reveal Codes. When Carl presses Alt-F3, WordPerfect puts the computer in the Reveal Codes mode. In this mode the screen shows the bracketed commands that tell WordPerfect how to display and print the text. While using the Reveal Codes mode, Carl can edit and format the document as usual. When Carl wants to hide the commands, he presses Alt-F3 again.

```
                        CARL WADE
                    18 LEROY STREET
                   BINGHAMTON, NY 10037
                      600-623-4667
           CAREER OBJECTIVE

           Challenging position with an advertising agency as an
           entry-level account representative. Seeking the
           experience that leads to a career as an accounts
           manager.
 B: CLETTER                          Doc 1 Pg 1 Ln 1" Pos 1"
   ▲    ▲    ▲    ▲    ▲    ▲    ▲    ▲    ▲    ▲    ▲  } ▲      ▲
[Center Pg] [L/R Mar:1.75",1.5"] [Center]CARL WADE[HRt]
[Center]18 LEROY STREET[HRt]
[Center]BINGHAMTON, NY 10037[HRt]
[Center]600[—]623[—]4667[HRt]
[HRt]
[BOLD]CAREER OBJECTIVE[bold][HRt]
[HRt]
Challenging position with an advertising agency as an [SRt]
entry[—]level account representative. Seeking the[SRt]
experience that leads to a career as an accounts[SRt]

Press Reveal Codes to restore screen
```

Carl wants to hide the codes, he presses Alt-F3 again. Any time the screen output is not what you expect, you can select Reveal Codes and see what the problem is.

Text Blocks

A **text block** is a unit of text in a document. It can consist of one or more characters, words, phrases, sentences, paragraphs, or even pages. Text blocks can be moved, deleted, copied, saved, and inserted. You can manipulate text blocks by using just a few keystrokes. To appreciate the power of these commands, imagine trying to move a paragraph to another place in a paper if your only tool were a typewriter.

The Survey Example

Barbara Crim is taking her first sociology course at California College. Halfway through the term, she is asked to write a survey that evaluates people's eating and exercising habits. After class Barbara goes to the school's computer lab and sits down to use WordPerfect to write the survey.

After reading the first draft of her survey (Figure 9-17), Barbara decides that it needs some changes. She wants to reverse the order of questions 4 and 5 so all of the eating-habit questions will be together. She also wants to eliminate question 9, since it deals with hobbies rather than eating or exercising. And finally, she needs to type the Never–Always scale for questions 2 through 8. Before Barbara can do any of these tasks, however, she must first define—or **mark**—the blocks she wants to manipulate.

Figure 9-17 The first draft of Barbara's survey. Barbara enters this draft of her survey.

```
Newspapers, magazines, and TV shows are filled with
stories on health and fitness.  But just how healthy
are people today?  An  introductory sociology course at
California College is conducting a survey to evaluate
community attitudes and activities.  We would
appreciate your helping us by answering the following
questions.  Please circle the number that corresponds
to the answer that best describes your behavior.

1.   Do you eat a variety of foods from each of the
     four food groups each day?
     Never       1     2     3     4     5       Always

2.   Do you limit the amount of fat and cholesterol you
     eat?

3.   Do you limit the amount of salt you eat?

4.   Do you maintain your desired weight--being neither
     overweight nor underweight?

5.   Do you limit the amount of sugar you eat?

6.   Do you exercise vigorously for 15-30 minutes at
     least 3 times a week?

7.   Do you walk to nearby locations rather than
     driving your car?

8.   Do you take part in leisure activities that
     increase your level of fitness?

9.   Do you participate in group activities or hobbies
     that you enjoy?

10.  What is your age?
     a. under 18 b. 18-21 c. 22-35 d. 36-50 e. over 50

11.  What is your sex?
     a. male          b. female

12.  What is your marital status?
     a. single        b. married        c. divorced
```

Marking a Block

Marking a block of text is done in different ways with different word processing software. In general, you move the cursor to the beginning of the chunk of text that constitutes the block. Then you either press a function key or use the keys to place block markers there. You do the same thing at the end of the block. Once the block is marked, it can be subject to a variety of block commands.

Since Barbara is using WordPerfect, she positions the cursor at the beginning of question 4 (just under the "4"), and presses Alt and F4 at the same time. This activates the Block command. WordPerfect reminds Barbara that the command is on by flashing the words "Block on" in the lower-left corner of the screen. Next Barbara moves the cursor until the entire question is highlighted. Now the block is marked (Figure 9-18).

Notice that the marked block stands out on the screen. Many word processing programs present marked blocks in **reverse video**—the print in the marked area is the color of the normal background and the back-

Figure 9-18   Marking a block of text.
Barbara uses the Alt and F4 keys to mark question 4.

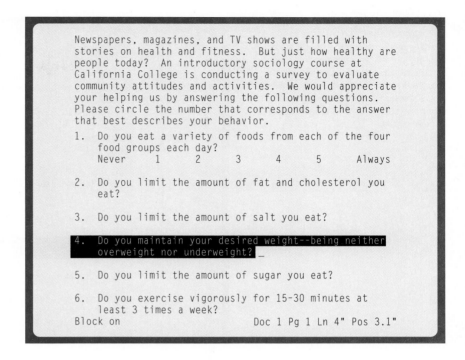

```
Newspapers, magazines, and TV shows are filled with
stories on health and fitness.  But just how healthy are
people today?  An introductory sociology course at
California College is conducting a survey to evaluate
community attitudes and activities.  We would appreciate
your helping us by answering the following questions.
Please circle the number that corresponds to the answer
that best describes your behavior.
1.  Do you eat a variety of foods from each of the four
    food groups each day?
    Never     1     2     3     4     5      Always

2.  Do you limit the amount of fat and cholesterol you
    eat?

3.  Do you limit the amount of salt you eat?

4.  Do you maintain your desired weight--being neither
    overweight nor underweight? _

5.  Do you limit the amount of sugar you eat?

6.  Do you exercise vigorously for 15-30 minutes at
    least 3 times a week?
Block on                        Doc 1 Pg 1 Ln 4" Pos 3.1"
```

ground is the color of the normal print. If, for example, the screen normally has black letters on a white background, the marked portion of the text shows white letters on a black background.

Moving a Block

Once the block is marked, Barbara can use the Block Move command. The **Block Move command** removes a block of text from its original location and places it in a second location—the block still occurs only once in the document. Moving a block from one location to another is also called *cutting and pasting,* a reference to what literally would have to be done if you were using a typewriter.

Different word processing packages move text blocks in different ways. Some packages require only that you move the cursor to the new location; then, when you press a certain key or keys, the block disappears from its old location and is inserted at the location of the cursor. However, other word processing packages, such as WordPerfect, have separate commands: one that means "cut"—or delete the block from the old location—and another that means "paste"—or insert the block in the new location.

To move question 4 under question 5, Barbara has marked question 4—the block she wants to move. Now she presses Ctrl and F4 simultaneously to make the Block command options appear (Figure 9-19a). Next she presses 1 to indicate she is working with a block, then 1 to move the block (that is, question 4). Question 4 disappears from the screen (Figure 9-19b). Barbara now moves the cursor to the position where she wants to insert question 4—under question 5. She presses Enter to move the text to the current cursor location. Figure 9-19c shows the survey after the question has been moved. Barbara then adjusts the space between

Figure 9-19   Easy moves. (a) After Barbara marks the text she wants to move, she accesses the Block command options by pressing Ctrl-F4. (b) Barbara selects Move and the text disappears from the screen. Barbara then directs the cursor to the spot where she wants to insert the question. (c) When she presses Enter, the text appears in its new location.

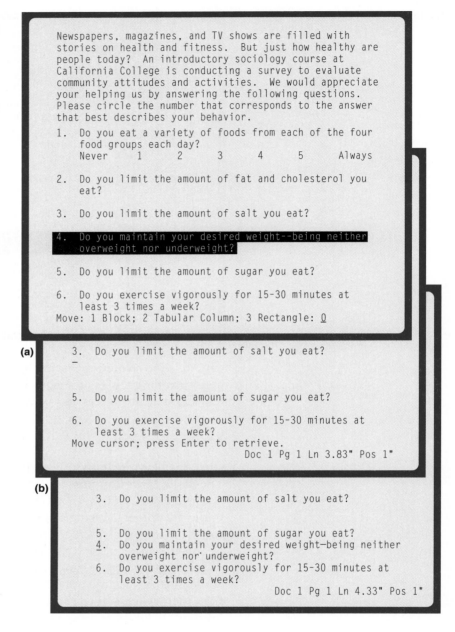

lines as necessary and changes the question numbers so the order is correct. If Barbara were an advanced user, she might have used an automatic numbering feature that would renumber the questions for her.

Deleting a Block

Barbara is not finished yet; she must get rid of question 9. One way to do this is to mark the question as a block and then use the **Block Delete command.** In WordPerfect the Block Delete command is the first half of the Block Move command—the "cut" part of "cut and paste." Other word processing programs may have a separate command for deleting blocks.

As before, Barbara marks the block—in this case, question 9. Then she presses Ctrl and F4 simultaneously, presses 1 to indicate she is working with a block, and then presses 3 to delete the block. An alternate method of deleting a block is to mark the block and then press Del.

As you can see, the Block Delete command makes it easy to remove chunks of unwanted text from a document. Although the same thing can be accomplished with character-by-character deletions, this approach is not very efficient for removing a large amount of text.

Copying a Block

Now Barbara wants to add the Never–Always scales. Since they will all be the same, she can do this easily by using the Block Copy command. The Block Copy command is similar to the Block Move command. The **Block Copy command** copies the block of text into a new location. However, the block also stays in its original location—that is, the same text appears twice (or more) in the document. The Block Copy command comes in handy when similar material is needed repeatedly in the same document, since you have to key in the text only once.

Barbara has already typed the scale once, as shown in Figure 9-17. Now she marks the block of text and presses Ctrl and F4 simultaneously. She presses 1 to indicate she is working with a block, then Barbara presses 2 to select the copying function. Next she moves the cursor to the position where she wants to insert the text—under question 2—and presses Enter to copy the text. She repeats these steps to copy the scale under question 3 through question 8. The final draft of her survey is shown in Figure 9-20.

 ## Some Other Important Features

Popular word processing packages offer more features than most people use. One of the main items of interest for newcomers is a tutorial; many packages include an introduction to its capabilities. The tutorial may consist of an elaborate context-sensitive Help index or on-line instructions. Other vendors also provide tutorial materials, such as supplemental software, videos, cassettes, and books. All these materials will help you learn about the many capabilities the software offers. We cannot discuss every feature here, but we want to mention three that you will find handy—help, spacing, and searching.

Help

Most word processing programs, like all of the best software, offer a **Help index** that provides on-screen reference material for assistance with the program. When you are uncertain about what to do, you may not have a manual nearby to give you guidance. If you want to add a footnote to a

Newspapers, magazines, and TV shows are filled with
stories on health and fitness. But just how healthy
are people today? An introductory sociology course at
California College is conducting a survey to evaluate
community attitudes and activities. We would
appreciate your helping us by answering the following
questions. Please circle the number that corresponds
to the answer that best describes your behavior.

1. Do you eat a variety of foods from each of the
    four food groups each day?
    Never   1   2   3   4   5   Always

2. Do you limit the amount of fat and cholesterol
    you eat?
    Never   1   2   3   4   5   Always

3. Do you limit the amount of salt you eat?
    Never   1   2   3   4   5   Always

4. Do you limit the amount of sugar you eat?
    Never   1   2   3   4   5   Always

5. Do you maintain your desired weight--being neither
    overweight nor underweight?
    Never   1   2   3   4   5   Always

6. Do you exercise vigorously for 15-30 minutes at
    least 3 times a week?
    Never   1   2   3   4   5   Always

7. Do you walk to nearby locations rather than
    driving your car?
    Never   1   2   3   4   5   Always

8. Do you take part in leisure activities that
    increase your level of fitness?
    Never   1   2   3   4   5   Always

9. What is your age?
    a. under 18 b. 18-21 c. 22-35 d. 36-50 e. over 50

10. What is your sex?
    a. male   b. female

11. What is your marital status?
    a. single   b. married   c. divorced

Figure 9-20 The final draft. Barbara has made all the changes she wants at this time, so she prints the final draft of her survey.

document, for instance, you will need to create a superscript numeral—a numeral whose base is above the usual text baseline. Unfortunately, nothing on the template tells you how to do this. You need help.

To invoke the Help feature in WordPerfect, you press F3. As the screen indicates in Figure 9-21a, you press S to get information on features that begin with the letter *s*. To create a superscript, the screen tells you to begin by pressing Ctrl and F8 simultaneously (Ctrl-F8), menu choice 1, then choice 1 from the next menu (Figure 9-21b). Press Enter when you want to leave Help and return to your document.

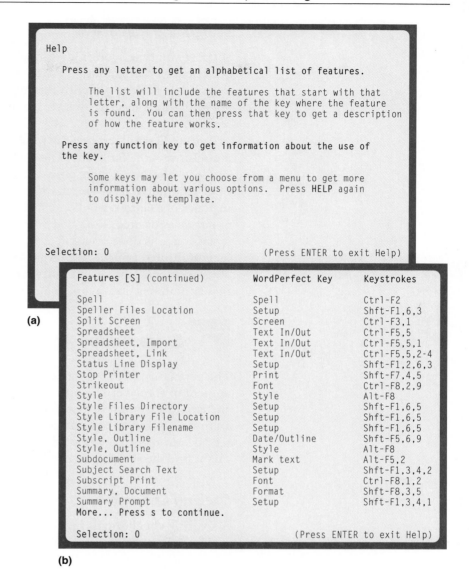

Figure 9-21   Getting help. At any point in a WordPerfect session, you can get help by pressing F3. (a) The Help screen displays directions to get you to the specific help you need. (b) If you press S, a list of features beginning with that letter appears. To exit Help, you press Enter.

Spacing

Most of the time you will want your documents—letters, memos, reports—to be single-spaced. But there are occasions when it is convenient or necessary to double-space or even triple-space a document. Word processing lets you do this with ease. In fact, a word processing program lets you switch back and forth from one type of spacing to another, just by pressing a few keys. A writer, for example, can single-space a printed copy of a new chapter for ease of reading. Then he or she can double-space the same document for the editor, who will appreciate the space to write in notes and changes.

Search and Replace

Suppose you type a long report in which you repeatedly spell the name of a client as "Mr. Sullavan." After you submit the report to your boss, she sends it back to you with this note: "Our client's name is Sullivan, not Sullavan. Please fix this error and send me a corrected copy of the report."

You could scroll through the whole report, looking for "Sullavan" and replacing it with "Sullivan." Then you could save and reprint the report. There is, however, a more efficient way—the **search and replace function.** This function can search through a document quickly, finding each instance of a certain word or phrase and replacing it with another word or phrase as desired. Note that you make the request just once, but the replacement is done over and over. Most word processing programs offer **conditional replace,** which asks you to verify each replacement. In other instances, the search function can be used by itself to find a particular item in a document.

 ## Extra Added Attractions

The popularity of word processing programs has encouraged the development of some very helpful enhancements. These added attractions are used to analyze text that has already been entered; to check spelling, grammar, and style; to find words in a thesaurus; and to write form letters. If your reports are riddled with spelling errors and typos, then you might find the spelling checker especially helpful.

Spelling Checkers

A **spelling checker** will find spelling errors you may have made when typing. The program compares each word in your document to the words it has in its "dictionary." A spelling checker's dictionary often contains more than 100,000 correctly spelled words. If, while looking through your document, the spelling checker program finds a word that is not on its list, it assumes that you have misspelled or mistyped that word. Some spelling checker programs are available only outside the word processing program. To use such a checker, you load it, then load and search your saved document file. WordPerfect, and most popular word processors, contain their own spelling checkers inside the program. When you invoke the spelling checker, it searches through the document you are typing. It then presents each misspelled word and provides suggestions for replacement spellings. You can set spelling checkers to ignore words beginning with uppercase letters, so they do not recognize proper names, such as Ms. Gillen, or acronyms, such as NASA. Otherwise, you must decide if the name is actually misspelled.

When a typical spelling checker highlights a word that it believes is misspelled, it tries to help you out by displaying all the words that it thinks you may be trying to spell (Figure 9-22). If you recognize the correct spelling of the word in the list you are given, you can replace the incor-

Figure 9-22   Spelling checker. The highlighted word, "conjusion," is a misspelling, so the spelling checker offers some alternatives in the area below the dashed lines. In this case, pressing A replaces the misspelled word with the correct spelling.

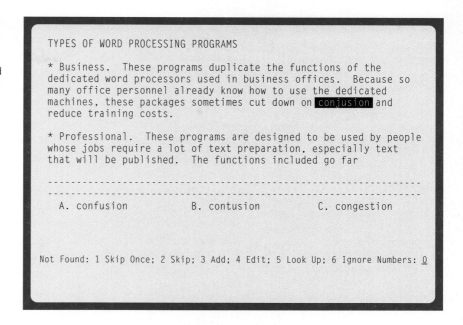

rect word with the correct word from the list. If the word highlighted is correct, you just leave it unchanged and continue searching through the document. Some spelling checkers can be set to check your spelling while you are typing. As soon as you type a word that the checker does not recognize, it causes the computer to sound a beep to catch your attention. Then it offers suggestions in the usual way.

The best spelling checkers let you create your own auxiliary dictionaries. If a word in your document is not in the spelling checker's main dictionary, the program then searches through your special dictionaries. This can be very useful. Suppose, for example, that you often write to a client named Mr. Mitchell and use computer jargon such as *byte* and *mainframe.* An ordinary dictionary would flag the words "Mitchell," "byte," and "mainframe" as misspelled. If you add these terms, which are correct in your environment, to your auxiliary dictionary, they will be considered correct in the future. If you have this type of spelling checker, you should add to your auxiliary dictionary the names of your friends and business associates and words that are often used in your job or field of study. In addition, many word processors let you use separately purchased dictionaries of technical terms for fields such as engineering, law, and medicine. When a word processing program like WordPerfect offers its own spelling checker, it puts perfect spelling within everyone's reach. But perfection may be elusive when you consider that no spelling checker can recognize that you wanted "too" instead of "to," since both are correct spellings that differ in meaning. Such errors require the kind of checking program we look at next.

Grammar and Style Programs

A computer program cannot offer creativity, inspiration, class, elegance, or ingenuity. In short, no program will make you the next Shakespeare or Hemingway. But there are programs that can improve your writing:

Gettysburg Revisited

Some people are worried that grammar and style programs will remove true originality and give all prose an unattractive sameness. Consider the ringing words of Abraham Lincoln at Gettysburg: "Fourscore and seven years ago our fathers brought forth on this continent, a new nation, conceived in liberty, and dedicated to the proposition that all men are created equal."

When rewritten by a style program, this Gettysburg line became: "Eighty-seven years ago our ancestors started a free country here, where people are equal." Not exactly inspiring. Obviously, we need not always follow our computer's advice. The best grammar and style programs make suggestions and allow you to make the final determination.

They are called **grammar and style programs.** When you write using a word processing program, these extra programs can identify some of your grammatical or stylistic flaws. Let us consider some specific features of this kind of software.

A grammar and style program—sometimes called an editing program—can identify unnecessary words or wordy phrases. To help you eliminate repetition, it can check to see if particular patterns of words appear again and again. It also can check for sentences that seem too long (run-on sentences) and indicate that you should break them up into several short sentences for clearer writing.

Grammar and style programs can also identify spelling errors that a spelling checker program cannot pick up. For example, the word "four" is a correctly spelled word and would not be flagged by a spelling checker. However, "four example" is an incorrect use of the word "four," and thus a spelling error that an editing program can identify. Consider another error that many spelling checkers do not notice: double-typed words correctly spelled. For example, if you inadvertently typed "on the the table," most spelling checkers would pass right over the two occurrences of the word "the." Editing programs spot such errors for you. Even if you are not the next great American novelist, you can use these programs to produce correct and clear English.

Thesaurus Programs

Like everyone else, you may have racked your brain, trying to think of just the right word—a better word than the bland one that immediately came to mind. Perhaps you were energetic enough to get a thesaurus and look it up. A thesaurus is a book that gives synonyms (words with the same meanings) and antonyms (words with opposite meanings) for common words. But never mind the big books. Now you can have a great vo-

Figure 9-23   A thesaurus program. The words labeled A through K are synonyms for the highlighted word, "remove."

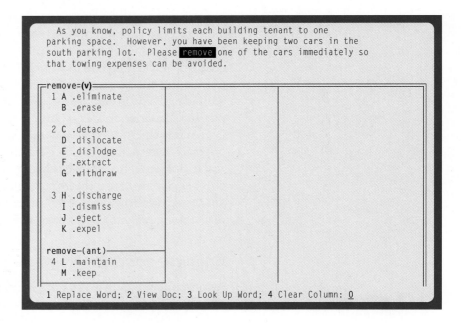

HOW TO BUY YOUR OWN PERSONAL COMPUTER

We cannot choose your new computer system for you any more than we might select a new car for you. But we can tell you to look for or avoid various features. We do not mean that we can lead you to a particular brand and model—so many new products are introduced every month that doing so would be impossible. If you are just starting out, however, we can help you define your needs and ask the right questions.

Where Do You Start?

Maybe you have already done some thinking and have decided that a personal computer offers advantages. Now what? You can start by talking to other personal computer owners about how they got started and how to avoid pitfalls. Or you can read some computer magazines, especially ones with evaluations and ratings, to get a feel for what is available. Next visit several dealers. Don't be afraid to ask questions. You are considering a major purchase, so plan to shop around.

Analyze Your Wants and Needs

Begin with a wants-needs analysis. Why do you want a computer? Be realistic: Will it probably wind up being used for games most of the time? Or for business ap-

plications? People use personal computers for a variety of reasons. Prioritize your needs; don't plan to do everything at once. At some point you will have to establish a budget ceiling. After you have examined your needs, you can select the best hardware-software combination for the money.

An Early Consideration

Although there are many brands of computers available, the business standard is an IBM or IBM-compatible machine; IBM-style computers account for approximately 75% of the market. If you will be using your computer for business applications and, in particular, if you need to exchange files with others in a business environment, consider sticking with the standard. However, the Apple Macintosh, with approximately 10% of the market, is an attractive alternative. The Macintosh is noted for ease of use, especially for beginners. It is also the system of choice for anyone working with graphics, including artists, illustrators, and desktop publishers.

What to Look for in Hardware

The basic personal computer system consists of a central processing unit (CPU) and memory, a monitor, a keyboard, a drive for a storage device (a 5¼-inch or 3½-inch diskette or hard disk), and a printer. Unless you know someone who can help you out with technical expertise, the best advice is probably to look for a packaged system—that is, one in which the preceding components (with the exception of the printer) are assembled and packaged by the same manufacturer. This gives you some assurance that the various components will work together.

The complete personal computer system. A complete personal computer system has a central processing unit and memory, monitor, keyboard, a drive for a storage device, and a printer.

Central Processing Unit

Today, most manufacturers make machines with 16-bit or 32-bit processors. More bits mean more power, faster processing, and more memory. If you plan to purchase an IBM or compatible machine, many software packages run most efficiently on computers using Intel's latest 386 or 486 microprocessors.

Operating System

An operating system is the means of control in a personal computer. Some 60 million PCs use the Microsoft disk operating system called DOS, making it the standard—particularly in business. In the last few years, competition among operating environments has arisen, especially with the release of Microsoft's Windows 3.1, a graphical user interface (GUI). A GUI promoted by IBM is OS/2, which can run programs written for DOS or Windows. Some nine million PC users purchased Microsoft Windows in its early years, encouraging developers to produce

more powerful versions of their DOS programs for Windows. If you want to buy into the ease of operations promised by the GUIs, you need to consider the added cost of extra memory and a pointing device, the mouse.

Memory

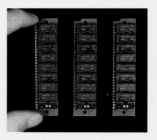

Memory is measured in bytes. The amount of memory you need in your computer is determined by the amount of memory required by the operating system and applications programs (like word processing or spreadsheets) that you want to use. For DOS machines, a minimum of 640 kilobytes (640,000

Adding memory. Simple plug-in modules called SIMMs (single in-line memory modules) have become the standard for adding memory to personal computers. Each SIMM provides 1, 2, 4, 8, or 16 MB of memory.

bytes) is recommended; Windows requires a minimum of 2 megabytes (2 million bytes) of memory; and OS/2, a minimum of 4 megabytes. Of course, the more memory you have the better, regardless of the operating system or applications. However, you would be wise to start out with the amount you can afford and feed your system's appetite for extra memory as the need develops. Memory has a tendency to become less expensive as time goes by.

Monitor

Sometimes called a video display screen, the monitor is a very important part of your computer system—you will spend most of your computer time looking at it. Before you buy any monitor, test it by using it to run some of the applications programs you intend to buy.

Color or Monochrome

Monochrome (green, amber, white on a black background, or black on a white background) monitors are often found in large institutions that employ people to input data all day. They may also appeal to the buyer who only wants to do light word processing. But the majority of computer users prefer color monitors. Such screens are required for graphics packages, entertainment programs, and many other applications. Since the color monitor is the most popular monitor among PC buyers, volume sales have driven down the cost considerably. Most first-time buyers would be wise to purchase a color monitor.

Monitor displays. (Top) Color monitors that let you see graphic displays and text in a multitude of colors are preferred by most computer users. (Bottom) A two-page screen display is useful for desktop publishing and graphics.

Screen Width

Although some Macintosh computers have a 9-inch screen, most monitors have a screen display of between 12 and 14 inches. Generally, a larger screen provides a display that is easier to read, so you will probably want at least a 12-inch screen. For most purposes, a screen that displays 25 lines of 80 characters each is standard.

Screen Readability

Be sure to compare the readability of different monitors. First, make certain that the screen is bright and has minimum flicker. Glare is another major consideration. Harsh lighting nearby can cause glare to bounce off the screen, and flat screens seem less susceptible to glare than others.

A key factor affecting screen quality is resolution, a measure of the number of dots, or pixels, that can appear on the screen. The higher the resolution—that is, the more dots—the more solid the text characters appear. For graphics, more pixels means sharper images. But do not be tempted to pay a higher price for the best resolution unless your applications need it.

Graphics Adapter Boards

If you want to use an application program that uses graphics and the computer you are considering does not come with the ability to display them, you will need to buy a graphics adapter board (sometimes called a graphics card) to insert into the computer. There are several different standards for graphics adapter boards: Video Graphics Adapter (VGA) and Super Video Graphics Adapter (SVGA), for example. Monitors designed for use with one type of card may not be capable of "understanding" the signals from a different type. Check carefully that you have the right monitor–graphics board combination, especially for Windows.

Ergonomic Considerations

Can the monitor swivel and tilt? If so, this will eliminate your need to sit in one position for a long period. The ability to adjust the position of the monitor becomes an important consideration when several users share the same computer. Another possibility is the purchase of add-on equipment that allows you to reposition the monitor. If you type for long periods, you might be wise to buy a wrist pad to support your hands and wrists.

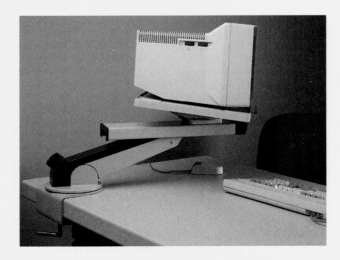

Ergonomic considerations. This monitor stand tilts and swivels so your neck does not have to.

Keyboard

Keyboards vary in quality. To find what suits you best, sit down in the store and type. Consider how the keys feel. Assess the color and layout of the keyboard, and find out whether it is detachable. You may be surprised by the real differences in the feels of keyboards. Make sure the keys are not crammed together; you will find that your typing is error-prone if your fingers are constantly overlapping more than one key. Ideally, keys should be gray with a matte finish. The dull finish reduces glare.

Most keyboards follow the standard QWERTY layout of typewriter keyboards. However, some have a separate numeric keypad. In addition, most keyboards have separate function keys, which simplify application program commands.

A detachable keyboard—one that can be held on your lap, for example—is desirable. You can move a detachable keyboard around to suit your comfort. This feature becomes indispensable when a computer is used by people of different sizes, such as large adults and small children.

Typewriter-style keyboard. Many keyboards now have 12 function keys along the top of the board, a numeric keypad on the right, plus an extra cursor movement pad.

Secondary Storage

You will need one or more disk drives to read programs into your computer and to store any programs or data that you wish to keep.

Diskettes

Most personal computer software today comes on disks. Modern diskettes are 3½ inches across. Although not necessary, you may find it helpful to have a 5¼-inch disk drive so you can use larger old-style diskettes. Many systems have at least one disk drive built into the computer.

Hard Disks

Although more expensive than diskettes, hard disks are fast and reliable and hold more data. These features make the hard disk increasingly important for

Secondary storage. (Top) The 3½-inch diskettes are standard on most IBM and IBM-compatible Macintosh computers. A diskette of this size is enclosed in a plastic case, which helps protect the disk. The 5¼-inch floppy diskette is still used on older IBM personal computers and compatibles and newer machines with the disk drives to accommodate the larger size. (Bottom) The inside of this hard disk drive shows the access arm hovering over the disk.

personal computer buyers. In fact, most computers are sold today with a built-in hard disk with a storage capacity of at least 40 million bytes—characters—of data. Greater capacities are available if you can afford them, and they are useful if you plan to work with graphics.

Printers

A printer is probably the most expensive piece of peripheral equipment you will buy. Although some inexpensive models are available, you will find that those costing $400 and up are the most useful. When choosing a printer, consider speed, quality, and cost. Verify that the printer will work with the applications software you intend to use. For example, will it print graphs created with Lotus 1-2-3?

For everyday printing, **a dot-matrix printer** capable of printing 250 characters per second will do very nicely. Each character is formed from a grid of dots,

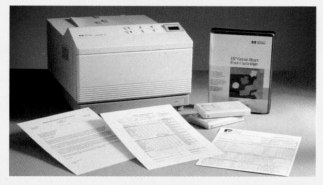

Printers. (Top) The 24-pin dot-matrix printers, such as this one, can produce results of near letter quality. (Middle) Laser printers are often used with desktop publishing software. (Bottom) Ink-jet printers can produce colorful graphic output.

A plotter. Plotters for personal computers can produce high-quality graphic output.

in the same way the lights on a temperature sign or stadium scoreboard spell out messages. Dot-matrix printers can also be used for printing computer-generated graphics. Near-letter-quality printers are dot-matrix printers that make a second pass at the characters or use a more dense array of dots to form the letters more fully.

Letter-quality printers use a daisy wheel, a device that can be removed (like a typewriter element) and replaced with a wheel that has a different type font on it. The disadvantage of this equipment is that it is relatively slow. These printers cannot print computer-generated graphics, but they do produce the sharp characters needed for business correspondence.

Although relatively slow, **ink-jet printers** are a popular, inexpensive alternative to dot-matrix printers. Color models can produce text and graphics whose color range and density usually surpass the color graphics of dot-matrix devices.

Laser printers are the top-of-the-line printers for quality and speed. They are also the most expensive. Laser printers are used by desktop publishers to produce text and graphics on the same page.

Plotters draw hard-copy graphics: maps, bar charts, engineering drawings, overhead transparencies, and even two- or three-dimensional illustrations. Plotters often come with a set of six pens in different colors.

Portability

Do you plan to let your computer grow roots after you install it, or will you be moving it around? Do you want a large video display, or will the smaller version on a laptop computer do? Portable computers have found a significant niche in the market, mainly because they are packaged to travel easily. A laptop computer is lightweight (often under 10 pounds) and small enough to fit in a briefcase. There are trade-offs, however, such as relatively poor screen readability and limited internal power.

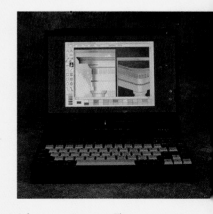

A laptop computer. These small computers, which often include built-in software, are an attractive option for users who travel.

Other Hardware Options

There are a great many hardware variations; we will mention a few here.

Communications Connections

If you wish to connect your computer via telephone lines to electronic bulletin boards, mainframe computers, or information utilities such as CompuServe or Prodigy, you will need a modem. This device converts computer data into signals that can be transmitted over telephone lines. The Hayes Smartmodem family of products has become the industry standard; most new modems claim some degree of Hayes compatibility.

Other Input Devices

If you are interested in games, you may wish to acquire a joy stick, which looks like the stick shift on a car. A joy stick allows you to manipulate a cursor on the screen. A more sophisticated device—and a must for GUIs—is a mouse, a gadget that you roll on a tabletop to move the cursor on the screen and make selections. Many software packages are designed to let you work more efficiently if your computer has a mouse attached. A scanner is useful if you need to store pictures and typed documents in your computer. Scanners are frequently purchased by people who want to use their computers for desktop publishing.

Surge Protectors

These devices protect against the electrical ups and downs that can affect the operation of your computer. Some of the more expensive models provide up to 10 minutes of full power to your computer if the electric power in your home or office is knocked out. This gives you time to save your work on disk (so that the work won't be lost if the power fails) or to print out a report you need immediately. If lightning storms or power fluctuations occur in your area, you would be well advised to purchase a surge protector.

What to Look for in Software

The current standard for operating systems is MS-DOS, made popular by IBM. Many applications programs that will do what you want to do are available for DOS-based computers. There are also many excellent programs written to run on the Apple Macintosh. Now let us consider hardware requirements, brand names, demonstrations, and languages.

Hardware Requirements for Software

Identify the type of hardware required before you buy software. Usually, the salesperson can advise you on hardware requirements for any software you purchase.

SYSTEM REQUIREMENTS

Operating Systems
MS-DOS (5.0 or higher for single user)

Hardware Requirements
IBM models and compatibles
Hard disk required

Main Memory
Minimum of 2MB of RAM

Printer
Any IBM-compatible printer

Read the directions. Make sure your hardware works with the software you are buying by reading the fine print on the software package.

QUESTIONS TO ASK THE SALESPERSON AT THE COMPUTER STORE

- Is the machine popular enough to have a user's group in my area?
- Is there anyone I can call about problems?
- Does the store offer classes on how to use this computer and software?
- Do you offer a maintenance contract for this machine?
- Can I expand the capabilities of the machine later?

Brand Names

In general, publishers of well-known software offer better support than lesser-known companies. Support may be in the form of tutorials, classes given by the vendor or others, and the all-important hot-line assistance. In addition, brand-name software usually offers superior documentation and upgrades to new and better versions of the product.

Software Demonstrations

Always ask for a demonstration before you buy. However, if you purchase your software through the mail from advertisements in computer magazines, you will not have an opportunity for a demonstration. In some cases, you can rely on a friend's recommendation, or you can consult the software reviews found in trade publications such as *InfoWorld*, *PC Magazine*, or *Macworld*.

Programming Languages

You may purchase programming languages on disk if you wish to write your own applications programs. BASIC is the most popular language for personal computers, but some personal computers can use FORTRAN, Pascal, C, and other languages such as LinkWay and ToolBook.

Shopping Around: Where to Buy

Where you buy is important, and usually the trade-off is between price and service—but not necessarily.

The Dealer

Remember that you are buying a relationship with the dealer as well as purchasing a computer. In a sense, you are also paying for your dealer's expertise. Answers to your questions, both now and later, may be the single most important part of your purchase. Vendors like IBM, Apple, and Hewlett-Packard have established nationwide organizations of authorized dealers. A vendor-authorized dealer usually has a well established business with recognized expertise in the product sold.

You might also decide to purchase a personal computer from a computer store, a discount house, or a bookstore. If you work for a large company or educational institution, ask whether your employer has made an employee purchase arrangement with a vendor. Substantial discounts are often available under such programs.

Service and Support

If you purchase your personal computer from a specialized computer store, you are usually ensured of service and support. The store's staff can help you through the rough spots. Remember, however, that the excellent computer store personnel who were available during your purchase decision may not be there when you need service. In addition, equipment and software change rapidly, and sometimes personnel are not as knowledgeable as you might hope. Many stores have other offerings, such as training classes, warranty service, or a loaner while your computer is being repaired.

Maintenance Contract

When purchasing a computer, you may wish to consider a maintenance contract, which should cover labor and parts. Such contracts vary in com-

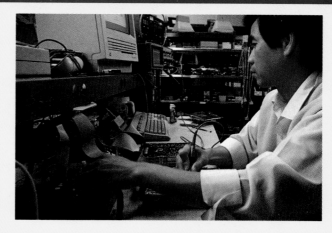

Repair. If your computer breaks down, you will probably need to take it to a repair center.

prehensiveness. Some cover on-site repairs (usually these contracts are available only to significant business customers); others require you to pack up the computer and mail it in.

Now That You Have It, Will You Be Able to Use It?

Once the proud moment has come and your computer system is at home or in the office with you, what do you do with it?

Documentation

Nothing is as important as documentation, the written manual and instructions that accompany hardware and software. Unfortunately, some documentation is inadequate. Ask to see the documentation before you buy. On a machine in the store,

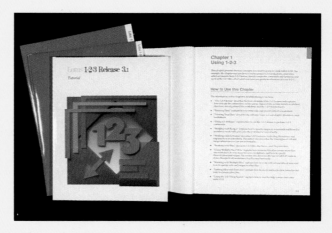

Documentation. Clear, easy-to-follow documentation is one of the most important features of a software package.

try performing one of the procedures the user's manual describes. The instructions should be simple to understand; too much jargon could cause you problems once you get your new hardware or software home.

Training

Can you teach yourself? In addition to the documentation supplied with your computer, numerous books and magazines offer help and answer readers' questions. Consult these sources. Other sources are classes offered by computer stores, local colleges, and hardware manufacturers and tutorials offered on diskettes by software vendors. These tutorials, offering hands-on participation right on your own computer, may be the most effective teaching method of all.

Survey for the Prospective Buyer

Identify the activities you would like to be able to do on your personal computer. Then read computer magazines, check with friends, and visit retail stores for hardware and software options. Select software with your computer hardware in mind,

Training. Hardware and software purchases, especially in business, sometimes include classes provided by the dealer.

and make certain that your software can be inexpensively and easily upgraded. Obtain comparative price information from many sources, including magazines, mail-order catalogs, and newspaper advertisements. Be prepared to comparison-shop.

SURVEY FOR THE PROSPECTIVE BUYER

1. Price Range
I can spend:

- ❏ Under $1000
- ❏ Up to $2000
- ❏ Up to $3500
- ❏ Up to $5000
- ❏ More

2. Hardware Features
I want the following features on my computer:

- ❏ MS-DOS compatibility
- ❏ Windows compatibility
- ❏ OS/2 compatibility
- ❏ Macintosh compatibility

- ❏ 16-bit processor
- ❏ 32-bit processor

- ❏ 256 kilobytes of memory
- ❏ 640 kilobytes of memory
- ❏ 1 megabyte of memory
- ❏ 2 megabytes of memory

- ❏ Monochrome screen
- ❏ Color screen
- ❏ 80-column screen

- ❏ Extra-large screen
- ❏ Excellent screen readability
- ❏ Color graphics capability
- ❏ EGA graphics standard
- ❏ VGA graphics standard
- ❏ Tilt-and-swivel screen
- ❏ Glare shield

- ❏ Wrist pad
- ❏ Numeric keypad
- ❏ Function keys
- ❏ Detachable keyboard

- ❏ Hard disk drive
- ❏ 3½-inch disk drive
- ❏ 5¼-inch disk drive

- ❏ Dot-matrix printer
- ❏ Letter-quality printer
- ❏ Ink-jet printer
- ❏ Laser printer
- ❏ Color printing capability

- ❏ Portability
- ❏ Modem
- ❏ Joy stick
- ❏ Mouse
- ❏ Scanner

- ❏ Surge protector
- ❏ Other

3. Software Features
I want the following software:

- ❏ Graphical user interface (GUI)
- ❏ Word processing
- ❏ Spreadsheet
- ❏ Database management
- ❏ Graphics
- ❏ Desktop publishing
- ❏ Communications
- ❏ Information services
- ❏ BASIC
- ❏ Other programming languages
- ❏ Games and recreation

4. Other Features
The following are important to me:

- ❏ Manufacturer's reputation
- ❏ Dealer's reputation
- ❏ Service and support
- ❏ Maintenance contract
- ❏ Documentation quality
- ❏ Training

cabulary at your fingertips—electronically, of course. Your access to this word supply is via a **thesaurus program,** which may be part of your word processing program or a separate program used in conjunction with it.

Suppose you find a word in your document that you have used too frequently or that just does not quite seem to fit. Place the cursor on the word. Then press the appropriate key to activate the thesaurus program. The program immediately provides a list of synonyms for the word you want to replace (Figure 9-23). You can then replace the old word in your document with the synonym you prefer. It is easy, and it is even painlessly educational.

Form Letters: Using the Merge Feature

A form letter used to be rather primitive, with your name typed—often in a different typeface—as an afterthought. No more. Now word processors like WordPerfect have **form letter** capabilities built-in. Using the Merge feature (Figure 9-24), you can send out masses of "personalized"

Figure 9-24   Using Merge for creating form letters. WordPerfect lets you create their own form letters quickly and easily. Three steps are involved: (a) First you insert codes in your letter, (b) then you put the names and addresses you want to send the letter to in a separate file, and (c) finally you use the Merge function to print the letters.

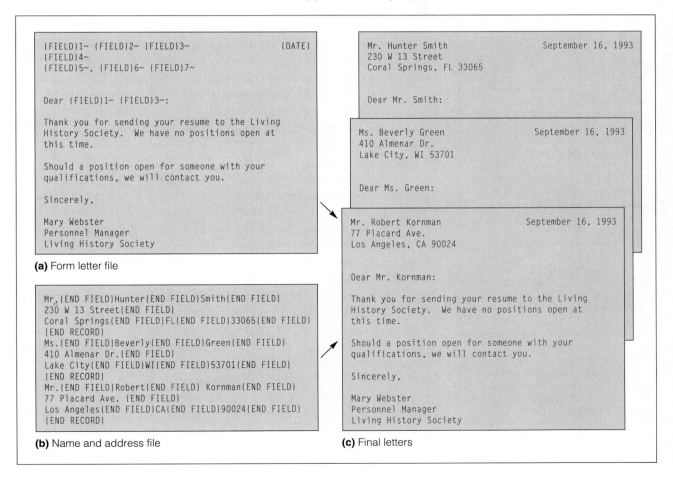

```
{FIELD}1~ {FIELD}2~ {FIELD}3~                    {DATE}
{FIELD}4~
{FIELD}5~, {FIELD}6~ {FIELD}7~


Dear {FIELD}1~ {FIELD}3~:

Thank you for sending your resume to the Living
History Society.  We have no positions open at
this time.

Should a position open for someone with your
qualifications, we will contact you.

Sincerely,

Mary Webster
Personnel Manager
Living History Society
```
(a) Form letter file

```
Mr.{END FIELD}Hunter{END FIELD}Smith{END FIELD}
230 W 13 Street{END FIELD}
Coral Springs{END FIELD}FL{END FIELD}33065{END FIELD}
{END RECORD}
Ms.{END FIELD}Beverly{END FIELD}Green{END FIELD}
410 Almenar Dr.{END FIELD}
Lake City{END FIELD}WI{END FIELD}53701{END FIELD}
{END RECORD}
Mr.{END FIELD}Robert{END FIELD} Kornman{END FIELD}
77 Placard Ave. {END FIELD}
Los Angeles{END FIELD}CA{END FIELD}90024{END FIELD}
{END RECORD}
```
(b) Name and address file

```
Mr. Hunter Smith                  September 16, 1993
230 W 13 Street
Coral Springs, FL 33065

Dear Mr. Smith:
```

```
Ms. Beverly Green                 September 16, 1993
410 Almenar Dr.
Lake City, WI 53701

Dear Ms. Green:
```

```
Mr. Robert Kornman                September 16, 1993
77 Placard Ave.
Los Angeles, CA 90024

Dear Mr. Kornman:

Thank you for sending your resume to the Living
History Society.  We have no positions open at
this time.

Should a position open for someone with your
qualifications, we will contact you.

Sincerely,

Mary Webster
Personnel Manager
Living History Society
```
(c) Final letters

The New Russian Revolution

The 1917 Russian Revolution placed the Soviet Union under Communist domination until a new democratic revolution—partially fueled by desktop publishing—resisted a hard-line crackdown. When Soviet President Mikhail Gorbachev was deposed by Communist hard-liners in a coup attempt on August 19, 1991, all major media—including newspapers—were closed down. To resist, the Russian government, led by President Boris Yeltsin, had to supply its own communications. New technologies—especially a desktop publishing system with an IBM PC with Aldus PageMaker software—made this essential communication possible.

Aldus had marketed a Russian version of PageMaker in the Soviet Union for little over a year before the political crackdown—a coup—occurred. One of its Moscow-based distributors, Juridical Literature Publishing House (JLPH), formerly state-owned, had been helping the Russian government set up an official newspaper called *Russia.* On the first day of the coup, JLPH graphic designer Yuri Tregubov helped assemble a special edition of the newspaper at Yeltsin's headquarters. The designer and his associates typed Yeltsin's emergency declaration into the Russian-language version of Microsoft Word 5.0, then imported it into PageMaker, and printed it on a LaserJet III laser printer. More than 1000 copies were photocopied and distributed among people who copied and passed it along to thousands of others.

Within 72 hours, President Yeltsin had restored order in the Soviet Union. But things would never be the same—especially with new technologies like desktop publishing to support the move toward democracy.

letters that cannot be distinguished from a letter produced by a professional printer. These programs have been a boon to fund-raising and political groups and a bane to the weary citizens who are tired of mounds of junk mail in their mailboxes. But, junk or not, these mailings are effective and, therefore, here to stay. In fact, you can join in and use them for your own group or organization. Here are the steps for creating form letters in WordPerfect:

- First, you create and store the form letter (Figure 9-24a). Instead of actually typing a person's name and address, you insert codes in the appropriate places in a *primary file.*

- Next, you create a file containing all the individual names and addresses in a *secondary file,* or *data file* (Figure 9-24b).

- Your last step is to use the Merge function to combine data in the primary and secondary files to generate a form letter for each name in the secondary file.

Each one of the letters looks as if it has been typed especially for the addressee (Figure 9-24c). This is the "personal touch" in the electronic age.

Desktop Publishing: An Overview

Would you like to be able to produce well-designed pages that combine elaborate charts and graphics with text and headlines in a variety of typefaces? Would you like to be able to do all this at your desk, without a ruler, pen, or paste? The technology that lets you do all this is here today, and it is called **desktop publishing,** or, sometimes, **electronic publishing.** You can use desktop publishing software to design sophisticated pages and, with a high-quality printer, print a professional-looking final document (Figure 9-25).

Until recently, people who wanted to publish documents had to use a traditional publishing process or a desktop publishing program. As word processing programs have become more sophisticated, however, the distinction between word processing and desktop publishing has become less clear. High-end word processing programs, along with a laser printer, can be used to create newsletters that have a fairly simple design—a few columns, a few boxes, a few graphic images, a few different type styles. But when you need something more elaborate—such as words flowing around and almost touching the petals of a daisy graphic, or automatic footnoting and indexing for your book—you need software specifically designed for desktop publishing. Boris Yeltsin, the president of Russia, used desktop publishing to help beat back a Communist coup in 1991 (see the essay "The New Russian Revolution").

But let us consider the more typical case of Cynthia Clark. Cynthia is a high school teacher who wants to interest her political science classes in the realities of politics by having the students create publications. She envisions her students preparing brochures to entice voters to the side

Figure 9-25   Desktop publishing. With desktop publishing software and a high-quality printer, you can create professional-looking newsletters and documents.

of one candidate or another—or, more generally, to get out the vote. In addition, she thinks creating a newsletter might boost students' interest in school politics. In the past Cynthia tried to have students create publications with the assistance of conventional publishing services. But timing was a problem: By the time the brochures or newsletters were printed, the semester was over. Furthermore, using outside help to produce publications was expensive.

With desktop publishing Cynthia can help her students produce a professional-looking publication by themselves, without the cost and delay of going to outside services. Sophisticated word processing and desktop publishing programs give the personal computer user the ability to do **page composition.** That is, Cynthia's students can decide where to place text and pictures on a page, what typefaces to use, and what other design elements to include. They can also insert graphics into the text. Cyn-

Figure 9-26   High-end desktop publishing. Steven R. Gilmore, a Vancouver, B.C. illustrator, used desktop publishing for all the graphics and type that went into this brochure for Vertigo Technology, Inc., manufacturers of 3-D animation systems.

Figure 9-27   The publishing process. Desktop publishing users can complete the writing, editing, design, and production cycles with the help of their personal computers.

thia sees desktop publishing as an affordable step between "plain vanilla" word processing and sophisticated professional typesetting services.

The Publishing Process

Sometimes we take the quality appearance of the publications we read for granted. A great deal of activity goes on behind the scenes to prepare a document for publication. Writers, editors, artists, designers, typesetters, and printers all contribute their knowledge and experience to complete a finished document (Figure 9-26). When you begin to plan your own publications, you will play several roles.

Figure 9-27 shows the main steps involved in publishing a newsletter. Desktop publishing makes it possible for the user to complete the writing, editing, design, and production cycles by using a personal computer. Desktop publishing also eliminates the time-consuming measuring, cutting, and pasting involved in traditional production techniques.

WRITING CYCLE

1. Write manuscript
2. Make preliminary illustration suggestions

EDITING CYCLE

1. Edit manuscript
2. Suggest illustrations
3. Copyedit manuscript
4. Prepare manuscript for production and design

DESIGN CYCLE

1. Estimate total length of manuscript
2. Design pages
3. Choose type
4. Design other page elements
5. Choose colors
6. Produce sample pages
7. Generate illustrations

PRODUCTION CYCLE

1. Typeset text
2. Proofread text
3. Place text on pages
4. Place illustrations on pages
5. Add finishing touches to prepare for printing

PRINTING CYCLE

1. Strip in halftones and four-color separations
2. Make plates
3. Print documents
4. Bind document if necessary

The Art of Design

If you are producing a brochure or newsletter, you probably want a sophisticated design. One part of the design is **page layout**—how the text and pictures are arranged on the page. For example, magazine publishers have found that text organized in columns and separated by a solid vertical line is an effective page layout. If pictures are used, they must be inserted into the text. Their size might need to be adjusted so they will fit the page properly. In addition to page layout, designers must take into account such factors as headings, type size, and typefaces. Are general headings used? Do separate sections or articles need their own subheadings? Does the size of the type need to be increased or decreased to fit a story into a predetermined space? What is the best typeface to use? Should there be more than one kind of typeface used on a page?

To help you understand how some of these decisions are made, we need to discuss some of the publishing terminology involved.

Typefaces: Sizes and Styles

The type that a printer uses is described by its size, typeface, weight, and style. **Type size** is measured by a standard system that uses points. A **point** equals about $\frac{1}{72}$ inch. Point size is measured from the part of the letter that rises the highest above the baseline (in letters such as h and l) and from the baseline to the part of the letter that descends the lowest (in letters such as g and y). The text you are now reading has been typeset in 10-point type. Figure 9-28 shows type in different sizes.

The shape of the letters and numbers in a published document is determined by the typeface selected. A **typeface** is a set of characters—letters, symbols, and numbers—of the same design. The typeface for the text you are now reading is called Trump Mediaeval. The typeface used in the margin essays is Frutiger. Some common typefaces are shown in Figure 9-29. Notice that a typeface can be printed in a specific **weight**—such as boldface, which is extra dark—or in a specific **style**—such as italic. These changes in typeface provide emphasis and variety. A **font** is a complete set of characters in a particular size, typeface, weight, and style.

Figure 9-28   Different point sizes. This figure shows a variety of different point sizes in the typeface called Helvetica.

Helvetica (12 pt)

Helvetica (18 pt)

Helvetica (24 pt)

Helvetica (36 pt)

Helvetica (48 pt)

Helvetica:
ABCDEFGHIJKLMNOPQRSTUVWXYZ
abcdefghijklmnopqrstuvwxyz
abcdefghijklmnopqrstuvwxyz
abcdefghijklmnopqrstuvwxyz

Times:
ABCDEFGHIJKLMNOPQRSTUVWXYZ
abcdefghijklmnopqrstuvwxyz
abcdefghijklmnopqrstuvwxyz
abcdefghijklmnopqrstuvwxyz

Avant Garde:
ABCDEFGHIJKLMNOPQRSTUVWXYZ
abcdefghijklmnopqrstuvwxyz
abcdefghijklmnopqrstuvwxyz
abcdefghijklmnopqrstuvwxyz

Garamond:
ABCDEFGHIJKLMNOPQRSTUVWXYZ
abcdefghijklmnopqrstuvwxyz
abcdefghijklmnopqrstuvwxyz
abcdefghijklmnopqrstuvwxyz

Palatino:
ABCDEFGHIJKLMNOPQRSTUVWXYZ
abcdefghijklmnopqrstuvwxyz
abcdefghijklmnopqrstuvwxyz
abcdefghijklmnopqrstuvwxyz

Frutiger:
ABCDEFGHIJKLMNOPQRSTUVWXYZ
abcdefghijklmnopqrstuvwxyz
abcdefghijklmnopqrstuvwxyz
abcdefghijklmnopqrstuvwxyz

Figure 9-29 Samples of typefaces. Shown here are different weights and styles of type-faces. Notice that changing the weight or the style of a typeface can change the impression it conveys.

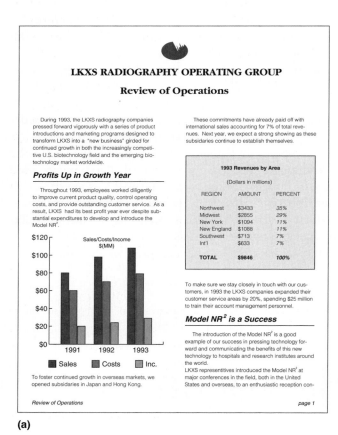

(a)

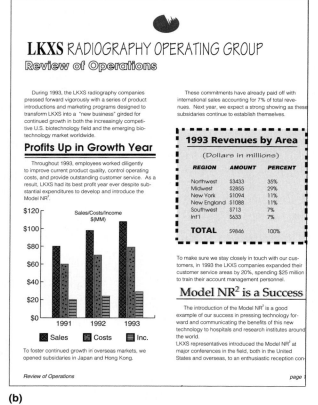

(b)

Figure 9-30 Sample designs. (a) This example uses complementary typefaces to produce a professional-looking document. (b) The same page created with clashing typefaces.

As shown in Figure 9-30a, varying the size and style of the type used can create an attractive appearance and draw attention to the most important sections of a page. However, using too many different fonts or using clashing fonts can create a page that is unattractive and hard to read (Figure 9-30b). Use different fonts with discretion.

Most printers used in desktop publishing store a selection of fonts in a ROM chip in the printer. These are called the printer's **internal fonts.** Also, most desktop publishing programs provide a **font library** on disk. A font library contains a wide selection of type fonts called **soft fonts.** A group of soft fonts can be sent—downloaded—to the printer. Then the printer can print text using these fonts.

Leading and Kerning

Two terms you will encounter when you begin desktop publishing are *leading* and *kerning.* **Leading** (pronounced "ledding") refers to the spacing between the lines of type on a page. Leading is measured vertically from the base of one line of type to the base of the line above it (Figure 9-31). Leading—just like type size—is measured in points. **Kerning** refers to the space between the characters in a line. In desktop software each font has a default kerning. Occasionally, you might want to change the kerning to improve the appearance of the final typeset work. An example of kerning is shown in Figure 9-32.

Solid leading (9/9)

When I wrote the following pages, or rather the bulk of them, I lived alone, in the woods, a mile from any neighbor, in a house which I had built myself, on the shore of Walden Pond, in Concord, Massachusetts, and earned my living by the labor of my hands only.
—Henry David Thoreau

+1-point leading (9/10)

When I wrote the following pages, or rather the bulk of them, I lived alone, in the woods, a mile from any neighbor, in a house which I had built myself, on the shore of Walden Pond, in Concord, Massachusetts, and earned my living by the labor of my hands only.
—Henry David Thoreau

+2-point leading (9/11)

When I wrote the following pages, or rather the bulk of them, I lived alone, in the woods, a mile from any neighbor, in a house which I had built myself, on the shore of Walden Pond, in Concord, Massachusetts, and earned my living by the labor of my hands only.
—Henry David Thoreau

Figure 9-31 Leading. Increasing the amount of leading between lines of type increases the amount of white space between lines.

(a) Unkerned:

WAVE

(b) Kerned:

WAVE

Figure 9-32 Kerning. (a) In this example, the space between the characters is not altered. (b) Kerning, or adjusting the space between the characters, can improve the overall appearance of the word.

Figure 9-33   Halftones. Halftones consist of a series of dots. Reducing the size of the dots makes the resulting halftone clearer.

Halftones

Halftones, which resemble photographs, appear in newspapers, magazines, books, and desktop publishing documents. Halftones are representations made up of black dots printed on white paper. Different numbers and sizes of dots in a given space produce shades of gray. As you can see in Figure 9-33, the smaller the dot pattern used, the clearer the halftone. Most printers used in desktop publishing produce halftones that meet professional standards.

Now let us put this publishing background to work by examining desktop publishing in more detail.

 ## Desktop Publishing Software

Desktop publishing systems let users create text and images, design the layout for a publication, move the text and images into the layout, and print the result. You have already studied how to create text with a word processing program. In chapters still ahead, you will learn that you can use spreadsheet and graphics programs to create images. Moving text and images and printing are straightforward once you become familiar with the desktop publishing software. It is the design of the pages, however, that is the heart of desktop publishing.

Imagine planning headlines not just in terms of what they say, but in terms of the size of the typeface and the spacing between the letters. Now try to decide just where a certain drawing should go, and how large it should be. Should the text be in columns? If so, how many columns and how wide? These are only some of the design issues to consider. But addressing these issues is easy with desktop publishing software; it lets you plan and change the page—right on your computer screen.

The software requirements for desktop publishing are:

- Word processing capabilities—either internal or external to the desktop publishing program—to create the text to be used in the publication

Figure 9-34   A desktop publishing menu. Most desktop publishing software lets you choose typefaces, type styles, and type sizes from a menu.

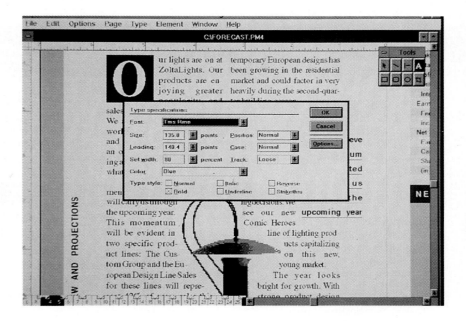

- A program to create or a scanner to capture graphics for the publication
- A desktop publishing program

Desktop publishing programs—also called **page composition programs,** or **page makeup programs**—make it possible for you to design the layout of each page of a publication on the computer screen. Using these programs, you can determine the number and the width of the columns of text to be printed on the page. You can also indicate where pictures, charts, graphs, and headlines should be placed.

Page composition programs provide boxes and pull-down menus, as shown in Figure 9-34, that let you specify the fonts you want to use in your publication. These programs also let you adjust the default leading, if necessary, to fit a block of text that is a little too long or too short into a column of your page layout.

Once you have created the design for each page, the desktop publishing program takes the text files you created and the graphics you produced (or brought in from another source such as using a scanner) and inserts everything into the page design that you have laid out. Page composition programs also let you move blocks of text and pictures around on your page. If you are not satisfied with the way the page looks, you can change the size of the type or the pictures or edit them.

Once the document is filled with words and graphics and in final designed form, you can print the document in a variety of ways. If only a few copies of the finished work are needed, you can print them on the laser printer attached to the computer. For high-quality output, some larger organizations, service bureaus (commercial shops that cater to desktop publishing users), and professional printers use **imagesetters,** which print at higher resolutions than laser printers and use resin-coated paper (laser printers use "plain" paper). Often, when the highest-quality copies are required, the file created by the desktop system can be stored

Macintosh

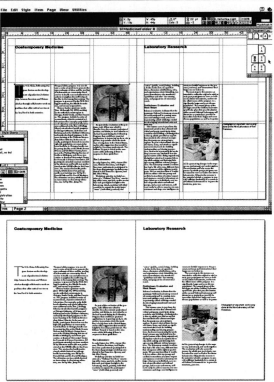

THE DESKTOP PUBLISHING COMPUTER

If there is one application that sets the Macintosh apart from other personal computers, it is desktop publishing. Businesses that invest in a Macintosh-based publishing environment may find themselves inundated with employee-produced publications—and without providing employees with much, if any, training.

Combining a Macintosh with a desktop publishing program (such as Aldus PageMaker or QuarkXpress) and a laser printer allows you to create attractive publications right on the screen. You can also move text and graphics around effortlessly, designing and redesigning on the fly. True to the Mac's graphical interface, most word processing and desktop publishing programs allow direct manipulation of such elements as margins, tabs, and graphics. You can set up master pages and lock in the column width and other guidelines—until you want to change things. On-screen rulers let you manipulate elements on each page, so your design can remain the same from page to page—or it can be changed independent of other pages.

You can use special features to snake your text around any graphic you choose. First you copy the graphic into the document, then have your program automatically surround it with a "text wrap" boundary. The next step is to "pour" text onto the page. Then all you do is watch while the program automatically prints tightly around the boundary of the graphic.

Designing pages electronically takes time to get used to, even for professional graphic artists. Although the process can be frustrating at times, the results can ultimately be gratifying. When your final version rolls off the laser printer, you can show it off with justifiable pride.

on disk and sent via modem (or hand-carried) to a sophisticated typesetting system to produce typeset copy. This can then be professionally printed if a large number of copies is needed.

Some of the best desktop publishing programs offer templates, prepared page layouts stored on disk. **Desktop publishing templates** provide predesigned outlines that are then filled in with text and graphics. Designed by experienced professional designers to guide the novice desktop publisher, templates suggest page design elements such as headline placement, the number and width of text columns, the best fonts to use, and image placement.

Hardware for Desktop Publishing

Computer hardware in general was described in detail in prior chapters. The discussion that follows focuses on the special needs of desktop publishing.

Input Devices

A number of input devices are used in desktop publishing, including the keyboard, mouse, scanners (black-and-white and color), art tablets, video (tape and disc), and CD-ROM players. Text is entered by using the keyboard, and the mouse is nearly essential in manipulating text and graphics. A scanner can be used to enter existing text and graphics in the desktop publishing system, and art tablets like the Wacom pressure-sensitive tablet can be used by artists to create graphics. For nonartists, **clip art**—images already produced by professional artists for public use—background patterning, borders, and even photography collections are sold by many publishers on CD-ROM. Such images on CD-ROM can be effortlessly copied and "pasted" right into publications. Figure 9-35 shows examples of the kinds of graphics included in such collections.

Figure 9-35   Clip art. A variety of clip art software can be purchased and used to improve the appearance of a document. Typical clip art is quite mundane—standard sketches of everyday items such as cars, flags, food, and household implements. The items pictured here offer a little more visual enhancement than the usual clip art software.

P E R S P E C T I V E S

DTP TREND: WORKGROUP PUBLISHING

A typical magazine office usually requires an editorial staff to write and edit copy, artists and photographers to create supportive illustrations, an ad group to handle advertisement space, an art director to lay out the stories, and a managing editor who plans and coordinates the whole issue. It is a swiftly changing world: Stories and pictures flow from desk to desk, then they are revised and get passed on again with more revisions. Priorities shift, layouts change, and story and ad sizes balloon up and down. In such offices nowadays, there is a trend toward workgroup publishing—publishing programs that allow a team of personal computer users to track, assemble, and control all the varied elements of a publication.

Workgroup publishing programs running on personal computers have begun to replace the proprietary, multimillion-dollar typesetting and production systems that for years have guided some of the country's largest magazines and newspapers. Unlike the large systems, most PC- and Macintosh-based publishing tools are designed for individual use. Even with the best word processing and desktop publishing software, however, creating a complex publication on a PC or Mac can still be still a large task.

Workgroup programs provide the ability to manage dozens of documents. The flow of work in a typical magazine office involves text that is entered and edited with off-the-

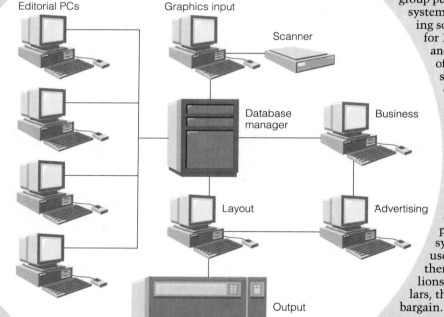

Editorial PCs   Graphics input

Scanner

Database manager   Business

Layout   Advertising

Output

Imagesetter

shelf word processing software, then poured into a desktop publishing program. Workgroup publishing programs combine and control all publishing activities through a centralized database manager, which tracks, updates, and stores all the elements. Everything eventually flows to imagesetter printers and emerges as a complete magazine. The programs keep all users up-to-date while providing security, control, and speedy access throughout the publishing process.

Two workgroup publishing programs, QuarkCopyDesk and QuarkDispatch, work as additions to popular desktop publishing programs (like the company's own QuarkXpress and Aldus PageMaker).

Quark estimates that a typical workgroup publishing system, including software for 10 users and 90 days of technical support, costs around $18,000. For newspapers and magazines whose proprietary publishing systems used to cost them millions of dollars, that's a bargain.

Work Flow of Workgroup Publishing
Workgroup publishing programs make it possible to create a complex and timely magazine using personal computers.

Monitors

For desktop publishing, the quality of the monitor is particularly important. The pages displayed on the screen must be very clear, so you need a high-resolution monitor. Since colorful images are essential to many publications, your monitor may need to be color. Some monitors, called full-page displays, can show an 8½ by 11-inch document in a vertical, or "standup," format. Still others can show a layout that spans two facing pages; magazine advertisements are often laid out in this way. These monitors look similar to 21-inch TVs.

Printers

The quality of the printer is one of the main factors in desktop publishing. Most desktop publishing systems include either a laser printer or a less expensive ink-jet or bubble-jet printer; the best laser printers are capable of producing text that closely resembles the quality of professional typesetting. If you need the quality of typesetting, an alternative is to send your file to a firm equipped with an imagesetter printer. Whether you use a printer that is part of a desktop system or you use an imagesetter, you can get a printout that is **camera-ready**—that is, it is ready to be photographed to make a plate for printing.

Printer Resolution   The characters and pictures you see in this book and other publications are actually made up of thousands of tiny dots. The smaller the dots that a device can print, the higher the **resolution.** The size and density of the dots are measured in dots per inch (dpi). The more dots per inch, the clearer and sharper the characters and graphics produced (Figure 9-36).

Service bureaus and professional printers usually use imagesetter printers to produce camera-ready originals with resolutions of 1200 to 2540 dots per inch; the dots are so small that they cannot be seen even under a magnifying glass. This level of resolution is called **typeset quality.** To approximate typeset quality, printers used in desktop publishing must be able to print text and graphics at resolutions of at least 300 dots per inch. Some laser printers can print at resolutions of 600 dots per inch and higher. Resolution is a factor to consider, since research has shown that text printed at a higher resolution is more readable and understandable than text printed at a lower resolution.

Page Description Languages   Printers used for desktop publishing must have a **page description language (PDL)**. PDLs let a page composition program tell the printer exactly how to use fonts, type sizes, text, and graphics. That is, after you compose a page on the computer, the desktop publishing program sends the correct instructions to the printer's PDL. Since your desktop publishing program is what gives the PDL its instructions, you do not need to worry about learning the PDL yourself.

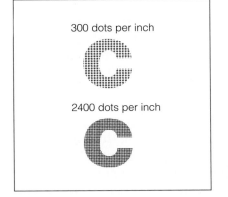

300 dots per inch

2400 dots per inch

Figure 9-36   Comparing dots per inch.
The greater the number of dots per inch (dpi), the greater the resolution of the text. Most laser printers produce output between 300 and 1200 dots per inch.

Desktop Publishing: The Payoff

The design, typesetting, and printing costs incurred by company publications are a major business expense. In fact, in American businesses, the cost of publications is second only to personnel costs. Many companies spend hundreds of thousands of dollars annually on publishing. Publications are a major expense for nonprofit organizations as well.

Most newsletters, advertising leaflets, technical manuals, and in-house business publications do not have to be of the finest quality. They can be designed, produced, and printed with desktop publishing. Even in cases where a large quantity of copies is needed and it is more practical to employ a professional printer, desktop publishing can still be used to design and produce the publication.

Because of their speed, flexibility, and output quality, desktop publishing systems can rapidly produce not only newsletters, business forms, and technical documents but also letterheads with company logos and manuals with magazine-style layouts. Users value the time and money savings, but what they value even more is the control—the ability to see exactly how a change in the type size or layout looks by observing the results immediately on a computer screen and the ability to decide if the change is appropriate. No more company newsletters filled with crooked lines and amateurish drawings—most offices are moving to the greener pastures of desktop publishing.

We Hope You Are Convinced

We hope you are convinced that word processing is a great time-saver, that it can be easy to learn, and that it is the best software tool—well, one of the best tools—for personal computers. Most of all, we hope you are convinced that word processing is essential for your career, no matter what it is.

Once you have mastered the basics of word processing, you may decide to expand your sights to include the desktop publishing features of word processing packages—or you may decide you are ready for the advantages of true desktop publishing software.

Word processing and desktop publishing are important software tools. But they are not the only important ones. Some people, in fact, are more interested in software that works with numbers rather than words. We are talking, of course, about spreadsheet software. This important topic is the subject of our next chapter.

R E V I E W   A N D   R E F E R E N C E

Summary and Key Terms

- **Word processing** is using a computer in the creation, editing, formatting, storing, and printing of a text document. The advantages of word processing over typing are that you can store your document, which makes it easier to incorporate changes, and you can see what you type before printing it.

- As you type, the screen displays a **cursor** to show where the next character you type will appear. You can move the cursor around on the screen by using **cursor movement keys** on the right side of the keyboard. The **PgUp** and **PgDn** keys let you move the cursor up or down a whole page at a time.

- Word processing programs treat the text you type as if it were on a long roll of paper, or scroll. You "roll the scroll" up or down on the screen by moving the cursor. This process is called **scrolling.**

- When a word that you type at the end of a line cannot fit on that line, the word processing program automatically starts that word on the next line. This feature is known as **word wrap.** Do not use a carriage return (that is, do not press Enter) at the end of a line unless you want to signal the end of a paragraph or provide a blank line.

- The use of each function key differs according to each application program. A paper or plastic **template,** which fits over the function keys, briefly describes the use of each key.

- To enter or edit text, use the keyboard as you would a typewriter. After completing the document and making corrections, save the document on a data disk. The **Insert mode** is the standard way of inserting corrections when using word processing. **Typeover mode** allows you to replace the existing text with new text. The Ins key acts as a **toggle switch,** allowing you to switch between the Insert mode and the Typeover mode.

- The **format** of a document is the way the document appears on the page. Factors affecting format are margin width, line spacing, use of boldface and underlining, and so on.

- To **center** text usually means to center text on a line. **Vertical centering,** however, adjusts the top and bottom margins so the text is centered vertically on the page.

- The original margin settings are called the **default settings.** Both the default left and right margins are usually 1 inch wide. The default top and bottom margins are also usually 1 inch each, allowing about 54 lines of text per page. When the margin settings are changed, most word processing software automatically adjusts the text to fit the new margins. This is called **automatic reformatting.**

- **Ragged right margin** means that the end of each line that calls for word wrapping does not end in the same position on the right side of the document. **Justified** text lines up neatly on the right side, creating an even margin.

- A word processing program that can show text style changes right on the screen is called a **wysiwyg** program—wysiwyg stands for *what you see is what you get.*

- **Boldface** words appear brighter, dimmer, or a different color than the surrounding words on the screen, depending on the word processing package and monitor used. When the document is printed, the marked words will appear darker than the rest of the text. To use **underlining** is to ensure that words are underscored when printed.

- Use the **Reveal Codes** mode to show on screen the codes that tell WordPerfect how to display and print the text.

- A **text block** is a unit of text—one or more characters, words, phrases, sentences, paragraphs, or even pages. Text blocks can be moved, deleted, copied, saved, and inserted. To manipulate a block of text, you must first define, or **mark,** the block. The marked block often stands out in **reverse video** on the screen.

- Use the **Block Move command** to move the text to a different location; this process is also known as cutting and pasting. The **Block Delete command** lets you delete a block of text. The **Block Copy command** copies the block of text into a new location, leaving the text in its original location as well.

- Use the **Help index** to access on-screen reference materials that provide assistance with the program.

- The **search and replace function** quickly searches through a document to find each instance of a certain word or phrase and replaces it with another word or phrase. Most programs offer **conditional replace,** which asks you to verify each replacement.

- A number of special programs work in conjunction with word processing software, analyzing text that has been entered already. These programs include **spelling checker programs,** which include a built-in dictionary, and **grammar and style programs,** sometimes called editing programs, which identify wordy phrases, repetition, run-on sentences, and spelling errors that cannot be identified by a spelling checker. There are also **thesaurus programs,** which include a reference that supplies synonyms and antonyms, and programs for creating **form letters.** Form letter programs let you create "personalized" letters automatically.

- **Desktop publishing,** or **electronic publishing,** can help you produce professional-looking documents containing both text and graphics. Desktop publishing can save time and money and can give you better control over the design and production of the final product.

- The publishing process includes writing, editing, designing, producing, and printing.

- One part of the overall design of a document is **page layout**—how the text and pictures are arranged on the page. Adding type to a layout is called **page composition.**

- Printers offer a variety of type. Type is described by **type size, typeface, weight,** and **style.** Type size is measured by a standard system based on the **point.** A **font** is a complete set of characters in a particular size, typeface, weight, and style.

- Most printers used in desktop publishing contain **internal fonts** stored in a ROM chip. Most desktop publishing programs provide a **font library** on disk, containing a selection of type fonts called **soft fonts.**

- **Leading** refers to the spacing between the lines of type on a page. **Kerning** refers to the space between the characters in a line.

- A **halftone**—a representation made up of dots—can be produced by desktop publishing printers.

- The software requirements for desktop publishing include a word processing program, a graphics program, and a page composition program. **Page composition programs**—also called **page makeup programs,** or **desktop publishing programs**—enable the user to design the page layout.

- Some page composition programs offer **desktop publishing templates**—prepared page layouts stored on disk. Page composition programs may also let a user integrate **clip art**—prepared drawings stored on disk.

- Devices used to input text and graphics in desktop publishing include the keyboard, mouse, scanners, art tablets, video (tape and disc), and CD-ROM.

- For the highest-quality publications, high-resolution monitors and printers should be used. Printer quality is particularly important if the user wishes to produce **camera-ready** printout. Some larger organizations, service bureaus, and professional printers use **imagesetters,** which print at higher resolutions than desktop printers and use resin-coated paper instead of the "plain" paper used by laser printers.

- Printed characters and pictures are actually made up of tiny dots. The smaller the dots printed, the higher the **resolution.** The size and density of the dots are measured in dots per inch (dpi). Resolutions of 1200 to 2540 dots per inch are called **typeset quality.**

- Printers used for desktop publishing must have a **page description language (PDL).**

Review Questions

1. What are the basic functions of word processing?
2. How is word processing different from typing?
3. What is meant by the term *word wrap?*
4. What is meant by the term *scrolling?* How do you use scrolling when you are viewing a long document on the screen?
5. What is the difference between the Insert mode and the Typeover mode when using word processing? How do you get into Insert mode?
6. When should Enter be pressed when entering text? Why?
7. How do you move the cursor up and down a line? How do you move the cursor from left to right?
8. How do you delete a character?
9. What happens to an unsaved file when you turn the computer off?
10. What is meant by the term *boldface?*
11. What is the format of a document? What is reformatting?
12. How is vertical centering different from centering?
13. What is meant by the term *text block?*
14. Name five operations that can be performed on a block of text.
15. What is the difference between a block move and a block copy operation?
16. How does a spelling checker recognize spelling errors in a document?
17. What is the function of a thesaurus program?
18. What is desktop publishing?
19. What advantages does desktop publishing have over word processing?
20. What advantages does desktop publishing have over traditional publishing methods?
21. How is the size of type specified?
22. What is a typeface, and does it differ from a font?
23. What is meant by the terms *leading* and *kerning?*
24. What are halftones?
25. What is a page composition program?
26. What are desktop publishing templates?
27. What is clip art?
28. What input and output hardware are needed for desktop publishing?
29. What is meant by the resolution of a printer?
30. What is the function of a page description language?

Discussion Questions

1. Why have professional writers taken to word processing programs?
2. If there are manuals available for word processing programs, why do some programs include a Help index?
3. Check your local software store for desktop publishing software. Consider asking these questions: a. What is the best-selling desktop publishing software? b. Which

printers are in most common use for desktop publishing? c. How many hours, approximately, does it take to learn how to use a particular desktop publishing software package? d. Are there classes available? e. Can you obtain samples of desktop publishing output?

4. Suppose you were familiar with a particular word processing package that is offered in a new version that includes some desktop publishing features. Would you be inclined to switch to the new version or to buy a separate desktop publishing package? There are many considerations. Take one position or the other and justify it.

True-False Questions

T F   1. Most of the advantages of word processing over typing are a result of separating typing from printing.

T F   2. The keystrokes required to underline text are the same in all word processing programs.

T F   3. While you are entering text in your word processing file, you should press Enter at the end of every line.

T F   4. You can save a file anytime you want.

T F   5. Formatting codes must be at the top of the document, before you begin typing any text.

T F   6. As you edit a file, you will see on the screen exactly what your document will look like when you print it.

T F   7. Leading must be the same throughout a document.

T F   8. Spelling checker programs correct your grammar, too.

T F   9. To do desktop publishing, you need a true desktop publishing program.

T F   10. *Leading* refers to how far apart text lines are; *kerning* refers to how close together letters are.

Spreadsheets: What if . . . ?

Alisha and Robert were working on a problem for their company. They

had assembled all the facts and figures regarding changing their com-

pany's telephone service. The costs of the existing phone service over

the past few years had been entered into a computer spreadsheet program,

along with the projected costs of the rival phone company. Now Alisha

and Robert were trying out different scenarios—changing the numbers

in different parts of the program—in an attempt to determine if the sav-

ings promised by the rival company were accurate. "What if," Alisha won-

dered aloud, "the costs per week increased because of growth in our west-

ern region?" She entered some new figures for the western region, and watched the software program calculate new information. "Not bad," Robert said. "Now what if the eastern region shrinks a bit while growth in the southern region increases along with growth in the West?" Alisha entered new figures for the eastern and southern regions, then watched as the spreadsheet program calculated the results again. This process went on for some time. Finally they had enough information to compile a report. Their figures showed that the new phone company's plan would save them at least 10% over the next five years—no matter how they looked at it.

Both large and small companies today rely on computers to help them make business decisions. The computer program that has done more for business than any other is the *spreadsheet*, an electronic version of the old ledger book used by Bob Cratchit in Charles Dickens's *A Christmas Carol.* You might remember how Bob spent his time shivering in Scrooge's business office, copying figures into ledger books by hand. The pages in such books, ruled into rows and columns, are called worksheets, or **spreadsheets** (Figure 10-1a). The manually constructed spreadsheet has been used as a business tool for centuries. Spreadsheets can be used to organize and present business data, thus aiding managerial decision making. But spreadsheets are not limited to businesses. Personal and family budgets, for example, are often organized on spreadsheets.

Unfortunately, creating a large spreadsheet is time-consuming and tedious, even when using a calculator or copying results from a computer printout. Another problem with manual spreadsheets is that it is too easy to make a mistake. You may not discover the mistake, and it could have serious consequences for the business and possibly your job. If you do discover the mistake after the spreadsheet is finished, you must manually redo the calculations that used the wrong number.

Electronic Spreadsheets

An **electronic spreadsheet** is a computerized version of a manual spreadsheet (Figure 10-1b). Working with a spreadsheet on a computer eliminates much of the toil of setting up a manual spreadsheet. In general, it works like this: You enter the data you want in your spreadsheet and then key in the types of calculations you need. The electronic spreadsheet program automatically does all the calculations for you and produces the results. The program does not make any calculation errors, and if you want a printed copy of the spreadsheet, a printer can produce it quickly. Also, you can store your electronic spreadsheet on a disk so that it can be used again. But the greatest labor-saving aspect of the electronic spreadsheet is that, when you change one value or formula in a worksheet, all the rest of the values on the spreadsheet are recalculated automatically to reflect the change.

Spreadsheet programs are very versatile. You saw how a spreadsheet helped Alisha and Robert analyze the costs of changing phone companies. Let us look at some other business applications.

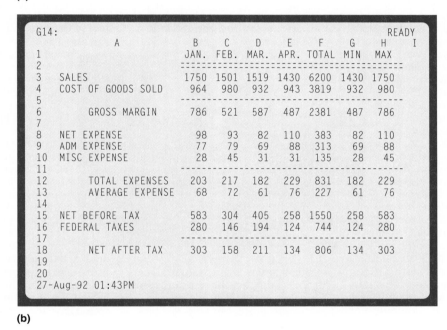

	JAN.	FEB.	MAR.	APR.	TOTAL	MIN	MAX
SALES	1750	1501	1519	1430	6200	1430	1750
COST OF GOODS SOLD	964	980	932	943	3819	932	980
GROSS MARGIN	786	521	587	487	2381	487	786
NET EXPENSE	98	93	82	110	383	82	110
ADM EXPENSE	77	79	69	88	313	69	88
MISC EXPENSE	28	45	31	31	135	28	45
TOTAL EXPENSES	203	217	182	229	831	182	229
AVERAGE EXPENSE	68	72	61	76	277	61	76
NET BEFORE TAXES	583	304	405	258	1550	258	583
FEDERAL TAXES	280	146	194	124	744	124	280
NET AFTER TAX	303	158	211	134	806	134	303

(a)

```
G14:                                                          READY
              A         B     C     D     E     F     G     H    I
1                      JAN.  FEB.  MAR.  APR.  TOTAL MIN   MAX
2                      ------------------------------------------
3   SALES              1750  1501  1519  1430  6200  1430  1750
4   COST OF GOODS SOLD  964   980   932   943  3819   932   980
5                      ------------------------------------------
6          GROSS MARGIN 786   521   587   487  2381   487   786
7
8   NET EXPENSE          98    93    82   110   383    82   110
9   ADM EXPENSE          77    79    69    88   313    69    88
10  MISC EXPENSE         28    45    31    31   135    28    45
11                     ------------------------------------------
12        TOTAL EXPENSES 203   217   182   229   831   182   229
13       AVERAGE EXPENSE  68    72    61    76   277    61    76
14
15  NET BEFORE TAX      583   304   405   258  1550   258   583
16  FEDERAL TAXES       280   146   194   124   744   124   280
17                     ------------------------------------------
18        NET AFTER TAX 303   158   211   134   806   134   303
19
20
27-Aug-92 01:43PM
```

(b)

Figure 10-1 Manual versus electronic spreadsheets. (a) This manual spreadsheet is a typical spreadsheet consisting of rows and columns. (b) The same spreadsheet created with a spreadsheet program.

- **Budget management.** You can use a spreadsheet in your business to list anticipated expenses and anticipated income. Then you can use the spreadsheet to analyze your expenditures by categories such as labor, office rent, and loan interest. When the business situation changes, you can easily see the effect. Suppose, for example, you hire more workers or increase the price of a product. You can quickly check the effect of your move on anticipated profits.

- **Competitive bidding.** Many industries use spreadsheet software to prepare bids to compete for contracts. In the construction industry, for example, you can enter into the spreadsheet the costs of the materials and resources needed to complete the project. Then you can explore "What if . . . ?" scenarios by changing types and costs of materials, delivery dates, equipment rentals, number and types of work-

P E R S P E C T I V E S

CAN ELECTRONIC LIGHTNING STRIKE TWICE?

Once in a great while an invention sparks an entire industry. Many people consider the electronic spreadsheet the linchpin of the personal computer industry. Now some are wondering if the two innovators who invented the spreadsheet—Dan Bricklin and Robert Frankston—might do the same thing for pen-based computers.

In 1977 Dan was a student at the Harvard School of Business. He spent most of his evenings working on case studies for his classes. This work required preparing manual spreadsheets for financial models. To make decisions about the way the case study businesses should be run, Dan had to prepare separate spreadsheets to analyze each alternative available to him as a manager. He often made errors and had to spend hours redoing his calculations. He, like other students and business managers around the world, was spending too much time doing and redoing arithmetic with a paper, pencil, and calculator. This left less time to study and understand the results of the calculations and to consider what they meant for business.

But what was the alternative? Dan toyed with the idea of doing the calculations for each case on the computer. However, each case study was so different that it would require a new computer program to analyze each one. This was just not possible. During the winter of 1978, Bricklin and Robert Frankston, a programmer friend, worked to develop a general-purpose program that could be used to solve any spreadsheet problem. This program evolved into the first electronic spreadsheet, called VisiCalc, for *Visible Calculator.*

When VisiCalc was modified to run on the inexpensive Apple II personal computer, the resulting combination was eagerly accepted by students, businesspeople, and professionals who used numbers in their work. In fact, VisiCalc is credited with being a major factor in making the Apple computer a popular success. The photo shows Bricklin (left) and Frankston running their Software Arts, Inc. booth at an early personal computer conference. For several years the program was the best-selling software for a personal computer. Since then, other companies have produced dozens of different spreadsheet programs—including the current market leader, Lotus 1-2-3, from Lotus Development Corporation.

The electronic spreadsheet placed the personal computer squarely in the business community, where it has grown and flourished. But what happened to its two creators? Bricklin and Frankston ended up selling VisiCalc to Lotus, and Bricklin even worked there for a while. But eventually they came back together, this time at Slate Computers, where they are working on software for the company's new pen-based computer. The duo's new product is called At Hand, one of the first spreadsheets to be announced for pen-based computers. If At Hand helps pen-based computers to the extent that VisiCalc helped personal computers, we would have to say that lightning does strike twice.

ers, and so forth. This is the way businesspeople determine what combination produces the best—and possibly lowest—bid.

- **Investments.** In the industries of finance and investment, spreadsheets are used to analyze the costs of borrowing money and the profits anticipated from lending money. Spreadsheets are used to analyze investment portfolios by keeping track of dividends and increases or decreases in the value of individual investments. By using spreadsheets to play out various stock-market and economic scenarios, the crucial question—Do I buy now or do I sell now?—is more easily answered. The spreadsheet program provides the tools to analyze masses of complex economic data accurately and quickly.

The tasks just described would be tedious and time-consuming if done with a calculator. Electronic spreadsheet programs reduce work for accountants, marketing managers, stockbrokers, contractors, and others who work with the flow of cash in a business.

 ## Spreadsheet Fundamentals

Before we can show you how to use a spreadsheet, we must first discuss some basic spreadsheet features. The characteristics and definitions that follow are common to all spreadsheet programs.

Cells and Cell Addresses

Figure 10-2 shows one type of spreadsheet—a teacher's grade sheet. Notice that the spreadsheet is divided into rows and columns, each labeled with a number or a letter. The rows have *numeric labels* and the columns have *alphabetic labels*. In Chapter 9 you learned that a word processing document can be far bigger than what the screen can show. The same is true of spreadsheets: Some spreadsheets have 8192 rows and 256 columns—or millions of places in which to enter data—certainly more than most of us will ever need to use. You can use the cursor movement keys to move around the spreadsheet, just as you can use them to scroll through a word processing document.

The intersection of a row and column forms a **cell.** Cells are the storage areas in a spreadsheet. When referring to a cell, you use the letter and number of the intersecting column and row. For example, in Figure 10-2, cell B7 is the intersection of column B and row 7. This reference name is known as the **cell address.**

Figure 10-2   Anatomy of a spreadsheet screen. This screen shows a typical spreadsheet—a teacher's grade sheet. It provides space for 20 rows numbered down the side and 8 columns labeled A through H. The intersection of a row and column forms a cell. When the cursor is on a cell, that cell is known as the active cell.

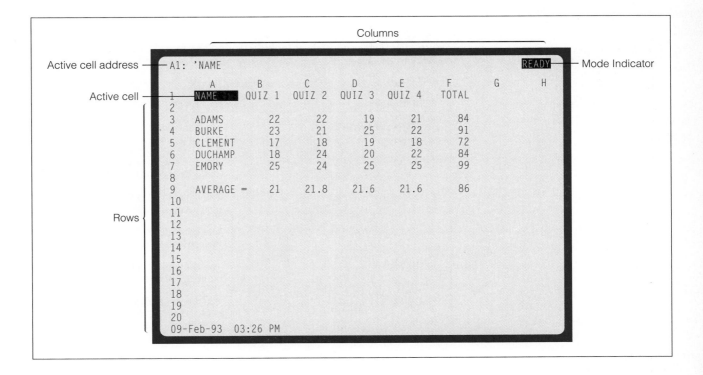

On a spreadsheet there is always one cell known as the **active cell,** or **current cell.** When a cell is active, you can enter data into it or edit its contents. The active cell is marked by a highlighted bar—the spreadsheet cursor. The spreadsheet cursor is also called a **pointer,** or **cell pointer.** The upper-left corner of the screen displays the active cell address. The active cell in Figure 10-2 is cell A1.

Contents of Cells: Labels, Values, Formulas, and Functions

Each cell can contain one of four types of entries: a label, a value, a formula, or a function. A **label** is a description. A cell that contains a label cannot be used to perform mathematical calculations. For example, in Figure 10-2, cells A1, A9, and F1 contain labels.

A **value** is a number entered into a cell to be used in calculations. A value can also be the result of a calculation. In Figure 10-2, for example, cell B3 contains a value.

A **formula** is an instruction to the program to perform a calculation. A formula generally contains cell addresses and one or more arithmetic operators: a plus sign (+) to add, a minus sign (-) to subtract, an asterisk (*) to multiply, and a slash (/) to divide. When you use a formula rather than entering the calculated result, the software can automatically recalculate the result if any of the values change. Formulas must be entered without spaces between the characters. Figure 10-3 shows some common formulas.

A **function** is a preprogrammed formula. Functions let you perform complicated calculations with a few keystrokes. Two common functions are the @SUM function, which calculates sums, and the @AVG function, which calculates averages. Most spreadsheet programs contain a number of different functions. Figure 10-4 shows some of the most common.

Figure 10-3 Some spreadsheet formulas. Spreadsheet formulas use arithmetic operators to perform calculations.

FORMULA	MEANING
(A1+A2) or +A1+A2	The contents of cell A1 plus the contents of cell A2
(A2–A1) or +A2–A1	The contents of cell A2 minus the contents of cell A1
(A1*A2) or +A1*A2	The contents of cell A1 times the contents of cell A2
(A2/A1) or +A2/A1	The contents of cell A2 divided by the contents of cell A1
+A1+A2*2	The contents of cell A2 times the number 2 plus the contents of cell A1
(A2–A1)/B1	The difference of the contents of cells A1 and A2 divided by the contents of cell B1

Figure 10-4 Some Lotus 1-2-3 functions. This figure shows some of the built-in functions available in Lotus 1-2-3. These functions let you perform difficult or repetitive calculations with just a few keystrokes.

FORMULA	MEANING
@SUM(range)	Calculates the sum of a group of numbers specified in an entire range. For example, the formula @SUM(A1..A10) calculates the sum of all numbers in cells A1 through A10.
@AVG(range)	Calculates the average of a group of numbers.
@SQRT(y)	Calculates the square root of a number. For example, @SQRT(A2) calculates the square root of the value contained in A2.
@COUNT(range)	Counts the number of *filled* cells in a range and displays the total number of cells containing a value or label.
@MIN(range)	Calculates and displays the smallest value contained in a range of values.
@MAX(range)	Calculates and displays the largest value contained in a range of values
@PMT(principal,interest,term)	Calculates the individual payments on a loan with known principal, interest rate, and term. The formula @PMT(A1, B1, C1) calculates the monthly payment by using the contents of A1 as the principal, the contents of B1 as the interest rate, and the contents of C1 as the term of the loan.
@IF(cond,x,y)	Determines what to display in a cell. *IF* the condition is true, *THEN* display x in the cell, *ELSE* display y.
@COS(y)	Calculates the cosine of the value y.
@SIN(y)	Calculates the sine of the value y.
@TAN(y)	Calculates the tangent of the value y.

Ranges

Sometimes it is necessary to specify a range of cells to build a formula or perform a function. A **range** is a group of one or more cells arranged in a block shape that the program treats as a unit during an operation. Figure 10-5 shows some ranges. To define a range, you must indicate the upper-left and lower-right cells of the block. The cell addresses need to be separated by one or two periods. For example, in Figure 10-2 the QUIZ 1 range is B3..B7 and the ADAMS range is B3..F3.

Moving the Cursor

To place data in a cell, you must first move the cursor to that cell. You can use the cursor movement keys to move (scroll) through the spreadsheet vertically or horizontally.

Figure 10-5 Ranges. A range is a group of one or more cells arranged in a rectangle. You can name a range or refer to it by using the addresses of the upper-left and lower-right cells in the group.

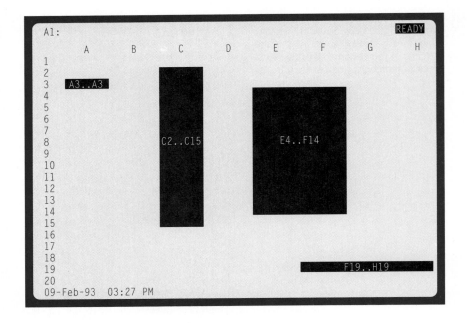

However, moving around a large spreadsheet by using the cursor movement keys can be tedious. Most programs let you zip around the spreadsheet by pressing predefined keys and function keys. For example, if you press the Home key, the cursor moves "home" to cell A1. Or, you can go directly to a cell by pressing the designated **GoTo function key,** also known as the **Jump-To function key.** When you press this key, the software asks you for the desired cell address. You type in the address—for example, D7—and press Enter. The cursor immediately moves to cell D7. This may sometimes be the fastest way to get to a cell.

Operating Modes

A **mode** is the condition, or state, in which the program is currently functioning, such as waiting for a command or allowing the selection of a menu item. Most spreadsheets have three main operating modes: the READY mode, the ENTRY mode, and the MENU mode. The Lotus 1-2-3 spreadsheet screen displays a **mode indicator**—a message that tells you the spreadsheet's current mode of operation—in the upper-right corner of the screen. In Figure 10-2 the mode indicator is labeled.

The READY Mode   Most spreadsheets are in the READY mode as soon as they are loaded into the system and the spreadsheet appears on the screen. The **READY mode** indicates that the program is ready for whatever action you want to take, such as moving the cursor, entering data, or issuing a command. As you begin entering data into a cell, you automatically leave the READY mode and enter the ENTRY mode.

The ENTRY Mode   When you are in the **ENTRY mode,** you can enter data into the cells. When a label is being entered, the word "LABEL" ap-

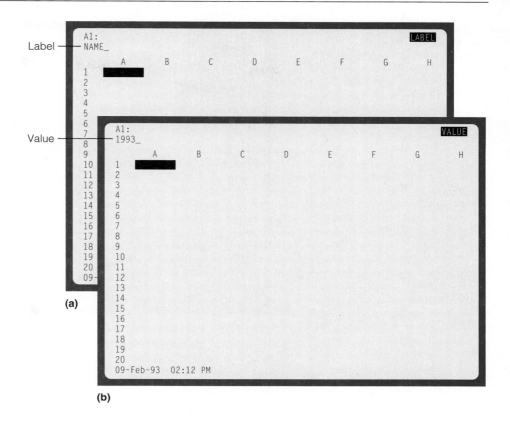

(a)

(b)

Figure 10-6 The ENTRY mode. When you are in the ENTRY mode, you can enter data into the cells. (a) When a label is being entered, the word "LABEL" appears in the mode indicator. (b) When a value is being entered, the word "VALUE" appears in the mode indicator.

pears in the mode indicator; the software assumes that any cell entry that begins with a letter (such as the N in "Name" in Figure 10-6a) is a label. The word "VALUE" appears in the mode indicator when a number, formula, or function is being entered into a cell (Figure 10-6b). After you key in the data and press Enter, the entry is stored in the cell and the program returns to the READY mode.

When you are in the ENTRY mode, the program does not let you jump or scroll around the spreadsheet—you can only enter data in a cell or edit a filled cell. The ENTRY mode lets you work on only one cell at a time. But sooner or later you will need to work on a whole group of cells. To do this, you need to enter the MENU, or command, mode.

The MENU Mode The **MENU mode** lets you use commands to manipulate a large number of cells at one time. Programs display commands in a **command menu,** which is shown near the top of the screen (Figure 10-7). The command menu contains a list, or menu, of options, such as Move and File. The commands are very important, and we will discuss them in more detail later in the chapter. To enter the MENU mode, you press the Slash (/) key.

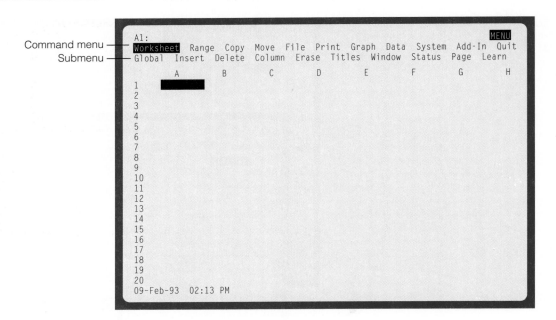

Command menu ——

Submenu ——

```
A1:                                                          MENU
Worksheet  Range Copy  Move  File   Print  Graph Data   System Add-In Quit
Global     Insert Delete Column Erase Titles Window Status Page   Learn

        A         B       C       D       E       F       G       H
 1
 2
 3
 4
 5
 6
 7
 8
 9
10
11
12
13
14
15
16
17
18
19
20
09-Feb-93  02:13 PM
```

Figure 10-7   The MENU mode. When you are in the MENU mode, a command menu appears near the top of the screen.

The Control Panel

Spreadsheets can get complicated. To help you keep track of what you are doing, most spreadsheet programs show a **control panel** at the top of the screen. The control panel usually consists of three lines.

The First Line   The first line of the control panel is the **status line** (Figure 10-8). This line tells you the cursor location (the cell address) and the contents of that cell. An apostrophe ('), quotation mark ("), or caret (^) at the beginning of the contents indicates that the active cell contains a label. At times the status line also shows information about the format—appearance—of the value or label in the cell and the width of the cell. (It is possible to change the appearance of the cell contents and the width of the cell, but that is beyond the scope of this text.)

To the far right of the status line is the mode indicator. As we mentioned earlier, this indicator tells you the current mode of operation.

The Second Line   The second line of the control panel is used in a variety of ways, depending on the operating mode. If you are in the ENTRY mode, the line displays the data you are typing in before it is actually entered into the cell (Figure 10-8a). This lets you make changes and corrections before entering the data. If you are in the MENU mode, the line shows the current menu options (Figure 10-8b). This line is also occasionally used for prompts—that is, questions to prompt you for further information needed by the program.

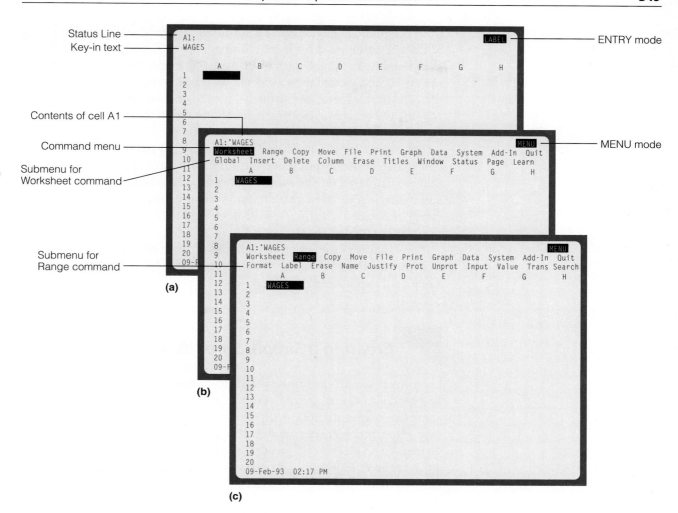

Figure 10-8 The Lotus 1-2-3 control panel. The first line of the control panel shows you the cursor location and the contents of that cell. (a) When you are in ENTRY mode, the second line of the panel displays the data you are typing in before it is entered into the cell. (b) When you are in the MENU mode, the second line of the panel shows the current menu options, and the third line shows the submenu for the command that the cursor is on. (c) When you move the cursor to another command, the submenu changes.

The Third Line The control panel's third line appears only when the program is in the MENU mode and you have placed the cursor over one of the options. This line shows a **submenu,** a list of options for the command you are choosing (Figure 10-8b), or information about the command if it has no submenus.

Let us look at menus and submenus in more detail.

Menus and Submenus

We have already mentioned that you can select spreadsheet commands by choosing from the command menu. Sometimes selecting a command from the menu does not cause a command to be executed; instead, you will see a submenu. This is an additional set of options that refer to the command you selected from the command menu. For example, in Figure 10-8b, the second menu row shows the subcommands—Global, Insert, Delete, Column, and so forth—for the major command Worksheet. Moving the cursor to another major command in the menu causes a different set of commands to appear (Figure 10-8c).

Submenus let you pick only the options that pertain to a particular command. Some of the choices on submenus have options of their own that are displayed on yet another submenu. This layering of menus and submenus lets you first give the computer the big picture with a general command such as "Print a spreadsheet" and then select a particular option such as "Print the first page."

Now that we have covered the basics of spreadsheets, let us pull this information together and see how you can use spreadsheet software for a practical application.

 ## Creating a Simple Spreadsheet

Learning to use an electronic spreadsheet program requires time. It might be a good idea to read the manual that comes with the program and spend some time experimenting with the software. Electronic spreadsheet programs have much greater capabilities than the average user will ever need. To explain an electronic spreadsheet program completely would require an entire book. However, you can understand how such programs work by studying some examples. The examples we will present use Lotus 1-2-3, Release 2.3. Lotus has established a standard approach to electronic spreadsheets; most popular spreadsheet programs work in a similar manner.

Lotus refers to the collection of data keyed into the program as a **worksheet.** Lotus emphasizes the term *worksheet* by saving spreadsheet files with the file name extension WK1 or WK3. We will use the terms *worksheet* and *spreadsheet* interchangeably.

The Expense Sheet Example

Lyle Mayes teaches a biology course at King High School. He recently bought the Lotus 1-2-3 program and uses it to keep track of his class's grades. Now he wants to use the program to keep track of his expenses. His expense sheet for the months of January through April is shown in Figure 10-9. Notice that each type of expense appears in a separate row of the expense sheet and each column is labeled with the name of a month. The amount of money spent on each item is entered in the cell at the intersection of the appropriate row and column.

The rightmost column of the spreadsheet contains the total amount spent on each item and the total income for the four-month period. At the bottom of each month column, Lyle enters the total amount spent

Figure 10-9   Lyle's expense worksheet.
This is Lyle's handwritten expense sheet.
Notice that if he makes any changes to one
of the values—for example, the March
food expense—he has to do numerous recalculations.

	JAN.	FEB.	MAR.	APR.	TOTAL
INCOME	2300	2300	2300	2300	9200
EXPENSES					
Rent	575	575	575	575	2300
Food	225	200	200	200	825
Phone	50	64	37	23	174
Heat	80	50	24	20	174
Insurance	100	100	100	100	400
Car	200	200	200	200	800
Leisure	105	120	95	125	445
TOTAL					
EXPENSES	1335	1309	1231	1243	5118
BALANCE	965	991	1069	1057	4082

and the balance of his account—the total amount of income minus the
total amount of the expenses. As you can see, creating an expense sheet
can be a time-consuming chore, and if a mistake is made, a number of
recalculations must be done.

Now let us follow the steps that Lyle takes to create this spreadsheet
with Lotus 1-2-3.

Loading the Program

To start his work, Lyle must boot the system. The actions he takes depend on the configuration of his computer system.

- If the system contains two floppy disk drives and Lotus Release 2.2,
  Lyle puts the Lotus System disk in drive A and a formatted data disk
  in drive B.
- If the system contains a hard disk drive and any version of Lotus, Lyle
  accesses the subdirectory in which he previously installed the Lotus
  program files.

Starting the Program   To start the program, Lyle types 123 or Lotus
depending on the version of the program he owns. Then he responds to
the program prompts until he sees an empty spreadsheet with the cursor positioned in cell A1 (Figure 10-10). Lyle's personal computer can
display 24 lines on a screen, with 80 characters per line. Regardless of
the size and capability of a particular screen, it will display only a small
part of all the rows and columns that are available in computer memory.
An electronic spreadsheet is like a piece of paper; you use only as much
as you need. For the expense sheet, Lyle needs to use only columns A
through F and rows 1 through 17.

Entering the Labels and Values

Since Lyle already knows what he wants to type into the spreadsheet, he
starts by entering the labels—the names of the months and the types of

expense. Starting with cell A3, Lyle types INCOME. As he types, the mode indicator display changes from "READY" to "LABEL." When Lyle finishes typing, the second line of the control panel displays the text: INCOME. Lyle then presses Enter to store his entry in the cell. When he does this, the mode indicator immediately returns to "READY" and the label he typed, INCOME, appears on the first line of the control panel.

To enter the rest of the labels and numbers, Lyle follows the same procedure, moving the cursor from cell to cell by using the cursor movement keys. If he makes a mistake as he is typing, he can use Backspace to make the correction before moving from the cell. Remember that the

Figure 10-10   A blank spreadsheet. The blank display indicates that Lotus 1-2-3 is loaded and ready to accept data.

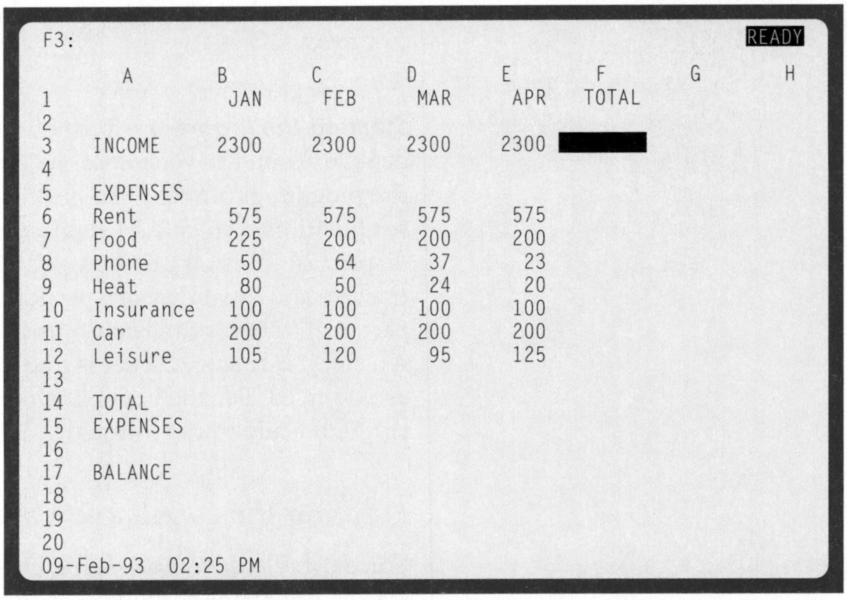

Figure 10-11   Entering labels and values. This screen shows Lyle's spreadsheet with all the labels and numbers entered.

1. Determine the results you want to display on your spreadsheet.
2. Determine the data you have to input to your spreadsheet to calculate the results you want.
3. Write down the rules for converting spreadsheet inputs to outputs. These are usually formulas that relate the input values to the output values.
4. Write down the names of the input and output values that you will use in your spreadsheet and the equations you will use. Record the exact form in which you will enter them into your spreadsheet. Then double-check this list to make sure it is completely correct.
5. Create the electronic spreadsheet by typing in the necessary data. Test your spreadsheet with a range of test values. Check the results produced by the spreadsheet against your own calculations that use the test data. If the results differ, go through your spreadsheet to find your mistake.

cursor must be in a cell to store data in that cell. Figure 10-11 shows Lyle's spreadsheet with all the labels and numbers entered in their cells.

Entering the Formulas and Functions

Lyle must enter the total income for the four months in cell F3. In cell F3 Lyle could type each value contained in row 3 in the formula to calculate total salary—(2300+2300+2300+2300). He would then press Enter and the spreadsheet would calculate the total for him and enter the result in F3. But, if any of the values in the equation changed, Lyle would have to change the formula. Instead, Lyle uses a formula that will add the contents of each of the four cells, regardless of their value. The formula he uses is (B3+C3+D3+E3). This formula tells the program to add the values that appear in the cells B3, C3, D3, and E3. Note that all formulas must be enclosed in parentheses or begin with an operation symbol; otherwise, the program will read the formula as a label. Lyle keys in the formula and presses Enter to store it in cell F3.

If you look at Figure 10-12, you see that cell F3 does not show the formula—instead, it shows the *result* of the formula. If the cursor is in the cell, then the formula appears in the upper-left corner of the screen. The result of the formula is the **displayed value** of the cell. The formula itself is the actual **cell content.** This is an important distinction to remember. Displayed values change if other values in the spreadsheet change. Formulas can be changed only if new data is entered into the cell.

To calculate the totals in the other rows, Lyle could enter the formula (B6+C6+D6+E6) for row 6, and so on, for each of the cells F6 to F12. However, Lotus 1-2-3 provides a simpler way of summing columns or rows—

Figure 10-12   Entering formulas. Lyle has entered the formula (B3+C3+D3+E3) into cell F3. Notice that the displayed value of the cell is the result of the calculation—9200. When the cursor is in cell F3, you can see the actual cell content in the upper-left corner of the screen.

```
          Cell contents                              Displayed value

F3: (B3+C3+D3+E3)                                                    READY
         A         B        C        D        E        F       G       H
1                  JAN      FEB      MAR      APR     TOTAL
2
3     INCOME      2300     2300     2300     2300     9200
4
5     EXPENSES
6     Rent         575      575      575      575
7     Food         225      200      200      200
8     Phone         50       64       37       23
9     Heat          80       50       24       20
10    Insurance    100      100      100      100
11    Car          200      200      200      200
12    Leisure      105      120       95      125
13
14    TOTAL
15    EXPENSES
16
17    BALANCE
18
19
20
09-Feb-93   02:27 PM
```

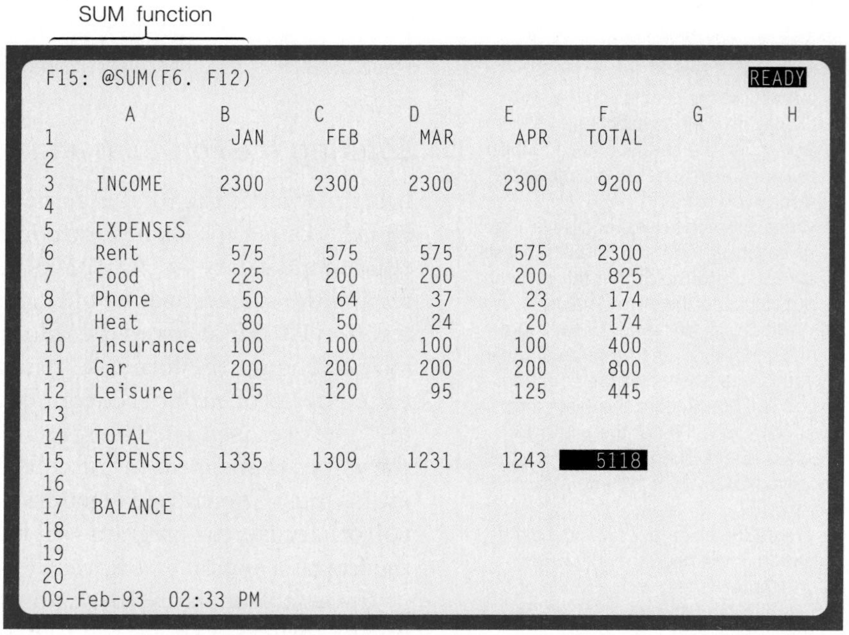

Figure 10-13 Entering functions. Lyle has entered the Lotus 1-2-3 function @SUM(F6..F12) in cell F15. In this function (F6..F12) is the range. As with formulas, the cell shows the result of the calculation, and the function is shown in the first line of the control panel.

SUM function

```
F15: @SUM(F6. F12)                                          READY

            A        B        C        D        E        F        G        H
1                   JAN      FEB      MAR      APR    TOTAL
2
3        INCOME    2300     2300     2300     2300     9200
4
5        EXPENSES
6        Rent       575      575      575      575     2300
7        Food       225      200      200      200      825
8        Phone       50       64       37       23      174
9        Heat        80       50       24       20      174
10       Insurance  100      100      100      100      400
11       Car        200      200      200      200      800
12       Leisure    105      120       95      125      445
13
14       TOTAL
15       EXPENSES  1335     1309     1231     1243     5118
16
17       BALANCE
18
19
20
09-Feb-93   02:33 PM
```

the @SUM function. For example, Lyle can key in @SUM(B6..E6) in cell F6. This tells Lotus to add up the contents of cells B6 through E6. The @ symbol tells Lotus that he is entering a function. The (B6..E6) part of the function is a range; recall that a range is a group of one or more cells arranged in a block. Lyle uses the @SUM function with the appropriate ranges for cells F6 through F12 and cells B15 through F15. Figure 10-13 shows the result.

Finally, Lyle needs to use a formula to compute the monthly balance. Remember, the monthly balance is the monthly income minus the monthly total expenses. So, for January, Lyle places the formula (B3-B15) in cell B17. This tells Lotus to take the value of cell B15 and subtract it from the value of cell B3. Lyle then fills in the rest of the balance row. Figure 10-14 shows the completed spreadsheet.

Making Corrections

Suppose that Lyle realizes that he made a mistake in his January food expense (the correct amount is 150). He also made a mistake in his April leisure expense (the correct amount is 123). Since the cells are already filled with incorrect data, Lyle needs to position the cursor in each filled cell and type in the new data; the keyed-in changes will appear in the second line of the control panel. When Lyle presses Enter, the old data in the cell will be replaced by the new data. Lyle begins by moving the cursor to cell B7 and typing in 150. He presses Enter. Then he moves the cursor to cell E12, types in 123, and presses Enter.

If the expense sheet were done manually, Lyle would also have to re-calculate the totals for row 7 and row 12, and the total expenses and balances for columns B, E, and F. But since the expense sheet is now entered

Figure 10-14   A complete spreadsheet.
This screen shows Lyle's spreadsheet with all the labels, values, formulas, and functions in place.

Balance formula

```
F17: (F3-F15)                                                    READY
         A        B       C       D       E       F       G      H
 1                JAN     FEB     MAR     APR     TOTAL
 2
 3      INCOME    2300    2300    2300    2300    9200
 4
 5      EXPENSES
 6      Rent      575     575     575     575     2300
 7      Food      225     200     200·    200     825
 8      Phone     50      64      37      23      174
 9      Heat      80      50      24      20      174
10      Insurance 100     100     100     100     400
11      Car       200     200     200     200     800
12      Leisure   105     120     95      125     445
13
14      TOTAL
15      EXPENSES  1335    1309    1231    1243    5118
16
17      BALANCE   965     991     1069    1057    4082
18
19
20
09-Feb-93  02:38 PM
```

Figure 10-15   Automatic recalculation.
Lyle has entered the changes for the January food expense and the April leisure expense. Lotus 1-2-3 automatically recalculates the affected totals and balances.

```
E12: 123                                                         READY
         A        B       C       D       E       F       G      H
 1                JAN     FEB     MAR     APR     TOTAL
 2
 3      INCOME    2300    2300    2300    2300    9200
 4
 5      EXPENSES
 6      Rent      575     575     575     575     2300
 7      Food      150     200     200     200     750
 8      Phone     50      64      37      23      174
 9      Heat      80      50      24      20      174
10      Insurance 100     100     100     100     400
11      Car       200     200     200     200     800
12      Leisure   105     120     95      123     443
13
14      TOTAL
15      EXPENSES  1260    1309    1231    1241    5041
16
17      BALANCE   1040    991     1069    1059    4159
18
19
20
09-Feb-93  02:39 PM
```

as an electronic spreadsheet, the spreadsheet program instantly recalculates these values. Figure 10-15 shows the result of typing only the two changed values. Nothing else had to be changed in the worksheet. Because Lyle used *formulas* to calculate these totals, the spreadsheet automatically adjusted all contents to reflect the changed values.

Automatic recalculation of the whole worksheet usually takes only a few seconds. This ability to recalculate a spreadsheet at the touch of a button has revolutionized the processes of budgeting and financial modeling. Now people who work with numbers can spend their time analyzing their results rather than doing arithmetic.

Now that Lyle has entered his worksheet, he can use the command menu to save, retrieve, and print it.

Using Spreadsheet Commands

Using the layered command menu can be a little tricky at first. To help make choosing the proper menus and submenus easier, you can create a command tree. A **command tree,** so called because it has a "trunk" at the top and many "branches," shows choices from the main command menu and choices from associated submenus (Figure 10-16). The main command menu line at the top forms the trunk of the tree. Making a command choice from this menu leads you down on a submenu branch. Some of the branches are short and simple, like the one for the Insert command. Others, like Worksheet, have many branches. Each successive branch is reached by selecting from the chain of submenus that appears on the screen.

To take some action—execute an instruction—on your spreadsheet, you must work your way out toward the tip of a branch. The commands along the way, as you go through the layers of menus, are merely vehicles for getting you to the instruction that will take the action you want. You must choose the right options from the submenus to get there. If

Figure 10-16 A command tree. This command tree shows the submenus associated with the Worksheet command. Notice that, if you follow the Worksheet-Erase path, there are no additional submenus. However, if you follow the Worksheet-Global path, there are many different choices you can make.

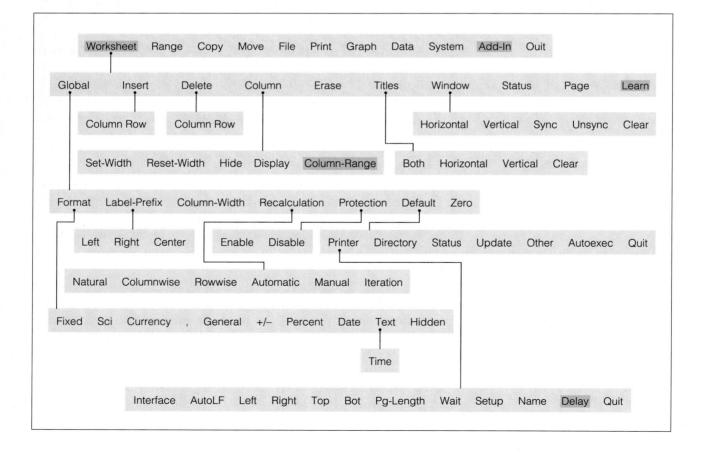

you make a false step (get into the wrong submenu), you can get back to the next higher menu by pressing Esc. In fact, you can get out of the MENU mode completely by continuing to press Esc until you see "READY" in the mode indicator. Remember that you work your way down through the levels of submenus by moving the menu cursor to a selection and pressing Enter. You can undo a selection and work your way back up to a previous menu by pressing Esc.

Now let us show you the steps Lyle takes to use several of the important commands on the main menu.

The File Command

The **File command** lets you manipulate the Lotus 1-2-3 files on your data disk. You can use the File command to perform such tasks as saving files, retrieving files, erasing files, and listing files. Figure 10-17 shows the command tree for the File command. We will look at how Lyle can use the File command to save, retrieve, and list files.

Saving a File   Since Lyle is finished with his spreadsheet, he can save it on his data disk by using the File command. To use this command with a new spreadsheet, Lyle must press / to obtain the command menu. Next he moves the menu cursor to the word "File" (Figure 10-18a). Notice that Save is one of the choices on the File submenu. With the cursor on File, Lyle presses Enter to access the File submenu. Now the submenu is the active menu. Lyle moves the cursor to Save. When he does, the bottom line of the control panel shows a description of the Save option (Figure 10-18b). Lyle presses Enter to select Save, and Lotus 1-2-3 prompts him for the file name he wishes to use (Figure 10-18c). Remember that file names can be up to eight characters long. Spreadsheet file names can contain letters, numbers, hyphens, and the underscore character. (If Lyle were saving a file that had already been saved once, he would see the file name displayed and just press Enter.) Lyle chooses the name B:EXPENSES,

Figure 10-17   The File command. This figure shows the command tree for the File command.

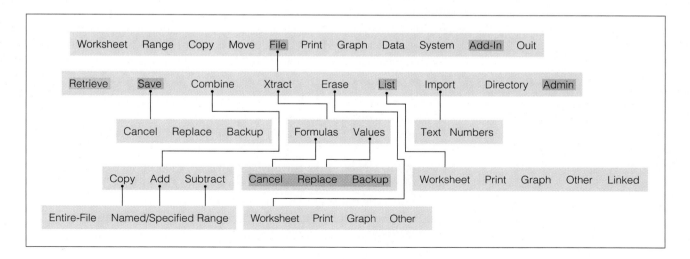

Figure 10-18   Saving a file. (a) To select the File command, Lyle moves the cursor to the option File. Note the submenu now shows options for the File command. Then Lyle presses Enter. (b) Now the submenu becomes the active menu. Lyle moves the cursor to the option Save and presses Enter. (c) Lotus 1-2-3 then asks him to enter a file name.

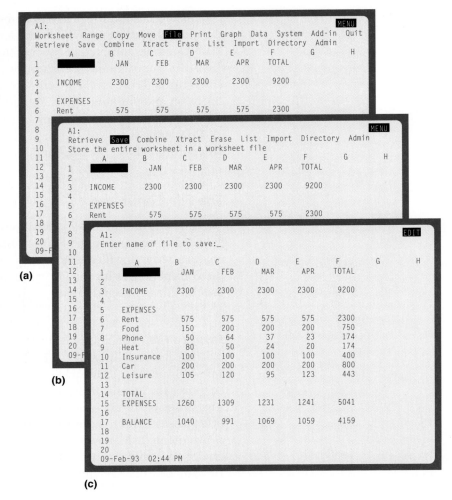

(a)

(b)

(c)

types it in, and presses Enter. (Lotus automatically adds an extension.) Since this is a new file, it is saved immediately.

There is another, faster, way to make these types of menu choices: Just type the first letter of the option you want to use, rather than moving the cursor. For example, Lyle can save his file more quickly by typing / (to access the MENU mode), then F (for *File*), S (for *Save*), followed by the disk drive location and file name. So Lyle could type:

    /FSB:EXPENSES

and press Enter to save his file. The shortcut method can be used for any of the menu commands.

Retrieving a File   Like the Save command, the Retrieve command is a File subcommand. If Lyle wants to retrieve the EXPENSES file, he presses / to obtain the command menu. Then he selects the File command and the Retrieve subcommand. Selecting the Retrieve command erases the current worksheet (if there happens to be one in memory) and then loads

Figure 10-19   Retrieving a file. When Lyle wants to retrieve a file, Lotus 1-2-3 displays a list of the worksheet files stored on the active drive.

```
A1:                                                              FILES
Name of file retrieve: B:\*.wk?
EXPENSES.WK1      GRADES1.WK1      GRADES2.WK1
           A          B          C          D          E          F          G          H
 1                   JAN        FEB        MAR        APR       TOTAL
 2
 3      INCOME       2300       2300       2300       2300       9200
 4
 5      EXPENSES
 6      Rent         575        575        575        575        2300
 7      Food         150        200        200        200        750
 8      Phone        50         64         37         23         174
 9      Heat         80         50         24         20         174
10      Insurance    100        100        100        100        400
11      Car          200        200        200        200        800
12      Leisure      105        120        95         123        443
13
14      TOTAL
15      EXPENSES     1260       1309       1231       1241       5041
16
17      BALANCE      1040       991        1069       1059       4159
18
19
20
09-Feb-93  02:46 PM
```

and displays the requested worksheet. Be sure to save any current worksheet before using Retrieve.

Lotus 1-2-3 then prompts Lyle for the name of the file he wants to retrieve. The program will jog Lyle's memory by listing the names of his stored files on the bottom line of the control panel (Figure 10-19). Lyle can either type in the name of one of the listed files and press Enter, or he can move the cursor to that file name and press Enter.

After Lyle enters the name of the file, the mode indicator flashes the word "WAIT"—this indicates that Lotus is loading the worksheet. When the worksheet appears on the screen, the mode indicator displays the word "READY."

Listing Files   If Lyle wants to check to see what worksheet files he has on his data disk, he can use the List subcommand. To do this, he types / and selects the File option. Then he selects List from the first submenu and Worksheet from the second submenu. Lotus then displays a list of the worksheet files. When Lyle wants to return to the worksheet, he presses Enter.

The Print Command

Spreadsheet programs generally let you print a copy of the spreadsheet at any time during the session. The **Print command** provides options for printing all or part of a spreadsheet on paper. Figure 10-20 shows the command tree for the Print command.

Lyle wants to print a copy of his spreadsheet. To do this, he must tell Lotus 1-2-3 what part of the spreadsheet he wants to print and whether he wants the spreadsheet printed on paper or stored on a disk.

Figure 10-20   The Print command. This figure shows the command tree for the Print command.

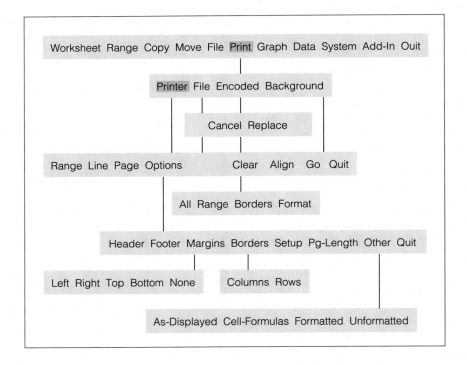

Figure 10-21   Printing a worksheet. After Lyle chooses the Print option from the menu and the Printer option from the first submenu, another submenu appears. This submenu lets Lyle describe the range he wishes to print, start the printing process, and leave the Print menu.

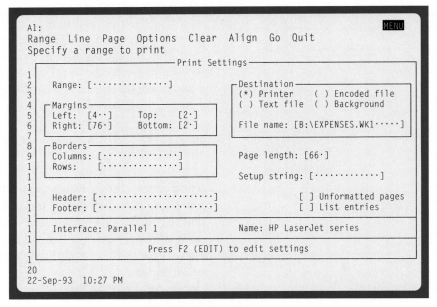

Lyle begins by selecting the Print option from the menu. Then he selects Printer from the first submenu because he wants to have a printed copy of the spreadsheet. When Lyle selects Printer, another submenu appears (Figure 10-21).

Now Lyle must tell Lotus how much of the spreadsheet he wants to print. Notice in Figure 10-19 that Lyle's work does not occupy the whole spreadsheet. Rather, it is clustered in a small block. The upper-left corner of the block is cell A1; the lower-right corner is cell F17.

Try Lying on Your Side

Printing spreadsheets—especially long ones—can be a challenge. When you are displaying a spreadsheet on the computer screen, you can move along a row to see all the columns of data in that row. However, when a wide spreadsheet is printed, the columns that will not fit across the page appear on a separate page. This means that you will have to cut and paste—literally—your printed copy of the spreadsheet.

Most printers produce 80 characters per line but can also print 132 characters in compressed mode. If this is still not sufficient to print all the columns in your spreadsheet, you can purchase software that will turn your spreadsheet sideways, printing the spreadsheet along the length of the printer paper. (Some of the sideways-printing programs are included with newer versions of Lotus 1-2-3 and some must be purchased separately.) The Microsoft Windows and Macintosh versions of Lotus 1-2-3 allow sideways printing. With the output in this form, all the rows run continuously—but you must tape pages together unless you use a printer that can take fanfold paper.

The two cell addresses define the range of the worksheet that needs to be printed.

To tell Lotus the range, Lyle selects the Range command. Then he types A1 (the cell in the upper left of his worksheet) followed by one or two periods and F17 (the cell in the lower right of his worksheet). Lyle then presses Enter. This returns him to the menu he just left. Next Lyle makes sure that his printer is on and ready to print. Then he selects Go from the second submenu to begin the printing. Figure 10-22 shows the final printed spreadsheet.

When the printing is completed, the second submenu is still the active menu. To return to the READY mode, Lyle must select the Quit command from the submenu.

Like the other commands we have discussed, the commands involved in the printing task can be entered quickly by typing:

```
/PPRA1.F17
```

pressing Enter, and then typing G for Go. When you want to leave the PRINT mode, type Q for *Quit*.

The Worksheet Erase Command

If Lyle wants to start another worksheet without leaving and reentering the Lotus 1-2-3 program, he can use the **Worksheet Erase command.** This command clears the worksheet in computer memory of any data that has been entered, and an empty worksheet appears on the screen. The Worksheet Erase command does not erase any worksheets saved on a disk.

To use the Worksheet Erase command, Lyle presses the / key. Then he selects Worksheet from the menu and Erase from the submenu. When Lotus asks if he really wants to erase the worksheet, Lyle types Y for *Yes*. If he has changed the file since the last time he saved it, Lotus warns him

Figure 10-22   The printed worksheet. For Lyle, getting a printed spreadsheet that shows his revisions takes only a few keystrokes. If he had been working with a handwritten ledger, making revisions would have been tedious and the result less attractive than this printed spreadsheet.

	JAN	FEB	MAR	APR	TOTAL
INCOME	2300	2300	2300	2300	9200
EXPENSES					
Rent	575	575	575	575	2300
Food	150	200	200	200	750
Phone	50	64	37	23	174
Heat	80	50	24	20	174
Insurance	100	100	100	100	400
Car	200	200	200	200	800
Leisure	105	120	95	123	443
TOTAL EXPENSES	1260	1309	1231	1041	5041
BALANCE	1040	991	1069	1259	4159

and asks if he really wants to erase it. The new worksheet appears on the screen.

The Quit Command

To leave the spreadsheet program and return to DOS, you must use the **Quit command** from the command menu. If you have changed your file since you last saved it, Lotus will warn you that the changes will not be saved if you quit now. The program will ask if you want to end the Lotus 1-2-3 session anyway.

Since Lyle has already saved his file, he selects the Quit command. Lotus 1-2-3 asks him to confirm the command with a Y (Yes, leave the program) or a N (No, do not leave the program). Lyle presses Y, and the DOS prompt appears.

Using the Help Key

The wide assortment of commands can be bewildering to the novice user. In fact, command choices can be confusing to an experienced user, too. But help is as close as your computer. When you are lost or confused, Lotus 1-2-3 uses F1 as the **Help key.** Pressing F1 places you in the HELP mode. You can press the Help key anytime, even in the middle of a command.

The HELP mode is useful in two ways. First, it is **context-sensitive**—that is, it offers helpful information related to the command you are using when you press the Help key. Second, you can select the **Help index,** which—for all practical purposes—gives you access to a reference manual right on your screen. Use the Help index to select a topic, and the spreadsheet program supplies aid on that topic. It is easy to get out of the HELP mode: Press Esc once.

Integrated Packages

Put word processing, spreadsheet, database, and graphics programs into one package, and the result is an **integrated package** of programs—an all-in-one set. Integrated packages are especially useful when numeric data must be included in textual reports or when a graphic representation of numbers can more easily show what the numbers mean.

Furthermore, with an integrated package you do not need to learn completely different programs that use different commands. Perhaps the most difficult steps you have to take when you learn to use a new program are the first few. After that, you have oriented yourself to the "feel" of the program and can start being productive with it. Programs in an integrated package share a common methodology and command structure so that you do not have to begin anew to use a particular program in the pack-

Superstar of Application Software

Lotus 1-2-3, which has sold more than eight million copies since 1983, is the most popular software *application* ever. Only two other products—both operating systems—Microsoft DOS (over 60 million copies) and Microsoft Windows (nearly nine million copies) have outsold Lotus 1-2-3. All computers must have an operating system, but not all computer users need a spreadsheet. Only Microsoft's Excel spreadsheet application outsells Lotus 1-2-3 in the Windows market. To encourage the appeal of Lotus 1-2-3, Lotus Development Corporation has generated a number of versions of the program to suit users with different needs and hardware.

age; each program has a familiar flavor. This reason for using an integrated package is similar to one of the reasons for using versions of spreadsheets with the Microsoft Windows graphical user interface.

Another advantage of an integrated package is the fast, easy transfer of data among the programs in the package. For example, it is easy to move a table of spreadsheet numbers into a word processing report. Graphs can be prepared using the graphics program, then easily inserted into text prepared using the word processing program. However, if you are using a separate word processing program and separate spreadsheet and graphics programs, you will find that moving data from one program to another program is not simple. And even though there are certain standard file types, they cannot always store exactly what you want to pass to the second program. Ease of data transfer among programs and a common command structure has created a demand for integrated packages.

The First Integrated Package: Lotus 1-2-3

Although Version 2.3 of Lotus 1-2-3 does not have word processing capability, it does integrate a very powerful spreadsheet program with a business graphics program and a limited database program. All three functions in the package are based on storing data in a spreadsheet. After you enter the data into the spreadsheet, you can view the data graphically by using the graphics program. You can also use commands available through the database program to sort the data in your spreadsheet or to find rows in the spreadsheet that match certain conditions.

Each of the programs has a menu that lets you choose what task you want to perform. You can also move instantly from one program to another by making a selection from a menu. Furthermore, once your graphs and database are set up, you can stay in the spreadsheet program and see graphs of your data or select records from your database by simply pressing one key. Lotus also stores the graphs and database with the spreadsheet file on which they are based.

To Integrate or Not?

The popularity of Lotus 1-2-3 has led to the development of a number of different packages that integrate program functions. Two different approaches have been taken by software developers:

- One approach involves including word processing, spreadsheet, graphics, and database capabilities in one program package. Some of the more popular programs of this type are Microsoft Works, Enable, and Symphony for the IBM PC, and Microsoft Works, Claris Works, and Microsoft Excel for the Apple Macintosh.

- The other approach allows a user to purchase the individual word processing, spreadsheet, graphics, and database programs that are most appealing to that user. These **standalone programs** are then integrated by a **universal manager program,** which coordinates the separate software, presents a common interface to the user, and handles data transfer among the programs. Microsoft Windows is an example of a universal manager program.

Despite their many advantages, sales of integrated packages have not skyrocketed. There are a couple of reasons for this. First, the individual functions—like word processing or graphics—within an all-in-one package are not usually as strong as those in standalone packages. If you need state-of-the-art word processing and state-of-the-art database management, you would probably be better served by buying two standalone programs. Second, integrated packages are rather expensive, and you pay for all the functions in the package even if you really need only two or three.

 ## *Business Graphics*

The change from numbers to pictures is a refreshing variation. But graphics used in business are not toys. In fact, graphics can show words and numbers and data in ways that are meaningful and quickly understood. This is the key reason they are valuable.

Personal computers give people the capability to store and use data about their businesses. These same users, however, sometimes find it difficult to convey this information to others—managers or clients—in a meaningful way. **Business graphics**—graphics that represent data in a visual, easily understood format—provide an answer to this problem.

Why Use Graphics?

Graphics generate and sustain the interest of an audience by brightening up any lesson, report, or business document. In addition, graphics can help get a point across by presenting an overwhelming amount of data in one simple, clear graph (Figure 10-23). What is more, that simple graph can reveal a trend that could be lost if buried in long columns of numbers. To sum up, most people use business graphics software for one of two reasons: (1) to view and analyze data and (2) to make a positive impression during a presentation. To satisfy these different needs, two types of business graphics programs have been developed: analytical graphics and presentation graphics.

Analytical Graphics

Analytical graphics programs are designed to help users analyze and understand specific data. Sometimes called analysis-oriented graphics programs, these programs let you use already-entered spreadsheet or database data to construct and view line, bar, and pie-chart graphs (Figure 10-24a–c).

Although analytical graphics programs do a good job of producing simple graphs, these programs are too limited and inflexible for a user who needs to prepare elaborate presentations. Lotus 1-2-3, for example, lets you choose from only a small number of graph types, and the program's

Figure 10-23   Business graphics. (a) A large amount of data can be translated into (b) one simple, clear graph.

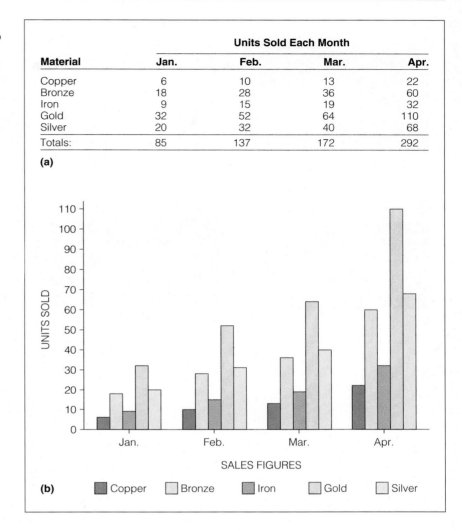

Material	Units Sold Each Month			
	Jan.	**Feb.**	**Mar.**	**Apr.**
Copper	6	10	13	22
Bronze	18	28	36	60
Iron	9	15	19	32
Gold	32	52	64	110
Silver	20	32	40	68
Totals:	85	137	172	292

(a)

(b)   Copper   Bronze   Iron   Gold   Silver

formatting features—which allow different graph sizes, different color possibilities, and different types of lettering—are limited. These limitations may be of little concern to some users. But those who require sophisticated graphics will want to consider presentation graphics.

Presentation Graphics

Presentation graphics programs are also called **business-quality graphics programs,** or presentation-oriented desktop graphics programs. These programs let you produce charts, graphs, and other visual aids that look as if they were prepared by a professional artist (Figure 10-24d–f). However, you can control the appearance of the graphics when you do them yourself, and you can produce them faster and make last-minute changes if necessary.

Most presentation graphics programs help you do three kinds of tasks:

● Edit and enhance charts created by other programs, such as the analytical graphics produced by Lotus 1-2-3.

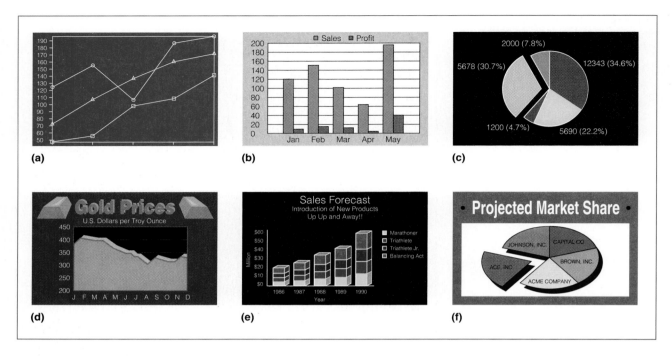

Figure 10-24   Analytical graphics compared to presentation graphics. Analytical graphics (a, b, and c) are certainly serviceable, but they lack the clarity and appeal of presentation graphics (d, e, and f). Compare the line graphs (a and d), bar graphs (b and e), and pie charts (c and f).

- Create charts, diagrams, drawings, and text slides from scratch.
- Use a library of symbols, drawings, and pictures—called clip art (Figure 10-25)—that comes with the graphics program. Because the computer produces the drawings and manipulates them, even a nonartist can create professional-looking illustrations. In this chapter, the essay called "Presentation Graphics Everywhere" introduces some samples of presentation graphics.

Presentation graphics increase the impact of your message. They make the information you are presenting visually appealing, meaningful, and understandable. High-quality graphics have been shown to increase both the amount that a listener learns in a presentation and the length of time that the information is retained by the listener. Also, an audience perceives you as more professional and knowledgeable when you include overhead graphics and slides in your presentation.

You can produce high-quality output on a variety of media: video screens, printers, plotters, overhead transparencies, or slides for projection. Some presentation graphics programs, such as Harvard Graphics (Software Publishing Corporation), let you store pictures, text slides, charts, and graphs on disk. This means you can use the computer to present a series of text or graphic images, one after the other, on your display. When you make a presentation, you can run the display manually or have the screens presented by the computer automatically, in time increments

Figure 10-25   Enhancing graphics with symbols. Presentation graphics programs provide a library of symbols, which users can choose from. As shown on the left in this graphic, such symbols can add interest to columns of numbers.

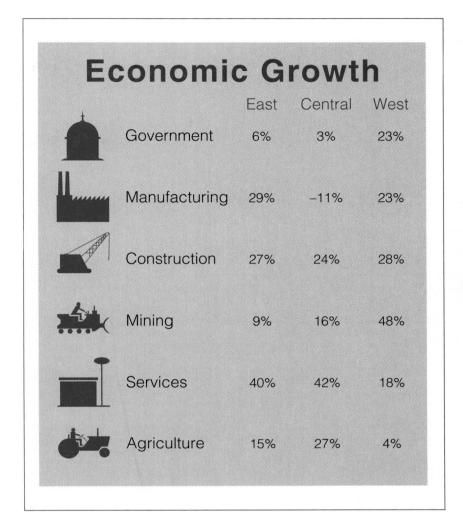

Economic Growth

		East	Central	West
Government		6%	3%	23%
Manufacturing		29%	–11%	23%
Construction		27%	24%	28%
Mining		9%	16%	48%
Services		40%	42%	18%
Agriculture		15%	27%	4%

ranging from four seconds to four minutes per image. A few programs let you animate your images. For example, graph bars might grow as product sales increase.

 ## Some Business Graphics Terminology

To use a graphics program successfully, you should know some basic concepts and design principles. Let us begin by exploring the types of graphs you can create.

Line Graphs

One of the most useful ways of showing trends or cycles over the same period of time is to use a **line graph.** For example, the graph in Figure 10-26a shows company costs for utilities during a four-month period.

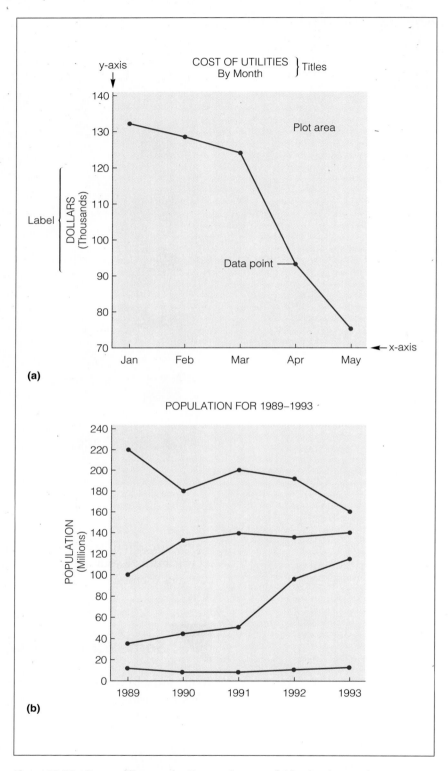

Figure 10-26   Types of line graphs. Line graphs are useful for showing trends over a period of time. In many analytical programs, a different symbol is used for each variable's range. (a) The one line in the plot area of a single-range graph shows only one variable. (b) Multiple-range graphs show several different variables or lines.

Line graphs are appropriate when there are many values or you need to graph complex data. In the business section of the newspaper, line graphs are used to show complex trends in gross national product, stock prices, or employment changes over a period of time. Also, corporate profits and losses are often illustrated by line graphs.

In the line graph in Figure 10-26a, notice the lines that run vertically along the left edge and horizontally along the bottom. Each line is called an **axis.** (The plural of *axis* is *axes.*) The horizontal line, called the **x-axis,** normally represents units of time, such as days, months, or years. The vertical line, called the **y-axis,** usually shows measured values or amounts, such as dollars, staffing levels, units sold, and so on. The area inside the axes is called the **plot area**—the space in which the graph is plotted, or drawn.

Graphics programs automatically scale (arrange the units or numbers on) the x-axis and y-axis so that the graph of your data is nicely proportioned and easy to read. When you become proficient with a graphics program, you can select your own scales for the axes.

Each dot or symbol on a line graph represents a single numeric quantity called a **data point.** You must specify the data to be plotted on the graph. This data is usually referred to as the *values.* The items that the data points describe are called **variables.** Most graphs are produced from the data stored in the rows and columns of spreadsheet files. Recall from the spreadsheet discussion that you can refer to particular rows or columns of a spreadsheet as a *range.* A graph that plots the values of only one variable is sometimes referred to as a **single-range graph** (Figure 10-26a). If more than one variable is plotted on the same graph, it is referred to as a **multiple-range graph** (Figure 10-26b).

To make the graph easier to read and understand, **labels** identify the categories along the x-axis and the units along the y-axis. **Titles** summarize the information in the graph and are used to increase comprehension.

Bar Graphs

Bar graphs are used for graphing the same kinds of data that line graphs represent. Notice in Figure 10-27 that, in **bar graphs,** areas shaded up to the height of the point being plotted create a bar. These graphs can be striking and informative when they are simple. They are often used to illustrate multiple comparisons such as sales, expenses, and production activities. Bar graphs are useful for presentations, since the comparisons are easy to absorb. However, if there is a lot of data for several variables, the bars on the graph become narrow and crowded, making a confusing and busy graph; in such a case, a line graph is preferable.

In Figure 10-27, there are three different types of bar graphs. The first is a **single-range bar graph,** in which only one variable is involved; in this example, the single variable is monthly expenses. The second type of bar graph is a multiple-range bar graph called a **clustered-bar graph.** In this type of graph, data values for three different variables—supplies, utilities, and travel—are plotted next to each other along the x-axis. Be-

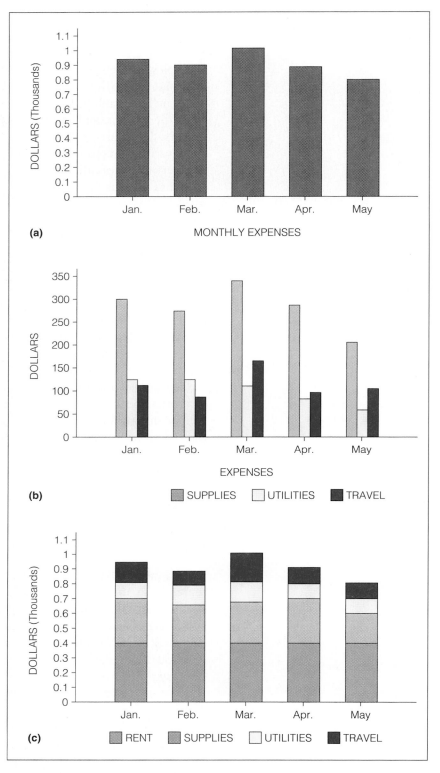

Figure 10-27   **Types of bar graphs.** (a) A single-range bar graph shows only one variable—in this case, monthly expenses. Multiple-range bar graphs show several variables. The other two graphs in this figure show the two basic types of multiple-range bar graphs: (b) A clustered-bar graph shows several variables. (c) A stacked-bar graph shows the different variables stacked on top of one another.

Figure 10-28   Types of pie charts. Pie charts are used to show how various values make up a whole. (a) A regular pie chart. (b) An exploded pie chart.

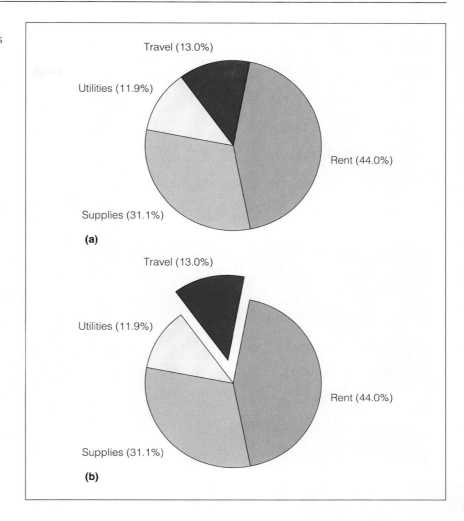

cause clustered-bar graphs contain so much information, it is important to label each cluster clearly. You can create a **legend,** or list, that explains different colors, shadings, or symbols in the graph. A legend is used at the bottom of Figure 10-27b. The third type of bar graph, the **stacked-bar graph,** is also a multiple-range bar graph. In this graph, however, the different variables are stacked on top of one another. All the data common to a given row or column appear in one bar.

Pie Charts

Representing just a single variable, a **pie chart** shows how various values make up a whole. These charts really look like pies; the whole amount is represented by a circle, and each wedge of the pie represents a value. Figure 10-28a shows a pie chart.

Pie charts can show only the data for one variable—January in this example. However, this pie chart does the best job of showing the proportion of the "pie" dollar that goes for rent, supplies, and so forth during that one month. Notice that pie charts often have the written per-

Personal Computers in Action

PRESENTATION GRAPHICS EVERYWHERE

Why are people taking the trouble to get information all gussied up with fancy graphics when the unembellished numbers would be quite acceptable? The answer is that graphics are worth the trouble. The most effective way to make a presentation is to take advantage of visual aids. Studies show that graphics—especially color graphics—increase persuasiveness by as much as 50%. They also communicate complex information faster. As you can see from the samples here, colorful graphics can be given a three-dimensional look and enhanced with drawings of related objects, such as people and phones.

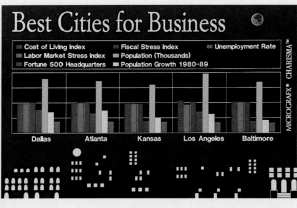

centage shown by each separate wedge of the pie. It is best to keep pie charts simple; if the pie contains more than eight wedges, you might consider using a bar graph or line graph instead.

Figure 10-28b shows one of the wedges pulled slightly away from the pie, for emphasis. This type of pie chart is called an **exploded pie chart.** This technique loses its effectiveness if more than one or two "slices" are separated. Not all graphics programs have the ability to produce an exploded pie chart.

On to Storing Data

Thus far in our discussion of software applications, we have moved from words to numbers to pictures. We will devote more attention to graphics in Chapter 12. But first we turn to another powerful computer application, storing data so it is easily accessible in databases—the subject of our next chapter.

R E V I E W   A N D   R E F E R E N C E

Summary and Key Terms

- Forms that are used to organize data into rows and columns are called **spreadsheets.** An **electronic spreadsheet** is a computerized version of a manual spreadsheet. An electronic spreadsheet program quickly and automatically performs calculations to reflect changes in values or formulas. In Lotus 1-2-3, an electronic spreadsheet is called a **worksheet.**

- The intersection of a row and column forms a **cell.** Cells are the storage areas in a spreadsheet. When referring to a cell, you use the letter and number of the intersecting column and row. This reference name is the **cell address.**

- There is one cell known as the **active cell,** or **current cell.** The active cell is marked by the spreadsheet's cursor, also called a **pointer,** or **cell pointer.**

- Each cell can contain one of four types of data. A **label** provides descriptive information about entries in the spreadsheet. A **value** is an actual number entered into a cell. A **formula** is an instruction to the program to perform a calculation. A **function** is a preprogrammed formula. Sometimes you must specify a **range** of cells to build a formula or perform a function.

- You can use the cursor movement keys to scroll through the spreadsheet horizontally or vertically. You may also use a **GoTo function key,** also known as the **Jump-To function key.**

- A **mode** is the condition, or state, in which the program is currently functioning. Most spreadsheets have three main operating modes: the **READY mode,** the **ENTRY mode,** and the **MENU mode.** The spreadsheet screen displays a **mode indicator,** which tells you the current mode.

- Spreadsheet programs display commands in a **command menu** shown near the top of the screen. The command menu contains a list, or menu, of different options.

- Most spreadsheet programs display a **control panel** to help you keep track of what you input. The control panel usually consists of three lines. The first line is the **status line;** the second line is used in a variety of ways; and the third line shows a **submenu,** which lists options for the command you are choosing.

- To create a spreadsheet, you enter labels, values, formulas, and functions into the cells. Formulas and functions do not appear in the cells; instead, the cell shows the result of the formula or function. The result is called the **displayed value** of the cell. The formula or function is the **cell content.** To make corrections to data in a cell, you must move the cursor to that cell.

- A **command tree** shows all the choices from the main command menu and all the choices from associated submenus.

- The **File command** lets you manipulate the Lotus 1-2-3 files on your data disk. You can use the File command to save, retrieve, list, and erase files.

- The **Print command** provides options for printing all or part of a spreadsheet on paper. It also lets you store a "printed" spreadsheet on disk.

- The **Worksheet Erase command** clears the current worksheet out of memory, providing you with a blank worksheet. This command does not affect already-saved worksheets.

- To leave the spreadsheet program and return to DOS, you must use the **Quit command** from the command menu. Always save your file before you quit, since many spreadsheet programs do not automatically save files.

- The **Help key** places you in the HELP mode. This mode is **context-sensitive**—that is, it offers helpful information related to the command you were using when you pressed the Help key. While in HELP mode, you can select the **Help index,** which gives you access to an on-screen reference manual.

- Programs in an **integrated package** share a common methodology and command structure, which make learning and data transfer easier. **Standalone programs** can be integrated by a **universal manager program** that presents a common interface to the user and handles data transfer among the programs.

- **Business graphics** represent business data in a visual, easily understood format. They help users analyze data, and they help make business reports more interesting.

- **Analytical graphics programs** help users analyze and understand specific data. **Presentation graphics programs,** or **business-quality programs,** produce sophisticated graphics that are appropriate for formal presentations. Presentation graphics programs also contain a library of symbols and drawings called clip art.

- A **line graph** has lines that define a period of time and the units measured. Each line is called an **axis.** The horizontal line is called the **x-axis,** and the vertical line is called the **y-axis.** The area inside the x-axis and y-axis is the **plot area.** Each dot or symbol on a line graph is a **data point.** Each data point represents a value. The items that the data points describe are called **variables.**

- Graphs that plot the values of only one variable are called **single-range graphs.** A **multiple-range graph** plots more than one variable.

- **Bar graphs** show data comparisons by presenting bars of different lengths or heights. In a **single-range bar graph,** only one variable is involved. A **clustered-bar graph** shows more than one variable. A **stacked-bar graph** also shows multiple variables, but the bars are stacked on top of one another. You can create a **legend** to explain the colors or symbols on a complex graph. **Labels** identify the categories along the x-axis and the units along the y-axis. **Titles** summarize the information in the graph.

- A **pie chart** represents a single variable and shows how different values make up a whole. Each wedge of the pie represents a value. On an **exploded pie chart,** a wedge is pulled slightly away from the pie for emphasis.

Review Questions

1. In a spreadsheet, what is the intersection of a row and column called?
2. Where are the entries in a spreadsheet stored?
3. How are individual columns and rows identified on an electronic spreadsheet?
4. What is a range?
5. What is meant by the formula @AVG(B1..B10)? Where will the result of calculating this formula be displayed on the screen?
6. What is another way to write the formula A1+A2+A3+A4+A5?
7. Regardless of the cursor's location in the spreadsheet, what are three ways in which you can move the cursor to cell A1?
8. What are three of the modes in which Lotus 1-2-3 operates?
9. What mode must you be in to make an entry in a cell? Can you make an entry in a cell when you see the command menu on the screen?
10. What key do you press to access the command menu?
11. What is displayed in the mode indicator when you start to enter a value in a cell? What is displayed in the mode indicator when you start to enter a label in a cell?
12. What are some of the commands available in the command menu?
13. What is a submenu? How do you access a submenu? How do you make a choice from a submenu?
14. What is automatic recalculation?
15. What command in Lotus 1-2-3 lets you store, retrieve, list, or erase your worksheet files?

Discussion Questions

1. Why are personal computer graphics used in business?
2. Explain the difference between analytical and presentation graph- ics.
3. Describe the similarities and differences between a single-range bar graph, a clustered-bar graph, and a stacked-bar graph. For what purpose is each best suited?
4. What is an exploded pie chart, and why is it used?
5. What are some advantages for using an integrated package over a dedicated spreadsheet application?

True-False Questions

T F 1. A cell is the amount of a spreadsheet you can see on the screen.

T F 2. The formulas @SUM(A1..B3) and @SUM(A1..B3) generate the same result.

T F 3. You can bring up the Lotus 1-2-3 menu by pressing / or \.

T F 4. The formulas B3+B4+B5+B6 and @SUM(B3..B6) generate the same result.

T F 5. The command sequence /Worksheet Erase Yes erases a file from the screen but not from the disk.

T F 6. Integrated packages allow you to use a common methodology and command structure to link software from different manufacturers.

T F 7. Presentation graphics packages allow users to create graphics that are more elaborate than those produced by analytical graphics packages.

T F 8. Line graphs are frequently used to display changes in variables over time.

T F 9. Bar graphs and stacked-bar graphs can both be multiple-range graphs.

T F 10. A pie chart can be a multiple-range graph.

11

Database Management Systems

Getting Data Together

Cecile's parents are frantic when they bring her to the hospital emergency room. She has been bitten by a poisonous snake. The treatment seems obvious: an anti-poison drug. However, the situation is not that simple. Cecile suffers from a rare blood disorder and therefore needs special care. Fortunately, the hospital can access a computerized database of medical information—MEDLINE, at the National Library of Medicine—to find out what the appropriate treatment should be. A hospital aide uses a computer terminal to call the MEDLINE database, which is in Bethesda, Maryland. The computer searches through millions of medical journal articles, and the doctors select pertinent ones from the titles

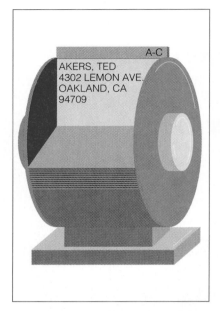

Figure 11-1 An index-card database.
Each card in this index-card file contains one person's name and address. The cards are arranged alphabetically by last name.

that appear on the terminal screen. The anti-poison drug will not help, they learn, but a blood transfusion will. In no time, doctors have the information to save Cecile's life.

MEDLINE services are available in emergency rooms, operating rooms, and wherever else doctors need help in a hurry. The service is especially helpful in rural areas, where a doctor may not have seen a particular set of symptoms before. Medical expertise is as close as the terminal and as fast as the computer.

Storing and accessing data is absolutely vital in today's society. A **database** is an organized collection of related data. In a loose sense you are using a database when you use a phone book, look in a library's card catalog, or take a file out of a file cabinet. Unfortunately, as the amount of data increases, creating, storing, changing, sorting, and retrieving data become overwhelming tasks. For example, suppose you had a collection of names and addresses, each on a separate card stored in an index-card file (Figure 11-1). If you had only 25 cards, putting the cards in alphabetical order or even finding all the people who have the same zip code would be fairly easy. But what if you had 100, or 1000, or 10,000 cards? What if you had several different index-card files—one organized by names, one by cities, and one by zip codes? What if you had different people adding more cards each day, not knowing if they were duplicating other cards in the file? And what if you had another set of people trying to update the data on the cards? As you can see, things might get out of hand—and you would be pulling out your hair trying to deal with it. Enter computers and database management software.

Getting It Together: Database Programs

A **database management system (DBMS)** is software that helps you organize data in a way that allows fast and easy access to the data. In essence, the program acts as a very efficient and elaborate file system. With a database program you can create, modify, store, and retrieve data in a variety of ways. Some benefits of database management system software are:

- **Integrated files.** Using a database, files that would be physically separated in a paper system can be joined together. For example, consider two file drawers, one for customers and one for sales representatives. Suppose you needed data—perhaps the address of a sales rep who helped a particular customer. You would have to look first in the customer drawer to find the name of the sales rep and then in the sales rep drawer to find the sales rep's address. Database programs smooth the way for these types of searches by storing the relationships needed to combine data from different files stored on disk.

- **Reduced redundancy.** When businesses have many different files, the same data is often stored in several different places. In a database, data is usually stored in just one place. This reduces the amount of duplicate data in the system. In addition, updating can be done quickly and efficiently—without having to track down the repeated data.

Personal Computers in Action

NOT JUST FOR DOCTORS ANYMORE

Susan Corning watched her elderly father slowly fading, his body racked by a rare form of cancer. For 18 months, she stood by feeling helpless, wondering why the doctors had no answers. Then she decided to take matters into her own hands.

In her work as a management consultant, Susan had frequently accessed computerized information systems to obtain answers. She decided to spend some money on a computerized search of the type doctors use to find the latest medical data. Through a reference in an obscure journal, she found a University of California doctor who was experimenting successfully with a new drug. She soon arranged for her father to see the doctor and get the drug. Within weeks, her dad had resumed an active lifestyle that included skiing and golf.

Medical databases are not just for doctors anymore. Anyone can access them—not just medical professionals and skilled computer users, as in the past. New industries have sprung up, giving consumers access to the same information as the experts. Dozens of public health agencies and health resource libraries, clinics, and hospitals nationwide have installed the Health Reference Center (HRC), a hardware system made by Information Access of Foster City, California. HRC offers consumers a personal computer to locate and print out disease-specific articles. For a fee, a number of organizations will run computer searches on a medical topic and supply the results. Su-

about such new services, expressing concern that patients may substitute a database search for critical medical care. But some doctors think providing public access to medical databases is a good idea, because the systems provide patients with information that is educational and supportive.

In any case, do not expect your insurance to pick up the tab for such information searches—they can cost as much as $1500. To avoid high costs, searches must be specific. Remember, you cannot sim-

san Corning used the services of Medical Information Service, and within 24 hours she had a bound report that included up to 200 references.

Not surprisingly, the American Medical Association is cautious

ply request information about red eyes and a runny nose if you want insight on your allergy. Such a search might provide too much general information and end up draining more than your sinuses.

- **Shared data.** Data in files can be shared by different people. Separate files for each department or function are unnecessary. Data can be stored once and accessed by authorized people using computers.
- **Centralized security.** When data is all in one place, you have better control over access to it. Scattered files are more difficult to protect. Security is particularly important for personnel files, restricted product information, customer credit ratings, marketing plans, and similar sensitive data.

In this chapter we will show you how to create and modify a database. But first we need to discuss some of the general terms used with databases.

Using a Database Management System

There are a large number of DBMS programs on the market today. Some databases focus exclusively on text-based information, others include graphics and photographs, such as pictures of the earth recorded by government weather satellites (see the essay "On a Clear Day," which appears later in this chapter). Covering all the operations, features, and functions of every individual package would be impossible. Therefore, throughout this chapter, we will discuss the characteristics and features of one of the most popular database programs—dBASE IV, which we will call dBASE for short. This program has many features in common with other database software packages.

Database Organization

In a paper file system, data on different topics is stored in segregated files. A paper file system cannot store information about how data in one file is related to data in another file. A database, however, can store data relationships, so files can be integrated. Data stored in integrated files can be combined. The way the database organizes data depends on the type, or **model,** of the database.

The three main database models are hierarchical, network, and relational. Each type structures, organizes, and uses data differently. Hierarchical and network database systems are usually found on mainframes and minicomputers. Hierarchical systems are databases in which some records are subordinate to others in a structure resembling a tree. Network systems are databases in which subordinate records can be subordinate to more than one record; this involves "child" records which may have more than one "parent." We will focus here on relational database systems, which are more common on personal computers.

A **relational database** organizes data in a table format consisting of related rows and columns. Figure 11-2a shows an address list; in Figure 11-2b, this data is laid out as a table. In a relational system, data in one file can be related to data in another, allowing you to tie together data from several files. Relating files is an advanced topic beyond the scope of this book. This chapter will focus on creating and updating one file.

Fields, Records, and Files

In a relational database a table is called a **relation.** Notice in Figure 11-2b that each box in the table contains a piece of data, known as a **data item.** Each column of the table represents a **field,** or **attribute.** The specific data items in a field may vary, but each field contains the same type of data—for example, first names or zip codes. In a given relation there

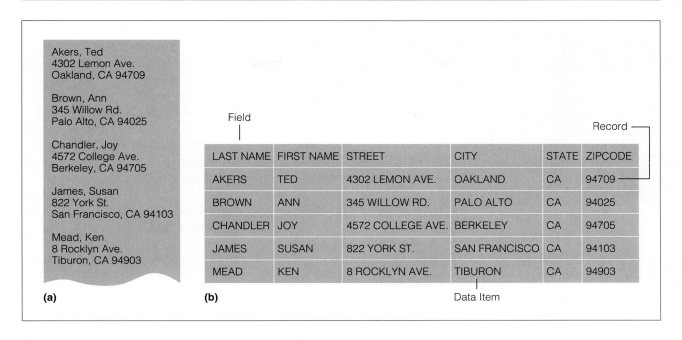

Akers, Ted
4302 Lemon Ave.
Oakland, CA 94709

Brown, Ann
345 Willow Rd.
Palo Alto, CA 94025

Chandler, Joy
4572 College Ave.
Berkeley, CA 94705

James, Susan
822 York St.
San Francisco, CA 94103

Mead, Ken
8 Rocklyn Ave.
Tiburon, CA 94903

Field

Record

LAST NAME	FIRST NAME	STREET	CITY	STATE	ZIPCODE
AKERS	TED	4302 LEMON AVE.	OAKLAND	CA	94709
BROWN	ANN	345 WILLOW RD.	PALO ALTO	CA	94025
CHANDLER	JOY	4572 COLLEGE AVE.	BERKELEY	CA	94705
JAMES	SUSAN	822 YORK ST.	SAN FRANCISCO	CA	94103
MEAD	KEN	8 ROCKLYN AVE.	TIBURON	CA	94903

(a)

(b)

Data Item

Figure 11-2   A relational database. In this example the address list in (a) is organized as a relational database in (b). Note that the data is laid out in rows and columns; each field is equivalent to a vertical column and each record is equivalent to a horizontal row.

is a fixed number of fields. All the data in any given row is called a **record,** or **tuple.** Each record has a fixed number of fields, but there can be a variable number of records in a given relation. Figure 11-2b shows five records—one for each person. A relation—a table—is also called a **file.** Furthermore, a database file can be considered a collection of records. Although we have introduced the formal terms *attribute, tuple,* and *relation* in this discussion, we will be referring to them by their more common names: *field, record,* and *file,* respectively.

File Structure

There are two steps to creating a database file: designing the structure of the file and entering the data into the file. To create the file structure, you must choose meaningful fields. The fields you choose should be based on the data you will want to retrieve from the database. For example, if you are creating a list of addresses, you might define fields for name, street address, city, state, and zip code. After you load the program and tell the software that you want to create a file structure, you see a structure input form on the screen. The program asks for several types of information. Let us take a look at each one.

Field Names   Names of the types of data you want to use are called **field names.** For example, a field called PHONE could be used to contain a phone number. A field name can be up to ten characters long, must begin with a letter, and cannot contain a space or any punctuation. Letters, numbers, and underscores are permitted.

Field Types   There are four commonly used **field types:** character fields, numeric fields, date fields, and logical fields. **Character fields** contain descriptive data such as names, addresses, and telephone numbers. **Nu-**

Why Do They Call It a Card Catalog?

Not long ago, libraries had card catalogs—dozens (and in some large libraries, hundreds of thousands) of little drawers, each filled with hundreds of little cards, each containing information about one book. Each book had three little cards: one each in the title, author, and subject catalogs. The catalogs took up a lot of space and required a lot of effort to maintain.

Some libraries still have these card catalogs, but more often today they have a computerized database that contains the catalog. A library visitor uses a computer terminal to request information on a specific title, author, or general subject.

Some libraries even allow users to call up the catalog from home by phone. In Gainesville, Florida, the phone book listing the Alachua County Library includes a phone number for the Dial-Up Catalog, along with the modem settings. All you need is a personal computer and an understanding of modem terminology.

However, one thing has not changed at your local library. Whether they have an old-fashioned set of catalog drawers or a new computerized database, you will still find little scraps of paper and stumps of pencils to write down what you discover in your search.

meric fields contain numbers used for calculations. When you enter a numeric field, you must specify the number of decimal places you wish to use. **Date fields** are automatically limited to eight characters, including the slashes used to separate the month, day, and year. **Logical fields** accept only single characters. Logical fields are used to keep track of true or false conditions. For example, if you want to keep track of whether a bill has been paid, you could use a logical field and enter Y for *Yes* or N for *No*. Other types of fields available in dBASE are **floating-point fields,** for speeding up calculations when using extremely precise numbers, and **memo fields,** for holding comments and other information.

Field Widths   The **field width** determines the maximum number of characters or digits to be contained in the field, including decimal points. Most database programs let you enter up to 128 fields in each record. Each character-type field can be up to 254 characters; each numeric-type field can be up to 20 characters wide.

Relational Operators

You will need to use a **relational operator** when entering instructions that involve making comparisons. Table 11-1 shows the relational operators that are commonly used. These operators are particularly useful when you want to locate specific data items. For example, to instruct a program to search through an address database and find the records of all the people who live in Wisconsin, you would enter the command:

```
LIST FOR STATE = "WI"
```

This command tells the program to look for the characters WI at the beginning of the state field.

Now we can move on to using a DBMS to design and create a database. Consider Rita Chung's problem—a problem that needs a database solution.

A Problem for a Database

Rita works as an intern for a public television station. One of her jobs is to keep track of the people who have pledged to donate money to the sta-

Table 11-1

Relational operators.

Operator	Explanation
<	Less than
>	Greater than
=	Equal to
<=	Less than or equal to
>=	Greater than or equal to
<>	Not equal to

Figure 11-3   Designing the file structure. Rita sketches the way she wants to set up her database. Note that she has seven fields—LNAME, FNAME, CITY, PHONE, AMOUNT, DATE, and PAID.

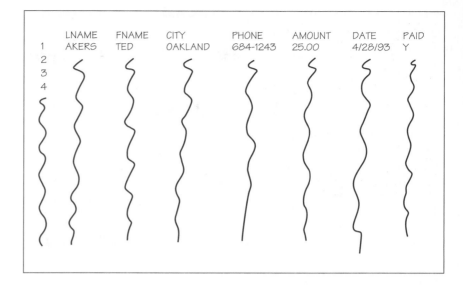

tion. Currently, each person's name, city, and phone number is kept on a separate card, along with the amount pledged and the date the pledge was made. Rita wants to place this data into a computer by using dBASE. She also wants to add another column of data—the PAID field—that tells whether each person has actually paid the amount he or she pledged.

First Rita sketches on paper the structure of the database—what kind of data she wants in each row and column (Figure 11-3). Her next step is to enter this structure into the computer. A copy of dBASE is stored on Rita's hard disk. She loads the dBASE program and sees the copyright notice; she presses Enter to begin using the program.

 ## Building a Database

dBASE uses a system of menus called **work surfaces.** These menus let you edit, display, and manage your data. The most important menu is called the **Control Center.** This is the first menu Rita sees after loading dBASE. The Control Center provides access to nearly all of the features of the program. As shown in Figure 11-4, the Control Center menu consists of six **panels** that display various options. Users do most of their work by using the Control Center. It is worth noting the options across the top of the screen: Catalog, Tools, Exit. Each of these options represents a submenu. As Rita works, she will often press F10 to activate the submenu display. Then she will type the first letter of the desired submenu, such as C for Catalog.

The menu system of the Control Center saves users from having to remember commands and from the typing errors that could result if they had to enter commands from the keyboard. However, some experienced users prefer the Command mode, which allows them to type dBASE commands. These users may be familiar with previous versions of dBASE and do not need menu cues to remember the commands. Rita can access the Command mode by pressing the Escape key, Esc, while the cur-

Figure 11-4 dBASE Control Center screen. The dBASE Control Center screen lets you access nearly all the features included in dBASE.

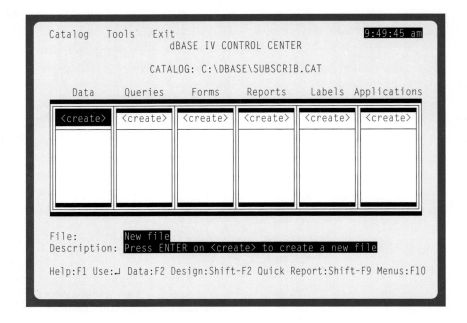

sor is in the Control Center. In response, the **dot prompt**—a period—appears on the screen. After the dot prompt, Rita can type the dBASE command she desires. To return to the Control Center from the Command mode, Rita can type Assist or press F2. This chapter will show how to use the Control Center menus.

Any time Rita needs help in dBASE, she can press F1 for **Help.** If the Control Center is on the screen, she can get information about each choice shown by using the cursor movement keys to highlight a choice on the menu. Once she has highlighted the appropriate choice, she presses F1; a screen describing that choice appears. She can press Esc to leave the Help screen and resume her work with the Control Center.

Creating a Catalog

dBASE allows users to keep a **catalog,** a group of related files. For instance, once Rita has created the database she is planning, she could create several reports that are associated with the database, and perhaps also design special forms for mailing labels. She would want to store all such files in the same catalog. Files can be added to or deleted from the catalog, and a single file can belong to more than one catalog. A file that is deleted from a catalog listing is not deleted from the disk.

Before Rita creates the database file structure she sketched in Figure 11-3, she needs to create a catalog. Beginning from the Control Center, which is the first work surface that appears after dBASE is loaded, she presses F10 and the Catalog menu appears (Figure 11-5a). The menu selection Use a different catalog—the option that lets her make a new catalog—is already highlighted, so she presses Enter. A new menu appears in the upper right of the screen (Figure 11-5b). The option <create> is already highlighted, so Rita presses Enter. dBASE then prompts her for a

Figure 11-5   Creating a catalog. (a) Rita creates a new catalog by pressing F10 and C to access the Catalog menu. She chooses the highlighted option, Use a different catalog, by pressing Enter. (b) A new menu pops up. Rita presses Enter to choose <create>. dBASE prompts her to type a catalog name. (c) Rita types SUBSCRIB and presses Enter.

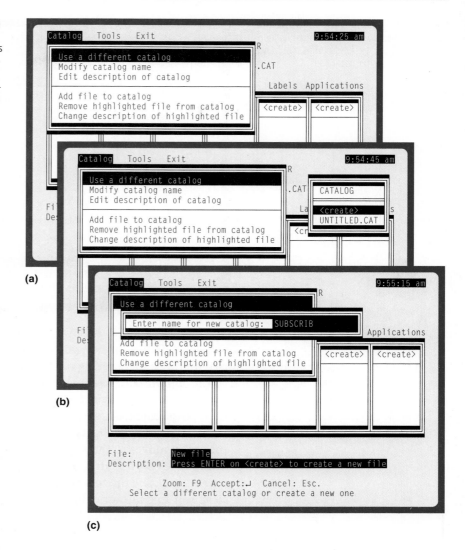

(a)

(b)

(c)

catalog name. A catalog name, which must begin with a letter, can be from one to eight characters in length and can contain letters, numbers, and underscores. Rita enters SUBSCRIB (Figure 11-5c) and presses Enter. The screen again displays the unobstructed Control Center.

Creating the File Structure

Next Rita will create a file structure. In the Control Center, in the Data panel, <create> is already highlighted, so Rita presses Enter. dBASE then displays the database design work surface (Figure 11-6). Rita has already decided how to organize the database (recall her sketch in Figure 11-3), so she begins by entering the first field name.

Rita has decided to use the field name LNAME to stand for *last name* (dBASE does not accept spaces in field names). She types LNAME in the Field Name column and presses Enter. The cursor moves to the Field Type column. In this column, Rita must specify whether the field will be a

Figure 11-6 Creating the file structure.
To create a file structure, Rita must fill in information about the field names, field type,
and file width in her database.

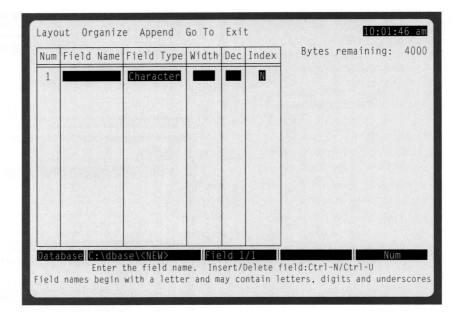

character field, a numeric field, a date field, or a logical field. There are
two methods for entering the field type. Rita can press the Spacebar until the appropriate field type name is displayed in the column—Character is the first field type name to appear, as shown in Figure 11-6—and
then press Enter. Or, she can enter the first character of the field type.
Rita types C for Character (but does not press Enter); the cursor automatically moves to the Field Width column. Rita enters 10 and presses
Enter. The column after Field Width is Dec. The column name stands
for *Decimal*, and the column is used to enter the number of decimal places
to appear in a numeric field. Because Rita defined the LNAME field as
a character field, she does not have to specify the number of decimal places;
the cursor automatically bypasses Dec and moves to the Index column.
This column can be used to specify dBASE capabilities beyond the scope
of this discussion. The N in the index column means there is no index.
For the purposes of this chapter, we can ignore the index column from
this point. Rita presses Enter to begin a new line and a new field definition.

Rita continues to enter the fields. The completed field structure is
shown in Figure 11-7. Notice that she defined the PHONE field as a character field, since a phone number is not used in mathematical calculations. Furthermore, phone numbers may contain hyphens and parentheses that dBASE would misread as mathematical operators in a numeric
field. Notice also that Rita does not have to define a width for the DATE
field or the PAID field. When a user specifies a date field or logical field,
dBASE enters the appropriate field width automatically.

As Rita finishes defining each field, dBASE automatically puts a new
numbered line on the screen so she can define the next field. After Rita
has defined the last of her fields, the cursor is on a blank line, ready to
accept field 8. Instead of entering a field name, Rita presses Enter. dBASE

Figure 11-7 The completed file structure. Rita has completed the file structure. Note the different field types. To save this structure, Rita presses Enter. dBASE prompts her for a file name. Rita types PLEDGE and presses Enter.

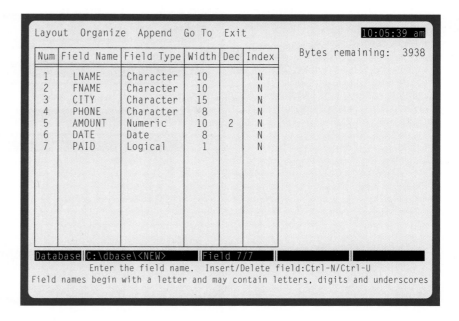

recognizes this as a signal to stop defining fields. It then asks Rita to name the database file. She types PLEDGE and presses Enter. dBASE asks if she wants to input data now. She chooses N because she wants to do other things first. The Control Center reappears, this time with the file name PLEDGE shown in the Data column and at the bottom of the screen after the word "File:". The new database file PLEDGE will be listed in the catalog SUBSCRIB.

Now Rita wants to enter a database description, which will be displayed in the file description area whenever the file name is highlighted on the Control Center screen. With the cursor on the file name PLEDGE in the Data column of the Control Center, Rita presses Enter. A dialog box offers three choices: Close file, Modify structure/order, and Display data. Rita uses the cursor movement keys to highlight

    Modify structure/order

and presses Enter. The Organize menu appears.

Rita uses the cursor movement keys—the left arrow—to pull down the Layout menu. She types E—for Edit database description—to display a prompt box. As Figure 11-8 shows, Rita types

    List of pledge name, address, telephone, and amount
    donated

and presses Enter, which causes a return once again to the design structure.

Rita signals dBASE that she is finished by pressing F10 and then using Right Arrow—to display the Exit menu, on which the option Save changes and exit is highlighted. dBASE displays the file name PLEDGE at the bottom of the screen. Rita presses Enter twice, and the Control Center reappears. The description now appears below the file name at the bottom of the screen.

Figure 11-8 Entering the database description. Once Rita completes the structure, she must enter a description of the database. To do so, Rita uses the cursor movement keys to pull down the Layout menu. Then she types E and dBASE prompts her for the database description. Rita types the description shown in the figure and presses Enter.

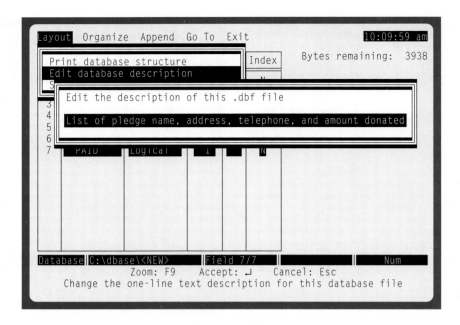

Figure 11-9 Viewing the structure. Rita views the completed file structure by pressing Shift-F2 to display the Organize menu. Rita presses Esc, and the file structure appears.

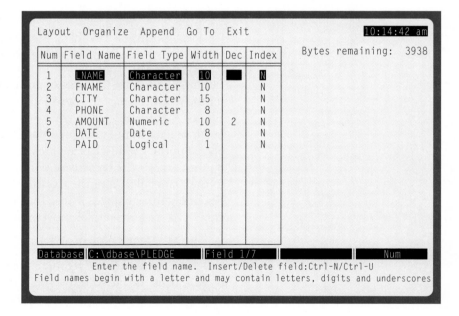

Viewing the Structure

Rita can view the completed file structure from the Control Center by pressing Shift-F2 to display the Organize menu. Rita presses Esc, which clears the screen of the Organize menu and displays the structure of PLEDGE, as shown in Figure 11-9. After reviewing the structure, Rita presses Esc to return to the Control Center. dBASE responds with "Are you sure you want to abandon this operation?" Rita types Y and the Control Center appears again.

Entering the Data

To enter records into the database, Rita must first specify the catalog to be used. She was previously using the SUBSCRIB catalog, and it is still in use. The file name PLEDGE appears in the Data panel, on the left side of the Control Center. Since the name of the file she wants to use is already highlighted, Rita presses F2, causing dBASE to display the Edit screen.

The Edit screen presents the field vertically to provide an on-screen input form (Figure 11-10a). The designated width for each field is highlighted. Rita fills in the blanks of the input form, beginning with data about Ted Akers (Figure 11-10b). If the data item is shorter than the field length, Rita presses Enter to move to the next field. However, if the width of the entry is exactly the size of the field, the program beeps and automatically advances to the next field. If Rita makes a mistake while she is typing, she can use Backspace or the cursor movement keys to make corrections. After AMOUNT, she types 25 followed by a decimal point; dBASE adjusts the field properly. In the DATE field, if the day or month is a single digit, Rita must press Right Arrow to shift the number to the right one place or type 0 before entering the single-digit number.

Once Rita has filled in all the data for the first record, dBASE automatically saves the record and displays another blank input form, so she

(a)

(b)

Figure 11-10   The data input form.
(a) Rita uses the Edit screen to access an on-screen input form for her file. The highlighted areas show the designated field width for each field. (b) Rita has filled in the data for the first record.

Macintosh

ELECTRONIC DATABASES BY PHONE

Macintosh users, like many computer users, often have tough questions about their computers. Apple Computer, Inc. thinks AppleLink is the answer. Based on a mainframe computer at Apple headquarters in Silicon Valley, AppleLink is a system of electronic libraries, bulletin boards, and electronic mail services accessible by telephone. Armed with only a modem and the special AppleLink software, a Macintosh user can log into the AppleLink system and find a vast array of reference material.

AppleLink on-line libraries are actually databases that the user can search for information related to a given problem. If the answer is not there, the user can send an electronic mail inquiry directly to an expert at Apple. If the problem is particularly thorny, perhaps involving products from several vendors, experts from many sources can be called in to collaborate on a solution through AppleLink electronic conferencing.

Some support issues do not involve problems with hardware or software; they focus instead on which new or improved products should be purchased for a given task. Sales and marketing-related information—pricing, product descriptions, promotional offers, and so on—is available for items pro-

duced by Apple and third-party vendors. AppleLink also provides demonstration versions of the latest software. Using the telephone lines, AppleLink users can download these programs to their "in basket" and then run the programs to get a feel for how they work.

One of the most useful features of the AppleLink environment is the user-to-user bulletin boards, where any Mac user can talk on-line to any other Mac user. Users, as well as hardware and software personnel from all over the world, can listen to each other's problems and offer advice, encouragement, and—when those are not enough—sympathy. AppleLink also offers special access to Apple technical

people to developers of Macintosh hardware and software.

AppleLink access is not free. There is an hourly charge—higher during business hours than non-business hours. But with the special software provided for transferring information—and its compression capabilities—users can prepare much of their work off-line and then upload it to the mainframe via their "out basket" in seconds.

As desktop computers become more powerful and as telecommunications networks become faster and more reliable, a limitless variety of information will become available through networked electronic databases and services like AppleLink.

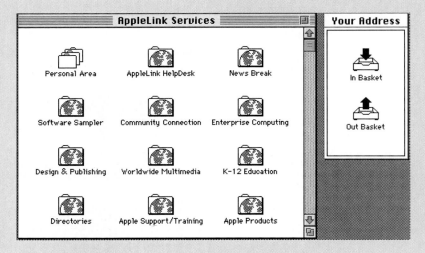

---

can enter the data items for the fields in the second record. When Rita completes the very last record, dBASE expects still another and again moves to a new empty form. To indicate that she has finished entering data, Rita presses Enter. dBASE recognizes this as a signal that Rita does not have any more data to enter now. It automatically saves all the records she created and displays the Control Center.

Listing the Records

Rita wants to review the records she just entered, to look for errors. The Browse screen will allow her to list the records horizontally on the

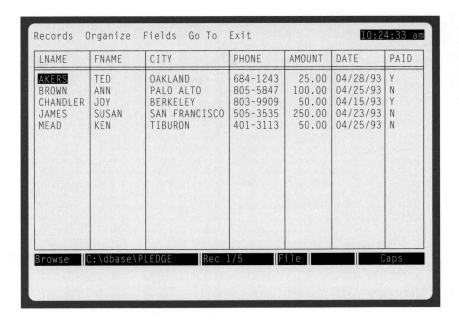

```
 Records  Organize  Fields  Go To  Exit                     10:24:33 am

 LNAME      FNAME    CITY             PHONE     AMOUNT   DATE      PAID

 AKERS      TED      OAKLAND          684-1243   25.00  04/28/93  Y
 BROWN      ANN      PALO ALTO        805-5847  100.00  04/25/93  N
 CHANDLER   JOY      BERKELEY         803-9909   50.00  04/15/93  Y
 JAMES      SUSAN    SAN FRANCISCO    505-3535  250.00  04/23/93  N
 MEAD       KEN      TIBURON          401-3113   50.00  04/25/93  N




 Browse     C:\dbase\PLEDGE        Rec 1/5       File              Caps
```

Figure 11-11   Viewing the records in Browse. Rita uses the Browse screen to view the records in her database. The Browse screen displays the records horizontally.

screen. Rita presses F2. The Edit screen of the last record she used appears. Rita presses F2 again to switch to the Browse screen. She then uses Up Arrow to move up to the top of the file and reveal all the records (Figure 11-11).

If she likes, Rita can print the field by using the **quick report** feature. She presses Shift-F9 to display a submenu for printing, then B for Begin printing. Her printer produces a list of the records she has just entered, and the Browse screen reappears. Rita leaves the Browse screen by pressing F10 to get to the Browse menu. After using the cursor movement keys to move to Exit, she presses Enter. The Control Center reappears.

Listing Specific Fields

dBASE provides a method to create listings of selected records and fields, called **queries.** Rita decides she wants to see a list that shows just the LNAME, PAID, and PHONE fields, in that order. Rita begins from the Control Center. She moves to the second column, Queries; highlights <create>; and presses Enter. The PLEDGE database file is still active, so its fields are displayed (Figure 11-12a). Notice that not all the fields fit across the bottom of the screen; those hidden to the right will appear when Rita uses Tab. Rita must mark the fields in the order in which she wants them to appear. She can use Tab to move right and Shift-Tab to move left.

Rita could automatically select all the fields in the database file for her query by pressing Enter within the first column, Pledge.dbf. However, Rita wants to select specific fields only, so she must mark the fields

Figure 11-12   Listing specific fields.
(a) Rita can list specific fields using Query menu. To do this, she highlights <create> in the Queries panel and the Query screen appears. (b) She then selects LNAME, PHONE, and PAID by using the F5 function key to un-select the other fields.

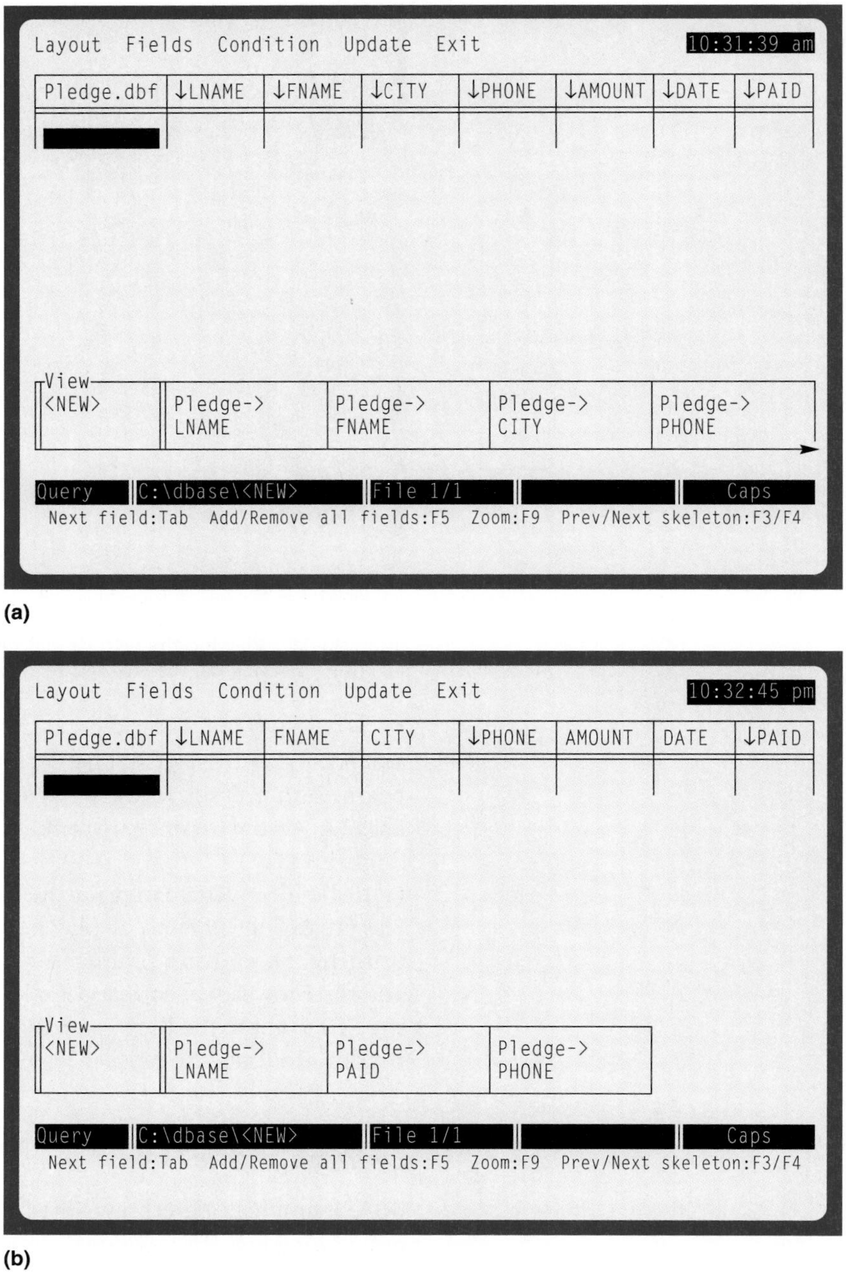

```
 Layout  Fields  Condition  Update  Exit           10:31:39 am
┌──────────┬───────┬───────┬───────┬───────┬────────┬───────┬───────┐
│Pledge.dbf│↓LNAME │↓FNAME │↓CITY  │↓PHONE │↓AMOUNT │↓DATE  │↓PAID  │
├──────────┼───────┼───────┼───────┼───────┼────────┼───────┼───────┤
│███████   │       │       │       │       │        │       │       │
│                                                                    │
│                                                                    │
│ ┌View────┬──────────┬──────────┬──────────┬──────────┐             │
│ │<NEW>   │ Pledge-> │ Pledge-> │ Pledge-> │ Pledge-> │             │
│ │        │ LNAME    │ FNAME    │ CITY     │ PHONE    │─────────▶   │
│ └────────┴──────────┴──────────┴──────────┴──────────┘             │
│ Query  C:\dbase\<NEW>      File 1/1                    Caps         │
│ Next field:Tab  Add/Remove all fields:F5  Zoom:F9  Prev/Next skeleton:F3/F4 │
└────────────────────────────────────────────────────────────────────┘
```

(a)

```
 Layout  Fields  Condition  Update  Exit           10:32:45 pm
┌──────────┬───────┬───────┬───────┬───────┬────────┬───────┬───────┐
│Pledge.dbf│↓LNAME │FNAME  │CITY   │↓PHONE │AMOUNT  │DATE   │↓PAID  │
├──────────┼───────┼───────┼───────┼───────┼────────┼───────┼───────┤
│███████   │       │       │       │       │        │       │       │
│                                                                    │
│                                                                    │
│ ┌View────┬──────────┬──────────┬──────────┐                        │
│ │<NEW>   │ Pledge-> │ Pledge-> │ Pledge-> │                        │
│ │        │ LNAME    │ PAID     │ PHONE    │                        │
│ └────────┴──────────┴──────────┴──────────┘                        │
│ Query  C:\dbase\<NEW>      File 1/1                    Caps         │
│ Next field:Tab  Add/Remove all fields:F5  Zoom:F9  Prev/Next skeleton:F3/F4 │
└────────────────────────────────────────────────────────────────────┘
```

(b)

she does *not* want. Rita uses Tab to move across the fields. As the cursor rests on each field, she presses F5 if she does not want to include that field in her query. If she does want to include that field, she simply presses Tab to pass over it. As each unmarked field is passed, its name appears in the structure on the lower half of the screen. After the fields have been marked, the screen should look like Figure 11-12b. To print the contents of the selected fields, Rita uses the Quick Report menu. She presses Shift-F9 and presses Enter.

After reviewing the list, she decides to save the query. She presses F10 to return to the query menu, which then shows the Layout menu already highlighted, and highlights Save this query. dBASE prompts her to save the query under a name. She types PHONELST and presses Enter. Rita then presses F10 to bring up the query menu and uses Right Arrow to go to the Exit option. She selects Save changes and exit and dBASE returns her to the Control Center. The Control Center now includes the file name PHONELST in the Queries panel.

Closing the Files and Exiting the Program

In general, a file is *open* when it is available for commands and *closed* when it is not. dBASE automatically closed the PLEDGE database file at the completion of the querying process just described. However, Rita will open it again so that you can see how a user directs dBASE to close a file. To open the file, Rita highlights the file name, PLEDGE, in the Data panel. She presses Enter. A prompt box appears containing the highlighted option Use file, which allows her to specify the file she wants to use (Figure 11-13a). She presses Enter to open PLEDGE, the file whose name is highlighted.

Rita uses a similar process to close the file: She highlights PLEDGE and presses Enter. Because the file is open, dBASE expects a closure request. So, in the prompt box that appears, the Close file option is highlighted (Figure 11-13b). Rita presses Enter to close the file without terminating the dBASE session. At this point, Rita can reopen the file or create another database file by highlighting <create> in the Data panel. Or, she can exit the program.

Now Rita wants to exit the program and return to DOS. She does this by pressing F10 and using Right Arrow to access the Exit menu. Rita highlights Quit to DOS (Figure 11-13c) and presses Enter.

Changing a Database

Over a period of time, changes usually need to be made to any database. New records must be added, others modified or deleted. dBASE allows you to add, delete, and change records by using the Edit and Browse menus. Rita has some changes to make to the PLEDGE database.

Opening Files

Rita once again loads dBASE. To add, edit, or delete data in a file, she must tell dBASE which file to use. From the Control Center, Rita uses the cursor movement keys to highlight the name of the PLEDGE database file. Then she presses Enter. The program opens the database file and a menu containing the options Use file, Modify structure/order, and Display data appears (Figure 11-14). Rita highlights Display data and presses Enter. The records are displayed within the Browse screen. Rita can use either

Figure 11-13   Closing a file and exiting dBASE. (a) dBASE closed the file automatically when Rita saved the query. She knows this because, when she highlights PLEDGE, the menu that appears contains the option use file. (b) If the file had been open, the menu would have displayed the option Close file. (c) To exit dBASE, Rita presses F10 to access the Exit menu. Then she highlights Quit to DOS and presses Enter.

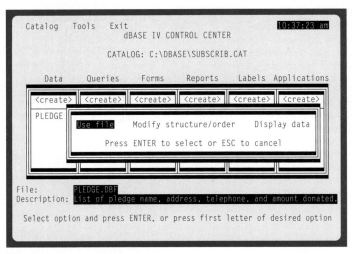

(a)

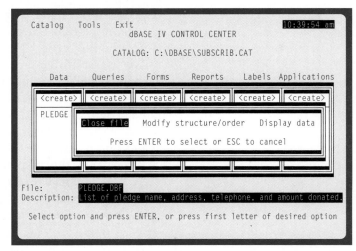

(b)

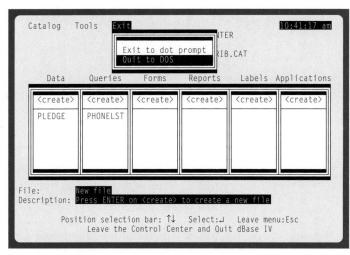

(c)

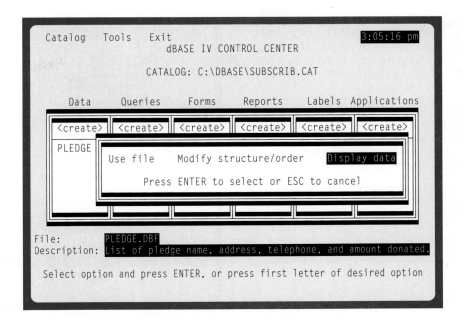

```
 Catalog   Tools   Exit                                    3:05:16 pm
                          dBASE IV CONTROL CENTER

                      CATALOG: C:\DBASE\SUBSCRIB.CAT


      Data      Queries     Forms      Reports     Labels  Applications

   <create>    <create>    <create>    <create>    <create>    <create>

   PLEDGE
               Use file    Modify structure/order    Display data

                      Press ENTER to select or ESC to cancel




 File:         PLEDGE.DBF
 Description:  List of pledge name, address, telephone, and amount donated.

   Select option and press ENTER, or press first letter of desired option
```

Figure 11-14   Opening a file and displaying the data. Rita wants to modify the records in the PLEDGE file. She highlights the file name in the Control Center and presses Enter. dBASE displays a menu; Rita highlights Display data and presses Enter.

The records are displayed within the Browse screen. Rita can use either Browse or Edit to make changes to the file.

Modifying Existing Records

Rita receives a list of pledge activity for the week from one of her co-workers. She needs to update record 1—Ted Akers has a new phone number. Also, Ann Brown has paid, so Rita needs to record the payment in record 2. She decides to use the Edit screen for the first change and the Browse screen to change the other.

Using the Edit Screen   Rita presses F2 to move to the Edit screen. The Edit screen allows editing of a data item in an individual record. In some cases, you must access the record you want to see. There are several ways to access a record so it can be modified; the easiest is to move down the file by using Down Arrow. In Rita's case, however, record 1, the first record she wants to modify, already appears on the screen (Figure 11-15a). Rita moves the cursor to the PHONE field, then types in the new phone number. (If necessary, she can also use the Ins and Del keys to make additional changes to the data.) Notice in Figure 11-15b that, in record 1, the new data has replaced the old data.

After Rita has used the Edit screen to access a particular record, she can edit previous or succeeding records in the file by pressing PgUp or PgDn. The PgUp key moves the cursor to the previous record; the PgDn key moves the cursor to the next record. If Rita wanted to save these

Figure 11-15   Modifying records by using the Edit screen. (a) Rita uses the Edit screen to make changes to record 1. (b) As she types in changes to Ted Akers' phone number, the new number is written over the old.

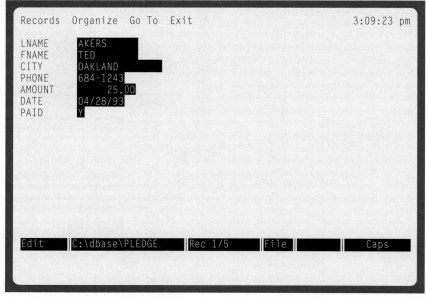

(a)

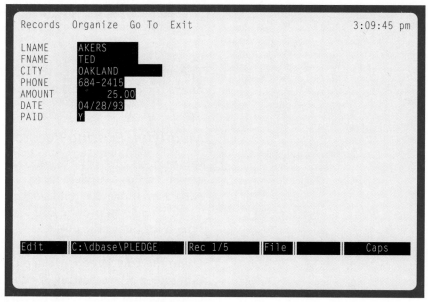

(b)

changes now, she would press Ctrl-End. Instead, Rita has decided to use the Browse menu to change the next record before saving.

Using the Browse Screen   The Browse screen provides the same editing capabilities as the Edit screen. However, Browse displays a record across one line on the screen, and displays as many records as will fit on the screen—usually about 17. To see records not shown on the screen, you can scroll up or down by using PgUp or PgDn. If there were a number of

On A Clear Day . . .

When a weather satellite records a photograph of the earth on a clear day, that picture may someday become part of the latest *National Geographic Atlas of the World*. Weather satellite photos are electronically recorded back on Earth and placed in a database of images maintained by the National Oceanic and Atmospheric Administration (NOAA). To produce the National Geographic Society's atlas, private firms and government agencies from around the world contribute to the NOAA database. Seven photographic mosaics of continents make up the final atlas, and each mosaic is made available to the public at cost by the National Geographic Society.

The team that writes software and reviews images for the North American mosaic works at the Environmental Research Institute of Michigan. Matching one swath of the continent to another to create a single mosaic is "a lot like putting together a jigsaw puzzle," says team member Chris Chiesa (pictured).

Today thousands of databases are available to anyone who can afford the access price—which is often fairly low. Many databases can be accessed on-line—that is, from a computer linked to a modem. The cost to a personal computer user may be as little as $5 a month, plus the minimal charge of a local phone call. Whole new businesses have sprung up around databases and the research expertise needed to use them. Computer databases have become essential tools in the Information Age.

```
 Records  Organize  Fields  Go To  Exit                    3:12:03 pm

 LNAME     FNAME    CITY          PHONE     AMOUNT  DATE      PAID

 AKERS     TED      OAKLAND       684-2415   25.00  04/28/93  Y
 BROWN     ANN      PALO ALTO     805-5847  100.00  04/25/93  N
 CHANDLER  JOY      BERKELEY      803-9909   50.00  04/15/93  Y
 JAMES     SUSAN    SAN FRANCISCO 505-3535  250.00  04/23/93  N
 MEAD      KEN      TIBURON       401-3113   50.00  04/25/93  N




 Browse  C:\dbase\PLEDGE    Rec 1/5      File         Caps
```

Figure 11-16   Modifying records by using the Browse screen. Rita can also use the Browse screen to make changes. She will change record 2 to indicate that the subscriber has paid.

fields in a record, Rita could **pan**—move horizontally across the screen—to the right by using Tab or Enter or to the left by using Shift-Tab.

The file is still open, so Rita presses F2 to use the Browse screen to display the records. Since there are currently only five records in her file, the screen displays all the records (Figure 11-16). To update record 2, Rita moves the cursor down to record 2 and presses Enter to move over to the PAID field. Then she types Y. After she has made the change, she presses Ctrl-End to save the data and return to the Control Center.

Adding Records

Rita wants to add two new subscribers—Mary Schwartz and Ted Greenlee. She can do this within the Browse screen or Edit screen. The menus and options both screens offer are the same, so Rita can use the same steps in either screen.

To add the first new record—the record about Mary Schwartz—Rita presses F2 twice to get back to the Edit screen. She then presses F10 to move to the Edit menu. The Records submenu is shown with the choice Add new records highlighted (Figure 11-17a), so she simply presses Enter. A blank data entry form for the PLEDGE file—just like the one used to enter the original records—appears on the screen (Figure 11-17b). Rita types in the data about Mary Schwartz and Ted Greenlee. The completed screens are shown in Figures 11-17c and 11-17d. When Rita finishes the second new record and sees a blank template, she uses Up Arrow to re-

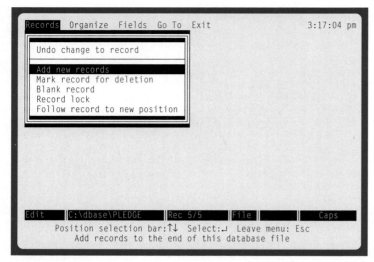

(a)

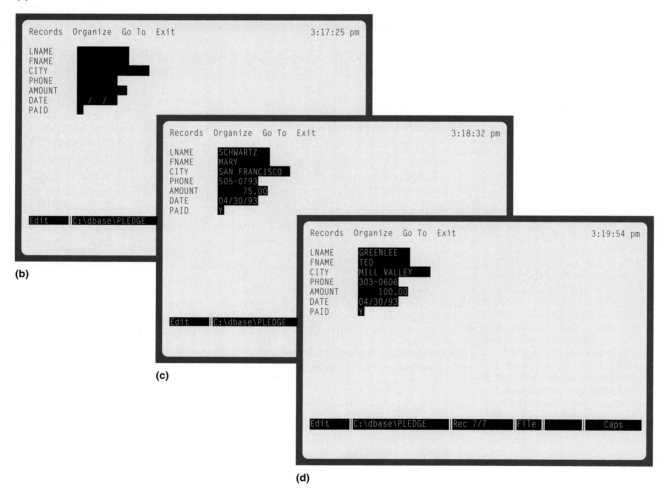

(b)

(c)

(d)

Figure 11-17   Adding records with the Edit screen. (a) Rita wants to use the Edit screen to add records. Because Add new records is already highlighted in the Records menu, Rita simply presses Enter. (b) dBASE presents her with a new input form. (c) Rita uses the Edit screen to add data about Mary Schwartz and (d) Ted Greenlee.

DO YOU WANT YOUR PICTURE IN THE COMPUTER?

Take the concept of a database one step further: In addition to storing data about an object, the computer can store its picture. The idea is a natural for computers that have high-resolution screens. It is also a good fit for any application where visual images enhance knowledge. But what if the "object" whose picture is stored is a person?

For example, personnel records often include a photo database. Employers use such files for employee identification and a host of other applications. Consider this scenario: Company executives gather in the boardroom to discuss promoting several employees to partner status. At one point the discussion focuses on Robert Smith. However, an executive from a different division cannot recall who Robert is. No problem. In moments the face of Robert Smith, along with related career information, is retrieved from the company database and flashed on the overhead screen. Ah, yes, Robert is the fellow who gave the dynamic presentation on new marketing directions at the annual meeting. Robert is in.

There certainly are advantages

in having photos of employees available from the computer. This is especially true of large firms with offices in several states or even countries. Some companies have found computer retrieval useful for the employee review process. Companies who used to rely on slide presentations were constrained by a prescribed presentation order; a database system permits any employee record to be retrieved at any time.

However, photo identification presents a new set of problems. First on the list is privacy. Think of all the computer files that contain your name and address, and then consider how that information is shared and sold, with very little control. The net result is in your mailbox. Although many of us have resigned ourselves to losing control over our addresses, having our pictures passed from computer to computer is another matter.

turn to the last record. Then she saves the file and exits by pressing Ctrl-End. The Control Center reappears.

Deleting Records

Sometimes a record must be removed—deleted—from a database file. Deleting records from a file is a two-step process. The steps to delete records are the same within the Browse and Edit screens. First, the specific records must be marked for deletion by using the Records submenu. Second, they must be permanently removed from the file by using the Organize submenu. Note that once you remove a marked record by erasing it, the record cannot be recovered.

Rita has been notified that Joy Chandler has moved and no longer wishes to donate to the station; Chandler's record needs to be deleted from the PLEDGE file. The file name is already highlighted in the Control Center, so Rita presses F2 twice. The Browse screen appears. Then

Figure 11-18   Deleting records with the Browse screen. (a) To delete a record, Rita moves to the record she wants to remove and presses F10 to move to the Records menu. (b) She then highlights Mark record for deletion and presses Enter.

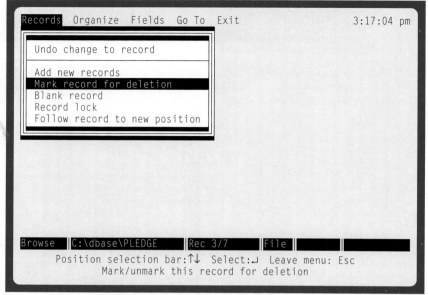

(a)

(b)

she moves the cursor to Chandler's record and presses F10 to see Browse submenus. The Records option is already highlighted. She presses Enter then uses Down Arrow to move, on the menu that appears, to Mark record for deletion (Figure 11-18a). Rita presses Enter. The word "Del" appears in the lower-right corner of the screen as the cursor rests on Chandler's record (Figure 11-18b). The record is now marked for deletion.

The process of deleting marked records in dBASE is called "packing the file." To actually delete the record Rita must now "pack" her file. She presses F10 to move to the Browse submenu. She moves to the Organize menu and, using the cursor movement keys, highlights Erase marked records (Figure 11-19a). dBASE displays the message "Are you

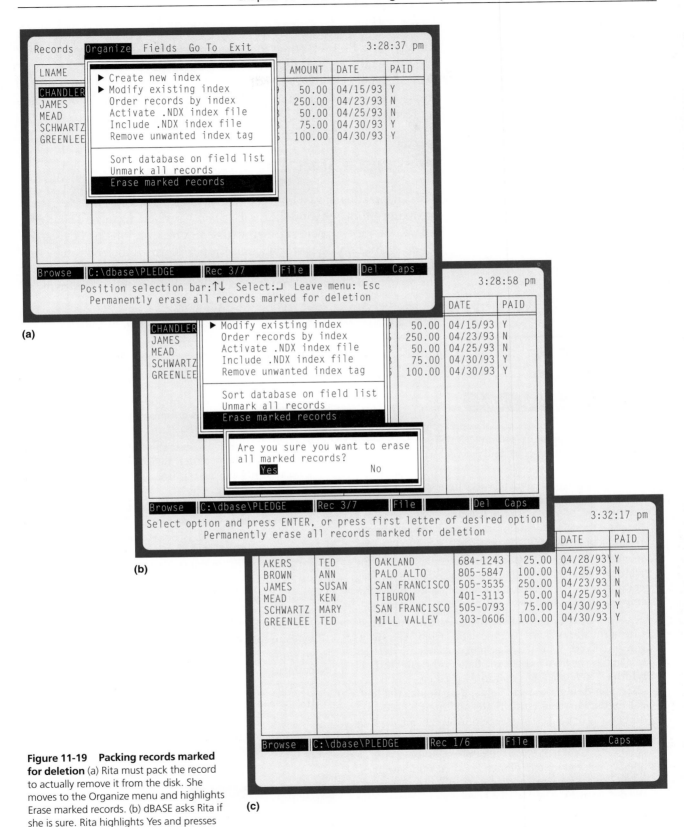

Figure 11-19 Packing records marked for deletion (a) Rita must pack the record to actually remove it from the disk. She moves to the Organize menu and highlights Erase marked records. (b) dBASE asks Rita if she is sure. Rita highlights Yes and presses Enter. The Browse screen verifies that the record has been deleted.

sure you want to erase all marked records?" Rita highlights Yes and presses Enter (Figure 11-19b). When the operation is complete, the display panel shows the message "⅙" (Figure 11-19c). This tells Rita that there are now only six records in the PLEDGE file. The Chandler record is not one of them. Rita saves these changes by pressing Ctrl-End. The Control Center reappears and Rita exits dBASE and returns to the DOS prompt.

Just a Start

This chapter has shown how powerful a database can be. However, there are many options beyond the basic capacities of setting up and changing a database—the capacities illustrated here. These options are beyond the scope of this book, but we encourage you to learn all the bells and whistles of whatever database management package you may use in the future—the payoff in time-saving convenience will make your efforts worthwhile.

R E V I E W   A N D   R E F E R E N C E

Summary and Key Terms

- A **database** is an organized collection of related data. A **database management system (DBMS)** is software that creates, manages, protects, and provides access to a database.

- A database can store data relationships so that files can be integrated. The way a database organizes data depends on the type, or **model,** of the database. There are three database models—hierarchical, network, and relational.

- In a **relational database,** data that is organized logically in a table is called a **file,** or **relation.** Each "box" in the table contains a piece of data known as a **data item.** Each column of the table represents a **field,** or **attribute.** All the data in any given row is called a **record,** or **tuple.**

- There are two steps to creating a file: designing the structure of the file and entering the data. When a file structure is defined, many database programs require the user to identify the **field names,** the **field types,** and the **field widths.** There are four commonly used types of fields: **character fields, numeric fields, date fields,** and **logical fields. Floating-point** fields and **memo fields** are other types of fields available in dBASE. The field width determines the maximum number of letters, digits, or symbols to be contained in the field.

- dBASE IV uses a system of menus called **work surfaces.** Some experts prefer to enter commands directly, using the **dot prompt,** a period displayed on the screen. The most important menu is the **Control Center,** which provides access to nearly all of the features of dBASE. Users can also work in the Command mode, in which the menu disappears and a dot prompt appears.

- In dBASE, a **catalog** is a group of related files. dBASE allows you to store a database file and files associated with it (such as reports) under the same identifier, which is like a family name; within a catalog each file has a unique file name.

- Like most database programs, dBASE has a number of commands that let you create a file structure, enter records, update records, delete records, edit records, and list records. dBASE offers a feature called **quick report** for printing a file. A **query** is a method of creating a listing of selected records and fields.

- Deleting records from a file is a two-step process. The specific records must be marked for deletion by using one command. Then the record is removed from the file by using another command.

- At times, a **relational operator** is needed when making comparisons or when entering instructions. Common relational operators include =, <, and >.

- If you need help when using dBASE, you can press F1 to access a Help screen.

- At times you may have to **pan**—move sideways across the screen—to view all the fields in a database.

Review Questions

1. What is a database?
2. What is a database management system?

3. Explain how a database management system benefits users.
4. Explain how a relational database organizes data.
5. Define the following database terms: *field, record, file.*
6. What is the database prompt that tells you that you are in Command mode?
7. List the three field specifications a database program needs to create a file structure.
8. List the four most common types of fields.
9. How can you add a record to a database file?
10. What steps must you take to delete a record from a file?

Discussion Questions

1. How much information do you think is available in electronic databases concerning you and your family?
2. What kinds of information would you want to keep in a database? Give several examples.
3. Do you think Rita's database of subscribers should be made available to local businesses by the public television station to help it raise funds for new programs?
4. Should businesses be allowed to keep database information about your buying habits?
5. Why might you *not* want your picture kept in your company's database?

True-False Questions

T F 1. A database management system allows fast and easy access to data.
T F 2. The type of database most often used on personal computers is the relational database.
T F 3. The Control Center in dBASE allows you access to nearly all features of dBASE.
T F 4. Within a database, each record may contain a different number of fields.
T F 5. Field types are largely arbitrary—the user can choose any field type for most types of data.
T F 6. The first step in creating a database is to enter data.
T F 7. In dBASE a catalog comprises all the files on one floppy disk.
T F 8. A file can be in only one catalog at a time.
T F 9. Browse and Edit allow a user to make the same types of changes.
T F 10. Once you enter data records into a database file, you can add more records but you cannot delete old records.

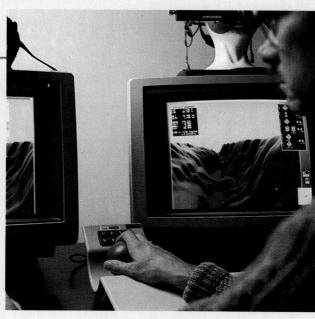

CHAPTER

12

Computer Graphics

From Art to Animation and Beyond

Jed McReynolds and his family were looking forward to their annual
vacation. For as long as he could remember, Jed had visited his local
AAA auto club office for help in planning his driving route. But this
year was different. His neighbor, Frank Lee, invited him over to see his
new IBM personal computer and try out a program called Automap Road
Atlas, which offers details on more than 52,000 cities and nearly 360,000
miles of roads in the U.S. After Jed typed in his starting point, departure time, and destination, the software displayed a colorful map of his
route and plotted both the shortest and fastest routes, including an estimated time of arrival for each stop along the way. The output was

405

based on Jed's preferred driving speeds and preferred route. The software even mentioned points of interest he might want to see. A printout provided the map and directions he needed. Jed was so pleased with the convenience of the software, he canceled his visit to the AAA office and mused about buying his own PC when he got back from his trip.

 ## *The Rise of Computer Graphics*

Computer graphics only recently emerged in their own right as a major—and sometimes spectacular—part of the computer industry. But, you may ask, who uses computer graphics? The answer is just about everyone. What reader could possibly be unaware of video games? Who has not seen television station logos, commercials, news programs, or movies that use computer-produced animated graphics? Computer graphics can also be found in education, art, science, sports—in fact, just about everywhere (see Figure 12-1).

Figure 12-1   Computer graphics. Both the world of science and the world of art benefit from the power of computer graphics.

Anyone who wants to communicate effectively in today's world must take into consideration society's reliance on visual communication. Think of the many professionals who use computers to create their wares: architects, engineers, illustrators, and designers. In the past, these professionals have used a drawing board, pen, and paper in a process that involved relatively low cost, ready access, and total control over graphics production. But consider the *process*—especially the repetition of drawing and erasing, painting, and starting over. There is much to be said for electronic programs that allow you to undo or erase quickly, eliminate the need to repeat physical strokes, speed up tasks by using preset formulas, and provide lightning-fast delivery.

There are many reasons why you might want to use computer graphics. The precision of the computer allows you to produce an image just the way *you* want it. The ease with which the computer lets you experiment with templates allows you to replace designs, layouts, and palettes quickly and efficiently. Artwork that you create digitally is easy to store and retrieve. And don't forget: Electronic colors never fade!

We start our introduction to computer graphics with a look back at early efforts.

Early Computer Graphics

Long before personal computers appeared on the scene, computer graphics consisted of text characters arranged to look like figures. For example, you can easily recognize how text characters were used to recreate the popular "Kilroy was here" drawing, which adorned the walls of many public places beginning in the 1940s.

During the 1970s, some "graphic" standards emerged in computer communications. Compact symbols evolved to provide the emphasis or context that would normally be "lost in the translation" from spoken to written communications. The symbols, such as those that follow, use just three punctuation marks each to create expressive faces. (Look at them sideways.)

:-) Smiling face

:-] Smirking face

;-) Winking face

:-(Frowning face

The use of those text-based symbols continues in E-mail conversations and telecommunications today. But graphics standards have emerged that allow us to produce spectacular high-resolution pictures that rival—and even go beyond—anything done by hand with paint or other traditional media.

With the emergence of quality displays and printers capable of superhigh resolution and millions of colors, the level of graphics available today is amazing. Just *how* amazing is a subject that we will discover as we turn to the matter of how computers create pictures.

How Do Computers Create Graphics?

Computers are by nature "number machines." Their power with numbers must be used creatively to generate pictures. A computer can produce pictures because a computer monitor consists of **pixels** (*pic*ture *el*ements, or individual dots). A pixel can be either on or off—lighted or not. A monitor's **resolution**—its ability to display fine details in pictures—is based on a number of factors, chief among them being the number, size, and type of pixels (Figure 12-2). Pixels can be small or large, round or square (or even rectangular). In general, the smaller the pixel, the higher the resolution. And, because small square pixels can be set closer together than small round ones, square pixels produce higher resolution than round ones. When perceived by the human eye, tiny pixels form the pictures we see; examine a newspaper photo closely and you can see that, like a monitor, it is made up of dots. Changing the pixel-lighting sequence rapidly creates animated pictures.

What you see on a computer monitor also depends on the way the hardware displays pixels. Most computer operating systems have the capacity to display numbers, characters, and symbols quickly. The pixels that make them up are accessed in groups, so "pixel pictures" can be created with little delay.

In early personal computers, graphics capabilities evolved as their markets grew. For example, the IBM PC began life as a text-based system; graphics came as an afterthought. IBM added on graphics capa-

Figure 12-2 Pixel. Think of your computer screen as a Cartesian coordinate system. That simply means it is a grid, allowing you to pinpoint a location on the screen. The screen shown is 1024 pixels × 800 pixels, or 819,200 pixels. With so many pixels, this screen has very high resolution. The round pixel (colored dot) shown is at the intersection of 7,2. When that pixel is turned on, a dot will light up on your screen—and disappear when turned off.

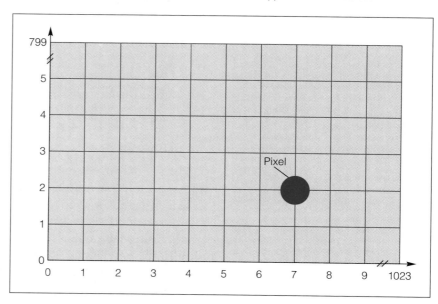

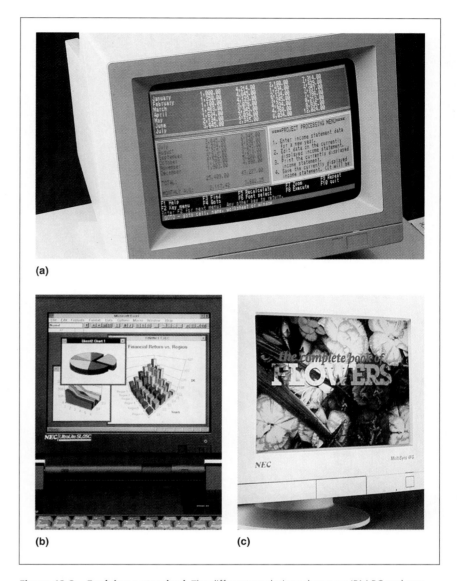

(a)

(b) (c)

Figure 12-3 Evolving a standard. The different resolutions shown on IBM PC and compatible monitors illustrate the evolution of graphics standards from the original text-based IBM operating system. Three generations are represented: (a) the color graphics adapter (CGA), (b) the video graphics adapter (VGA), and (c) the super video graphics adapter (SVGA).

bility by evolving new resolution standards and the hardware to support them. As Figure 12-3 shows, **CGA** (color graphics adapter), **EGA** (extended graphics adapter), and **VGA** (video graphics adapter) represented advances in graphics. Subsequent improvements—**SVGA** (super VGA adapter) and **XGA** (extended VGA adapter)—have made computer graphics even better. The Apple II line of personal computers also evolved higher screen resolutions with each new generation. When Apple released the Macintosh in 1984, it shifted to a fully graphical environment. The standard 9-inch monochrome screen of the Macintosh Classic family has a resolution of 512×342 pixels. The Macintosh II

Figure 12-4   Graphics systems. Popular computer graphics systems are manufactured by (a) Apple, (b) NeXT, and (c) Sun. All feature graphics capabilities favored by architects, engineers, and scientists, among others.

family offers a color monitor with a resolution of 640 × 480 pixels—the same as IBM's VGA standard. Higher-resolution monitors can be added with hardware changes; they are usually standard on Apple's Macintosh Quadra computers, NeXT systems, and Sun workstations (Figure 12-4).

Graphics Fundamentals

There are two fundamental types of graphic images created by computers: bitmapped (raster) graphics and object (vector) graphics. Another type we will look at briefly is PostScript graphics, which have emerged as the most popular graphics for high-quality printing and publishing. Each type has its advantages and disadvantages.

Bitmapped Graphics   When you want to "paint" a line or swash on a monitor, you can use bitmapped graphics. With **bitmapped graphics** pictures are created by turning individual pixels on and off in a coordinate grid that divides the display area. Another name for this type of graphics is **raster graphics,** based on **raster-scan technology,** in which electric beams cause the screen to emit light to produce a screen image. The Macintosh and Microsoft Windows operating environments display text; graphics; and icons, menus, and on-screen windows as bitmapped graphics. The resolution of the image corresponds to the resolution of the monitor.

Graphics software packages that use bitmapping are called **paint programs.** The MacPaint program (originally released with the first Macintosh) set the standard for paint programs. It offered a palette of tools for drawing lines, boxes, circles, and text, along with tools like a "paint bucket" that let you fill enclosed areas with patterns and an "eraser" that let you rub out anything you dragged it over. For IBM PCs and computers compatible with them, a popular paint program is PC Paintbrush Plus (Figure 12-5).

Most paint programs contain on-screen icons that represent tools. The tools mimic traditional drawing and painting tools—pencil, paint-

Figure 12-5   Paint program. Paint programs like PC Paintbrush Plus offer a palette of tools represented by icons. You select the tool that is appropriate for creating the graphic element you need. For example, to draw lines, you select the tool represented by the pencil icon; to fill in enclosed sections of the screen with a color or pattern, you select the paint bucket icon.

brush, pen, paint bucket, and paint spray can. Some even provide special tools for smearing, blending, and other advanced techniques. To create an image, you move a pointing device across the screen, turning pixels on or off. In color programs, each pixel contains closely spaced red, green, and blue pixels whose intensity can be varied to provide different colors. Paint programs do not "remember" that a shape is a shape, a line is a line, or even that a character of text is simply that. Once something has been painted on the screen, it is merely a collection of pixels. Therefore, shapes cannot be altered except by painting over them, and text cannot be edited except by painting more text over it. If you do not plan to make changes to your picture later, then bitmapped graphics may meet your needs.

However, you as artist can express just about any feeling you want in a paint program. You just cannot change things as you could in an object graphics program, where such drawbacks disappear.

Object Graphics   When you want to experiment or you are not sure if the image you are creating will be the final one, you need a graphics program that "remembers." A system that creates **object graphics** can remember what is drawn. Creating object graphics involves turning on and off pixels by plotting **vectors**—points that define lines and geometric shapes, such as circles, rectangles, ellipses, and trapezoids. These plots are actually mathematically computed formulas called **algorithms**—the basic building blocks of the tools used to create object graphics. Since individual pixels are turned on and off by means of formulas (which can easily be recalled to repeat the graphic or adjusted to begin the image at another location or resize the image), object graphics are very flexible. The essential difference between bitmapped and object graphics is in the way the software forms them (Figure 12-6), but to users the striking distinction is that object graphics software allows the computer to remember images, so the images can be changed. Systems that remember need large amounts of memory.

Graphics programs that produce object graphics are called **draw pro-**

Figure 12-6   Bitmapped vs. object graphics. The computer creates graphics in two fundamentally different ways. Using a traditional drawing of a house as the original (a), a paint program (b) creates an image by using raster-scan technology, or bitmapping—in other words, by turning on individual pixels in a grid. A draw program (c) uses the vector method; it connects lines between individual points to form an object graphic.

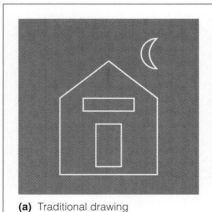

(a) Traditional drawing

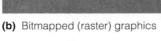

(b) Bitmapped (raster) graphics

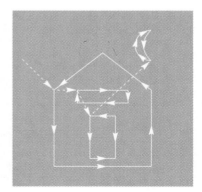

(c) Object (vector) graphics

Figure 12-7   Draw program. Draw programs like CorelDRAW allow you to use tools just like a paint program—with several additions, especially the ability to remember what is drawn for easier revision at a later time.

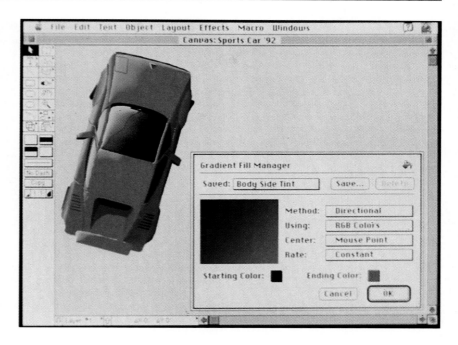

grams. The tools of such programs like CorelDRAW (Figure 12-7) let the user create perfect circles, squares, rectangles, or any other closed geometric shape. One of its most popular capabilities is the ability to produce **fractal graphics.** These images are derived from fractal geometry, which uses special formulas to calculate complex equations quickly. Computer artists use fractal graphics when they need to draw lines that resemble natural boundaries, such as mountain ranges or coastlines (Figure 12-8). Such shapes can be filled with colors, patterns, or shades of gray. In addition, since text created with object graphics is remembered, it can be edited and changed easily. Because the shape, position, and parts of objects are recallable, their starting points can be relocated easily; moreover, the original size of a graphic can be changed proportionally or kept in perspective while changed in size. Some programs—such as SuperPaint from Aldus—offer both object and paint graphics.

PostScript Graphics   The enormous amount of memory required to create very elaborate graphics has inspired product developers to find ways to cut down memory use. That is what PostScript graphics are all about. **PostScript** is a specific *language* that describes computer graphics in a way that uses much less memory than other methods. PostScript was developed to drive high-resolution output devices such as laser printers, imagesetters, and film processors. Like draw programs, PostScript graphics programs remember what they draw, but they do more than merely convert lines and shapes into algorithms. PostScript creates a kind of outline of a character, then uses special "hints" to round out rough edges. This produces precise and readable characters— of just about any size—that can be resized quickly without a loss of quality. PostScript is often called a *page description language* because

Spaceballs: 3-D Mouse Input

Perhaps you have seen one of the 3-D movies that came out of the 1950s. The theater audience wore special colored glasses and nearly jumped out of their seats because monsters looked as if they were crashing right out of the screen.

The techniques of 3-D have come a long way since then. Today there is 3-D visualization technology at work in modeling, flight simulation, multidimensional geometry, and other aspects of computer graphics. Input devices for 3-D include the spaceball, which is like a mouse or trackball that the user can move in space.

Figure 12-8   Fractal graphics. Fractal images are popular because the formulas that draw them do an excellent job of portraying the jagged boundaries of mountain ridges as well as more abstract patterns.

you can use it to save a whole page as a graphic image.

PostScript has become the standard for graphics output devices. In addition, it is important for anyone who plans to create publications using high-resolution monitors to understand one of the popular ways of saving and sending graphics, called *Encapsulated PostScript (EPS)*. An EPS file allows a publisher to preview the placement of a low-resolution image on a page, while saving space in the final product by including the PostScript code only in the file sent to a printer.

Now we turn to input devices used with graphics software.

Graphics Input Devices

There are many ways to produce and interact with computer graphics. The following are some of the most common. Some of these devices can also be used for input other than graphics.

Light Pens   For direct interaction with your computer screen, few devices beat a light pen. It is versatile enough to modify graphics on-screen or to choose from a menu of activities on the screen. A **light pen** has a light-sensitive cell at the end. When it is placed against the screen, the light pen closes a photoelectric circuit and so pinpoints the place on-screen where pictures or data can be entered or modified.

Game Sticks   The best known of this category of input device is the **joystick** that appeared with the first computer games. But joysticks have evolved into many styles of input devices, including hand grips, steer-

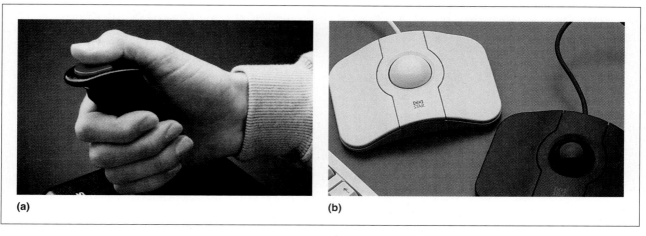

(a)   **(b)**

Figure 12-9   Game sticks. The original input device for commercial computer games was the joy stick. Today there are any number of variations, including (a) grips that look like they belong in jet fighters and (b) combination joy stick–and–mouse devices.

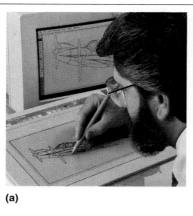

(a)

(b)

Figure 12-10   Digitizers. (a) An engineer uses a digitizing tablet to input his drawing and sees the results immediately on the computer screen. (b) Artists also benefit from digitizers, which can offer a means of natural, pressure-sensitive input. The digitizer shown here is the Wacom graphic tablet.

ing wheels, and even combination mouse-joysticks (Figure 12-9). The joystick for games was the first popular input device used for graphics. Today there are even 3-D devices that let you control more than a single dimension of space (see the accompanying essay, "Spaceballs: 3-D Mouse Input"). Most graphics programs require a mouse or digitized pen to provide input.

Digitizers   An image—whether a drawing or a photo—can be scanned by a device called a **digitizer,** which converts the image into digital data that the computer can accept and represent on the screen. A **digitizing tablet** lets you create your own images. This device has a special stylus that can be used to draw or trace images, which are then converted to digital data that can be processed by the computer (Figure 12-10a). With a pressure-sensitive device like the pen used with the Wacom graphic tablet (Figure 12-10b), software can emulate many of the aspects of traditional artistic media.

Synthesizers   Another graphics input device—better known among musicians—is the piano-like instrument called a **synthesizer,** which can sound like any musical instrument. Combined with music software, synthesizers can not only imitate any instrument, but they can also be used to compose music—the result appears on-screen as musical notation, which a laser printer can output as sheet music. In some cases, the composition process can be a very graphic one (in this chapter, see the essay called "A New Face for Your Interface").

Scanners   You probably have seen pictures that strike you as perfect for supplementing something you are writing. If you are using a word processor, you can capture the picture in digitized form and then add it to your document. To do this, you need to use an input device called

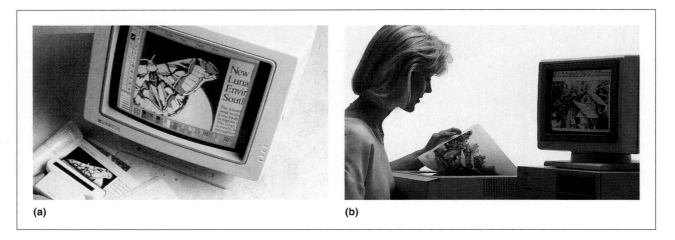

(a)   **(b)**

Figure 12-11   Scanners. (a) As this hand-held scanner is moved over a picture, the image appears on the computer screen. (b) A picture is laid face down on this desktop scanner, which looks somewhat like a small copy machine. Both black-and-white and color images can be scanned. The resulting resolution can be up to 600 dots per inch or higher.

a **scanner.** A scanner photographs—on a line-by-line basis—anything it can view. For example, as you move a handheld scanner over a news clipping, the same text and picture in that clipping appear on the screen of your personal computer; when you finish, the image can be moved into a graphics program and further manipulated, stored on a disk, or even placed in a word processing/desktop publishing document. Scanners come in many forms (Figure 12-11). There are even inexpensive, personal scanners that can translate slides—either negative or positive film—into video signals and send the signals to a computer monitor for use in a presentation program such as PowerPoint. All such input devices can scan black and white, several shades of gray, and color. Files created by scanning are really graphics files, not text files. Before you can edit scanned-in text, you must use optical character recognition (OCR) software to read it; this process converts the graphics characters into the codes necessary for text characters. Such conversions may introduce minor errors, so someone usually reviews scanned-in text for accuracy. Once converted, files created by scanning can be used like any other files: They can be edited, printed, and so forth, making the scanner a very useful device.

Who needs a scanner? Anyone who dislikes typing—or wants to avoid adding typographical errors to a document. This usually occurs when long documents or book-length treatises must be retyped—scanning to the rescue! For example, teachers can scan text in books for use in classroom exercises, lawyers can scan contracts, and publishers can save the cost of retyping manuscripts.

Figure 12-12   Touch screen. A pointing finger interrupts light beams emitted from the edges of the screen. The computer translates the interruption into a point on the screen.

Touch Screens   If you disdain pens and mice, perhaps you would prefer the direct human touch—your finger. **Touch screens** accept input data by letting you point at the screen to select your choice (Figure 12-12). Sensors on the edges of the screen pinpoint the touched location and cause a corresponding action on the screen.

Digital Still Cameras   Cameras like Logitech's Fotoman (Figure 12-13a) let you snap up to 32 digital images, which can then be transferred di-

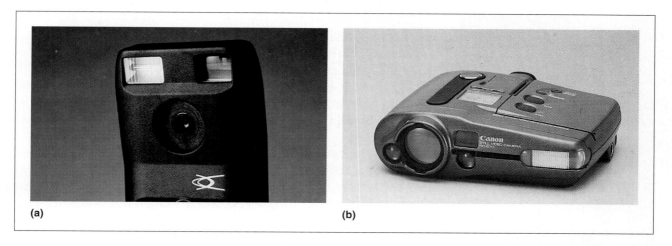

(a)   (b)

Figure 12-13   Digital still cameras.
(a) Fotoman from Logitech Corporation was the first inexpensive digital camera to allow a picture to be piped directly into a personal computer. At about $800, Fotoman is a black-and-white camera that does not need special digitizing equipment, as (b) Xapshot from Canon, does.

rectly to your personal computer. No film is involved. You can use software to manipulate your pictures and then move them into a letter, memo, report, electronic mail message, fax, or overhead transparency. The $799 Fotoman can be used for real estate, inventory, ID, and other purposes—wherever low resolution black-and-white images are acceptable. But high resolution color photographs are more the reserve of Canon's Xapshot Still Video Camera (Figure 12-13b), which captures up to 50 images on a diskette, then uses special equipment to transfer them to a personal computer for manipulation, a process which clears the Xapshot's floppy disk for reuse.

Digital Video Imaging   With the emergence of techniques that squeeze graphics into smaller chunks of memory suitable for personal computers, you have the ability to show movies or television right on your computer screen. In the past this has only been possible with costly equipment additions, so few personal computers have had access to this technology. Today, the process involves first obtaining the pictures through video cameras, videodiscs, or television; using a high resolution video board to digitize them; manipulating the digitized images with a software program (such as Adobe's Premiere); and compressing or decompressing them with a program like QuickTime, from Apple, which is fast enough to run the images as movies. Film-making on the desktop seems to be in sight.

Graphics Output Devices

Just as there are many different ways to input graphics to the computer, there are many different ways to output graphics. Essentially, graphics can be output on a screen, paper, an overhead transparency, or a 35mm slide. We have already discussed screens, so now we will look at other graphics output devices.

Plotters   Plotters draw hard-copy graphics output in the form of maps, bar charts, engineering drawings, and even two- or three-dimensional illustrations. Plotters often come with a set of four pens in four differ-

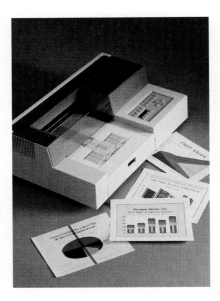

Figure 12-14 A plotter. Designers of circuit boards, street maps, schematic diagrams, and similar products can work in fine detail on a computer screen, then print the results on a plotter.

ent colors. Most plotters also offer shading features. Plotters are of two types: flatbed and drum.

A **flatbed plotter** looks like a drafting table with a sheet of paper on it and a mechanical pen suspended over it (Figure 12-14). The pen is at an angle to the table and moves around on the paper under the control of a computer program. The flatbed is commonly used for engineering drawings. Small flatbed plotters are also available for personal computers.

The paper for a **drum plotter** is rolled around a cylinder—the drum—instead of being flat on a table. A pen is poised over the drum. If the pen is placed on the paper while the drum unrolls the paper (which is taken up temporarily on another drum), a straight line is drawn along its length. On the other hand, if the pen is moved across the paper while the paper remains in place, a line is drawn across the paper. You can visualize the various diagonal lines and curves that can be drawn with combinations of drum and pen movement. One advantage of a drum plotter is that the sheet of paper can be quite long, which is necessary in certain scientific work.

Printers As we noted earlier, some printers are capable of producing graphics. Although graphics are most dramatic on a screen or on a slide produced from a screen, many users need to include graphics in reports, so printers that can produce graphics play an important role.

Overhead Transparencies When making a presentation to a group, fancy graphics are not much help when they appear only on your computer screen or on paper. Transparencies used on an overhead projector are one way to present information to a group. Some plotters and printers are capable of producing overhead transparencies because they can print on a sheet of acetate instead of paper. Laser printers do an excellent job of creating overhead transparencies.

Overhead Projection Devices A number of overhead projection devices have evolved, though for some reason a clever, hi-tech name for them has not. These devices are really flatpanel, liquid-crystal displays (LCDs) connected to a personal computer. They can be placed atop an overhead projector, just like a transparency, allowing a roomful of people to view what is on the computer screen. Instead of showing static overheads, you can use a standard personal computer to create a dynamic presentation. These overhead devices can project both black-and-white and color displays. And, because it is difficult to manipulate the computer and point out things on the screen at the same time, you can use the mouse to point on the computer screen if you are near it. If you are not near the computer, you might use one of the new pointing instruments that can be used like an old-fashioned ruler. From anywhere in the room, these fairly inexpensive pen-like devices use a laser beam to cast a red dot on the screen.

35mm-Slide Makers We mentioned the slide scanner in the section about input, but when it comes to creating slides in the first place, you no longer have to depend on a professional graphic artist to produce them. With the emergence of personal computers that create screens for use in presentations, a number of production alternatives have arisen. If you can save screen graphics on disk, you can take the disk in (or mail it) to a processing service that will provide slides of your computer graphics. In addition, there are various devices available that allow you to produce your own 35mm slides of computer screens. Some use a camera that attaches to your computer—one end of a cone-shaped device fits over the camera, and the wide rectangular end fits exactly over the screen. Just click, and you capture your computer graphic on film that can be developed by standard processing. One device, the Polaroid Palette, produces instant slides. This system does not photograph your screen; instead, it uses graphics data to produce a digital image. It can even colorize your graphics by creating color slides from a black-and-white computer monitor.

Video Cassette Recorders   Permanent graphic output does not have to be still. Specially designed video cassette recorders (VCRs) and video recorders can be hooked into computer systems. You can then edit the tape by computer before storing the final product on videotape.

CD-ROM   The same technology that gave us CD music provides the capability of delivering, on CD-ROM, enormous amounts of data to your personal computer. As sales of CD music exploded, the price of manufacturing came down, encouraging developers of large programs to take advantage of CD-ROM's enormous capacity. With about 600 megabytes of space available—the same capacity as 500 high-density, 5¼-inch floppy disks—a CD-ROM disc can hold music, sound, animation, graphics, video, and even movies. For example, when packed on a CD-ROM, a computerized encyclopedia like *Compton's Multimedia Encyclopedia* can offer the usual textual information about a U.S. president and also include sound excerpts from interviews, photographs, and even a video clip of a famous speech—all adding to the excitement of learning. In addition, CD-ROM has multiple audio tracks that allow developers to include more than one language for the same sound bites.

For several years now, CD-ROM drives and discs have been moving into businesses, government agencies, and libraries, where they have replaced file cabinets and microfiche readers. More recently, the general public has started to buy into the technology, encouraged by pioneering titles like Microsoft's Multimedia Beethoven: The Ninth Symphony and Broderbund's interactive book *Just Grandma and Me.*

Although most CD-ROM disc drives are made in Japan by companies like Toshiba, Hitachi, Sony, NEC, Pioneer, and Matsushita, there is one major exception—Philips NV, the Dutch electronics conglomerate that helped Sony pioneer compact disc technology in the late 1970s. But some U.S. companies are also involved. In spring 1991, Microsoft, Tandy, NCR, and eight other major computer firms formed the Multimedia PC Marketing Council to promote CD-ROM and establish multimedia standards. Since then, computers bearing the council's MPC

A NEW FACE FOR YOUR INTERFACE

Some computer researchers believe that consumers may soon find it no harder to operate a computer than to talk to a clerk or an information agent. But it may take an unusual change in the user interface—the way we interact with computers. A notion once considered radical is now being tried at Sony's research and development labs in Tokyo. And Sony is getting encouragement from several American companies, including Apple Computer. What is this interface? A face.

Picture the scenario: Seated at a synthesizer, a young lady improvises on the keyboard of an electric piano hooked up to a high-powered computer graphics system. On the

screen before her is a face only a mother could love—the face was derived from a No mask. (No is classical Japanese dance-drama known for heroic subjects and measured movements and chants.) In any case, the face can show a wide range of emotions. As the woman improvises on the keyboard, the face responds to changes in tempo or melody, providing feedback. If it "likes" the sounds, it shows joy; if not, it shows perplexity or dislike. It can even stick out its tongue or provide a smack—a kiss—of support.

One reason for its realism is that each part of the face is programmed to tense up or relax independently, but each can act smoothly in combination with others. The software already has been used to demonstrate a new

graphics system called System G, which Sony sells to TV producers. It creates such special effects as wrapping the face of the commentator around a football and "kicking" it through the goalposts.

Within a decade, according to those who follow user interface designs, computers may appear more human-like, and your interaction with them may be almost pleasurable. Speech recognition software may enable the machine to understand you, and the machine may provide the right facial expressions in response. Also—as strange as it may seem—you may not have to talk to your computer at all. Research under way may lead to computers that can gauge your mood and even read your lips. George Bush would like that.

logo are required to have at least a 386SX microprocessor; 2 megabytes of RAM; a 30-megabyte hard drive; a VGA display; a mouse and a keyboard; serial, parallel, MIDI (music interface), and joystick ports; headphones or speakers; and DOS.

CD-ROM is also helping Kodak counter the influence of the Fotoman and Xapshot cameras (mentioned in "Digital Still Cameras" above) in the photography market. Kodak's new Photo CD system does an end-run around the expense of digital imaging cameras by giving the installed base of 35mm camera users a way to digitize their film onto CD-ROM. You bring your regular film roll into a photofinishing outlet and in one to three days you get a gold compact disc with your digitized photos and set of color proofs (small picture replicas) as the cover. A set of 24 color exposures costs about $18. You can also order sets of prints from either your negatives or the Photo CD.

The CD-ROM is often confused with CD-I (Philips) and CDTV (Commodore), two rival media. Philips recently announced a joint venture with Nintendo, the maker of the popular video game units, to produce a CD-ROM system that would be compatible with Super Nintendo units and CD-I (the "I" stands for *Interactive*) technology. Commodore launched its product, CDTV (a digital disc player that connects to a television set), in January 1991. Its relatively high price ($995) and a lack of software have kept sales down. Sega and NEC have also announced video game units with add-on CD-ROM drives. Later in this chapter we will take a brief look at the rise of video games and their impact on the world of computer graphics.

Graphics Formats

Once you have used a graphics software program or various input devices to create a computer graphic, you may want to save the image for later use. **Graphics formats** determine the way a picture is stored on disk. A picture created by PostScript code is saved in a different format than a picture saved by a paint program (which only copies the pixels that form the image). Some common examples of graphics formats include the PICT format, which almost every Macintosh graphics program can use, and the PCX format, which is a standard graphics format for IBM and IBM-compatible machines and the format used by PC Paintbrush Plus. Some format names, such as PICT, describe the purpose of the format; others are initials. TIFF (.TIF for DOS computers) stands for *Tagged Image File Format*. The TIFF format is used by most scanners and has been widely adopted for creating bitmapped graphics. In fact, graphics formats run the gamut from simple to incredibly complex. The complex ones use compression techniques to limit memory use. The best graphics software programs can be used with many graphic formats.

If you want to move a picture from one graphics program to another (or even from one word processing or desktop publishing program to another), you need to know what format the program uses. If you add the more complex step of transferring graphics between computers with different operating systems, you also need to be able to convert the files from one system to the other. Depending on the programs involved, this can be relatively easy or impossible. For example, the PageMaker program runs on both the Macintosh and IBM machines, so the documents—including most graphics created with one machine—can be transferred easily to the other by using an external conversion program like MacLink PC Plus.

However, converting a picture from one graphic format to another may involve the loss of data, precision, color fidelity, or other critical factors. Some formats—such as GIF, a compressed graphics format used for sending color images over phone lines—are designed to use space efficiently. Other formats—TIFF, for example—require vast amounts of disk storage and may take a while to load or convert. Color graphics formats are often described in terms of the number of bits used per pixel to represent data about color: 4-bit graphics allow up to 16 colors, 8-bit graphics allow 256 colors, and 24-bit graphics provide millions of colors and can achieve photographic realism. Keep in mind that 24-bit, for instance, means 24 bits for each pixel. Therefore, the more bits of data graphics require, the more space they take up when stored on disk. Some color images can take up all the space on an 80-megabyte (or larger) hard disk drive. Now let us take a closer look at color graphics.

Color Graphics

What many artists learn when they first dip their electronic brushes into a computer graphics color palette is that the fire-engine red they

Printing Documents with Custom Colors

The first time you print a document with colors, you will notice that there is a difference between the printed colors and the colors on your monitor. Not only that, if you print the same document on two different output devices, you may also see color variations. How do you control this?

Many software programs allow you to create a customized set of colors called a palette. It is best to use a swatch book to do this. For documents that will be printed, the most helpful systems are either the PMS (Pantone Matching System) or CMYK modes. You can buy the *Pantone Formula Guide* for PMS samples, or the *Pantone Process Color Selector* for CMYK samples at any art store with a graphic arts department. The Process Color Selector shows every possible combination of the four basic colors—from one to all four (cyan, magenta, yellow, and black)—in incremental variations from 0% to 100%. You can then enter these numbers onto your palette. Choosing colors based on what you see in your books instead of what is shown on the monitor is the best way to envision the final output.

If it is critical to get the output color just right, you can create your own sample swatches. After you select the colors in your palette, you make a document showing at least one square inch of each color and print it on your intended output device. If you feel the need to recalibrate any color, you can make changes before the bulk of your work has begun. You can then complete your document, confident that your control of color has been as precise as possible.

paint or draw on a screen turns weak or faded when printed on paper—or worse, ends up purple when output to a slide. Why? There are a number of reasons, but the basic problem stems from the difference between how color is created on a screen and how it is created on paper or film.

First of all, different output devices vary in the way they represent color. A monitor displays color by lighting up phosphors on the screen. A color printer may transfer patterns of colored dots on paper, and printing presses overlay various tints of ink to produce a desired color. Color slides are made by exposing color film. These are different technologies, so each has a different way of achieving the same color.

Second, color representation is further complicated by the various **color models**—systematic ways for describing color. For example, computers describe color numerically and people describe color visually. The most well-known model is probably the **red-green-blue (RGB)** model used by TV screens, computer monitors, and slide recorders (which create slides from computer output). The RGB model is based on an additive process, meaning that light is *added* to create various colors. The opposite—a subtractive process—is the basis of the **cyan-magenta-yellow-black (CMYK)** model. This is the model used by printing presses and color printers, and it involves subtracting light to create color. Human vision uses a model called **hue-saturation-brightness (HSB),** which generally defines *hue* as our ability to distinguish different colors, *saturation* as our ability to see various shades of the same color, and *brightness* as our ability to distinguish the brightness of each color. Since HSB values can be transformed to RGB values through an arithmetic calculation, you can easily set your RGB screen by using your own visual capabilities. The best graphics software support these and many other models.

To ensure color correspondence among screens, some professionals use a **swatch book,** a collection of colors produced by a printer. Others use **calibration devices** to help ensure that what appears on one monitor is the same as what appears on the monitor down the hall and that color output from devices such as color printers corresponds closely to the color on the screen. Since most programs and devices contribute only partial solutions to the problem of "color-tuning" different pieces of equipment, graphics users eagerly await a **device-independent color standard.** This standard will allow effortless transfer from the screen to paper or film and vice versa.

Using Computer Graphics

Depending on how you plan to use computer graphics—for personal or business uses; for presentations, illustrations, mapping, or design; in multimedia; or for games and entertainment—creating computer graphics requires different amounts of memory and power, as well as different levels of monitor and printer resolution. Let us look at some of the ways graphics are being used.

Personal Graphics

Perhaps you are a visual learner. Nowadays, when many homes often have more than one television, it is hard *not* to grow up as a visual learner. Most of us spend more time watching television, videotapes, and movies than reading books, magazines, or newspapers. Whether good or bad, our daily contact with TV and computer monitors is helping us to develop a visual vocabulary as impressive as our verbal vocabulary. Most of us are rapidly becoming very sophisticated about graphic images. Our maturity shows when we start using graphics to *communicate* rather than simply to *decorate*.

Personal graphics programs let you create professional-quality greeting cards, flyers, banners, stationery, and even awards and certificates (Figure 12-15). Even if your artistic talent has not been tapped since you made your last finger painting in kindergarten, you can create an artistic impression by using the collections of **clip art**—ready-made images that you can "clip" and drop into your document—available with many graphics programs. With these programs you can electronically cut and paste your way around your own computerized print shop.

Business Graphics

Business graphics give you the ability to supplement numeric text with graphic depictions. Colorful graphics, maps, and charts help managers compare data more easily, spot trends, and make decisions more quickly. The use of color also has an impact that helps people get the picture—literally. And, although color graphs and charts have been around businesses for years, the computer allows users to create, automatically, graphs based on facts in spreadsheet or database files or on data input

Figure 12-15 Personal graphics. Programs like Print Shop allow nonartists to create artistic greeting cards, banners, flyers, and other printed materials. With collections of templates available, users select from menus of options, type in personal messages, and add clip art—ready-made, copyable pictures. Then they print out professional-quality pieces.

Figure 12-16 Business graphics. (a) A large amount of data can be translated into (b) one simple, clear graph.

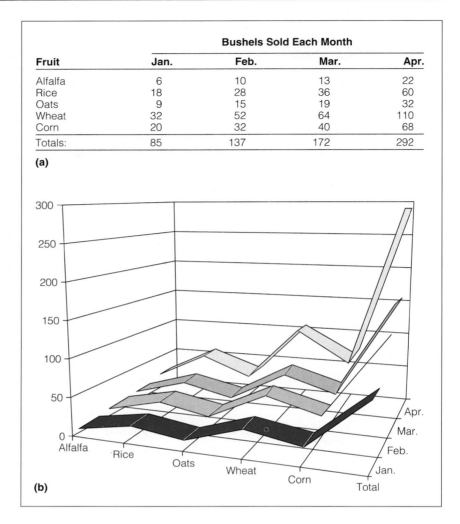

Fruit	Bushels Sold Each Month			
	Jan.	Feb.	Mar.	Apr.
Alfalfa	6	10	13	22
Rice	18	28	36	60
Oats	9	15	19	32
Wheat	32	52	64	110
Corn	20	32	40	68
Totals:	85	137	172	292

(a)

(b)

into the program itself (Figure 12-16). For example, a stockbroker can view stock-market price and volume charts of data from sales transactions completed that very day. One user refers to business graphics as "computer-assisted insight."

When the boss says you are in charge of presenting the latest company report to a committee, you panic first—then you remember you can do it easily with programs like Hollywood, PowerPoint, Persuasion, or Harvard Graphics. These kind of programs are generally referred to as **presentation graphics** programs because they have "slide show" capabilities that allow you to create colorful slides efficiently and present them on a computer screen or project them by connecting an overhead projector to your computer (in this chapter see the Macintosh essay, "Presentation Graphics"). Presentation programs let you create with ease large stylized text, organization charts, art and graphics in many textures and patterns, blends, and fills. Each also offers access to business clip-art collections for illustrating ideas. This area of graphics is changing rapidly, as new products like Action! and Magic emerge—products that combine the attraction of presentation graphics with the versatility of multimedia. See Chapter 10 for additional information on the use of presentation graphics in the business environment.

MACINTOSH

PRESENTATION GRAPHICS: MIXING BUSINESS WITH PLEASURE

The Macintosh is justly famous for its graphics capabilities. Little wonder, then, that the Mac has become the machine of choice for producing high-quality presentation graphics. If you need to make a presentation, graphics can make the crucial difference between communicating and not communicating. Products now available for the Mac—and rapidly becoming available for Windows on the IBM—go far beyond merely dressing up spreadsheet charts. Mac graphics products are highly integrated systems for organizing a presentation: designing illustrations; editing text and visual images; and producing colorful slides, overhead transparencies, and paper materials.

Here is a rundown of the basic features of good presentation graphics software for the Macintosh:

- Outlining tools supplied with many packages get you off to a good start, helping you organize—and easily *re*organize—your thoughts before you commit them to paper.
- Standard templates provide basic layouts that you can copy, modify, and reuse. The templates guide you in using logos, titles, text, and illustrations effectively.
- Easy-to-learn tools allow you to create, edit, and embellish graphics that are based on the data in a spreadsheet.
- An "overview" feature displays 20 or more reduced illustrations on the screen. You can access this feature while working on a specific graphic, and you are free to arrange and rearrange the reduced images in any sequence you like. Most packages also let you create speaker's notes and handouts based on these reduced images.
- Compatibility with a wide variety of devices allows output from black-and-white printers to color ink-jet, thermal, and laser printers that produce images of near-photographic quality. Service bureaus in most major cities can take the files produced by presentation graphics software and, using machines called film recorders, create dazzlingly clear and colorful 35mm slides.

As computers become commonplace resources for creating visual aids, audiences will expect more and more of presenters. You can take some comfort, then, in knowing that easy-to-use software is available to help you create a polished, first-class presentation.

ANGLES COMPANY

First Quarter Summary

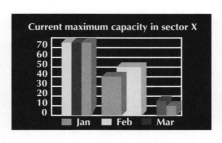

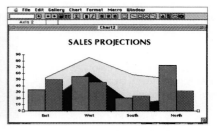

Illustration Graphics

Professional artists can fulfill their fantasies with illustration software such as CorelDRAW!, Adobe Illustrator, or Aldus FreeHand. **Illustration graphics** programs provide the quality tools a professional demands to approximate traditional approaches. These programs can produce smooth curves and subtle shading effects. In addition to providing a choice of millions of colors, patterns, and shades, illustration graphics programs support pressure-sensitive devices that make creating com-

Computer Artist . . . or just Artist?

Many people criticize computer graphics, saying they are not as good as what *real* artists can create with natural paints and brushstrokes. But Chelsea Sammel, California artist, does not consider this an issue. She calls herself an illustrator, not a *computer* illustrator. One look at her work is convincing. There is hardly any way to tell her electronic art from her own traditionally-rendered canvases.

To create "Kim Reading" (shown here), Sammel works with a 32-bit video capture and display card and a combination of tools, including a Drawing Board II digitizing tablet. She uses Painter and Oasis, paint programs designed for use with pressure-sensitive devices.

"My goal is to have something like a digital sketchboard," Sammel says. "The further I can get away from the keyboard, the better." She usually starts by sketching a simple black-and-white outline with a low-density brush. Then she creates a color palette—choosing browns, sage, and reds for highlights—and adding color with customized, heavy-density brushes set to resemble oil paints.

Sammel says digitizing tablets and pressure-sensitive devices have allowed illustrators to return to the way they used to work while providing advantages not found in traditional media. She can produce the look she wants, then send it to a client on disk for fast feedback. With computers, "the ease of moving information is greater, and it's much faster to make changes."

---

puter graphics feel more like drawing. Programs such as Aldus Photo-Shop even provide users with tools for touching up and revising photographs and other images that can be scanned in from many different media.

Mapping Graphics

Information systems used to describe geographic data take advantage of **mapping graphics** programs that combine computer graphics, spatial modeling capabilities, and database management (Figure 12-17). Such graphics programs are encouraging a new generation of mapmakers who specialize in merging crisp photo imagery from satellites and aircraft with vast available databases, providing a new kind of map that offers "layers" of information. Such maps can meet the needs of just about anyone—from a city politician who needs information about voter registration to plan for re-election, to an astronaut who needs information about the stars to determine present location in space. Envisioning data with mapping graphics lets you *see* things in a form you can understand immediately.

Video Graphics

Unbounded by the fetters of reality, graphics on the computer can be as creative as a Disney cartoon. Although **video graphics** operate on the same principle as moving pictures—one frame at a time appears in quick succession—they are produced by computer programs that com-

Figure 12-17   Mapping graphics. Mapping graphics provide more than a picture of an area viewed from above. In this case, there are layers of data available about tax base, sewer and electricity lines, population density, and just about anything you want to learn about the area. With mapping graphics, information is immediately available and interconnected.

Figure 12-18   Video graphics. This television commercial for LifeSavers Holes uses computer-generated video graphics to bring the playground scene to life.

bine graphics, animation, sound, and video into one event. Programs like Macromind Director and FilmMaker have made quite a hit in the video market, in movies, and on TV. Many people do not even realize they are watching video graphics at work (Figure 12-18). The next time you watch television, skip the snack and pay special attention to the commercials. Even when there is a live human in the advertisement, there is a good chance that the moving objects you see—cars that "morph" (turn slowly) into tigers and camera lenses that cut through solid walls with a swishing sound—are the work of computers.

Multimedia

Multimedia programs provide the capabilities of a professional mixing studio right on the desktop. Using a personal computer, you can combine computer graphics, animation, sound, and video or film into one multimedia program that can be used interactively (Figure 12-19). Many schools use such programs as MediaMaker and MediaTracks to involve students in making their own educational multimedia productions. Students learn to *repurpose* video—to cut out digitized sections from existing videodiscs and use them for their own purposes. Then they add their own sound, computer graphics, video, and even homemade movies—combining everything into a full-scale production. For example, students at one school repurposed ABC News Interactive's Quake 1989, which provides professionally produced clips of the 1989 San Francisco earthquake. By combining their own videos of school interviews with the professional clips, the students ended up with a personally involving, vivid multimedia show on earthquake safety. Students at San Francisco State University created a multimedia program called *Newcomers.* The result is an appealing look into the lives of newly arrived, foreign-born students who pass along insights to ease the frustration and isolation of newcomers who will come after them.

Multimedia graphics do not have to be commercial or educational, of course. Some multimedia artists produce beauty for its own sake

Figure 12-19   Multimedia. At the California Academy of Sciences, visitors use an interactive computer system called LifeMap to learn about evolution. This multimedia system uses a videodisc to give museum patrons access to huge amounts of information, photographs, charts, and drawings. Users can decide for themselves what and how much they want to learn.

Figure 12-20   Art for art's sake. This may look like a colorful photograph of bustling life under the sea, but it is really a computerized graphic rendering from an artist's imagination.

(Figure 12-20). An important scientific use of graphics is to construct moving models of structures too small for the human eye to see—structures such as the DNA molecule, whose atoms, represented by gleaming spheres, can be made to twist and fold. As virtual reality comes to science and astronomy, the use of multimedia graphics becomes essential for researchers who want to use these tools to "fly" through a 3-D map of Mars or "walk" through a molecule of a chemical to realize a new sense of patterning.

Computer-Aided Design/Computer-Aided Manufacturing

Computer graphics are also an essential part of a field known by the abbreviation **CAD/CAM**—short for **computer-aided design/computer-aided manufacturing.** In this area, computers are used to create two- and three-dimensional images of every kind of product from hand tools to tractors. CAD/CAM provides a bridge between design and manufacturing. Personal computer software like AutoCAD has become dominant in this field; it is used by architects and engineers in place of the traditional drawing board and drafting tools. We will examine CAD/CAM in more detail in Gallery 3, which describes manufacturing systems.

Games and Entertainment

One of the first uses of computer graphics in personal computers was for video games. In 1972, Atari Corporation began placing video games in bars around Silicon Valley in California. Pong, the first video game, was simply a table-tennis game in which a white dot randomly moved around the screen like a Ping-Pong ball. You tried to keep it on the screen by operating "paddles" on the side of the screen (two players could also play, each controlling a paddle). Pong was a big hit, catapulting Atari into home computers. After Atari introduced the superhit game Pac-Man, it became a multibillion-dollar company.

Two decades later, Nintendo, the leading video game maker in the world, can boast sales of nearly 29 million video game machines that attach to TV monitors. Nintendo's competitors, Sega and NEC, have introduced 16-bit machines that provide increased graphics resolution and new capabilities for even more astounding graphics. But Nintendo has rallied to release a 16-bit contender of its own: Super Nintendo.

Meanwhile, personal computer games and entertainment programs have continued to garner admiration and success—as well as some controversy. New offerings continue to challenge computer games enthusiasts. With the success of Pac-Man came many sequels, such as Ms. Pac-Man. In fact, most superhits are followed quickly by sequels—just as in the movies.

Entertainment offerings have certainly gone beyond Pac-Man. Some games are Star Trek–like shoot'-em-ups and some offer adventure-style interaction (where you pick the next step from a number of choices, one of which may kill you off). Of recent interest are the new education/entertainment combinations like SimEarth and SimAnt (in this chapter, see the essay "Games Galore"). Some let you control jet planes, train sets, or race cars. The interactive Cosmo Ozmo and space adventure Spaceship Warlock are so large they are best offered on CD-ROM. But,

Personal Computers in Action

GAMES GALORE

Literally thousands of computer games have emerged as screen resolution has improved, the number of screen colors has increased, and computer memory has skyrocketed.

One superstar computer game is Russian import Tetris, an amazingly addictive game that has become almost as popular as Pac-Man, the most popular computer game of all time. Invented by a young Russian hacker, Tetris won a number of awards for its tantalizing approach: It taps the player's need to create order out of chaos. In the center of the Tetris game screen, the player is presented with a series of different boxes, that appear in a steady pattern. The idea is to use the keyboard or mouse to maneuver the different shapes into place, with minimum

wasted space. Each filled line across the bottom disappears, leaving space for more boxes to fall. The game ends when the space available fills to the stop and cuts off further falling boxes. Sequels are Welltris (which uses 3-D effects) and Wordtris (which uses words).

Another award winner is SimEarth, which challenges the player's ability to control the geosphere, biosphere, hydrosphere, atmosphere, and population and avoid environmental catastrophe. Another winner from the same company, Maxis Software, is SimAnt. This game

is based on the Pulitzer prize–winning book *The Ants*. Players must learn the ant way of life, beat rival red ants, and overrun a suburban backyard and house, forcing the occupants to flee.

Spaceship Warlock is considered the first "cyberpunk" work of art on a CD-ROM. More fascinating for its artistic style than its game, the program was created by computer artist Mike Saenz. Co-designed by Joe Sparks, the program is a new kind of multimedia science-fiction novel. Like a comic book, its goal seems to be to provide an experience akin to that of the movie *Bill and Ted's Excellent Adventure*.

as in the movies, adult games like Leisure Suit Larry in the Land of Lounge Lizards threaten to bring down controversy on the industry; some are suggesting that computer games be given ratings that could restrict their purchase by children.

One way to consider change in computer graphics is to compare early video games with today's offerings. Pong was a simple square white dot you batted between two vertical white lines on the screen. Early 8-bit Nintendo game machines could show only 16 colors at one time from a total of 52. By comparision, Super Nintendo (16-bit) machines can display a set of up to 256 colors—numerous other sets are available in a library that features more than 32,000 different shades. On personal computers today, CD-ROM access and SVGA screen capabilities offer photographic-quality resolution and more than 16 million colors.

Personal In-flight TV

In the past, many people embarked on long airline trips with a book to wile away the hours. If they wanted to see a movie, they had to wait for the flight attendants to get around to setting it up for all to view. But things are changing. Today on some airlines you can sit back and pass the time by watching your own personal TV set, lodged in the back of the seat ahead of you.

Personal in-flight TV has become popular among such international airlines as Cathay Pacific, Singapore, and British Airways. BE Avionics has installed nearly $29 million worth of video systems in their aircraft for first-class and business-class travelers. But soon, all travelers will be flipping through the channels of their personal television sets. In fact, many believe the airline video systems will become a top revenue generator as smart features and functions are added to the service. BE Avionics already controls more than 70% of the world market for "passenger control units"—those armrest buttons you push to turn on lights, signal a flight attendant, or listen to music. The company foresees a day when airline passengers will be able to shop duty-free, order food and drinks, and even fax the office—without leaving their seats.

Another way to look at change is to study the speed of video games. In early computer games, the characters appeared to move through molasses. As computing power grew, so did the quickness of computer game displays. Now, characters can actually move faster than a speeding bullet. Although screen resolution and speed are factors in the advance of game technology, the primary trend in computer games today involves the challenges. Games are becoming more interactive, collaborative, and competitive in the midst of increasing artistry and realism.

A Graphic Future

During the last decade, the field of computer graphics has made incredible progress. Software has offered more and more features and tools and hardware has offered increased processor speed and memory size, so the typical graphics program has grown tremendously. But that's just the beginning. Soon, we are told, the desktop will get some assistance from *smart* features and tools. These features may be found on the TV set of the future—even on airline flights (see "Personal In-Flight TV," an essay in this chapter).

Decades of academic research into artificial intelligence is finally beginning to pay off with features. For example, the "Drafting Assistant" promoted in Ashlar Vellum—a graphics program available for Macintosh, Windows, and Silicon Graphics computers—is capable of supplementing a designer's skills. Running constantly in the background, this software "knows" geometric rules and can generate continuous feedback to the user about points, lines, and relationships in the drawing. The effect is to anticipate all that you may want to do—and help you do it more quickly and efficiently. (For more on artificial intelligence, see Chapter 16.)

Other examples include bells and whistles that may support a gentler human interface. For example, a program like Kid Pix—a low-cost paint program for children—features "smart" painting tools that have built-in special effects, such as stamp tools with numerous pictures, shapes and patterns. What could be smart about a paintbrush tool? How about a "tree brush" to create lines that spontaneously branch out, or a "drip brush" to leave a random trail of drops, or "wacky brushes" to accompany strokes with sounds—all adding excitement to the act of creativity.

Imagine what artists of the future may conceive when they draw or paint with a brush that "knows" the principles of good design. If you want to utilize these principles, you can. If not, you can turn them off. Such options may benefit the novice or act as reference tools for the expert. We all can use good advice, so it may benefit art in general to have tools that can help us determine style or impact and tools that can suggest still other tools, sets, palettes, or global transformations. Smart programs may help you find what you need when you need it—without your having to take time out to seek help elsewhere.

With pressure-sensitive graphic tablets, software can emulate many of the more concrete aspects of traditional artistic media. As 3-D graphic modeling comes into its own and virtual reality provides new media, the tools of the sculptor and machinist will become available in electronic form. What shape they might take or how they might allow users to interact with the environment may be as exciting and challenging as art itself.

Now that we have learned about the most popular applications, we will turn to how people use computers on the job. In Part IV, we will focus on how business harnesses the power of workplace computing, the importance of security, and how artificial intelligence is beginning to pay off.

R E V I E W A N D R E F E R E N C E

Summary and Key Terms

- Computer graphics are used in many areas—such as TV commercials, logos, movies, games, art, science, and education—but perhaps are most common in business.

- **Pixels** are the picture elements, or dots, that make up a computer screen. A monitor's **resolution** depends on the number of pixels and their size and type, among other factors.

- **CGA, EGA,** and **VGA** are graphics standards and accompanying hardware that evolved for IBM personal computers and machines compatible with them. As each new standard—CGA (color graphics adapter), EGA (enhanced graphics adapter), and VGA (video graphics adapter), **SVGA** (super VGA adapter), and **XGA** (extended VGA)—was developed, resolution improved.

- **Bitmapped graphics** are created by turning individual pixels on or off. This type of representation is also referred to as **raster graphics,** which is based on **raster-scan technology.** This technology involves dividing, with a coordinate grid, the display area of a monitor. **Paint programs** use bitmapped graphics, which differ from object graphics.

- **Object graphics** involve drawing on a monitor by connecting points with precise lines and forming geometric shapes. This type of graphic representation involves turning pixels on and off by plotting **vectors** and by computing mathematical formulas called **algorithms.** Unlike bitmapped graphics, object graphics programs can remember what they have created, so the user can revise it. **Draw programs** create object graphics.

- **Fractal graphics** are based on mathematical formulas. Fractals allow artists to quickly draw lines that resemble natural boundaries, such as mountain ridges or seacoasts.

- **PostScript** is a standard language created by Adobe Systems and used for displaying and outputting graphics quickly and efficiently.

- Besides the mouse, common graphics input devices include **light pens, digitizers, digitizing tablets, joysticks, synthesizers, scanners, touch screens,** and **digital cameras** (still and video).

- Besides screens, graphics output devices include **plotters, printers, overhead transparencies, projection devices, 35mm-slide makers, VCRs,** and **CD-ROM players.**

- Plotters draw graphics output on paper. **Flatbed plotters** look like drafting tables, but on **drum plotters** the paper is rolled on a cylinder instead of being flat on a table.

- **Graphics formats** allow users to transfer pictures from one program to another, or from one computer system to another.

- **Color models** are systematic ways to describe color produced by computers, printers, and slide recorders. **RGB (red-green-blue)** is the model used for color on screens and film, and **CMYK (cyan-magenta-yellow-black)** is the model used by computer printers. **HSB (hue-saturation-brightness)** is a model that describes the human way of envisioning color. A **device-independent color** standard will allow effortless transfer of color images from the screen to paper or film and vice versa.

- To help achieve the same colors on different types of equipment, some professionals use a **swatch book,** a collection of colors produced by a final-output press or printer. Some professionals use **calibration devices** that are attached directly to screens to ensure that one produces the same colors as another.

- **Personal graphics** let you create your own professional-quality greeting cards, banners, signs, letterheads, and certificates. Many personal graphics programs offer **clip art,** images created by professional artists, to provide that professional look.

- **Business graphics** offer businesses a way to enhance numbers with pictures. Graphics help readers understand text and presentations.

- **Presentation graphics** programs offer "slide show" capabilities. With one of these programs, anything that appears as a graphic on the computer screen can be part of a slide show.

- **Illustration graphics** programs are professional paint and draw programs used mainly by professionals. They provide the tools artists, illustrators, and graphic designers demand.

- **Mapping graphics** combine computer graphics, spatial modeling, and huge databases. The result is a "map" that depicts an area and can offer "layers" of information.

- **Video graphics** operate on the same principle as moving pictures—one frame appears after another in quick succession. When video graphics are produced by the computer, however, graphics, animation, sound, and video can be controlled by a computer program.

- **Multimedia** programs allow a user to combine computer graphics, animation, sound, and video or film in one production. With these programs users can *repurpose* sounds, video, and even film by extracting pieces from other sources and putting them together in a new production.

- In **computer-aided design/computer-aided manufacturing (CAD/ CAM),** computers are used to create two- and three-dimensional pictures of manufactured products from hand tools to robots.

- Computer games started the computer graphics industry and continue to advance the state of the art. Video game machines from Nintendo, Sega, and NEC offer more power and new ideas while computer games offer challenges that are increasingly interactive, collaborative, and competitive. The size and artistry of some computer games demand the space available only on CD-ROM.

Review Questions

1. What is a pixel and how does its shape affect screen resolution?
2. How do bitmapped and object graphics differ?
3. What is the color model used by a computer monitor?
4. Name one way a business can use graphics.
5. Name five graphics input devices and explain how each one works.
6. Name a device that is both an input and output device.

7. What is CAD/CAM, and how is CAD/CAM technology used?
8. Name two types of plotters. How do they differ?
9. Describe how a synthesizer can be classified as a graphics device.
10. What is HSB and how is it used?
11. Why is the RGB color model called additive?
12. Why is the CMYK color model called subtractive?

Discussion Questions

1. What are some advantages of creating movies entirely on computers?
2. Imagine that you have to write a term paper. What kind of graphics would be useful to add to your paper? Discuss how you might use different types of graphics for different subject areas (science, economics, history, and so on).
3. Which kind of graphics program would you use to illustrate a business report?
4. If you wanted to design a car, what kind of graphics program would you select? Why?

True-False Questions

T F   1. Computer-produced artwork can be quickly erased, revised, stored, and retrieved, so it is very appealing to artists.

T F   2. Pixels are on-screen dots that can be illuminated individually.

T F   3. The higher the resolution of the screen, the more closely the pixels are crowded together and the finer the definition of the screen image.

T F   4. The two fundamental ways computers create graphic images is through raster and vector graphics, also called bitmapped and object graphics.

T F   5. A popular way of drawing natural boundaries such as coastlines and mountain ranges involves animation graphics.

T F   6. QuickTime is a compression-decompression capability that allows a Macintosh computer to display movies.

T F   7. Digital still video cameras allow a photographer to take color pictures without using film.

T F   8. Graphic formats are the borders on computer graphics.

T F   9. Artists who use computers use calibration devices to maintain color consistency on computer screens when moving color graphics from one machine to another.

T F   10. Multimedia combines computer graphics, animation, sound, and video or film into one interactive computer program.

WORKPLACE TOOLS

13

Computers on the Job
How Workers Use Computers

When Sally Kelley was studying for her degree in accounting, she took on computers too. She knew she had to master spreadsheet software so she could propose "What if . . . ?" scenarios to her clients. Furthermore, she was convinced that word processing would be useful for memos and reports. When she was hired by an international bank, she anticipated that she would use a personal computer on a fairly regular basis. What she did not anticipate was that the computer would be the major tool on her desk and that she would use it constantly for everything she did.

On a typical work morning, Sally turns on her desktop computer, which is part of a network of office computers, as soon as she walks into her office. While she removes her coat and unpacks her briefcase, the computer is displaying a list of options. She selects "Today's Calendar," and the screen displays "10:30 AM—Carston meeting re new trust" and "1:00 PM—lunch with T. Morales, Lakeside Cafe." The meeting notice reminds her to ask accountant Amy McKenna to bring the latest Carston reports to the meeting. She uses word processing to compose a memo quickly, then sends it to Amy via the office computer network. Next, she selects the option "Read Mail" from the screen and checks the list of incoming messages. Sally sees that her computer has received a memo from her boss. She decides that it needs immediate attention and displays it on the screen. She sees that he is calling for an emergency meeting in the conference room at 9:00. Sally stores the other messages so she can read them later, and she heads for her first meeting of the day.

As the day moves on, Sally uses the computer to fetch client data from her database, to retrieve information about a company via a data communications system, and to plot client strategies by using spreadsheet software. She prints reports on the laser printer. And, finally, she takes home diskettes of office data to work with that evening on her computer at home. Sally can use all this technology as casually as she uses the telephone or the copy machine. Sally is a prime example of a personal computer user on the job. Her employer is committed to a full range of computers—from supercomputers through mainframes and minicomputers, to—literally—thousands of personal computers networked around the world. There are few limits to the uses of computers in a complex business enterprise.

Big Guys: Users of Large Computer Systems

The companies that use large computer systems today are mostly the same companies that used them 30 or 40 years ago: corporations that have big budgets. These organizations—typically banks, insurance firms,

Figure 13-1   Mainframe computer.

and aerospace companies—were the pioneers (Figure 13-1). The computers they used were potent by then-current standards, even though today's personal computers are more powerful. In the 1950s and early 1960s, many companies obtained big computers because they believed that computers would provide a competitive edge. This turned out to be true, but it was a long time before managers really understood the true promise of computers.

Early users were somewhat uncertain about how to use the new tool. In fact, to them the computer was useful for no more than clerical tasks. Pioneering applications for many companies were payroll and accounting systems. The idea was to save labor costs by having the computer do some of the work. Many organizations, including the government, used computers as "number crunchers," machines that ground away at formulas. When computers began to be used interactively, businesspeople saw that the computer could be used as a service tool, giving instant reservations or bank balances.

Today large computer systems are used in every conceivable way, from research to manufacturing. Mid-range computers make number crunching and computerized services available to medium-size companies. But it is the highly affordable personal computer that has really opened up computing for the worker.

Personal Computers in the Workplace

Figure 13-2 Personal computer users. Personal computers support businesspeople in a variety of ways. (a) This international recruiting agency uses a database to keep track of client records and to match employers with the right job candidates. (b) This scuba gear vendor uses a computerized database to check inventory.

Personal computers are everywhere in the workplace, no matter the industry: retail, finance, insurance, real estate, health care, education, government, legal services, sports, politics, publishing, transportation, manufacturing, agriculture, construction, and on and on (Figure 13-2). It would be easier to ask where computers are excluded in the workplace. No industry interested in increasing productivity and helping workers and man-

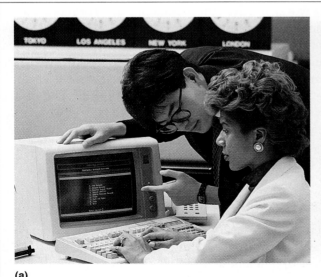

(a)

(b)

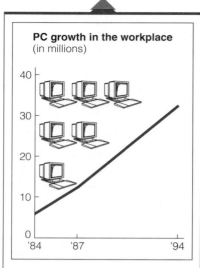

PC growth in the workplace
(in millions)

A Personal Computer on Every Desk

The number of personal computers in business has skyrocketed. At the end of 1987, the year personal computers took off, there were about 11 million personal computers in use in business. The number of units climbed to over 31 million by 1991. Politicians in the past have sought to reassure us with talk of "a chicken in every pot" or "a car in every garage." Perhaps they should now talk about "a computer on every desk."

agers would exclude them—and expect to compete in today's marketplace. It was not always that way.

Evolution of Personal Computer Use

Personal computer use seems to have evolved in three phases. Personal computers were first used in business by individual users to transform work tasks. Constantly retyped full documents, for example, gave way to quickly modified word-processed documents. The much-erased manual spreadsheet became the automatically recalculated electronic spreadsheet. And overflowing file drawers were transformed into automated databases. These changes gave a significant boost to individual productivity and can be considered the first phase of the evolution of personal computer use. Some organizations are still in this phase.

Many more organizations have entered the second phase. That is, they have gone beyond personal computer use by individuals. The second phase involves transforming a work group or department. This department-oriented phase probably embraces a network and may also include personal computer access to large computer systems. This phase requires planning and structure.

The third phase of personal computer evolution is the most dramatic, calling for the transformation of the entire business. Practically speaking, however, the third phase is really just an extension of the earlier phases: Each individual and each department uses computers to enhance the company as a whole. Few companies have come close to this idyllic state. This three-stage transformation—individual, department, and business—broadly describes a company's progress at blending its computer and business goals.

The Impact of Personal Computers

In the decades to come, personal computers will continue to radically alter the business world, much as the automobile did. For more than 50 years, the automobile fueled the economy, spawning dozens of industries, from oil companies to supermarkets. Other businesses, like real estate and restaurants, were transformed by the mobility provided by the car. Personal computers are having a similar effect, for two reasons: (1) They have brought the cost of computing down to the level of a mass-produced consumer product and (2) they have worked their way into most business organizations.

Now that they are in businesses, let us consider who in business really needs to use them.

Where PCs Are Almost a Job Requirement

Who must know how to use a personal computer to perform some part of a job? As we have already implied, the answer may soon be *everyone*. But we are not close to that landmark yet. Even if you can see that your intended job is in the must-know category, it is likely that you can receive some on-the-job training. Let us look at some of the jobs that might require PC knowledge. Notice that many of the jobs mentioned would probably fit in more than one category.

- Real estate broker, attorney, doctor, auto mechanic, or anyone who needs to search for information in a variety of ways
- Accountant, tax planner, medical researcher, farmer, psychologist, budget manager, financial planner, stockbroker, or anyone who needs to analyze data
- Advertising copywriter, secretary, author, teacher, student, legislator, reporter, or anyone who needs to write and change documents
- Designer, editor, nurse, members of the military, retail sales manager, or anyone who needs to share data with other workers
- Project leader, construction manager, reservations agent, trucker, factory supervisor, or anyone who must keep track of schedules
- Insurance salesperson, fitness consultant, political candidate, sports manager, or anyone who needs to give a compare-the-results sales pitch

This list may make you pause; you may not have seen computers in some of these roles. But there is no question that computers are changing the way we work.

How Computers Change the Way We Work

Computers are changing the way both individuals and organizations work. By providing timely access to data, computers let us spend less time checking and rechecking data and more time getting work done. In addition to increasing overall productivity, computers have had a fundamental impact on the way some people approach their jobs.

Executives were among the first to notice the change. An oil company executive noted that her secretary is no longer the keeper of all knowledge because many documents now get prepared without the secretary even seeing them. In fact, a lot of professionals use their computers in lieu of yellow pads. The net result is that work is done much more effectively (Figure 13-3).

The Name of the Game Is Speed

Not the computer game—the *business* game. From California to Maine, a principal topic among management consultants and business school professors is speed. Why? Who cares? And, if there really is a good reason for speed, how is it gained?

The *why* question has the most straightforward answer: Speed kills the competition. If your product gets to market first, you get the sale. Lag behind and get left out.

Who cares? Managers, of course, and—perhaps surprisingly—employees. Employee satisfaction improves when employees are working

Figure 13-3 Many professionals and executives make continual use of computers.

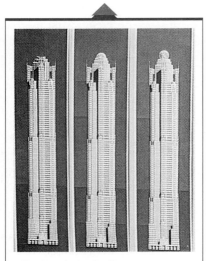

Skyscrapers by Computer

Planning a skyscraper is a complicated business. Part of that complication comes from the need for many architects, with various specialties, to communicate with each other. At the Chicago architectural firm of Skidmore, Owings & Merrill, long known as a designer of high-tech skyscrapers, the communication problem has been solved: Each architect has a personal computer, and the computers are hooked together in networks.

Skidmore has local area networks on several floors of a downtown office building; the networks are linked together by yards and yards of fiber optics cable. Project managers can divide a job of designing a building into several manageable pieces, and individual architects can pick up their slice of the job via the network. Architects working on the same job can use the network to exchange files and even complex drawings. The network allows them to do multiple activities, without getting in each others' way.

In addition, since the firm is working on about 100 buildings at a given time, one architect may be working on several jobs at once. Once a portion of a job is done, that segment can be sent electronically to the centralized printing facility.

Skidmore, the high-tech architect, has gone one high-tech step further.

for a responsive, successful company. Also, using computers to speed up operations gives employees more responsibility and flexibility.

So, how is speed achieved? Do we just put out an order to step on the gas? Probably not—that would just speed up the mess and burn out machines and workers. There are many ways to speed up operations, including providing worker incentives, reducing the number of approvals needed for action, and—of course—putting the computer to work whenever possible.

A new software tool for speeding up work is called **groupware,** network software designed to be used by many individuals at the same time. Groupware allows teams of workers to communicate more quickly and efficiently (Figure 13-4). The Boeing Company recently cut the time needed to complete a wide range of team projects by an average of 91%— or one-tenth of the time they had taken before. In one case, a group of engineers, designers, machinists, and manufacturing managers used an IBM groupware product called TeamFocus to design a standardized control system for complex machine tools in several plants. Managers say such a job would normally take more than a year; with 15 electronic meetings, it was done in 35 days. The computer is not the only answer, but it is a major factor in shaping business.

By providing timely access to data, computers let us spend less time checking and rechecking data—and more time getting things done. This inspires informed decision making and improves overall productivity. Today's computer systems speed memos, documents, and graphs to workers throughout the organization. This kind of direct people-to-people communication enriches every aspect of a business.

Figure 13-4   Computers speed up teamwork. A networked meeting at Boeing involves team members sitting at personal computers and talking to one another through the screen. Anyone can contradict the boss, since nobody knows who is saying what. Boeing claims measurable productivity gains.

The Electronic Supervisor

Did you work hard at the office today? Most people, when surveyed, report a full day's work. But managers have long suspected that this is not so. In fact, many employees spend more time at the coffee machine or in personal conversations than they realize. Others may be daydreaming while giving the appearance of working at their desks. Those days may be over for employees monitored by software right inside their computers—and such changes may be raising stress levels as well as ethical issues.

The computer is a see-all, tell-all supervisor. Surveillance software can count the number of keystrokes (and number of typos), keep track of how much time you actually spend working on the computer, monitor your telephone calls, and compare your keying speed with that of other employees.

Those who work directly with computers most of the day, such as data entry operators or word processors, are the most vulnerable to such a system. But others who work at machines are exposed, too. Check sorters and mailroom employees, for example, work with machines that can be outfitted with computers to keep track of the amount of work processed in a given time period, such as an eight-hour shift. Workers such as telemarketers, who make outgoing phone calls as part of their jobs, are often monitored by computers.

Already, about five million workers are so monitored. Some experts have predicted that, as the number of computer-monitored workers increases, so will related personnel problems, such as increased stress and lowered morale. In fact, critics say that computer-monitored work settings amount to "electronic sweatshops," where employees must do boring, fast-paced work that requires constant alertness and attention to detail. And worst of all, the supervisor is not even human.

The Portable Worker

Many workers attribute their success to plain hard work—and they want the potential to take their work with them wherever they go. These days, taking work along means taking the computer along.

The Tools of Portability   For ideal portability, a worker needs this set of machines: a notebook, palmtop, or laptop computer—with fax and modem; a laser printer; and a cellular phone or built-in satellite transmission capabilities. Some workers, especially managers, have these machines at home as well as in the office. With the appropriate software, these machines can help the worker with any routine task—from answering electronic mail to writing reports to comparing financial options for a possible merger—and do it anywhere. Many workers carry a laptop in the field or when traveling (Figure 13-5). Workers can use technology to send electronic and voice mail messages that can be picked up at the recipient's convenience. A report prepared at home or on the road can be sent via communications devices to the office, where it is printed on a laser printer and then sent by fax to other interested parties. These electronic tools are catching on rapidly, and they are spreading beyond the traditional office.

The New Convenience   Some say the new technology goes beyond providing convenience. Some say what computers provide is *liberation*—liberation from the confines of the office, from the stressful 9-to-5 commute, from frustrating telephone tag, and even from time zone barriers. Telecommuting, as we have mentioned, is ideal for some workers. But

Figure 13-5   Computers on the go. This sales representative uses a desktop personal computer at the office, but she carries a laptop on sales calls to provide on-the-spot product information and prices for the pharmacist.

BUSINESS SOFTWARE SAMPLER

Beyond the standard business software—spreadsheets, general ledger, payroll, desktop publishing, and so on—there are many interesting offerings for individuals in business. Brand names change, so we will describe software categories.

- **Personal information manager (PIM).** This type of software can help any office worker, but especially a manager, cope with information overload. The basic idea behind a PIM is that most people live in a world overburdened with telephone messages, Post-it notes, newspaper clippings, expense tabs, appointment cards, and other scraps of paper. A PIM can store appointment data and travel plans, phone numbers, and various lists and memos. Some PIMs offer quite sophisticated features, organizing diverse text-based data for project management or business analysis. A PIM is sometimes referred to generically as a productivity tool, because it helps the user make order out of chaos. As one office worker put it, "It allows me to keep all these balls in the air without getting hit on the head."

- **Personnel.** Some software packages allow businesses to keep all personnel data, including photographs, on-line for easy updating. The on-line photos make employee identity checks more effective because an employee's picture appears on the screen along with employment verification.

- **Security.** Combine computerized fingerprint scanning with a door lock, and the result is enhanced security. The computer will admit you to an area only if your fingerprints are in a database. Similarly, some computers scan retinas to enforce security: You look into a monitor and the machine scans your eyes with a laser beam to identify you.

- **Client/Tracker.** This type of package is for any business that has a customer sales component. A typical client tracker keeps a complete, up-to-date record of all business contacts—a record that is available at a moment's notice. The software stores data about clients, sets up daily call lists, prepares sales reports, prints mailing labels, and may even remind you about a client's personal quirks.

- **Employee training tutorials.** Some managers think that the computer can be an effective and relatively inexpensive way to train employees. Software is available, by product brand name, to train people at their own pace in word processing, spreadsheets, database management, and other commonly used applications. More and more such packages include voice, music, video and animation stored on CD-ROM or interactive videodisc.

- **Banner and certificate makers.** Get employee attention by announcing events in a big way. Banner software can produce interesting output on a simple dot-matrix printer. The printed signs are great for office parties. Certificate software can produce impressive-looking certificates of accomplishment. Choose from numerous borders, enter your message, and leave space for the gold-foil seal, which is included in the package.

- **Label makers.** Some handy programs create professional-looking labels of all sorts, from mailing or file labels to stickers for diskettes. For example, a program reads the files on a diskette in a given drive and then prints a label listing all the files; you can attach the label to your diskette for easy identification. Businesses can also create their own signs, stationery, and even business cards with similar programs.

- **Name tag kits.** With these packages you can prepare professional-looking tags inexpensively, so all conference goers, for example, can have a badge shouting "HI! I'M MADGE!" or whatever the tag wearer's name is. These kits are flexible enough to permit you to include last-minute attendees. Complete kit includes software, blank name tags, and plastic holders.

- **Organization charts.** Here is the fastest way to create professional-looking organization charts. Just type in names, titles, departments, and so on, and let the software do the rest. The charts can be updated easily when the personnel roster changes.

- **Career software.** Paralyzed at the thought of finding your first job? Bored with the job you have and not sure how to look for a new one? You are a good candidate for career software, which will help you conduct a thorough and organized job search. A typical package takes you by the hand and teaches you how to assess your skills, develop career objectives, and write your resume and cover letters.

the liberation being described here is not a pattern of being at home—it is the lack of a pattern. Workers can, for all practical purposes, stay in touch with the office and the action 24 hours a day, seven days a week—from any location.

 Software at Work

Consider some specific business applications for the software tools in the marketplace.

Communications Software

If you have a computer, a modem, and some communications software, you have the capability to access any other computer system similarly configured. Businesses are the major users of communications software. There are as many applications as there are entrepreneurs to devise them and users to buy them. Here are some on-line services that workers value.

On-Line Reservations   Need a reservation? Don't call your travel agent—reach for your computer. The American Airlines reservation system, called Sabre, is one of the major reservations systems used by travel agents and airlines around the world. Now, for a fee, any business can have direct access to the Sabre system through that business's own computer. Individuals can have access to Sabre too. Those who use Sabre for business or personal travel have immediate access to airfares at any hour of any day. Sabre reports an airline's on-time performance, uses a personalized profile to sort through flights and seating arrangements, spells out applicable restrictions, and summarizes travel arrangements. Of course, anyone can get all this free from an airline or travel agent, but some people prefer the convenience of making their own arrangements.

Weather Forecasting   We have long relied on the media, both television and print, to keep us informed about the weather. This service is adequate for most of us. Some businesses, however, are so dependent on the weather that they need constantly updated information. On-line services offer analysis of live weather data, including air pressure, fog, rain, and wind direction and speed. Businesses that depend on the weather include agriculture, amusement parks, ski areas, and transportation companies, all of which make business decisions based on weather forecasts. (On-line weather forecasting services, by the way, are not intended for large airports, which have their own trained meteorologists on staff.)

On-Line to the Stock Exchange   Stock portfolios can be managed by software that takes quotations on-line directly from established market monitors such as Dow Jones. The software keeps records and offers quick and accurate investment advice. And, of course, the stock exchange itself is a veritable beehive of computers.

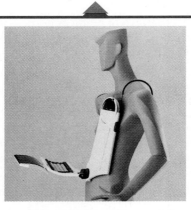

We must communicate by computer, but, increasingly, we must also use computer output in the form of pictures.

Graphics at Work

Computer graphics are an appendage that can delight and entertain and inform. Businesspeople can enhance a message by using graphics to express numbers in an easily understood form. But, sometimes, producing graphics is the chief function of a computer system or an integral part of the job of the worker who uses the system. In Chapter 12, we looked at computer graphics in depth. Here we list some of the many workers who depend on computer graphics to do their jobs.

Researchers   Some people worry a little about earthquakes; others get paid to worry about them. Researchers in the field of earthquake prediction use graphics in several different ways to help them visualize the forces that cause temblors. The "photo" in Figure 13-6a is a computer-generated graphic that helps scientists understand underground formations whose movements result in quakes. Computers can also digitize and assemble satellite photos, and the graphics that result help researchers spot geological patterns and shifts. These two examples are of government research, but private firms also do an enormous amount of research to strengthen their product lines.

Artists and Designers   As a tool of their craft, artists use sophisticated software to produce stunning computer art and animation. A clear business application of graphics is design. Everyone from architects to engineers to fashion designers can use the computer to design and simulate products (Figure 13-6b).

Musicians   The old movies feature inspired composers hanging over the piano in the middle of the night. First we see a few fingers dabbling at the keys, then a pause, a cocked ear, another bit of key tinkling, and—finally—a pencil writing the notes on paper. Many composers work that way today. But some do not. Composers still play the notes, but a computer equipped with listening software captures them and reproduces them as graphic images on the screen (Figure 13-6c). When the composition is completed, the composer will instruct the computer to print out the sheet music.

Doctors   How do you look inside the body to take its picture? X-rays are one way, of course. But amazing as X-ray technology is, it is far from perfect. X-ray films can be so fuzzy that interpreting them seems more an art than a science. Modern medical imaging has gotten quite a boost from the computer, however. Figure 13-6d shows how sharp an image can be when X-rays and computers are used together.

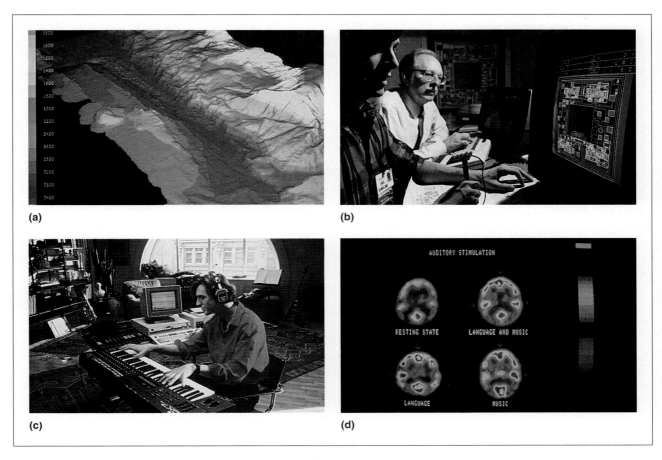

Figure 13-6   Graphics software at work. (a) Off the coast of Chile, three rocky plates that make up the ocean floor come together. Varying growth rates are causing one of the plates to slide under another, disappearing the way the steps at the bottom of an escalator seem to vanish. (b) This engineering team uses computer graphics to design a pressure-sensitive manifold. (c) This musician is using a computer system that translates sounds into musical notation, bridging the gap between the inspiration that creates new music and the laborious task of writing the notes down. (d) Computer-generated CAT scans give physicians and researchers information about the brain's activity. The uses of CAT scans vary from diagnosing mental illnesses to identifying the parts of the brain involved in speech.

Decision-Making Software

You have already studied in detail one important type of decision-making software: the computerized spreadsheet. You have seen how the ability of spreadsheet software to recalculate automatically lets decision makers explore different possibilities. Beginning with loan amortization, let us consider some of the significant ways that businesses use spreadsheets and other decision-making software.

Loan Amortization   Software for loan amortization determines due dates, payment number, payment amount, principal, interest, accumulated interest, and loan balance. Most loan amortization software also produces yearly and monthly reports.

Marketing by Computer

Buy your new car conveniently. Several car manufacturers offer personal computer users a full database of information on a disk. You will find everything you need to know about the cost, safety, design, and technology of the latest car models. *The Electronic Gallery* disk from Cadillac offers comprehensive technical information, as well as a feature that helps you to see if leasing might better fit your pocketbook. It will even help you sell your old car, providing a window sticker printout in the process. Of course, it will also write a letter to Cadillac for you, to arrange a test drive.

Break-Even Analysis   Can we afford the new equipment? Should we buy or lease? Should we try to compete in that market? Is the cost worth it? What is the payoff? At what point do we break even? Net present value and break-even software answers these questions and more—analyzing the relationships among variable costs, fixed costs, and income—and produces alternatives to consider. A computer-generated analysis based on actual conditions sure beats hunches scribbled on the back of an envelope.

Property Management   A type of program sometimes referred to as the landlord can be used to manage any income property, whether marina, apartment complex, or shopping mall. The software can record charges and payments for each renter and produce a variety of reports, such as a lease expiration list and tax analysis lists for each property.

No matter the business, getting a job done efficiently often depends on reliable access to stored data, our next topic.

Storage and Retrieval Software

Office workers and salespeople and manufacturers all use computers as tools in their businesses; most of these workers and many others rely on access to stored data.

Crime Detection   A lot of crime detection involves a process of elimination, which is often tedious work. A tedious task, however, is often the kind the computer does best. Once data is entered into a database, then searching by computer is possible. Examples: Which criminals use a particular mode of operation? Which criminals are associates of this suspect? Does license number AXB221 refer to a stolen car? And so on. One specific type of crime-detection computer system is the fingerprint-matching system, which can match crime-scene fingerprints with computer-stored fingerprints.

Sports Statistics   Here is the situation. Tied game, bases loaded, two outs, left-handed batter, bottom of the ninth. If you are coaching the team in the field, do you leave in the right-handed pitcher or pull him for a lefty? The seat-of-the-pants hunch is less common these days. Coaches and managers in professional sports want any help they can get. A wonderful source of help, one that can be carried right to the edge of the field, is the computer. In our current example, the bases-loaded scenario, the manager can check statistics from the batter's past performance against statistics about each available pitcher. All kinds of statistics can be stored in a database and retrieved on the spot (Figure 13-7).

Performing Arts   People in the performing arts use computers as standard business tools. They find databases particularly useful. Database software, for example, can search for the names of musical pieces—all 20-minute violin pieces by German composers, for example. The American Ballet Theater takes their computers on tour: One database plots

Computers at Work

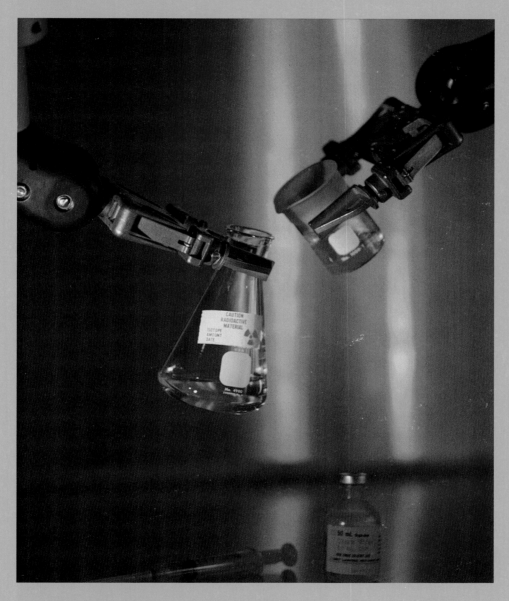

In this gallery, we will look at some of the ways in which workers put computers to use on the job. In the photo shown here, the "worker" is actually a robot, who is handling radioactive isotope solutions needed for human body scans.

CAD/CAE/CAM

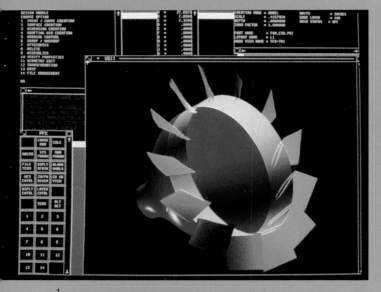

1

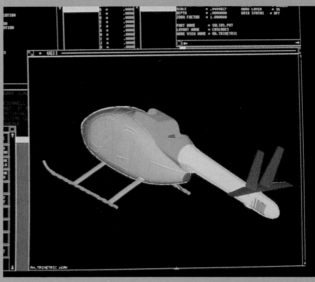

2

3

Factory products and even buildings can be devised and drawn on a computer-aided design (CAD) system, then transmitted electronically to a computer-aided engineering (CAE) system, where an engineer tests and modifies the design. The design may be sent to a computer-aided manufacturing (CAM) system, which uses the data to direct the production process.

(1, 2) These screens represent different design challenges in the creation of a McDonnell Douglas helicopter. **(3)** Special design software is used to consider aerodynamic factors for complex surfaces such as automobiles. **(4)** This computer-generated image shows a design plan for the Mall of America. The mall, which opened in summer 1992, is billed as the largest mall in the world. The designers cut approximately a year from the standard design and construction time by using automated drafting and management software.

4

Robots

5

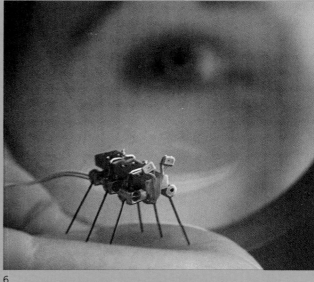

6

7

8

When most people think of robots, they probably have in mind the typical humanoid-shaped automaton of classic science-fiction movies. But robots of all shapes and sizes are performing a variety of serious tasks—without looking much like people.

(5) If you look closely at this picture, you can see the robotic "arm" reaching out to pick an apple. (6) This "insect robot" was developed at MIT. The advantage of a tiny robot is its potential for getting into very small places while being directed by the human controlling it. (7) The skills demonstrated by this robot artist indicate the dexterity being developed in robots. (8) Robots, who are running the whole show here, are most famous for their work in automotive factories. (9) A robot arm is sensitive enough to firmly grasp a delicate object, such as this integrated circuit, without injuring it.

9

Graphic Design

10

MEXICANA

11

13

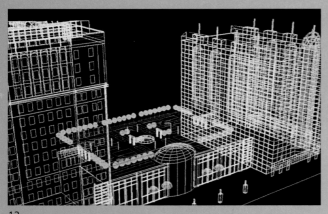

12

15

14

16

MOONLIT FLIGHT

17

18

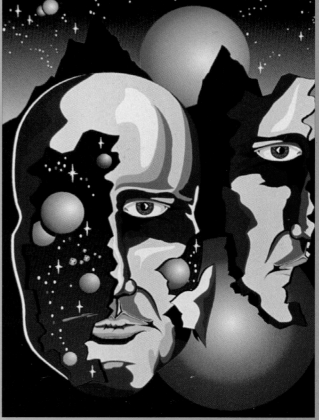

(10) In graphic design, image is everything. Computer graphics software lets designers choose from a wide range of colors and styles to create just the image they need, whether for advertising, architecture, or some other useful purpose. **(11)** This computer-generated image was created as an advertisement for Mexicana Airlines. **(12,13)** Architects use 3-D modeling software to draft building plans and to present design concepts to clients. These images represent two phases of an architect's concept of a block of buildings. **(14,15)** These computer graphic renderings were prize winners in a logo-design contest sponsored by software maker Corel Systems. **(16,17,18,19)** The graphic artists who designed these advertising images were first-place winners in a monthly contest sponsored by the makers of CorelDRAW, the graphics software the winners used.

19

Workers and Their Computers

20

21

22

(20) Using three-dimensional graphics software, these engineers review the design of a part for the Boeing 747-400 freighter airplane. The enlarged projection allows team members to view and discuss the design as a group. **(21)** This robotics engineer is testing the accuracy and sensitivity of a grasping robot arm. **(22)** This pizza chef keeps track of orders on a computer right in the kitchen. **(23)** This Federal Express package was labeled with a bar code at the sending point. Here, a worker runs a scanning pen over the bar code to computer-record the package's progress through the system.

23

24

25

27

(24) A police officer uses the computer to produce a simulated mug shot by compiling various features from descriptions of eyewitnesses. **(25)** A data processing manager in a hospital stands by a heap of patient folders that have been converted to computer-accessible form. **(26)** Workers in oil fields can use their laptop computers to record and analyze production data on-site. **(27)** Airline pilots use a computer-based cockpit simulator to practice their flying maneuvers.

26

Finance

28

29

30

31

(28) The New York Stock Exchange handles millions of transactions each business day with the very necessary help of computers. **(29)** Traders have their own computers, which they use to analyze data and place orders. **(30)** A bank teller uses a terminal to display customer account records and other information. **(31)** An investment broker relies on computer-produced charts that show data patterns.

Figure 13-7 Storage and retrieval in sports. Sports broadcasters use personal computers to store and retrieve facts immediately—keeping their audience informed and entertained.

rehearsal schedules; another keeps track of sets, lighting, and costumes. Some sophisticated organizations use databases to coordinate ticket sales with fund-raising; as a patron, this probably means that you will receive your tickets with great efficiency, then be solicited for a donation.

Legal Services   You have seen the formal photograph of the judge, the attorney, the politician—each with a solid wall of law books in the background. Those books are not just decoration, however. Workers in any law office need to be able to research legal precedents and related matters. But why not take the information in those books and just "drop it" into a computer? That is, in essence, what has been done. The books have been converted into computer-accessible databases, and the result is that legal research time has decreased significantly. Two common computerized legal research systems are LEXIS and WESTLAW, available in most law libraries and law firms.

Vertical Market Software

Vertical market software describes a program written especially for a particular group of customers, such as accountants or doctors. Some software makers specialize in computer systems for such markets (Figure 13-8). This user-oriented software usually presents options with a series of easy-to-follow menus that minimize training needed. Here are some examples of businesses where you might find vertical market software.

Figure 13-8   Vertical market software.
Some software is designed specifically for vertical markets—such as accountants, engineers, lawyers, or real estate agents. Scanning satellite images, geologists do some "oil prospecting" by computer.

Auto Repair Shops   Designed in conjunction with people who understand the auto repair business, this all-in-one software for an auto shop can prepare work orders, process sales transactions, produce invoices, evaluate sales and profits, track parts inventory automatically, print reorder reports, and update the customer mailing list.

Videotape Rental Stores   An important goal for a videotape rental store is fast service. One concept for fast service is simple enough: Let the computer match customers and tapes they rent. Here is how it works. Each regular customer receives a card with an identifying bar code on it; each rental tape is also bar-coded. At rental time, the customer's bar code and the tape's bar codes are scanned, causing an invoice to be printed. The entire transaction takes only a few seconds. (The scanning system can be overridden by typing in name and other data for new or cardless customers.) When the tape is returned, a clerk needs only to scan the tape label; the system automatically credits the proper customer with the return. The software can produce a variety of reports, such as reports of overdue rentals and mailing lists.

Beauty Salons   Does your hairdresser really remember exactly how to do your hair and that you like yard work and movies? Maybe. But it is more likely that a card is on file somewhere, listing your preferences. In some shops, that "card" is stored in the computer. Before you arrive, this data can be pulled up on a screen. After you leave, the hairdresser immediately updates your customer history. In addition, the computer credits your stylist for providing the service and uses this data to calculate the stylist's commission. The computer can also produce reports, include sales summaries by period, product inventories, appointment reminder cards, thank-you cards, and promotional letters.

PERSPECTIVES

THE DARK SIDE OF THE INFORMATION AGE

Even Information Age workers are not immune to the realities of economics. A growing number of U.S. firms are moving their data processing (DP) operations offshore or overseas, to places like Jamaica and Ireland. In these places, wages are lower, people speak English, and telecommunications allows instantaneous links to the host company's computers.

In Loughrea, Ireland, Cigna Corporation recently set up a data processing office, hiring 120 young Irish workers at $11,000 a year to process medical claims flown in daily from the U.S. Cheap labor also convinced McGraw-Hill to set up operations in Ireland. At an office across town from Cigna, the company hired 40 full-time and a dozen part-time workers. The employees work at computer terminals, maintaining the worldwide circulation files of 16 McGraw-Hill magazines. Their terminals are linked directly to mainframes in Hightstown, New Jersey.

In the Philippines and Singapore, other U.S. firms have established offices and hired local labor to handle data entry jobs ranging from accounting, medical transcription, and telemarketing, to technical support of high-tech products.

"All you need is office space," says Robert Ady, head of PHH Fautus, a Chicago relocation consultant. Computers allow employers "a chance to tap talent anywhere in the world," says Sunil Tagare, vice president of Kessler Marketing Intelligence, a consulting firm based in Newport, Rhode Island. Tagare thinks the U.S. will lose "a lot of white-collar jobs."

Unions are concerned. Dennis Chanut, an AFL-CIO official in Washington, D.C., believes America has already lost several thousand jobs because of the relocation of computer-based facilities. He fears that once the U.S. economy recovers, employers will step up relocation as a means of cutting labor costs.

Obviously, not everyone sees relocation as a bad thing. Robert Crawford, North American director of the Locate in Scotland program, believes that the U.S. would have lost the jobs anyway, as newer technologies (such as electronic scanning of printed materials) make data entry jobs obsolete. His group works to create jobs in Scotland by focusing on manufacturing and deliberately shies away from data processing.

Mailing List Services   Traditionally, managers ignored the cost of mailings as a nickel-and-dime expense. Now, managers view their company mailing list as a target for cost reduction. There are many software packages to generate mailing lists; cost savings can result from trimming and focusing them. "Hunter-killer" software roots out incomplete addresses and duplicates, even if they are not quite identical in appearance. This kind of software can also use addresses "intelligently." For example, if the mailing consists of a lawn care circular, the software can eliminate addresses that include "Apt."

 ## What Could Possibly Be Next?

The future is already in sight. Soon workers will wonder how today's mute, passive boxes were ever called computers. Already some personal computers, or terminals hooked up to bigger machines, can talk, listen, and display live images. No computer is an island: They can call one another and send faxes, mail, and messages. People who cannot leave their computers at home are taking them along—and may even wear them one day. Some computers are disappearing altogether—into the furniture to become part of the desk, the cabinet, the blackboard. It seems to be the fate of the computer to move into the background—and to be everywhere.

Which brings up the subject of our next chapter: Just how do you manage information systems when they are both in and out of the office and even disappearing into the woodwork?

R E V I E W   A N D   R E F E R E N C E

Summary and Key Terms

- The companies that use mainframe computers today are mostly the same companies that were computer pioneers, large corporations that have large budgets. Early users used computers for clerical tasks. When computers began to be used interactively, businesspeople saw that the computer could be used as a service tool.

- Mid-range computers made "number crunching" and computerized service available to medium-size companies. But it was the highly affordable personal computer that really opened up computing for the worker.

- A partial list of where computers are used includes retail, finance, insurance, real estate, health care, education, government, legal services, sports, politics, publishing, transportation, manufacturing, agriculture, and construction.

- Personal computer use seems to evolve in three phases: transformation of an individual's productivity, transformation of a department, and transformation of a business.

- Personal computers will radically alter the business world for two reasons: (1) They have brought the cost of computing down to the level of a mass-produced consumer product, and (2) they have worked their way into most business organizations.

- Many workers must know how to use a personal computer to perform some part of a job. If a job requires the use of a personal computer, it is likely that the worker will receive some on-the-job training.

- Computers are changing the way individuals and organizations work.

- There are many ways to speed up business operations, including putting the computer to work whenever possible. One especially exciting area involves **groupware**, networked software designed to be used by several individuals at the same time.

- By providing timely access to data, computers let us spend less time checking data and more time getting things done.

- The ideal set of machines for achieving worker portability consists of a laptop, notebook, or palmtop personal computer with fax and modem; a laser printer; and a cellular phone or satellite transmission capabilities.

- Businesses use software for communications, graphics, decision making, and storage and retrieval of information.

- **Vertical market software** is software for a group of similar customers, such as accountants or doctors.

- In just a few years, personal computers or terminals hooked up to bigger machines, will talk, listen, and display full-color life-like images. Computers will be able to talk to one another, taking calls and writing memos; they will provide easy guidance through vast amounts of data; and although they will move into the background, computers will be everywhere.

Review Questions

1. What distinguishes companies that use mainframe computers from other companies?
2. Describe some of the tasks computers were first assigned by pioneering businesses.
3. For what are computers used by businesses today?
4. Discuss the three phases through which businesses usually pass as they begin to use personal computers.
5. Describe how personal computers can change the way individuals and businesses work.
6. Describe some typical business software that workers might use today.
7. Describe an ideal set of computers and peripheral equipment for workers who travel.
8. Describe how vertical market software might be used by an auto repair shop.

9. If you were a construction engineer in the field, how might you use a laptop?
10. What do you think the future holds for using computers on the job?

Discussion Questions

1. Consider these five firms. What uses would each have for computers? Mention as many possibilities as you can: Security Southwestern Bank, a major regional bank with several branches; Azure Design, a small graphic-design company that produces posters, covers, and other artwork; Checkerboard Taxi Service, whose central office manages a fleet of 160 cabs that operate in an urban area; Gillick College, a private college that has automated all student services, such as registration, financial aid, testing, and more; Duffin Realty, a realty firm with multiple listings and 27 agents.
2. What careers are you considering? Discuss how computers are used currently in your field. How may their use change in the future?
3. What software applications do you feel you must learn before graduation?
4. Give examples of software you have seen used in various businesses.

True-False Questions

T F 1. Personal computers are not used in the workplace, since most companies already have mainframes.

T F 2. In 1987—the year personal computer use really began to take off—there were 11 million PCs in use in business.

T F 3. Many of the top management consultants and business school professors believe that pure speed is very important in business because it kills competition.

T F 4. Some experts believe that some personnel problems, such as stress in business, may be caused by using computers to monitor workers.

T F 5. The computer is a major factor changing all facets of business today.

T F 6. An ideal portable set of tools for a businessperson today includes a laptop computer (or one that is even lighter), a laser printer, a fax and/or modem, and cellular phone or satellite transmission capabilities.

T F 7. Earthquakes can be predicted by computers, so we need worry no longer.

T F 8. A PIM is software used as a personal information manager.

T F 9. Musicians no longer need to create or compose music, since computers can do it for them.

T F 10. Vertical market software is intended for a group of similar customers, such as accountants, lawyers, doctors, or auto repair shop owners.

Management Information Systems

Managing Computer Resources

Mark Dalton pursued a business degree with the goal of a career in management. He was uncertain, however, about his career ambitions. He thought that someday he would like to be at the very top of an organization, with—perhaps—an office with a stunning view. He thought it was more likely, however, that he would end up somewhere in the middle, reporting to the top bosses but with responsibilities for major activities below him. He assumed that his entry into management would be at the lowest rung on the ladder, in direct contact with the workers, supervising their operations and making sure they had what they needed to do the job.

As it happened, Mark did all these things, but not in the way he expected. While he was in college, he began a computer word processing service, typing up his classmates' term papers and resumes. He used part of his profits to buy a laser printer and desktop publishing software. Thus he was able to produce professional-looking documents and was able to offer his services to local small businesses. Mark's business-on-the-side grew beyond his expectations; he decided to go into business for himself full-time after graduation. Mark was his own boss and managed a group of employees. As the company grew, he managed at all levels and, eventually, had an office that overlooked the cityscape.

Whether managing your own company or someone else's—whether at the top, middle, or bottom level—the challenge is the same: to use available resources to get the job done on time, within budget, and to the satisfaction of all concerned. Let us begin with a discussion of how managers do this, then see how computer systems can help them.

Classic Management Functions

Managers have five main functions:

- **Planning,** or devising both short-range and long-range plans for the organization and setting goals to help achieve the plans
- **Organizing,** or deciding how to use resources, such as people and materials.
- **Staffing,** or hiring and training workers
- **Directing,** or guiding employees to perform their work in a way that supports the organization's goals
- **Controlling,** or monitoring the organization's progress toward reaching its goals

All managers perform these functions as part of their jobs. The level of responsibility regarding these functions, however, varies with the level of the manager. Often you will hear the terms *strategic, tactical,* and *operational* associated with top-level, middle-level, and low-level managers, respectively (Figure 14-1a).

Whether the head of General Electric or an electrical appliance store or of a large company or a small one, a top-level manager must be concerned with the long-range view—the *strategic* level of management. For this manager, the main focus is **planning.** Consider a survey showing that Americans want family vacations and want the flexibility and economy of a motor vehicle; however, they also want more space than the family car provides. To the president of a major auto company, this information may suggest further opportunities for expansion of the recreational vehicle line.

The middle-level manager must be able to take a somewhat different view because his or her main concern is the *tactical* level of management. The middle manager will prepare to carry out the visions of the

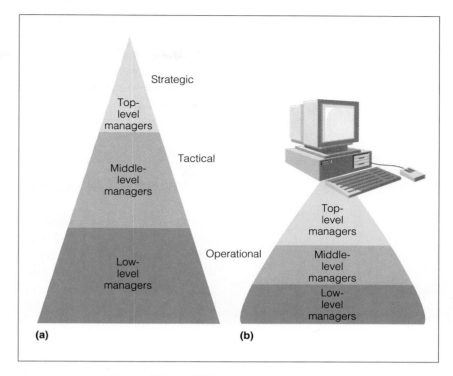

Figure 14-1   The management pyramid. (a) The classic view of management functions involves a pyramid featuring top managers handling strategic long-range planning, middle managers focusing on the tactical issues of organization and personnel, and low-level managers directing and controlling day-to-day operations. (b) The increasing use of personal computers in business is squeezing out mid- and low-level managers, thus flattening the pyramid.

top-level managers, assembling the material and personnel resources to do the job. Note that these tasks focus on **organizing** and **staffing.** Suppose the public is inclined to buy more recreational vehicles. To a production vice president, this may mean organizing production lines using people with the right skills at the right wage and perhaps farming out portions of the assembly that can be done by cheaper, less-skilled labor.

The low-level manager, usually known as a first-line supervisor, is primarily concerned with the *operational* level of management. For this manager, the focus is on **directing** and **controlling.** Personnel must be directed to perform the planned activities, and the low-level manager must monitor progress closely. The supervisor—an assembly-line supervisor in our recreational vehicle example—is involved in a number of issues: making sure that workers have the parts they need, checking employee attendance, maintaining quality control, handling complaints, keeping a close watch on the schedule, tracking costs, and much more.

To make decisions about planning, organizing, staffing, directing, and controlling, managers need data that is organized in a way that is useful for them. An effective management information system can provide it.

With the entry of the personal computer into business, the classic view of management is changing. As more managers use computers to handle more management functions, middle-level and low-level managers are being squeezed out. The *downsizing* of business involves not just an elimination of many middle-management jobs, but the takeover by the personal computer and local area networks of work previously done by minicomputers and mainframes. This is occurring in many developed countries, not just the United States. What is actually happening, according to the experts, is that the pyramid is being flattened (Figure 14-1b).

MIS for Managers

A **management information system** (**MIS**) may be defined as a set of formal business systems designed to provide information for an organization. (Incidentally, you may hear the term *MIS system,* even though the *S* in the abbreviation stands for *System;* this is an accepted redundancy.) Whether or not such a system is called an MIS, every company has one. Even managers who make hunch-based decisions are operating with some sort of information system—one based on their experience. The kind of MIS we are concerned with here includes a computer as one of its components. Information serves no purpose until it gets to its users. Timeliness is important, and the computer can act quickly to produce information.

The extent of a computerized MIS varies from company to company, but the most effective kinds are those that are integrated. An integrated MIS incorporates all five managerial functions—planning, organizing, staffing, directing, and controlling—throughout the company, from typing to top-executive forecasting. An integrated management computer system uses the computer to solve problems for an entire organization, instead of attacking them piecemeal. Although in many companies the complete integrated system is still only an idea, the functional aspects of MIS are expanding rapidly in many organizations. Some of the traditional functional areas of MIS are:

- Accounting
- Finance
- Marketing
- Personnel
- Research and development (R&D)
- Legal services
- Operations and production management
- Informational systems

Each area involves its own information requirements and support for decision making, but they also share common information needs.

The **MIS manager** runs the MIS department. This person's position has been called information resource manager, director of information services, chief information officer, and a variety of other titles. In any case, whoever serves in this capacity should be comfortable with both computer technology and the organization's business.

The Scope of Responsibility: Turf Wars

Is the MIS manager responsible for the whole company? Not really, but sometimes it seems that way. If computers are everywhere—and they are—can the MIS department be far behind? For a long time—through the 1960s and 1970s—anyone who needed computer services made a formal request to the computer professionals. That is, employees had to present their needs to the official keepers of automated power, where information was dispensed. A great deal of power, both computer and political, was concentrated in one place. Distribution of power has come in a variety of ways. As we noted in Chapter 5, for example, placing smaller computers in remote locations, such as branch offices, gave computer users better access and, consequently, more control. But the biggest change was made by placing personal computers directly in the hands of users.

In many ways, however, this distribution of power is an illusion. Users are constrained by their needs for the corporate data, and the data is still firmly in the hands of the MIS department. Many personal computers are plugged into networks that the MIS department must control and monitor. Also, users rely heavily on MIS-run information centers, which help them with computer-related problems. It certainly seems that a lot of power still rests with the MIS manager.

And recently, manufacturing has become an area of focus for the MIS department. The demand from top management to increase productivity in the manufacturing arena is escalating, and computer technology is considered the answer. So, there is one more set of technologies for the MIS manager to contend with. What this will probably mean, however, is a battle over territory. Manufacturing managers would prefer to keep the MIS department out of the production process but, as more technologies are introduced, they have no choice but to include MIS—that is, if they want to meet their end goal of increasing productivity.

The MIS manager is gaining authority over an empire that is getting more and more unruly, with computers and computer users spread all over the company. The role of the MIS department is changing from the caretaker of large computers to the supporter of computers and their networks right in the user's environment. And there is a more subtle change: MIS managers can no longer hide behind the protective cloak of technical mystery because their users have become more sophisticated. In effect, even the interpersonal style of the MIS manager is changing.

There are two issues here: control of power and the nature of the MIS manager's job. Although it is clear that the MIS department dominates the company's use of computers, ultimate control lies with the users themselves, who pay the bills for computer services. As for the MIS manager, his or her focus is now on service and support. As technology changes, so will the focus and scope of the job.

MIS Reports for Managers

A computer system can produce different kinds of reports, which can be described as summary, exception, or detail reports. Reports can also be categorized as periodic or on-demand. **Periodic reports** are produced on a regular schedule, such as daily or monthly, and are preplanned to produce detail, summary, or exception data. These reports are printed. **On-demand reports** do as their name suggests: They provide information in response to an unscheduled demand—a request—from a user. On-demand reports are often produced directly on a terminal or personal computer screen, although the report can be printed as well. Let us look more closely at these reports in the context of their value to managers.

- **Top-level managers.** For strategic planning, high-level managers need to be able to see historical information—an analysis of data trends—not for just some parts of their business but for the total business. Moreover, such managers must be able to make decisions about things that happen unpredictably. The MIS, therefore, must be able to produce on-demand reports that integrate information and show how factors affecting various departments are related to each other. An on-demand report might show the impact of strikes or energy shortages on all parts of the company.

- **Middle-level managers.** To do their tactical planning and organizing functions, middle-level managers need to be aware of trends—to know what the business is doing and where it is going. Thus, these managers are most in need of summary reports and exception reports. **Summary reports** are limited to totals or trends. Examples of summary reports showing trends are those showing past and present interest rates or sales data (Figure 14-2a). **Exception reports** show only data that reflects unusual circumstances. Examples of exception reports are those showing depleted budgets, payments being made to temporary employees, and books temporarily out of stock or not yet published (Figure 14-2b).

- **Low-level managers.** Concerned mainly with day-to-day operations, low-level managers need **detail reports,** which give complete, specific information on routine operations; these reports help keep offices and plants running. Examples are overtime information from this week's payroll, spare parts that need to be ordered, quality-control results of yesterday's inspections at Dock B, and books to be shipped (Figure 14-2c). Many computer-based MISs are self-determining—that is, they can take some preplanned actions on their own. An MIS can, for example, automatically reorder depleted stock as directed by an inventory management program or automatically issue bonuses for salespeople when incoming orders reach a certain level.

It should be clear that an MIS must be capable of delivering both detailed and general information not only on a regular schedule but also to fill unpredictable requests.

Figure 14-2   Three kinds of reports.
These are examples of the kinds of reports a book publisher might use. (a) This report summarizes the sales of math books over the previous four years. (b) This exception report lists titles temporarily out of stock or not yet published. (c) This report provides the details on books to be shipped.

```
FOUR-YEAR SALES TITLE REPORT AS OF 1/31/94
MATHEMATICS-AUTHOR & TITLE

50239 LYON TRIGONOMERTY
1993 QTY         1992 QTY          1991 QTY          1990 QTY
  15,813           16,239            20,871            23,918

50240 SMITH LINEAR MATH
1993 QTY         1992 QTY          1991 QTY          1990 QTY
  25,031           25,502            29,193            22,108

50241 ANDREWS COLLEGE MATH
1993 QTY         1992 QTY          1991 QTY          1990 QTY
  20,013           18,925            19,931            23,206
```

(a) Summary report

```
AVAILABILITY DATE LISTING-
TITLES TEMP OUT OF STOCK OR NOT YET PUBLISHED 1/31/94

CODE AUTHOR & TITLE                    AVAILABLE

00089 BYRNE ELEM STATISTICS            APR  2, 94
00093 BLUESTONE ANTHROPOLOGY           MAR  3, 94
00156 ALBRIGHT INFECTIOUS DISEASES     APR 28, 94
```

(b) Exception report

```
DAILY SALES REGISTER BY TYPE OF SALES 1/31/94 PAGE 1

SHIP-TO ADDRESS        CODE AUTHOR&   LIST    QTY  TOTAL
                       TITLE          PRICE        AMOUNT

THE SOUTH MAIN         36980 WILSON   22.95   100  2295.00
BOOKSTORE              ANATOMY &
209 SOUTH MAIN         PHYSIOLOGY
CHICAGO, IL 60625

UNIVERSITY BOOKSTORE   50239 LYON     17.95   300  5385.00
OLD STATE COLLEGE      TRIGONOMETRY
800 W VICTORIA ST
STAMFORD, CT 06903

EASTERN ARCATA UNIV    34102 SPENCE   17.95   400  7180.00
BOOKSTORE              GENETICS
PO BOX 8769
ARCATA, CA 95521
```

(c) Detail report

Managing Personal Computers

Personal computers burst on the business scene in the early 1980s with little warning and less planning. The experience of the Rayer International Paper Company is typical. One day a personal computer appeared on the desk of engineer Mike Burton—he had brought his in from home. Then accountants Sandy Dean and Mike Molyneaux got a pair of ma-

Personal Computers in Action

A LOOK AT COMPUTERS IN BUSINESS

Personal computers are in businesses big and small. Here is a cross section of some computer applications.

- **Hotel management.** The Hilton Hotel chain uses a micro-to-mainframe link to connect its hotels to the main headquarters system. The system gives hotels two-way communication; the reservation system, for example, can both send and receive data.

- **Newspaper reporting.** The *Dallas Morning News* has over 100 laptop computers assigned to reporters, who take them everywhere from ballparks to inaugurations. In the office, computers are used for the extensive graphics imagery the paper uses on each page.

- **In-store shopping.** The Macy's department store chain offers a computerized bridal registry. Spouses-to-be register their gift preferences by entering them into the store's computer database. A touch screen lets store customers call up a list of gift choices by selecting the bride's or groom's name and a preferred price range. The computer system keeps track of which items have already been purchased and which are still desired, avoiding the problem of duplicate gifts. However, the system designers have still not found a way to prevent people from purchasing identical gifts at stores other than Macy's.

- **Baseball records.** The Baseball Hall of Fame in Cooperstown, New York—yes, it is a business—features a user-interactive computer. Visitors can spend hours comparing the baseball statistics of their heroes.

- **Car manufacturing.** The Ford Motor Company uses computers for every aspect of making a new car—engineering, manufacturing, assembling, and testing. Personal computers are used by people in all parts of the company to access data.

- **Stock trading.** Many brokerage houses let customers use their own computers to call up instant information. To gain access to these services, a customer needs only a personal computer and a modem. Software is provided by the brokerage firm.

- **Door-to-door selling.** Amway distributors—who sell cosmetics, detergents, and other household products nationwide—now have personal computers they can use to place orders directly with the headquarters office in Michigan.

- **Restaurant management.** Las Casuelas Terraza, a restaurant in Palm Springs that seats 200 people, uses personal computers to automate the cashier system, keep track of food inventory, design and print the menus, monitor employee comings and goings, and keep track of employee tips.

chines—they had squeezed the money for them out of the overhead budget. Keith Wong, the personnel manager, got personal computers for himself and his three assistants in the company's far-flung branch offices. And so it went, with personal computers popping up all over the company. Managers realized that the reason for runaway purchases was that personal computers were so affordable: Most departments could pay for them out of existing budgets, so the purchasers did not have to ask anyone's permission.

Managers, at first, were tolerant. There were no provisions for managing the purchase or use of personal computers, and there certainly was no rule *against* them. And it was soon apparent that these machines were more than toys. Pioneer users had no trouble justifying their purchases— their increased productivity spoke for them. In addition to mastering software for word processing, spreadsheets, and database access, these users declared their independence from the MIS department.

Managers, however, were soon faced with several problems. The first was incompatibility—the new computers came in an assortment of brands and models and did not mesh well. Software that worked on one machine did not necessarily work on another. Second, users were not as independent of the MIS department as they had thought—they needed assistance in a variety of ways. In particular, they needed data that was in the hands of the MIS department. And, finally, no one person was in charge of the headlong plunge into personal computers. Many organizations solved these management problems in these ways:

- They addressed the compatibility problem by establishing acquisition policies.
- They solved the assistance problem by creating information centers.
- They corrected the management problem by creating a new position called the personal computer manager.

Let us examine each of these solutions.

Personal Computer Acquisition

In an office environment managers know they must control the acquisition and use of personal computers, but they are not always sure how to do it. As we noted, workers initially purchased personal computers before any company-wide or even office-wide policies had been set. The resulting compatibility problems meant that they could not easily communicate or share data. Consider this example: A user's budgeting process calls for certain data that resides in the files of another worker's personal computer or perhaps involves figures output by the computer of a third person. If the software and machines these people use do not mesh, compatibility becomes a major problem.

In many companies MIS departments have now taken control of personal computer acquisition. The methods vary, but they often include the following:

- **Standards.** Most companies now have established standards for personal computers, for the software that will run on them, and for data communications. Commonly, users must stay within established standards so they can tie into corporate resources. For example, if IBM PS/2 architecture is the standard, then a compatible machine is acceptable.

- **Limited vendors.** Some companies limit the number of vendors—sellers of hardware and software—from whom they allow purchases. MIS managers have discovered they can prevent most user complaints about incompatibility by allowing products from just a handful of vendors.

- **Limited support.** MIS departments generally control a company's purchases by specifying which hardware and software products will be supported by the MIS department.

As you can see, these methods overlap. But all of them, in one form or another, give the MIS department control. In other words, users are being told, "If you want to do it some other way, then you're on your own." Despite the above measures, however, many companies have given in to employee preference for one computer or another. For example, the adoption of the Macintosh for projects demanding presentation graphics and desktop publishing has encouraged a limited erosion of the IBM standard in many businesses.

The Information Center

If personal computer users compared notes, they would probably find that their experiences are similar. The experience of budget analyst Donna Sanchez is typical. She convinced her boss to let her have her own personal computer so she could analyze financial data. She purchased a popular spreadsheet program and, with some help from her colleagues, learned to use it. She soon thought about branching out in other areas. She wanted a statistics software package but was not sure which one was appropriate. She thought it would be useful to have a modem but did not feel she was equipped to make a hardware decision. And, most of all, she felt her productivity would increase significantly if she could get her hands on the data in the corporate data files.

The company **information center** is the MIS solution to these kinds of needs. Although no two are alike, a typical information center gives users support for the user's equipment. The information center is devoted exclusively to giving users service. And, best of all, user assistance is immediate, with little or no red tape.

Information center services often include the following:

Figure 14-3   The information center.
Classes are held at the information center to teach managers and other employees how to use the company's computers.

- **Software selection.** Information center staff helps users determine which software packages suit their needs.

- **Data access.** If appropriate, the staff helps users get data from the large corporate computer systems for use on the users' computers.

- **Training.** Education is a principal reason for an information center's existence. Classes are usually small, frequent, and on a variety of topics (Figure 14-3).

- **Technical assistance.** Information center staff members stand ready to assist in any way possible, short of actually doing the users' work for them. That help includes advising on hardware purchases, aiding in the selection and use of software, finding errors, helping submit formal requests to the MIS department, and so forth.

To be successful, the information center must be placed in an easily accessible location. The center should be equipped with personal computers and terminals, a stockpile of software packages, and perhaps a library. It should be staffed with people who have a technical background but whose explanations feature plain English. Their mandate is the user comes first.

The Personal Computer Manager

And who is going to manage the revolution? The users-get-computers revolution, that is. The benefits of personal computers for the individual user have been clear almost from the beginning: increased productivity, worker enthusiasm, and easier access to information. But once personal computers move beyond entry status, standard corporate accountability becomes a factor; large companies are spending millions of dollars on personal computers and top-level managers want to know where all this money is going. Company auditors begin worrying about data security. The company legal department begins to worry about workers illegally copying software. Before long, everyone is involved, and it is clear that someone must be placed in charge of personal computer use. That person is the **personal computer manager**.

There are four key areas that need the attention of this manager:

- **Technology overload.** The personal computer manager must maintain a clear vision of company goals so that users are not overwhelmed by the massive and conflicting claims of aggressive vendors plying their wares. Users engulfed by phrases like *network topologies* and *file gateways* or a jumble of acronyms can turn to the personal computer manager for guidance with their purchases.

- **Cost control.** Many people who work with personal computers believe the initial costs are paid back rapidly, and they think that should satisfy managers who hound them about expenses. But the real costs entail training, support, hardware and software extras, and communications networks—much more than just the computer itself. The personal computer manager's role includes monitoring *all* the expenses.

- **Data security and integrity.** Access to corporate data is a touchy issue. Many personal computer users find they want to **download** (or access) data from the corporate mainframe to their own machines, and this presents an array of problems. Are they entitled to the data? Will they manipulate the data in new ways, then present it as the official version? Will they expect MIS to take the data back after they have done who-knows-what with it? The answers to these perplexing questions are not always clear-cut, but at least the personal computer manager will be tuned in to the issues.

- **Computer junkies.** And what about employees who are feverish with the new power and freedom of the computer? When they are in school, these user-abusers are sometimes called hackers; on the job they are often called junkies because their fascination with the computer seems like an addiction. Unable to resist the allure of the machine, they overuse it and neglect their other work. Personal computer managers usually respond to this problem by setting down guidelines for computer use.

The person selected to be the personal computer manager is usually from the MIS area. Ideally, this person has a broad technical background, understands both the potential and limitations of personal computers, and is well known to a diverse group of users.

One way that the personal computer manager can keep the support of top-level managers is to make sure those managers have their own computers.

When the Boss Gets a Computer

All over this land business executives—frustrated by the backlog of unfinished work in their corporate MIS departments—have opted for do-it-yourself, buying their own personal computers and packaged software. Sometimes these executives are even the heads of companies (in this chapter, see the essay "Executives Stay on Top with PCs").

One chief executive officer of a pharmaceutical company, for instance, wanted direct access to company finance and sales data. With some assistance from a computer specialist within the company, he purchased personal computers for himself and his staff. They took classes in software applications, particularly spreadsheet software. This software let them examine issues of business strategy, such as the level of sales discounts and advertising support needed to reach the company's sales targets. Earlier strategic planning was fairly informal: "We just eyeballed the numbers and made our best guesses." Now all that has changed. In fact, computers make a very significant difference in how managers do their jobs. In companies with offices around the world, managers may not be able to get together very often, but they are staying in touch daily through their personal computers (Figure 14-4).

How Computers Affect Managers

People who dismiss the impact of the personal computer sometimes say, "It's just another tool." Some tool. The personal computer is making profound changes in the work lives of businesspeople who use it, though some seem unaware of what is going on.

Regional business manager Augusta Green, for example, stoutly insists, "The computer hasn't changed *my* life." But listen to the changes.

Figure 14-4   Programming wizard CEO. Philippe Kahn, founder and CEO of Borland International, Scotts Valley, California, is the programming wizard behind one of the top-selling programming languages, Turbo Pascal. A French-born mathematician, Kahn keeps abreast of the competition by continually testing equipment and competitor's products. When he's on the road, he relies on laptops and telecommunications, running Borland by electronic mail from wherever he happens to be—Paris; New York; or Auckland, New Zealand. Kahn says he is fighting the "meetingomania" of American business. Borland managers around the world seldom meet in person but are always on-line—electronically connected.

When asked how she uses her machine, she begins by describing her early personal computer projects. One was drawing up a budget and the other was designing a compensation package for the 80 people under her supervision. Later, she added hardware and software to send electronic messages to people in the office, dispatch electronic mail to other parts of the country, and call up articles from the business press. She also uses her computer to write memos and reports—"a piece of cake," she says.

Augusta eventually succumbed to a second personal computer at home, which she uses to do office work in the evening. She finds it easier to carry diskettes to and fro than to lug a briefcase full of paper. Most mornings, in fact, Augusta tosses her diskettes into her out-box, knowing the secretary will take it from there. Finally, Augusta reflects on all this activity. "Everything I do on the computer," she says, "I do ten times faster than I used to do it."

For many managers, the machine that is "just a tool" speeds analysis to a breakneck pace, answers all sorts of "What if . . .?" questions,

PERSPECTIVES

EXECUTIVES STAY ON TOP WITH PCS

What do James E. Clark, Patricia Seybold, and W. Thomas Stephens have in common? They are all executives who stay on top of their businesses daily, no matter where they are—anywhere in the world—through highly portable personal computers and telecommunications devices that liberate them from the constraints of the office. These executives praise their new-found freedom and believe their use

neglected to pack a printer. Spying two fax machines side by side in the hotel's business office, he asked to use them—both. "You want to send a fax to yourself?" the questioner looked at him, surprised. After explaining the trick in mind, he got his way—and a printout of his presentation. Clark also found a solution to the lack of phone jacks (for telecommunications) in hotel rooms. His new Safari notebook computer from AT&T includes the first "wireless mailbox"—a small pager that can store as many as 20

fact that she is tapping away on a Safari notebook—bespeak another high-tech executive at work. "It's the only place I could find a plug," she explains. This much-traveled management consultant likes the instant interaction provided by telecommunications with her equally nomadic staff at her Office Computing Group in Boston. She hopes to start using a pen-based computer soon. "You could project the image on an overhead screen so that a group could see it and work together to make that particular process more efficient."

In Manhattan traffic, CEO W. Thomas Stephens of Manville Corporation, uses a laptop to catch up on his work. When he goes on business trips in the U.S., he usually packs fax capabilities and a small printer along with his laptop. On overseas trips, he travels lighter, with an 11-ounce palmtop. At his office and at home, he uses IBM-

of personal computers has made them infinitely more productive—and saved them large amounts of time in the office, on the road, and at home.

James E. Clark, a vice president for medium-size computers at AT&T's new NCR subsidiary, found himself in a predicament recently on a trip to Bombay, India. He needed a printout of a presentation stored on his laptop. But he had

messages of about 40 words each. The messages are bounced off the SkyTel satellite and onto the pager's screen. Clark calls it "anytime, anywhere computing" using "a post office in the sky."

Patricia Seybold sits on the floor between two elevators at the Phoenix Sky Harbor airport, looking almost like a homeless person. But her dress and manner—and the

compatible machines. Stephens relies heavily on the personal computer to analyze acquisitions for his multibillion dollar company: "It gives you an opportunity to be a lot more powerful and to focus on being creative rather than spending your time making charts and that sort of thing." But, he says, his daughter Anne, eight, still beats him at computer chess.

sends and receives mail, and lets executives get out of the office more. In earlier chapters we discussed some of the key software packages—word processing and desktop publishing, spreadsheets, database management, and graphics—that help make these things possible. Now we want to take a closer look at software of special significance to managers: decision support systems.

Decision Support Systems

Imagine yourself as a top-level manager trying to deal with a constantly changing environment, having to consider changes in competition, in technology, in consumer habits, in government regulations, in union demands, and so on. How are you going to make decisions about those matters for which there are no precedents? In fact, making one-of-a-kind decisions—decisions that no one has had to make before—is the real test of a manager's mettle. In such a situation, you would probably wish you could turn to someone and ask a few "What if . . .?" questions (Figure 14-5).

"What if . . .?" That is the question businesspeople want answered, especially for those important decisions that have no precedent. A **decision support system** (**DSS**) is a computer system that supports managers in nonroutine decision-making tasks. The key ingredient of a decision support system is a modeling process. A **model** is a mathematical representation of a real-life system. A mathematical model can be computerized. Like any computer program, the model can use inputs to produce outputs. The inputs to a model are called **independent variables** because they can change; the outputs are called **dependent variables** because they depend on the inputs.

Consider this example. Suppose, as a manager, you have the task of deciding which property to purchase for one of your manufacturing processes. You have many factors to consider: the asking price, interest

Figure 14-5 Making decisions with the help of a computer. Businesspeople use computers to try out different scenarios, without investing a great deal of time and money.

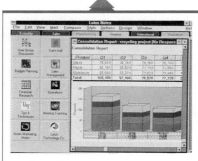

Gains for Groups at All Levels

Harnessing the ideas of a group is tough for group decision makers when everyone speaks at once. But when groupware like Lotus Notes enters the picture, brainstormers around a table can all express their ideas—and still expect to be heard. This groupware cousin to spreadsheet standard Lotus 1-2-3 lets participants type their ideas on networked personal computers. Anyone can respond to any idea at anytime, and all responses will be displayed and maintained in a coherent fashion. Lotus Notes differs from an electronic mail system, in which senders must specify the recipients of their messages—Notes lets anyone with an interest in a subject have access to the information. A company's employees around the globe may respond, forming small, networked groups to help each other make better-informed decisions. Proponents of groupware say that team members stay abreast of one another's progress whether they are in a meeting room or scattered. As the flow of knowledge becomes democratized, many firms with senior executives who might otherwise avoid computers find these kinds of interactions not only useful but important. For example, before they started using Lotus Notes, only four members of Price Waterhouse's senior executive committee used personal computers—now all do.

rate, down payment required, and so on. These are all independent variables—the data that will be fed into the computer model of the purchase. The dependent variables, computed on the basis of the inputs, are the effect on your cash resources, long-term debt, and ability to make other investments. To increase complexity, we could add that the availability of workers and nearness to markets are also input factors. Increasing the complexity is appropriate, in fact, because decision support systems often work with problems that are more complex than any one individual can handle.

Using a computer model to reach a decision about a real-life situation is called **simulation.** It is a game of "let's pretend." You plan the independent variables—the inputs—and you examine how the model behaves based on the dependent variables—the outputs—it produces. If you wish, you may change the inputs and continue experimenting. This is a relatively inexpensive way to simulate life situations, and it is considerably faster than the real thing.

A decision support system does not replace MIS; instead, a DSS supplements MIS. There are distinct differences between them. MIS emphasizes planned reports on a variety of subjects; DSS focuses on decision making. MIS is standard, scheduled, structured, routine; DSS is quite unstructured and available on request. MIS is constrained by the organizational system; DSS is immediate and friendly.

The decision-making process must be fast, so the DSS is interactive: The user is in direct communication with the computer system and can affect its activities. In addition, most DSSs cross departmental lines so that information can be pulled from the databases of a variety of sources, such as marketing and sales, accounting and finance, production, and research and development. A manager trying to make a decision about developing a new product needs information from all these sources.

In fact, managers may spend half of their working hours in group decision-making meetings. Such meetings require software that can help them make informed and competent decisions quickly. The **group decision support system** (**GDSS**) consists of hardware, software, people, procedures, and databases needed to support decision making by groups. GDSS goes beyond traditional DSS by trying to build consensus and by acknowledging that special procedures, devices, and approaches are needed in group settings. Such procedures are used to spur creative thinking and to foster clear communications and effective group decision-making techniques.

GDSS requires immediate access to huge amounts of information residing throughout company databases. Special software products have emerged to support GDSS, called **groupware**—software to encourage group strategies in word processing, spreadsheets, database search-and-retrieval, graphics, and communications, as well as decision-making. GDSS may also require alternative settings, such as decision room facilities, local-area and wide-area decision networks, or even teleconferencing capabilities.

Top-level executives and decision makers face unique decision-making problems and pressures. An **executive support system** (**ESS**) is a DSS or GDSS especially made for senior-level executives, including all the

Keeping in Touch

Bernard Krisher, an American journalist-entrepreneur in Tokyo, composes a message on his palmtop personal computer while visiting Mt. Fuji. Krisher is an advisor to *Focus,* a popular weekly; writes speeches for Japanese executives; runs a jewelry salon on the Ginza; advises a PC users network; runs a database service for businesses; and travels a lot on assignments. To do all that, he employs only electronic help, using personal computers and modems, cellular phones, and faxes. Recently, he was in New York for six weeks. "Many of my clients didn't even know I wasn't in Tokyo," he says.

necessary hardware, software, data, procedures, and people. The unique concern of an ESS involves the leadership position of the participants and how their decisions affect an entire organization. An ESS must take into consideration:

- The overall vision or broad view of company goals
- Strategic, long-term planning and objectives
- Organizational structure
- Staffing and labor relations
- Crisis management
- Strategic control and monitoring of overall operations

Executive decision-making also requires access to outside information from competitors, federal authorities, trade groups, consultants, and news gathering agencies, among others. There is also a high degree of uncertainty and a future orientation involved in most executive decisions. Successful ESS software must therefore be easy to use, flexible, and customizable. It must offer a wide range of computing resources and a high degree of specialization, support all aspects of decision making, and allow a focus on external conditions. In addition, to respond to the high degree of uncertainty involved, the use of modeling is important.

Several commercial software packages are available for specific modeling purposes. The purpose might be marketing, sales, or advertising. Other packages that are more general provide rudimentary modeling but let you customize the model for different purposes—budgeting, planning, or risk analysis, for example.

There is another possibility. Suppose that a full-scale decision support system is not needed. In fact, let us say that the key decisions that need support involve exploring a number of alternatives by varying assumptions about market size, market share, selling prices, manufacturing costs, and expenses. Sound familiar? Right, we are talking about a perfect application for a spreadsheet program. Today's most widely used decision support system is spreadsheet software. In Chapter 16 we will look at more comprehensive ways to solve business problems—with expert systems and artificial intelligence.

Leading Business into the Future

Who will manage businesses in the future? Someone once remarked, somewhat facetiously, that all top management—presidents, chief executive officers (CEOs), and so forth—should be drawn from the MIS ranks. After all, the argument goes, computers pervade the entire company, and people who work with computer systems can bring broad experience to the job. Today, most presidents and CEOs still come from legal, financial, or marketing backgrounds. But as the computer industry and its professionals mature, that pattern could change.

Another challenge looming as personal computer use increases in business is the security and integrity of corporate data. We investigate ethical issues in the next chapter.

R E V I E W   A N D   R E F E R E N C E

Summary and Key Terms

- All managers have five main functions: planning, organizing, staffing, directing, and controlling. Top-level managers focus primarily on strategic functions, especially long-range **planning;** middle-level managers focus on the tactical, especially the **organizing** and **staffing** required to implement plans; and low-level managers are concerned mainly with operational functions, **controlling** schedules, costs, and quality as well as **directing** the personnel.

- A **management information system (MIS)** is a set of business systems designed to provide information for decision making. A computerized MIS is most effective if it is integrated.

- The **MIS manager,** a person familiar with both computer technology and the organization's business, runs the MIS department.

- An MIS can produce detail, summary, and exception reports, either on a regular schedule (**periodic reports**) or in response to unscheduled requests from users (**on-demand reports**). **Detail reports** provide complete, specific information; **summary reports** are limited to totals or trends. **Exception reports** show only data that reflects unusual circumstances.

- Top-level managers frequently require information that aids strategic planning. They often request on-demand reports about the impact of unpredictable occurrences. Middle-level managers usually need summary reports showing expenses and sales trends and exception reports about unexpected expenses and projects behind schedule. Low-level managers typically require detail reports about factors affecting routine operations.

- When personal computers first became popular in the business world, most businesses did not have general policies regarding them, which led to several problems. Many businesses developed acquisition policies to solve the compatibility problem, established information centers to provide assistance to users, and created the position of personal computer manager to ensure coordination of personal computer use.

- Personal computer acquisition policies may include establishing standards for hardware and software, limiting the number of vendors, and limiting the hardware and software that the MIS department will support.

- An **information center** typically offers employees classes on a variety of computer topics, advice on selecting software, help in getting data from corporate computer systems, and technical assistance on such matters as hardware purchases and requests to the MIS department.

- The main concerns of a **personal computer manager** are (1) avoiding technology overload, (2) monitoring all the expenses connected with personal computers, (3) being aware of potential data security problems when users **download** data from the corporate mainframe to their own personal computers, and (4) setting guidelines for personal computer use to combat user-abusers.

- An increasing number of business executives use their own personal computers to assist them in strategic planning (mainly through spreadsheets, database access, and graphics) and communication (mainly through electronic mail and word processing).

- A **decision support system (DSS)** is a computer system that supports managers in nonroutine decision-making tasks. A DSS involves a **model,** a mathematical representation of a real-life situation. A computerized model allows a manager to try various "What if . . .?" options by varying the inputs (**independent variables**) to see how they affect the outputs (**dependent variables**). The use of a computer model to reach a decision about a real-life situation is called **simulation.** Since the decision-making process must be fast, the DSS is interactive, allowing the user to communicate directly with the computer system and affect its activities.

- A **Group decision support system (GDSS)** consists of hardware, software, people, procedures, and databases needed to support decision making by groups. GDSS goes beyond DSS by trying to build consensus among groups. Special software products have emerged to support GDSS, especially **groupware,** software that encourages group interaction in word processing and other applications. An **executive support system (ESS)** is a DSS or GSSS especially made for senior-level executives.

Review Questions

1. Describe the five main functions of managers, explaining how the emphasis varies with the level of management.

2. What terms are used generally to describe the functions of managers at the top, middle, and low levels?

3. What is an MIS? Why is an integrated MIS the most effective type?

4. Define the following: detail report, summary report, exception report, periodic report, and on-demand report.

5. Explain how the various types of MIS reports are related to the different management levels and functions.

6. Explain why the MIS manager can be regarded as a powerful person within a company.

7. Name the three main personal computer management problems and explain how they arose.

8. Describe three common methods through which MIS departments control personal computer acquisition.

9. Describe some of the functions of an information center.
10. Describe four ways in which a personal computer manager can help a company.

Discussion Questions

1. Discuss why an executive might buy a personal computer.
2. Why do experts believe the classic management pyramid is flattening today?
3. Do you feel a personal computer manager is necessary in business today? Provide examples from businesses you know to help explain your feelings.
4. Why do you think user-created programs worry PC managers?
5. Describe a problem situation that could be simulated through a decision support system. Specify the input factors and the types of output.

True-False Questions

T F   1. The main goals of a manager at any level precludes his or her use of a personal computer.

T F   2. Directing and controlling are the primary functions of low-level managers.

T F   3. An MIS department usually handles service and support functions for personal computers in a company.

T F   4. A main reason for a company's information center is to train employees to use their personal computers and run software.

T F   5. Data security and integrity are touchy issues faced by businesses when personal computer users want access to corporate data.

T F   6. On-demand reports provide data in response to unusual circumstances.

T F   7. A personal computer manager is in charge of the acquisition of all personal computers in a company.

T F   8. One of the hidden costs of bringing personal computers into the office is the additional cost of connecting them to networks.

T F   9. DSSs are computer systems that support managers in nonroutine decision-making tasks.

T F   10. Fewer executives are using personal computers today than in the past.

15

Security, Privacy, and Ethics

Protecting Hardware, Software, and Data

 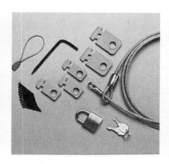 

On March 6, 1991, personal computer users all over the world turned on

their machines in fear and trepidation. In most cases, nothing unusual

happened; the computers started up just fine. But in some cases, a mes-

sage flashed on the screen and the computer began to erase all files and

data stored on the hard disk. Unless backup copies were available, the

data was lost irretrievably. Financial data, subscriber names and addresses,

church membership and donation records, real estate records, and hun-

dreds of other types of computer data—the very foundations of many

businesses—had become victims.

What had happened? A virus called Michelangelo had somehow spread

Taking Computer Crime Seriously

The U.S. Supreme Court's refusal to hear the case of Cornell graduate student Robert T. Morris, Jr., convicted of passing a virus that ended up shutting down more than 6000 computers on the Internet network, sent a message to high-tech criminals: Times are changing. Shortly afterward, the Justice Department revealed plans for a five-person Computer Crime Unit, dedicated to investigating and prosecuting computer crimes—and pushing for harsher penalties and a general tightening of the laws in this area.

The Justice Department believes the original Computer Fraud and Abuse Act needs shoring up with a provision to make it a crime to insert a virus of any type into a computer system. It also wants to expand its breadth with "reckless" as well as "intentional" damages as grounds for conviction.

The act originally gave the Justice Department the muscle it needed to crack down on hackers. In November 1990, three persons were convicted for breaking into a Bell South computer system; they were sentenced to 21 months in jail and ordered to pay $230,000 in restitution. Prior to that, in May, Operation Sundevil enlisted 150 Secret Service agents in raids on 27 suspected hackers and resulted in the seizure of 23,000 computer disks and 40 computers. Few prosecutions came of it. On the contrary, a raid on Steve Jackson Games of Austin, Texas, left the company on the verge of bankruptcy, so it is suing the Secret Service, with the help of the Electronic Frontier Foundation, a group that supports hackers on First Amendment grounds.

However, the Supreme Court's action, as well as the Justice Department's new unit, tells high-tech criminals that harsher penalties and longer sentences lie ahead.

throughout the personal computer community around the world. A **virus** is a set of illicit instructions that passes itself on to other programs with which it comes in contact. In this case, the Michelangelo virus was spread on IBM and IBM-compatible personal computers by unsuspecting users who shared diskettes that carried the virus instructions. Michelangelo was first spotted in Europe in March 1990. Within a year it had spread to the United States and the rest of the world. Named after the famous artist born on March 6, 1475, the Michelangelo virus—and its threat to annihilate hard disk data—caught the interest of newspaper editors all over the globe. They ran stories about the virus for several days before its attack. The publicity was credited with alerting most users to the dangers and saving their data.

Whoever created the virus was never caught. But one thing became evident: A virus can strike at any time because few computer systems are totally secure. A dramatic story about a virus may make fascinating reading, but a virus is only a small part of the security problem. Computer systems are vulnerable in a variety of ways (Figure 15-1). The security of computers and computer-related data is a critical issue. Let us begin by examining the most fascinating of security breaches: computer crime.

Computer Crime

Most of us have read about teenage hackers who create programs like viruses that cause havoc when run on computers. Originally, *hacker* was a term used to describe self-taught, enthusiastic computer users, but the word has become a term of derision. Now, it usually describes a person who gains access to computer systems illegally. Hackers are a real annoyance, but the most serious losses are caused by electronic pickpockets who are a good deal older and not half so harmless. Consider these examples.

- A small business operator and a salesman were arrested by police in a sting operation that netted more than $200,000 worth of counterfeit packages of Microsoft's latest DOS software.

- A brokerage clerk sat at his terminal in Denver and, with a few taps of the keys, transformed 1700 shares of his own stock, worth $1.50 per share, to the same number of shares in another company worth ten times that much.

- A keyboard operator in Oakland, California, changed some delivery addresses to divert several thousand dollars' worth of department-store goods into the hands of accomplices.

- A ticket clerk at the Arizona Veteran's Memorial Coliseum issued full-price basketball tickets for admission, then used her computer to record the sales as half-price tickets and pocketed the difference.

These stories point out that computer crime is not always the flashy, front-page news about geniuses getting away with millions of dollars.

Figure 15-1   Is your computer secure?
The computer industry, which is vulnerable to both natural and man-made disasters, has been slow to protect itself.

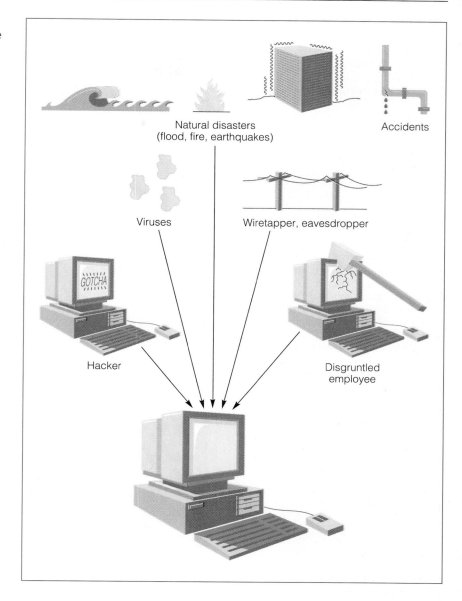

Stories about computer crime continue to fascinate the general public. They are "clean" white-collar crimes; no one gets physically hurt. They often feature people beating the system—that is, beating an anonymous, faceless, presumably wealthy organization. Sometimes the perpetrators even fancy themselves as modern-day Robin Hoods, taking from the rich to give to the poor—themselves and their friends. One electronic thief, in fact, described himself as a "one-man welfare agency."

The problems of computer crime have been aggravated in recent years by increased access to computers (Figure 15-2). More employees now have access to computers on their jobs. Many more people are using personal computers. And more students are taking computer training. Computer crime is serious business and deserves to be taken seriously by everyone.

Disgruntled or militant employee could

- Sabotage equipment or programs
- Hold data or programs hostage

Competitor could

- Sabotage operations
- Engage in espionage
- Steal data or programs
- Photograph records, documentation, or CRT screen displays

Data control worker could

- Insert data
- Delete data
- Bypass controls
- Sell information

Clerk/supervisor could

- Forge or falsify data
- Embezzle funds
- Engage in collusion with people inside or outside the company

System user could

- Sell data to competitors
- Obtain unauthorized information

Operator could

- Copy files
- Destroy files

User requesting reports could

- Sell information to competitors
- Receive unauthorized information

Engineer could

- Install "bugs"
- Sabotage system
- Access security information

Data conversion worker could

- Change codes
- Insert data
- Delete data

Programmer could

- Steal programs or data
- Embezzle via programming
- Bypass controls

Report distribution worker could

- Examine confidential reports
- Keep duplicates of reports

Trash collector could

- Sell reports or duplicates to competitors

Figure 15-2 The perils of increased access. By letting your imagination loose, you can visualize many ways in which people can compromise computer security. Computer-related crime would be far more rampant if all the people in these positions took advantage of their access to computers.

A Glossary for Computer Crooks

Although the emphasis in this chapter is on preventing rather than committing crime, being familiar with the terms and methods computer criminals use is part of being a prudent computer user. Many of these words or phrases have made their way into the general vocabulary.

Bomb: A virus that sabotages a program to trigger damage based on certain conditions; it is usually set to go off at a later date—perhaps after the perpetrator has left the company.

Data diddling: Changing data before or as it enters the system.

Data leakage: Removing copies of data from the system without a trace.

Piggybacking: Using another person's identification code or using that person's files before he or she has logged off.

Pirate: A person who copies software illegally.

Salami technique: Using a large financial system to squirrel away small "slices" of money that may never be missed.

Scavenging: Searching trash cans for printouts and carbons containing not-for-distribution information.

Trapdoor: Leaving, within a completed program, an illicit program that allows unauthorized—and unknown—entry.

Trojan horse: A virus that covertly places illegal instructions in the middle of a legitimate program. In other words, it appears to do something useful but actually does something destructive in the background. An example is the "Sexy Ladies" HyperCard stack on the Macintosh, which erases the hard drive while you check the cheesecake.

Virus: A piece of software that attaches itself to applications or files. When run, the application or file provides a pathway for the virus to spread to your system files and other software, or from one system to another.

Worm: A virus that replicates and spreads.

Zapping: Using an illicitly acquired software package to bypass all security systems.

Who Is the Computer Criminal?

Here is what a computer criminal is apt to be like. He (we will use *he* here, but of course *he* could be *she*) is usually someone occupying a position of trust in an organization. Indeed, he is likely to be regarded as the ideal employee. He has had no previous law-breaking experience and, in fact, will not see himself as a thief but as a "borrower." He is apt to be young and to be fascinated with the challenge of beating the system. Contrary to expectations, he is not necessarily a loner; he may operate well in conjunction with other employees to take advantage of the system's weaknesses.

What motivates the computer criminal? The causes are as varied as the offenders. However, a few frequent motives have been identified. A computer criminal is often the disgruntled employee, possibly a long-time loyal worker out for revenge after being passed over for a raise or promotion. In another scenario an otherwise model employee may commit a crime while suffering from personal or family problems. Not all motives are emotionally based. Some people simply are attracted to the challenge of the crime. In contrast, it is the ease of the crime that tempts others. An experienced security consultant noted that computer crime is nothing but white-collar crime with a new medium: Every time an employee is trained to use a computer at work, he or she also gains knowledge that could be used to harm the company.

In many cases the criminal activity is unobtrusive; it fits right in with regular job duties. One offender noted that his colleagues would never ask what he was doing; instead, they would make comments like, "That turkey, that technician, all he ever does is talk his buzzwords, can't talk to him," and walk away. So the risk of detection is often quite low. Computer criminals think they can get away with it. And they do—some of the time.

Types and Methods of Computer Crime

Computer crime falls into three basic categories:

- Theft of computer time for development of software, either for personal use or with the intention of selling it
- Theft, destruction, or manipulation of programs or data
- Alteration of data stored in a computer file

Although it is not our purpose to write a how-to book on computer crime, the essay called "A Glossary for Computer Crooks" mentions some criminal methods as examples, in addition to defining terms like *virus*, *worm*, and *trojan horse*.

Discovery and Prosecution

Prosecuting the computer criminal is difficult because discovery is often difficult. Many times the crime simply goes undetected. In addition, crimes that are detected are—an estimated 85% of the time—never reported to the authorities. By law, banks have to make a report when their computer systems have been compromised, but other businesses do not. Often they choose not to report because they are worried about their reputations and credibility in the community.

Most discoveries of computer crimes happen by accident. For example, a bank employee changed a program to add 10¢ to every customer service charge under $10 and $1 to every charge over $10. He then placed this overage into the last account, a bank account he opened himself in the name of Zzwicke. The system worked fairly well, generating several hundred dollars each month, until the bank initiated a new marketing campaign in which they singled out for special honors the very first depositor—and the very last. In another instance some employees of a city welfare department created a fictitious work force, complete with Social Security numbers, and programmed the computer to issue paychecks, which the employees would then intercept and cash. They were discovered when a police officer investigated an illegally parked overdue rental car—and found 7100 fraudulent checks inside.

Even if a computer crime is detected, a prosecution is by no means assured. There are a number of reasons for this. First, some law enforcement agencies do not fully understand the complexities of computer-related fraud. Second, few attorneys are qualified to handle computer crime cases. Third, judges and juries are not always educated about computers and may not understand the value of data to a company.

In short, the chances of committing computer crimes and having them go undetected are, unfortunately, good. And the chances that, if detected, there will be no ramifications are also good: A computer criminal may not go to jail, may not be found guilty if prosecuted, and may not even be prosecuted.

But this situation is changing. Since Congress passed the **Computer Fraud and Abuse Act** in 1986, there has been a growing awareness on the national level. Prosecutors complain, however, that the law is loose, ill-defined, and an easy target for sharp defense attorneys. This law, however, is supplemented by state statutes. Most states have passed some form of computer crime law. The number of safe places for computer desperadoes is dwindling fast.

 ## Security: Playing It Safe

As you can see from the previous section, the computer industry has been extremely vulnerable in the matter of security. Computer security once meant the physical security of the computer itself—guarded and locked doors. Computer screens were given dark filters so others could not easily see the data on the screen (Figure 15-3). But filters and locks by no means prevent access, as we have seen. Management interest in security has been heightened, and managers are now rushing to purchase more sophisticated security products.

Biometrics and High-Tech Crime

U.S. businesses and government agencies lose more than $1 billion a year to hackers and high-tech criminals. How to fight it? Many say that there is only one way: Limit access to files and databases.

But there are other, newer ways involving biometrics—the science of measuring body parts. Biometrics can recognize your voice, inspect your eyes—to compare the map of blood vessels on the back of your eyeball—and check your fingerprints and even your kisser. That's right, you kiss the screen and the computer matches this input with a file that contains your unique lip patterns.

Each means of biometric recognition has advantages and drawbacks:

- **Voice.** Using speech recognition capabilities, the computer recognizes your voice. This method allows access from a phone; however, it is expensive, and static can interfere.

- **Eyes.** As shown here, a laser beam scans the map of the blood vessels of your eye. Many wonder if it is safe for the eyes.

- **Fingerprints.** This means of identification has worked for police for years. The technology is unwieldy, however, unless the reading device is portable.

- **Lip prints.** After the user kisses the screen, the computer checks the kisser's unique lip patterns against those on file. This technology is still unproved, and makeup, cold sores, chapped lips can interfere with print recognition.

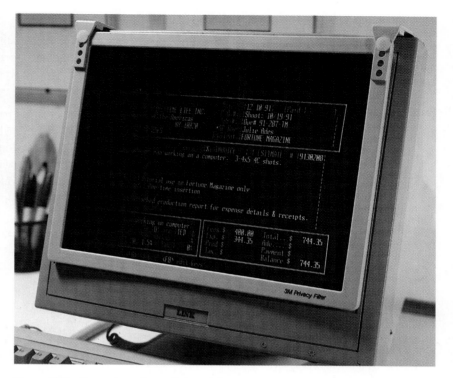

Figure 15-3 Computer privacy. To keep information private, some companies use darkened filters over the personal computer screens in open offices. This Privacy Filter by 3M shields work from people on either side. The filter is clear for the person using the computer, but move 30 degrees to either side and it appears black.

What is computer security? We may define it as follows: **Security** is a system of safeguards designed to protect a computer system and data from deliberate or accidental damage or access by unauthorized persons. That means safeguarding the system against such threats as burglary, vandalism, fire, natural disasters, theft of data for ransom, industrial espionage, and various forms of white-collar crime.

Identification and Access: Who Goes There?

How does a computer system detect whether you are the person who should be allowed access to it? Various means have been devised to give access to authorized people—without compromising the system. These means fall into four broad categories: what you have, what you know, what you do, and who you are.

- **What you have.** You may have a key, badge, token, or a plastic card to give you physical access to the computer room or a locked-up terminal. A card with a magnetized strip, for example, can give you access to your bank account via a remote cash machine.

- **What you know.** Standard what-you-know items are a system password or an identification number for your bank cash machine. Cipher locks on doors require that you know the correct combination of numbers.

- **What you do.** In our daily lives we often sign documents as a way of proving who we are. Though a signature is difficult to copy, forgery is not impossible. For this and other reasons, signatures lend themselves to human interaction better than machine interaction.

- **What you are.** Now it gets interesting. Some security systems use **biometrics,** the science of measuring individual body characteristics. Fingerprinting is old news, but voice recognition is relatively new. Even newer is the concept of identification by the retina of the eye and the patterns of your lips, but all have drawbacks (in this chapter, see the essay "Biometrics and High-Tech Crimes"). These techniques enable a machine to recognize a properly authorized person.

Some systems use a combination of the preceding four categories. For example, access to an automated teller machine requires both something you have—a plastic card—and something you know—a personal identification number.

When Disaster Strikes: What Do You Have to Lose?

In New York, a power outage shut down computer operations and effectively halted business, air traffic, and transportation throughout the United States. In Italy, armed terrorists singled out corporate and state computer centers as targets for attack and, during a ten-month period, bombed ten such centers throughout the country. In California, a poem, a pansy, a bag of cookies, and a message, "Please have a cookie and a nice day," were left at the Vandenberg Air Force Base computer installation—along with five demolished mainframe computers. Computer installations of any kind can be struck by natural or man-made disasters that can lead to security violations. What kinds of problems might this cause an organization?

Your first thoughts might be of the hardware, the computer and its related equipment. But loss of hardware is not a major problem in itself; the loss will be covered by insurance, and hardware can be replaced. The true problem with hardware loss is the diminished processing ability that exists while managers find a substitute facility and return the installation to its former state. The ability to continue processing data is critical. Some information industries, such as banking, could literally go out of business in a matter of days if their computer operations were suspended.

Loss of software should not be a problem if the organization has heeded industry warnings—and used common sense—to make backup copies.

A more important problem is the loss of data. Imagine trying to reassemble lost or destroyed master files of customer records, accounts receivable, or design data for a new airplane. The costs would be staggering. We will consider software and data security in more detail later in this chapter. First, however, let us present an overview of disaster recovery, the steps to restoring processing ability.

Disaster Recovery Plan

A **disaster recovery plan** is a method of restoring data processing operations if those operations are halted by major damage or destruction. There are various approaches. Some organizations revert temporarily to manual services, but life without the computer can be difficult indeed. Others arrange to buy time at a service bureau, but this is inconvenient for companies in remote or rural areas. If a single act, such as a fire, destroys your computing facility, it is possible that a mutual aid pact will help you get back on your feet. In such a plan, two or more companies agree to lend each other computing power if one of them has a problem. This would be of little help, however, if there were a regional disaster and many companies needed assistance.

Banks and other organizations with survival dependence on computers sometimes form a **consortium,** a joint venture to support a complete computer facility. Such a facility is completely available and routinely tested but used only in the event of a disaster. Among these facilities, a **hot site** is a fully equipped computer center, with hardware, environmental controls, security, and communications facilities. A **cold site** is an environmentally suitable empty shell in which a company can install its own computer system.

The use of such a facility or any type of recovery at all depends on advance planning—specifically, the disaster recovery plan. The idea of such a plan is that everything except the hardware has been stored in a safe place somewhere else. The storage location should be several miles away, so it will not be affected by local physical forces, such as a hurricane. Typical items stored at the backup site are program and data files, program listings, program and operating systems documentation, hardware inventory lists, output forms, and a copy of the disaster plan manual.

The disaster recovery plan should include these items:

- **Priorities.** A list of priorities identifies the programs that must be up and running first. A bank, for example, would give greater weight to account inquiries than to employee vacation planning.
- **Personnel requirements.** The plan should comprise procedures for notifying employees of changes in locations and procedures.
- **Equipment requirements.** A list of needed equipment and where it can be obtained will speed recovery efforts.
- **Facilities.** Most organizations cannot afford consortiums, so the recovery plan should include a list of alternative computing facilities.
- **Capture and distribution.** This part of the plan outlines how input and output data will be handled in a different environment.

Computer installations actually perform emergency drills. At some unexpected moment a notice is given that "disaster has struck," and the computer professionals must run the critical systems at some other site.

Software Security

Software security has been an industry concern for years. Initially, there were many questions: Who owns a program? Is the owner the person who

P E R S P E C T I V E S

THE WORLD OF VIRUSES

A computer with a disease? No, not really. A virus actually affects a computer program, not the machine. And, like a biological virus, a software virus is contagious. That is, a virus passes itself on to other programs with which it comes in contact, if the conditions are right.

Viruses come in many forms and from all over the world. The first recognized virus was created by Fred Cohen while a student at the University of Southern California. His doctoral thesis proved that computer code could replicate itself, attach itself to other files, and change the behavior of the computer. At a 1983 seminar on computer security—to the chagrin of the government agents in the audience—he presented findings that proved that small strings of code could, among other things, make a hard disk "suicidal."

The National Computer Security Association (NCSA) reports that only four viruses were discovered in all of 1986, compared with one every few days in 1990. Edward Wilding, editor of *Virus Bulletin*, an international newsletter on virus prevention and removal, reported that 20 to 30 new viruses appeared each month during 1991.

Viruses from Everywhere

Viruses come from all over the world. The Virus Information Summary List (VSUM), a hypertext-based virus reference program created by Patricia M. Hoffman, covers viruses from 33 countries, including the top virus producers: the United States (which has contributed 41), Bulgaria (38), and what used to be called the Soviet Union (26). Besides the Michelangelo and Jerusalem viruses, some other infamous viruses are:

- **Peace (Canada).** A benign virus released by a computer magazine in Canada, it affected only the Macintosh community and revealed itself on the anniversary of the release of the Macintosh II, displaying a peace sign.

- **Red Cross (Germany).** Also known as the Ambulance virus, it is a nondestructive virus that shows itself on occasion by blaring a "siren" and displaying an ambulance driving along the bottom of the screen.

- **Dark Avenger (Bulgaria).** A destructive virus whose B strain installs itself in memory; writes "Eddie lives. . . . Somewhere in Time!"; and overwrites a data file or program, damaging it beyond repair.

- **Stealth (Israel).** A destructive virus that, among other things, attacks the File Allocation Table (FAT)—your hard disk map—leaving your personal computer inoperable.

- **Joshi (India).** On January 5, your computer displays a sign asking you to "Say Happy Birthday, Joshi." If you do not type exactly those words, this destructive virus erases your hard disk.

---

wrote the program or the company for which the author wrote the program? What is to prevent a programmer from taking copies of programs from one job to another? Or, even simpler, what is to prevent any user from copying personal computer software onto another diskette?

Many of these perplexing questions have been answered. If a programmer is in the employ of the organization, the program belongs to the organization, not the programmer. If the programmer is a consultant, however, the ownership of the software produced should be spelled out specifically in the contract—otherwise, the parties enter extremely murky legal waters.

According to a U.S. Supreme Court decision, software can be copyrighted. Unfortunately, however, reality seems out of synch with the decision: Although unauthorized duplication is specifically prohibited by law, very little can be done to prevent it. Software continues to be copied as blatantly as music cassettes. We will examine this issue more closely when we consider ethics, later in the chapter.

Data Security

We have discussed the security of hardware and software. Now let us consider the security of data, which, as we said, is one of an organization's most important assets. Here too there must be planning for security. Usually, this is done by security officers who are part of top management. There are five critical planning areas for data security:

- Determination of appropriate policies and standards. A typical statement of policy might read: "All computer data and related information will be protected against unauthorized disclosure and against alteration or destruction."
- Development and implementation of security safeguards, such as passwords.
- Inclusion of security precautions at the development stage of new automated systems, rather than after the systems are in use.
- Review of state and federal laws related to security. This is particularly significant in banking.
- Maintenance of historical records associated with computer abuse.

What steps can be taken to prevent theft or alteration of data? There are several data protection techniques; these will not individually (or even collectively) guarantee security, but at least they make a good start.

Secured Waste   Discarded printouts, printer ribbons, and the like can be sources of information to unauthorized persons. This kind of waste can be made secure by the use of shredders or locked trash barrels.

Passwords   Passwords are the secret words or numbers that must be typed on the keyboard to gain access to a computer system. In some installations, however, the passwords are changed so seldom that they become known to many people. And some users even tape paper with their password written on it right on the terminal. (In a case prosecuted by the federal government, the defendant admitted that he got a secret code by strolling into the programmers' area and yelling, to no one in particular, "Hey, what's the password today?" He got an answer.) Good data protection systems change passwords often and also compartmentalize information by passwords, so that only authorized persons can have access to certain data.

Internal Controls   Internal controls are controls that are planned as part of the computer system. One example is a transaction log. This is a file of all accesses or attempted accesses to certain data.

Auditor Checks   Most companies have auditors go over the financial books. In the course of their duties, auditors frequently review computer

Some Gentle Advice on Security

Being a security expert is an unusual job because, once the planning is done, there is not a lot to do except wait for something bad to happen. Security experts are often consultants who move from company to company. They sometimes write books and articles for the trade press, in which they usually include long and detailed checklists. Do this, do that, and you will be OK. We cannot attempt such a long set of lists here, but we offer a brief subset that includes some of the most effective approaches.

Beware of disgruntled employees. Ed Street was angry. Seething. How could they pass over him for a promotion again? Well, if they were not going to give him what he deserved, he would take it himself. Ah, the tale is too common. Be forewarned.

Sensitize employees to security issues. Most people are eager to help others. They must be taught that some kinds of help, such as assisting unauthorized users with passwords, are inappropriate. Most security breaches are possible because people are ignorant, careless, or too helpful.

Call back all remote-access terminals. Don't call us, we'll call you. If you arrange a computer-kept list of valid phone numbers for access to your system, you eliminate most hackers. With such a system the computer has to call the caller back for the user to gain remote access, and it will do so only if the user's number is valid. The fact that the hacker has the computer's phone number is irrelevant. What matters is whether the computer has the hacker's.

Keep personnel privileges up to date. And, we might add, make sure they are enforced properly. "Hi, Bill, how ya doin'?" "Pretty good, Frank, good to see you." Bill, the guard, has just swept unauthorized Frank into the computer area. Some of the biggest heists have been pulled by people who *formerly* had legitimate access to secured areas. Often, they can still get in because the guard has known them by sight for years.

programs and data. From a data security standpoint, auditors might also check to see who has accessed data during periods when that data is not usually used. They are also on the lookout for unusual numbers of corrected data entries, usually a trouble sign. What is more, the availability of off-the-shelf audit software—programs that assess the validity and accuracy of the system's operations and output—promotes tighter security because it allows auditors to work independently of the programming staff.

Cryptography   Data being sent over communications lines may be protected by scrambling the messages—that is, putting them in code that can be broken only by the person receiving the message. The process of scrambling messages is called **encryption.** The American National Standards Institute has endorsed a process called the **Data Encryption Standard (DES),** a standardized public key by which senders and receivers can scramble and unscramble their messages. Although the DES code is well known, companies still use it because the method makes it quite expensive to intercept coded messages. Thus interlopers are forced to use other methods of gathering data—methods that carry greater risk of detection. Encryption software is available for personal computers. A typical package, for example, offers a variety of security features: file encryption, keyboard lock, and password protection.

Applicant Screening   The weakest link in any computer security system is the people in it. At the very least, employers should verify the facts that job applicants list on their resumes to help weed out dishonest applicants before they are hired.

Separation of Employee Functions   Should a programmer also be a computer operator? That would put him or her in the position of being able not only to write unauthorized programs, but also to run them. By limiting employee duties so that doubling up on job functions is not permitted, a computer organization can restrict the amount of unauthorized access. That is, in an installation where the computers—mainframes or minis—are behind locked doors, only operators have physical access to them. Unfortunately, separation of functions is not practical in a small shop; usually one or more employees perform multiple functions. And, of course, separation of functions does not apply in a personal computer environment.

Built-In Software Protection   Software can be built into operating systems in ways that restrict access to the computer system. One form of software protection system matches a user number against a number assigned to the data being accessed. If a person does not get access, it is recorded that he or she tried to tap into some area to which they were not authorized. Another form of software protection is a user profile: Information is stored about each user, including the files to which the user has legitimate access. The profile also includes each person's job func-

Personal Computers in Action

CHECKING YOUR OWN SECURITY

A Personal Checklist for Hardware

With the subject of security fresh in your mind, now is a good time to consider a checklist for your own personal computer and its software. We will confine this list to a computer presumed to be in the home.

1. No eating, drinking, or smoking near the computer.
2. Do not place the computer near open windows or doors.
3. Do not subject the computer to extreme temperatures.
4. Clean equipment regularly.
5. Place a cable lock on the computer.
6. Use a surge protector.
7. Store diskettes properly in a locked container.
8. Maintain backup copies of all files.
9. Store copies of critical files off site.

A Personal Checklist for Software

A word of prevention is in order. Although there are programs that can prevent virus activity, protecting yourself from viruses depends more on common sense than on building a "fortress" around the computer. Here are a few common-sense tips:

1. If your software allows it, follow write-protect measures for your floppy disks before installing any new software. If it does not allow it, write-protect the disks immediately after installation.

(a)

(b)

Security devices. (a) Locking up your computer can help minimize theft. (b) A surge protector can protect your computer system and files from unpredictable electrical problems. An uninterruptible power system (UPS) maintains your system with power even during power outage; it is designed to give you extra time to do an orderly shutdown (not to keep your system running for hours after the failure of the regular power source).

2. Do not install software unless you know it is safe. Viruses tend to show up on free software acquired from sales representatives, resellers, computer repair people, power users, and consultants.
3. Make your applications (and other executable files) read-only. This will not prevent infection, but it can help contain those viruses that attack applications.
4. Stop the so-called sneakernet crowd. This is the group that moves around the office (in sneakers, of course) and prefers to transfer files quickly via floppy disk.
5. Make backups. This is a given: Always back up your hard disk and floppies.

Laptops and Security

Computer security is causing concern among corporate and government agencies. Especially frightening is the growth in laptop computer thefts, as criminals discover a new path into corporate and government secrets.

Security experts warn that thieves can use stolen laptops to:

- enter viruses or faulty data into corporate and government databases
- steal secrets from the disk drive
- get passwords to access secrets in mainframes

One occurrence that helped raise awareness involved a *former* Wing Commander in Great Britain's Royal Air Force who learned the hard way about laptop theft. Stopping to look at new cars in an automobile showroom, David Farquhar left his laptop in his car. It only took a few minutes for someone to break in and walk off with his laptop computer—containing U.S. General Norman Schwarzkopf's plans for the upcoming Allied strike against Iraq. Farquhar paid dearly; he was demoted and slapped with a substantial fine. The laptop, anonymously returned a week later, had its disk drive and war plans still intact. But no trace of the thief was ever found.

Computer security experts suggest that laptop users protect themselves by:

- encrypting the data disks on their laptops,
- setting up security protocols between the laptop and mainframe,
- and keeping the laptop locked up or out of sight when not in use.

tion, budget number, skills, areas of knowledge, access privileges, supervisor, and loss-causing potential. These profiles are available for checking by managers if there is any problem.

Security Considerations for Personal Computers

One summer evening two men in coveralls with company logos backed a truck up to the building that housed a university computer lab. They showed the lab assistant, a part-time student, authorization to move 23 personal computers to another lab on campus. The assistant was surprised but not shocked, since lab use was light in the summer quarter. The computers were moved, all right, but not to another lab.

There is an active market for stolen personal computers and their internal components. As this unfortunate tale indicates, personal computer security breaches can be pretty basic. One simple, though not foolproof, remedy is to lock personal computer hardware in place.

In addition to theft, personal computer users need to be concerned about the computer's environment. Personal computers in business are not coddled the way bigger computers are. They are designed, in fact, to withstand the wear and tear of the office environment, including temperatures set for the comfort of people. Most manufacturers discourage eating and smoking near computers and recommend some specific cleaning techniques, such as vacuuming the keyboard and cleaning the disk drive heads with a mild solution. The enforcement of these rules is directly related to the awareness level of the users.

Most personal computer data is stored on diskettes, which are vulnerable to sunlight, heaters, cigarettes, scratching, magnets, theft, and dirty fingers. The data is vulnerable as well. Hard disks used with personal computers are subject to special problems too. If a computer with a hard disk is used by more than one person, your files on the hard disk may be available for anyone to browse through.

There are several precautions that can be taken to protect disk data. One is to use a **surge protector,** a device that prevents electrical problems from affecting data files. The computer is plugged into the surge protector, which is plugged into the outlet. Another precaution is to back up all files. Hard disk files should be backed up onto diskettes or tape. Diskettes should be under lock and key.

Awareness of personal computer security needs is gradually rising. However, security measures and the money to implement them are directly related to the amount of the expected loss. Since the dollar value of personal computer losses is often relatively low, personal computer security may be less than vigorous.

Viruses and Vaccines

The terms *viruses* and *vaccines* have entered the jargon of the computer industry to describe some of the bad things that can happen to computer systems and programs. Unpleasant occurrences like the March 6, 1991, attack of the Michelangelo virus will be with us for years to come. In fact, from now on, you need to check your IBM or IBM-compatible personal computer for the presence of Michelangelo before March 6 every year—or risk losing all the data on your hard disk when you turn on your machine that day. And Macintosh users need to do the same for another intruder, the Jerusalem virus, before each Friday the 13th, or risk a similar fate for their data.

A virus, as its name suggests, is contagious. As we said in the introduction to this chapter, it is a set of illicit instructions that infects other programs and may spread rapidly (Figure 15-4). The Michelangelo virus went worldwide within a year. Some types of viruses include the **worm,** a program that spreads by replicating itself; the **bomb,** a program intended to sabotage a computer by triggering damage based on certain conditions— usually at a later date; and the **trojan horse,** a program that covertly places illegal, destructive instructions in the middle of an otherwise legitimate program. A virus may be dealt with by means of a **vaccine,** or **antivirus,** program, a computer program that stops the spread of and often eradicates the virus.

Transmitting a Virus   Consider this typical example. A programmer secretly inserts a few unauthorized instructions in a personal computer operating system program. The illicit instructions lie dormant until three events occur together: (1) The disk with the infected operating system

Figure 15-4   An example of a virus invasion.

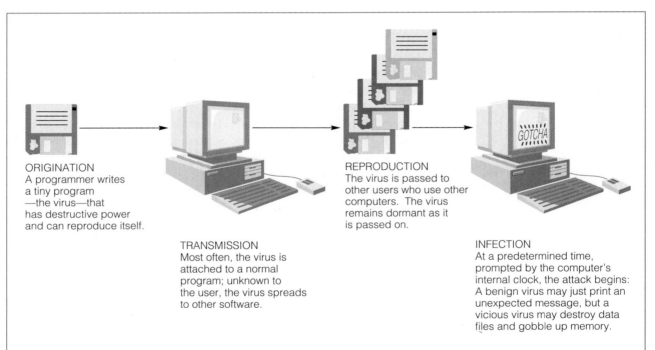

ORIGINATION
A programmer writes a tiny program —the virus—that has destructive power and can reproduce itself.

TRANSMISSION
Most often, the virus is attached to a normal program; unknown to the user, the virus spreads to other software.

REPRODUCTION
The virus is passed to other users who use other computers. The virus remains dormant as it is passed on.

INFECTION
At a predetermined time, prompted by the computer's internal clock, the attack begins: A benign virus may just print an unexpected message, but a vicious virus may destroy data files and gobble up memory.

Worm Research Wriggles Awry

Robert T. Morris, Jr., the son of one of the nation's top government cryptologists, was convicted of unleashing a virus—more accurately, a worm—over the Internet network that eventually shut down more than 6000 computers. He was sentenced to three years probation, given a $10,000 fine, and required to perform 400 hours of community service. Some have argued it was a light sentence for the damage caused, but others say it was research and certainly not maliciously intended.

It all happened in November 1988, when Morris's research project on viruses got away from him. Morris was unable to explain to the court's satisfaction just how his virus got into Internet, a network that connects hundreds of universities and government agencies, linking thousands of computers around the world. What happened next shocked much of the computer world. Within 24 hours, his virus—more accurately, a worm because it would replicate itself over and over—effectively brought Internet to its knees.

Morris's worm made a meal of any vacant computer memory, until all of the memory in any VAX or Sun computer encountered had been used up, knocking it out of service. Only the cooperation and around-the-clock efforts by a number of students and faculty at U.C. Berkeley, MIT, and other schools ended what could have been a nightmare scenario for many universities, businesses, and government agencies.

is in use; (2) a disk in another drive contains another copy of the operating system and some data files; and (3) a command, such as COPY or DIR, from the infected operating system references a data file. Under these circumstances, the virus instructions are now inserted into the other operating system. Thus the virus has spread to another disk, and the process can be repeated again and again. In fact, each newly infected disk becomes a virus carrier.

Damage from Viruses   We have explained how the virus is transmitted; now we come to the interesting part—the consequences. In this example, the virus instructions add 1 to a counter each time the virus is copied to another disk. When the counter reaches 4, the virus erases all data files. But this is not the end of the destruction, of course; three other disks have also been infected. Although viruses can be destructive, some are quite benign; one simply displays a peace message on the screen on a given date. Others may merely be a nuisance, like the Ping-Pong virus that bounces a "Ping-Pong ball" around your screen while you are working. But a few could result in disaster for your disk, as in the case of Michelangelo.

Prevention   A word about prevention is in order. Although there are programs called vaccines that can prevent virus activity, protecting your computer from viruses depends more on common sense than on building a "fortress" around the machine. Although there have been occasions where commercial software was released with a virus, these situations are rare. Viruses tend to show up most often on free software acquired from friends. Even commercial bulletin board systems, once considered the most likely suspects in transferring viruses, have cleaned up their act and now assure their users of virus-free environments. But not all bulletin board systems are run professionally. So you should always test diskettes you share with others by putting their write-protection tabs in place. If an attempt is made to write to such a protected diskette, a warning message appears on the screen. It is not as easy to protect hard disks, so many people use antivirus programs, such as those available from Central Point and Symantec. Before any diskette can be used with a computer system, the antivirus program scans the diskette for infection. The drawback is that once you buy into this type of software, you must continuously pay the price for upgrades as new viruses are discovered.

Privacy: Keeping Personal Information Personal

Think about the forms you have willingly filled out: paperwork for loans or charge accounts, orders for merchandise through the mail, magazine subscription orders, applications for schools and jobs and clubs, and on and on. There may be some forms you filled out with less delight—for taxes, military draft registration, court petitions, insurance claims, or a stay in the hospital. And remember all the people who got your name and address from your check—fund-raisers, advertisers, and petitioners. We have only skimmed over the possibilities, but we can say with certainty where all this information went: straight to a computer file.

Where is that data now? Is it passed around? Who sees it? Will it ever be deleted? Or, to put it more bluntly, is *anything* private anymore? In some cases we can only guess at the answers. It is difficult to say where your data is now, and bureaucracies are not often eager to enlighten you. Without your knowledge the data may have been moved to other files. In fact, much of the data is most definitely passed around, as anyone with a mailbox can attest. As for who sees your personal data, the answers are not comforting. Government agencies, for example, regularly share data that was originally filed for some other purpose. IRS records, for example, are compared with draft registration records to catch draft dodgers, and also with student loan records to intercept refunds to former students who defaulted on their loans. The IRS created a storm of controversy by announcing a plan to use commercial direct-mail lists to locate tax evaders. Many people are worried about the consequences of this kind of sharing (Figure 15-5). For one thing, few of us can be certain that data about us, good or bad, is deleted when it has served its legitimate purpose.

But we should not doubt the power of public outrage to fight such goings-on. Three notable attempts at computerizing private information have been derailed by public outrage. The first two involved the U.S. Postal Service, which decided that it would be useful to keep customers' mailing lists on disk, to generate address labels. In addition, the service wanted to sell to businesses the lists of mailing addresses that it computerized. (One of the results would have been enormous revenue for the postal service.) A third incident involved Lotus Development Corporation's effort to create a CD-ROM filled with data concerning just about everyone in the United States—a CD-ROM intended for sale to marketers. After the public heard of these efforts—and complained—all three projects were canceled.

But the fact remains that, for very little money, anybody can learn anything about anybody—through massive databases. And there are matters you want to keep private. You have the right to do so. Although there is little you can do to stop data about you from circulating through computers, there are some laws that give you access to some of it. Let us see what kind of protection is available to help preserve privacy.

Legislation: Protecting Your Right to Privacy

Significant legislation relating to privacy began with the **Fair Credit Reporting Act** in 1970. This law allows you to have access to and gives you the right to challenge your credit records. In fact, this access must be given to you free of charge if you have been denied credit.

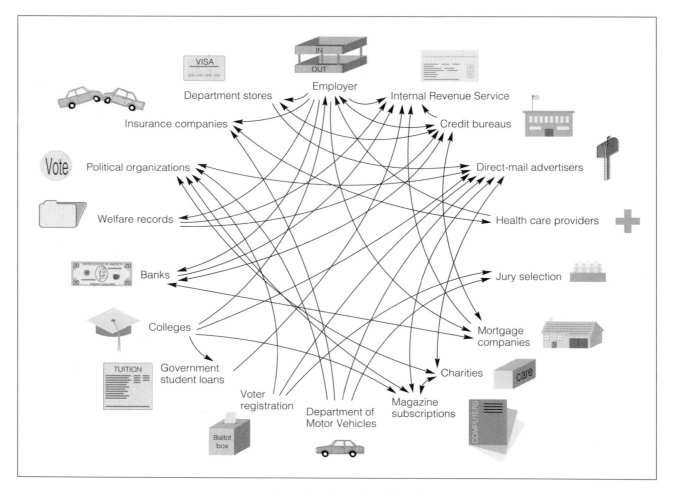

Figure 15-5   Potential paths of data. When an organization acquires data about you, it is often shared with—or sold to—other organizations.

Businesses usually contribute financial information about their customers to a community credit bureau, which gives them the right to review a person's prior credit record with other companies. Before the Fair Credit Reporting Act, many people were—without explanation—turned down for credit because of inaccurate financial records about them. Because of the act, people may now check their records to make sure they are accurate. The **Freedom of Information Act** was also passed in 1970. This landmark legislation allows ordinary citizens to have access to data about them that was gathered by federal agencies (although sometimes a lawsuit has been necessary to pry data loose).

The most significant legislation protecting the privacy of individuals is the **Federal Privacy Act** of 1974. This act stipulates that there can be no secret personnel files; individuals must be allowed to know what is stored in files about them, and how the data is used, and be able to correct it. The law applies not only to government agencies but also to private contractors dealing with government agencies. These organizations cannot obtain data willy-nilly, for no specific purpose; they must justify obtaining it.

A more recent law is the **Video Privacy Protection Act** of 1988, which prevents retailers from disclosing a person's video rental records without a court order; privacy supporters want the same rule for medical and insurance files. Another step in that direction is the **Computer Matching and Privacy Protection Act** of 1988, which prevents the government from comparing certain records in an attempt to find a match. However, most comparisons are still unregulated. For example, the government routinely compares IRS records with draft registration records to catch those who have failed to register.

 ## A Matter of Ethics

There has always been the problem of professional computer personnel having access to files. In theory, they could do something as simple as snooping into a friend's salary on a payroll file or as complex as selling military secrets to foreign countries. But the problem has become more tangled as everyday people—not just computer professionals—have daily contact with computers. They have access to files, too. Many of those files are on diskettes and may be handled in a careless manner. As we noted earlier, data is the resource most difficult to replace, so increased access is the subject of much concern among security officers.

Where do you come in? As a student you could easily face ethical problems involving access and much more. Try some of these. A nonstudent friend wants to borrow your password to get access to the school computer. Or, you know of a student who has bypassed computer security and changed grades for himself and some friends. Perhaps a "computer freak" pal collects software and wants you to copy a software disk used in one of your classes. And so on.

The problems are not so different in the business world. You will recognize that, whether you are a computer professional or a user, you have a clear responsibility to your own organization and its customers to protect the security and privacy of their information. Any compromise of data, in particular, is considered a serious breach of ethics. Many corporations have formal statements saying as much and present them to employees individually for their signatures.

If you plan to be a computer professional, you will be bombarded by articles on ethics in the trade press. Professional ethics for the computer industry is also a key topic at conferences and a lament in the halls of lawmakers. Any theme that gets this much attention usually results in action.

Most experts talk of self-regulation via the professional computer organizations. Several organizations, such as the Data Processing Management Association (DPMA) and the Association for Computing Machinery (ACM), already have a code of ethics. Handling this "among ourselves" is considered preferable to regulation imposed by a federal agency.

Copying Software

Let us move from general principles of ethics to a very individual problem—copying software. Have you ever copied a friend's music tape onto your own blank tape? Many people do so without much thought. It is also possible to photocopy a book. Both acts are clearly illegal, but there is much more fuss over illegal software copying than over copying music or books. Why is this? Well, to begin with, few of us are likely to undertake the laborious task of reproducing *War and Peace* on a copy machine. The other part of the issue is money. A pirated copy of a top-20 tape will set the recording company—and the artist—back about $10. But pirated software may be valued at hundreds of dollars. The problem of stolen software has grown right along with the personal computer industry. Before we discuss industry solutions, we must distinguish among various kinds of software, based on its availability to the public.

OK If I Copy That Software?

Some software is considered to be in the **public domain** because its generous maker, probably an individual at home or an educator, chooses to make it free to all. Software called **shareware** is also given away free even though it is copyrighted; the maker hopes for voluntary monetary compensation—that is, he or she hopes that you like it well enough to send a contribution. Both public domain software and shareware may be copied freely and given to other people. But the software that people use most often, such as WordPerfect or Lotus 1-2-3, is **copyrighted software,** software that costs money and must not be copied without permission from the manufacturer. Making illegal copies of copyrighted software is called **software piracy.**

Consider this incident. Bill Huston got his computer education at a local community college. One of his courses taught him how to use software on personal computers. He had access to a great variety of copyrighted software in the college computer lab. After graduating, he got a job at a local museum, where he used database software on a personal computer to help them catalog museum wares. He also had his own computer at home.

One day Bill stopped back at the college and ran into a former instructor. After greetings were exchanged, she asked him why he happened to drop by. "Oh," he said, "I just came by to make some copies of software." He wasn't kidding. Neither was the instructor who, after she caught her breath, replied, "You can't do that. It's illegal." Bill was miffed, saying "But I can't afford it" and, finally, "I'm sorry I mentioned it!" But the instructor was not sorry at all. She immediately alerted the computer lab. As a result of this encounter, the staff strengthened policies on software use and increased the vigilance of lab personnel. In effect, schools must protect themselves from people who lack ethics or are unaware of the law.

There are many people like Bill. He did not think in terms of stealing anything; he just wanted to make copies for himself. But, as the software industry is quick to point out, unauthorized copying *is* stealing because the software makers do not get the revenues to which they are entitled. Furthermore, if software developers are not properly compensated, they may not find it worthwhile to develop new software for our use.

Why Those Extra Copies?

Copying software is not always a dirty trick—there are lots of legitimate reasons for copying. To begin with, after paying several hundred dollars for a piece of software, you will definitely want to make a backup copy in case of disk failure or accident. You might want to copy the program onto a hard disk and use it—more conveniently—from there. Or you might want to have one copy at the office and another to use at home. Many software publishers have no trouble with any of these types of copying. But thousands of computer users copy software for another reason: to get the program without paying for it. And therein lies the problem.

Software publishers first tried to solve the problem by placing **copy protection** on their software—a software or hardware roadblock to make it difficult or impossible to make pirated copies. In effect, copy protection punishes the innocent with the guilty. There was vigorous opposition from software users, who argued that it was unfair to restrict paying customers just to outsmart a few thieves. Most software vendors have now dropped copy protection from their software, but they are still vigilant about illegal copies. For example, Lotus Development Corporation, a leading purveyor of software, has brought million-dollar lawsuits against some companies, charging them with making illegal copies of Lotus 1-2-3. AutoDesk, Inc., fiercely protective of its best-selling AutoCAD, has hired an outside law firm to prosecute suspected pirates—recovering more than $6 million in some 3500 cases. But the most widespread solution seems to be vendor permission to copy software *legally*, an approach called site licensing.

Site Licensing

Although there is no clear definition industrywide, in general a **site license** permits a customer to make multiple copies of a given piece of software. The customer needing all these copies is usually a corporation, which can probably obtain a significant price discount for volume buying. The exact nature of the arrangement between the user and the software maker can vary considerably. Typically, however, a customer obtains the right to make an unlimited number of copies of a product, agrees to keep track of who uses it, and takes responsibility for copying and distributing manuals to its own personnel.

The advantages seem to be all on the user's side:

- A big price break, sometimes as high as 50%
- The availability of as many copies as needed

COPY SOFTWARE ILLEGALLY AND YOU COULD GET THIS HARDWARE ABSOLUTELY FREE.

Don't Copy That Floppy

Figure 15-6 Capturing your attention. The Software Publishers Association, an organization that supports software developers, has launched an advertising campaign to warn personal computer users about the possible "rewards" for copying software illegally.

- Freedom from potential lawsuits from the software vendor

But why does the software maker subscribe to this? The main reason is pressure from corporate customers with enormous clout. Who can ignore General Electric or Chevron?

Know Your Legal Rights (and Wrongs)

Some people justify their actions in copying software as the "higher good of learning" or "only to test it out." One organization, the Software Publishers Association (SPA), has launched a campaign to help educate the public on the rights and wrongs of copying (Figure 15-6).

Stealing software is simple. You just copy it for the wrong reasons. However, calling the SPA anti-piracy hotline is also simple. Anyone— disgruntled employee or dissatisfied client—can call (800) 388-7478 and report you. Before you know it, you could be facing legal action, stiff fines, and even a prison term.

The SPA encourages personal computer users to understand the laws. As we have mentioned, not all copying is illegal. Some software developers (Microsoft, WordPerfect, Claris, and Borland) even allow you to use your copy of a program wherever you want—as long as you do not allow others to copy it. Other companies, like Aldus Corporation, limit their license to use on one personal computer; once PageMaker is loaded on one computer, for example, it must be removed before it can be used on another computer. Under Aldus's terms, only one person at a time can use the program over a network, even though the product remains on one machine (a file server).

EDUCOM, an educational organization, offers the following advice in its brochure, *Using Software: A Guide to the Ethical and Legal Use of Software for Members of the Academic Community.*

1. ***What do I need to know about software and the U.S. Copyright Act?***
   Unless it has been placed in the public domain, software is protected by copyright law. The owner of a copyright holds exclusive right to the reproduction and distribution of his or her work. Therefore, it is illegal to duplicate or distribute software or its documentation without the permission of the copyright owner. If you have purchased your copy, however, you may make a backup for your own use, in case the original is destroyed or fails to work.

2. ***Can I loan software I have purchased myself?***
   If your software came with a clearly visible license agreement, or if you signed a registration card, READ THE LICENSE CAREFULLY before you use the software. Some licenses may restrict use to a specific computer. Copyright law does not permit you to run your software on two or more computers simultaneously unless the license agreement specifically allows it. It may, however, be legal to loan your software to a friend temporarily as long as you do not keep a copy.

3. ***If software is not copy-protected, do I have the right to copy it?***
   Lack of copy protection does NOT constitute permission to copy software in order to share or sell it. "Non–copy-protected" software enables you to

protect your investment by making a backup copy. In offering non–copy-protected software to you, the developer has demonstrated significant trust in your integrity.

4. *May I copy software that is available through facilities on my campus so that I can use it more conveniently in my own room?*
   Software acquired by colleges and universities is usually licensed. The licenses restrict how and where the software may be legally used by members of the community. This applies to software installed on hard disks in microcomputer clusters, software distributed on disks by a campus lending library, and software available on a campus mainframe or network. Some institutional licenses permit copying for certain purposes. Consult your campus authorities if you are unsure about the use of a particular software product.

5. *Isn't it legally "fair use" to copy software if the purpose in sharing it is purely educational?*
   No. It is illegal for a faculty member or student to copy software for distribution among the members of a class, without permission of the author or the publisher. You should check carefully each piece of software and the accompanying documentation yourself. In general, you do not have the right to do these things:

   - receive and use unauthorized copies of software, or
   - make unauthorized copies of software for others.

Now you know the facts. The effort to uphold the law also pays off in other ways. It is a well-recognized fact that no software is ever completely bug-free. In addition, manufacturers of hardware often introduce new operating environments that may undermine the efficiency of your software. For that reason, registered owners of programs are assured timely information regarding bug fixes or changes to their programs. Software developers also revise their programs to add new features from time to time and offer registered owners a reduced, upgrade price.

Paying Attention Because We Must

The issues raised in this chapter are often the ones we think of after the fact—that is, when it is too late. The security and privacy factors are somewhat like insurance that we wish we did not have to buy. But we do buy insurance for our homes and cars and lives because we know we cannot risk being without it. The computer industry also knows that it cannot risk being without safeguards for security and privacy. As a computer professional, you will share responsibility for addressing these issues. As a computer user, in whatever capacity, you can take comfort in the fact that the computer industry recognizes their importance.

Next we turn to the final chapter and the cutting edge of the Information Age: how artificial intelligence, expert systems, and robotics may open the doors to the future.

R E V I E W   A N D   R E F E R E N C E

Summary and Key Terms

- Computer criminals are likely to be trusted employees with no previous law-breaking experience. Many are motivated by resentment toward an employer, by personal or family problems, by the challenge of beating the system, or the tempting ease with which the crime can be committed.

- Three basic types of computer crime are (1) theft of computer time for development of software; (2) theft, destruction, or manipulation of programs or data; and (3) alteration of data stored in a computer file.

- The word *hacker* originally referred to an enthusiastic, self-taught computer user, but now the term usually describes a person who gains access to computer systems illegally.

- Prosecution of computer crime is often difficult because law enforcement officers, attorneys, and judges are unfamiliar with the issues involved. However, in 1986 Congress passed the latest version of the **Computer Fraud and Abuse Act,** and most states have passed some form of computer crime law.

- **Security** is a system of safeguards designed to protect a computer system and data from deliberate or accidental damage or access by unauthorized persons. Common threats include burglary, vandalism, fire, natural disasters, theft of data for ransom, industrial espionage, and various forms of white-collar crime.

- The means of giving access to authorized people are divided into four general categories: (1) what you have (a key, badge, or plastic card), (2) what you know (a system password or identification number), (3) what you do (such as signing your name), and (4) what you are (by making use of **biometrics,** the science of measuring individual body characteristics such as fingerprints, voice, retina, and lips).

- Loss of hardware and software is generally less of a problem than loss of data. Loss of hardware should not be a major problem, provided that the equipment is insured and a substitute processing facility is found quickly. Loss of software should not be critical, provided that the owner has taken the practical step of making backup copies. However, replacing lost data can be quite expensive.

- A **disaster recovery plan** is a method of restoring data processing operations if they are halted by major damage or destruction. Common approaches to disaster recovery include relying temporarily on manual services; buying time at a computer service bureau; making mutual assistance agreements with other companies; or forming a **consortium,** a joint venture with other organizations to support a complete computer facility.

- A **hot site** is a fully equipped computer facility with hardware, environmental controls, security, and communications equipment. A **cold site** is an environmentally suitable empty shell in which a company can install its own computer system.

- A disaster recovery plan should include (1) priorities indicating which programs must be running first, (2) personnel requirements specifying where employees should be and what they should do, (3) equipment requirements, (4) information about an alternative computing facility, and (5) specifications for how input and output data will be handled in a different environment.

- Software can be copyrighted. If a programmer is employed by an organization, any program written for the organization belongs to the employer. If the programmer is a consultant, however, the contract must clearly state whether it is the organization or the programmer that owns the software.

- There are five critical planning areas for data security: (1) determination of appropriate policies and standards, (2) development and implementation of security safeguards, (3) inclusion of security precautions during development of new automated systems, (4) review of state and federal laws related to security, and (5) maintenance of historical records associated with computer abuse.

- Common means of protecting data are securing waste; separating employee functions; and implementing passwords, internal controls, auditor checks, cryptography, applicant screening, and **copy protection** (a software or hardware roadblock to piracy).

- Data sent over communications lines can be protected by **encryption,** the process of scrambling messages. The National Standards Institute has endorsed a process called **Data Encryption Standard (DES).**

- Personal computer security includes such measures as locking hardware in place; providing an appropriate physical environment; and using a **surge protector,** a device that prevents electrical problems from affecting data files.

- **Virus** is the name generally given to software that causes malicious or nonmalicious alteration of computer files. A virus attaches itself to applications or files. A **vaccine,** or **antivirus** is a computer program that stops the spread of the virus and eradicates it. Some types of viruses are the **worm,** a program that spreads by replicating itself; the **bomb,** a program intended to sabotage a computer by triggering damage based on certain conditions—usually at a later date; and the **trojan horse,** a program that covertly places illegal, destructive instructions in the middle of an otherwise legitimate program.

- The security issue extends to the use of information about individuals that is stored in the computer files of credit bureaus and government agencies. The **Fair Credit Reporting Act** allows individuals to check the accuracy of credit information about them. The **Freedom of Information Act** allows people access to data that federal agencies have gathered about them. The **Federal Privacy Act** allows individuals access to information about them that is held not only by government agencies, but also by private contractors working for the government. Individuals are also entitled to know how that information is being used. The **Video Privacy Protection Act** and the **Computer Matching and Privacy Protection Act** have extended federal protections.

- Some software is considered to be in the **public domain** because it is free. **Shareware** software is copyrighted software that is given away on the honor system, with the author asking for voluntary compensation.

- **Copyrighted software** costs money and must not be copied without permission from the manufacturer. Making illegal copies of copyrighted software is called **software piracy.** Many software publishers offer a **site license,** which permits a customer to make multiple copies of a given piece of software.

Review Questions

1. What are some common motivations for computer crime?
2. What are the three main categories of computer crime?
3. What are four types of computer viruses and how do they differ?
4. Name and describe the four general techniques for identifying authorized users.
5. Why is loss of data a more serious problem than loss of software or hardware?
6. What should a disaster recovery plan include and why?
7. Name five critical planning areas for data security.
8. Describe the security considerations for personal computers.
9. Name three privacy laws and explain why each one was enacted.
10. What is site licensing?

Discussion Questions

1. Before accepting a particular patient, a doctor might like access to a computer file listing patients who have been involved in malpractice suits. Before accepting a tenant, the owner of an apartment building might want to check a file that lists people who have previously sued landlords. Should computer files be available for such purposes? Explain your answer.
2. Discuss your reaction to the following statement: "Some software is just too expensive for the average personal computer owner to buy. Besides, I am only copying my friend's disk for personal use."
3. Why do some people consider computer viruses important? Discuss your answer from the point of view of the hacker, the professional programmer, and the MIS manager.

True-False Questions

T F 1. A virus is always lethal to your hard disk.
T F 2. One means of achieving computer security is by physically restricting access.
T F 3. One category of computer crime is the manipulation of programs or data.
T F 4. The loss of hardware is the most serious potential security problem.
T F 5. It is legitimate to make a copy of software for backup purposes.
T F 6. Software can be copyrighted.
T F 7. A site license permits you to make multiple copies of a software program and even run it on a network.
T F 8. The process of scrambling a message is called encryption.
T F 9. A surge protector can keep worms out of your personal computer.
T F 10. Shareware works on the honor system. You can copy it freely, but if you want to keep and use it you must pay for it.

CHAPTER

16

Modern Trends

Artificial Intelligence, Expert Systems, and Robotics

John Kelly had 30 years on the job as a metal fabricator for a jetliner manufacturer. His job was to align crucial jet engine components in a precise way, then spot-weld them together. Both John and his employers knew that the safety of thousands of airline passengers rested on his shoulders. He was a dedicated, conscientious worker who was extremely careful each time he made a weld.

John had heard about industrial robots for years. He had seen them move into the automotive industry and knew people who had lost their jobs to them. But he felt that his job was secure. It required too much precision and too much human judgment—and getting it right was simply too important to trust to a machine.

John's employers did not share his views. They were convinced that modern industrial robots could position metal parts more precisely than humans and that, with careful adjustment, their welds would be more consistently sound. Despite the pleas of John and his co-workers—and against the wishes of their union—the company contracted for a prototype robot-based welding system to test their views.

To John's surprise and discomfort, management assigned him to work on the robot project. They asked him to provide the robot manufacturer's representatives with input on the design and programming of the machine. With abundant skepticism, but with a fair amount of curiosity, too, John agreed to help.

The robot system designers first watched John work, then they videotaped his movements—the way he manipulated the jigs holding the parts and the way he positioned the weld. Later they sat down with him and discussed the cues he looked for while working: how he knew when the parts were seated properly, what told him the weld was complete and sound, and so on.

It was several months before the robot system was ready, and several more before all the bugs were out, its video camera "eyes" adjusted, and its welds perfect. But when the robot turned out product, it was as fast and as good as any 10 John Kellys. And John was happily surprised: The robot needed his help. The engine parts had to be tested and certified before they could be used. In other words, John stayed on the job. With the increased pace of production, even more personnel were required to carry out the testing.

Although he often mused about the "old days," John was impressed by the consistent high quality of the parts produced by the robot. In fact, he felt a tinge a pride when his old co-workers referred to the robot as "John Junior."

Not all workers have been as fortunate as John. But it is obvious that we need to come to terms with artificial intelligence, expert systems, and robots before we can understand their impact on our lives. We will start with artificial intelligence.

 ## *The Artificial Intelligence Field*

Artificial intelligence (AI) is a field of study that explores how computers can be used for tasks that require the human characteristics of intelligence, imagination, and intuition. Computer scientists sometimes prefer a looser definition, calling AI the study of how to make computers do things that—at the present time—people can do better. The phrase "at the present time" is significant because artificial intelligence is an evolving science: As soon as a problem is solved, it is moved off the artificial intelligence agenda. A good example is the game of chess, once considered a mighty AI challenge. But now that most computer chess programs can beat most human competitors, chess is no longer an object of study by scientists and thus no longer on the artificial intelligence agenda.

Today the term *artificial intelligence* encompasses several subsets of interests (Figure 16-1):

- **Problem solving.** This area of AI includes a spectrum of activities, from playing games to planning military strategy.
- **Natural languages.** This facet involves the study of the person/computer interface in unconstrained English language.
- **Fuzzy logic.** This is a type of artificial intelligence that allows machines to "think" more like humans, providing a method of precisely measuring vague concepts. (If that sounds kind of fuzzy, read on.)
- **Expert systems.** These AI systems present the computer as an expert on some particular topic.

Figure 16-1 The artificial intelligence family tree.

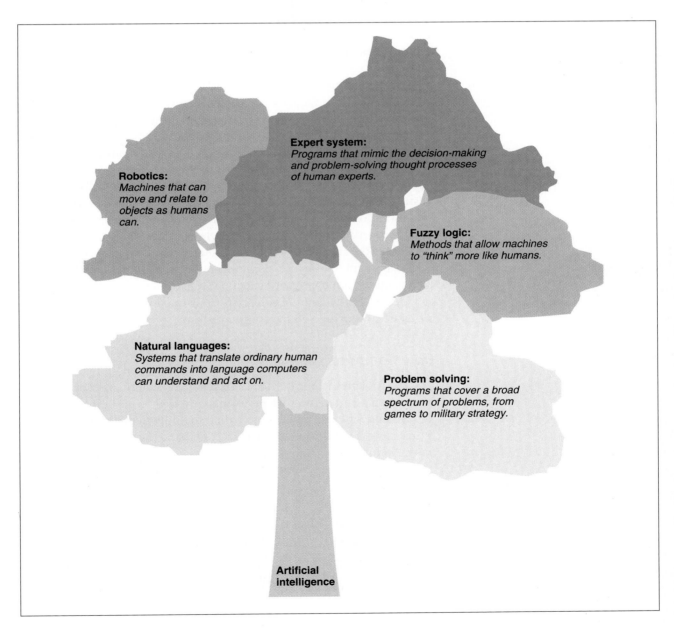

Robotics:
Machines that can move and relate to objects as humans can.

Expert system:
Programs that mimic the decision-making and problem-solving thought processes of human experts.

Fuzzy logic:
Methods that allow machines to "think" more like humans.

Natural languages:
Systems that translate ordinary human commands into language computers can understand and act on.

Problem solving:
Programs that cover a broad spectrum of problems, from games to military strategy.

Artificial intelligence

- **Robotics.** This field involves endowing computer-controlled machines with electronic capabilities for vision, speech, and touch.

Although considerable progress has been made in these sophisticated fields of study, early successes did not come easily. Before we examine current advances in these areas, let us pause to consider some early moments in the development of artificial intelligence.

Early Mishaps

In the early days of artificial intelligence, scientists thought that the computer would experience something like an electronic childhood, in which it would gobble up the world's libraries and then begin generating new wisdom. Few people talk like this today because the problem of simulating intelligence is far more complex then just stuffing facts into the computer. Facts are useless without the ability to interpret and learn from them.

An artificial intelligence failure on a grand scale was the attempt to translate human languages via the computer. Although scientists were able to pour vocabulary and rules of grammar into the computer, the literal word-for-word translations often produced ludicrous output. In one infamous example, the computer was supposed to demonstrate its prowess by translating a phrase from English to Russian and then back to English. Despite the computer's best efforts, "The spirit is willing, but the flesh is weak" came back "The vodka is good, but the meat is spoiled."

An unfortunate result of this widely published experiment was the ridicule of artificial intelligence scientists, considered dreamers who could not accept the limitations of a machine. Funding for AI research disappeared, plunging the artificial intelligence community into a slump from which it did not recover until expert systems emerged in the 1980s. Nevertheless, a hardy band of scientists continued to explore artificial intelligence, focusing on how computers learn.

How Computers Learn

The study of artificial intelligence is predicated on the computer's ability to learn—and to improve performance based on past errors. The two key elements of this process are called the knowledge base and the inference engine. A **knowledge base** is a set of facts and rules about those facts. An **inference engine** accesses, selects, and interprets a set of rules. The inference engine applies the rules to the facts to make up new facts—thus the computer has learned something new. Consider this simple example:

FACT: Barbara is George's wife.
RULE: If X is Y's wife then Y is X's husband.

The computer—the inference engine—can apply the rule to the fact and come up with a new fact: George is Barbara's husband. Although the result of this simplistic example may seem of little value, it is indeed true that the computer now knows two facts instead of just one. Rules, of course, can be much more complex and facts more plentiful, yielding more sophisticated results. In fact, artificial intelligence software is capable of searching through long chains of related facts to reach a conclusion—a new fact.

Further explanation of the precise way computers learn is beyond the scope of this book. However, we can use the learning discussion as a springboard to the question that most people ask about artificial intelligence: Can a computer really think?

The Artificial Intelligence Debate

To imitate the functioning of the human mind, a machine with artificial intelligence would have to be able to examine a variety of facts, address multiple subjects, and devise a solution to a problem by comparing new facts to its existing storehouse of data from many fields. So far, artificial intelligence systems cannot match a person's ability to solve problems through original thought instead of using familiar patterns as guides.

There are many arguments for and against crediting computers with the ability to think. Some say, for example, that computers cannot be considered intelligent because they do not compose like Beethoven or write like Shakespeare; the rejoinder is that neither do most ordinary human musicians or writers—you do not have to be a genius to be considered intelligent.

Look at it another way. Suppose you rack your brain over a problem, and then—Aha!—the solution comes to you all at once. Now, how did you do that? You do not know, and nobody else knows either. A big part of human problem solving seems to be that jolt of recognition, that ability to see things suddenly as a whole. Experiments have shown that people rarely solve problems using step-by-step logic, the very thing that computers do best. Most modern computers still plod through problems one step at a time. The human brain beats computers at "Aha!" problem solving, because it has millions of neurons working simultaneously. Now some scientists are taking that same approach with computers.

Brainpower: Neural Networks

A microprocessor chip is sometimes referred to as the "brain" of a computer. But, in truth, computers have not yet come close to matching the human brain, which has trillions of connections between billions of neurons. What is more, the most sophisticated conventional computer does not "learn" the same way the human brain learns. But let us consider an unconventional computer, one whose chips are actually designed to mimic the human brain. These computers are called **neural networks,** or, simply, neural nets.

If a computer is to function more like the human brain and less like an overgrown calculator, it must be able to experiment and to learn from its mistakes. Researchers are developing computers with a few thousand brain-like connections. Instead of the computer circuits following the usual step-by-step series of instructions, the circuits in a neural net computer form a grid, much like a nerve cell in the brain. The grid is used to recognize patterns. For instance, a neural network with optical sensors, shown in Figure 16-2, could be "trained" to recognize the letter *A*.

At best, today's neural networks consist of only a few thousand connections—still a far cry from the billions found in the human brain.

The Famous Turing Test

So, can a computer think or not? Listen to Alan Turing. Several decades ago, this English mathematician proposed a test of thinking machines. In the **Turing test,** a human subject is seated before two terminals that

Figure 16-2   Neural nets. This figure shows how a neural network with optical sensors is trained to recognize the letter *A*. 1) When the system makes an incorrect choice, the incorrect circuits are weakened. 2) When a correct choice is made, those circuits are strengthened. 3) After several attempts with different forms of the letter *A,* in which the correct circuits are repeatedly strengthened, the neural net is able to identify the letter accurately.

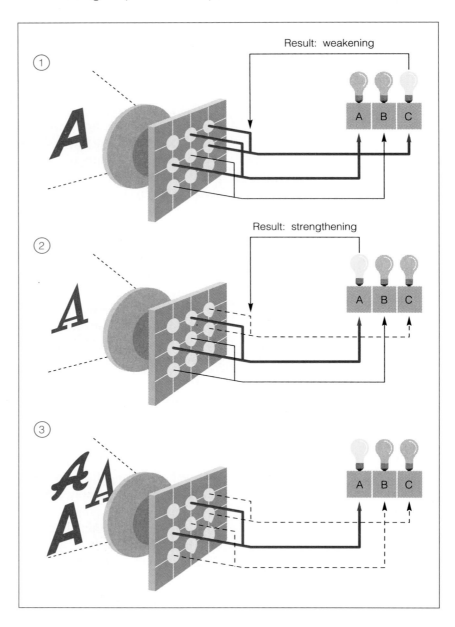

Eliza, The First Computer Psychologist

In the 1960s, a computer scientist named Joseph Weizenbaum wrote a little program as an experiment in natural language. He named the program after Eliza Doolittle, the character in *My Fair Lady* who wanted to learn to speak proper English. The software allows the computer to act as a benign therapist who does not talk much but, instead, encourages the patient—the computer user—to talk.

The Eliza software has a storehouse of key phrases to be dragged out when triggered by the patient. For example, if a patient types "My mother never liked me," the software—cued by the word "mother"—can respond "Tell me more about your family." If there are no key words from the patient, the computer responds neutrally, with a phrase such as "I see" or "That's very interesting" or "Why do you think that?" If a patient gives yes or no answers, the computer may respond "I prefer complete sentences." With party tricks like these, the program is able to move along quite nimbly from line to line.

Weizenbaum was astonished to discover that people were taking his little program seriously, pouring out their hearts to the computer. In fact, what he viewed as misuse of the computer radicalized Weizenbaum, who spent the next several years giving speeches and writing articles against artificial intelligence.

are connected to hidden devices. One terminal is connected to a terminal run by another person, and the second terminal is connected to a computer. The subject is asked to guess, by carrying out conversations through the terminals, which is the person and which is the computer. If the human judge cannot tell the difference, the computer is said to have passed and is considered, for all practical purposes, a thinking machine. Every year, the Boston Computer Museum hosts a contest offering a $100,000 prize to anyone who writes a program for a computer that passes the Turing test. No one has ever won the full prize (see the essay, "The Whimsical, but not quite *Thinking* machine").

But perhaps we are asking the wrong question: Will a computer ever *really* think? One possible answer: Who cares? If a machine can perform a task really well, does it matter if it *really* thinks? Still another answer is: Yes, machines will really think, but not as humans do. They lack the sensitivity, appreciation, and passion that are intrinsic to human thought.

Meanwhile, scientists are getting rather good at developing related areas of artificial intelligence. We will focus on some of the more visible results of recent research in natural languages, expert systems, and robotics.

The Natural-Language Factor

The language people use on a daily basis to write and speak is called a **natural language.** Natural languages are associated with artificial intelligence because humans can make the best use of artificial intelligence if they can communicate with the computer in natural language. Furthermore, understanding natural language is a skill thought to require intelligence.

Some natural-language words are easy to understand because they represent a definable item: *horse, chair, mountain*. Other words, however, are much too abstract to lend themselves to straightforward definitions: *justice, virtue, beauty*. But this kind of abstractness is just the beginning of the difficulty. Consider the word "hand" in these statements.

- Tim had a hand in the robbery.
- Tim had a hand in the cookie jar.
- Tim is an old hand at chess.
- Tim gave Dick a hand with his luggage.
- Tim asked Mary for her hand in marriage.
- All hands on deck!
- Look, Ma! No hands!

As you can see, natural language abounds with ambiguities; the word "hand" has a different meaning in each statement. In contrast, sometimes statements that appear to be different really mean the same thing:

- Alan sold Judy a book for five dollars.
- Judy bought a book for five dollars from Alan.

Personal Computers in Action

THE WHIMSICAL, BUT NOT QUITE *THINKING,* MACHINE

To learn more about artificial intelligence, the Boston Computer Museum holds an annual contest—with a $100,000 prize—for the first computer program that can fool people into thinking they are really dealing with a human instead of a machine.

The event features the Turing test—in which people must decide if they are dealing with humans or machines—and involves about 10 judges and several hidden contestants that are either computers or people. The computers are programmed by researchers to converse like people on certain restricted topics, such as martinis or romantic relationships. The judges are Boston-area residents without computer training. After 14-minute dialogues with each of the hidden entities, the judges have to guess which ones are computers.

A recent test provided this exchange: "What can you say about martinis?" asked the judge. "I'm not sure," responded the machine, "Those martinis must have taken their toll on me."

To the surprise of many experts, several of the computers were successful in passing themselves off as humans. One that passed the Turing test most often was programmed to make whimsical conversation. Five judges—50 percent—thought the computer was human, and this feat won its author a $1500 award. Three other computer programs fooled at least one judge.

"I thought the whimsical program was a human because I was at ease with it and it made me laugh," said 22-year-old judge Martha Gruppe. The winning program was PC Therapist II, commercially available from Thinking Software, Inc. of Woodside, NY.

Conversely, two of the judges thought one of the humans was a computer. Shakespeare expert Cynthia Clay provided such knowledge of the literary luminary that one judge said, "I didn't expect a human would have that amount of knowledge about Shakespeare."

The annual event is partially supported by MIT and Dr. Joseph Weizenbaum, creator of the Eliza computer program that fooled many early users by mimicking a psychologist. Eliza's initial success was based on the strategy of using the questioner's own words in responses.

No computer program has been able to pass the Turing test completely—yet.

- Judy gave Alan five dollars in exchange for a book.
- The book that Judy bought from Alan cost five dollars.

It takes very sophisticated software (not to mention enormous computer memory) to unravel all these statements and see them as equivalent. A key function of the AI study of natural languages is to develop a computer system that can resolve ambiguities.

Feeding computers the vocabulary and grammatical rules it needs to know is a step in the right direction. However, as you saw earlier in the account of the language translation fiasco, true understanding requires more: Words must be taken in context. Humans begin acquiring a context for words from the day they are born. Consider this statement: Jack cried when Alice said she loved Bill. From our own context, we can draw several possible conclusions: Jack is sad, Jack probably loves Alice, Jack probably thinks Alice doesn't love him, and so on. These conclusions may not be correct, but they are reasonable interpretations based on the context we supply. On the other hand, it would *not* be reasonable to conclude from the statement that Jack is a carpenter or that Alice has a new refrigerator.

One of the most frustrating tasks for AI scientists is providing the computer with the sense of context that humans have. Scientists have attempted to do this in regard to specific subjects and found the task daunting. For example, a scientist who wrote software so the computer could have a dialogue about restaurants had to feed the computer hundreds of facts that any small child would know, such as the fact that restaurants have food and that you are expected to pay for it.

Fuzzy Logic

What is "fuzzy" about fuzzy logic? Intelligence itself—*human* intelligence, that is. As humans, we deal with many vague notions in arriving at decisions. In contrast, machine intelligence is very precise. According to Michio Sugeno, a Tokyo engineer considered to be among the most important researchers in this field, machine intelligence—like classical logic—is based on either/or thinking. This is the kind of thinking that places you either *in* the set of thin people or *not* in. You are either thin or fat, at least to standard methods of artificial intelligence.

Fuzzy logic expands AI thinking so it more closely resembles the way humans deal with the gray areas of rationalization. Sugeno says fuzzy logic can measure vagueness—in the *precise* way required by a machine. In other words, you can be 1.00 thin (100 percent)—or 0.98, or just .02 thin. At the same time, other categories that help define the concept can be measured similarly to encompass the whole concept of thinness.

Fuzzy logic was invented more than 25 years ago and has been used successfully in electronically controlled devices ranging from vacuum cleaners and automobile transmissions to subway systems and rocket-docking systems. It is the logic underlying a video camera's ability to steady an image even when the camera is jostled during filming. In a washing machine, fuzzy logic assesses the size and untidiness of the load, then decides how long to run. It also helps guide self-guidance systems in robots.

Ever since Sugeno attached more importance to human *subjectivity* than *objectivity*, his research interests have been focused on artificial intelligence in hopes of designing computers that are patterned after the brain. His first success came in the early 1980s, when he designed a water purification plant that used fuzzy logic to handle the complexities involved in the range of impurities in the water. For several years he analyzed the rules of fuzzy logic, then applied them to robotics. He came up with a fuzzy algorithm to control a remote, voice-controlled, self-parking car. Next he turned fuzzy logic to the problem of controlling unmanned helicopter flight.

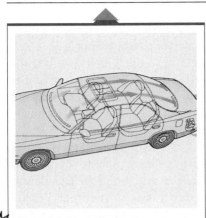

Smart Car Cruising

Cruising along a long stretch of highway is more relaxing in cars equipped with automatic cruise and climate control. Cruise control allows you to set the speed you want your car to maintain down long stretches of highway. This lets you remove your foot from the gas pedal and settle into a more restful position while driving. Professional drivers swear by it. It is safe, since cruise control will automatically disengage when you push the brake pedal.

Yet, both are conveniences that many occasional drivers seldom take advantage of—even though they may have paid extra for both. Now new car models—smart cars—are emerging that might take over such decisions for them. Fuzzy logic, and its ability to handle situations that call for more humanlike thinking strategies, has already been employed by some car manufacturers. Take the latest Mazda 929 sedan—as well as controlling inside climate with its solar-powered "moonroof" ventilation system, its fuzzy logic handles cruise control which lets it respond more quickly and precisely than conventional units to the changing demands on the engine.

Sugeno and others in the field are working on the first natural-language computer, one that can be controlled and programmed easily by human operators. The computer will be able to recognize and respond to complex commands in the spoken language of the operator.

Currently, a less formidable task is to give a computer enough data to answer questions on a given topic. For instance, a stockbroker's computer does not need to know what a stock is, only if factors indicate it is time to buy. Such systems, a subset of artificial intelligence, are called expert systems.

Expert Systems

An **expert system** is a software package used with an extensive set of organized data that presents the computer as an expert on a particular topic. For example, a computer could be an expert on where to drill oil wells, or what stock purchase looks promising, or how to cook soufflés. The user is the knowledge seeker, usually asking questions in a natural—that is, English-like—language format. An expert system can respond to an inquiry about a problem—What will happen if the bill of particulars is not received before the adjourned deadline?—with both an answer and an explanation of the answer. (This is a legal question using a lawyer's "natural language," and the answer is probably "Prepare a motion to dismiss the case.") The expert system works by figuring out what the question means, then matching it against the facts and rules that it "knows" (Figure 16-3). These facts and rules, which reside on disk, originally come from a human expert.

Expert Systems in Business

For years, expert systems were no more than bold experiments, the exclusive property of the medical and scientific communities. Special programs could offer medical diagnoses or search for mineral deposits or examine chemical compounds. But, in the early 1980s, expert systems began to make their way into commercial environments. Consider these examples:

- The Campbell Soup Company has an expert system nicknamed Aldo, for Aldo Cimino, the human expert who knows how to fix cooking machines. Aldo was getting on in years and being run ragged, flying from plant to plant whenever a cooker went on the blink. Besides, how would the company manage when he retired? Now Aldo's knowledge has been distilled into an expert system that can be used by workers in any location.

- Nordstrom, a chain of stores selling high-quality clothing, uses an expert system to extend customer credit limits. Suppose, for example, that a customer wants to charge a coat whose cost pushes the to-

Figure 16-3 An expert system on the job. This expert system helps Ford mechanics track down and fix engine problems.

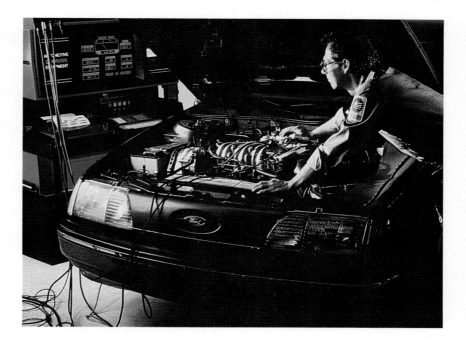

tal debt beyond the current credit limit. In the past, the salesperson phoned a human expert who reviewed credit records and made a decision. Meanwhile, the customer waited. The decision process has been transferred to an expert system, which is faster, less expensive, and accomplishes the same job.

- Factory workers at The Boeing Company use an expert system to assemble electrical connectors for airplanes. In the old days, workers had to hunt through 20,000 pages of cross-referenced specifications to find the right parts, tools, and techniques for the job—approximately 42 minutes per search. The expert system lets them do the same thing in about 5 minutes.

- Employees at Coopers and Lybrand, a "Big Eight" accounting firm, use an expert system called ExperTax to help clients with tax planning. The knowledge of tax planning experts is available to inexperienced accountants, and it is as close as their computers.

- The United Airlines terminal at O'Hare Airport in Chicago handles 400 flights per day, which must be distributed among 50 gates. Complications include the limitations of jumbo jets, which do not maneuver easily into some gates. Furthermore, both the weather and heavy runway traffic can affect how quickly planes can get in and out. Airline employees, who used to track planes on a gigantic magnetic board, now keep track of gate positions with an expert system that takes all factors into account (Figure 16-4).

The cost of an expert system can usually be justified in situations where there are few experts but great demand for knowledge. It is also worthwhile to have a system that is not subject to human failings, such as fatigue.

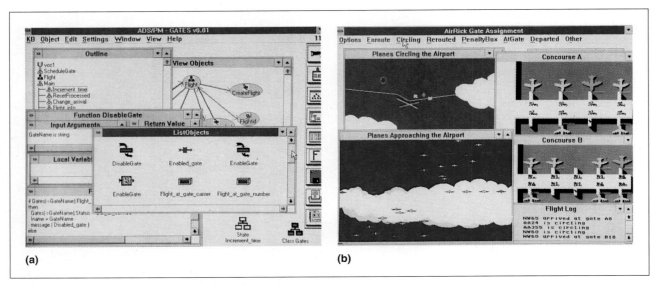

(a)   **(b)**

Figure 16-4   Airline scheduling program produced with the aid of an expert system.
This system offers a graphical user interface to help solve a complex airport scheduling problem. (a) This screen illustrates the system's ability to display multiple views of objects and the
relationships between them. (b) Various screen windows show planes circling the airport, the
number of planes approaching the airport, gate information, and two concourses with planes
at their gates. *Courtesy of Aion ® Development System.*

Building an Expert System

Some organizations choose to build their own expert systems to perform
well-focused tasks that can easily be crystallized into rules. A simple example is a set of rules for a banker to use when making decisions about
whether to extend credit. But very few organizations are capable of building an expert system from scratch. The sensible alternative is to buy an
expert shell, a software package that consists of the basic structure used
to find answers to questions. It is up to the buyer to fill in the actual knowledge on the chosen subject. You could think of the expert shell as an empty
cup that becomes a new entity once it is filled—a cup of coffee, for instance, or a cup of sugar.

The most challenging task of building an expert system often is deciding who the appropriate expert is and then trying to pin down his or
her knowledge. Experts often believe that much of their expertise is in-
stinctive and thus find it difficult to articulate just why they do what
they do. However, the expert is usually following a set of rules, even if
the rules are only in his or her head. The person ferreting out the information, sometimes called a **knowledge engineer,** must have a keen eye
and the skills of a diplomat. Sometimes cameras are used to observe the
expert in action.

Once the rules are uncovered, they are formed into a set of IF-THEN
rules: IF the customer has exceeded a credit limit by no more than 20%
and has paid the monthly bill for six months, THEN extend further credit.
After the system is translated into a computerized version, it is reviewed,
changed, tested, and changed some more. This repetitive process can take

A Bath for the Big Guy

Some of us spend part of an afternoon attacking a dirty car with a sponge and a pail of sudsy water. But how would you like the job of washing a jumbo jet? About once a month, airlines must remove the accumulated grime that can cause flight drag and cut into fuel efficiency. As a manual job, a jet bath takes 20 workers about four hours. Enter the robots. A robot cleaning system, using 35 brushes and 17 TV cameras, can restore the plane's luster in approximately 80 minutes.

months or even years. Finally, it is put into the same situations as the human expert would face, where it should give equal or better service but much more quickly.

The Outlook for Expert Systems

Some industry analysts feel that expert systems are beginning to mimic the analytic processes of humans and that, as a result, these programs border on true artificial intelligence. Putting together the facets we have discussed so far, a computer having artificial intelligence should understand the facts it knows, come up with new facts, and be able to engage in a wide-ranging conversation about them in a natural language. By these standards, expert systems today are still rather dim-witted. Furthermore, each system has intelligence only in one specific area.

Expert systems will infiltrate companies department by department, much as personal computers did before them. Some expert systems are now available on personal computers. The main limitation of using an expert system on a personal computer is that the expert system requires a substantial amount of memory. In addition, a large amount of rules, facts, and program code must be stored, requiring the use of a hard disk. Even so, it seems likely that more expert systems for personal computers will appear in the near future.

Robotics

Many people smile at the thought of robots, perhaps remembering the endearing C-3PO of *Star Wars* fame and its "personal" relationship with humans. But vendors have not made even a small dent in the personal robot market—the much-heralded domestic robots have never materialized. So, where are the robots today? Mainly in factories.

Robots in the Factory

Most robots are in factories, spray-painting and welding—and taking away jobs. The Census Bureau, after two centuries of counting people, has now branched out and today is counting robots as well. About 15,000 robots existed in 1985, and double that number in 1990. What do robots do that merits all this attention?

A loose definition of *robot* is a type of automation that replaces human presence. But a **robot** is more completely defined as a computer-controlled device that can physically manipulate its surroundings. Some robots, as we will see later, can also manipulate themselves. There are a wide variety of sizes and shapes of robots, each designed with a particular use in mind. Often these uses are functions that would be tedious or even dangerous for a human to perform. The most common industrial robots sold today are mechanical devices with five or six axes of motion, so they can rotate into proper position to perform their tasks (Figure 16-5).

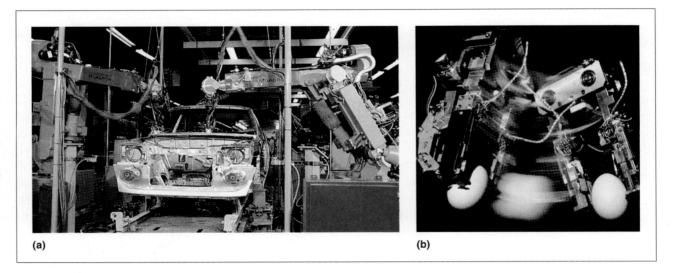

(a)

(b)

Figure 16-5   Industrial robots. (a) These standard robots are used in the auto industry to spray-paint new cars. (b) This robot is not making breakfast. Hitachi uses the delicate egg, however, to demonstrate that its visual-tactile robot can handle fragile objects. The robot's sensors detect size, shape, and required pressure, attaining sensitivity almost equal to that of a human hand.

We mentioned spray-painting and welding, but a more intelligent robot can adapt to changing circumstances. For example, with the help of a TV-camera eye, a robot can see components it is meant to assemble. It is able to pick them up, rearrange them in the right order, or place them in the right position before assembling them.

Robot Vision

Recently, **vision robots** have been taught to see in living color—that is, to recognize multicolored objects solely from their colors. This is a departure from the traditional approach, whereby robots recognize objects by their shapes (Figure 16-6), and from vision machines that "see" only a dominant color. For example, a robot in an experiment at the University of Rochester was able to pick out a box of Kellogg's Sugar Frosted Flakes from 70 other boxes. Among the anticipated benefits of such visual recognition skills is supermarket checkout. You cannot easily bar code a squash, but a robot might be trained to recognize it by its size, shape, and color.

Field Robots

Just think of some of the places you would rather not be: inside a nuclear power plant, next to a suspected bomb, at the bottom of the sea, or in the middle of a chemical spill. But robots readily go to all those places. Furthermore, they go there to do some dangerous and dirty jobs. These days, robots "in the field" inspect and repair nuclear power plants, dispose of bombs, inspect oil rigs for undersea exploration, clean up chemical accidents, and much more. Space researchers look forward to the day when "astrobots" can be stationed in orbit, ready to repair faulty satellites.

Only a few years ago there were just a handful of field robots commercially employed. Now there are hundreds, and soon there will be thousands. Field robots may be equipped with wheels, tracks, legs, fins, or

Figure 16-6   The seeing robot. Robots "see" by casting light beams on objects and identifying them by matching their shapes to those of already "known" objects. In this machine-vision sequence, (a) the object is seen by the robot, (b) the object is matched to known shapes, (c) inappropriate shapes are eliminated, and (d) the object is recognized.

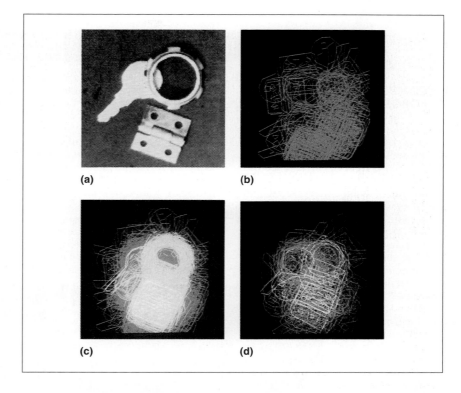

(a)   (b)

(c)   (d)

even wings (Figure 16-7). Field robots have been largely overshadowed by factory robots, mainly because they lack the independent glamour of their manufacturing counterparts; field robots must be remotely controlled by human operators. Now, however, the poor relative status of field robots is changing because enough computer power can be packed into a field robot to enable it to make most decisions independently. Field robots need all the power they can get. Unlike factory robots, which are bolted to the ground and blindly do the same tasks over and over again, field robots must often contend with a highly unstructured environment.

Controlling Your Destiny

The immediate prospects for expert systems and robots is growth and more growth. We can anticipate both increased sophistication and more diverse applications. The progress in the more esoteric applications of artificial intelligence will continue to be relatively slow. No one need worry that any computer can capture the wide-ranging sophistication of a human just yet. People are in charge of computers, not the other way around.

In the Information Age, understanding computers and learning to use them will help us manage our lives more profitably. Marshall McLuhan once alerted us to the role that tools play in our lives: They are not just separate or distinct from us; they are extensions of our inner selves. In the past, managing our daily existence has had more to do with how we handle relationships with people than anything else. In the future, our relationships with technology will become just as important.

Figure 16-7   Flying robot. Can a robot really fly? Yes. Flying robots have both military and civilian uses. This Sentinel robot can soar up to 10,000 feet to spy on an enemy or to inspect high-voltage wires or spot forest fires.

PERSPECTIVES

COMPUTERS IN YOUR WORLD: ROBOT TALES

Like computers before them, robots will soon be everywhere. Here are some samples.

Robots fight oil fires. It seems most fitting that robots should do dangerous work and replace the humans who might otherwise have to sacrifice their lives. Fighting the oil well fires in Kuwait after the Persian Gulf war with Iraq claimed a number of lives until robot firefighters were brought in. The last oil well fire was doused in early 1992—months ahead of schedule, thanks in part to the robot firefighters.

Robby the Robot steps out. NASA has developed a robot vehicle, Robby, designed to explore Mars. Without human help, Robby can successfully pick its

way along a rocky dry riverbed. Eventually, Robby will be sent on its own to Mars to scout possible landing spots for a human mission.

Robots on display. If you care to see robots in the workplace, here is your chance. At the General Motors manufacturing plant in Flint, Michigan, state-of-the-art robots labor side by side with their human co-workers on an assembly line. Seam-sealing robots can stretch their torches into out-of-the-way places quickly. Others can place car seats on a conveyor belt, using an

electronic eye to match each seat with the appropriate car model. Still others may install windshields. Tours are available to the public every Tuesday and Thursday.

Lending a hand. Robots may soon be of significant use to the disabled. Researchers have already developed a robot for quadriplegics. The machine can respond to a dozen voice commands, including those that tell them to answer the door, get the mail, and serve soup.

Let the robots fight the next war. It has been suggested by some artificial intelligence researchers that countries send their most sophisticated robots into battle, declare a winner, and get on with living. Although this seems rather preposterous, it is food for thought.

REVIEW AND REFERENCE

Summary and Key Terms

- **Artificial intelligence (AI)** is a field of study that explores how computers can be used for tasks that require the human characteristics of intelligence, imagination, and intuition. AI has also been described as the study of how to make computers do things that—at the present time—people can do better.

- *Artificial intelligence* is considered an umbrella term to encompass several subsets of interests, including problem solving, natural languages, expert systems, and robotics.

- In the early days of AI, scientists thought that it would be useful just to stuff facts into the computer; however,

facts are useless without the ability to interpret and learn from them.

- An early attempt to translate human languages by providing a computer with vocabulary and rules of grammar was a failure because the computer could not distinguish the context of statements. This failure impeded the progress of artificial intelligence.

- The study of artificial intelligence is predicated on the computer's ability to learn—and to improve performance based on past errors.

- A **knowledge base** is a set of facts and rules about those facts. An **inference engine** accesses, selects, and interprets a set of rules. The inference engine applies rules to the facts to make up new facts.

The Programming Process

Planning the Solution

In Chapter 6, we described the five steps of the programming process in a general way. We noted that the first step, defining the problem, is related to the larger arena of systems analysis and design, a subject we examined closely in Chapter 8. The second step involves planning the solution, and the last three steps—coding, testing, and documenting the program—are really done in the context of a particular programming language, such as BASIC.

This appendix will look more closely at the planning phase, detailing the steps to help you understand how to develop program logic. First you will be introduced to three different approaches to program planning—*flowcharting, structure charts,* and *pseudocode*—and examples of each. Normally, a programmer would use only one or two to reach a solution. We present all three here—side by side—so you can compare them.

Flowcharts, which present a map of a solution, were the primary planning device for many years. They were favored over other methods because logic is easier to follow with pictures than with words. But flowcharts have some drawbacks: They are not easy to change, and they tend to be too detailed. A programmer draws a flowchart, then writes a program based on that flowchart; both the flowchart and the program listing are part of the program documentation. As the program changes—and it will—corresponding changes should be made on the flowchart. And therein lies the problem: Most programmers simply do not keep flowcharts up-to-date. However, there is a new wrinkle that makes flowcharts more palatable: They can be drawn and revised using flowcharting software.

A structure chart illustrates the structure of a program by depicting its parts as independent hierarchical modules. The resulting picture identifies a program's major functions at a high level, making it fairly easy to gain an overview quickly.

Pseudocode is easier to maintain than a flowchart. Since pseudocode is just words, it can be kept on a computer file and changed easily, using word processing. Although pseudocode is not a visual tool, it is nevertheless an effective vehicle for stating and following program logic. For these reasons, flowcharts have fallen out of favor and pseudocode has become popular. But flowcharts are often used as teaching devices, so we include them here.

In this appendix we will also examine another important topic: structured programming, an accepted standard of programming that minimizes logic complexity. Let us begin with the pictures—flowcharts.

 ## *Flowcharts*

A flowchart presents a visual map of a program. The flowchart uses *arrows* to represent the direction of the program flow and *boxes* and other shapes to display actions. Note that in this discussion we are talking about a **logic flowchart,** a flowchart that represents the flow of logic in a program. A logic flowchart is different from a **systems flowchart,** which shows the flow of data through an entire computer system. We examined systems flowcharts in Chapter 8.

We will use the ANSI flowchart symbols introduced in Chapter 6 (see Figure 6-1). Templates of ANSI symbols (Figure A-1) are available in many office-supply stores and college bookstores and are helpful in drawing flowcharts by hand. They are also found in popular flowcharting software such as MacFlow (Figure A-2). The most common symbols you will use represent process, decision, connector, start/stop, input/output, and direction of flow. Now let us use flowcharting to show just what programming is all about.

Figure A-1   A template containing standard ANSI flowchart symbols. Templates like this one are used as drawing aids.

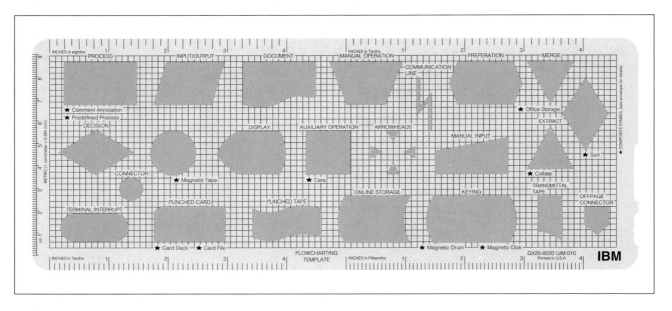

Figure A-2 Flowcharting software. A flowcharting software product called MacFlow offers ANSI symbols (left) to use in creating a flowchart on a Macintosh.

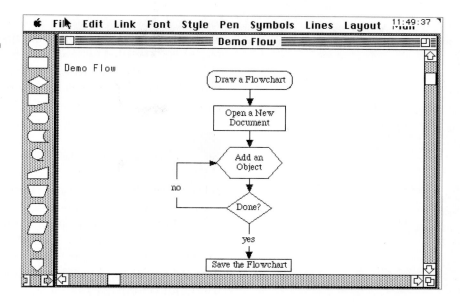

Example: Summing Numbers from 1 through 100

Figure A-3 shows how you might flowchart a program to find the sum of all numbers between 1 and 100. There are a number of things to observe about this flowchart.

First, the program uses two places in the computer's memory as storage locations, or places to keep intermediate results. In one location is a counter, which might be like a car odometer: Every time a mile passes, the counter counts it as a 1. In the other location the computer stores a sum—that is, a running total of the numbers counted. The sum location will eventually contain the sum of all numbers from 1 through 100: $1 + 2 + 3 + 4 + 5 + \ldots + 100$.

Second, as we start the program, we must initialize the counter and the sum. When you **initialize,** you set the starting values of certain storage locations, usually as the program execution begins. We will initialize the sum to 0 and the counter to 1.

Third, note the looping. You add the counter to the sum and a 1 to the counter, then come to the decision diamond, which asks if the counter is greater than 100. If the answer is No, the computer loops back around and repeats the process. The decision box contains a **compare operation;** the computer compares two numbers and performs alternative operations based on the comparison. If the result of the comparison is Yes, the computer produces the sum as output, as indicated by the print instruction. Notice that the parallelogram-shaped symbol is used for printing the sum, because printing is an output process.

A **loop**—also called an **iteration**—is the heart of computer programming. The beauty of the loop, which may be defined as the repetition of instructions under certain conditions, is that you, as the programmer, have to describe certain instructions only once rather than describing them repeatedly. Once you have established the loop pattern and the conditions for concluding (exiting from) the loop, the computer continues

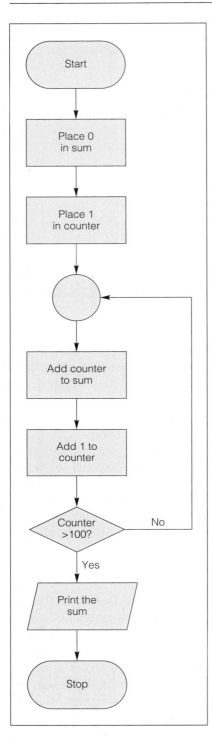

Figure A-3   A loop example. This flow-chart uses a loop to find the sum of numbers from 1 through 100.

looping and exits as it has been instructed to do. The loop is considered a powerful programming tool because the code is reusable; once written, it can be called upon many times. Notice also that the flowchart can be modified easily to sum the numbers from 1 through 1000 or 500 through 700 or some other variation. Now let us look at how structure charts are formed.

Structure Charts

A **structure chart** graphically illustrates the structure of a program by showing independent hierarchical steps. This high-level picture identifies major functions that are the initial component parts of the structure chart. Each major component is then broken down into subcomponents, which are, in turn, broken down still further until sufficiently detailed components are shown. Since the components are pictured in hierarchical form, a drawing of this kind is also known as a **hierarchy chart.** A structure chart is easy to draw and easy to change, and it is often used to supplement or even to replace a logic flowchart.

Example: Payroll Processing

An example of a structure chart is shown in Figure A-4. As the illustration shows, the top level of the structure chart gives the name of the program, Payroll process. The next level breaks the program down into its major functions: read inputs, compute pay, and write outputs. One set of program statements performs each function. Each of these major functions is then subdivided further into smaller pieces. (We could break them down even further, but space does not permit it.)

The major functions are repeatedly subdivided into smaller pieces of manageable size. Each of these components is also, according to plan, as independent of the others as possible. For example, step 4.1, Write master, can be executed independently of any activity in step 4.3, Write paychecks.

We will use fairly small, concise structure charts in the examples in this appendix.

Pseudocode

As you have learned, **pseudocode** is an English-like way of representing the solution to a problem. It is considered a "first draft" because the pseudocode eventually has to be translated into a programming language. Although pseudocode is like English and has some precision to it, it does not have the very definite precision of a programming language. Pseudocode cannot be executed by a computer. When using pseudocode to plan a program, you can concentrate on the logic and not worry about the rules of a specific language. It is also easy to change pseudocode if you discover a flaw in your logic—once it is coded in a programming lan-

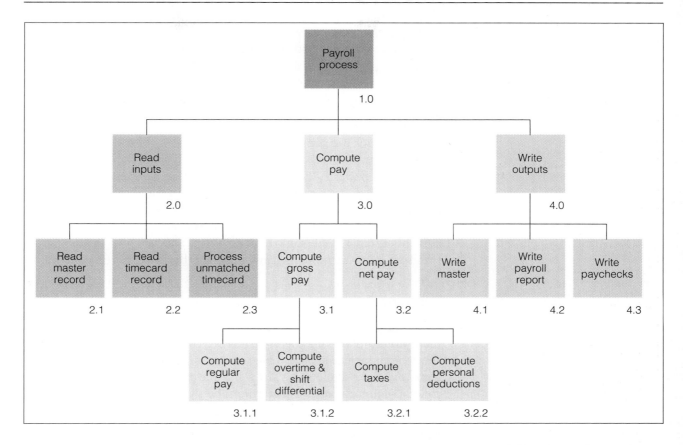

Figure A-4   A structure chart. The numbers outside the boxes refer to more detailed diagrams of these functions.

guage, most people find that it is more difficult to change logic. Pseudocode can be translated into a variety of programming languages, such as Pascal or COBOL. It is helpful to introduce pseudocode in relation to flowcharting. Before doing so, however, let us consider structured programming.

 ## Structured Programming

Structured programming is a technique that emphasizes breaking a program into logical sections by using certain universal programming standards. Structured programming makes programs easier to write, check, read, and maintain. The computer industry widely accepts structured programming as a productive way of programming. We will examine the rationale and concepts of structured programming more thoroughly later in this appendix. For now we just introduce some basic concepts of structure in this discussion of flowcharts, structure charts, and pseudocode. Note, however, that a programmer would use flowcharting, structure charts, *or* pseudocode to plan a solution. We present them together here so you can see how each method can be used to solve the same problem.

In a program, **control structures** control how the program executes. Structured programming uses a limited number of control structures to minimize the complexity of programs and thus cut down on errors. There are three basic control structures in structured programming:

- Sequence
- Selection
- Iteration

These three are considered the basic building blocks of all program construction. You will see that we have used some of these structures already, in Figures A-2 and A-3.

Before we discuss each control structure in detail, it is important to note that each structure has only one **entry point** (the point where control is transferred to the structure) and one **exit point** (the point where control is transferred from the structure). This property makes structured programs easier to read and to debug than unstructured programs.

Sequence

The **sequence control structure** is the most straightforward: One statement simply follows another in sequence. The left side of Figure A-5 shows the general format of a sequence control structure as it is used in flowcharting or in pseudocode. The right side of Figure A-5 shows an example of a sequence control structure: The two steps follow in sequence.

Selection

The **selection control structure** is used to make logical decisions. This control structure has two forms: IF-THEN-ELSE and IF-THEN. The IF-THEN-ELSE control structure works as follows: IF (a condition is true), THEN (do something), ELSE (do something different). For instance, IF

Figure A-5   Sequence. (a and b) The general format of the sequence control structure. (c and d) An example of sequence control structure. To compute the total of movie extras' wages, ① determine one extra's salary for that week's shooting by multiplying the hourly rate times the number of hours worked on the picture that week. ② Add that extra's salary to those of other extras to find the total.

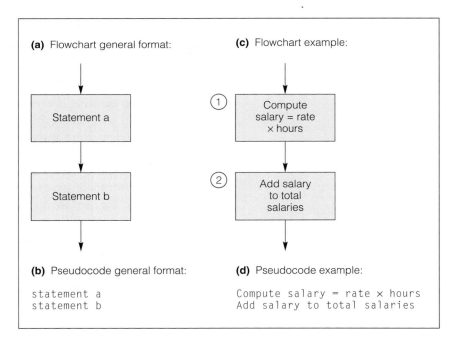

the alarm clock goes off and it is a weekend morning, THEN just turn it off and go back to sleep, ELSE get up and go to work. Or, to use a more specific example, IF a student is a resident, THEN the fee equals number of credits times $450, ELSE fee is number of credits times $655. Figure A-6 shows the general format and an example of IF-THEN-ELSE in both a flowchart and in pseudocode.

IF-THEN is a special case of IF-THEN-ELSE. The IF-THEN selection is less complicated: IF the condition is true, THEN do something—but if it is not true, then do nothing. For example, IF the shift worked is shift 3, THEN add bonus of $50. Note that there will always be some action that results from using IF-THEN-ELSE; in contrast, IF-THEN may or may not produce action, depending on the condition. The IF-THEN variation is shown in Figure A-7.

Figure A-6   IF-THEN-ELSE. (a and b) The general format of the IF-THEN-ELSE control structure. There can be one or more statements for each of the two paths, True and False. (c and d) An example of an IF-THEN-ELSE control structure. A trucker orders tires at a truck-tire warehouse. IF ① the quantity of tires ordered is greater than the quantity on hand (q.o.h.), THEN ② the computer prints "Incomplete stock," ELSE ③ it prints "Reordered" and subtracts the quantity ordered from the quantity on hand.

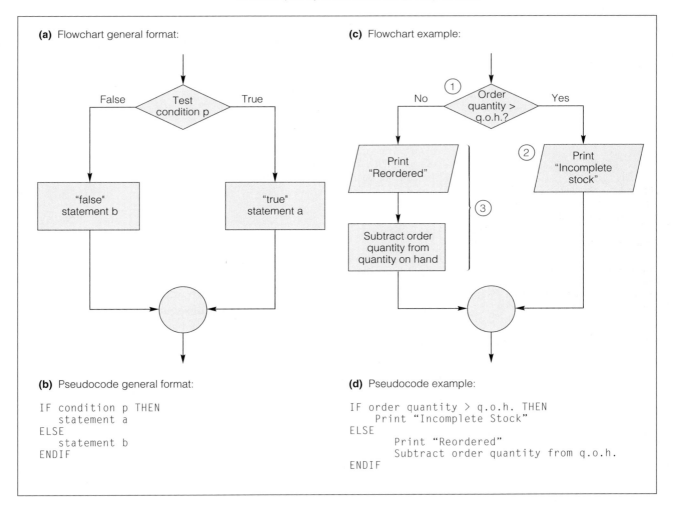

(a) Flowchart general format:

(c) Flowchart example:

(b) Pseudocode general format:

```
IF condition p THEN
   statement a
ELSE
   statement b
ENDIF
```

(d) Pseudocode example:

```
IF order quantity > q.o.h. THEN
     Print "Incomplete Stock"
ELSE
       Print "Reordered"
       Subtract order quantity from q.o.h.
ENDIF
```

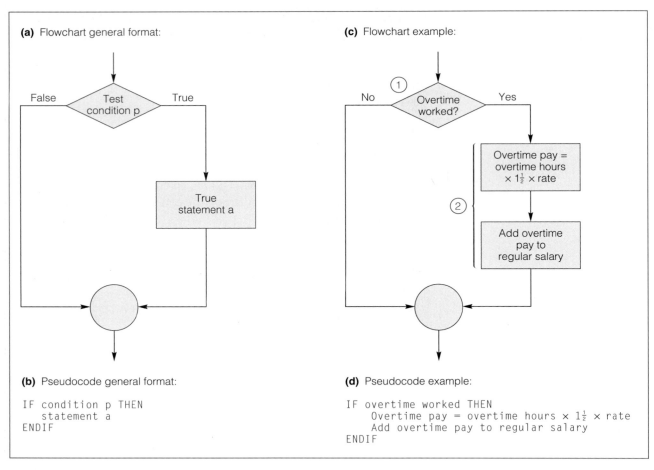

(a) Flowchart general format:

(c) Flowchart example:

(b) Pseudocode general format:

```
IF condition p THEN
    statement a
ENDIF
```

(d) Pseudocode example:

```
IF overtime worked THEN
    Overtime pay = overtime hours × 1½ × rate
    Add overtime pay to regular salary
ENDIF
```

Figure A-7 IF-THEN. (a and b) The general format of the IF-THEN control structure. (c and d) An example of an IF-THEN control structure. IF ① a department store employee worked overtime, THEN ② the program computes overtime pay by multiplying the overtime hours by 1½ times the hourly rate; the total is added to the employee's regular salary.

Iteration

The **iteration control structure** is a looping mechanism. The only necessary iteration structure is the DOWHILE structure, which is shown in Figure A-8. An additional form of iteration is called DOUNTIL; DOUNTIL is really just a combination of sequence and DOWHILE. Although DOUNTIL is not one of the three basic control structures, it is convenient to introduce the DOUNTIL structure now, and it is shown in Figure A-9.

When looping, you must give an instruction to stop the repetition at some point; otherwise, you could—theoretically—go on looping forever and never get to the end of the program. There is a basic rule of iteration, which is related to structured programming: *If you have several statements that need to be repeated, a decision about when to stop repeating has to be placed either at the beginning of all the loop statements or at the end of all the loop statements.*

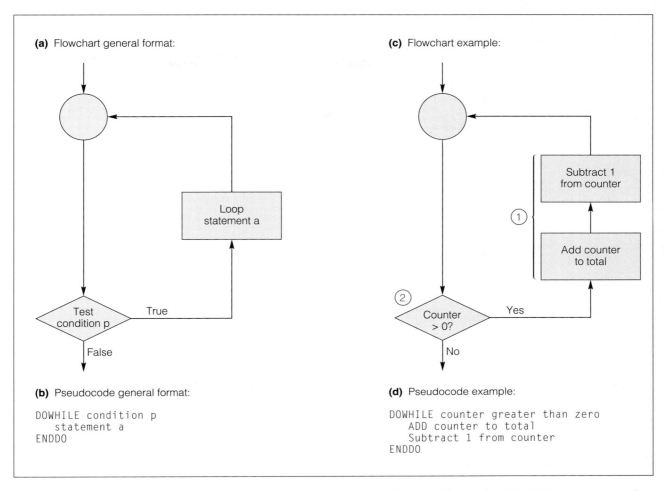

(a) Flowchart general format:

Loop
statement a

Test
condition p

True

False

(b) Pseudocode general format:

```
DOWHILE condition p
   statement a
ENDDO
```

(c) Flowchart example:

Subtract 1
from counter

Add counter
to total

①

② Counter
> 0?

Yes

No

(d) Pseudocode example:

```
DOWHILE counter greater than zero
   ADD counter to total
   Subtract 1 from counter
ENDDO
```

Figure A-8   DOWHILE. (a and b) The general format of the DOWHILE control structure. (c and d) An example of a DOWHILE control structure. DO ① add counter to total and subtract 1 from counter WHILE ② counter is greater than 0.

If you put the loop-ending decision at the beginning, it is called a **leading decision;** if you put it at the end, it is called a **trailing decision.** The position of the decision constitutes the basic difference between DOWHILE and DOUNTIL. As Figure A-8 shows, DOWHILE tests at the beginning of the loop—the diamond-shaped decision box is the first action of the loop process. The DOUNTIL loop tests at the end, as you can see in Figure A-9. The DOUNTIL loop, by the way, guarantees that the loop statements are executed at least once because the loop statements are executed before you make any test about whether to get out. This guarantee is not necessarily desirable, depending on the program logic. Also note that the test condition of DOUNTIL must be False to continue the loop—this is an important difference from the DOWHILE loop.

These basic control structures may seem a bit complex in the beginning, but it is worth taking your time to learn them. In the long run, they are the most efficient models for programming.

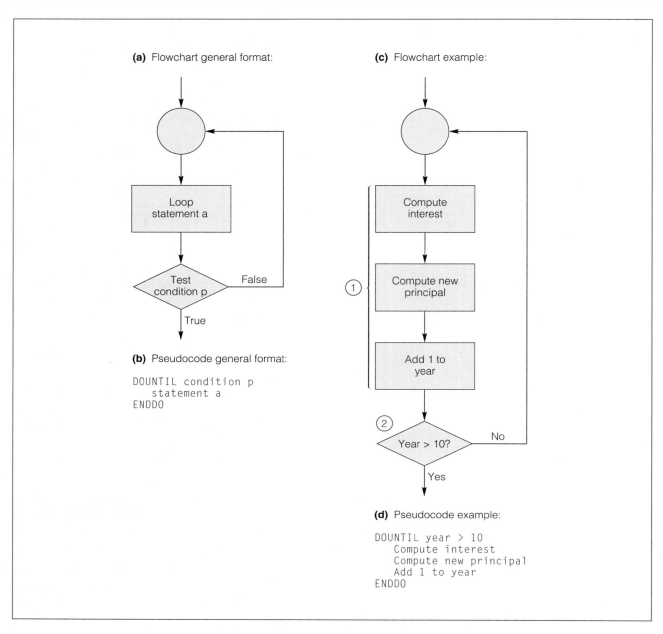

(a) Flowchart general format:

Loop statement a

Test condition p — False

True

(b) Pseudocode general format:

```
DOUNTIL condition p
   statement a
ENDDO
```

(c) Flowchart example:

Compute interest

Compute new principal ①

Add 1 to year

② Year > 10? — No

Yes

(d) Pseudocode example:

```
DOUNTIL year > 10
   Compute interest
   Compute new principal
   Add 1 to year
ENDDO
```

Figure A-9   DOUNTIL. (a and b) The general format of the DOUNTIL control structure. (c and d) Example of a DOUNTIL control structure. DO ① compute interest, compute principal, and add the number 1 to the total years UNTIL ② the number of years is greater than 10.

Using Flowcharts, Structure Charts, and Pseudocode

Let us now consider four extended examples. In each example, solutions are shown in flowchart, structure chart, and pseudocode form. Keep in mind that only one approach would normally be selected.

Some Pseudocode Rules

Although pseudocode is not as formal as a programming language, many programmers follow rules like these:

- Begin each program or program section with "Start" and finish with "End."

- Capitalize control words, such as IF and THEN.

- Write sequence statements in order, one under the other.

- Use IF-THEN-ELSE for decisions. Begin the decision with IF and end with ENDIF. THEN goes at the end of the IF line. If an ELSE is needed, align it with the IF and ENDIF. Indent the statements that go under THEN or ELSE.

- Use DOWHILE or DOUNTIL for iteration (looping). Indent the statements after the DO statement. End each DO with ENDDO, in the same margin as the DO.

Example: Counting Salaries

Suppose you are the manager of a personnel agency that has 50 employees. You want to know how many people make over $30,000 a year, $20,000 to $30,000, and under $20,000.

Figure A-10 shows a solution to your problem. Let us go through the flowchart in Figure A-10a first. The circled numbers in the text that follows correspond to the circled numbers in the illustration. Use the structure chart and pseudocode in parts b and c of the figure for comparison.

① The program begins by initializing four counters to 0. The employee counter will keep track of the total number of employees in the company; the other counters—the high-salary counter, the medium-salary counter, and the low-salary counter—will count the numbers of employees in the salary categories.

② In the parallelogram-shaped input box, we indicate that the computer reads the salary at this point. A **Read** statement may be defined as code that brings something that is outside the computer into memory; to *read*, in other words, means to *get*. The Read statement causes the computer to get one employee's yearly salary; since the instruction is in a loop, the computer will eventually get all salaries.

③ The first of the diamond-shaped decision boxes is a test condition that can go either of two ways—Yes or No. Note that if the answer to the question "Salary > $30,000?" is Yes, then the computer will process this answer by adding 1 to the high-salary counter. If the answer is No, the computer will ask, "Salary < $20,000?"—and so on.

④ For every decision box, no matter what decision is made, program control flows to a connector. And, as the flowchart shows, each decision box has its own connector. Note that, in this case, each connector is directly below the decision box to which it relates.

⑤ Whatever the kind of salary, the machine adds 1 (for the employee) to the employee counter, and a decision box then asks, "Employee counter = 50?" (the total number of employees in the company).

⑥ If the answer is No, the computer makes a loop back to the first connector and goes through the process again. Note that this is a DOUNTIL loop because the decision box is at the end rather than at the beginning of the computing process (DO keep processing UNTIL employee counter equals 50).

⑦ When the answer is finally Yes, the computer then goes to an output operation (a parallelogram) and prints the salary count for each of the three categories. The computing process then stops.

Review the flowchart and observe that every action is one of the three control structures we have been talking about: sequence, selection, or iteration.

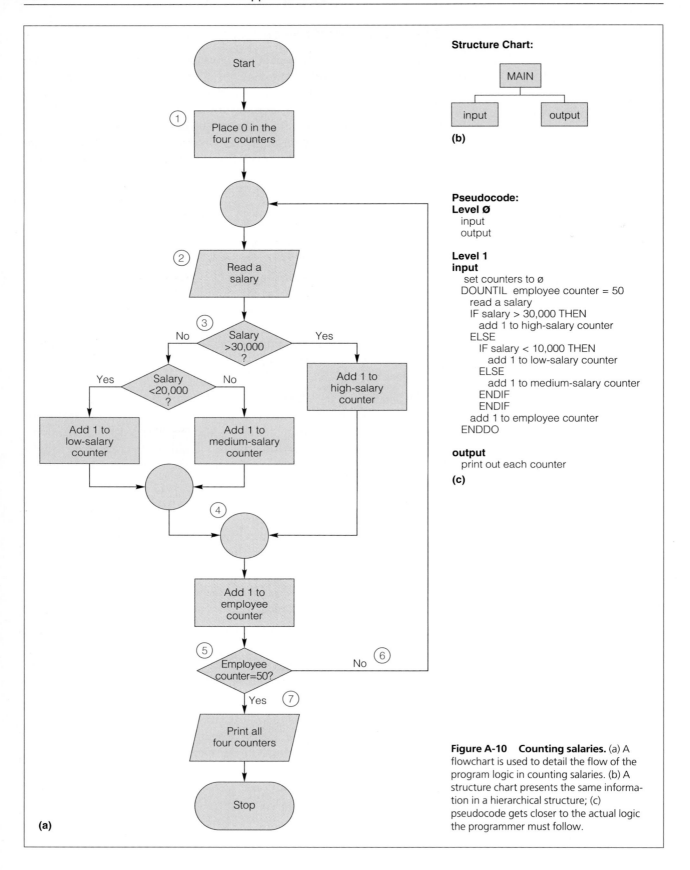

Structure Chart:

MAIN

input   output

(b)

Pseudocode:
Level Ø
input
output

Level 1
input
  set counters to ø
  DOUNTIL employee counter = 50
    read a salary
    IF salary > 30,000 THEN
      add 1 to high-salary counter
    ELSE
      IF salary < 10,000 THEN
        add 1 to low-salary counter
      ELSE
        add 1 to medium-salary counter
      ENDIF
    ENDIF
    add 1 to employee counter
  ENDDO

output
  print out each counter

(c)

Figure A-10   Counting salaries. (a) A flowchart is used to detail the flow of the program logic in counting salaries. (b) A structure chart presents the same information in a hierarchical structure; (c) pseudocode gets closer to the actual logic the programmer must follow.

Example: Customer Credit Balances

In the example in this section, we will consider a flowchart that describes the process of checking a retail customer's credit balance (Figure A-11a). The structure chart in Figure A-11b gives an overview. The pseudocode (Figure A-11c) provides another way to view the process. The file of customer records is kept on some computer-accessible medium, probably disk. This is a more true-to-life example than the previous salary example because, rather than a file with exactly 50 records, the file here contains

Figure A-11   Checking a credit balance. (a) A flowchart details the program logic in checking a customer's credit balance. (b) The structure chart and (c) pseudocode each show a different method of detailing the same procedures.

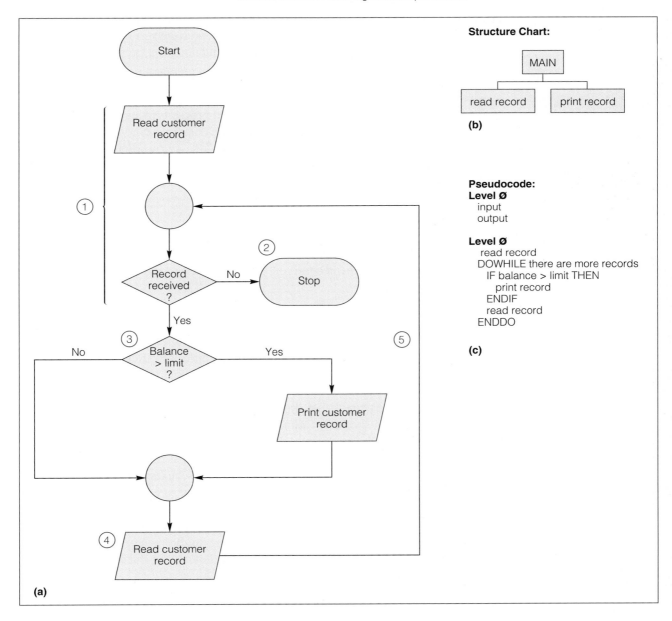

Structure Chart:

MAIN

read record   print record

(b)

Pseudocode:
Level Ø
  input
  output

Level Ø
  read record
  DOWHILE there are more records
    IF balance > limit THEN
      print record
    ENDIF
    read record
  ENDDO

(c)

an unknown number of records. The program has to work correctly no matter how many customers there are.

As store manager, you need to check the customer file and print out the record of any customer whose current balance exceeds the credit limit, so salesclerks will not ring up charge purchases for customers who have gone over their credit limits. (Recall that a record is a collection of related data items; a customer record would likely contain customer name, address, account number, and—as indicated—current balance and credit limit.) The interesting thing about this flowchart is that it contains the same input operation, "Read customer record," twice (see the parallelograms). We will see why this is necessary. Let us proceed through the flowchart:

① After reading the first customer record and proceeding through the connector, you have a decision box that asks, "Record received?" This is a test to see if you have run out of all customer records (which you probably would not have the first time through).

② If the answer is No, you have reached an **end of file**—there are no more records in the file—and the process stops.

③ If the answer is Yes, the program proceeds to another decision box, which asks a question about the customer whose record you have just received: "Balance > limit?" This is an IF-THEN type of decision. If the answer is Yes, then the customer is over the limit and, as planned, the computer prints the customer's record and moves on to the connector. If the answer is No, then the computer moves directly to the connector.

④ Now we come to the second Read statement, "Read customer record." Why are two such statements needed? Couldn't we just forget the second one and loop back to the first Read statement again?

The answer lies in the rules of structure. As we stated, a loop requires a decision either at the beginning or at the end. If we omitted the second Read statement and looped back to the first Read statement, then the decision box to get us out of the loop ("Record received?") would be in the middle, not the beginning or the end, of the loop. Why not put "Record received?" at the end? That strategy will not work either, because then the instructions would tell the computer to do the processing before the program had ascertained if there were a record to process.

In summary: The decision box cannot go at the end, and the rules say it cannot be in the middle; therefore, the decision must go at the beginning of the processing. Thus, the only way to read a second customer record after the computer has read the first one is to have the second Read statement where you see it. The first Read statement is sometimes called the **priming read.** This concept of the double Read may seem complicated at first, but it is very important. Reviewing the description of this flowchart may help.

⑤ Next, the program loops back to the connector and repeats the process. Incidentally, this is a DOWHILE loop because the decision box is at the beginning rather than at the end of the computing process (DO keep processing WHILE records continue to be received).

Note that, as before, each action in the program is either a sequence, a selection, or an iteration. In fact, since you have now seen two totally different examples—counting salaries and checking credit balances—you can begin to see how the control structures can be used for different applications. That is, the subject matter of the program may change, but the structured programming principles remain the same.

Example: Shift Bonus

Here is a description of the problem whose solution is represented in Figure A-12. The problem concerns awarding employees bonuses based on the shift worked. The example is a little more elaborate because it involves moving data—employee number, name, and bonus—to a report line to set it up before printing. As the figures show, a first-shift employee gets a bonus of 5% of regular pay, but employees who work the second or third shift get a 10% bonus. Also, the program counts the employees on the second or third shifts—that is, it performs one count for both shifts. If the shift is not 1, 2, or 3, then the program produces an error message.

Example: Student Grades

Now let us translate a flowchart—and accompanying structure chart and pseudocode—into a program. You could type this program in on a computer terminal connected to a mainframe computer or key it directly into your personal computer. The computer would deliver back to you, on a terminal screen or in printout form, the answers you seek. Figure A-13 on page 537 shows the flowchart, structure chart, pseudocode, program, and output.

The program is written in BASIC, a programming language similar to English in many ways. So, even with no knowledge of BASIC, you can understand the program. There are several "dialects" of the BASIC language, but we have chosen to use simple generic BASIC in this example.

The numbers in the far left column of the BASIC program are called statement numbers. In the program, REM stands for a remark, a statement that simply documents the program. The REMs briefly describe what the program is supposed to do, or the REMs list variable names. Variable names are symbolic names of locations in main storage. The PRINT statement tells the computer what message or data to print out, the READ statement reads the data to be processed, the GOTO (go to) statement tells which statement the computer is to go to, and DATA statements list the data to be read by the computer.

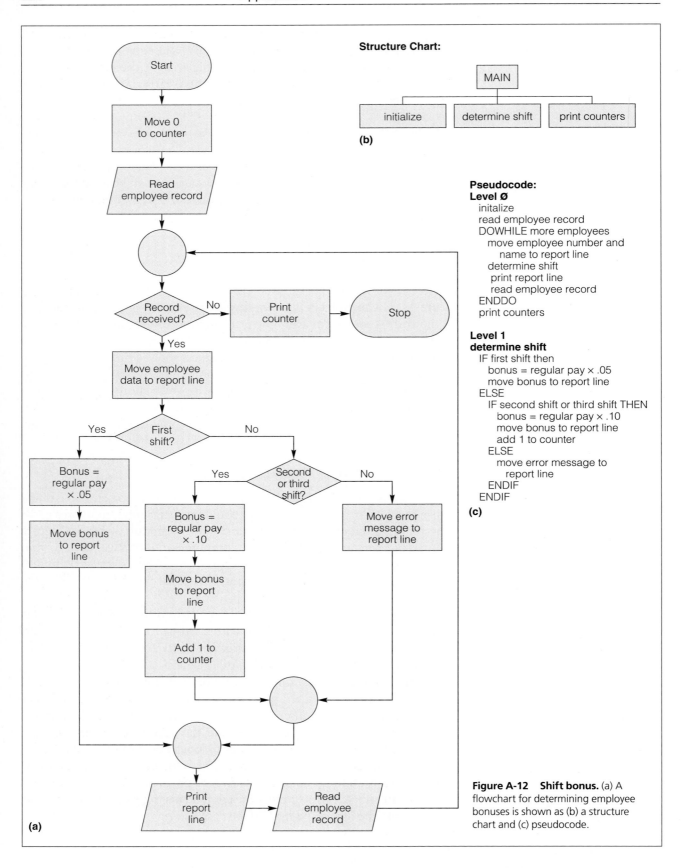

Structure Chart:

MAIN
- initialize
- determine shift
- print counters

(b)

Pseudocode:
Level Ø
initalize
read employee record
DOWHILE more employees
  move employee number and
    name to report line
  determine shift
  print report line
  read employee record
ENDDO
print counters

Level 1
determine shift
IF first shift then
  bonus = regular pay × .05
  move bonus to report line
ELSE
  IF second shift or third shift THEN
    bonus = regular pay × .10
    move bonus to report line
    add 1 to counter
  ELSE
    move error message to
      report line
  ENDIF
ENDIF

(c)

Figure A-12   Shift bonus. (a) A flowchart for determining employee bonuses is shown as (b) a structure chart and (c) pseudocode.

Our problem is, first, to compute the student grades (ranging from 0 through 100) for six students, and, second, to count the number of students who have scored fewer than 60 points. The grade points are based on student performance on two tests, a midterm exam, and a final exam, the scores of which have been weighted in a certain way.

Let us conceive of the problem in terms of input, processing, and output.

Input   The circled numbers in the text correspond to the circled numbers in the flowchart, but you may follow the pseudocode if you prefer. Corresponding statement numbers from the program follow in parentheses.

① **Print headings** (lines 240 through 300). This statement refers to the headings on the report (skip ahead to Figure A-13e to see what they look like). The first is the overall heading, "STUDENT GRADE REPORT." Lines that contain only the word PRINT, as line 240 does, cause blank lines to print on the output; this provides better spacing. Next the coding instructs the printer to print the three column headings.

② **Place 0 in counter** (line 310). This line does not accept input; this line causes the initialization process that is required here, at the outset. The counter will count the number of students who score fewer than 60 points, as you will see later.

③ **Read number, name, scores** (line 320). The input data is given in lines 420 through 480.

Processing

④ **Record received?** (line 330). Note that this is a DOWHILE loop because the decision box is at the beginning of the process. In generic BASIC, DOWHILE is implemented with IF-THEN-ELSE. The decision box asks if the particular student number, name, and scores read are the last ones in the file. How will the computer know this? Because the numeral -9999 will tell it "end of file." You will note that the student numbers are four digits other than -9999 (see lines 420 through 470). The -9999 decision instructs the computer to advance to statement 390 when the end of the file is reached.

⑤ **Compute total points** (line 340). The scores are weighted 20% for the first test, 20% for the second test, 25% for the midterm, and 35% for the final exam. The total of these weighted scores gives the course grade. In the program, these percentages are documented in remark statements (lines 80 through 110). The formula that totals the scores and incorporates the weightings is stated in line 340. Here the expression $.20*S1$ means 20% times the first test score (S1). In BASIC, the asterisk symbol ($*$) is used as the multiplication symbol.

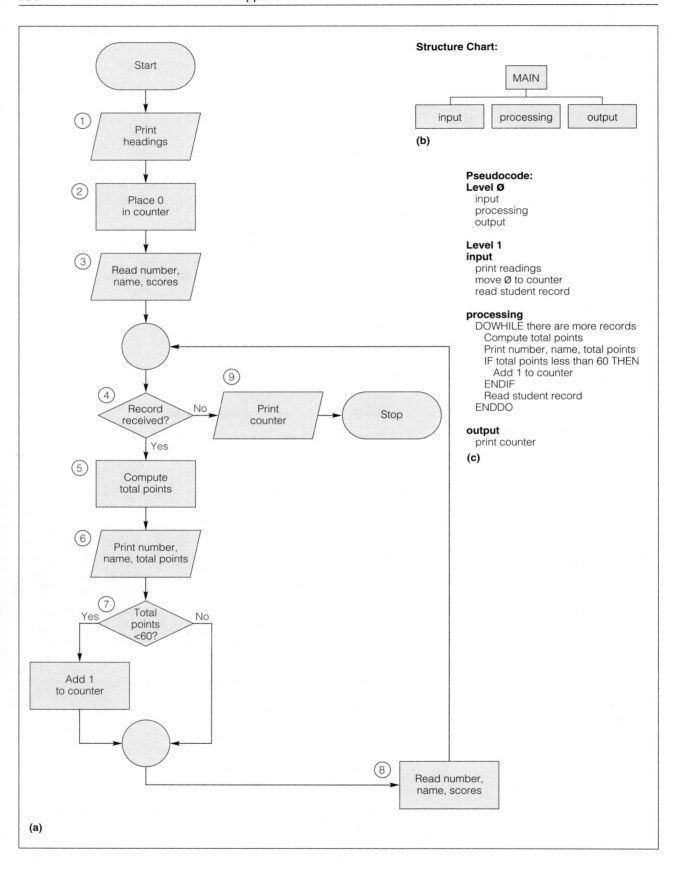

Structure Chart:

MAIN

input | processing | output

(b)

Pseudocode:
Level Ø
  input
  processing
  output

Level 1
input
  print readings
  move Ø to counter
  read student record

processing
  DOWHILE there are more records
    Compute total points
    Print number, name, total points
    IF total points less than 60 THEN
      Add 1 to counter
    ENDIF
    Read student record
  ENDDO

output
  print counter

(c)

Start

① Print headings

② Place 0 in counter

③ Read number, name, scores

④ Record received? — No → ⑨ Print counter → Stop

Yes

⑤ Compute total points

⑥ Print number, name, total points

⑦ Total points <60? — Yes / No

Add 1 to counter

⑧ Read number, name, scores

(a)

```
10    REM PROGRAM TO COMPUTE STUDENT POINTS
20    REM
30    REM THIS PROGRAM READS, FOR EACH STUDENT,
40    REM   STUDENT NUMBER, STUDENT NAME, AND
50    REM   4 TEST SCORES. THE SCORES ARE TO
60    REM   BE WEIGHTED AS FOLLOWS:
70    REM
80    REM      TEST 1: 20 PERCENT
90    REM      TEST 2: 20 PERCENT
100   REM      MIDTERM: 25 PERCENT
110   REM      FINAL: 35 PERCENT
120   REM
130   REM VARIABLE NAMES USED:
140   REM
150   REM   COUNT   COUNT OF STUDENTS SCORING LESS THAN 60
160   REM   NUM     STUDENT NUMBER
170   REM   NAM$    STUDENT NAME
180   REM   S1      SCORE FOR TEST 1
190   REM   S2      SCORE FOR TEST 2
200   REM   S3      SCORE FOR MIDTERM
210   REM   S4      SCORE FOR FINAL
220   REM   TOTAL   TOTAL STUDENT POINTS
230   REM
240   PRINT
250   PRINT "    STUDENT GRADE REPORT"
260   PRINT
270   PRINT "STUDENT","STUDENT","TOTAL"
280   PRINT "NUMBER","NAME","POINTS"
290   PRINT
300   PRINT
310   LET COUNT = 0
320   READ NUM,NAM$,S1,S2,S3,S4
330   IF NUM = -9999 THEN 390
340   LET TOTAL = .20*S1+.20*S2+.25*S3+.35*S4
350   PRINT NUM,NAM$,TOTAL
360   IF TOTAL < 60 THEN COUNT = COUNT+1
370   READ NUM,NAM$,S1,S2,S3,S4
380   GOTO 330
390   PRINT
400   PRINT "NUMBER OF STUDENTS WITH POINTS < 60:";COUNT
410   STOP
420   DATA 2164,ALLEN SCHAAB,60,64,73,78
430   DATA 2644,MARTIN CHAN,80,78,85,90
440   DATA 3171,CHRISTY BURNER,91,95,90,88
450   DATA 5725,CRAIG BARNES,61,41,70,53
460   DATA 6994,RAOUL GARCIA,95,96,90,92
470   DATA 7001,KAY MITCHELL,55,60,58,55
480   DATA -9999,XXX,0,0,0,0
490   END
```

(d)

```
                  STUDENT GRADE REPORT

STUDENT           STUDENT                      TOTAL
NUMBER            NAME                         POINTS


2164              ALLEN SCHAAB                 70.4
2644              MARTIN CHAN                  84.4
3171              CHRISTY BURNER               90.5
5725              CRAIG BARNES                 56.5
6994              RAOUL GARCIA                 92.9
7001              KAY MITCHELL                 56.8

NUMBER OF STUDENTS WITH POINTS < 60:2
```

(e)

Figure A-13 Student grades. (a) A flowchart, (b) structure chart, and (c) pseudocode that produce a student grade report. (d) The resulting BASIC program is presented, along with (e) a sample printout.

⑥ **Print number, name, total points** (line 350). Printing is really an output operation; we include it here for convenience because it is part of the loop.

⑦ **Total points < 60?** (line 360). This decision box is given as an IF-THEN statement. If a student has fewer than 60 points, 1 is added to COUNT.

⑧ **Read number, name, scores** (line 370). As in the customer credit example, we have here an instance of a repeated Read statement. A GOTO statement is used to close the loop. That is, the input instruction given in step 3 is repeated.

We now make the loop back to the first connector and continue to DO this processing WHILE the answer to the question Record received? is Yes.

Output

⑨ **Print counter** (line 400). When the program reaches the end of the file, the computer prints the total number of students who have fewer than 60 points. The printout of results is shown in Figure A-13e.

All this is probably a bit confusing if you are a beginner. Practice helps.

Programmers Emerge

In the 1950s the programmer was hardly noticed, according to Edsger Dijkstra (pronounced "DIKE-stra"), one of the first to spotlight the importance of the programmer in computing. For one thing, the computers themselves were so large and so cantankerous to maintain that they attracted most of the attention. For another, Dijkstra said, "The programmer's somewhat invisible work was without any glamour: you could show the machine to visitors and that was several orders of magnitude more spectacular than some sheets of coding." Programmers flourished, nevertheless, as the demand for software grew.

In the 1960s, hardware overreached software. The development of hardware and storage capabilities proceeded apace, but software development could not keep up. Hardware costs had decreased, but software projects ran over budget and did not meet their deadlines. And, when projects were finally completed, they often did not meet the users' needs.

In the 1970s, software costs continued to rise. It was apparent that, if money was to be saved, software had to improve. No longer would programmers be allowed to produce programs that were casually tested or that only the programmer could read. The use of obscure coding in an attempt to shave a microsecond of computer time began to be discouraged. Programmers had to develop new, more organized approaches to the complex problems that, in the '70s, now seemed routine. The programmer's job was no longer "invisible work."

Early Programming

How did people go about programming in the early '60s? One computer scientist wrote: "Computer programming was so badly understood that hardly anyone even thought about proving programs correct; we just fiddled with a program until we knew it worked." Dijkstra, in fact, has nagged and cajoled programmers since the early years to think in advance instead of using a rearguard action for finding errors *after* a program is written.

Finding program errors after the fact was—and still is, in some quarters—an accepted way of programming. That is, a programmer wrote a program that seemed to solve the problem, then the program was put to the test. As soon as an error turned up, that one was fixed. This would continue until, eventually, the programmer got the program working well enough to use. To Dijkstra, this seemed a shoddy way of doing things. "Program testing," he said, "is a very convincing way of demonstrating program errors but never their absence."

In 1966 C. Bohm and G. Jacopini introduced structured programming in a paper in *Communications of the ACM* (the journal of the Association for Computing Machinery). In their paper, which had been published previously in Italy, they proved mathematically that any problem solution could be constructed using only three basic control structures—the three structures that we have been calling *sequence, selection* (IF-THEN-ELSE), and *iteration.* It is interesting to note that the concept of structured programming has remained unchanged since it was proposed more than two decades ago.

These three control structures—sequence, selection, and iteration—were, of course, used before 1966. But other control structures were also used. The most notable was the transfer structure, also known as the GOTO. After Bohm and Jacopini proved the need for only the three basic control structures, however, the time had come to cut down on the number of GOTO statements.

The idea of structured programming was given a boost in March 1968, when Dijkstra published a now famous letter in *Communications of the ACM.* Under the heading "Go To Statements Considered Harmful," Dijkstra contended that using the GOTO statement was an invitation to making a mess of one's program and that reducing the number of GOTOs reduced the number of programming errors. GOTOs, he said, could be compared to pasta. If a person took a program and drew a line from each GOTO statement to the statement to which it transferred, the result would be a picture that looked like a bowl of spaghetti. Since then, people have referred to excessive GOTOs in a program as "spaghetti code." Note the comparison of programs with and without GOTOs in Figure A-14.

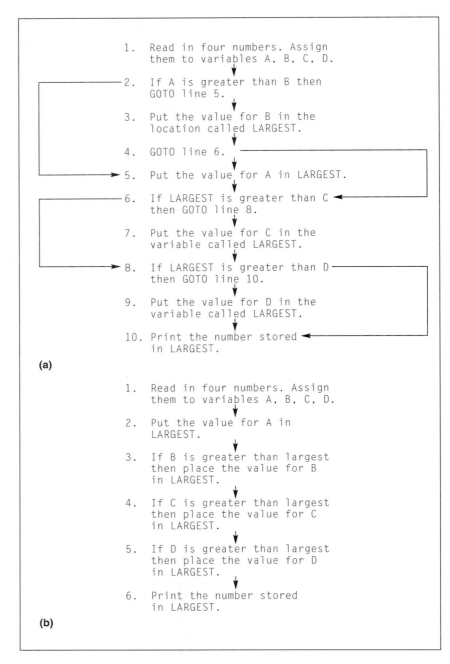

(a)

(b)

Figure A-14   With and without GOTO statements. These two programs, written here in plain English, do the same thing: Each finds the largest of four numbers. Such a task could be used, for example, to locate the salesperson with the greatest dollar value of sales for the month. (a) An illustration of GOTO programming. Even this small example demonstrates how confusing GOTO programming can be. (b) A solution for the same problem in GOTOless programming; it does the job in a tidy, sequential manner.

Structured Programming Takes Off

The results of the first major project using structured programming were published in 1972. The project involved automating the clipping file of the *New York Times* in such a way that, using a list of index terms, users could browse through abstracts (summaries) of all the paper's articles, automatically retrieve the text of an article, and display it on a terminal. The project involved 83,000 lines of source code and took 22 calendar months and 11 person-years to produce, yet it was delivered under budget and ahead of schedule. Equally important, there was an amazingly low error rate: Only 21 errors were found during the five weeks of acceptance testing, and only 25 additional errors appeared during the first year of the system's operation.

In December 1973 *Datamation*, one of the principal trade journals of the computer industry, devoted an entire issue to structured programming. This issue brought the subject to the attention of many programmers in the United States. One article hailed structured programming as a programming revolution.

And a revolution it has been. The theory—if not total practice— has been universally accepted in the computer industry. One obvious proof of this acceptance is the number of programming language text-books on the market with the word *Structure* in the title. No one would even consider publishing a text for unstructured COBOL (a popular programming language for business). So trainees coming into the industry have "structure" fresh in their heads, and what do they find? For some, the purest of structured shops. Many, however, are shocked to find existing programs—fat, messy, programs—dripping with GOTOs. Why is this? These programs were written in the '60s and even the '70s, before structured programming had taken hold. Managers would love to have them redone in structured code, but there often seem to be more pressing priorities or budget constraints. Occasionally, a trainee is welcomed with open arms as the savior who is going to convert some of the program dinosaurs to structured code. This may be the ultimate challenge—structuring a 5000-line program that has been massaged by perhaps 50 different programmers over the last 15 years. The biggest problem may be that no one really understands how the program works anymore!

Managers have estimated that structured techniques increase programming productivity by approximately 25%. This is so because structured programming:

- Increases the clarity and readability of programs (partly because you can read the program sequentially instead of hopping all over with GOTOs)
- Reduces the time required to test programs
- Decreases the time required to maintain programs (because increased clarity means less time spent in trying to read and understand code)

So far, we have discussed the historical significance and rationale for structured programming and tied it to the three fundamental structures: sequence, selection, and iteration. But the issue of structure cuts deeper.

Expanding the Structured Programming Concept

When the concept of program structure was first introduced, some people thought their programs would be structured if they simply got rid of GOTOs. There is more to it than that. Structured programming is a method of designing computer system components and their relationships to minimize complexity. So, in addition to limited control structures (again: sequence, selection, and iteration), two important aspects of structured programming are (1) top-down programming design and (2) module independence through coupling and cohesion. Before we describe these concepts, let us pause for an expanded formal definition: **Structured programming** is a set of programming techniques that uses a limited number of control structures, top-down design, and module independence.

One of the first steps in **top-down design** is to identify basic program functions. These functions are further divided into smaller and smaller subfunctions of more manageable size. These subfunctions are called *modules*. The structure charts we discussed earlier are good examples of top-down design, and using structure charts to plan programs is a means to achieving it.

Now let us look more closely at the way modules are planned.

Modularity

Computer professionals recognize that the way to efficient development and maintenance is to work on a program as a series of manageable pieces. The way that a program is divided has a significant effect on how it works. We have already noted, in the discussion of structure charts, that structured design involves organizing the pieces of a program in a hierarchical way. Lower-level components are called modules. Once converted to programmed form, a **module** is a set of logically related statements that performs a specific function.

One relationship between modules is called **coupling,** which is the measure of the strength of the relationship between two modules. Ideally, that relationship should be weak so that the modules are independent; then, if a change is made in one module, it will not affect other modules. Another relationship is called **cohesion,** the measure of the inner strength of an individual module. The best relationship here is a strong one; a module should have a single function, although that is not always possible. An example of a single function is the computation of withholding tax. This function would not be included with other functions, such as computing insurance deductions. Strong cohesion encourages module independence, which—in turn—makes future changes easier.

In addition, a module should have a **single entry** and a **single exit.** In a single-entry module, execution must always begin at the same place, usually at the beginning; the module can be entered at only a single point. Similarly, the module may be exited from only one place, as shown in Figure A-15. Keeping track of what is going on in

Figure A-15   Single entry, single exit. The program control module executes module B by transferring to its entry point. After the instructions in module B are executed, the module is exited via its exit point. Program control returns, in this case, to the point of departure, the control module.

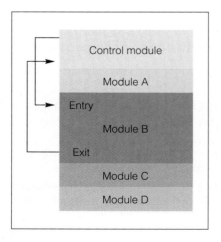

a program is easier if there is only one way to get in and one way to get out of each module in it.

A module should be of manageable size. A single page of coded program instructions is often considered an ideal size.

Is There a Future for Structured Programming?

We have focused on structure and its acceptance in the computer community. We have industry-wide agreement on this important issue and can consider it settled, right? No, not quite. Structured programming makes sense if you are using what is called a **procedural language**—that is, a language that presents a step-by-step process for solving a problem, as in the Pascal or C languages. It is the steps— program statements—of the procedure that need structuring. But nothing stays the same for long in the computer industry. When the focus shifts from *how* to accomplish a task—the step-by-step way—to *what* you want to accomplish, **nonprocedural languages** are preferred. Object-oriented languages (discussed in Chapter 6) are the most popular nonprocedural languages. New, easy-to-use languages will continue to be introduced as the industry evolves.

A Career in Programming?

In this appendix you have seen some of the habits of mind and the care required to write programs. But remember that what you have seen is just an overview. When deciding on programming as a career, you can only be sure about your choice after you have tried learning and using a programming language. After the brief glimpse we have just shown you, perhaps you will want to give programming a try.

R E V I E W   A N D   R E F E R E N C E

Summary and Key Terms

- The planning phase of programming involves the steps necessary to help you understand how to develop program logic. Programmers and others can use flowcharting, structure charts, and pseudocode to plan a solution for a problem.

- Flowcharts are symbolic pictorial representations of step-by-step solutions to problems. They consist of arrows representing the direction a program takes and boxes and other symbols representing actions. A **logic flowchart** represents the flow of logic in a program; a **systems flowchart** shows the flow of data through an entire computer system.

- To **initialize** means to set the starting values of certain storage locations, usually as the program begins to execute.

- A **compare operation** occurs when the computer compares two numbers and performs alternative operations based on the comparison.

- A **loop**—also called an **iteration**—is defined as the repetition of instructions under certain conditions; once established, the loop is considered a powerful programming tool because the code is reusable.

- A **structure chart** graphically illustrates the structure of a program by showing independent hierarchical modules. It is also known as a **hierarchy chart**.

- **Pseudocode** is a way of representing the solution to a problem by using English to express the logic. It is considered a "first draft" for solving the problem because eventually it must be translated into a programming language.

- **Structured programming** is a technique that emphasizes breaking a program into logical sections by using certain universal programming standards. In more formal terms, structured programming is a set of programming techniques that includes a limited number of control structures, top-down design, and module independence.

- Structured programming uses **control structures** to handle execution. The **sequence control structure** involves one statement following another in sequence. A **selection control structure** can take one of two forms: IF-THEN-ELSE and IF-THEN. An **iteration control structure** is a looping mechanism that uses DOWHILE for **leading decisions** and DOUNTIL for **trailing decisions.** Each structure has only one **entry point** (the point where control is transferred to the structure) and one **exit point** (the point where control is transferred from the structure). These characteristics make structured programs easier to read and debug than unstructured programs.

- A **Read** statement brings something that is outside the computer into memory; *reading,* in other words, means *getting.* The first Read statement is sometimes called the **priming read.** When you read to the **end of file,** there are no more records in the file, so the reading process stops.

- **Top-down design** identifies basic program functions before dividing them into subfunctions called modules. Structure charts illustrate top-down design.

- When converted to program form, a **module** is a set of logically related statements that performs a specific function.

- **Coupling** is the measure of the strength of the relationship between two modules. Weak coupling is ideal because a change in one module does not affect other modules. **Cohesion** is the measure of the inner strength of a module. Strong cohesion makes modules more independent, a characteristic that facilitates future changes. A module should also have a **single entry** and a **single exit** so that it is easier to keep track of the flow of logic in the program.

- A **procedural language,** such as COBOL, is a language that presents a step-by-step process of solving a problem. **Nonprocedural languages,** such as object-oriented languages, simply state what task is to be accomplished.

Review Questions

1. What are three programming aids used in planning solutions for problems? How do two of the aids differ from the third? Which one is more hierarchical than the others?

2. What is the main drawback for using flowcharting in programming?

3. Which one of the three programming aids is considered a "first draft" for programming?

4. Describe the three main control structures in structured programming. Name and describe the specific types of statements.

5. Explain how the three control structures are evident in the flowchart for counting salaries (Figure A-10) and in the flowchart for checking credit balances (Figure A-11).

6. Write the pseudocode for this problem: Read a file of records and, if the account type is business, check further. (Hint: You must create an IF statement within an IF statement, as in Figure A-10.) If the order amount is greater than 1000, then set the discount rate to the maximum; otherwise, set the discount rate to the minimum. But if the account type is other than business—an ELSE situation—then set the discount rate to 0. After making these checks, compute the discount, compute the amount due, and write the record and the amount due. Note also that, as in Figure A-11, you need a priming read. And remember to start and end the program.

7. Explain the debt programmers owe to Edsger Dijkstra and what structured programming owes to the team of C. Bohm and G. Jacopini.

8. How did structured programming differ from the way programming had been done previously?

9. State the benefits of structured programming.

10. Explain how maintaining a limited number of control structures helps to make structured programming less complex.

11. Describe top-down design.

12. Explain the concept of modularity.

13. Describe a procedural language. How does it differ from a nonprocedural language?

Discussion Questions

1. Should students be required to take a programming course, even if they are not going to become programmers?

2. Why might programmers be more inclined to use structure charts than flowcharting or pseudocode? Would you say this reflects a laziness in record keeping, a preference for more relevant material, or some other tendency?

3. Do you think pseudocode is *really* like English? Why or why not?

4. Having seen some of the tasks they perform, would you say that programmers are better described as "geniuses" or detail-minded individuals? Support your choice.

True-False Questions

T F   1. Flowcharts are non-visual representations of programs.

T F   2. *Structure chart* is another name for pseudocode.

T F   3. The standard symbols used in flowcharting are called ANSI symbols.

T F   4. A loop is used to set a starting value in a certain storage location in memory.

T F   5. Structured programming is used in procedural languages.

T F   6. Selection control structures involve test conditions like DOUNTIL.

T F   7. A leading decision for a loop can use DOWHILE.

T F   8. To bring something in from outside a program, you use a WRITE instruction.

T F   9. Top-down design requires you to identify basic program functions first.

T F 10. COBOL is a procedural language.

History and Industry

The Continuing Story of the Computer Age

Figure B-1 The Altair. The term *personal computer* had not even been invented yet, so Ed Roberts's small computer was called a "minicomputer" when it was featured on the cover of *Popular Electronics.*

Although the story of computers has diverse roots, the most fascinating part—the history of personal computers—is quite recent. The beginning of this history turns on the personality of Ed Roberts the way a watch turns on a jewel. It began when his foundering company took a surprising turn.

Like other entrepreneurs before him, Ed Roberts had taken a big risk. He had already been burned once, and now he feared being burned again. The first time, in the early 1970s, he had borrowed heavily to produce microprocessor-based calculators, only to have the chip producers decide to build their own product—and sell it for half the price of Ed's calculator.

Ed's new product was based on a microprocessor too—the Intel 8080—but it was a *computer.* A little computer. The "big boys" at the established computer firms considered computers to be industrial products; who would want a small computer? Ed was not sure, but he found the idea so compelling that he decided to make the computer anyway. Besides, he was so far in debt from the calculator fiasco that it did not seem to matter which project propelled him into bankruptcy. Ed's small computer and his company, MITS, were given a sharp boost by Les Solomon, who promised to feature the new machine on the cover of *Popular Electronics.* In Albuquerque, New Mexico, Ed worked frantically to meet the publication deadline, and he even tried to make the machine pretty, so it would look attractive on the cover (Figure B-1).

Making a good-looking small computer was not easy. This machine, named the Altair (after a heavenly "Star Trek" destination), looked like a flat box. In fact, it met the definition of a computer in only a minimal way: It had a central processing unit (on the chip), 256 characters (a paragraph!) of memory, and switches and lights on a front panel for input/output. No screen, no keyboard, no storage.

But the Altair was done on time for the January 1975 issue of *Popular Electronics,* and Roberts made plans to fly to New York to demonstrate the machine for Solomon. He sent the computer on ahead by railroad express. Ed got to New York but the computer did not—the very first personal computer was lost! There was no time to build a new computer before the publishing deadline, so Roberts cooked up a phony version for the cover picture: an empty box with switches and lights on the front panel. He also placed an inch-high ad in the back of the magazine: Get your own Altair kit for $397.

Ed was hoping for perhaps 200 orders. But the machine—that is, the box—fired imaginations across the country. Two thousand customers sent checks for $397 to an unknown Albuquerque, New Mexico, company. Overnight, the MITS Altair personal computer kit was a runaway success.

Ed Roberts was an important player in the history of personal computers. Unfortunately, he never made it in the big time; most observers agree that his business insight did not match his technical skills. But other entrepreneurs did make it. In this chapter, we will glance briefly at the early years of computers and then examine more recent history.

Babbage and the Countess

Born in England in 1791, Charles Babbage was an inventor and mathematician. When solving certain equations, he found the hand-done mathematical tables he used filled with errors. He decided a machine could be built that would solve the equations better by calculating the differences between them. He set about making a demonstration model of what he called a **difference engine** (Figure B-2). The model was so well received that in about 1830 he enthusiastically began to build a full-scale working version, using a grant from the British government.

Figure B-2 Charles Babbage's difference engine. Babbage's Difference Engine #2 was never completed during his lifetime. The one shown here was built in 1991 by the London Science Museum, according to Babbage's original designs. The engineers, Barrie Holloway (left) and Reg Crick (right), built it in honor of Babbage's 200th birthday.

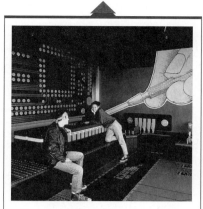

The Computer Museum

The Computer Museum in downtown Boston, Massachusetts, is the world's first museum devoted solely to computers and computing. The museum illustrates how computers have affected all aspects of life: science, business, education, art, and entertainment. Over half an acre of hands-on and historical exhibits chronicle the enormous changes in the size, capability, applications, and cost of computers over the past 40 years. Two mini-theaters show computer classics as well as award-winning computer-animated films.

The Computer Museum Store offers a large selection of such unique items as state-of-the-art silicon chip jewelry and chocolate "chips" as well as books, posters, cassettes, and more.

Figure B-3   The Countess of Lovelace. Augusta Ada Byron, as she was known before she became a countess, was Charles Babbage's colleague in his work on the analytical engine and has been called the world's first computer programmer.

However, Babbage found that the smallest imperfections were enough to throw the machine out of whack. Babbage was viewed by his own colleagues as a man who was trying to manufacture a machine that was utterly ridiculous. Finally, after spending its money to no avail, the government withdrew financial support.

Despite this setback, Babbage was not discouraged. He conceived of another machine, christened the **analytical engine,** which he hoped would perform many kinds of calculations. Although it was never built in his time, a model was eventually put together by his son. It was not until 1991 that a working version of the analytical engine was built and put on public display in London. It embodied five key features of modern computers:

- An input device
- A storage place to hold the number waiting to be processed
- A processor, or number calculator
- A control unit to direct the task to be performed and the sequence of calculations
- An output device

If Babbage was the father of the computer, then Ada, the Countess of Lovelace, was the first computer programmer (Figure B-3). The daughter of English poet Lord Byron and of a mother who was a gifted mathematician, Ada helped develop the instructions for doing computations on the analytical engine. Lady Lovelace's contributions cannot be overvalued. She was able to see that Babbage's theoretical approach was workable, and her interest gave him encouragement. In addition, she published a series of notes that eventually led others to accomplish what Babbage himself had been unable to do.

Herman Hollerith: The Census Has Never Been the Same

The hand-done tabulation of the 1880 United States census took seven and a half years. A competition was held to find some way to speed the counting process of the 1890 United States census. Herman Hollerith's tabulating machine won the contest. As a result of his system's adoption, an unofficial count of the 1890 population (62,622,250) was announced only six weeks after the census was taken.

The principal difference between Hollerith's and Babbage's machines was that Hollerith's machine used electrical rather than mechanical power (Figure B-4). Hollerith realized that his machine had considerable commercial potential. In 1896 he founded the successful Tabulating Machine Company, which, in 1924, merged with two other companies to form the International Business Machines Corporation—IBM.

Watson Smart? You Bet!

Just as computers were getting off the ground, Thomas Watson, Sr., saw the best and brightest called to arms in World War II. But he did not just bid his employees a sad adieu. He paid them. Each and every one received one quarter of his or her annual salary, in twelve monthly installments. The checks continued to arrive throughout the duration of the war. Every month those former employees thought about IBM and the generosity of its founder.

The result? A very high percentage of those employees returned to IBM after the war. Watson got his brain trust back, virtually intact. The rest is history.

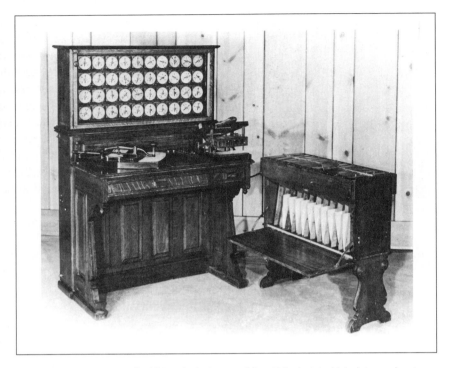

Figure B-4   Herman Hollerith's tabulating machine. This electrical tabulator and sorter was used to tabulate 1890 census data.

 ## Watson of IBM: Ornery but Rather Successful

For over 30 years, from 1924 to 1956, Thomas J. Watson, Sr., ruled IBM with an iron grip. Cantankerous and autocratic, supersalesman Watson made IBM a dominant force in the business machines market, first as a supplier of calculators, then as a developer of computers.

IBM's entry into computers was sparked by a young Harvard professor of mathematics, Howard Aiken. In 1936, after reading Lady Lovelace's notes, Aiken began to think that a modern equivalent of the analytical engine could be constructed. Because IBM was already such a power in the business machines market, with ample money and resources, Aiken worked out a careful proposal and approached Thomas Watson. In one of those make-or-break decisions for which he was famous, Watson gave him $1 million. As a result, the Harvard Mark I was born.

 ## The Start of the Modern Era

Nothing like the **Mark I** had ever been built before. It was 8 feet high and 55 feet long, made of streamlined steel and glass, and it emitted a

Figure B-5   The ABC. John Atanasoff and his assistant, Clifford Berry, developed the first digital electronic computer, nicknamed the ABC for *Atanasoff-Berry computer.*

sound during processing that one person said was "like listening to a roomful of old ladies knitting away with steel needles." Unveiled in 1944, the Mark I was never very efficient. But the enormous publicity it generated strengthened IBM's commitment to computer development. Meanwhile, technology had been proceeding elsewhere on separate tracks.

American military officials approached Dr. John Mauchly at the University of Pennsylvania and asked him to build a machine that would rapidly calculate trajectories for artillery and missiles. Mauchly and his student J. Presper Eckert relied on the work of Dr. John V. Atanasoff, a professor of physics at Iowa State University. During the late 1930s Atanasoff had spent time trying to build an electronic calculating device to help his students solve mathematical problems. He and an assistant, Clifford Berry, succeeded in building the first digital computer that worked electronically; they called it the **ABC,** for **Atanasoff-Berry computer** (Figure B-5).

After Mauchly met with Atanasoff and Berry in 1941, he used the ABC as the basis for the next step in computer development. From this association ultimately came a lawsuit, based on attempts to get patents for a commercial version of the machine Mauchly built. The suit was finally decided in 1974, when a federal court determined that Atanasoff had been the true originator of the ideas required to make an electronic digital computer actually work. (Some computer historians dispute this court decision.) Mauchly and Eckert were able to use the principles of the ABC to create the **ENIAC,** for **Electronic Numerical Integrator and Calculator.** The main significance of the ENIAC is that, as the first general-purpose computer, it was the forerunner of the UNIVAC I, the first computer sold on a commercial basis.

The Computer Age Begins

The remarkable thing about the computer age is that so much has happened in so short a time. We have leapfrogged through four generations of technology in about 40 years—a span of time whose events are within the memories of many people today. The first three computer "generations" are pinned to three technological developments: the vacuum tube, the transistor, and the integrated circuit. Each has drastically changed the nature of computers. We define the timing of each generation according to the beginning of commercial delivery of the hardware technology. Defining subsequent generations has become more complicated because the entire industry has become more complicated.

The First Generation, 1951–1958: The Vacuum Tube

The beginning of the commercial computer age may be dated June 14, 1951. This was the date the first **UNIVAC—*Uni*ver*sal Automatic Computer***—was delivered to a client, the U.S. Bureau of the Census, for use in tabulating the previous year's census. The date also marked the first

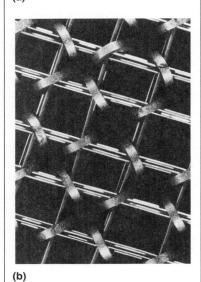

(a)

(b)

Figure B-7   Magnetic cores. (a) A 6- by 11-inch magnetic core memory. (b) Close-up of a magnetic core memory. A few hundredths of an inch in diameter, each magnetic core was mounted on a wire. When electricity passed through the wire on which a core was strung, the core could be magnetized as either "off" or "on." These states represented a 0 (off) or a 1 (on). Combinations of 0s and 1s could be used to represent data. Magnetic cores were originally developed by IBM, which adapted pill-making machinery to produce them by the millions.

Figure B-6   Vacuum tubes. Vacuum tubes were used in the first generation of computers. Vacuum tube systems could multiply two ten-digit numbers together in one-fortieth of a second.

time that a computer had been built for business applications rather than for military, scientific, or engineering use. The UNIVAC was really the ENIAC in disguise and was, in fact, built by Mauchly and Eckert, who in 1947 had formed their own corporation.

In the first generation, **vacuum tubes**—electronic tubes about the size of light bulbs—were used as the internal computer components (Figure B-6). However, because thousands of such tubes were required, they generated a great deal of heat, causing many problems in temperature regulation and climate control. In addition, although all the tubes had to be working simultaneously, they were subject to frequent burnout—and the people operating the computer often did not know whether the problem was in the programming or in the machine.

Another drawback was that the language used in programming was machine language, which uses numbers. (Present-day higher-level languages are more like English.) Using numbers alone made programming the computer difficult and time-consuming. The UNIVAC used **magnetic cores** to provide memory. These consisted of small, doughnut-shaped rings about the size of pinheads, which were strung like beads on intersecting thin wires (Figure B-7). To supplement primary storage, first-generation computers stored data on punched cards. In 1957 magnetic tape was introduced as a faster, more compact method of storing data.

The Second Generation, 1959–1964: The Transistor

Three Bell Lab scientists—J. Bardeen, H. W. Brattain, and W. Shockley—developed the **transistor,** a small device that transfers electric signals across a resistor. (The name *transistor* began as a trademark concocted from *trans*fer plus re*sistor.*) The scientists later received the Nobel prize for their invention. The transistor revolutionized electronics in general and computers in particular. Transistors were much smaller than vacuum tubes, and they had numerous other advantages: They needed no warm-up time, consumed less energy, and were faster and more reliable.

During this generation, another important development was the move from machine language to **assembly languages**—also called **symbolic languages.** Assembly languages use abbreviations for instructions (for example, L for LOAD) rather than numbers. This made programming less cumbersome.

After the development of symbolic languages came **high-level languages,** such as **FORTRAN** (1954) and **COBOL** (1959). Both languages, still widely used today (in updated forms), are more English-like than assembly languages. High-level languages allowed programmers to give more attention to solving problems. Also, in 1962 the first removable disk pack was marketed. Disk storage supplemented magnetic tape systems and enabled users to have fast access to desired data.

All these new developments made the second generation of computers less costly to operate—and thus began a surge of growth in computer systems. Throughout this period computers were being used principally by business, university, and government organizations. They had not filtered down to the general public. The real part of the revolution was about to begin.

The Third Generation, 1965–1970: The Integrated Circuit

One of the most abundant elements in the earth's crust is silicon, a nonmetallic substance found in common beach sand as well as in practically all rocks and clay. The importance of this element to Santa Clara County, which is about 30 miles south of San Francisco, is responsible for the county's nickname: Silicon Valley. In 1965 Silicon Valley became the principal site for the manufacture of the so-called silicon chip: the integrated circuit.

An **integrated circuit** (abbreviated **IC**) is a complete electronic circuit on a small chip of silicon. The chip may be less than ⅛ inch square and contain thousands or millions of electronic components. Beginning in 1965 integrated circuits began to replace transistors in computers. The resulting machines were now called third-generation computers. An integrated circuit was able to replace an entire circuit board of transistors with one chip of silicon much smaller than one transistor.

Integrated circuits are made of silicon because it is a **semiconductor.** That is, it is a crystalline substance that will conduct electric current when it has been "doped" with chemical impurities implanted in its lattice-like structure. A cylinder of silicon is sliced into wafers, each about 6 inches in diameter, and the wafer is etched repeatedly with a pattern of electrical circuitry. Several layers may be etched on a single wafer. The wafer is then divided into several hundred small chips, each with a complete circuit so tiny it is half the size of a human fingernail—yet under a microscope it looks as complex as a railroad yard.

The chips were hailed as a generational breakthrough because they had desirable characteristics: reliability, compactness, and low cost. Mass-production techniques have made possible the manufacture of inexpensive integrated circuits.

Personal Computers in Action

THE SOFTWARE ENTREPRENEURS

Ever thought you'd like to run your own show? Make your own product? Be in business for yourself? Entrepreneurs are a special breed. They are achievement-oriented; like to take responsibility for decisions; and dislike repetitive, routine work. They also have high levels of energy and a great deal of imagination. But perhaps the key is that they are willing to take risks.

Entrepreneurs often have still another quality—a more elusive quality—that is something close to charisma. This charisma is based on enthusiasm, and it allows them to lead people, form an organization, and give it momentum. Study these real-life entrepreneurs, noting their paths to glory and—sometimes—their falls.

Steve Jobs

Of the two Steves who formed Apple Computer, Steve Jobs was the true entrepreneur. Although they both were interested in electronics, Steve Wozniak was the technical genius, and he would have been happy to have been left alone to tinker. But Steve Jobs would not let him alone for a minute—he was always pushing and crusading. In fact, Wozniak had hooked up with an evangelist, and they made quite a pair.

When Apple was getting off the ground, Jobs wanted Wozniak to quit his job so he could work full-time on the new venture. Wozniak refused. His partner begged and cried. Wozniak gave in. While Wozniak built Apple computers, Jobs was out hustling, finding the best marketing man, the best venture capitalist, and the best company president. This entrepreneurial spirit paid off in a spectacular way as Apple rose to the top of the list of microcomputer companies.

Bill Gates

When Bill Gates was a teenager, he swore off computers for a year and in his words, "tried to act normal." His parents, who wanted him to be a lawyer, must have been relieved when Bill gave up the com-

The beginning of the third generation was trumpeted by the IBM 360 series (named for 360 degrees—a full circle of service), first announced April 7, 1964. The System/360 family of computers, designed for both business and scientific use, came in several models and sizes. The equipment housing was blue, leading to IBM's nickname, Big Blue.

The 360 series was launched with an all-out, massive marketing effort to make computers business tools—to get them into medium-size and smaller business and government operations where they had not been used before. The result went beyond IBM's wildest dreams. The reported $5 billion the company invested in the development of the System/360 quickly repaid itself, and the system rendered many existing computer systems obsolete. Big Blue was on its way.

Software became more sophisticated during this third generation. Several programs could run in the same time frame, sharing computer resources. This approach improved the efficiency of computer systems. Software systems were developed to support interactive processing, which used a terminal to put the user in direct contact with the computer. This kind of access caused the customer service industry to flourish, especially in areas such as reservations and credit checks.

puter foolishness and went off to Harvard in 1974. But Bill started spending weekends with his friend Paul Allen, dreaming about personal computers, which did not exist yet. When the MITS Altair, the first personal computer for sale, splashed on the market in January 1975, both Bill and Paul moved to Albuquerque to be near the action at MITS. But they showed a desire even then to chart their own course. Although they wrote software for MITS, they kept the rights to their work and formed their own company. Their company was called Microsoft.

When MITS failed, Gates and Allen moved their software company to their native Bellevue, Washington. They employed 32 people in 1980 when IBM came to call. Gates recognized the big league when he saw it and put on a suit for the occasion. Gates was offered a plum: the chance to develop the operating system (a crucial set of software) for IBM's soon-to-be personal computer. Although he knew he was betting the whole company, Gates never hesitated to take the risk. He and his crew worked feverishly for many months to produce MS-DOS—Microsoft Disk Operating System. It was this product that sent Microsoft on its meteoric rise.

Mitch Kapor

Kapor did not start out on a direct path to computer fame and riches. In fact, he wandered extensively, from being a disk jockey to piano teacher to counselor. He had done some programming, too, but did not like it much. But, around 1978, he found he did like fooling around with personal computers. In fact, he had found his niche.

In 1983 Kapor introduced a software package called Lotus 1-2-3, and there had never been anything like it before. Lotus added the term *integrated package* to the vocabulary; the phrase described the software's identity as a combination spreadsheet, graphics, and database program. Kapor's product catapulted his company to the top of the list of independent software makers in just two years.

Bill Millard

Bill Millard believed that nothing was impossible. It was his habit, for example, to give employees of his IMSAI company impossible assignments and then exhort them to "make a miracle." IMSAI made one of the early personal computers. IMSAI employees were inspired and they did work hard, but nobody worked harder than Bill. Sales were phenomenal. The computer, unfortunately, was not. Quality control caught up with Bill and the company eventually failed.

But not Bill. He just struck out in a new direction. He realized that people would buy personal computers in stores, and he founded the Computerland chain in 1976. His net worth now is in the *billions,* and he describes himself as "the biggest winner of all in the microcomputer industry."

Champions of Change

Entrepreneurs thrive on change. Jobs, Wozniak, and Kapor all left their original companies to start new companies. When Steve Jobs lost control of Apple Computer in 1986, he went out and started NeXT Computer, Inc. Stay tuned for future breakthroughs from these and other personal computer entrepreneurs.

Large third-generation computers began to be supplemented by mini-computers, which are functionally equivalent to a full-size system but are somewhat slower, smaller, and less expensive. These computers have become a huge success with medium-size and smaller businesses.

The Fourth Generation, 1971–Present: The Microprocessor

Through the 1970s computers gained dramatically in speed, reliability, and storage capacity, but entry into the fourth generation was evolutionary rather than revolutionary. The fourth generation was, in fact, an extension of third-generation technology. That is, in the early part of the third generation, specialized chips were developed for computer memory and logic. Thus, all the ingredients were in place for the next technological development, the general-purpose processor-on-a-chip, otherwise known as the **microprocessor,** which became commercially available in 1971.

Nowhere is the pervasiveness of computer power more apparent than in the explosive use of the microprocessor. In addition to the common applications of digital watches, pocket calculators, and personal computers, you can expect to find microprocessors in virtually every machine in the home or business—microwave ovens, cars, copy machines, television sets, and so on. Computers today are 100 times smaller than those of the first generation, and a single chip is far more powerful than ENIAC.

The Fifth Generation: Japan's Challenge

The term *fifth generation* was coined by the Japanese to describe the powerful, "intelligent" computers they wanted to build by the mid-1990s. Since then, however, it has become an umbrella term, encompassing many research fields in the computer industry. Key areas of ongoing research are artificial intelligence, expert systems, and natural language—topics discussed in detail in Chapter 16.

Japan's original announcement of the fifth generation captivated the computer industry. Some view the fifth generation as a race between Japan and the United States, with nothing less than world computer supremacy as the prize. However, the Japanese budget has been cut significantly in recent years, and enthusiasm over the project has waned somewhat.

The Special Story of Personal Computers

Personal computers are the machines you can "get closest to," whether you are an amateur or a professional. There is nothing quite like having your very own personal computer. Its history is very personal too, full of stories of success and failure and of individuals with whom we can readily identify.

I Built It in My Garage

As we noted in the beginning of the chapter, the very first personal computer was the MITS Altair, produced in 1975. But it was a gee-whiz machine, loaded with switches and dials—and no keyboard or screen. It took two teenagers, Steve Jobs and Steve Wozniak, to capture the imagination of the public with the first Apple computer. They built it in that time-honored place of inventors, a garage, using the $1300 proceeds from the sale of an old Volkswagen. Designed for home use, the Apple was the first to offer an easy-to-use keyboard and screen. Founded in 1977, Apple Computer was immediately and wildly successful. When its stock was offered to the public in December 1980, it started a stampede among investors eager to buy in. Apple has introduced an increasingly powerful line of computers, including the Macintosh, which continues to sell well. (Figure B-8 shows early documentation for the first commercial Apple computer.)

The other major player in those early years was Tandy Incorporated, whose worldwide chain of Radio Shack stores provided a handy sales outlet for the TRS-80 personal computer. Other manufacturers who enjoyed more than moderate success in the late 1970s were Atari and Commodore. Their number was to grow.

Figure B-8   Apple manual. Shown here is a collector's item: the very first manual for operation of an Apple computer. Unfortunately, the early manuals were a hodgepodge of circuit diagrams, software listings, and handwritten notes. They were hard to read and understand and almost guaranteed to frighten away all but the most hardy souls.

Figure B-9   The IBM PC. Launched in 1981, the IBM PC took just 18 months to rise to the top of the best-seller list.

The IBM PC Phenomenon

IBM announced its first personal computer in the summer of 1981. IBM captured the top market share in just 18 months, and even more important, its machine became the industry standard (Figure B-9). This was indeed a phenomenal success.

IBM did a lot of things right, such as including the possibility of adding memory. IBM also provided internal expansion slots, so that peripheral equipment manufacturers could build accessories for the IBM PC. In addition, IBM provided hardware schematics and software listings to companies who wanted to build products in conjunction with the new PC. Many of the new products accelerated demand for the IBM machine.

Other personal computer manufacturers have hurried to emulate IBM, producing "PC clones," copycat computers that can run software designed for the IBM PC. Meanwhile, IBM has offered both upscale and downscale versions of its personal computer: PC XT, PC Portable, PC AT, the ill-fated PCjr, and various models of the PS/2 (Personal System/2). Because of increasing competition, IBM faces some stiff challenges in the 1990s to retain its position as the leader in the PC marketplace.

The story of personal computer history is ongoing, with daily fluctuations reflected in the trade press. The effects of personal computers are far-reaching, and they remain a key topic in the computer industry.

 ## The Story Continues

History is still being made in the computer industry, of course, and it is being made incredibly rapidly. A book cannot possibly pretend to describe all the very latest developments. Nevertheless, as we indicated earlier, the four areas of input, processing, output, and storage describe the basic components of a computer system—whatever its date.

R E V I E W   A N D   R E F E R E N C E

Summary and Key Terms

- Charles Babbage, a nineteenth-century mathematician, is called the father of the computer because of his invention of two computation machines. His **difference engine,** which could solve equations, led to another calculating machine, the **analytical engine,** which embodied the key parts of a computer system—an input device, a processor, a control unit, a storage place, and an output device. Countess Ada Lovelace helped develop instructions for carrying out computations on Babbage's device.

- The first computer to use electrical power instead of mechanical power was Herman Hollerith's tabulating machine, which was used in the 1890 census in the United States. Hollerith founded a company that became the forerunner of International Business Machines Corporation (IBM).

- Thomas J. Watson, Sr., built IBM into a dominant force in the business machines market. He also gave Harvard professor Howard Aiken research funds with which to build an electromechanical computer, the **Mark I,** unveiled in 1944.

- John V. Atanasoff, with assistant Clifford Berry, devised the first digital computer to work by electronic means, the **Atanasoff-Berry Computer (ABC).**

- The **ENIAC (Electronic Numerical Integrator and Calculator),** developed by John Mauchly and J. Presper Eckert at the University of Pennsylvania in 1946, was the world's first general-purpose electronic computer.

- The first computer generation began June 14, 1951, with the delivery of the **UNIVAC (UNIVersal Automatic Computer)** to the U.S. Bureau of the Census. First-generation computers required thousands of **vacuum tubes,** electronic tubes about the size of light bulbs. First-generation computers had slow input/output, were programmed only in machine language, and were unreliable. The main form of memory was **magnetic core.** Magnetic tape was introduced in 1957 to store data compactly.

- Second-generation computers used **transistors,** developed at Bell Laboratories. Compared to vacuum tubes, transistors were small, needed no warm-up, consumed less energy, and were faster and more reliable. During the second generation, **assembly languages,** or **symbolic languages,** were developed. They used abbreviations for instructions, rather than numbers. Later, **high-level languages,** such as **FORTRAN** and **COBOL,** were also developed. In 1962 the first removable disk pack was marketed.

- The third generation emerged with the introduction of the **integrated circuit (IC)**—a complete electronic circuit on a small chip of silicon. Silicon is a **semiconductor,** a substance that will conduct electric current when it has been "doped" with chemical impurities.

- With the third generation, IBM announced the System/360 family of computers. During this period more sophisticated software was introduced that allowed several programs to run in the same time frame and supported interactive processing, in which the user, by using a terminal, has direct contact with the computer.

- The fourth-generation **microprocessor**—a general-purpose processor-on-a-chip—grew out of the specialized memory and logic chips of the third generation.

- The term fifth generation was coined to describe the machines the Japanese wanted to create by the mid-1990s—"intelligent" machines more powerful than those on the market so far. The term now encompasses computer systems involving artificial intelligence, expert systems, and natural language.

- The first microcomputer, the MITS Altair, was produced in 1975. However, the first successful computer to include an easy-to-use keyboard and screen was offered by Apple Computer, founded by Steve Jobs and Steve Wozniak in 1977. IBM entered the microcomputer market in 1981 and captured the top market share in just 18 months.

- In the third generation, software became more sophisticated. Programmers learned how to make several programs run at the same time, and interactive processing became common, especially in service industries that provided reservations and credit checks.

Review Questions

1. What was *different* about the difference engine?
2. Who conceived of the analytical engine? Was it ever built?
3. What five key features of modern computers were embodied in the original analytical engine?
4. Who is considered to be the first computer programmer?
5. What company later became International Business Machines Corporation (IBM)?
6. Who is said to have been most responsible for the success of IBM?
7. What was the name of the first digital computer to work electronically?
8. Which small device marked the start of the second generation of computers?
9. Which two entrepreneurs built a personal computer in a garage—and, in the process, launched the personal computer business as we know it?
10. How did the IBM PCjr differ from the IBM PC in the marketplace?

Discussion Questions

1. What explains the fact the first person to successfully build a personal computer has been more or less forgotten by history?
2. What was the main difference between the machines designed by Hollerith and Babbage? What influence do you think this factor had on the relative potential for their machines?
3. Describe the influence of the 1890 census on the evolution of computers.
4. Explain how the invention of the integrated circuit influenced the development of the personal computer.
5. Explain the evolution of computers in terms of generations.

True-False Questions

T F 1. The computer was first conceived by a person born in the late 18th century.

T F 2. Thomas Watson, Sr., started IBM's entry into computers with a $1 million grant to a young Harvard professor.

T F 3. The first commercial computer was called ENIAC.

T F 4. The MITS Altair is said to have been the first personal computer.

T F   5. PC clones are copycat personal computers that can use software designed for the IBM PC.

T F   6. The third generation of computers evolved from the invention of the integrated circuit.

T F   7. The UNIVAC's memory consisted of small doughnut-shaped rings strung like beads on intersecting thin wires.

T F   8. The IBM PCjr failed in the marketplace.

T F   9. Three IBM scientists are credited with the invention of the transistor.

T F   10. Research into Fifth-generation computers stimulated interest in artificial intelligence.

Number Systems

Data can be represented in the computer in one of two basic ways: as **numeric data** or as **alphanumeric data.** The internal representation of alphanumeric data—letters, digits, special characters—was discussed in Chapter 2. Recall that alphanumeric data may be represented using various codes; EBCDIC and ASCII are two common codes. Alphanumeric data, even if all digits, cannot be used for arithmetic operations. Data used for arithmetic calculations must be stored numerically.

Data stored numerically can be represented as the binary equivalent of the decimal value with which we are familiar. That is, values such as 1050, 43218, and 3 that we input to the computer will be converted to the binary number system. In this appendix you will study the binary number system (base 2) and two related systems, octal (base 8) and hexadecimal (base 16).

Number Bases

A number base is a specific collection of symbols on which a number system can be built. The number base familiar to us is base 10, upon which the **decimal** number system is built. There are ten symbols—0 through 9—used in the decimal system.

Since society uses base 10, that is the number base most of us understand and can use easily. It would theoretically be possible, however, for all of us to learn to use a different number system. This number system could contain a different number of symbols and perhaps even symbols that are unfamiliar.

Base 2: The Binary Number System

Base 2 has exactly two symbols: 0 and 1. All numbers in the **binary** system must be formed using these two symbols. As you can see in column 2 of Table 1, this means that numbers in the binary system become long

Table 1   Number bases 10, 2, 8, 16: First values

Base 10 (decimal)	Base 2 (binary)	Base 8 (octal)	Base 16 (hexadecimal)
0	0000	0	0
1	0001	1	1
2	0010	2	2
3	0011	3	3
4	0100	4	4
5	0101	5	5
6	0110	6	6
7	0111	7	7
8	1000	10	8
9	1001	11	9
10	1010	12	A
11	1011	13	B
12	1100	14	C
13	1101	15	D
14	1110	16	E
15	1111	17	F
16	10000	20	10

quickly; the number 1000 in base 2 is equivalent to 8 in base 10. (When different number bases are being discussed, it is common practice to use the number base as a subscript. In this case we could say $1000_2 = 8_{10}$.) If you were to continue counting in base 2, you would soon see that the binary numbers were very long and unwieldy. The number 5000_{10} is equal to 10011100010000_2.

The size and sameness—all those zeros and ones—of binary numbers make them subject to frequent error when they are being manipulated by humans. To improve both convenience and accuracy, it is common to express the values represented by binary numbers in the more concise octal and hexadecimal number bases.

Base 8: The Octal Number System

The **octal** number system uses exactly eight symbols: 0, 1, 2, 3, 4, 5, 6, and 7. Base 8 is a convenient shorthand for base 2 numbers because 8 is a power of 2: $2^3 = 8$. As you will see when we discuss conversions, one octal digit is the equivalent of exactly three binary digits. The use of octal (or hexadecimal) as a shorthand for binary is common in printed output of main storage and, in some cases, in programming.

Look at the column of octal numbers in Table 1. Notice that, since 7 is the last symbol in base 8, the following number is 10. In fact, we can count right through the next seven numbers in the usual manner, as long as we end with 17. Note, however, that 17_8 is pronounced "one-seven," not "seventeen." The octal number 17 is followed by 20 through 27, and so on. The last double-digit number is 77, which is followed by 100. Although it takes a little practice, you can see that it would be easy to learn to count in base 8. However, hexadecimal, or base 16, is not quite as easy.

Base 16: The Hexadecimal Number System

The **hexadecimal** number system uses exactly 16 symbols. As you have just seen, base 10 uses the familiar digits 0 through 9, and bases 2 and 8 use a subset of those symbols. Base 16, however, needs those ten symbols (0 through 9) and six more. The six additional symbols used in the hexadecimal number system are the letters A through F. So the base 16 symbols are: 0, 1, 2, 3, 4, 5, 6, 7, 8, 9, A, B, C, D, E, and F. It takes some adjusting to think of A or D as a digit instead of a letter. It also takes a little time to become accustomed to numbers such as 6A2F or even ACE. Both of these examples are legitimate numbers in hexadecimal.

As you become familiar with hexadecimal, consider the matter of counting. Counting sounds simple enough, but it can be confusing in an unfamiliar number base with new symbols. The process is the same as counting in base 10, but most of us learned to count when we were too young to think about the process itself. Quickly—what number follows 24CD? The answer is 24CE. We increased the rightmost digit by one—D to E—just as you would have in the more obvious case of 6142 to 6143. What is the number just before 1000_{16}? The answer is FFF_{16}; the last symbol (F) is a triple-digit number. Compare this with 999_{10}, which precedes 1000_{10}; 9 is the last symbol in base 10. As a familiarization exercise, try counting from 1 to 100 in base 16. Remember to use A through F as the second symbol in the teens, twenties, and so forth (. . . , 27, 28, 29, 2A, 2B, and so on).

Conversions Between Number Bases

It is sometimes convenient to use a number in a base different from the base currently being used—that is, to change the number from one base to another. Many programmers can nimbly convert a number from one base to another, among bases 10, 2, 8, and 16. We will consider these conversion techniques now. Table 2 summarizes the methods.

To Base 10 from Bases 2, 8, and 16

We present these conversions together because the technique is the same for all three.

Let us begin with the concept of positional notation. **Positional notation** means that the value of a digit in a number depends not only on its own intrinsic value but also on its location in the number. Given the number 2363, we know that the appearance of the digit 3 represents two different values, 300 and 3. Table 3 shows the names of the relative positions.

Table 2   Summary conversion chart

		To Base		
From Base	**2**	**8**	**16**	**10**
2		Group binary digits by 3, convert	Group binary digits by 4, convert	Expand number and convert base 2 digits to base 10
8	Convert each octal digit to 3 binary digits		Convert to base 2, then to base 16	Expand number and convert base 8 digits to base 10
16	Convert each hexadecimal digit to 4 binary digits	Convert to base 2, then to base 8		Expand number and convert base 16 digits to base 10
10	Divide number repeatedly by 2; use remainders as answer	Divide number repeatedly by 8; use remainders as answer	Divide number repeatedly by 16; use remainders as answer	

Table 3   Digit positions

Digit	2	3	6	3
Position	Thousand	Hundred	Ten	Unit

Using these positional values, the number 2363 is understood to mean:

$$
\begin{array}{r}
2000 \\
300 \\
60 \\
\underline{3} \\
2363
\end{array}
$$

This number can be expressed as:

$(2 \times 1000) + (3 \times 100) + (6 \times 10) + 3$

We can express this expanded version of the number another way, using powers of 10 (note that $10^0 = 1$).

$2363 = (2 \times 10^3) + (3 \times 10^2) + (6 \times 10^1) + (3 \times 10^0)$

Once you understand the expanded notation, the rest is easy: You expand the number as we just did in base 10, but use the appropriate base of the number. For example, follow the steps to convert 61732_8 to base 10:

1. Expand the number, using 8 as the base:
$61732 = (6 \times 8^4) + (1 \times 8^3) + (7 \times 8^2) + (3 \times 8^1) + (2 \times 8^0)$

2. Complete the arithmetic:
$$61732 = (6 \times 4096) + (1 \times 512) + (7 \times 64) + (3 \times 8) + 2$$
$$= 24576 + 512 + 448 + 24 + 2$$

3. Answer: $61732_8 = 25562_{10}$

The same expand-and-convert technique can be used to convert from base 2 or base 16 to base 10. As you consider the following two examples, use Table 1 to make the conversions. (For example, A in base 16 converts to 10 in base 10.)

Convert $C14A_{16}$ to base 10:

$$C14A_{16} = (12 \times 16^3) + (1 \times 16^2) + (4 \times 16^1) + 10$$
$$= (12 \times 4096) + (1 \times 256) + (4 \times 16) + 10$$
$$= 49482$$

So $C14A_{16} = 49482_{10}$.

Convert 100111_2 to base 10:

$$100111_2 = (1 \times 2^5) + (1 \times 2^2) + (1 \times 2) + 1$$
$$= 39$$

So $100111_2 = 39_{10}$.

From Base 10 to Bases 2, 8, and 16

These conversions use a simpler process but more complicated arithmetic. The process, often called the *remainder method,* is basically a series of repeated divisions by the number of the base to which you are converting. You begin by using the number to be converted as the dividend; succeeding dividends are the quotients of the previous division. The converted number is the combined remainders accumulated from the divisions. There are two points to remember:

1. Keep dividing until the quotient is zero.
2. Use the remainders in reverse order.

Consider converting 6954_{10} to base 8:

```
8|6954
  8|869      2
    8|108    5
      8|13   4
        8|1  5
          0  1
```

Using the remainders backwards, $6954_{10} = 15452_8$.

Now use the same technique to convert 4823_{10} to base 16:

```
16|4823
   16|301     7
      16|18   13 (=D)
        16|1  2
           0  1
```

The remainder 13 is equivalent to D in base 16. So $4823_{10} = 12D7_{16}$.

Convert 49_{10} to base 2:

```
2|49
2|24        1
2|12        0
2|6         0
2|3         0
2 1         1
  0         1
```

Again using the remainders in reverse order, $49_{10} = 110001_2$.

To Base 2 from Bases 8 and 16

To convert a number to base 2 from base 8 or base 16, convert each digit separately to three or four binary digits, respectively. Use Table 1 to make the conversion. Leading zeros may be needed in each grouping of digits to fill out each to three or four digits.

Convert 4732_8 to base 2:

4	7	3	2
100	111	011	010

So $4732_8 = 100111011010_2$.

Now convert $A046B_{16}$ to base 2:

A	0	4	6	B
1010	0000	0100	0110	1011

Thus $A046B_{16} = 10100000010001101011_2$.

From Base 2 to Bases 8 and 16

To convert a number from base 2 to base 8 or base 16, group the binary digits from the right in groups of three or four, respectively. Again use Table 1 to help you make the conversion to the new base.

Convert 111101001011_2 to base 8 and base 16:

In the base 8 conversion, group the digits three at a time, starting on the right:

111	101	001	011
7	5	1	3

So $111101001011_2 = 7513_8$.

For the conversion to base 16, group the digits four at a time, starting on the right:

1111	0100	1011
F	4	B

$111101001011_2 = F4B_{16}$.

Sometimes the number of digits in a binary number is not exactly divisible by 3 or 4. You may, for example, start grouping the digits three at a time and finish with one or two "extra" digits on the left side of the number. In this case, just add as many zeros as you need to the front of the binary number.

Consider converting 1010_2 to base 8. By adding two zeros to the front of the number to make it 001010_2, we now have six digits, which can be conveniently grouped three at a time:

001	010
1	2

So $1010_2 = 12_8$.

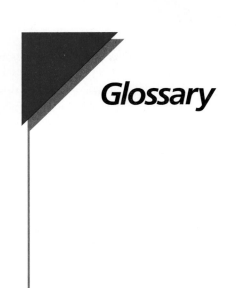

Glossary

Access arm A mechanical device that can access all the tracks of one cylinder in a disk storage unit.

Accumulator A register that collects the results of computations.

Acoustic coupler A modem that connects to a telephone receiver rather than directly to a telephone line.

Active cell The cell currently available for use in a spreadsheet. Also called the current cell.

Ada A structured programming language, named for Countess Ada Lovelace, that encourages modular program design.

Address A number used to designate a location in memory.

Address register Helps locate where instructions and data are stored in memory.

ALGOL (ALGOrithmic Language) A language, developed primarily for scientific programming, that has limited file-processing capabilities.

Algorithm 1. A mathematically computed formula. 2. The instructions that define a process and generate a result in a finite number of steps. For example, in graphics there are algorithms that calculate a Bezier curve, a straight line, a line of any thickness, and a pattern or color.

ALU Arithmetic logic unit.

Amplitude The height of the carrier wave in analog transmission. Amplitude indicates the strength of the signal.

Amplitude modulation A change of the amplitude of the carrier wave in analog data transmission to represent either the 0 bit or the 1 bit.

Analog transmission The transmission of computer data as a continuous electric signal in the form of a wave.

Analytical engine A mechanical device of cogs and wheels, designed by Charles Babbage, that embodied the key characteristics of modern computers.

Analytical graphics Traditional line graphs, bar charts, and pie charts; used to illustrate and analyze data.

ANS-COBOL A version of COBOL standardized in 1974 by the American National Standards Institute (ANSI).

ANSI American National Standards Institute.

APL (A Programming Language) A powerful, interactive, easily learned language introduced by IBM.

Applications management tools Software that allows a manager to review software versions across networks and update them automatically.

Applications software Programs designed to perform specific tasks and functions.

Arithmetic/logic unit (ALU) The electronic circuitry in a computer. The ALU executes all arithmetic and logical operations.

Arithmetic operations Mathematical calculations the ALU performs on data.

Artificial intelligence The field of study that explores computer involvement in tasks requiring intelligence, imagination, and intuition.

ASCII (American Standard Code for Information Interchange) A coding scheme using 7-bit characters to represent data characters.

Assembler program A translator program used to convert assembly language programs to machine language.

Assembly language A second-generation language that uses abbreviations for instructions. Also called symbolic language.

Assistant menu The first menu that appears when accessing dBASE.

Asynchronous transmission Data transmission in which each group of message bits is preceded by a start signal and ended with a stop signal.

Atanasoff-Berry Computer (ABC) The first electronic digital computer, designed by John V. Atanasoff and Clifford Berry, in the late 1930s.

ATM Automated teller machine.

Attribute Column of a relation in a relational database. Also called a field.

Audio-response unit A device that converts data in main storage to vocalized sounds understandable to humans. Also called a voice synthesizer, or a voice output device.

Audit trail A method of tracing data from the output back to the source documents.

Auto-answer The feature of a modem that allows it to automatically answer incoming calls from another modem.

Auto-dial The feature of a modem that allows it to automatically call another modem.

Auto-disconnect The feature of a modem that allows it to automatically disconnect communication from another modem when it receives a disconnect message or when the other party hangs up.

Automated teller machine (ATM) Input/output device connected to a computer used by bank customers for financial transactions.

Automatic redial Automatic redialing by a modem when it receives a busy signal.

Automatic reformatting In word processing, automatic adjustment of text to accommodate changes.

Auxiliary storage Storage, often disk, for data and programs. Auxiliary storage is separate from the CPU and memory. Also called secondary storage.

Average access time The average time that it takes to move the read/write head to data on a disk or tape.

Axis A reference line of a graph. The horizontal axis is the x-axis. The vertical axis is the y-axis.

Background In large computers, the memory area for programs with low priorities.

Backlighting Lighting installed to shine through a screen, such as an LCD, to make it more legible.

Backup system A way of protecting data by copying it and storing it in more than one place.

Bacteriorhodopsin A bacterial protein, first isolated in the 1970s, that is similar to a protein on the retina of the eye. Bacteriorhodopsin converts light energy into chemical energy. It is said to hold the key to molecular miniaturization and photonic computing.

Band printer An impact printer using a horizontally rotating band containing characters that are struck by hammers through paper and ribbon.

Bandwidth The number of frequencies that can fit on one communications line or link at the same time.

Bar code reader A stationary photoelectric scanner that reads bar codes by means of reflected light.

Bar codes Standardized patterns (Universal Product Code) of vertical marks that identify products.

Bar graph A graph made up of filled-in columns or rows that represent the change of data over time.

BASIC (Beginners' All-purpose Symbolic Instruction Code) A high-level programming language that is easy to learn and use.

Batch file A service program, or utility, that runs the same set of programs automatically each time the computer starts up. See also *Command file.*

Batch processing A data processing technique in which transactions are collected into groups, or batches, for processing.

BBS Bulletin board system.

Binary system A system in which data is represented by combinations of 0s and 1s, which correspond to the two states off and on.

Biometrics The science of measuring individual body characteristics; used in some security systems.

Bit A binary digit.

Bitmapped display A graphics display screen that is divided into dots, each of which can be illuminated individually.

Bitmapped graphics Images produced by turning on or off an individual pixel. Paint programs involve bitmapped graphics and do not "remember" that rectangles are rectangles or text is text. Once something has been painted, it is just a collection of pixels. You can erase part of a word created with bitmapped graphics, but you cannot edit it. Also called raster graphics or paint graphics. See also *Object graphics.*

Block A collection of logical records. Also called a physical record.

Block copy command The command used to copy a block of text into a new location.

Block delete command The command used to erase a block of text.

Blocking The process of grouping logical records into one physical record, or block.

Blocking factor The number of logical records in one physical record.

Block move command The command used to remove a block of text from one location in a document and place it elsewhere.

Boldface Printed characters in darker type than the surrounding characters.

Bomb An application that sabotages a computer by triggering damage—usually at a later date. Also called a logic bomb.

Booting Loading the operating system into memory.

bpi Bytes per inch.

Branch In a flowchart, the connection leading from the decision box to one of two possible responses. Also called a path.

Bridge A device that recognizes and transmits packets to be sent to other similar networks.

Brouter A device that combines the functions of a bridge and a router, routing those packets whose protocol it can recognize.

Bubble-jet printer A printer that uses a rising and falling bubble to force drops of ink onto paper.

Bulletin board system (BBS) Telephone-linked personal computers that provide public-access message systems.

Bursting The separation of continuous-form computer paper into individual sheets.

Bus, buses, or **bus lines** Collections of wires connecting the parts of a computer. Also called data buses.

Business graphics Graphics that represent data in a visual, easy-to-understand format.

Business-quality graphics program A program that allows a user to create professional-looking business graphics. Also called a presentation graphics program.

Bus network A network that assigns a portion of network management to each computer but preserves the system if one component fails.

Byte Strings of bits (usually 8) used to represent one data character—a letter, digit, or special character.

Bytes per inch (bpi) An expression of the amount (density) of data stored on magnetic tape.

C A sophisticated programming language invented by Bell Labs in 1974.

C++ An object-oriented programming language; a version of C.

Cable interface unit Electronic components in a box outside a computer; it sends and receives signals on the network cable.

Cache The temporary storage location used in caching.

Caching Using an area of semiconductor memory (a cache) to speed access to data. Data that the computer is most likely to request is kept in a cache. If the data is found there, the computer does not have to access the disk, which takes longer than accessing a cache.

CAD/CAM Computer-aided design/computer-aided manufacturing.

Calibration devices Equipment that helps ensure visual consistency of output from different monitors or printers.

Camera-ready In publishing, ready to be photographed to create printing plates.

Candidates Alternative plans offered in the preliminary design phase of a project.

Carrier sense multiple access with collision detection (CSMA/CD) The line control method used by Ethernet. Each node has access to the communications line and can transmit if it hears no communication on the line. If two stations transmit simultaneously, they will wait and retry their transmissions.

Carrier wave An analog signal used in the transmission of electric signals.

Carterfone decision The Federal Communications Commission decision allowing competitors in the formerly regulated domain of AT&T.

CASE Computer-aided software engineering.

Cathode ray tube (CRT) The most common type of computer screen.

CCITT Consultative Committee on International Telegraphy and Telephony.

CD-ROM Compact disk read-only memory.

Cell The intersection of a row and a column in a spreadsheet. Entries in a spreadsheet are stored in individual cells.

Cell address In a spreadsheet, the column and row coordinates of a cell.

Cell contents The label, value, formula, or function contained in a spreadsheet cell.

Centering Placing a line of text midway between the left and right margins.

Centralized computer system A system that does all processing at one location.

Centralized data processing Keeping hardware, software, storage, and computer access in one location.

Central processing unit (CPU) Electronic circuitry that executes stored program instructions. It consists of two parts: the control unit and the arithmetic/logic unit.

Chain printer An impact printer consisting of characters on a chain that rotate past all print positions.

Change agent The role of the systems analyst in overcoming resistance to change within an organization.

Channel On magnetic tape, a row of bits that runs the length of the tape. Also called a track.

Character A letter, number, or special character (such as $).

Character printer An impact printer, similar to a typewriter, that prints character by character.

Characters per inch (cpi) An expression of the amount (density) of data stored on magnetic tape.

Check bit A bit added to each byte to alert the computer to an error in data transmission. Also called a parity bit.

Chief Information Officer (CIO) Manager of an MIS department.

Circuit One or more conductors through which electricity flows.

CISC Complex instruction set computer.

Classify To categorize data according to characteristics that make it useful.

CLI Command-line interface.

Client 1. An individual or organization contracting for systems analysis. 2. In a client/server network, a program on the personal computer or workstation that allows that node to communicate with the server.

Client/server A network setup that involves a server, which controls the network, and a client, who accesses the network and its services.

Clip art Illustrations already produced by professional artists for public use. Computerized clip art is stored on disk and used to enhance a graph or document.

Clock A component of the CPU that produces pulses at a fixed rate to synchronize all computer operations.

Clock speed The number of times that a computer's clock ticks per second.

Clone A personal computer that closely imitates the operation and architecture of the IBM Personal Computer.

Closed architecture Personal computer design that limits add-ons to those that can be plugged into the back of the machine.

Clustered-bar graph Bar graph comparing several different but related sets of data.

CMOS Complementary metal oxide semiconductor.

Coaxial cable Bundles of insulated wires within a shielded enclosure. Coaxial cable can be laid underground or undersea.

COBOL (COmmon Business-Oriented Language) An English-like programming language used primarily for business applications.

CODASYL (COnference of DAta SYstem Languages) The organization of government and industrial representatives that introduced COBOL.

Cohesion A measure of the inner "strength" of a program module.

Cold site An environmentally suitable empty shell in which a company can install its own computer system.

Collaborative software Educational and other software that allows users on networked or linked computers to participate in a cooperative or competitive way in an on-line activity. See also *Workgroup computing software*.

Collision The problem that occurs when two records have the same disk address.

COM Computer output microfilm.

Command A name that invokes the correct program or program segment.

Command file A service program, or utility, that may contain control statements and automatically run programs whenever it is invoked. See also *Batch file*.

Command-line interface (CLI) An operating system interface in which commands are issued to the operating system by typing them in at the DOS prompt.

Command menu The list of commands in an application program such as Lotus 1-2-3.

Command mode One of two options for entering commands in dBASE; commands are typed in at the dot prompt.

Command tree A hierarchical diagram that shows all the choices from a main command menu and the associated submenus.

Common carrier An organization approved by the FCC to offer communications services to the public.

Communications The ability of computer users to communicate via networks and/or modems.

Compact disk read-only memory (CD-ROM) Optical data storage technology using disk formats identical to audio compact disks.

Compare operation An operation in which the computer compares two data items and performs alternative operations based on the comparison.

Compatible A personal computer that can run software designed for the IBM Personal Computer.

Compiler A translator that converts the symbolic statements of a high-level language into computer-executable machine language.

Complementary metal oxide semiconductor (CMOS) A semiconductor device that does not require a large amount of power to operate. The CMOS is often found in devices that require low power consumption, such as portable computers.

Complex instruction set computer (CISC) A CPU design that contains a large number of instructions of varying kinds.

CompuServe A major information utility that offers program packages, text editors, encyclopedia references, games, and a software exchange, as well as services such as banking, travel reservations, and legal advice.

Computer A machine that accepts data (input) and processes it into useful information (output).

Computer-aided design/computer-aided manufacturing (CAD/CAM) The use of computers to create two- and three-dimensional pictures of manufactured products.

Computer-aided software engineering (CASE) Software that provides an automated means of designing systems.

Computer anxiety The fear of computers.

Computer conferencing A method of sending, receiving, and storing typed messages within a network of users.

Computer doctor Jargon for a computer repairperson.

Computer Fraud and Abuse Act A law passed by Congress in 1984 to fight computer crime.

Computer literacy The awareness, knowledge of, and capacity to interact with computers.

Computer mart A large building that houses dozens of high-tech vendors.

Computer operator A person who monitors the console screen, reviews procedures, and keeps peripheral equipment running.

Computer output microfilm (COM) Computer output produced as very small images on sheets or rolls of film.

Computer phobia See *Computer anxiety*.

Computer programmer A person who designs, writes, tests, and implements programs.

Computer system A system that has a computer as one of its components.

Computing Performing arithmetic operations.

Computing Services A department that manages computer resources for an organization. Also called Information Services, or Management Information Systems.

Conditional replace A word processing function that asks the user whether to replace text each time the program finds a particular item.

Connector A symbol used in flowcharting to connect paths.

Console The front panel of a computer system; it alerts the operator when something needs to be done.

Consortium A joint venture to support a complete computer facility to be used in an emergency.

Consultative Committee on International Telegraphy and Telephony (CCITT) An agency of the United Nations; it is involved in development of communications standards.

Context sensitivity A software feature that allows a user to access information about the application or command the user is currently using.

Continuous form paper Sheets of paper attached end to end to form a continuous folded sheet, with sprocket holes along the sides that help feed the paper evenly through the printer.

Continuous word system A speech recognition system that can understand sustained speech, so users can speak normally.

Control panel The upper portion of a spreadsheet screen; it consists of status, entry, and prompt lines.

Control structure The pattern for controlling the flow of logic in a program. The three basic control structures are sequence, selection, and iteration.

Control unit The circuitry that directs and coordinates the entire computer system in executing stored program instructions.

Coordinating Orchestrating the process of analyzing and planning a new system by pulling together the various individuals, schedules, and tasks that contribute to the analysis.

Copy protection Software or hardware that makes it difficult or impossible to make unauthorized copies of software.

Copyrighted software Software that costs money and must not be copied without permission from the manufacturer.

Coupling A measure of the strength of the relationship between program modules.

cpi Characters per inch.

CPU Central processing unit.

CRT Cathode ray tube.

CSMA/CD Carrier sense multiple access with collision detection.

Current cell The cell currently available for use in a spreadsheet. Also called the active cell.

Current drive The disk drive currently being used by the computer system. Also called the default drive.

Cursor An indicator on the screen; it indicates where the next character will be inserted. Also called a pointer.

Cursor movement keys Keys on the computer keyboard that allow the user to move the cursor on the screen.

Cyberphobia See *Computer anxiety*.

Cylinder A set of tracks on a magnetic disk. These tracks can be accessed by one positioning of the access arm.

Cylinder method A method of organizing data on a magnetic disk. This method organizes data vertically, which minimizes seek time.

Daisy-wheel printer A letter-quality character printer that has a removable wheel with a set of spokes, each containing a raised character.

DASD Direct-access storage device.

DAT Digital audio tape.

Data Raw material to be processed by a computer.

Database A collection of interrelated files stored together with minimum redundancy.

Database management system (DBMS) A set of programs that create, manage, protect, and provide access to the database.

Data buses See *Bus*.

Data collection device A device that allows direct data entry in such places as factories and warehouses.

Data communications The process of exchanging data over communications facilities.

Data communications systems Computer systems that transmit data over communications lines, such as public telephone lines or private network cables.

Data compression A class of techniques that attempts to decrease the number of bits required to represent data. This is useful for saving both storage space and transmission time.

Data Encryption Standard (DES) The standardized public key by which senders and receivers can scramble and unscramble their messages.

Data entry operator A person who prepares data for computer processing.

Data flow diagram (DFD) A diagram that shows the flow of data through an organization.

Data item Data in a relational database table.

Data transfer The transfer of data between memory and secondary storage.

Data transfer rate The speed with which data can be transferred to or from a disk and a computer.

Data point A single value represented by a bar or symbol in a graph.

Date field A field used for dates and automatically limited to eight characters, including slashes used to separate the month, day, and year.

DBMS Database management system.

Deadlock The condition in which each of two programs needs resources held captive by the other and neither is willing to release the resource it has until it gets the one the other has.

DDP Distributed data processing.

Debugging The process of detecting, locating, and correcting mistakes in a program.

Decentralized computer system A system in which the computer and some storage devices are in one location, but the devices that access the computer are elsewhere.

Decision box The standard diamond-shaped box used in flowcharting; it indicates a decision.

Decision logic table A standard table of the logical decisions that must be made regarding potential conditions in a given system. Also called a decision table.

Decision support system (DSS) A computer system that supports managers in nonroutine decision-making tasks.

Decision table A standard table of the logical decisions that must be made regarding potential conditions in a given system. Also called a decision logic table.

Decollating The process of removing carbon paper from between the layered copies of multiple-copy computer paper.

Default drive 1. The disk drive to which commands refer in the absence of any specified drive. Unless instructed otherwise, an application program stores files on the memory device in the default drive. 2. The disk drive currently being used. Also called the current drive.

Default settings The settings automatically used by a program unless the user specifies otherwise.

Demodulation The reconstruction of the original digital message after analog transmission.

Density The amount of data stored on magnetic tape; expressed in number of characters per inch (cpi) or bytes per inch (bpi).

Dependent variable Output of a model, so called because it depends on the inputs.

DES Data Encryption Standard.

Desk-checking A programming phase in which a programmer mentally checks the logic of a program to ensure that it is error-free and workable.

Desktop publishing Using a personal computer, special software, and a laser printer to produce very high-quality documents that combine text and graphics. Also called electronic publishing.

Desktop publishing program A software package for designing and producing professional-looking documents. Also called a page composition program, or page makeup program.

Desktop publishing template A pre-prepared page layout stored on disk.

Detail design A systems design subphase in which the system is planned in detail.

Detail report A report that provides complete, specific information on routine operations.

Device-independent color A standard designed to allow consistent results when an image is transferred from the screen to paper or film and vice versa.

DFD Data flow diagram.

Diagnostic message A message that informs the user of programming language syntax errors.

Diagnostics Error messages provided by the compiler as it translates a program.

Difference engine A machine designed by Charles Babbage to solve polynomial equations by calculating the successive differences between them.

Digital audio tape (DAT) A type of tape or a recording format that involves the digitization of analog data and allows near-perfect reproduction.

Digital transmission The transmission of data as distinct pulses.

Digitizer A graphics input device that converts images into digital data that the computer can accept.

Digitizing tablet A graphics input device that allows the user to create images. It has a special stylus that can be used to draw or trace images, which are then converted to digital data that can be processed by the computer.

Direct access Immediate access to a record in secondary storage, usually on disk. Also called random access.

Direct-access storage device (DASD) A storage device in which a record can be accessed directly.

Direct-connect modem A modem connected directly to the telephone line.

Direct conversion A system conversion in which the user simply stops using the old system and starts using the new one.

Direct file organization An arrangement of records so each is individually accessible.

Direct file processing Processing that allows the user to access a record directly by using a record key.

Disaster recovery plan Guidelines for restoring data processing operations if they are halted by major damage or destruction.

Discrete word system A speech recognition system limited to understanding isolated words.

Disk controller A device that converts the computer's requests to read from or write to a disk into the action of the access arms and read/write heads.

Disk drive A device that allows data to be read from a disk and written on a disk.

Diskette A single magnetic disk on which data is recorded as magnetic spots. Available in both 5¼-inch and 3½-inch format.

Disk mirroring Simultaneously writing the same data to two identical disks. This leaves one disk as a backup if the other should fail.

Disk pack A stack of magnetic disks assembled together.

Displayed value In a spreadsheet cell, the calculated result of a formula or function.

Distributed data processing (DDP) A data processing system in which processing is decentralized, with the computers and storage devices in dispersed locations.

Documentation 1. In a program, a detailed written description of the programming cycle and specific facts about the program. 2. The instruction manual for packaged software.

Dot-addressable display See *Bitmapped display.*

Dot-matrix printer A printer that constructs a character by activating a matrix of pins to produce the shape of a character on paper.

Dot prompt In dBASE, the prompt that tells the user that the program is ready for a command.

Download To transfer data from a mainframe or large computer to a smaller computer. See also *Upload.*

DRAM Dynamic random-access memory.

Drum plotter A graphics output device in which paper is rolled on a drum with a computer-controlled pen poised over it.

Drum printer A printer consisting of a cylinder with embossed rows of characters on its surface. Each print position has a complete set of characters around the circumference of the drum.

DSS Decision support system.

Dumb terminal A terminal that does not process data. It is merely a means of entering data into a computer and receiving output from it.

Dynamic random-access memory (DRAM) A type of RAM that stores its memory in a charge that must be constantly refreshed. It is the most common memory in personal computers because of its size and cost. See also *SRAM.*

EBCDIC (Extended Binary Coded Decimal Interchange Code) A coding scheme established by IBM and used in IBM mainframe computers.

EDI Electronic data interchange.

EFT Electronic fund transfer.

Electronic data interchange (EDI) A set of standards by which companies can electronically exchange items such as invoices and purchase orders.

Electronic disk See *RAM disk.*

Electronic fund transfer (EFT) Paying for goods and services by transferring funds electronically.

Electronic mail (e-mail) Sending messages directly from one terminal or computer to another. The messages may be sent and stored for later retrieval.

Electronic publishing Using a personal computer, special software, and a laser printer to produce very high-quality documents that combine text and graphics. Also called desktop publishing.

Electronic spreadsheet A computerized worksheet used to organize data into rows and columns for analysis.

E-mail Electronic mail.

Encryption The process of encoding communications data.

End of file The point in a program or module where all files have been read.

End-user The person who buys and uses computer software or who has contact with computers.

End-user revolution The trend of computer users becoming more knowledgeable about computers and less reliant on computer professionals.

ENIAC (Electronic Numerical Integrator And Computer) The first general-purpose electronic computer, which was built by Dr. John Mauchly and J. Presper Eckert, Jr., and was first operational in 1946.

Entry mode The spreadsheet mode that lets the user enter data.

Entry point The point in a module where control is transferred. Each module has only one entry point.

Equal to (=) condition A logical operation in which the computer compares two numbers to determine equality.

Erasable optical disc An optical disc on which data can be stored, moved, changed, and erased, just as on magnetic media.

Erase head The head in a magnetic tape unit that erases any data previously recorded on the tape.

Ergonomics The study of human factors related to computers.

Ethernet A popular local area network; this system accesses the network by listening for a free carrier signal.

E-time The execution portion of the machine cycle.

Event-driven Refers to multiprogramming; programs share resources based on events that take place in the programs.

Exception report A report that shows only data reflecting unusual circumstances.

Exit point The point in a module from which control is transferred. Each module has only one exit point.

Expansion slots The slots inside a computer that allow a user to insert additional circuit boards.

Expert shell Software having the basic structure to find answers to questions; the questions themselves can be added by the user.

Expert system A software package that presents the computer as an expert on some topic.

Exploded pie chart A pie chart with a "slice" that is separated from the rest of the chart.

External direct-connect modem A modem that is separate from the computer, allowing it to be used with a variety of computers.

External DOS commands Commands that access DOS programs residing on the DOS disk as program files. The programs must be read from the disk before they can be executed. These program files are not automatically loaded into the computer when it is booted. See also *Internal DOS commands*.

Facsimile (fax) technology The use of computer technology to send digitized graphics, charts, and text from one facsimile machine to another.

Fair Credit Reporting Act Legislation, passed in 1970, allowing individuals access to credit records and the right to challenge them.

Fax board A circuit board that fits inside a personal computer and allows the user to transmit computer-generated text and graphics without interrupting other applications programs.

FCC Federal Communications Commission.

Feasibility study The first phase of systems analysis, in which planners determine if and how a project should proceed. Also called a system survey or a preliminary investigation.

Federal Communications Commission (FCC) The federal agency that regulates communications facilities.

Federal Privacy Act Legislation, passed in 1974, stipulating that government agencies cannot keep secret personnel files and that individuals can have access to all government files that contain information about them.

Fiber optics Technology that uses light instead of electricity to send data.

Field A set of related characters. In a database, also called an attribute.

Field name In a database, the unique name describing the data in a field.

Field type A category describing a field and determined by the kind of data the field will accept. Common field types are character, numeric, date, and logical.

Field width In a database, the maximum number of characters that can be contained in a field.

Fifth generation A term coined by the Japanese to refer to new forms of computer systems involving artificial intelligence, natural language, and expert systems.

File A repository of data or a collection of related records. In word processing, a document created on a computer.

File command A command selection on the main menu of Lotus 1-2-3. The File command allows file manipulation: saving, retrieving, and erasing.

File server A computer exclusively dedicated to making files available on a network.

File transfer software Data communications software that lets the user transfer files between connected computers.

Firmware See *Read-only memory*.

Flash memory A type of PROM that has characteristics that make it useful as a replacement for disk storage in some applications. Flash memory is nonvolatile, can be written to by the computer, and uses less power than a disk drive.

Flatbed plotter A graphics output device that resembles a table with a sheet of paper on it and a mechanical pen suspended over it. The pen moves around on the paper under control of the computer program.

Flat-panel display A display screen that is much thinner and lighter and generally consumes less power than a CRT. The most popular type is an LCD, but TFT active matrix displays are gaining in popularity.

Floppy disk A flexible magnetic diskette on which data is recorded as magnetic spots.

Flowchart The pictorial representation of an orderly step-by-step solution to a problem.

Font A complete set of characters in a particular size, typeface, weight, and style.

Font library A variety of type fonts stored on disk.

Foreground An area in memory for programs that have a high priority.

Format The specifications that determine the way a document or worksheet is displayed on the screen or printer.

Formatting The process of organizing the magnetic particles on the surface of a disk and preparing the disk to store data. Formatting also erases a disk.

Form letter program A program that can be designed to send out "personalized" letters that look like letters produced on a typewriter.

Formula In a spreadsheet, an instruction to calculate a value.

FORTH A language, released by Charles Moore in 1975, that was designed for real-time control tasks, as well as business and graphics applications.

FORTRAN (FORmula TRANslator) The first high-level language, introduced in 1954 by IBM; it is scientifically oriented.

Fourth-generation language A nonprocedural language. Also called a 4GL, or a very high-level language.

Freedom of Information Act Legislation, passed in 1970, that allows citizens access to personal data gathered by federal agencies.

Frequency The number of times an analog signal repeats during a specific time interval.

Frequency modulation The alteration of the carrier wave frequency to represent 0s and 1s.

Front-end processor A communications control unit designed to relieve the central computer of some communications tasks.

Full-duplex transmission Data transmission in both directions at once.

Function A built-in spreadsheet formula.

Function keys Special keys programmed to execute commonly used commands.

Fuzzy logic A type of artificial intelligence that resembles human thinking in that it can measure imprecise, or vague, entities.

Gallium arsenide Material used as a substitute for silicon in chip making.

Gantt chart A bar chart commonly used to depict schedule deadlines and milestones.

Gateway A device that connects two dissimilar networks, allowing machines in one network to communicate with those in the other.

GB Gigabyte.

General-purpose register A register used for several functions, such as arithmetic and addressing purposes.

Generic operating system An operating system that works with different computer systems.

Gesture-based interface In pen-based computer system, a user interface (such as a stylus) that transforms the *gestures*, or motions, made by the user to electronic input.

Gigabyte (GB) One billion bytes.

GIGO Garbage in, garbage out: The quality of the output is directly dependent on the quality of the input.

GoTo function key In a spreadsheet, the key used to get to another cell. Also called the Jump-To function key.

Grammar and style program A word processing program that identifies unnecessary words and wordy phrases in a document.

Graphical user interface (GUI) An image-based interface in which the user sends directions to the operating system by selecting icons from a menu or manipulating icons on the screen by using a pointing device such as a mouse. The most popular GUI is Microsoft Windows.

Graphics Pictures or graphs.

Graphics adapter board A circuit board that enables an IBM Personal Computer to display pictures or graphs as well as text. Also called a graphics card.

Graphics card See *Graphics adapter board*.

Graphics formats Information that describes a picture in an electronic file.

Greater than (>) condition A comparison operation that determines if one value is greater than another.

Green-bar paper Computer paper with green bands.

Groupware Workgroup or collaborative computing.

GUI Graphical user interface.

Hacker 1. An enthusiastic, largely self-taught computer user. 2. Currently, a person who gains access to computer systems illegally, usually from a personal computer.

Half-duplex transmission Data transmission in either direction, but only one way at a time.

Halftone A reproduction of a black-and-white photograph; it is made up of tiny dots.

Hardcard A board that provides the capacity of a 20- or 40-megabyte hard disk. A hardcard fits into an expansion slot inside a personal computer.

Hard copy Printed paper output.

Hard disk An inflexible disk. Hard disks are usually in a pack, often in a sealed module.

Hard magnetic disk A metal platter coated with magnetic oxide and used for magnetic storage.

Hard-sectored disk A disk with a hole in front of each sector, near the center of the disk.

Hardware The computer and its associated equipment.

Hashing Applying a formula to a record key to yield a number that represents a disk address. Also called randomizing.

Hayes compatible Modems that use the command set originated for the Hayes Smartmodem.

Head switching Activation of a particular read/write head over a particular track.

Helical recording Placing data on tape by placing it in tracks that run diagonally across the tape. This method has several advantages over conventional linear recording, including higher data density and longer tape life.

Help index On-screen reference material providing assistance with a program.

Help key The key that, when pressed, accesses on-screen reference material.

Hierarchy chart See *Structure chart*.

High-level languages English-like programming languages that are easier to use than older symbolic languages.

Hit rate The percentage of time that the data being sought is found in a cache.

Home computers An early name given to personal computers. Also known as microcomputers.

Home controls Personal computer–controlled devices that receive their instructions over existing household wiring and perform some household tasks.

Host computer The central computer in a network.

Hot site For use in an emergency, a fully equipped computer center with hardware, communications facilities, environmental controls, and security.

Hybrid A computer with its own unique design that will also simulate that of another computer manufacturer, notably IBM.

IBG Interblock gap.

Icon A small picture on a computer screen; it represents a computer activity.

Impact printer A printer that forms characters by physically striking the paper.

Implementation The phase of systems analysis that includes training, equipment conversion, file conversion, system conversion, auditing, evaluation, and maintenance.

Independent variable Input to a model. It is called independent because it can change.

Indexed file organization The combination of sequential and direct file organization.

Indexed file processing A method of file organization that represents a compromise between sequential and direct methods.

Indexed processing See *Indexed file processing*.

Information Processed data; data that is organized, meaningful, and useful.

Information center A company unit that offers employees computer and software training, help in getting data from other computer systems, and technical assistance.

Information Services A department that manages computer resources for an organization. Also called Computing Services or Management Information Systems.

Information utilities Commercial consumer-oriented communications systems, such as The Source and CompuServe.

Initializing Setting the starting values of certain storage locations before running a program.

Ink-jet printer A printer that sprays ink from jet nozzles onto the paper.

Input Raw data that is put into the computer system for processing.

Input device A device that puts data in machine-readable form and sends it to the processing unit.

Inquire To use a computer terminal to ask questions about data in a mainframe computer.

Inquiry A request for information.

Insert mode In word processing, a text input mode in which text is inserted at the current cursor position without overwriting any text already in the document.

Instruction set The commands that a CPU understands and is capable of executing. Each type of CPU has a fixed group of these instructions, and each set usually differs from that understood by other CPUs.

Integrated circuit A complete electronic circuit on a small chip of silicon.

Integrated package A set of software that typically includes related word processing, spreadsheet, database, graphics, and telecommunications programs.

Integrated Services Digital Network (ISDN) A communications link that allows digital transmission of voice and data.

Intelligent terminal A terminal that can be programmed to perform a variety of processing tasks.

Interactive Data processing in which the user communicates directly with the computer, maintaining a dialogue.

Interactive tablet Pen-based computer.

Interblock gap (IBG) On magnetic tape, the blank space that separates records. Also called an interrecord gap.

Interlaced A description of a video display in which every other line is scanned; it takes two passes to refresh the screen.

Internal DOS commands Commands that access DOS programs that are loaded into the computer when the system is booted. See also *External DOS commands*.

Internal font A font built into the read-only memory of a printer.

Internal modem A modem on a circuit board. An internal modem can be installed in a computer by the user.

Internal storage The electronic circuitry that temporarily holds data and program instructions needed by the CPU. Also called memory, main memory, primary memory, primary storage, or main storage.

International Standards Organization (ISO) A group that has developed protocols for data communications. See *Open Systems Interconnection*.

Internet A public communications network used by private companies, government bodies, and academic institutions in over 30 countries.

Interpreter A program that translates and executes high-level languages one instruction at a time.

Interrecord gap (IRG) On magnetic tape, the blank space that separates records. Also called an interblock gap.

Interrupt A condition that suspends normal program processing temporarily.

Interview The data-gathering operation in systems analysis.

IRG Interrecord gap.

ISDN Integrated Services Digital Network.

ISO International Standards Organization.

Iteration The repetition of program instructions under certain conditions. Also called a loop.

Iteration control structure A looping mechanism.

I-time The instruction portion of the machine cycle.

Joystick A graphics input device that allows fingertip control of figures on a CRT screen.

Jump-To function key The key used to get to a distant part of a file. Also called the GoTo function key.

Justification Aligning text along left and/or right margins.

K, or KB Kilobyte.

Kerning Adjusting the space between characters to create a more attractive or readable appearance.

Key A unique identifier for a record.

Keyboard A common input device similar to the keyboard of a typewriter.

Kilobyte (K, or KB) 1024 bytes.

Knowledge-based system A collection of facts stored in a computer and accessed by natural language.

Label In a spreadsheet, data consisting of a string of text characters.

LAN Local area network.

Laptop computer A small portable computer that can weigh less than 10 pounds.

Large-scale integration (LSI) A chip containing a large number of integrated circuits.

Laser printer A printer that uses a light beam to transfer images to paper.

LCD Liquid crystal display.

Leading The vertical spacing between lines of type.

Leading decision The loop-ending decision that occurs at the beginning of a DOWHILE loop.

Leased line A communications line dedicated to one customer. Also called a private line.

Legend In regard to a graph, text that explains the colors, shading, or symbols used to label the data points.

Less than (<) condition A logical operation in which the computer compares values to determine if one is less than another.

Letter-quality printing High-quality output produced by some printers, such as the daisy wheel.

Librarian A person who catalogs processed disks and tapes and keeps them secure.

Light pen A graphics input device that allows the user to interact directly with the computer screen.

Line graph A graph made by connecting data points with a line.

Line printer A printer that assembles all characters on a line at one time and prints them out practically simultaneously.

Link A physical data communications medium.

Liquid crystal display (LCD) The flat display screen found on some laptop computers.

LISP (LISt Processing) A language designed to process nonnumeric data; popular for writing artificial-intelligence programs.

Local area network (LAN) A network designed to share data and resources among several computers.

Logical field A field used to keep track of true and false conditions.

Logical operations Comparing operations. The ALU is able to compare numbers, letters, or special characters and take alternative courses of action depending on the result of the comparison.

Logical record A record written by an application program.

Logic bomb See *Bomb.*

Logic chip A general-purpose processor on a chip, developed in 1969 by an Intel Corporation design team headed by Ted Hoff. Also called a microprocessor.

Logic error A flaw in the logic of a program.

Logic flowchart A flowchart that represents the flow of logic in a program.

Logo A language developed at MIT by Seymour Papert; it features commands that move a "turtle" on the CRT screen.

Loop The repetition of program instructions under certain conditions. Also called iteration.

LSI Large-scale integration.

Machine cycle Combination of I-time and E-time.

Machine language The lowest level of language; it represents information as 1s and 0s.

Magnetic core Flat doughnut-shaped metal used as an early memory device.

Magnetic disk An oxide-coated disk on which data is recorded as magnetic spots.

Magnetic-ink character recognition (MICR) A method of machine-reading characters made of magnetized particles.

Magnetic tape A magnetic medium with an iron-oxide coating that can be magnetized. Data is stored on the tape as extremely small magnetized spots.

Magnetic tape unit A data storage unit used to record data on and retrieve data from magnetic tape.

Main circuit board Hosts the main circuits of the computer hardware, including the central processing unit. Also called motherboard by technicians.

Mainframe A large computer that has access to billions of characters of data and is capable of processing data very quickly.

Main memory The electronic circuitry that temporarily holds data and program instructions needed by the CPU. Also called memory, primary memory, primary storage, main storage, or internal storage.

Main storage The electronic circuitry that temporarily holds data and program instructions needed by the CPU. Also called memory, main memory, primary memory, primary storage, or internal storage.

MAN Metropolitan area network.

Management Information System (MIS) A set of formal business systems designed to provide information for an organization.

Management Information Systems A department that manages computer resources for an organization. Also called Computing Services, or Information Services.

Mark To define a block of text before performing block commands.

Mark I An early computer; built in 1944 by Harvard professor Howard Aiken.

Master file A semi-permanent set of records.

MB Megabyte.

Megabyte (MB) One million bytes.

Megaflops One million floating-point operations per second. A measure of a computer's ability to process mathematical operations.

Megahertz One million cycles per second. Often used as the measure for clock speed.

Memory The electronic circuitry that temporarily holds data and program instructions needed by the CPU. Also called main memory, primary memory, primary storage, main storage, or internal storage.

Memory management The process of allocating memory and keeping the programs in memory separate from one another.

Memory protection The process of keeping a program from straying into other programs and vice versa.

Menu An on-screen list of choices.

Menu mode The spreadsheet mode that allows the user access to command menus.

Metropolitan area network (MAN) A network operating in an area the size of a city. A MAN is smaller than a wide area network and larger than a local area network.

MICR Magnetic-ink character recognition.

MICR inscriber A device that adds magnetic characters to a document.

Microcode Permanent instructions inside the control unit that are executed directly by the machine's electronic circuits.

Microcomputer The smallest and least expensive class of computer. Also called a personal computer.

Microcomputer manager The manager in charge of personal computer use.

Microfiche Sheets of film (4 × 6 inches) that can be used to store computer output.

Microprocessor A general-purpose processor on a chip, developed in 1969 by an Intel Corporation design team headed by Ted Hoff. Also called a logic chip.

Microsecond One-millionth of a second.

Micro-to-mainframe link Connection between microcomputers and mainframe computers.

Microwave transmission Line-of-sight transmission of data signals through the atmosphere from relay station to relay station.

MICR reader/sorter A machine that reads and sorts documents imprinted with magnetic characters.

Millisecond One-thousandth of a second.

Minicomputer A computer with storage capacity and power less than a mainframe's but greater than a personal computer's.

Minifloppy A 5¼-inch floppy disk.

MIPS Millions of instructions per second. A measure of how fast a CPU can process information.

MIS Management Information System.

MIS manager The manager of the MIS Department.

MITS Altair The first microcomputer kit, offered to computer hobbyists in 1975.

Mode The state in which a program is currently functioning. In a spreadsheet program, there are usually three modes: Ready mode, Entry mode, and Menu mode.

Mode indicator The message displayed on the screen by a spreadsheet program; it tells the user the program's current mode of operation.

Model 1. A type of database, each type representing a particular way of organizing data. The three database models are hierarchical, network, and relational. 2. In a DSS, an image of something that actually exists or a mathematical representation of a real-life system.

Modem Short for *mo*dulate/*dem*odulate. A device that converts a digital signal to an analog signal or vice versa. Used to transfer data between computers over analog communications lines.

Modula-2 A Pascal-like language designed for writing systems software.

Modulation The process of converting a signal from digital to analog.

Module A set of logically related statements that perform a specific function.

Monochrome A computer screen that displays information in only one color, usually black or white.

Monolithic Refers to the inseparable nature of memory chip circuitry.

Mouse A handheld computer input device whose rolling movement on a flat surface causes corresponding movement of the cursor on the screen.

Motherboard See *main circuit board*.

Multimedia A combination of hardware and software that is capable of providing many different forms of output integrated into one presentation. Output may consist of text, sound, graphics, animation, video, and movies—all available at the same time.

Multiple-range graph A graph that plots the values of more than one variable.

Multipoint line A line configuration in which several terminals are connected on the same line to one computer.

Multiprogramming The concurrent execution of two or more programs on a computer and the sharing of the computer's resources.

Multiuser, multitasking personal computer A supermicro with a high-speed microprocessor and significantly increased memory and hard-disk capacity.

Nanosecond One-billionth of a second.

Natural language A programming language that resembles human language.

NCR paper Multiple-copy computer paper that, without using carbon paper, produces copies.

Near letter quality The appearance of printing produced by dot-matrix printers with 24-pin printheads.

(handwritten annotations in top margin: "Star ≠ office building", "Ring ≠ building", "bus = can hook anything onto it— very flexible = large company!")

Network A computer system that uses communications equipment to connect two or more computers and their resources.

Network cable For some LANs, the cable used to connect nodes to the LAN.

Network interface card A circuit board that can be inserted into a slot inside a personal computer to allow it to send and receive messages on a LAN.

Node A device—such as a personal computer, hard disk, printer, or another peripheral—that is connected to a network.

Noise Electrical interference that causes distortion when a signal is being transmitted.

Nonimpact printer A printer that prints without striking the paper.

Nonprocedural language A language that states what task is to be accomplished but does not state the steps needed to accomplish it.

Notepad computer A pen-based computer about the size of a notepad of paper.

Numeric field A field that contains numbers used for calculations.

Object graphics Images produced by turning on and off pixels by plotting vectors (points) that define lines and geometric shapes (such as circles, rectangles, ellipses, Bezier curves, and trapezoids). These plots are actually mathematically computed formulas called algorithms, which form the basis of all object-oriented drawing programs. Also called vector graphics, or draw graphics. See also *Bitmapped graphics*.

Object module A machine-language version of a program; it is produced by a compiler or assembler.

OCR Optical character recognition.

OCR-A The standard typeface for optical characters.

Office automation The use of technology to help achieve goals in an office.

OMR Optical mark recognition.

On-demand report A report that provides information in response to an unscheduled demand from a user.

On-line Processing in which terminals are directly connected to the computer.

Open architecture Personal computer design that allows additional circuit boards to be inserted in expansion slots inside the computer.

Open Systems Interconnection (OSI) A set of communications protocols defined by the International Standards Organization (ISO).

Operating environment An operating system designed so the user does not have to memorize or look up commands.

Operating system A set of programs through which a computer manages its own resources.

Operating system function See *System call*.

Operating system routine See *System call*.

Optical character-recognition (OCR) Using a light source to read special characters and convert them to electrical signals to be sent to the CPU.

Optical disk Storage technology that uses a laser beam to store large amounts of data at relatively low cost.

Optical mark recognition (OMR) Using a light beam to recognize marks on paper.

Optical read-only memory (OROM) An optical medium that can be read, but not written to, by the user.

Optical recognition system A system that converts optical marks, optical characters, handwritten characters, and bar codes into electrical signals to be sent to the CPU.

Organization chart A hierarchical diagram depicting management by name and title.

Organizing Determining resource allocation for an organization.

OROM Optical read-only memory. An optical memory that can be read, but not written to, by the user.

Orphans Personal computers that have been discontinued and are no longer supported by their manufacturers.

OSI Open Systems Interconnection.

Output Raw data that has been processed into usable information.

Output device A device, such as a printer, that makes processed information available for use.

Packaged software Software that is packaged and sold in stores.

Packet A combination of data and address items sent over a packet-switching network.

Packet switching A method of sending data between computers that does not require a continuous connection. The data is combined with information about the address of the data; the two items together form a packet. The packet is routed through the network until it reaches its destination.

Page composition Adding type to a layout.

Page composition program A software package for designing and producing professional-looking documents that combine text and graphics. Also called a page makeup program, or desktop publishing program.

Page description language (PDL) A language built into printers used in desktop publishing. Used by a desktop publishing program to control the way a printer prints a page.

Page frame The space in main memory in which to place a page.

Page layout In publishing, the process of arranging text and graphics on a page.

Page makeup program A software package for designing and producing professional-looking documents that combine text and graphics. Also called a page composition program, or desktop publishing program.

Pages Equal-size blocks into which a program is divided for storage.

Paging Keeping program pages on disk and calling them into memory as needed.

Paint graphics See *Bitmapped graphics.*

Palmtop computer The smallest computer available, weighing less than 1 pound.

Pan To move the cursor across a spreadsheet.

Parallel conversion A method of systems conversion in which the old and new systems are operated simultaneously until the users are satisfied that the new system performs to their standards.

Parallel processing Using many processors, each with its own memory unit, that work at the same time to process data.

Parity bit A bit added to each byte to alert the computer to an error in data transmission. Also called a check bit.

Participant observation A form of observation in which the systems analyst temporarily joins the activities of the group.

Pascal A structured, high-level programming language named for Blaise Pascal, a seventeenth-century French mathematician.

Path 1. In a file directory, the path from the root disk, through nested subdirectories, to the current location of a file. 2. In a network, any route between two nodes. 3. In a flowchart, the connection leading from the decision box to one of two possible responses. Also called a branch.

PDL Page description language.

Peer-to-peer A network setup in which there is no controlling server computer; all computers on the network share programs and resources.

Pen-based computer A computer whose primary input is handwriting, which is entered by means of a pen-like stylus. The computer employs a flat screen and employs gesture recognition technology.

Periodic report A report produced on a regular schedule and preplanned to produce detail, summary, or exception data.

Peripheral equipment Hardware devices attached to a computer.

Personal computer The smallest and least expensive type of computer. Also called a microcomputer.

Personal information manager (PIM) Productivity software that can help office workers, especially managers, cope with information overload.

PgDn key The key used to advance the document one full screen.

PgUp key The key used to back up to the previous screen.

Phantom disk See *RAM disk.*

Phase The relative position in time of one complete cycle of a wave.

Phased conversion A systems conversion method in which the new system is phased in gradually.

Photonics The science of light-sensitive computing. As opposed to electronic- or silicon-based computing, photonic computing involves light as the on-off medium. Photonics research currently points toward faster, three-dimensional, and miniaturized computing in the future.

Physical record A collection of logical records. Also called a block.

Picosecond One-trillionth of a second.

Pie chart A pie-shaped graph used to compare values that represent parts of a whole.

PILOT A programming language invented in 1973; used most often to write computer-aided instruction in various subjects.

Pilot conversion A systems conversion method in which a designated group of users try the system first.

PIM Personal information manager.

Pipelining Speeding up a CPU by allowing several instructions to begin executing before prior instructions are finished.

Pixel A picture element on a computer display screen.

PL/I (Programming Language One) A free-form and flexible programming language designed as a compromise between scientific and business programs.

Plot area The area in which a graph is drawn.

Point A typographic measurement equaling approximately $1/72$ inch.

Pointer An indicator on a screen; it shows where the next user-computer interaction will be. Also called a cursor.

Point-of-sale (POS) terminal A terminal used as a cash register in a retail setting. It may be programmable or connected to a central computer.

Point-to-point line A direct connection between each terminal and the computer or between computers.

Portable computer A self-contained computer that can be easily carried and moved.

POS Point of sale.

Preliminary design The subphase of systems design in which the new system concept is developed.

Preliminary investigation The first phase of a systems analysis, in which planners determine if and how a project should proceed. Also called a feasibility study, or a system survey.

Presentation graphics program A program that allows a user to create professional-looking business graphics. Also called a business-quality graphics program.

Primary memory The electronic circuitry that temporarily holds data and program instructions needed by the CPU. Also called memory, primary storage, main storage, internal storage, and main memory.

Primary storage The electronic circuitry that temporarily holds data and program instructions needed by the CPU. Also called memory, primary memory, main storage, internal storage, and main memory.

Priming read The first read statement in a program.

Print command A command that provides options for printing a spreadsheet.

Printer A device for generating output on paper.

Printer spacing chart A chart used to determine and show a report format.

Print server A part of a network application that controls and provides access to networked printers and spooling.

Private line A communications line dedicated to one customer. Also called a leased line.

Procedural language A language used to present a step-by-step process for solving a problem.

Process An element in a data flow diagram that represents actions taken on data: comparing, checking, stamping, authorizing, filing, and so forth.

Process box In flowcharting, a rectangular box that indicates an action to be taken.

Processor The central processing unit (CPU) of a computer.

Prodigy A communications service introduced by Sears and IBM. It is aimed at providing information, personal communication, and shopping services desired by home users.

Program A set of step-by-step instructions that directs a computer to perform specific tasks and produce certain results.

Programmable read-only memory (PROM) Chips that can be programmed with specialized tools called ROM burners.

Programmer/analyst A person who performs systems analysis functions in addition to programming.

Programming language A set of rules that can be used to tell a computer what operations to do.

PROLOG (PROgramming in LOGic) An artificial-intelligence programming language invented in 1972 by Alan Colmerauer at the University of Marseilles.

PROM Programmable read-only memory.

Prompt A signal that the computer or operating system is waiting for data or a command from the user.

Protocol A set of rules for the exchange of data between a terminal and a computer or between two computers.

Prototype A limited working system or subset of a system that is developed to test design concepts.

Pseudocode An English-like way of representing structured programming control structures.

Public domain software Software that is free and not copyrighted.

Questionnaire In the data-gathering phase of systems analysis, a source of facts to be input as data.

Queues Areas on disk in which programs waiting to be run are kept.

Ragged right margin Nonalignment of text at the right edge of a document.

RAID Redundant array of inexpensive disks.

RAM Random-access memory.

RAM disk A chip that lets the computer regard part of its memory as a third disk drive. Also called an electronic disk or a phantom disk.

RAM-resident program A program that stays in the background of memory, ready to be activated when needed.

Random access Immediate access to a record in secondary storage, usually on disk. Also called direct access.

Random-access memory (RAM) Memory that provides temporary storage for data and program instructions.

Randomizing Applying a formula to a key to yield a number that represents a disk address. Also called hashing.

Range A group of one or more cells, arranged in a rectangle, that a spreadsheet program treats as a unit.

Raster-scan technology A video display technology in which electric beams cause the CRT screen to emit light to produce a screen image.

Raster graphics See *Bitmapped graphics.*

Read To bring data outside the computer into memory.

Read-only media Media recorded on by the manufacturer that can be read from but not written to by the user.

Read-only memory (ROM) Memory that can be read. Data in it remains after the power is turned off. Also called firmware.

Read/write head An electromagnet that reads the magnetized areas on magnetic media and converts them into the electrical pulses that are sent to the processor.

Ready mode The spreadsheet mode indicating that the program is ready for whatever action the user specifies.

Real storage That part of memory that temporarily holds part of a program pulled from virtual storage.

Real-time processing Processing in which the results are available in time to affect the activity at hand.

Record A collection of related fields in a database. Also called a tuple.

Reduced instruction set computer (RISC) A computer that offers only a small subset of instructions.

Redundant array of inexpensive disks (RAID) A class of storage that uses several connected disks that act as a unit. Using multiple disks allows manufacturers to improve data security, access time, and data transfer rates.

Reformat To readjust paragraphs that have been altered during word processing.

Refresh To maintain the image on a CRT screen.

Register A temporary storage area for instructions or data.

Relation A table in a relational database model.

Relational database A database in which the data is organized in a table format consisting of columns and rows.

Relational model A database model that organizes data logically, in tables.

Relational operator An operator (such as <, >, or =) that allows a user to make comparisons and selections.

Repeater A device to relay a signal from one network to another. Both devices must use a similar physical transmission method.

Resolution The clarity of a video display screen or printer output.

Resource allocation The process of assigning resources to certain programs.

Response time The time between a typed computer request and the response of the computer.

Retrieval The recovery of data stored in a computer system.

Reverse video The feature that highlights on-screen text by switching the usual text and background colors.

Ring network A "circle" of point-to-point connections between computers at local sites. A ring network does not contain a central host computer.

RISC Reduced instruction set computer.

Robot A computer-controlled device that can physically manipulate its surroundings.

ROM Read-only memory.

ROM burner A specialized device used to program read-only memory chips.

Rotational delay For disk units, the time it takes for a record on a track to revolve under the read/write head.

Round-robin scheduling A system of having users take turns using the processor.

Router A device that can direct a packet toward its destination.

RPG (Report Program Generator) A problem-oriented language designed to produce business reports.

Sampling Collecting a subset of data relevant to a system.

Satellite transmission Data transmission from earth station to earth station via communications satellites.

Scanner A device that reads text and images directly into the computer.

Scan rate The number of times a CRT screen is refreshed in a given time period.

Screen A television-like output device that can display information.

Scrolling A word processing feature that allows the user to move to and view, in 24-line chunks, any part of a document on the screen.

SDLC Systems development life cycle.

Sealed module A disk drive containing the disks, access arms, and read/write heads sealed together. Also called a Winchester disk.

Search-and-replace function A word processing function that finds and changes each instance of a repeated item.

Secondary storage Additional storage, often on disk, for data and programs. Secondary storage is separate from the CPU and memory. Also called auxiliary storage.

Sector method A method of organizing data on a disk in which each track is divided into sectors that hold a specific number of characters.

Security A system of safeguards designed to protect a computer system and data from deliberate or accidental damage or access by unauthorized persons.

Seek time The time required for an access arm to position over a particular track on a disk.

Selection bar The submenu that appears when a command is chosen in the Assistant menu of dBASE.

Selection control structure A control structure used to make logic decisions.

Semiconductor A crystalline substance that conducts electricity when it is "doped" with chemical impurities.

Semiconductor storage Data storage on a silicon chip.

Sequence control structure A control structure in which one statement follows another in sequence.

Sequential file organization The arrangement of records in ascending or descending order by key.

Sequential file processing Processing in which records are usually in order according to a key field.

Serial processing Processing in which one program must finish running before another can begin.

Server The central computer in a network; it is responsible for managing the network and its services.

Service bureaus Commercial shops that cater to desktop publishing users.

Service program A prewritten program that performs routine file-handling tasks, such as file conversion and sort-merges. Also called a utility program.

Shareware Software that is given away free, although the maker hopes that satisfied users will voluntarily pay for it.

Shell An operating environment layer that separates the operating system from the user.

SIMM Single in-line memory module.

Simplex transmission Transmission of data in one direction only.

Simulation The use of computer modeling to reach decisions about real-life situations.

Simultaneous processing Execution of more than one program at the same time, each program using a separate CPU.

Single entry The unique point where execution of a program module begins.

Single exit The unique point where termination of a program module occurs.

Single in-line memory module (SIMM) A circuit board that holds RAM (in increments of 1, 2, 4, 16, or more megabytes) for easy installation of extra memory in a personal computer.

Single-range bar graph A bar graph that plots the values of only one variable.

Single-range graph A graph that plots the values of only one variable.

Sink In a data flow diagram, a destination for data going outside an organization.

Site license A license permitting a customer to make multiple copies of a piece of software.

Smalltalk An object-oriented language in which text is entered into the computer by using the keyboard, but all other tasks are performed using a mouse.

Smart terminal A terminal that can do some processing, usually to edit data it receives.

SNA Systems Network Architecture.

SNOBOL A powerful string-processing language used by text editors and language processors.

Soft font A font that can be downloaded from the disk in a personal computer to a printer.

Software Instructions that tell a computer what to do.

Software piracy Unauthorized copying of computer software.

Sort An operation that arranges data into a particular sequence.

Source In a data flow diagram, an origin outside the organization.

Source data automation The use of special equipment to collect data and send it directly to the computer.

Source document Paper containing data to be prepared as input to a computer.

Source module A program as originally coded, before being translated into machine language.

Source program listing The printed version of a program as the programmer wrote it.

Speech recognition Converting the spoken word to instructions a computer can use.

Speech recognition device A device that accepts the spoken word through a microphone and converts it into digital code that can be understood by a computer.

Speech synthesis The process of enabling machines to talk to people.

Spelling checker program A word processing program that checks the spelling in a document.

Spooling A process in which files to be printed are placed temporarily on disk.

Spreadsheet A worksheet divided into rows and columns that can be used to analyze and present business data.

SRAM Static random-access memory.

Stacked-bar graph A bar graph in which all data common to a given row or column appears stacked in one bar.

Standalone programs Individual programs, such as word processing and spreadsheet programs.

Standard A format or method accepted by a majority of users. In the computer world, for example, the standard operating system among IBM personal computer users is MS-DOS or PC-DOS.

Star network A network consisting of one or more smaller computers connected to a central host computer.

Start/stop symbol An oval symbol used to indicate the beginning and end of a flowchart.

Start/stop transmission Asynchronous data transmission.

Static random-access memory (SRAM) A type of RAM that requires a continuous current to hold data. SRAM is usually faster, but larger and more expensive than dynamic RAM. See also *DRAM*.

Status line The first line of the control panel in a spreadsheet program like Lotus 1-2-3. The status line tells the cursor location (the cell address) and the contents of that cell.

Stock tab Printer paper that is like newsprint.

Storage register A register that temporarily holds data taken from or about to be sent to memory.

Storing Retaining data that has been processed.

Structure chart A chart that illustrates the top-down design of a program and is often used to either supplement or replace a logic flowchart.

Structured interview An interview in which only planned questions are used.

Structured programming A set of programming techniques that includes a limited number of control structures, top-down design, and module independence.

Style The way a typeface is printed, for example, in *italic*.

Submenu An additional set of options related to a prior menu selection.

Summarize To reduce data to a more concise, usable form.

Summary report A management information system report limited to totals or trends.

Supercomputer The largest and most powerful category of computers.

Supermicro A multiuser, multitasking microcomputer that has a high-speed microprocessor, increased memory, and hard-disk storage.

Supermini A minicomputer at the top of its class in terms of capacity and price.

Supervisor program An operating system program that controls the entire operating system and calls in other operating system programs from disk storage as needed.

Supply reel A reel that has tape with data on it or on which data will be recorded.

Surge protector A device that prevents electrical problems from affecting data files.

Swatch book A collection of colors on paper produced by a final output press or printer. Used to standardize color.

Switched line A communications line that connects through a switching center to a variety of destinations.

Symbolic language A second-generation language that uses abbreviations for instructions. Also called assembly language.

Synchronous transmission Data transmission in which characters are transmitted together in a continuous stream.

Syntax The rules of a programming language.

Syntax errors Errors in the use of a programming language.

Synthesis by analysis Speech synthesis in which a device analyzes the input of an actual human voice, stores and processes the spoken sounds, and reproduces them as needed.

Synthesis by rule Speech synthesis in which a device applies linguistic rules to create an artificial spoken language.

System An organized set of related components established to perform a certain task.

System call Also called an operating system function, or operating system routine. A command that a program sends to the operating system to instruct it to perform a task related to the hardware or the operating environment.

System journal A file whose records represent real-time transactions.

Systems analysis The process of studying an existing system to determine how it works and how it meets user needs.

Systems analyst A person who plans and designs individual programs and entire computer systems.

Systems design The process of developing a plan for a system, based on the results of the systems analysis.

Systems development The process of programming and testing to bring a new system into being.

Systems development life cycle (SDLC) The multi-phase process required for creating a new computer system.

Systems flowchart A drawing that depicts the flow of data through a computer system.

Systems Network Architecture (SNA) A set of communications protocols made commercially available by IBM.

System survey The first phase of systems analysis, in which planners determine if and how a project should proceed. Also called a feasibility study, or a preliminary investigation.

System testing A testing process in which the development team uses test data to determine whether programs work together satisfactorily.

Take-up reel A reel that always stays with the magnetic tape unit.

Tape backup system A tape cartridge or cassette is used to duplicate data from a hard disk to ensure data preservation in the event of hard disk failure.

Tape drive The drive on which reels of magnetic tape are mounted when their data is ready to be read by the computer system.

Tariff A list of services and rates to be charged for data communications services.

Telecommunications The union of communications and computers.

Telecommuting Using telecommunications and computers at home as a substitute for working outside the home.

Teleconferencing A system of holding conferences by linking geographically disbursed people together through computer terminals or personal computers.

Teleprocessing A system in which terminals are connected to the central computer via communications lines.

Template 1. A plastic sheet placed over the function keys to help a user remember the tasks performed by each key. 2. In a spreadsheet program, a worksheet that has already been designed for the solution of a specific type of problem.

Terminal A device that consists of an input device, an output device, and a communications link to the main terminal.

Terminal emulation software Data communications software that makes a personal computer act like a terminal that communicates with a larger computer.

Text block A continuous section of text in a document.

TFT Thin-film-transistor.

Thesaurus program With a word processing program, this program provides a list of synonyms and antonyms for a word in a document.

Thin-film-transistor (TFT) active matrix screen A flat-panel display used with laptop and notebook computers that produces extremely sharp output because each pixel has its own transistor to control brightness.

Time delay A modem feature that allows a computer to call another computer and transfer a file at a future time.

Time driven Refers to the round-robin system of scheduling multiprogramming.

Time sharing Concurrent use of one machine by several people, who are given time "slices" by turns.

Time slice In time sharing, a period of time—usually a few milliseconds or microseconds—during which the computer works on a user's tasks.

Title The caption on a graph that summarizes the information in the graph.

Toggle switch A keystroke that turns a function of a program on or off.

Token passing The protocol for controlling access to a Token Ring Network. A special signal, or token, circulates from node to node, allowing the node that "captures" the token to transmit data.

Token Ring Network An IBM network that uses token passing to access the shared network cable.

Top-down design A design technique that identifies basic program functions before dividing them into subfunctions called modules.

Topology The physical layout of a local area network.

Touch screen A computer screen that accepts input data by letting the user point at the screen to select a choice.

Track 1. On magnetic tape, a row of bits that runs the length of the tape. Also called a channel. 2. On magnetic disk, one of many data-holding concentric circles.

Trackball An input device often described as an upside-down mouse; a user rolls a ball to move the cursor on the screen.

Trailing decision The loop-ending decision that occurs at the end of a DOUNTIL loop.

Transaction file A file that contains all changes to be made to the master file: additions, deletions, and revisions.

Transaction processing The technique of processing transactions one at a time, in the order in which they occur.

Transistor A small device that transfers electrical signals across a resistor.

Transponder A device in a communications satellite that receives a transmission from earth, amplifies the signal, changes the frequency, and retransmits the data to a receiving earth station.

Trojan horse An application that covertly places destructive instructions in the middle of a legitimate program but appears to do something useful.

Tuple See *Record*.

Twisted pairs Wires twisted together in an insulated cable. Twisted pairs are frequently used to transmit data over short distances. Also called wire pairs.

Typeface A set of characters—letters, symbols, and numbers—of the same design.

Typeover mode A text-entry mode in which each character typed overwrites the character at the cursor position.

Typeset quality Printer resolution of 1200 to 2540 dots per inch.

Type size The size, in points, of a typeface.

ULSI Ultra large-scale integration.

Ultra large-scale integration (ULSI) A 10-megabit chip.

Ultramicro disk A 2½-inch 500-kilobyte diskette.

Underlining Underscoring text.

Unicode A coding scheme using 16 bits to represent characters. It is designed to provide enough codes to represent the characters of all the languages of the world.

Unit testing Testing a program by using test data.

UNIVAC I (Universal Automatic Computer I) The first computer built for business purposes.

Universal manager program A program that uses a common interface to coordinate separate standalone programs.

Universal Product Code (UPC) A code number unique to a product. The UPC code is the bar code on the product's label.

UNIX A generic multiuser, time-sharing operating system developed in 1971 at Bell Labs.

Unstructured interview An interview in which questions are planned in advance, but the systems analyst can deviate from the plan.

Update To keep files current by changing data as appropriate.

Upload To send a file from one computer to a larger computer. See also *Download*.

User A person who uses computer software or has contact with computer systems.

User friendly A term to refer to software that is easy for a novice to use.

User interface The type of communication that occurs between the computer and user—the way the user works with the computer. Common types are MS-DOS's command-line interface, the graphical user interface of Microsoft Windows and the Macintosh, and the gesture-based interface of pen-based computers.

User involvement The involvement of users in the systems development life cycle.

User's guide An instruction manual that holds the printed software documentation.

Utility program A prewritten program that performs routine file-handling tasks, such as conversion and sort/merges. Also called a service program.

Vacuum tube An electronic tube used as a basic component in the first generation of computers.

Value In a spreadsheet, data consisting of a number representing an amount, a formula, or a function.

Value-added network (VAN) A communications system in which a value-added carrier leases lines from a common carrier. The lines are then enhanced by adding error detection and faster response time.

Variable On a graph, the items that the data points describe.

VDT Video display terminal.

Vectors The arrows—lines with directional notation—used in data flow diagrams.

Vertical centering Adjusting the top and bottom margins so that text is midway between the top and the bottom of the page.

Vertical market A market consisting of a group of similar customers.

Vertical market software Software for a group of similar customers, such as accountants or doctors.

Very high-level language A fourth-generation language.

Very large-scale integration (VLSI) A 1-megabit chip.

Videoconferencing Computer conferencing combined with cameras and wall-size screens.

Video display terminal (VDT) A terminal with a screen.

Video graphics Computer-produced animated pictures.

Videotex Data communications merchandising.

Virtual memory See *Virtual storage.*

Virtual reality A computer interface that places the user in an artificial world. Virtual reality programs detect the user's actions and instantly change the user's perceptions as a result. The input and output devices involved provide enough sensory feedback to the user to allow him or her to act as if what they experience were real.

Virtual storage A technique in which part of the program is stored on disk and is brought into memory only as needed.

Visualization technology A recent development in engineering that uses shape, location in space, brightness, color, and motion to create and manipulate sophisticated graphics representing complex numeric data.

VLSI Very large-scale integration.

Voice input Using the spoken word as a means of entering data.

Voice mail A system in which a spoken message is digitized and stored in the recipient's voice mailbox. Later the recipient can dial the mailbox, and the system delivers the message in audio form.

Voice output device See *Voice synthesizer.*

Voice synthesizer A device that converts data in main storage to vocalized sounds understandable to humans. Also called an audio-response unit, or voice output device.

Volatile Subject to loss when electricity is interrupted or turned off. Data in semiconductor storage is volatile.

Volume testing The testing of a program by using real data in large amounts.

WAN Wide area network.

Wand reader An input device that scans the special letters and numbers on price tags in retail stores.

Weight The variation in the visual heaviness of a typeface; for example, words look much heavier when in **boldface** type.

Wide area network A network of geographically distant computers and terminals.

Winchester disk A disk drive in which the disks, access arms, and read/write heads are combined in a sealed module.

Wire pairs Wires twisted together in an insulated cable. Wire pairs are frequently used to transmit data over short distances. Also called twisted pairs.

Word The number of bits that constitute a common unit of data, as defined by the computer system.

Word processing Computer-based writing, editing, styling, storing, and printing of text.

Word processing/desktop publishing Using computer programs that involve both word processing and desktop publishing.

Word wrap A word processing feature that automatically starts a word at the left margin of the next line if there is not enough room for it on the line.

Workgroup computing software A class of software designed to improve the ability of people to work in teams. It can include such applications as electronic mail, calendar systems, and document annotation programs. See also *Collaborative software.*

Worksheet Erase command The command that clears the current spreadsheet from memory, leaving a blank worksheet.

Workstation 1. A supermicro. 2. A GUI terminal attached to a large mainframe computer. 3. A personal computer attached to a LAN.

Work surfaces A system of menus used in the dBASE database application that lets you edit, display, and manage data.

WORM Write-once, read-many media.

Worm A program, often called a virus, that spreads and replicates.

Write-once, read-many media (WORM) A medium that can be written on only once; then it becomes a read-only medium.

WYSIWYG "What you see is what you get"—a phrase used in word processing to describe the ability of the program to show, on the screen, text styles such as italic and boldface. Non-wysiwyg programs cannot show the actual style on the screen but only on the paper printout.

x-axis The horizontal reference line of a graph, often representing units of time.

y-axis The vertical reference line of a graph, usually representing values or amounts, such as dollars, staffing levels, or units sold.

Credits

Front Matter

Frontispiece Photo
©Vibeke Sorensen, San Diego Computer Company, "Reflection Study".
Title Page ©Jim Cambo/Tony Stone Worldwide.
vi: Norman Millar.
Detailed Table of Contents viii: Courtesy of International Business Machines. **ix:** Left, Courtesy of Computer Support Corporation. Middle, Courtesy of International Business Machines. Right, Courtesy of International Business Machines. **xi:** Courtesy of Compaq Computer Corporation. **xii:** Courtesy of Hewlett-Packard Company. **xiii:** Courtesy of NASA. **xiv:** Courtesy of International Business Machines. **xv:** Courtesy of Urban Taylor & Associates.
xvi: Reprinted with the permission of Compaq Computer Corporation. All rights reserved. **xvii:** "Without Borders" graphic opening. Courtesy of TBS Productions, Inc. **xviii:** Courtesy of International Business Machines. **xix:** Courtesy of GMFanuc.
xx: Gallery 1, ©Ed Kashi.
xxi: Gallery 2, ©Peter Sibbald. Gallery 3, Courtesy of International Business Machines. B-G: Courtesy of Comp U.S.A., The Nation's largest Computer Superstore.
Part Openers
Pt. I: Gregory MacNicol. (2 Photos).
Pt. II: Left, Patricia Corrigan, "Tic Tac Toe". Right, David Sherwin, "Portrait". **Pt. III:** David Sherwin, Left, "Go", Right, "Landscape".
Pt. IV: Left, Larry Cohn. Right, Vibeke Sorensen.

Introduction

Chapter Openers Left, Blair Seitz/Rainbow. Right, Image Created by Craig Rosenberg, University of Washington. Photo Courtesy of Silicon Graphics, Inc. **1:** Right to left, Joe Sohm/The Image Works. ©Tom Wolf. Courtesy of International Business Machines. ©Frank Siteman 1987/Rainbow.
Text Page 3: 1(a) Left, ©Mark Antman/The Image Works. 1(a) Right, ©George Haling/Photo Researchers, Inc. 1(b) Left, Courtesy of International Business Machines. 1(b)-Right, ©Joe Sohm/The Image Works. 1(c) Left, ©Michael P. Gadomski/Photo Researchers, Inc. 1(c) Right, ©Blair Seitz/Photo Researchers, Inc. 1(d) Left, ©Lawrence Migdale/Photo Researchers, Inc. 1(d) Right, Courtesy of International Business Machines.
4: 2 Bottom left, Courtesy of International Business Machines. 2 Upper left, Courtesy of International Business Machines. 2 Right, ©Richard Tauber. **5:** Courtesy of International Business Machines. **6:** ©Richard Tauber. **7:** Courtesy of International Business Machines. **8:** Courtesy of International Business Machines. **9:** 3 ©Frank Siteman 1987/Rainbow.
11: 4(a,b) Horace Hefner. **12:** 5 Image created by Craig Rosenberg, University of Washington. Photo courtesy of Silicon Graphics, Inc. **13:** Left, Courtesy of Amtech Corporation. 6 Image produced by NCSA using Wavefront's Advanced Visualizer.™ **14:** ©1990 Peter Menzel. **15:** 8 ©Hank Morgan/Photo Researchers, Inc. **17:** 9 Courtesy of U.C.S.F. Computer Graphics Lab. **18:** 10 ©Tom Wolf.

Chapter 1

Chapter Openers 22: Right, Courtesy of Hewlett-Packard Company.
22, 23: Left to right, Courtesy of International Business Machines. Courtesy of Intel Corporation. Reprinted with the permission of Compaq Computer Corporation. Courtesy of GRID System.
Text 26: 1-2 Top, middle, bottom left, bottom right, Courtesy of International Business Machines. 1-2 Bottom middle, Courtesy of Intel Corporation. **28:** 1-3(a) Reprinted with permission of Compaq Computer Corporation. All rights reserved. 1-3(b) Courtesy of GRID System. 1-3(c) Courtesy of Articulate Systems, Inc. 1-3(d) Logitech, Inc. **30:** 1-4(a) ©The Stock Solution. 1-4(b) Courtesy of Texas Instruments. **31:** 1-5(a-c) Courtesy of International Business Machines. 1-5(d) Courtesy of Quantum Leap Technologies. **32:** Michael Fayl. **33:** 1-6 Lower right, Courtesy of Sperry Corporation. 1-6 Top, Courtesy of International Business Machines. 1-6 Lower left, Reprinted with permission of Compaq Computer Corporation. All rights reserved. **34:** 1-7(a) Courtesy of International Business Machines. 1-7(b) Photo by Paul Shambroom, Courtesy of Cray Research, Inc. 1-7(c) Courtesy of International Business Machines. 1-7(d) Courtesy of Hewlett-Packard Company. **35:** Courtesy of Hewlett-Packard Company. **36:** Courtesy of Thinking Machines Corporation. **39:** Courtesy of International Business Machines. **40:** 1-9 Richard Tauber. **41:** 1-10(a) Courtesy of

Brøderbund Software. **44:** 1-12(a) Courtesy of Claris Corporation. 1-12(b) Courtesy of Micrografx, Inc. **45:** ©Stephen Collins/Photo Researchers, Inc. **46:** Logo Courtesy of United Way of America, Jillian Elliott.

Chapter 2

Chapter Openers 50: Left, ©Drake Sorey. Right, Courtesy of Intel. **51:** Left to right, Courtesy of International Business Machines. ©Ed Kashi. Courtesy of Intel. (2 photos) **Text 62:** 2-9(a) Courtesy of Texas Instruments. 2-9(b) Courtesy of Intel. **52:** ©Ira Wyman/The Computer Museum. **64:** ©Ed Kashi. **65:** ©Drake Sorey.

Chapter 3

Chapter Openers 74: Left, Courtesy of Hewlett-Packard Company. Right, ©Gerry Gropp. **75:** Left to right, Courtesy of Spectra-Physics. Courtesy of Inmac. Courtesy of Hewlett-Packard Company. Courtesy Logitech. **Text 76:** 3-1 Courtesy of Hewlett-Packard Company. **77:** Courtesy of A.D.A.M. Software, Inc. **78:** 3-2(a) Reprinted with permission of Compaq Computer Corporation. All rights reserved. 3-2(b) ©1989 McDonald's Corporation. 3-2(c) Courtesy of International Business Machines. **79:** 3-3 Courtesy of Apple Computer, Inc. **84:** 3-6 Courtesy of International Business Machines. **86:** 3-8 Courtesy of Spectra-Physics. 3-8(b) Courtesy of International Business Machines. **87:** 3-9 Photo Courtesy of NCR Corporation. **88:** 3-10 Courtesy of International Business Machines. **90:** 3-11(a,b) Courtesy of International Business Machines. 3-11(c) Courtesy of NEC. **91:** ©Drake Sorey. **93:** Courtesy of Logitech. **94:** 3-12 ©Gerry Gropp. **98:** 3-15 Courtesy of Hewlett-Packard Company. **99:** 16(a) Courtesy of Hewlett-Packard Company. **100:** 3-17 Courtesy of Inmac.

Chapter 4

Chapter Openers 106: Left to right, Photo Courtesy of Seagate Technology, Inc. **107:** Left to right, Photo Courtesy of Unisys Corporation. Courtesy of Iomega. Courtesy of Microelectronics & Computer Tech Cor-

poration. Courtesy of Storage Technology Corporation. **Text 112:** 4-2 Photo Courtesy of Unisys Corporation. **116:** 4-4(a) Courtesy of Memorex. 4-4(b) Courtesy of 3M. 4-4(c) Courtesy of Inmac. 4-4(d) Courtesy of BASF. **118:** 4-6 Courtesy of Memorex Computer Supplies. **120:** Courtesy of Storage Technology Corporation. **121:** 4-9(a) Nashua Computer Products. 4-9(b) BASF Systems Corporation. 4-9(c) Courtesy of KAO Infosystems Company. **122:** 4-11 Courtesy of Hewlett-Packard Company. **123:** 4-12(a) Photo Courtesy of Seagate Technology, Inc. 4-12(c) Anacodyne, Inc. **136:** 4-22(a) Courtesy of International Business Machines. 4-22(b) Microscience International Corporation **137:** 4-23(a) Courtesy of PLI. 4-23(b) Courtesy of Iomega. **138:** 4-24(a,b) Courtesy of Quantam Corporation. **139:** 4-25 Courtesy of PSION. 4-26 Courtesy of Tallgrass Technologies. **141:** Courtesy of Encyclopedia Britannica. Courtesy of Microsoft Corporation. **142:** Courtesy of Microelectronics & Computer Tech. Corporation.

Chapter 5

Chapter Openers 146: Left & right, Courtesy of International Business Machines. **147:** Left to right, Courtesy of Compaq Computer Corporation. ©Robert Holmgren. Courtesy of Murata. Hayes Modem. **Text 149:** 5-1 Courtesy of Compaq Computer Corporation. **150:** 5-2 Courtesy of the Government of Alberta Technology, Research and Telecommunications. **153:** 5-4(b) Hayes Modem. 5-4(c) Global Village Modem. 5-4(d) Courtesy of Mitsubishi International Corporation. **157:** 5-7(a) Courtesy of National Wire and Cable Corporation. 5-7(b,c) Inmac. **159:** ©Robert Holmgren. **164:** Courtesy of International Business Machines. **170:** Courtesy of Minitel. **172:** 5-14 Left & right, Courtesy of International Business Machines. **174:** 5-15 Courtesy of Videotelecom Corporation **175:** 5-16 Courtesy of Murata/Muratec. **177:** 5-17(a,b) Prodigy. **178:** Courtesy of International Business Machines.**179:** 5-18(a,b) Prodigy.

Chapter 6

Chapter Openers 188: Right, ©Tim Brown/Tony Stone Worldwide.

189: Left to right, Courtesy of Microsoft Corporation. Department of the Navy. ©Tim Brown/Tony Stone Worldwide. **Text 191:** Department of the Navy. **195:** Department of the Navy. **197:** ©Tim Brown/Tony Stone Worldwide. **203:** ©Tom Tracy. **220:** 6-16 Courtesy of Microsoft Corporation.

Chapter 7

Chapter Openers 24: Left, Courtesy of International Business Machines. Right, ©George Lange. **225:** Left to right, ©Stella Johnson. Courtesy of International Business Machines. Courtesy of Microsoft Corporation. Courtesy of NeXT Step. **Text 238:** Top, Courtesy of International Business Machines. Bottom, Courtesy of Apple Corporation. **241:** ©Stella Johnson. **244:** ©George Lange. **247:** 7-10 Courtesy of International Business Machines. **248:** 7-11(a,b) Courtesy of Microsoft Corporation **249:** 7-12(a) Courtesy of International Business Machines. 7-12(b) Courtesy of Hewlett-Packard Company. 7-12(c) Courtesy of NeXT Step. **250:** (a,b) ©John Greenleigh/Apple Computer, Inc.

Chapter 8

Chapter Openers 254: Left, Courtesy of International Business Machines. Right, ©Koji Horiuchi. **255:** Courtesy of International Business Machines. Courtesy of Microsoft Corporation. **Text 257:** New Yorker Magazine. **265:** Courtesy of International Business Machines. **281:** ©Koji Horiuchi.

Chapter 9

Chapter Openers 290: Left, ©Rick Friedman/Black Star. Right, Image provided courtesy of Silicon Graphics, Inc. **291:** Left to right, W. Laski/Sipa Press. Courtesy of Apple Computer, Inc./John Greenleigh. Amy Snyder. Main title and supporting graphics for the world famous Academy Awards by artist C. David Pina in 1991. Oscar statuette ©A.M.P.A.S. Photo Courtesy of Wacom. **Text 323:** 9-25 Courtesy of Rick Binger/Pentagram Design. **324:** 9-26 ©Steven Gilmore, designer. **328:** 9-33 ©Adam Zakin. **293:** Amy Snyder. **304:** ©Rick Friedman/Black Star. **322:** W. Laski/Sipa Press.

Chapter 10

Chapter Openers 338: Left, Courtesy of Micrografx. Right, ©Ira Wyman. **339:** Left to right, Courtesy of Harvard Graphics. Courtesy of Computer Support Corporation. Courtesy of Claris Corporation. Software Publishing Corporation has granted permission to use this illustration of the software screen capture from Harvard 3.0.

Text 342: ©Ira Wyman. **363:** Courtesy of Lotus Development Corporation. **372:** Top right, Courtesy of Micrografx. Top left, Courtesy of Harvard Graphics. Bottom left, Courtesy of Computer Support Corporation. Center right, Courtesy of Claris Corporation. Bottom right, Software Publishing Corporation has granted permission to use this illustration of the software screen capture from Harvard 3.0.

Chapter 11

Chapter Openers 376: Right, ©Andy Sacks/Tony Stone Worldwide. Left, Courtesy of Sperry Corporation. **377:** Left to right, U.C.S.F. Photo by David Powers. Courtesy of Sun Microsystems, Inc. Reprinted with permission of Compaq Computer Corporation. All rights reserved. ©Peter Menzel 1990.

Text 379: Reprinted with permission of Compaq Computer Corporation. All rights reserved. **382:** U.C.S.F. Photo by David Powers. **397:** ©Andy Sacks/Tony Stone Worldwide. **399:** Picture Power is a PC base image database from Picture Ware, Inc.

Chapter 12

Chapter Openers 404: Left, Courtesy of Hewlett-Packard Company. Right, ©Rollo Silver, AMYDALA, Box 214, San Cristobal, NM 87564 USA. **405:** Left to right, Courtesy of Dycam, Inc. ©Steve Niedorf/The Image Bank. "Without Borders" graphic opening. Courtesy of TBS Productions Inc. Photo Courtesy of Danny Mitchell.

Text 406: 12-1 Top Left, Courtesy of International Business Machines. 12-1 Top right, bottom, Time Arts, Inc. (2) **409:** 12-3(a) Courtesy of Sperry Corporation. 12-3(b,c) Courtesy of NEC U.S.A., Inc. **410:** 12-4(a)

Courtesy of Apple Computer, Inc./John Greenleigh. 12-4(b) Image provided courtesy of Silicon Graphics, Inc. 12-4(c) Courtesy of Sun Microsystems, Inc. **411:** 12-5 Electronic Arts. Studio 34. **413:** 12-7 Courtesy of Deneba Software. **414:** 12-8 ©Rollo Silver, AMYDALA, Box 214, San Cristobal, NM 87564 USA. Left, ©Peter Menzel 1990. **415:** 12-9(a) Courtesy of Advanced Gravis Computer Technology Ltd. 12-9(b) Stingray Trackball is a registered trademark of CoStar Corporation. 12-10(a) Courtesy of Inmac. 12-10(b) Main title and supporting graphics for the world famous Academy Awards by artist C. David Pina in 1991. Oscar statuette ©A.M.P.A.S. Photo Courtesy of Wacom Technology Corporation. **416:** 12-11(a) Logitech, Inc. 12-12 Courtesy of Hewlett-Packard Company. **417:** 12-13(a) Courtesy of Dycam, Inc. 12-13(b) Canon U.S.A., Inc. **418:** 12-14 Courtesy of Hewlett-Packard Company. **423:** 12-15 Courtesy of Brøderbund Software, Inc. **426:** 12-17 ©Steve Niedorf/The Image Bank. Left, "Kim Reading" created by Chelsea Sammuel on CalComp's Drawing Board 2 graphics tablet. **427:** 12-18 Pixar/Colossall Pictures 1990. (3 Photos) **428:** 12-19 ©Caroline Kopp/California Academy of Sciences 1990. 12-20 "Without Borders" graphic opening. Courtesy of TBS Productions Inc. **430:** Courtesy of Maxis. **431:** Photo Courtesy of Danny Mitchell.

Chapter 13

Chapter Openers 436: Left, ©Joseph Poberskin/Tony Stone. Right, ©Hank Morgan/Rainbow. **437:** Left to right, ©Robert Holmgren. Courtesy of Compaq Computer Corporation. Courtesy of International Business Machines. ©Peter Menzel 1990.

Text 438: 13-1 Courtesy of Unisys Corporation. **439:** 13-2(a) ©Joseph Poberskin/Tony Stone. 13-2(b) ©Robert Holmgren **441:** 13-3 Courtesy of Hewlett-Packard Company. **442:** 13-4 ©Phil Schofield. Left, ©Ralf-Finn Hestoft/Picture Group. **443:** 13-5 Courtesy of Compaq Computer Corporation. **444:** Courtesy of Window Phone. **446:** NEC U.S.A., Inc. **447:** 13-6(a) Courtesy of Stephen C. Cande, Stephen Lewis/Lamont-Doherty Geological Observatory;

Joyce Miller, Scott Fergusson/URI. 13-6(b) ©Peter Menzel 1990. 13-6(c) Cardiff University/Australian Information Service. 13-6(d) Courtesy of Siemans. **448:** ©Drake Sorey. **449:** 13-7 Courtesy of Hewlett-Packard Company. **450:** 13-8 ©Hank Morgan/Rainbow. **451:** Courtesy of International Business Machines.

Chapter 14

Chapter Openers 454: Left, ©Steven W. Lewis. Right, ©John Harding. **455:** Left to right, ©Peter Sibbald. Courtesy of International Business Machines. ©Nina Barnett 1992. ©Paul L. Meredith 1992.

Text 464: 14-3 Courtesy of International Business Machines. **467:** 14-4 ©John Harding. **469:** 14-5 Courtesy of International Business Machines. **462:** Courtesy of International Business Machines. (3 photos) **468:** Top Left, ©Paul L. Meredith 1992. Bottom Left, ©Nina Barnett 1992. Right, ©Steven W. Lewis. **471:** ©Peter Sibbald. **470:** Courtesy of Lotus Development Corporation.

Chapter 15

Chapter Openers 474: Right, ©Ted Morrison. **475:** Left to right, Courtesy of Curtis Manufacturing Company, Inc. Courtesy of Software Publishers Association. Courtesy of Curtis Manufacturing Company, Inc. Courtesy of Symantec Corporation.

Text 481: 15-3 ©Ted Morrison. Left, Courtesy of Eyedentify, Inc. **484:** Courtesy of Symantec Corporation. **487:** (a) Courtesy of Curtis Manufacturing Company, Inc. (b) Misco, Inc. **496:** 15-6 Courtesy of Software Publishers Association.

Chapter 16

Chapter Openers 500: Left, The Computer Museum Boston. Right, Courtesy of GMFanuc Robotics Corporation. **501:** Left to right, Courtesy of Japan Airlines. The Computer Museum/Boston. Mazda Motor of America. Photo Courtesy of Canadair.

Text 511: 16-3 Courtesy Ford Motor Company. **512:** 16-4(a,b) Courtesy of Aion ® Development System. **514:** 16-5(a) Courtesy of Cincinnati Milacron. 16-5(b) Hitachi, Ltd.

515: 16-6 (a-d) Thinking Machines Corporation. **515:** 16-7 Photo courtesy of Canadair. **508:** The Computer Museum/Boston. **510:** Mazda Motor of America. **513:** Courtesy of Japan Airlines. **516:** Courtesy of GMFanuc Robotics Corporation.

Appendix B
547: B-1 Reprinted from POPULAR ELECTRONICS, January 1975. ©1975, Ziff-Davis Publishing Company. **548:** B-2 Courtesy of Science Museum Library, London. **549:** B-2 ©D. Bohl/The Computer Museum/Boston. **549:** B-3 Culver Pictures. **550:** Left and B-4, International Business Machines Archives. **551:** B-5 Iowa State University of Science and Technology. **552:** B-6 International Business Machines Archives. **552:** B7(a&b) International Business Machines Archives. **554:** B-5 Courtesy of NeXT, Inc. B Microsoft Corporation. **555:** B Lotus Development Corporation. **556:** B-8 Margaret and Jerry Wozniak. **557:** B-9 Courtesy of International Business Machines.

Buyer's Guide
BG-1: Courtesy of Comp U.S.A., The Nation's largest Computer Superstore. **BG-2:** Left, Courtesy of International Business Machines. Right, ©Drake Sorey. **BG-3:** Top left, Courtesy of International Business Machines. Bottom left, Courtesy of Super Mac Technology. Bottom right, Courtesy of Microcomputer Accessories. **BG-4:** Left, Courtesy of International Business Machines. Top right, Courtesy of BASF Corporation. Bottom right, Courtesy of Microscience International Corporation. **BG-5:** Top left, Courtesy of Panasonic Communications & Systems Company. Left middle, bottom, & top right, Courtesy of Hewlett-Packard Company. Bottom right, Courtesy of Dell Computer Corporation. **BG-7:** ©Drake Sorey. (2 Photos) **BG-8:** Courtesy of International Business Machines.

GALLERIES

Gallery 1
Frontispiece: Photo courtesy of Hewlett-Packard Company. **2:** Courtesy of International Business Machines. **3:** Precision Visuals International/Science Photo Library/Photo Researchers, Inc. **4:** ©Robert Holmgren 1991. **5:** Courtesy of Motorola, Inc. **6:** Courtesy of AT&T. **7:** Courtesy of International Business Machines. **8:** Sperry Corporation. **9:** Courtesy of TRW, Inc. **10:** Courtesy of Micron Technology, Inc. **11:** ©Dan McCoy/Rainbow. **12:** ©Dr. Jeremy Burgess/Science Photo Library/Photo Researchers, Inc. **13:** Courtesy of AT&T. **14-16:** Courtesy of Hewlett-Packard Company. **17:** ©Astrid & Hanns-Frieder Michler/Science Photo Library/Photo Researchers, Inc. **18:** Courtesy of Advanced Micro Devices, Inc., Sunnyvale, CA. **19:** Courtesy of National Semiconductor. **20:** ©The Telegraph Colour Library/FPG International. **21** Courtesy of Advanced Micro Devices, Inc., Sunnyvale, CA. **22:** Courtesy of Quantum Corporation. **23:** ©Alfred Pasieka/Science Photo Library/Photo Researchers, Inc.

Gallery 2
Frontispiece: ©Peter Menzel. **1:** Drawing Board 2 is a product of the Scottsdale, Arizona-based Digitizer Products Group of Cal Comp Inc., which is a Lockheed Company. **2:** Courtesy of International Business Machines. **3 :** ©Michael Freeman. **4:** Courtesy of Wolfram Research, Inc. **5:** Courtesy of International Business Machines. **6:** Reprinted with permission of Compaq Computer Computer Corporation. All rights reserved. **7:** Courtesy of Maxis Software. **8:** Courtesy of International Business Machines. **9:** ©Howard Sochurek. **10:** ©Michael Freeman. **11:** Courtesy of Siemans Medical Systems. **12:** David Umberger, Purdue News Service. **13:** Courtesy of U.C.S.F. Computer Graphics Laboratory. **14:** Courtesy of Sport Sense. **15:** Courtesy of Buena Vista Software. **16:** Courtesy of Nintendo of America, Inc. **17:** Courtesy of U.S. Olympic Committee. **18:** ©Peter Menzel **19:** ©Dan McCoy/Rainbow. **20:** Courtesy of International Business Machines. **21:** From Invisible Site and George Coates Performance Works. **22:** Courtesy of MTV/XAOS Inc.

23: Courtesy of Silicon Graphics, Inc. **24:** Courtesy of ILM/SOFTIMAGE, Inc. **25:** ©Jay Blacksberg. **26:** ©Peter Menzel. **27, 28:** Courtesy of International Business Machines. **29:** ©Hank Morgan/Rainbow. **30:** ©Ed Kashi. **31:** Courtesy of XAOS Inc. **32:** Courtesy of Berkeley Systems. **33:** ©Cynthia Rubin/Electronic Arts. **34:** Rollo Silver /Amygdala, Box 219, San Cristobal, New Mexico, 87564. **35:** Image by Imagic, USA. Provided Courtesy of SOFTIMAGE, Inc. **36:** Daniel Langlois, SOFTIMAGE, Inc. **37:** Courtesy of AXS /Optical Technology Resource. **38-40:** ©Gregory MacNicol. **41:** ©Chris Renaldi, Graphic Plan-it! **42:** Photography; George Fry, Photocomposition; Raphaele/Digital Transparencies, Inc. **43:** Courtesy of Silicon Graphics, Inc.

Gallery 3
Frontispiece: ©Will and Deni McIntyre/Photo Researchers, Inc. **1, 2:** Photo Courtesy of Hewlett-Packard Company. **3, 4:** Courtesy of Computer Vision, a Prime Computer Company. **5:** ©Philippe Plailly/Science Photo Library/Photo Researchers, Inc. **6, 7:** ©1991 Peter Menzel. **8:** ©C.J. Howard 1990/FPG. **9:** ©T.J. Florian/Rainbow. **10:** Courtesy of Mathematica/Tempura program. **11:** ©Corel Systems Corporation **12, 13:** Courtesy of Autodesk Multimedia, created with 3D Studio, Release 2 on a 486-based PC. **14, 15, 16, 17, 18, 19:** ©Corel Systems Corporation **20:** ©Boeing Computer Services. **21:** ©Hank Morgan/Rainbow. **22:** ©Window Phone. **23:** ©T. Tracy/FPG International. **24:** ©Ed Kashi. **25, 26:** ©Andy Freeberg. **27:** ©James King-Holmes/SPL/Photo Researchers, Inc. **28:** ©John Neubauer. **29:** ©Alan Dorow. **30:** Courtesy of International Business Machines. **31:** ©Frank Siteman/Rainbow.

Index